Building an Outstanding Police Service:

Understanding the Police Effectiveness, Efficiency, and Legitimacy (PEEL) Inspection Framework

Eric Halford
https://orcid.org/0000-0002-3913-1679
Rabdan Academy, UAE

IGI Global
Scientific Publishing
Publishing Tomorrow's Research Today

Vice President of Editorial Melissa Wagner
Director of Acquisitions Mikaela Felty
Director of Book Development Jocelynn Hessler
Production Manager Mike Brehm
Cover Design Jose Rosado

Published in the United States of America by
IGI Global Scientific Publishing
701 East Chocolate Avenue
Hershey, PA, 17033, USA
Tel: 717-533-8845 | Fax: 717-533-7115
Website: https://www.igi-global.com E-mail: cust@igi-global.com

Library of Congress Cataloging-in-Publication Data

Names: Halford, Eric, 1980- editor.
Title: Building an outstanding police service : understanding the Police Effectiveness, Efficiency, and Legitimacy (PEEL) inspection framework / [edited by] Eric Halford.
Description: Hershey, PA : IGI Global Scientific Publishing, 2026. | Includes bibliographical references and index. | Summary: "The book's primary aim is to explore and outline what it takes for UK police forces to achieve an "outstanding" PEEL rating"-- Provided by publisher.
Identifiers: LCCN 2025011216 (print) | LCCN 2025011217 (ebook) | ISBN 9798337327570 (hardcover) | ISBN 9798337327587 (paperback) | ISBN 9798337327594 (ebook)
Subjects: LCSH: Police administration--Great Britain.
Classification: LCC HV8195.A3 B84 2026 (print) | LCC HV8195.A3 (ebook) | DDC 353.3/60941--dc23/eng/20250515
LC record available at https://lccn.loc.gov/2025011216
LC ebook record available at https://lccn.loc.gov/2025011217

British Cataloguing in Publication Data
A Cataloguing in Publication record for this book is available from the British Library.

Table of Contents

Detailed Table of Contents

Vision and mission statements are critical for defining an organization's identity, aligning its objectives, and guiding both internal culture and public expectations. This chapter explores their importance within policing, where clarity in purpose and values is essential for performance, accountability, and public trust. Despite their significance, a review of UK police services found that many either lack clear vision and mission statements or fail to make them accessible. Drawing on evidence from business and public sector research, the chapter outlines how well-crafted statements enhance resource efficiency, employee engagement, and service delivery. It distinguishes vision from mission, detailing their distinct roles and proposing a structured approach for their development. Emphasizing the need for collaboration, the chapter argues that inclusive processes yield statements that are meaningful and actionable. Finally, it highlights best practices in integrating these statements into governance and daily policing operations to drive sustained improvement.

This chapter explores the effectiveness of police forces in building, developing and maintaining an inclusive workforce. It highlights the requirement for organisations to audit their workforce and demand profile to ensure that both align. It uses case studies of the two forces rated as outstanding by the PEEL Assessment process. The key concepts explored include the psychological contract, employer value proposition (EVP) and an inclusive workforce. The critical role of executive sponsorship and commitment to these programmes designed to support these concepts is identified

Introducing higher education routes into policing has raised controversy in recent years (Brown, 2018, Simmel-Binning and Tower 2017). Many argue that having educated officers particularly given the complexity of the role they now engage in is a necessity (NPCC 2016). Research also suggests in can increase public satisfaction and reduce complaints, increase cultural diversity, reduce the use of force and enhance legitimacy (Brown, 2018; Paoline and Terrill, 2015; Paterson, 2011). This chapter will discuss the role of education and development in ensuring police officers have the relevant skills to do their job, including initial training routes and continuous professional development. It will outline what 'good' looks like and why forces need to adapt their approaches and invest more in their people.

This chapter presents a case study examining the sustainability of the Police Education Qualifications Framework (PEQF) by exploring its origins and assessing the future potential of a more highly educated police workforce. It analyses the College of Policing's professionalisation agenda and the introduction of a standardised national curriculum, considering concerns around creating an increasingly educated and potentially perceived as 'elitist' police service. The chapter evaluates the operational implications of the rapid influx of young and inexperienced officers and identifies key barriers to embedding evidence-based policing within current organisational cultures. Finally, it highlights opportunities to reduce police–academic bureaucracy and strengthen long-term collaborative partnerships essential for meaningful and enduring reform.

Policing is an increasingly complex occupation, shaped by evolving crime, public attitudes, resource constraints, and policy shifts. This chapter explores occupational stressors affecting police officers' mental health and morale, examining both organizational and operational pressures. Key stressors include trauma exposure,

This chapter critically explores how UK police forces can build and sustain an ethical workforce. It examines the erosion of public trust following high-profile cases, such as the 2021 murder of Sarah Everard by a serving officer, and the systemic failures these cases exposed in vetting, leadership, and culture. It highlights the role of ethical leadership in the HMICFRS PEEL inspection regime and the central importance of the College of Policing's Code of Ethics, updated in 2024. Case studies illustrate that positive leadership and clear standards support ethical policing, while misconduct, misogyny, and racism can flourish under an ineffective leadership regime. Key areas covered include vetting, misconduct management, and counter-corruption, with discussion of AI innovations, confidential reporting, and reforms in forces like Cleveland and South Yorkshire. Drawing on the Angiolini Inquiry and Casey Review, the chapter concludes that meaningful reform relies on ethical, consistent leadership and a proactive, values-driven culture across all levels of policing.

This chapter explores how UK police services use demand-based strategic planning through the Force Management Statement (FMS) process to ensure efficiency, effectiveness, and sustainability under the HMICFRS inspection framework. Achieving an "outstanding" rating requires a strong commitment to understanding and managing demand. Historically, police services employed forecasting, technology, and prioritization strategies (Walley & Adams, 2019). However, recent analysis highlights new enablers: data-driven insights, demand visualization, systematic use of technology, and evidence-based methodologies. Effective management relies on prioritization, resource alignment, agile performance structures, and workforce development. This chapter examines these enablers, detailing how outstanding services optimize strategic planning to meet evolving demands.

its innovative practice in the most recent series of PEEL inspections, demonstrating the potential of novel approaches to police business.

This chapter examines the evolution of police performance management in the UK, highlighting the challenges posed by shifting oversight models and the limitations of traditional performance metrics. It explores the distinction between targets and measures, emphasizing the need for ethical performance assessment to prevent distortions caused by target-driven policing. The chapter outlines evidence-based methodologies such as Data Envelopment Analysis (DEA), Crime Harm Indexes, and Proactive Policing Indexes to provide a more nuanced understanding of police effectiveness. A performance management model is proposed, integrating strategic objectives, accountability, and ethical oversight to enhance transparency, efficiency, and public trust in policing.

This chapter provides an overview of the ways in which police services can translate evidence into practice. It explores the emergence of the evidence-based policing agenda, its influence, challenges, and opportunities. Based on this exploration, the chapter presents a different model, evidence-informed practice, to highlight other important ways in which police could and should engage in knowledge creation, translation and evaluation. It is suggested that police services would benefit from reflecting on adult and organisational learning theories to develop as learning organisations which can help police services to more naturally and sustainably translate evidence into practice in partnership with others. By further developing as learning organisations, it is hoped that a learning sector emerges supporting the holistic whole-system responses required to address the challenges police, partners and communities are facing.

This chapter provides an overview of effectiveness within policing, considering the roles of various agencies and how specific metrics are utilised to provide insight. It explores the limitations of certain frameworks and highlights how these could be advanced and considers the role in which effectiveness holds in our understanding of policing. Considering public perceptions of policing and how the model of policing by consent informs our interpretation of effectiveness. This introduction to effectiveness within policing consider the framework utilised by His Majesty's Inspectorate of Police and Fire & Rescue Services (HMICFRS), PEEL assessments.

This chapter examines the effectiveness of police response to public calls for service, drawing on national PEEL (Police Effectiveness, Efficiency, and Legitimacy) assessments, procedural justice theory, and empirical research. It explores how the timeliness, fairness, and professionalism of police responses shape public perceptions of legitimacy, trust, and operational competence. Through a structured analysis of call handling, response capability, public engagement, and case studies, the chapter identifies key operational and cultural factors that enable effective response policing. Emphasis is placed on triage systems like THRIVE, officer communication, technological infrastructure, and the growing complexity of non-crime demand such as mental health and safeguarding incidents. The chapter highlights examples of promising practice from forces and contrasts them with underperforming services to illuminate barriers such as staffing shortfalls, inconsistent supervision, and outdated systems.

This chapter explores the critical role of custody services in policing, highlighting their influence on police legitimacy, public trust, and detainee welfare. It examines how outstanding custody practices - aligned with the PEEL assessment framework - can enhance operational efficiency, transparency, and ethical standards. Key components such as staff training, safeguarding, facility management, and technology integration are discussed alongside best practices from UK police forces. The chapter also addresses recurring challenges, such as disproportionate use of force and inadequate healthcare, offering forward-looking recommendations to support continuous improvement and excellence in custody service delivery.

Effective criminal investigation is fundamental to public confidence and the legitimacy of policing. This chapter examines the principles, structures, and practices that underpin high-quality investigations within police forces in England and Wales, drawing upon recent HMICFRS PEEL inspection findings. It explores how robust investigative governance is achieved through clear accountability and experienced supervision, to drive consistency and quality across all levels of investigation. Key themes include maximising investigative opportunities, embedding an investigative mindset across the workforce, and advancing victim-focused, evidence-led prosecutions. Short-term reforms focus on improving oversight, documentation, and compliance with the Victims' Code of Practice, while long-term reforms call for leadership development, workforce planning, and a learning culture centred on reflective practice. The chapter argues that forces achieving investigative excellence are those that balance procedural fairness, victim engagement, and organisational learning.

Crime prevention is a fundamental principle of UK policing, embedded in the HMICFRS inspection framework. To achieve an "outstanding" rating, police services must demonstrate leadership in prioritising crime and anti-social behaviour (ASB) prevention at local, regional, and national levels. This chapter presents a strategic framework for achieving excellence through five key themes: prioritisation, preparation, understanding, response, and evaluation. Drawing on case studies of outstanding police services, it explores how proactive leadership, structured problem-solving, community engagement, and data-driven evaluation enhance effectiveness. By embedding crime prevention into strategic and operational priorities, police services can drive sustainable reductions in crime and ASB.

This chapter examines how UK police forces manage offenders and suspects, based on findings from the 2022–2025 HMICFRS PEEL inspection reports. No force achieved an "Outstanding" grade in this area, despite high public concern over violent and sexual crime. Focusing on seven forces rated "Good," the chapter

better protect the public by understanding the often-sophisticated business of crime, not just to arrest it but destroy it from the inside out. At a time of restructures for increased efficiency and productivity, policing aspires to work smarter. It is only by exploring bold thinking about the adoption of an OCB mindset, and by investing in additional skillsets, that a new performance growth can be unleashed. Such new ways of thinking about the business of crime offer a transformational opportunity to turn policing funding and performance crises into a generational opportunity.

Given that Fraud accounts for more than 40% of reported crime in the UK, which is rising year over year, this chapter will provide an overview of fraud. The focus will be on understanding the current landscape, offender type, fraud type, key organisations and government agencies and their strategic response to this growing problem. This topic has been added to the HMICFRS PEEL inspections from 2025 and the chapter aims to provide the reader with a better understanding of the problem and the part they play as a member of a police service that will be subject to an HMICFRS Fraud inspection at some point during which they hope to achieve an 'outstanding' rating. The author has extensive experience in this complex crime from both public and private sector organisations and brings that experience to the chapter by drawing upon a combination of key literature and range of industry and government reports. Education is a key theme throughout the chapter as knowledge gaps exist and impact the reporting process.

This chapter summarises key theoretical ideas on police legitimacy and explores how elements of the HMICFRS PEEL assessment framework may influence police practices that affect legitimacy. While PEEL inspections reference legitimacy, chief officers often prioritise trust and confidence, which are linked but not identical concepts. Legitimacy is complex, shaped by internal and external factors, with no single solution. It is best understood as a by-product of police behaviour and activity (Hough, 2020; McGregor, 2024; O'Reilly, 2024), and remains a topic more widely examined in academic than operational contexts. This chapter offers an overview and highlights how PEEL may help identify areas for improvement. For a deeper analysis, further reading is recommended.

This chapter traces the rise and recent decline of public confidence in policing in England and Wales, using Crime Survey data, PEEL inspection findings, and Dorset Police's Project Genesis. It links falling trust to misconduct scandals, budget cuts, and the routine abstraction of neighbourhood officers, which erodes visible engagement. Forces graded "outstanding" protect neighbourhood resources, employ two-way communication, and embed structured problem-solving. Project Genesis found community engagement occupied under five percent of recorded activity, prompting 44 evidence-based recommendations that later boosted HMICFRS ratings. The chapter contends that sustained, evidence-led investment in local engagement, clear accountability metrics, and protected staffing are vital to restore legitimacy, satisfaction, and confidence, and to future-proof policing against changing public expectations and fiscal pressures.

This chapter critically examines how police forces in England and Wales engage with the public in ways that are fair, appropriate, and respectful, as framed by PEEL Q2. It explores the role of Neighbourhood Policing Teams (NPT), procedural justice, and community involvement in fostering legitimacy and trust. Drawing on empirical research, national surveys, and key reviews such as the Lammy and Casey Reports, the chapter analyses current practices, identifies barriers to effective engagement, and highlights opportunities for reform. Particular attention is given to the experiences of minoritised communities and the perspectives of police practitioners. The chapter incorporates recent developments in conflict management training, unconscious bias awareness, and the evolving expectations outlined in the HMICFRS 2025–29 consultation. It concludes by proposing future directions grounded in co-production, cultural competence, and sustainable leadership.

The chapter explores the shift towards whole systems partnership working in UK police forces, and how partnership approaches are helping to address HMICFS PEEL assessment criteria. In discussing this issue, the chapter focuses on three inspection questions: (1) How good is the police force at preventing and deterring crime, antisocial behaviour and reducing vulnerability (2) How good is the police force at protecting

Preface

His Majesty's Inspectorate of Constabulary and Fire and Rescue Services (HMICFRS) play a central role in shaping police improvement in England and Wales. Through its PEEL framework, focused on police effectiveness, efficiency, and legitimacy, HMICFRS provides evidence-informed assessments intended to strengthen performance, improve stewardship of resources, and enhance public trust. Yet despite the prominence of PEEL in professional discourse, there remains a notable gap. There is no dedicated, practitioner-facing resource that systematically supports police leaders and operational specialists to understand what "outstanding" looks like across the full inspection landscape, and crucially, how to translate that aspiration into delivery. This edited volume is designed to fill that gap.

OVERVIEW OF THE SUBJECT MATTER AND WHERE IT FITS TODAY

This book is concerned with a practical question that sits at the centre of contemporary policing governance: how can forces build and sustain the organisational capability and capacity required to perform at the highest level across the breadth of PEEL expectations, while remaining lawful, ethical, and publicly trusted. The current operating environment makes this question more urgent than at any point in recent decades. Forces face ever increasing complex and overlapping demands, including vulnerability and safeguarding, cyber-enabled offending and fraud, serious and organised crime threats, and high levels of repeat service contact. Alongside this, workforce pressures relating to recruitment, retention, training capacity, supervision, wellbeing, and resilience are persistent. Public scrutiny is also more intense, with recent high profile incidents involving police officers nationally creating a focus on policing that has rarely been seen. In this context legitimacy needs to shaped not only by outcomes, but by fairness, professionalism, transparency, integrity, and the quality of service delivered to victims and communities.

In this environment, "outstanding" cannot be achieved through isolated excellence or short-term performance spikes. It must be achieved through consistent organisational capability built across people, systems, practice, leadership, governance, and ethics. PEEL can be approached narrowly as a compliance instrument, but its greater value lies in its role as an improvement architecture. When interpreted properly, it signals what high-performing services do differently and what they are able to demonstrate consistently, not simply what they can prepare for inspection. This volume therefore treats PEEL as a practical route map for building sustainable performance both now, and in the future, across the domains that matter most to the public and to policing itself.

TARGET AUDIENCE

This volume is written for a deliberately mixed audience. It is intended for chief officers, senior leaders, heads of department, governance and performance leads, analysts, operational specialists, and professional staff who hold accountability for improvement and need a structured reference point for shaping capability and evidencing impact. It is equally relevant for educators and trainers designing professional development programmes, and for students and researchers seeking a consolidated understanding of inspection as a driver of practice rather than simply a reporting mechanism. Each chapter has been commissioned to be operationally usable, but with sufficient conceptual and evidential grounding to be credible within both professional and academic settings.

STRUCTURE OF THE BOOK

To support coherence across a wide inspection terrain, the book is organised into four sections that reflect the practical conditions required for outstanding performance: People, Efficiency, Effectiveness, and Legitimacy. These sections are interconnected rather than independent. People strategies fail without sustainable demand planning. Operational effectiveness is fragile without legitimacy. Legitimacy cannot be protected without workforce integrity, ethical decision-making, and reliable information governance. The structure is designed to provide a clear reader journey through these dependencies, while still allowing chapters to be read as stand-alone resources when depth is required in a particular area.

What follows is a brief description of each chapter and its contribution.

Chapter 1, Creating an Organisational Vision

Opening the volume, Chapter 1 establishes the strategic foundation for outstanding performance by treating organisational vision as a practical leadership discipline rather than a rhetorical statement. It considers how vision shapes priorities, behaviours, investment decisions, and organisational standards, and how leaders can ensure that improvement intent is translated into consistent delivery across the service. The chapter provides the starting point for the volume by setting out why clarity and coherence are prerequisites for sustainable improvement.

Chapter 2, Recruitment, Selection and Talent Management

Focusing on capability at source, Chapter 2 explores how forces build workforce strength through recruitment, selection, and talent management. It addresses workforce pipelines, leadership development, specialist skills acquisition, and the organisational mechanisms needed to ensure selection decisions reduce risk while improving performance. The contribution of the chapter is to demonstrate that "outstanding" is not only an operational outcome, but a workforce design consequence built through deliberate choices about who is recruited, how they are developed, and how talent is retained and deployed.

Chapter 3, The Recruitment and Retention of Special Constables

Chapter 3 examines the Special Constabulary as a distinct workforce opportunity and challenge. It considers how forces recruit, train, and retain special constables, and how they can build a sustainable model that supports resilience, local engagement, and operational capacity. The chapter contributes by addressing a frequently under-developed area of workforce strategy and by linking volunteer capability to wider organisational performance and legitimacy.

Chapter 4, Police Education

Positioning education as a core capability lever, Chapter 4 argues that police education is now central to workforce professionalism and legitimacy, aligning with the NPCC Policing Vision 2030 and the PEEL focus on building, developing, and supporting an ethical and inclusive workforce. It traces the development of UK police education reforms, including the PEQF and police–HEI partnerships, and explains why implementation has been uneven due to cultural resistance, variable delivery models, and fragile collaboration between academia and policing. The chapter highlights retention and wellbeing pressures for student officers and shows that programme success depends heavily on organisational and supervisory support. It concludes that HMICFRS should assess education and CPD more explicitly within PEEL, because current inspection coverage does not yet support robust judgements on whether forces are meeting future skills demands.

Chapter 5, Sustainability of the PEQF and Associated Potential Challenges

Chapter 5 examines the development and long-term viability of the Police Education Qualifications Framework as a central strand of police professionalisation in England and Wales. It situates the framework within a wider context of declining confidence, cultural reform pressures, and increasing operational complexity, arguing that a more educated workforce has the potential to strengthen competence, ethics, and legitimacy. The chapter explains how PEQF pathways emerged, how they interacted with rapid recruitment and changing demand, and why implementation has been uneven, including concerns about elitism, organisational resistance, limited capacity to embed evidence-based practice, and strain on student officers balancing study with frontline work. It concludes that sustainability depends on supportive leadership, credible police–academic partnerships, improved retention, and a stronger commitment to continuing professional development.

Chapter 6, Occupational Mental Health in Policing

Drawing on survey findings from police officers in the United Kingdom and Ireland, Chapter 6 examines occupational mental health in policing in line with PEEL expectations on workforce wellbeing and effective action to address stress-related harms. It distinguishes operational stressors, arising from frontline exposure to traumatic incidents, from organisational stressors such as bullying, excessive workloads, inadequate support, and workplace culture. The chapter reports that officers in both jurisdictions rated their mental health significantly more positively before joining policing than at the time of the survey, and it identifies common impacts including anxiety, depression, burnout, and trauma-related symptoms. While formal support mechanisms exist, the chapter shows that stigma, lack of trust in management, and a culture of stoicism can inhibit help-seeking and reduce confidence in organisational support. It concludes that improving wellbeing requires prevention-oriented strategies that address avoidable organisational stressors, strengthen leadership and supervision, and embed mental health support into everyday practice rather than relying solely on post-incident interventions.

Chapter 7, Capacity and Capability Building to Support and Protect the Workforce

Chapter 7 explains why capacity and capability building are essential to achieving outstanding performance in the PEEL area concerned with building, supporting and protecting the workforce. It clarifies the distinction between capacity building as an organisation-wide ability to sustain resources, systems and resilience, and capability building as the targeted development of skills and competence required for effective practice. The chapter positions the Force Management Statement as a central mechanism for integrating both concepts through evidence-informed workforce planning, training, and investment decisions. It also introduces key theories that underpin workforce development and implementation and draws on applied case studies of Cumbria Constabulary and Humberside Police to illustrate how outstanding forces operationalise wellbeing, retention, inclusion, and workload management. The chapter concludes with practical guidance on designing and implementing sustainable workforce development programmes.

Chapter 8, Police Values, Ethics, Diversity and Inclusion

With legitimacy rooted in internal culture as well as external performance, Chapter 8 argues that ethical, lawful, and inclusive workplace practice is foundational to operational delivery and public confidence, aligning directly with PEEL expectations on building, developing, and looking after the workforce. It explains how workforce experiences, particularly in the early stages of service, shape professional identity, standards, and retention, and why forces must prioritise inclusive tutoring, mentoring, and psychologically safe supervision. Drawing on recent national inquiries and thematic findings, the chapter highlights how cultural failures, weak supervision, and tolerated misconduct erode internal trust and external confidence. It then identifies core features of high-performing forces, including values-based leadership, robust first and mid-line leadership development, meaningful wellbeing support, and data-informed action on disproportionality in progression and misconduct outcomes. It concludes that policing must rebuild legitimacy from within by protecting its people, challenging harmful behaviour early, and embedding inclusion as routine practice.

Chapter 9, Achieving and Maintaining Workforce Integrity

Chapter 9 applies systems thinking to criminal investigation, arguing that forces improve investigative effectiveness by optimising the investigative system as a whole rather than relying on isolated fixes such as technology, outsourcing, or further specialisation. Drawing on Seddon's Vanguard Method, it explains how clarity of purpose, understanding demand and failure demand, improving flow, and building capability can reduce avoidable work and strengthen investigative quality and organisational learning. Using Cumbria Constabulary's Principles of Investigation as a case study, the chapter demonstrates how a consistently applied investigative framework can improve planning, supervisory oversight, handovers, victim updates, and case closure through clear minimum standards. It also draws lessons from other safety-critical sectors, particularly aviation, to show how structured checklists and post-event learning can improve reliability. The chapter concludes that systems thinking is fundamentally a cultural and leadership endeavour that requires reflective practice, learning over blame, and consistent organisational adoption.

SECTION TWO: EFFICIENCY

Chapter 10, Demand Based Strategic Planning

Grounding efficiency in evidence of demand, Chapter 10 explains how demand based strategic planning underpins police efficiency, effectiveness, and sustainability within the PEEL framework. It is based on a scoping review of PEEL inspections, drawing practical lessons from forces graded outstanding and focusing on how they use the Force Management Statement as a structured annual self-assessment and planning mechanism. The chapter distinguishes external demand from internal demand that drains frontline capacity, and sets out contemporary enablers for understanding and managing both. These include data-driven demand awareness, visualisation tools, responsible use of technology (including AI), evidence-based methods that consider volume, harm and effort, robust prioritisation models, mature governance and accountability frameworks, and workforce development aligned to future demand. It concludes with clear recommendations to help forces embed the FMS as a "living" planning system rather than a compliance exercise.

Chapter 11, Achieving Maximal Efficiency Using Systems Thinking

Chapter 11 applies systems thinking to criminal investigation, arguing that forces improve investigative performance by optimising the whole investigative system rather than relying on isolated fixes such as new technology, outsourcing, or increased specialisation. Drawing on Seddon's Vanguard Method, it explains how clarity of purpose, understanding demand (including failure demand), improving flow, and strengthening capability can reduce avoidable work and improve investigative quality and organisational learning. Using Cumbria Constabulary's

Principles of Investigation as a case study, the chapter illustrates how a consistent, organisation-wide investigative framework can strengthen supervision, improve handovers, support victim updates, and reduce rework. It concludes that systems thinking is fundamentally a leadership and culture endeavour, requiring reflective practice, learning over blame, and consistent adoption.

Chapter 12, An Introduction to Artificial Intelligence and Machine Learning in Policing

Providing a baseline for informed adoption, Chapter 12 introduces artificial intelligence and machine learning in policing and explains why these technologies are increasingly central to investigative capability, workforce development, and advanced analytics. It notes that no UK force has yet been graded outstanding for AI and ML under PEEL and argues that achieving excellence requires more than procurement. Forces must demonstrate measurable value, robust evaluation, and sustainable integration into operational workflows. The chapter outlines key policing applications, including digital investigation support, automated analysis of large data volumes, and leverage analytics such as geospatial intelligence. It also foregrounds the ethical and legitimacy risks, including privacy, surveillance concerns, bias, transparency, and data manipulation, and emphasises the need for strong governance, interoperability, and a digitally capable workforce supported through strategic leadership and partnerships.

Chapter 13, Using Innovation in Policing

Chapter 13 explores innovation as a coordinated organisational practice, defined as the conception, development, implementation and evaluation of novel approaches that create value for stakeholders. It explains that innovation in PEEL is not graded as a standalone criterion but is typically reflected through case examples across inspection themes, and it reports an analysis of recent PEEL outcomes to identify where innovation most commonly appears and where it is least evident. The chapter then examines the main barriers and enablers of innovation in law enforcement, including bureaucracy, resource constraints, cultural resistance, risk aversion, and the importance of collaboration, diversity, education, and supportive leadership. It offers practical guidance for leaders seeking to foster an innovation culture through clear strategy, communication, psychological safety, experimentation, and recognition of learning, illustrated through operational case examples.

Chapter 14, Delivering and Assessing High Performance

Chapter 14 examines how police services can deliver and assess high performance in a way that is consistent, evidence-based, and ethically robust. It outlines how police performance management in the UK has evolved through repeated cycles of centralisation and decentralisation and explains why this has generated confusion about what "good" performance looks like and how it should be measured. The chapter distinguishes between targets and measures, showing how target-driven approaches can distort priorities, increase bureaucracy, reduce professional discretion, and incentivise unethical practices such as gaming crime data. It then sets out the components of ethical performance management, emphasising integrity in crime recording, balanced performance indicators, transparency, and leadership culture. Finally, it introduces a practical performance model that links organisational mission, officer activity, and outcomes, and highlights evidence-based methods for assessing efficiency, effectiveness, harm reduction, public confidence, and victim experience.

Chapter 15, Turning Research into Evidence Based Practice

Translating evidence into routine practice is the focus of Chapter 15, which argues that forces need deliberate mechanisms so that "what works" becomes embedded in day-to-day decision making rather than remaining external guidance. It introduces evidence-based policing as a key driver of this agenda, but also critiques its limitations, including debates about hierarchies of evidence, politicisation, and the risk of narrowing what counts as usable knowledge in complex policing contexts. The chapter then sets out practical enablers for translation, including clearer organisational purpose and support mechanisms, critical appraisal skills, and structured approaches to assessing interventions (for example, EMMIE), while emphasising that evidence may also sit within local organisational knowledge and partnerships. It concludes that sustained impact depends on trusted partnerships, upskilling the workforce to create and appraise evidence, and ongoing evaluation and monitoring so forces become genuine learning organisations.

SECTION THREE: EFFECTIVENESS

Chapter 16, Effectiveness within Policing

Chapter 16 introduces the concept of effectiveness in policing and explains how it is understood, measured, and debated within England and Wales. It distinguishes effectiveness from efficiency, arguing that effectiveness concerns outcomes and impact, while efficiency concerns how resources and processes are used to deliver those outcomes. The chapter outlines how HMICFRS uses the PEEL framework to assess effectiveness across core functions, while recognising both the advantages of standardisation and criticisms relating to validity, contextual differences between forces, and the risk of inspection becoming a compliance exercise. It also reviews wider measures of effectiveness, including crime statistics and public surveys, highlighting limitations such as under-reporting and data quality issues. The chapter concludes by emphasising that effectiveness must incorporate adaptability to emerging threats, evidence-based practice, and the maintenance of legitimacy and public trust.

Chapter 17, Police Responding

One of the most visible determinants of public confidence is the focus of Chapter 17, which examines police responding as a core component of service delivery shaped by both timeliness and the quality of interaction. It explains how PEEL assessments scrutinise call handling, risk and vulnerability assessment, deployment decisions, and professional conduct at the point of contact, emphasising that response quality is not defined by speed alone. The chapter situates response policing within contemporary demand, including mental health, missing persons, safeguarding, and public welfare, often under constrained resources. It draws on procedural justice theory and operational guidance to show why fairness, communication, empathy, and clear explanations matter, particularly when outcomes are limited. It identifies practice features associated with stronger performance, including consistent triage models, effective supervision, demand-led resourcing, reliable technology, and systematic attention to public feedback and follow-up.

Chapter 18, Delivering Outstanding Custody Services

Chapter 18 argues that custody is a pivotal bridge between frontline policing and the criminal justice system, and that custody practice directly shapes perceptions of fairness, legitimacy, and trust. It explains why custody is becoming more prominent within PEEL, particularly in the proposed 2025 to 2027 framework, where it will be inspected more explicitly and assessed against expectations such as lawful and humane detention, safeguarding of vulnerable detainees, ethical use of force, access to healthcare, and protection of legal rights. The chapter sets out core components of outstanding provision, including continuous staff development, robust risk assessment and vulnerability management, safe and dignified environments, effective internal and external scrutiny, and the careful use of technology to strengthen transparency and evidential integrity. It also highlights recurring weaknesses identified through inspections and oversight, such as inconsistent healthcare access, unreliable use of force recording, estate limitations, and governance gaps, before concluding with recommendations focused on training, partnerships, policy assurance, ethical governance, and continuous improvement.

Chapter 19, Conducting Quality Investigations

Chapter 19 argues that high-quality investigations are fundamental to public confidence and police legitimacy, particularly as charge outcomes have declined and victim trust in criminal justice processes has weakened. It explains that investigative success is shaped heavily by early actions, including preserving "golden hour" opportunities, adopting an investigative mindset across call handling and first response, and ensuring clear ownership of enquiries. The chapter emphasises consistent compliance with investigative governance and disclosure duties, clear guidance on "reasonable lines of enquiry", and strong supervisory oversight, especially given reduced workforce experience and high caseloads. It also highlights victim-focused practice, auditable management of withdrawals, and evidence-led prosecutions, alongside the growing importance and risks of digital evidence. The chapter concludes with practical recommendations on supervision, workload, continuity, and operating models to make investigative quality sustainable.

Chapter 20, Reducing and Preventing Crime and Anti-social Behaviour

Chapter 20 positions crime prevention as a foundational policing purpose and a core inspection expectation, arguing that outstanding performance is achieved through organisational capability rather than isolated tactics. It explains what HMICFRS requires for forces to be graded good and how outstanding forces differentiate themselves by demonstrating leadership, influence, and demonstrable impact across prevention and anti-social behaviour reduction. Rather than cataloguing interventions, the chapter sets out five essential themes that underpin effective prevention and reduction: understanding, prioritisation, preparation, response, and evaluation. It defines key concepts and situates prevention within established criminological and public health frameworks, then uses practice examples from forces graded outstanding to illustrate how prevention is embedded through protected neighbourhood policing, structured problem-solving, partnership models, and evidence-led use of powers. The chapter concludes by emphasising that rigorous evaluation and learning are decisive for credibility, improvement, and sustained reductions in harm.

Chapter 21, Managing Dangerous Offenders

Chapter 21 examines how UK police forces manage offenders and suspects by analysing HMICFRS PEEL findings from 2022 to 2025. It highlights that no force achieved an "Outstanding" grade in this area, despite high public concern about violent and sexual crime and the centrality of offender management to public protection. Focusing on the small group of forces graded "Good", it identifies common strengths that appear to underpin stronger performance, including effective use of technology, consistent risk assessment, proactive enforcement activity, purposeful resource management, and robust use of ancillary orders. It also considers emerging tools and approaches, such as digital monitoring, polygraph-informed supervision, and early exploration of AI, and proposes a composite model designed to help raise national standards.

Chapter 22, The Desistance Model for Offender Management

A co-produced case study is presented in Chapter 22, outlining a project designed to help public protection teams adopt desistance-focused practice when supervising people with sexual convictions under MAPPA and notification requirements. It explains how rising caseloads and long-term supervision demands require approaches that balance public protection with rehabilitation and human rights. Using participatory action research, the project brought together MOSOVO officers, police leaders, people with lived experience of sexual convictions, and academics to develop three practical resources: a Desistance Practice Framework, a Desistance Management Plan, and a set of Twelve Principles for Assisting Desistance. The chapter summarises the development process and the principles, emphasising constructive relationships, strengths-based supervision, person-centred language, appropriate training and supervision, and force-wide consistency. It concludes by positioning the work as a formative stage of a wider pilot programme and sets out recommendations to strengthen national guidance and continuing professional development.

Chapter 23, Disrupting Serious and Organised Crime

Chapter 23 proposes a shift in how policing targets serious and organised crime by reframing some organised crime groups as organised crime businesses, where profit, supply chains, and business infrastructure are the true centre of gravity. It argues that conventional approaches often blunt impact by focusing primarily on nominal disruption and prosecution, while the business of crime continues largely uninterrupted. The chapter introduces the "Think OCB" approach, combining intelligence and investigation with business modelling, financial and market analysis, and multi-agency expertise to expose hidden enterprise structures, exploit vulnerabilities, and disrupt criminal operations more permanently. It sets out an operating model centred on mapping, profiling, forming a cross-disciplinary "one-team", and implementing disruption strategies that target revenue flows, business dependencies, and enabling infrastructures, including the strategic use of tax, regulatory, and proceeds-of-crime mechanisms. It concludes that stronger outcomes require workforce skills, playbooks, and analytical tools that enable business-like disruption alongside traditional enforcement.

Chapter 24, Responding to and Investigating Fraud

Chapter 24 argues that fraud and wider economic crime now represent one of the fastest-growing threats in the UK and will increasingly attract inspection scrutiny as HMICFRS strengthens its focus on fraud from 2025 onwards. It explains that contemporary fraud is often cyber-enabled, frequently linked to serious organised crime, and rarely bounded by geography, which increases investigative complexity and creates significant challenges for force-level policing. The chapter sets out what "good" looks like in an inspection-ready local response, emphasising clear ownership rather than displacement to national reporting systems, investigation where viable lines of enquiry exist, defined roles and governance, and a mature understanding of local fraud demand. Using identity fraud typologies and case examples, it shows how scenario-based learning can improve frontline triage, investigative decision-making, and victim safeguarding. It concludes by outlining practical expectations for intelligence-led practice, workforce capability, prevention, and public protection.

SECTION FOUR: LEGITIMACY

Chapter 25, Police Legitimacy

Chapter 25 provides an accessible foundation for understanding police legitimacy and its relevance to the PEEL framework, arguing that legitimacy is best understood as a by-product of police behaviour and activity rather than a discrete output that can be "fixed" through a single initiative. It clarifies legitimacy as the public granting the police authority to exercise power and expecting compliance and explains why procedural justice and policing by consent are central to sustaining that authority. The chapter distinguishes internal influences from external influences, highlighting how legitimacy can be destabilised by misconduct, historical failings, and the amplification of encounters through technology and social media, while recognising that some technologies can enhance accountability. It also evaluates how PEEL inspections support legitimacy indirectly through wider assessments of performance and ethical culture, but notes that legitimacy is not strongly captured in current judgement criteria. It concludes that legitimacy is strengthened through a professional workforce, procedural fairness, transparent engagement, and a focus on public safety outcomes.

Chapter 26, Strategies for Building Trust, Legitimacy, Confidence and Satisfaction

Chapter 26 examines how trust, legitimacy, confidence, and satisfaction are formed, measured, and strengthened in policing in England and Wales. It distinguishes confidence in policing as an institution from trust in police integrity and fairness, and explains how both are shaped by procedural justice, crime control performance, and wider social and political conditions. The chapter traces ideas such as policing by consent and reassurance policing, showing how neighbourhood policing, visible presence, and meaningful engagement can improve perceptions when delivered with consistency and quality. Using evidence from surveys, PEEL assessments, and case examples, it highlights how abstraction from neighbourhood roles and weakened engagement strategies can contribute to declining confidence. It concludes with practical approaches to protect engagement capacity, improve legitimacy, and respond to challenges such as controversial new technologies.

Chapter 27, Public Engagement

Chapter 27 examines public engagement as a core driver of trust, legitimacy, and public cooperation, positioning it as a practical measure of policing effectiveness rather than an optional add-on. It explains how fairness, appropriateness, and respect shape public confidence through everyday encounters, and it uses Neighbourhood Policing Teams as the primary delivery mechanism for sustained, localised engagement. The chapter highlights barriers such as abstraction of neighbourhood officers, resource constraints, negative public perceptions, and cultures that prioritise enforcement outputs over relational policing. It then sets out improvement opportunities focused on protected neighbourhood capacity, leadership accountability, performance measures that value engagement, and credible digital engagement that is interactive rather than one-way. It concludes that sustained, community-centred engagement is foundational to long-term legitimacy and effectiveness.

Chapter 28, Whole System Partnership Working

Chapter 28 examines how whole system partnership working supports PEEL expectations across prevention, vulnerability reduction, protection of vulnerable people, and offender management. It argues that modern demand is increasingly driven by complex need, including mental ill health, substance use, homelessness, trauma, and marginalisation, which frequently sits beyond the capacity of policing alone. The chapter explains why multi-agency and public health approaches have expanded, highlights promising models such as MASH, MARAC, violence reduction partnerships, and place-based prevention, and discusses initiatives such as Right Care, Right Person as part of a wider debate about police boundaries. It also sets out implementation challenges, including inconsistent partner engagement, data sharing constraints, unclear accountability, and weak shared outcome measurement, and concludes that effective collaboration depends on systems leadership, inclusive partnerships, sustained dialogue, and evaluation focused on collective impact rather than siloed outputs.

Chapter 29, Building Trust and Confidence Among Women and Girls

Chapter 29 offers a rare civilian perspective on rebuilding trust and confidence in policing, grounded in the author's journey from distrust to constructive partnership with police following the murder of Sarah Everard. Using the BE LADS campaign as a central case study, it shows how practical, non-accusatory guidance aimed at men and boys can contribute to violence against women and girls' prevention and to legitimacy-building. The chapter combines reflective narrative with applied recommendations for forces, emphasising authentic engagement, transparency, and communication that recognises women's rational safety concerns. It highlights lessons from delivering BE LADS training across UK forces, including a detailed organisational case study from City of London Police and examples from Guernsey Police. It concludes that trust is rebuilt through ordinary people taking responsibility, consistent openness, and visible action.

Chapter 30, Delivering Victim Focused Services

Finally, chapter 30 argues that the quality of police service to victims is a decisive test of performance and legitimacy, because victim experience shapes trust, cooperation, and the likelihood of achieving just outcomes. It explains how PEEL expectations relate to victim contact, safeguarding, crime recording, investigation quality, and ongoing victim care, and it sets these requirements within an evidence base on procedural justice, repeat victimisation, and victim engagement. The chapter emphasises trauma-informed policing as a practical approach to reducing re-traumatisation and improving victim cooperation, particularly for vulnerable victims and those affected by domestic abuse, sexual violence, hate crime, or online harms. It identifies systemic barriers including resourcing pressures, inconsistent recording and follow-up, and digital exclusion, and concludes with recommendations around communication, compliance with the Victims' Code, early identification of vulnerability, inclusive service design, and careful use of technology to improve transparency and victim support.

CONTRIBUTION TO THE FIELD

Taken together, this volume translates the concept of "outstanding" from a descriptor into a programme of organisational capability. It treats PEEL as a practical architecture for building sustainable performance across leadership, workforce development, governance, operational delivery, and legitimacy. Across the sections, the chapters reinforce that high performance cannot be separated from ethical foundations, workforce integrity, evidence-based practice, data reliability, and credible assurance. The aim is not to promote inspection compliance as an end in itself, but to support forces to deliver policing that is consistently effective, efficient, and legitimate, and that can be demonstrated transparently to the public and to professional scrutiny. In doing so, the book contributes a consolidated, practice-facing resource that strengthens the professional discipline of improvement in policing and supports better outcomes for victims, safer communities, and a more trusted policing system.

Eric Halford

Rabdan Academy, UAE

Acknowledgement

This edited volume has benefited from the time, expertise, and professional discipline of a substantial and diverse group of contributors. In total, the book brings together over 30 authors representing over 20 distinct organisations. Contributors span academic institutions, policing organisations, the third sector, and professional practice, reflecting the deliberately applied and practice-facing orientation of the volume. This breadth has been essential in ensuring that the chapters speak not only to theory and policy, but also to operational reality, leadership, and organisational delivery.

The volume also reflects a genuinely international contribution, with authors based in the United Kingdom alongside colleagues from the United Arab Emirates, the United States, and New Zealand. This international perspective has strengthened the book by enabling inspection, improvement, and performance themes to be considered across different policing systems, governance arrangements, and cultural contexts, while remaining grounded in the PEEL framework of England and Wales. I am sincerely grateful to the chapter authors for their time and contributions, and for their willingness to engage constructively with editorial guidance and peer review, which has been essential to the quality and coherence of the volume.

I would also like to acknowledge the support of the leadership at Rabdan Academy, whose trust and confidence in my work has provided the autonomy and enabling environment necessary to develop this book. Finally, I thank my family, whose patience and understanding, particularly through missed evenings and weekends, made the sustained effort of editing and coordinating this volume possible.

Eric Halford

Rabdan Academy, UAE

Section 1
People

Chapter 1
Creating a Vision, Driven by a Mission

Eric Halford
http://orcid.org/0000-0002-3913-1679
Rabdan Academy, UAE

ABSTRACT

Vision and mission statements are critical for defining an organization's identity, aligning its objectives, and guiding both internal culture and public expectations. This chapter explores their importance within policing, where clarity in purpose and values is essential for performance, accountability, and public trust. Despite their significance, a review of UK police services found that many either lack clear vision and mission statements or fail to make them accessible. Drawing on evidence from business and public sector research, the chapter outlines how well-crafted statements enhance resource efficiency, employee engagement, and service delivery. It distinguishes vision from mission, detailing their distinct roles and proposing a structured approach for their development. Emphasizing the need for collaboration, the chapter argues that inclusive processes yield statements that are meaningful and actionable. Finally, it highlights best practices in integrating these statements into governance and daily policing operations to drive sustained improvement.

INTRODUCTION

> *"We...define the core role of the police as being to promote public safety by maintaining order and upholding the law, which their unique powers enable them to do, and to carry out other activities which enable them to perform this core role legitimately, effectively and with minimum reliance on those powers" (The Police Foundation, 2022)*

DOI: 10.4018/979-8-3373-2757-0.ch001

Since the Royal Commission on Policing (1962–1964), which produced its final report in 1966, there has been no equivalent whole-system re-examination of police strategy in the United Kingdom (UK) (Oliver, 1987). The Royal Commission, therefore, represented the last genuine attempt to define policing as a strategic public service. In the decades that followed, national reviews tended to prioritise tactical reorganisation rather than long-term strategic renewal. For example, the Sheehy Inquiry (1993), the HMIC "Winning the Race" (Her Majesty's Inspectorate of Constabulary [HMIC], 2001) reforms, and later Home Office modernisation programmes of the 1990s and 2000s, each focused on efficiency, performance indicators, and managerial control, hallmarks of new public management, rather than on redefining policing's purpose.

This prolonged absence of strategic reflection has arguably produced a landscape in which mission and vision statements are either outdated or disconnected from operational reality. The Police Foundation's Strategic Review of Policing in England and Wales (2022) sought to fill this vacuum. Its analysis of legitimacy, complexity, and demand was both comprehensive and timely. Yet, despite its breadth, the review was largely diagnostic, identifying problems and proposing organisational adjustments without articulating a unifying strategic recalibration. The report's focus on redesigning 'policing and public safety for the twenty-first century' was framed through policy recommendations and capability reforms rather than through a cohesive mission that re-defines what policing *is for*.

In effect, the Police Foundation Review reflected a continuation of the post-1960s trend and emphasised structural efficiency and partnership models over a renewed sense of purpose. This gap underscores the central argument of this chapter, that without a clearly articulated vision and mission, policing reforms risk remaining transactional and reactive. A modern strategic framework for policing must therefore begin not with structure but with *purpose*, clarifying why the police exist, whom they serve, and how success should be understood in a democratic society. This chapter outlines the key components required to begin this journey.

PURPOSE VS. PERFORMANCE

Peter Drucker, widely regarded as one of the greatest business thinkers of the 20th century, emphasized the importance of vision and mission statements in his seminal works on modern organizational governance. Drucker (1973) firmly asserted that organizations are defined not by their industry, field, or services, but by their mission and purpose.

Drucker's (1973) notion that purpose defines an organisation's legitimacy aligns closely with the work of Deming (see the reissue published in 2018), whose 'system of profound knowledge' rejected the mechanistic assumptions of Frederick Taylor's scientific management outlined in the early 20th century (1911). Whereas Taylorism focused narrowly on efficiency through standardisation and control, Deming emphasised effectiveness through systems thinking, feedback, and continual improvement. Deming argued that organisations should view performance not as a set of isolated tasks but as the outcome of interdependent processes shaped by leadership, culture, and learning.

The legacy of Taylorism within policing remains visible in contemporary performance management regimes first introduced during the 1980s and 1990s, which prioritised measurable outputs such as arrests, detections, and response times, over systemic effectiveness and community outcomes. Through the 1990's and early 2000's, the focus of policing on *doing things right* began to eclipse the more strategic question of *doing the right things*. In this regard, Deming's quality-improvement philosophy, by comparison, demands a shift away from such compliance-driven controls to purpose-driven activity.

As Drucker (1973) and Chandler (2009) have both observed, *strategy must precede structure*. They believe that an organisation's design, systems, and hierarchy, should all be the consequence of its purpose, not the starting point. In policing, this principle has too often been reversed: structural reforms have been introduced in search of efficiency, often at the expense of strategic coherence. The goal should be to ensure that efficiency serves effectiveness, and that short-term metrics do not displace long-term legitimacy. By integrating the principles of Drucker and Deming, police organisations can move from a reactive, target-based culture toward one grounded in shared purpose, continuous learning, and meaningful improvement, hallmarks of what modern public-sector theory regards as strategic quality management.

VISION AND MISSION STATEMENTS IN POLICING

The key starting point for such a shift is the vision and mission statement. Policing, as a fundamental public service, stands out as a sector where well-crafted statements are particularly crucial as they not only help articulate organizational identity and priorities but also communicate values to the public and provide guidance to employees (Alegre & Berbegal-Mirabent, 2017). Despite their importance, research has consistently shown that many organizations either lack strategic vision and mission statements altogether or possess statements that fail to deliver meaningful value (Lundberg, 1984). In the context of public services, such shortcomings can have significant implications for performance, accountability, and stakeholder engagement. A review conducted for this book of the vision, mission, and values statements for UK police services revealed that very few prominently feature these on their public branding or websites. This finding aligns with research indicating that many organizations, particularly in the public sector, fail to prominently share such statements or even integrate them into performance reports (Leuthesser and Kohli, 2014). This is particularly concerning given that vision and mission statements, alongside a code of ethics, are pivotal in shaping organizational policies, processes, governance, and assessments of performance (Ostapski and Isaacs, 1992).

The purpose of the forthcoming sections is to explore the importance of vision and mission statements in policing and to outline evidence-based guidelines for their development. By examining their role in aligning organizational objectives with public expectations, I highlight how such statements can serve as a powerful tool for improving accountability, performance, and employee engagement. Furthermore, I provide practical insight into crafting vision and mission statements that not only reflect the unique identity of individual police services but also address the diverse needs of the communities they serve.

WHY DO THE POLICE NEED A VISION AND A MISSION?

By examining the websites of all 43 territorial police forces in England and Wales, it was established that 28% (n-12) did not clearly outline their mission, and 35% (n-15) also failed to outline the values for which their organisation stood. This illustrates that while some police services possess clear and focused vision and mission statements, their accessibility and prominence is not consistent, which suggests a lack of appreciation for their value. This is vital as services should "*use a variety of arrangements to give their workforces a clear understanding of their vision or values*" (Her Majesty's Inspectorate of Constabularies Fire and Rescue [HMICFRS], 2017, p12).

This disconnect is understandable, as much of the literature on their significance is rooted in the fields of business, marketing, and philosophy rather than criminology or policing (Hirota et al., 2010). As such, its is not an area that is well publicised in policing literature, thereby often neglected by practitioners and scholars alike. This is unfortunate, as evidence strongly supports the fact that well-crafted vision and mission statements can drive organizational success, with research consistently demonstrating that organizations with defined statements perform better across a range of metrics (Hirota et al., 2010). For instance, Bart and Baetz (1998) found that organizations with clear statements outperformed those without in terms of financial efficiency and resource allocation. Although police services do not pursue financial profits, fiscal responsibility and value for money are critical in a public sector context. In UK policing, the HMICFRS value-for-money profiles, which compare financial performance across police services, underscore the importance of such financial accountability (HMICFRS, 2024).

Efficient resource allocation is another key benefit of vision and mission statements. Bart and Baetz (1998) noted that organizations with well-defined statements allocate resources more effectively. This is particularly relevant for modern policing, where evolving demands such as the rise of cybercrime, complex vulnerability, and serious organised criminal networks, necessitate effective tactical, operational, and strategic resource management (National Police Chiefs Council, 2017). As Caneppele and Aebi (2017) observed, while traditional forms of 'offline' crime have declined in some areas, more complex criminal activities have increased, straining police resources.

Another critical function of vision and mission statements is their role in delivering value-added public services. Organizations with customer-focused mission statements are more likely to fulfil their promises, thereby enhancing customer satisfaction (Germain and Cooper, 1990). In policing, this translates to how victims and communities perceive their interactions with law enforcement.

Importantly, the benefits of vision and mission statements extend beyond external stakeholders to internal organizational culture. Studies show that these statements can positively influence employee motivation and engagement, particularly when employees participate in their development (Klemm et al., 1991; Bart and Baetz, 1998). This alignment fosters what is often referred to as discretionary effort, enhancing both performance and employee well-being (Hesketh et al., 2016). In policing, where the psychological demands of the job can be significant, this alignment is particularly valuable.

DISTINGUISHING VISION FROM MISSION

Recognizing the value of vision and mission statements is only the first step. Understanding their distinct roles and purposes is equally crucial. A key lesson from organisational science is that form follows function. Structural change, workforce design, and even cultural reform can only succeed when guided by a coherent strategic intent. For police services, this means that clarity of vision and mission must precede workforce models, command structures, or governance reforms. Otherwise, institutional change risks entrenching bureaucracy rather than building purpose.

Vision statements support the pursuit of clarity by focusing on the future, articulating an organization's aspirations and long-term goals. They are inherently broad and inspirational, capturing what the organization seeks to become (Taiwo et al., 2016). Fundamentally, the vision is a destination, encapsulating the essence of an organization's best self.

Mission statements, on the other hand, are more grounded in the present. They define the organization's core purpose, outlining what it does, how it does it, and why (Ostapski and Isaacs, 1992). A well-crafted mission statement provides clarity and focus, enabling an organization to prioritize activities while remaining flexible enough to accommodate evolving objectives (David, 2020).

Despite these distinctions, research reveals frequent confusion between the two, with leaders often using them interchangeably or blending their purposes (Pearce and David, 1987; Salem Khalifa, 2011). Effective development therefore requires a clear understanding of their unique roles and a commitment to crafting both statements in a manner that is complementary, and guides both strategic and operational priorities.

DEVELOPING A VISION AND MISSION STATEMENT

In policing, vision and mission statements are not always accurate descriptions of what the police do (action), but they do express what they want to be perceived as doing by the public (Dario et al., 2022). This is dangerous disconnect as it can create the situation whereby the police service's employee behaviours may be distinct to their outlined vision and mission (Rios et al., 2020). This is most easily exemplified by misuse of force or stop and search practices, which are often driven by aggressive and/or discriminatory policing practices that frequently go against the stated goals of policing (Richardson and Goff, 2012; Trinkner et al., 2019).

This distinction between the mission, vision and action of police services can be attributed to role conflict, with individuals, teams or departments prioritizing legal or occupational responsibilities over the organisation's ambitions (Dario et al., 2022). As such, it is vital that the strategic goals of the police service sufficiently map across the operational and tactical level reality experienced by front line employees, which can be achieved by pursuing certain key principles in their development.

Co-Creation

Mapping vision and mission statements across the frontline reality is often problematic, as their generation has traditionally followed a top-down approach, where senior leaders craft statements in isolation (Alegre & Berbegal-Mirabent, 2017). In hierarchical institutions like policing, this approach is unsurprising. However, research suggests that inclusive, collaborative processes yield better outcomes (David, 2020; Williams et al., 2014). This fact is highlighted by HMICFRS who have identified that *"In higher-performing forces, these had been developed in collaboration with members of the workforce and were widely recognized and adopted"* (HMICFRS, 2017, p12).

It is therefore vital that as a foundational principle, personnel at all levels, from community support officers to chief constables, contribute to their development. This is because frontline officers occupy a unique position and are responsible for translating abstract strategy into lived practice through their daily interactions with citizens. When these officers are included in the design and refinement of mission and vision statements, they help anchor them in operational reality, making them more than aspirational rhetoric. Such participation also enhances their internal legitimacy by fostering a sense of ownership, empowerment, and alignment with shared organisational purpose. As the saying commonly goes, "*If they don't weigh in, they won't buy in*".

Community Involvement

Collaboration in developing vision and mission statements is particularly important in public service organizations, where statements possess a dual-purpose and must balance operational effectiveness with social expectations (Moss et al., 2011). For policing, this encompasses maintaining public trust, confidence, and legitimacy, which have been foundational to UK policing for over a century (The Police Foundation, 2022), while simultaneously delivering effective law enforcement, crime investigation, prevention, and reduction (Dario et al., 2022). Therefore, developing vision and mission statements in policing cannot be the sole domain of senior leadership, or be constructed entirely by service employees alone. Equally important is the principle of inclusion, specifically community voices, and particularly those from groups historically underrepresented or over-policed. This extends to youth groups, faith communities, women's networks, and minority associations, ensuring that the collective vision of policing mirrors the pluralism of modern society.

For the vision and mission statements to gain authenticity, they must be co-created with those who interact with the organisation's values on the ground. This inclusive approach reflects the principle that legitimacy derives from participation, whilst also ensuring that the statements reflect both the internal reality of police work and the external expectations of the public. As Tyler (2006) and Bradford and Jackson (2018) observe, procedural justice and legitimacy in policing depend not simply on effectiveness, but on fairness, voice, and respect.

Involving community representatives, advisory boards, and local partnerships in the development process reinforces and enables each factor (fairness, voice, and respect) as well as embracing diversity and facilitating representativeness, transparency and accountability. In this regard, outstanding police services increasingly recognise that inclusion is not only moral but strategic, as legitimacy cannot be sustained without visible equity and active community co-production.

THE COMPONENT PIECES

To translate strategy into structure and culture, organisations must first distinguish clearly between Mission, Vision, and Action. These three elements operate at different conceptual levels but are mutually dependent and are outlined in Table 1. In simple terms, the mission anchors legitimacy, the vision sets direction, and action ensures delivery. When the three are misaligned, such as when actions pursue numerical efficiency at the expense of purpose, the organisation loses coherence, credibility and legitimacy. Conversely, when every level of the service can trace its daily actions back to a shared mission and forward to a unifying vision, the result is strategic consistency, internal motivation, and improved public confidence. This triadic model reinforces the central argument that in policing, as in other complex public services, strategy must precede structure, and clarity of purpose must precede performance.

Table 1. A description of key features when creating a mission and vision statement.

Element	Core Question	Purpose in Policing	Temporal Focus
Mission (Why)	Why do we exist?	Defines the purpose of the police service	Present / Continuous
Vision (Where)	Where are we going?	Expresses the aspirational future state the police aims to help create.	Future / Aspirational
Action (How)	How will we get there?	Converts mission and vision into operational behaviours, policies, and performance frameworks.	Immediate / Practical

To construct these elements, vision and mission statements must include specific, evidence-based components. For vision statements, two core elements are essential (David, 2020):

1. Priority ambition: The overarching goal or aspiration of the organization.
2. Path to achievement: How the organization intends to achieve this goal.

Vision statements should be succinct, typically one sentence (David, 2020). For example, Durham Constabulary's vision, *"Delivering excellent policing to inspire confidence in victims and our communities,"* effectively conveys ambition, methodology, and stakeholder focus (Durham Constabulary, 2025).

For mission statements, up to nine components are recommended (David, 2020). These include: (1) the service's primary purpose, (2) its self-identity, (3) its key service users, (4) its geographic scope, (5) the core services delivered, (6) its ethical values, (7) its approach to employee well-being, (8) its approach to innovation, and (9) its economic goals. Within these components, it is further recommended that the mission statement contains an accurate description of what the organization does. To this end, a set of coded categories of police behaviours has been proposed for consideration of inclusion (Dario et al., 2022). These include: (1) order maintenance, (2) law enforcement and criminal justice, (3) community-oriented policing, (4) efficiency and productivity, (5) training and education, (6) multi-agency collaboration, (7) administrative services, (8) professionalism, (9) discretion, and (10) accountability.

The Metropolitan Police Service's mission statement provides a strong example of how a police service can encompass their commitment to community needs, technological innovation, employee well-being, and associated police behaviour.

> *"Focus on what matters most to Londoners. Work more closely with partners and the public. Achieve the best outcomes in the pursuit of justice and in the support of victims. Seize the opportunities of data and digital tech. Care for each other, work as a team and be an attractive place to work. Learn from experience, from others, and constantly strive to improve. Be recognised as a responsible, exemplary, and ethical organization".*
> *(Metropolitan Police, 2024)*

Leadership vs. Management as a Key Enabler

Even the best-crafted vision and mission statements require effective policies and culture to bring them to life, and in the forthcoming chapters of this book it will be explored in detail, how police services can embody both statements in their actions, thereby creating an outstanding service. Here, I conclude by briefly outlining how effective implementation of mission and vision statements depend not only on organisational design but on the human element that brings them to life. This is delivered through the final key component of strategic leadership.

The distinction between leadership and management has long been recognised in organisational theory, yet it remains a persistent challenge in policing. Management is primarily concerned with maintenance, and ensuring systems function efficiently, rules are followed, and short-term objectives are met. It is rooted in control, predictability, and the minimisation of risk. Managers preserve stability and enforce compliance, which are critical functions in any large bureaucracy, including policing. However, when management dominates at the expense of leadership, organisations can become process-driven and resistant to change and innovation. In policing, I suggest that decades of procedural reform and performance measurement have produced a service that is highly managed but insufficiently led. Targets, audits, and inspection frameworks have reinforced a culture of administrative compliance and governance, rather than strategic foresight. The result is what Deming (1987) described as activity without improvement, efficiency unmoored from effectiveness.

Leadership, by contrast, is about direction, and provides vision, inspiration, and meaning. It is inherently strategic rather than administrative. Leaders do not simply ensure that things are done right, they ensure that the right things are being done. As Drucker (1973) and Kotter (2008) both emphasised, leadership not only defines purpose, but it also motivates people to pursue it, whereas management ensures that existing systems serve that purpose efficiently. Strategic leadership, therefore, connects organisational purpose to management practice. Leaders who actively communicate and embody the service's mission and vision help bridge the gap between *why* the police exist and *how* they operate, fostering an alignment across all ranks.

As such, embedding strategic leadership throughout policing represents the final key component vital to enabling a shift from managing activity to delivering the purpose set out in clear vision and mission statements. When leaders at every level, from constable to chief constable, understand and champion the organisational vision and mission, police services evolve from a reactive organisation to a proactive institution of public trust, capable of delivering sustained quality outcomes and genuine legitimacy.

CONCLUSION

This chapter has demonstrated the importance of clear, well-defined vision and mission statements in policing. These statements are essential for aligning organizational performance with priorities, enhancing resource efficiency, and fostering employee motivation. However, many UK police services fail to fully leverage these tools, with unclear or inaccessible statements limiting their potential impact.

To address this gap, police services must adopt collaborative, evidence-based approaches to developing these statements, ensuring they reflect reality by considering both operational goals and social purpose. By embedding these statements into governance frameworks and aligning them with day-to-day practices, police services can lay a strong foundation for sustained success. Well-crafted vision and mission statements are not just administrative exercises but vital tools for driving meaningful change in modern policing.

REFERENCES

Alegre, I., & Berbegal-Mirabent, J. (2017). The real mission of the mission statement: A systematic review of the literature. *Academy of Management Proceedings, 2017*(1), 10729. Accessed online. Available at: DOI: 10.5465/ambpp.2017.10729abstract

Bart, C. K., & Baetz, M. C. (1998). The relationship between mission statements and firm performance: An exploratory study. *Journal of Management Studies, 35*(6), 823–853. Accessed online. Available at: DOI: 10.1111/1467-6486.00121

Bradford, B., & Jackson, J. (2018). Police legitimacy among immigrants in Europe: Institutional frames and group position. *European Journal of Criminology, 15*(5), 567–588.

Chandler, A. D. (2009). *Strategy and Structure: Chapters in the History of the industrial Enterprise*. MIT.

Dario, L. M., Cesar, G. T., & Crichlow, V. J. (2022). Reappreciating the varieties of police behavior: A national examination of contemporary police mission statements. *Policing, 45*(6), 893–907.

David, F. R. (1989). How companies define their mission. *Long Range Planning, 22*(1), 90–97. Accessed online. Available at: DOI: 10.1016/0024-6301(89)90055-1

David, F. R. (2020). Analysis of vision and mission statements characteristics and their association with Organizational Performance: A Guide to writing effective vision and mission statements. *Applied Studies in Agribusiness and Commerce, 14*(1-2), 87–95. Accessed online. Available at: DOI: 10.19041/apstract/2020/1-2/11

Deming, W. E. (2018). *Out of the Crisis, reissue*. MIT press.

Drucker, P. (1973). *Management: Tasks, Responsibilities and Practices*. Harper and Row.

Durham Constabulary. (2025) Our commitment. Accessed online. Available at: https://www.durham.police.uk/police-forces/durham-constabulary/areas/about-us/about-us/our-commitment/

Germain, R., & Cooper, M. B. (1990). How a customer mission statement affects company performance. *Industrial Marketing Management, 19*(1), 47–54. Accessed online. Available at: DOI: 10.1016/0019-8501(90)90027-s

Her Majesty's Inspectorate of Constabularies. (2001) Winning the Race: Embracing Diversity. Accessed online. Available at: https://hmicfrs.justiceinspectorates.gov.uk/publications/winning-the-race-embracing-diversity/

Hesketh, I., Cooper, C. L., & Ivy, J. (2016). Wellbeing and engagement in policing: The key to unlocking discretionary effort? *Policing*. Accessed online. Available at: DOI: 10.1093/police/paw021

Hirota, S., Kubo, K., Miyajima, H., Hong, P., & Won Park, Y. (2010). Corporate mission, corporate policies and business outcomes: Evidence from Japan. *Management Decision, 48*(7), 1134–1153. Accessed online. Available at: DOI: 10.1108/00251741011068815

His Majesty's Inspectorate of Constabularies Fire and Rescue. (2017) PEEL: Police leadership. A national overview. Accessed online. Available at: www.hmicfrs.justiceinspectorates.gov.uk

His Majesty's Inspectorate of Constabularies Fire and Rescue (2024) Value for money profiles. Accessed online. Available at: Value for money profiles - His Majesty's Inspectorate of Constabulary and Fire & Rescue Services

Klemm, M., Sanderson, S., & Luffman, G. (1991). Mission statements: Selling corporate values to employees. *Long Range Planning, 24*(3), 73–78. DOI: 10.1016/0024-6301(91)90187-S PMID: 10112154

Kotter, J. P. (2008). *Force for change: How leadership differs from management*. Simon and Schuster.

Leuthesser, L., & Kohli, C. (2014). Mission statements and corporate identity. *Proceedings of the 1996 Academy of Marketing Science (AMS) Annual Conference*, 145–148. DOI: 10.1007/978-3-319-13144-3_40

Lundberg, C. C. (1984). Zero-in: A technique for formulating better mission statements. *Business Horizons, 27*(5), 30–33. DOI: 10.1016/0007-6813(84)90038-7

Metropolitan Police. (2024) About the Met. Accessed online. Available at: https://www.met.police.uk/police-forces/metropolitan-police/areas/about-us/about-the-met/the-met-direction

Moss, T. W., Short, J. C., Payne, G. T., & Lumpkin, G. T. (2011). Dual identities in social ventures: An exploratory study. *Entrepreneurship Theory and Practice, 35*(4), 805–830. DOI: 10.1111/j.1540-6520.2010.00372.x

National Police Chiefs Council. (2017) Better Understanding Demand – Policing the Future. NPCC Performance Management Coordination Committee. Accessed online. Available at: https://www.researchgate.net/publication/356800726_Better_Understanding_Demand_-_Policing_the_Future

Oliver, I. (1987). The Royal Commission on the Police 1962. In: Police, Government and Accountability. Palgrave Macmillan, London. DOI: 10.1007/978-1-349-18557-3_2

Ostapski, S. A., & Isaacs, C. N. (1992). Corporate moral responsibility and the moral audit: Challenges for refuse relief inc. *Journal of Business Ethics*, *11*(3), 231–239. DOI: 10.1007/bf00871971

Pearce, J. A., & David, F. (1987). Corporate mission statements: The bottom line. *The Academy of Management Perspectives*, *1*(2), 109–115. DOI: 10.5465/ame.1987.4275821

Richardson, L. S., & Goff, P. A. (2012). Self-defense and the suspicion heuristic. *Iowa Law Review*, *98*, 293–336.

Rios, V. M., Prieto, G., & Ibarra, J. M. (2020). Mano suave–Mano Dura: Legitimacy policing and Latino stop-and-frisk. *American Sociological Review*, *85*(1), 58–75.

Salem Khalifa, A. (2011). Three F'S for the mission statement: What's next? *Journal of Strategy and Management*, *4*(1), 25–43. DOI: 10.1108/17554251111110104

Taiwo, A. A., Lawal, F. A., & Agwu, E. (2016). Vision and Mission in Organization: Myth or Heuristic Device? *International Journal of Business and Management*, *4*(3).

Taylor, F. W. (1911). *The principles of scientific management*. NuVision Publications, LLC.

The Police Foundation. (2022) The Final Report of the Strategic Review of Policing in England and Wales: A New Mode of Protection - Redesigning Policing and Public Safety for the 21st Century (pp. 1–192).

Trinkner, R., Kerrison, E. M., & Goff, P. A. (2019). The force of fear: Police stereotype threat, self-legitimacy, and support for excessive force. *Law and Human Behavior*, *43*(5), 421–435. PMID: 31305090

Tyler, T. R. (2006). *Why people obey the law*. Princeton university press.

Williams, R., & Morrell, L., D., & V. Mullane, J. (2014). Reinvigorating the mission statement through Top Management Commitment. *Management Decision*, *52*(3), 446–459. DOI: 10.1108/md-10-2012-0736

Chapter 2
Recruitment Selection and Talent Management

Andy Wilson
http://orcid.org/0000-0001-7269-2606
Abertay University, UK

Denise Martin
http://orcid.org/0000-0002-9890-8011
Northumbria University, UK

Neil Leslie
http://orcid.org/0000-0003-0277-9356
Abertay University, UK

ABSTRACT

This chapter explores the effectiveness of police forces in building, developing and maintaining an inclusive workforce. It highlights the requirement for organisations to audit their workforce and demand profile to ensure that both align. It uses case studies of the two forces rated as outstanding by the PEEL Assessment process. The key concepts explored include the psychological contract, employer value proposition (EVP) and an inclusive workforce. The critical role of executive sponsorship and commitment to these programmes designed to support these concepts is identified and discussed. Best practice programmes are identified in the case study areas that have proven impact on early career retention and employee well-being. It is identified that Force Management Statements provide a valuable tool for workforce planning but recognised that additional employee lifecycle planning is required. The chapter call for law enforcement organisations to invest in talent development, leveraging data analytics, executive support and inclusive practices to enhance workforce efficiency.

DOI: 10.4018/979-8-3373-2757-0.ch002

INTRODUCTION

How good is the force at building, developing and looking after its workforce and encouraging an ethical, lawful and inclusive workplace?

The cornerstone of any outstanding organisation is its people; an organisation that neglects this vital resource and fails to implement effective management and strategic planning is likely to encounter significant challenges and potential failure. Efficient organisations recognise that there is a clear link between workforce planning and organisational performance (Walford-Wright & Scott-Jackson, 2018). The HMICFRS inspection framework (HMICFRS, 2025a) assesses forces in this area under the overarching question posed at the start of this chapter. This chapter identifies best practice across a range of public and private organisations to signpost ways that forces can increase their efficiency in this area. The 2021/2022 PEEL Assessments suggest that this is an area that forces need to develop, only two were rated as outstanding, the majority were rated adequate (HMICFRS, 2025b). Using Human Resource related concepts identified in a report prepared by the authors in conjunction with the College of Policing (Martin *et al*, 2022), this Chapter explores the good practice used by the outstanding forces to identify measures that can be implemented to improve performance in this area. The concepts identified are the psychological contract, the employer value proposition and an inclusive workforce.

FORCE MANAGEMENT STATEMENTS (FMS) AND WORKFORCE PLANNING

FMS are self-assessments conducted by Chief Constables (or their London equivalent) that feed the HMICFRS PEEL assessments but also provides a framework for strategic planning (HMICFRS, 2022). The FMS has four steps, Step 2 is dedicated to workforce planning, asking forces to consider capability, capacity, well-being, resilience and condition of their workforce and compare this with their own expectations and other forces across England and Wales. A more detailed explanation is provided by Halford in this volume, see Chapter 7.

Workforce planning is a challenge that is faced by many organisations; whilst police innovation in this area is welcomed, best practice from other organisations can be recognised and adopted. The authors were commissioned by the College of Policing to conduct a scoping review and qualitative research to assess the current position of talent development in policing and identify best practice in talent development across both policing and external organisations (Martin, Leslie, Wilson, van Deus Goss, & Durrant, 2022). Workforce planning encompasses an employee's lifecycle with an organisation, so whilst FMS provide medium term planning tools, policing organisations need to deploy longer foresight and planning models to encapsulate an employee's lifecycle.

Successful organisations employ data analytics[1] as part of their workforce planning; that is, critically analysing human resource data to highlight their demand profile and the skills and knowledge required to respond to said profile. Data analytics also provide a demographic breakdown of the organisation and highlight skills and knowledge gaps. However, there is a requirement to comprehend what is being analysed, *"what good looks like"* (Martin *et al*, 2022, p. 21). Detailed talent audits are required to identify the organisations extant skill capacity and effectively plan for future requirements (Pandita & Ray, 2018; Allegis, 2019; CIPD, 2022); these talent audits should be undertaken on a regular basis to illustrate how the workforce has changed and to help identify barriers that may hinder workforce development. The FMS provides a template for annual talent audits.

PSYCHOLOGICAL CONTRACT

Policing has, perhaps understandably, struggled to look inwardly and reflect on its performance at building and developing its workforce. The Peel Assessments identify that the majority of forces are adequate in this area, with a few graded as "Requiring Improvement" (HMICFRS, 2025a). The two forces awarded outstanding evaluations, Cumbria and Humberside, received this recognition for both their workforce planning and well-being interventions.

This concept refers to the unwritten set of expectations between employee and employing organisation, that encompasses mutual obligations, trust and fairness (Conway & Briner, 2005). Differing from formal contracts, these are subjective and dynamic, shaped by personal experiences and organisational culture. The HMICFRS (2025a) assessments highlight that for early career officers fulfilling this contract is critical for retention and motivation; when this is breached, for example, inadequate support or lack of development opportunities, it can lead to disengagement and attrition. The concept of psychological contracts is both complex and contested, with definitions varying across contexts (McDermott *et al*, 2013).

While some question the ability of a corporate body to form a psychological contract – given its abstract nature - research suggests that employees experience this contract primarily through their line manager, who is perceived as the organisation's representative (Conway & Briner, 2005; McDermott *et al*, 2013). Thus, if a supervisor prioritises performance over well-being, employees interpret this as reflecting the organisation's priorities and a breach of the psychological contract, leading to disengagement and potentially attrition.

HMICFRS (2025a) identified that outstanding forces implement workforce planning strategies focussing on onboarding and early career retention. These strategies recognise the psychological contract between the employee and organisation; fulfilling this contract is critical to the retention and motivation of talent especially during the early stages of a career (Clark-Ambrosini *et al*, 2023). Policing has sometimes struggled with fulfilling this contract, at times of accelerated recruitment emphasis is placed on achieving targets of new officers, overlooking early career development and retention. This brings the risk that negative experiences have an exponentially greater impact than positive ones

> *"if we don't identify them, nurture them, and develop them at the level that they need, then they become disenfranchised, disenchanted" (Police Officer, Research Participant) (Martin et al, 2022, p. 19)*

HMICFRS, through the PEEL assessments, has recognised that both forces awarded Outstanding grades in this area - Cumbria and Humberside - placed this contract at the forefront of their recruitment and early years retention strategies (HMICFRS, 2025a; HMICFRS, 2025c; HMICFRS, 2025d), although without explicitly stating that this is the case.

Both forces graded as outstanding implemented interventions designed to understand the individual concerns of those student officers who were considering leaving the force, designated "Say and Stay" conversations in Humberside and "Stay Conversations" in Cumbria. Unlike perfunctory exit interviews, these are solution focussed interventions, conducted by senior officers empowered to implement practical changes designed to address the concerns of the student officer. Cumbria Constabulary records the outcomes of these conversations on what it calls a "Fair Passport" that accompanies the officer if they move within the organisation, mitigating the need to repeatedly explain the reason for any adjustments. (HMICFRS, 2025c; HMICFRS, 2025d).

Effective talent management strategies require executive support, the senior leadership team must be committed to delivering successful interventions and take an active governance role (CIPD, 2022). In the two outstanding forces, there is clear evidence that student officer retention is recognised as an organisational risk with ownership sitting at Chief Officer level and governance boards monitoring and reviewing retention. Both forces employ data analytics to understand emerging patterns that may be impacting retention rates and seek to identify mitigating interventions (HMICFRS, 2025c; HMICFRS, 2025d).

The psychological contract between student officer and policing organisation is not fulfilled simply by an exit interview, indeed, reaching this stage is indicative of the contract breaking down. The outstanding forces employed a number of initiatives to support their student officers and promote retention in the organisation.

Both forces are proactive in identifying the needs of individual officers at an early stage in their career journey and providing a framework that accompanies the officer to minimise or eliminate the requirement for the student officer to constantly repeat and rehearse specific welfare needs or well-being issues. The needs of student officers are actively supported by a number of means. The traditional policing roles of Sergeant and Tutor Constable continue to form part of this support network, but with enhanced training to reflect different student officer pathways and the distinct requirements to fulfil these pathways. Student officers are allocated a dedicated Tutor Constable, responsible for preparing the student for independent patrol status, but also trained to identify well-being or welfare issues and signpost requisite support. In addition to the hierarchical support, Cumbria Constabulary offer all student officers a 'buddy;' this is an officer who can provide mentoring, advice or simply a different perspective, either for the duration of the officer's training or during times when the officer requires additional support (HMICFRS, 2025c; HMICFRS, 2025d).

Cumbria Constabulary operates a confidential support scheme where either student officers or their colleagues can raise issues and seek additional support for the student officer. This provides an alternative pathway for officers who may feel unwilling or uncomfortable speaking up about a concern, for example if the officer's first line manager (Sergeant) is not supporting the student appropriately. The learning and development team assess confidential referrals and can put additional support measures in place to support the student officer to be successful. The first line manager role is critical for early career officers; the post embodies the psychological contract with the supervisor being the interface between officer and organisation. Forces that received lower gradings in this area had inconsistent management standards with some suggesting that performance management was prioritised over well-being. This tends to undermine the psychological contract and impacts on officer retention (HMICFRS, 2025d).

EMPLOYER VALUE PROPOSITION (EVP)

Often referred to as employer branding, EVP is a critical aspect of employers looking after and developing their workforce, aligned with the psychological contract (see above). In simple terms, it describes the corporate values of an organisation that makes it an attractive employer. Vaiman, Scullion and Collings (2012) argue for an EVP that demonstrates corporate social responsibility, stressing the intrinsic rather than utilitarian rewards for potential employees. The authors contend that the ability to incorporate a strong sense of corporate social responsibility within an organisational EVP indicates to potential employees that the organisation takes seriously the development of an emotional bond with its staff, and the construction of workplace relationships predicated upon mutual respect and trust; factors held to be important in the motivation and retention of key staff.

Suggesting that current talent development strategies may be exacerbating workplace under-representation, Kwon and Jang (2022) advocate that an organisation's EVP must transmit unequivocal commitment to diversity to be effective in the acquisition and retention of talent. Similarly, Pandit and Ray (2018) propose a robust EVP that conveys corporate messages on ethical standards, professionalism, and transparency. Some commentators (see for example: Carpenter (2013); Pritchard (2014)) highlight the importance of producing talent development strategies that grasp the importance of understanding potential employees' attitudes towards the organisation and its brand, and which recognise how the candidate experience of potential employees impacts on brand confidence. In its recent review of policing in England and Wales, the Police Foundation (2022) promotes the idea of police recruitment campaigns that spotlight the elements of policing that centre on public service and the construction of social capital, rather than ones foregrounding the action-oriented, crime-fighting aspects of policing.

In the private sector, best practice organisations take a holistic view of rewarding and retaining talent to encourage talent to join and remain with the organisation extending beyond the financial (Kim *et al*, 2014). When esteem needs are fulfilled, there is greater job satisfaction and motivation (Bethke-Langenegger, Mahler, & Staffelbach, 2011). The public sector has less flexibility in offering holistic rewards packages due to organisational constraints but can satisfy esteem needs by aligning work activities to the strategic objective of public values (Kravariti & Johnston, 2020).

The two constabularies that received an outstanding grade for building, supporting and protecting the workforce demonstrated a number of the characteristics highlighted above as strong characteristics of the EVP; these are in addition to those discussed in the Psychological Contract, discussed above. The employee programmes discussed in this section are focussed more on the whole employee lifecycle and not early career officers. There was a clear feeling from HMICFRS that the forces had a comprehensive understanding of workforce well-being. (HMICFRS, 2025c; HMICFRS, 2025d)

Employee well-being is a critical characteristic of an ethical employer and both forces utilised programmes to enhance this area. Some of these initiatives seem rather simplistic, for example, Humberside's mental health video, *Strength in Being Blue,* but the value of this is in both senior and specialist officers sharing personal experience, both destigmatising mental health and signposting support services. This has been highlighted by Oscar Kilo[2] and the National Police Chiefs' Council (NPCC) as an example of good practice (HMICFRS, 2025d).

Similarly, Cumbria Constabulary's well-being support was praised by officers and staff; the Chief Constable prioritised this as one of four force priorities: 'care for colleagues.' One of the programmes which falls under this priority is Wiser Mind training programme that seeks to develop staff resilience using an evidence-based foundation and presented in a relaxed and informal manner. Like Humberside's video, this intervention has received praise from Oscar Kilo.

One of the strengths of these programmes is a visible and clear level of executive support. The CIPD (2022) recognise that organisational executive leaders are a critical element in delivering success and creating a climate whereby emotional bonds are stimulated between the workforce and the organisation (Pandita & Ray, 2018). Within policing specifically, it is recognised that without executive support, programmes are not actively embedded within the organisation and are less likely to succeed (Martin *et al*, 2022). A high level of executive support for well-being programmes is necessary for these to become part of the organisational branding or EVP.

A further aspect of the employee lifecycle EVP, one that attracted recognition for both outstanding forces, is their support for officers and staff who may be at risk from trauma. Cumbria Constabulary implemented programmes to incorporate managing stress and trauma into training for high-risk posts, complete with signposting to support services. Officers in such high-risk roles undertake psychological screening assessments, stress and risk assessments and open access to occupational health resources (HMICFRS, 2025c).

Humberside were identified for their support in dealing with major and critical investigations, using a case study of a major incident that had the potential to significantly impact well-being. The force set up and resourced a well-being hub with access to quiet rooms, well-being professionals and chaplaincy support. Trauma Risk Management (TRiM[3]) was offered on both initial attendance and after the deployment had been completed. The response to the incident included mutual aid[4] officers who naturally received the same level of well-being support however Humberside ensured that home forces were updated on the well-being support provided to officers so that they were in a position to continue the support and monitor officers. The provision of a well-being hub is recognised by the force as good practice and has been peer reviewed to identify ongoing improvements to the provision (HMICFRS, 2025d).

STRONG MANAGEMENT SKILLS

Effective management skills are also required to ensure efficient Talent Development; D'Annunzio-Green and Ramdhony highlight the place of line managers in providing role modelling and mentoring and development opportunities (2019), but managers can also hinder the development of high performing staff by failing to provide regular support, feedback and goal setting required for development (Kim, et al., 2014) First/second line management were identified as gatekeepers for Talent Development for their ability to identify and develop talent. Data from focus groups with police officers (Martin *et al,* 2022) suggested that line-managers were critical in whether an officer progressed in the service or not. There was recognition that line managers could be subjective when making decisions about who to support for promotion, tending to identify talent in their image and potentially creating a barrier to diversity, equality, and inclusion. There was an acknowledgement that unconscious bias played a role, and that management training required a focus on recognising and avoiding unconscious bias. Harris and Foster (2010), in their research, also found that managers found the equality agenda a challenging space when coming to supporting individuals.

Training and ongoing professional development should be provided to line managers who have a role in Talent Development; this should include the softer, human skills required rather than the processes (Kravariti & Jonston, 2019, Moreton, et al., 2022).

INCLUSIVE WORKFORCE

Policing has faced challenges over the years in developing an inclusive workforce, with police culture seen as a barrier when it came to creating equality of opportunities across the service. Literature on police culture suggests that there are certain characteristics that impact upon progression for those who are not part of the dominant culture; more importantly for talent development, there is a lack of understanding about specific skills and potential due to underlying prejudices and existing stereotypes (Bilkos, 2023). This was identified as a common issue raised in some of the interviews and focus groups, as stated by a respondent in Martin, Leslie, Wilson, van Dues Goss and Durrant (2022), '*but I think underlying some of the issues is the issue of culture, which cannot be challenged so easily.*' (p. 32).

One critical issue, that appeared to be impacting on the progression of females specifically, was the continuation of a macho culture; there was a perception that officers required to display masculine traits to seen as capable to undertake specific roles in the service. For example, research by Player et al (2019) highlight that there is substantial evidence suggesting that the stereotype of a typical leader is highly congruent with masculine traits, and this acts as a barrier to women progressing in leadership roles; specifically they argue that gender influences the perception, promotion, and development of leadership potential, something a respondent in Martin *et al* (2022) identified in policing, arguing that female officers felt they were unsuccessful in promotion processes because male officers were seen to have the requisite qualities.

Both outstanding forces were proactive in supporting student officers in this category, this has largely been discussed in the Psychological Contract section, above. Additionally, through their Say and Stay discussions, the forces were keen to understand the barriers to under-represented officers remaining within the organisation and actively sought to address these barriers.

Policing has often focussed on the recruitment of a diverse workforce, forgetting that it is necessary to retain that diverse workforce which has been recruited (Bury *et al*, 2018). In this aspect, both forces were proactive in supporting the retention and development of a diverse workforce. Humberside Constabulary were recognised for their innovative practice to support and develop women in policing and reducing the barriers to this, as with many such policies, it provides a menu of support rather than providing a 'one size fits all' type intervention and includes both officers seeking promotion and officers seeking access to specialist policing roles such as public order and firearms type roles. Whilst HMICFRS focussed on the development programme for women in policing, it recognised that Humberside support all under-represented groups (HMICFRS, 2025d).

Cumbria Constabulary similarly provides support to encourage representation amongst under reported groups. The force identified that under-represented officers were reticent about seeking developmental opportunities or promotion due to a lack of self-confidence and self-belief. The learning and development team actively supports under-represented candidates sitting national exams and offers mentoring support for interviews and assessments. When they recognised that officers leaving the force through retirement or promotion to other forces negatively impacted the gender balance of the senior leadership team and actively sought to redress this by promoting a female leadership day designed to encourage female staff to seek promotion in Cumbria (HMICFRS, 2025c).

CONCLUSION

Building, developing and sustaining an inclusive and motivated workforce is a core strategy to achieving excellence in policing. This chapter has explored three foundational pillars of effective talent management; fulfilling the psychological contract to strengthen retention and engagement, embedding a robust Employer Value Proposition to foster trust and organisational commitment, and creating an inclusive workforce that reflective of communities served. The success of these pillars, supported by evidence from outstanding organisations, is predicated upon proactive governance, data driven workforce planning and a culture of ownership and accountability at all levels. Talent development must be recognised as a strategic priority with Executive level ownership and governance, integrating well-being, diversity and leadership development into core organisational practice. This aligns with the College of Policing's (2024) *National talent development strategy for policing: Enabling a consistent strategic approach towards inclusive talent development in policing.*

REFERENCES

Allegis. (2019). *The New Meaning of Talent:Adapting to the Work and Workforce of Tomorrow*. Hanover: Allegis Group. Retrieved from https://www.bing.com/ck/a?!&&p=cdf4b8b4e96ad571108f261bb6d48f296c8f03c64d538e9e07153172d7268f3dJmltdHM9MTc2NzU3MTIwMA&ptn=3&ver=2&hsh=4&fclid=221231e9-f88e-672e-252f-27bcf9de6644&psq=The+New+Meaning+of+Talent%3aAdapting+to+the+Work+and+Workforce+of+Tomorr

Bethke-Langenegger, P., Mahler, P., & Staffelbach, B. (2011). Effectiveness of talent management strategies. *European Journal of International Management*, *5*(5), 524–539. DOI: 10.1504/EJIM.2011.042177

Bilkos, L. J. (2023). Taking the temperature: An intersectional examination of diversity acceptance in Canadian police services. *British Journal of Criminology*, *63*, 348–366. DOI: 10.1093/bjc/azac014

Bury, J., Pullerits, M., Edwards, S., Davies, C., & DeMarco, J. (2018). *Enhancing Diversity in Policing*. London: NatCen Social Research. doi:npcc.police.uk/documents/edhr/2018/NatCen%20Enhancing%20Diversity%20in%20Policing%20Report.pdf

Carpenter, L. (2013). Improving the candidate experience. *Strategic HR Review*, *12*(4), 203–208. DOI: 10.1108/SHR-03-2013-0017

CIPD. (2022). *Talent management: Understand the changing context and benefits of talent management, and the key features of a talent management strategy*. Retrieved May 01, 2025, from CIPD: https://www.cipd.co.uk/knowledge/strategy/resourcing/talent-factsheet#gre

Clark-Ambrosini, J. L., Ashleigh, M. J., Higgs, M., & Baruch, Y. (2023). Quid pro quo? The future for graduate development programmes through the lens of talent management. *International Journal of Human Resource Management*, *34*(17). Advance online publication. DOI: 10.1080/09585192.2022.2117991

College of Policing. (2024). *National talent development strategy for policing: Enabling a consistent strategic approach towards inclusive talent development in policing*. College of Policing. College of Policing. Retrieved from https://assets.college.police.uk/s3fs-public/2025-01/national-talent-development-strategy-for-policing.pdf

Conway, N., & Briner, R. B. (2005). *Understanding psychological contracts at work: A critical evaluation of theory and research*. Oxford University Press., DOI: 10.1093/acprof:oso/9780199280643.001.0001

Foley, J., & Massey, K. (2018). Police officers and post-traumatic stress disorder: Discussing the deficit in research, identification and prevention in England and Wales. *The Police Journal: Theory. Practice and Principles*, *92*(1), 23–34. DOI: 10.1177/0032258X18761284

HMICFRS. (2022, October 05). *Force management statement: Guidance and template for forces*. Retrieved from HMICFRS: https://hmicfrs.justiceinspectorates.gov.uk/publication-html/force-management-statement-guidance-for-forces/

HMICFRS. (2025a). *PEEL assessment 2023-2025*. Retrieved from HMICFRS: https://hmicfrs.justiceinspectorates.gov.uk/peel-assessments/what-is-peel/peel-assessments-2023-2025/

HMICFRS. (2025b, April 10). *PEEL Assessments*. Retrieved from HMICGRS: https://hmicfrs.justiceinspectorates.gov.uk/peel-reports-year/2023-25/

HMICFRS. (2025c). *PEEL 2023-2025 Police effectiveness, efficiency and legitimacy: An Inspection of Cumbria Police*. Retrieved from HMICFRS: https://s3-eu-west-2.amazonaws.com/assets-hmicfrs.justiceinspectorates.gov.uk/uploads/peel-assessment-2023-25-cumbria.pdf#page37

HMICFRS. (2025d). *PEEL 2023-2025 Police effectiveness, efficiency and legitimacy*. Retrieved from HMICFRS: https://s3-eu-west-2.amazonaws.com/assets-hmicfrs.justiceinspectorates.gov.uk/uploads/peel-assessment-2023-25-humberside.pdf#page37

Hunt, E., Jones, N., Hastings, V., & Greenberg, N. (2013). TRiM: An organizational response to traumatic events in Cumbria Constabulary. *Occupational Medicine*, *63*(8), 549–555. DOI: 10.1093/occmed/kqt113 PMID: 24174630

Kim, Y., Williams, R., Rothwell, W. J., & Penaloza, P. (2014). A Strategic Model for Technical Management: A Model Based on a Qualitative Case Study. *Performance Improvement Quarterly*, *26*(4), 93–121. DOI: 10.1002/piq.21159

Kravariti, F., & Johnston, K. (2020). Talent management: A critical literature review and research agenda for public sector human resource management. *Public Management Review*, *22*(1), 75–95. DOI: 10.1080/14719037.2019.1638439

Kwon, K., & Jang, S. (2022). There is no good war for talent: A critical review of the literature on talent management. *Employee Relations: The International Journal*, *44*(1), 94–120. DOI: 10.1108/ER-08-2020-0374

Martin, D., Leslie, N., Wilson, A., van Deus Goss, C., & Durrant, S. (2022). A National Strategy for Talent Development in Policing: Key Findings and Recommendations Report. Ryton-on-Dunsmore: College of Policing.

McDermott, A. M., Conway, E., Rousseau, D. M., & Flood, P. C. (2013). Promoting Effective Psychological Contracts Through Leadership: The Missing Link Between HR Strategy and Performance. *Human Resource Management*, *52*(2), 289–310. DOI: 10.1002/hrm.21529

Pandita, D., & Ray, S. (2018). Talent management and employee engagement–a meta-analysis of their impact on talent retention. *Industrial and Commercial Training*, *50*(4), 185–189. DOI: 10.1108/ICT-09-2017-0073

Player, A., Randsley de Moura, G., Leite, A. C., Abrams, D., & Tresh, F. (2019). Overlooked leadership potential: The preference for leadership potential in job candidates who are men vs. women. *Frontiers in Psychology*, *10*. Advance online publication. DOI: 10.3389/fpsyg.2019.00755 PMID: 31040804

Pritchard, K. (2014). Using employee surveys to attract and retain the best talent. *Strategic HR Review*, *13*(2), 59–62. DOI: 10.1108/SHR-10-2013-0100

The Police Foundation. (2022). *Strategic Review of Policing*. Retrieved September 22, 2022, from The Police Foundation: https://www.policingreview.org.uk/wp-content/uploads/srpew_final_report.pdf

Vaiman, V., Scullion, H., & Collings, D. (2012). Talent Management Decision Making. *Management Decision*, *50*(5), 925–941. DOI: 10.1108/00251741211227663

Walford-Wright, G., & Scott-Jackson, W. (2018). Talent Rising; people analytics and technology driving talent acquisition strategy. *Strategic HR Review*, *17*(5), 226–233. DOI: 10.1108/SHR-08-2018-0071

ENDNOTES

1. Data analytics refers to the systematic process of examining workforce-related data to identify patterns, trends, and insights that inform decision-making. In the context of policing, this involves analysing information such as recruitment figures, retention rates, demographic profiles, and skills inventories to forecast future workforce needs, highlight capability gaps, and support strategic planning (Kravariti & Johnston, 2020; HMICFRS, 2022)

2. Oscar Kilo is the National Police Well-being Service https://www.oscarkilo.org.uk

3 Trauma Incident Management (TRiM) is a peer support intervention designed to risk assess, support and educate after a traumatic event (Foley & Massey, 2018; Hunt *et al*, 2013).

4 The provision of support to another agency to ensure they have sufficient resources to meet demand. This is normally, but not exclusively, officers that have specific skills, for example authorised firearms officers.

Chapter 3

The Recruitment and Retention of Special Constables: A Case Study

Steven Wadley
http://orcid.org/0000-0003-4390-8265
Birmingham City University, UK

ABSTRACT

The following case study provides an overview of the challenges surrounding the recruitment and retention of Special Constables (SC) for the 43 police forces in England and Wales and proposes a set of recommendations for organisations to follow in order to maximise volunteer numbers and minimise attrition rates. Fundamentally, the challenges surrounding the recruitment and retention of SCs can be seen as early as the application and assessment stages of the joining process, where inconsistencies in the quality and accessibility of information from force to force, acts as a barrier to entry. Furthermore, a number of reported challenges such as significant time delays, poor communication from recruiting forces and limited support mechanisms are impacting applicant experience, potentially causing candidates to reconsider their decision to join. Further still, the early experiences of Special Constables, from recruitment to first operational deployment, plays a significant part in potentially determining the longevity and commitment to the role, with factors such as negative relationships between Specials and regulars often seen as a common demoralising theme. Focusing specifically on the following HMICFRS (2023b) PEEL inspection framework Question 9 - How good is the force at building, developing, and supporting its workforce and encouraging an ethical, lawful, and inclusive workplace? - this case study primarily explores the impact

DOI: 10.4018/979-8-3373-2757-0.ch003

to Special Constable candidates during the recruitment process but also considers how challenging working relationships and personal experiences may also damage volunteer officer retention levels. In particular, the PEEL 2023-25 cycle places a greater onus on inspecting, "...how forces are ensuring those newly recruited into the organisation are retained and how they develop into front-line leaders" (HMICFRS, 2023b: pg1) which can clearly be applied to both Special Constables as well as regular officers. Lastly, a set of simple and achievable recommendations including more support during the recruitment process, more timely updates from recruiting teams, a culture of respect and acceptance, greater use of conversations with potential leavers, plus the recognition of the value that Special Constables bring to the workforce will be detailed. By embracing these recommendations, police forces should help their respective organisations achieve the outstanding classifications they strive to meet as detailed in the HMICFRS judgement criteria.

INTRODUCTION

Special Constables are unpaid police volunteers who (after completing the requisite training and can demonstrate operational competence) hold the same warranted powers as their 'regular' counterparts (Caless et al., 2010; Callendar et al., 2018). Mostly indistinguishable from their salaried colleagues (the only significant visual difference being the SC lettering on epaulettes), Special Constables contribute to front-line, operational police work (Ramshaw and Cosgrove, 2020), supporting and supplementing full-time officers (Wolf et al., 2017). Each of the 43 forces in England and Wales, plus the British Transport Police have their own Special Constabulary (Britton et al., 2022) where volunteer officers will undertake core policing functions such as investigating crime, ensuring public safety, and delivering crime prevention initiatives (College of Policing, 2025).

Like their salaried colleagues, the Special Constabulary has its own ranking system, that loosely aligns with the standard rank structure of regular officers, namely Special Constable, Special Sergeant, Special Inspector, Special Superintendent and Specials Chief Officer, though multiple freedom of information requests demonstrates slightly differing ranks depending on force. For example, up until the 4th of December 2018, Devon and Cornwall Police had a Specials Chief Superintendent, though on the retirement of that individual, the force made the decision not to replace the rank (Devon and Cornwall Police, 2019), whilst Leicestershire Police (2019) state that they do not go above the rank of Special Chief Inspector. What this demonstrates is that there is a defined pathway for Specials seeking to develop their career and strive for promotion (and the associated roles and responsibilities that comes with it), though what the defined pathway looks like in practical terms, clearly changes based on the force an individual is volunteering with.

On an international scale, versions of the Special Constabulary exist in numerous countries throughout the world, although their core policing remit and functionality may differ to those in the United Kingdom (UK). For example, French reservist personnel focus their efforts on community policing (Thompson, 2022), whilst the Volunteer Special Constabulary (VSC) in Singapore (Singapore Police Force, 2025) has two pathways – one for the 'traditional' policing role and one for those who cannot pass the training and patrol requirements of an armed officer, but instead offer support within the community in areas such as engagement at events and roadshows, crowd control and traffic management.

A BRIEF HISTORY OF THE SPECIAL CONSTABULARY

From an historical context, the Special Constabulary has existed since 1831 when Parliament passed, "An act for amending the laws relative to the appointment of special constables, and for the better preservation of the police" (College of Policing, 2020 pg:1). It is linked to the formation of the first police forces in the early nineteenth century (Gaston and Alexander, 2001), though it can trace its history back further (Cambridgeshire Police, 2025). Over time, the role of the Special Constabulary changed, shifting from being utilised during times of civil unrest or emergency to the more current version of 'ordinary' citizens supporting the police in local neighbourhoods and communities (Home Office, 1967). At their peak in the 1950s, Special Constable numbers exceeded 67,000 (Rogers, 2025), with the highest numbers in the past 20 years being 20,343 in 2012 (Britton, 2020). As of September 2024, there are 5,818 Special Constables on record (Home Office, 2025), illustrating a significant decline in SC numbers, offering a potential warning to forces within the UK that their volunteer capability is rapidly diminishing.

Whilst Special Constables boost operational policing numbers for their adopted force, much of their core value comes from the external expertise that each individual possesses (National Police Chief's Council, 2018) and that they should be considered as a valued source of new experience and skills (Britton and Knight, 2016), that can strengthen policing effectiveness. Volunteers come with a plethora of knowledge and mastery in areas such as operational firefighters (Callendar et al., 2022) and medics (Glenny, 2016), plus they hold an additional intrinsic value as representatives of the communities they will go on to serve (Newburn, 2008; Pepper and Wolf, 2015).

The value of Special Constables (alongside other voluntary positions, (see Millie and Wells, 2019)) to the operational capacity of police forces in England and Wales is significant, with volunteers contributing their free time to support their local forces, equating to millions of hours per year (Britton et al., 2018). Whilst the number of serving Special Constables in each force differs significantly (often based on force size), a smaller force such as Warwickshire Police (2023) will have numbers in the 70 range, whilst larger forces such as West Midlands Police (2023) reporting approximately 245 officers and the greatest number shown by the Metropolitan Police (2023) at 1,466. What is important to take from these figures by way of illustration, is that the voluntary efforts and time given by the Special Constabulary across the 43 forces, roughly equates to 1600 staff members (Wadley, 2024) or a force the size of Cleveland or Gwent Police (Statista, 2024).

Furthermore, volunteers in all sectors are of incredible value, however when in periods of austerity or toughening budgetary restrictions, volunteers offer a much-needed resource that can only be of benefit to public services (Nesbit and Brudney, 2010; Colley, 2012). All of which serves to underpin the significant role the Special Constabulary must play within the broader policing remit and that the recruitment and retention of Special Constables must be considered as one of the keys to ensuring operational policing effectiveness for a modern police force.

KEY ISSUES AND FINDINGS

This case study provides an account of the challenges faced by police organisations tied to the recruitment and retention of volunteer officers of the Special Constabulary and reports to the key issues and findings from a growing body of literature from SC scholars, predominantly surrounding experiences, motivations and retention (see Callendar et al., 2018; Britton et al., 2022; Ramshaw and Cosgrove, 2020; Plimley and Krahenbuhl, 2019). Much less is known about the application and assessment process of joiners, highlighting a knowledge gap in this field of study, though Hesketh and Stubbs (2023) recent work focuses on the recruitment standards and stages with a focus on diversity, whilst Stubbs et al., (2023) looks at the derived value of support via existing social networks and how they can benefit an applicant during recruitment.

Of particular interest to this chapter is the topic wording under PEEL Q9 that states: *The force effectively supports its new recruits, encouraging them to remain* – this is pertinent to this piece as it seeks to reinforce the characteristics of 'good' through understanding: 1) *the challenges faced by new recruits*, 2) *how to make them feel included*, as well as 3) *the force taking the necessary steps to retain them* (HMICFRS, 2023b). By understanding, then applying the main factors detailed above, forces can put measures in place to ensure they are meeting, and exceeding, the PEEL expectations.

A challenging application and assessment process

As a sector with a multi-phased and rigorous application and assessment process, policing organisations most acknowledge the time and effort that volunteers give to recruitment activities – the various stages including the National Sift, in-force interview, bleep test and vetting (College of Policing, 2022) are testament to the depth of the recruitment activities that must all be passed satisfactorily. Where policing struggles and other sectors such as HM Prisons and Probation Service (2024) excels, is in the turnaround time to notify applicants of the outcomes of their assessments. Whilst there is a clear understanding that vetting decisions will rightly take their time, the other elements such as the situational judgement test and behavioural style questionnaire, could and ought to be resolved within a few days. Within Wadley's (2024) study, applicants commented upon the process being *'slow and disjointed'* and with the joining process to be *'a real test of commitment'* and in some instances, having to retake aspects such as the bleep test as they had lapsed during a protracted recruiting time. Comments included:

> *"At some points in the process I was waiting for months at a time with no feedback so maybe just some feedback as to what stage I am at and any progress being made. (R11)"*
>
> *"...You have to really really want to join despite the process and all its expense (travelling to assessments and occupational health) and the time it takes for vetting snd [and] waiting for a [space] in a course...(R3)"*
>
> *(Wadley, 2024: pg8)*

Marshall and Britton (2024), align with aspects of Wadley's (2024) work, and speak to the high rates of attrition due to a slow recruitment and onboarding process (in some instances up to 3 years (Wadley, 2024)) from the time of first application to completion of training. This is a significant factor as the feeling of being left somewhat abandoned was clearly felt by applicants, where the lack of progress updates and feedback on performance from recruiting teams, proving to be a barrier, with the applicant themselves having to show a true test of commitment to make it to the end of the process. Experiences such as these will not leave applicants with a favourable early impression of the force, with the real potential for a protracted and drawn-out process, potentially ending with an individual electing to remove themselves from the recruitment activities.

The need for better support and better information

In order to navigate through the various elements of the recruitment process, applicants must ensure that they are well-versed in the distinct stages and understand the expectations of what needs to be achieved at each step in a practical sense.

As there are a number of different elements to the process that arguably require a different set of skills (an interview is clearly different from a bleep test), it seems fair to state that support and guidance at each layer would prove to be valuable. New recruits alluded to the fact that they would benefit from support from Special Constables, their local force input, additional workshop sessions as well as online session, clearly speaking to the point that any support would be valuable and enhance their chances of success. Of note is the value that applicants put on the ability to engage with Special Constables themselves, showing real perceived benefit to be gleaned from people within the role, both on a practical level and from a peer support perspective, echoing the work of Stubbs et al., (2023).

Participants in Wadley's (2024) study, implied that some of the challenges they faced or pertinent questions they wanted answers to, could not easily be addressed for them, as the recruiting teams and training staff were not Special Constables themselves. They felt that having easy access to SCs would be hugely beneficial to their experience, where honest responses from people who had also gone through the same recruitment process, and were in the role they aspired to be, of immense value and help to allay some of their fears and concerns.

As previously stated, there are multiple layers to the application and assessment process, with each part different from the next. Websites such as the College of Policing (2023), provide a good overview of what a candidate should expect at each stage, plus a set of guidance notes and instructions, offering a satisfactory level of support to applicants. For some, this may prove to be enough, but for others who are less confident or with less experience, may find the process daunting. Therefore, there is a clear gap for forces and their respective recruiting teams, to develop a strong set of guidance documentation, revision material and explanatory videos, that candidates can access whenever needed. HM Government (2019) produced an employee guide to becoming a Special Constable, and whilst it is useful from a surface-level, information-sharing perspective, it does not provide the more comprehensive support applicants may need during the substantial recruitment process.

This is not to say that some of the support listed above does not already exist, merely that there is a discrepancy from force to force in the amount of depth to their recruitment material and that some form of standardisation needs to be put in place moving forwards. Guidance should be issued by the College of Policing, then promulgated down to force level, ensuring that future applicants can have the best support they need to enhance their chances of passing their assessments and taking up positions with their chosen forces.

The special/regular divide

For a newly qualified Special, the impact of being assigned to a station (or at least a group of officers) that have negative predispositions towards volunteer officers can be significant. Callendar et al., (2022) posit that there are numerous incidents where the management and behaviours towards volunteers are unwelcoming and disrespectful with responses from their study stating, "We all know teams, some stations, are wonderful [for Special Constables], and some are toxic. Look at the stats, you can see where they stay, [and] where they don't" (Callendar et al., 2022: pg. 702). Moreover, responses such as this are detrimental to an effective police force and goes against HMICFRS drivers to support new recruits and encouraging them to remain within the service.

In order to tackle this challenge, evidence of good practice was seen by forces such as Humberside Police, whose innovative approach to support new recruits and encourage them to stay in policing, is testament to the positive steps that organisations can take to ensure staff well-being and aid retention. Via their 'Say and Stay' strategy, conversations with their positive action team are used to gain an understanding of why people are considering leaving the force, with the end goal of working towards solutions to keep them in post (HMCIFRS, 2023a). Similarly, Cumbria Police were also recognised as outstanding within the building, supporting, and protecting the workforce category, where a similar strategy encouraging new recruits to stay via one-to-one conversations and support in the areas such as coaching, mentoring, and flexible working arrangement (HMCIFRS, 2023), are further evidence of positive, practical resolutions being utilised. No specifics relating to the Special Constabulary were seen within the wording of the two PEEL assessments, however, it is evident to see that some forces are taking proactive steps to address retention issues, which can be easily replicated for the voluntary element of policing.

Within their work on the experiences of being a Special Constable in the UK, Plimley and Krahenbuhl (2019) refer to a number of their findings that speak positively to their experiences such as participants being proud to be a Special and the rewarding feeling they get from carrying out the role. Conversely, they report on the negative aspects of their experience referring to the 'line of division' that is encountered by Specials from their regular police officer counterparts. Sadly, this is a common theme throughout broader policing with numerous authors (see Gaston and Alexander, 2001; Mirrlees-Black and Byron, 1994; Marshall and Britton, 2024; Callendar et al., 2021) reporting this as a fundamental barrier to the acceptance and development of the Special Constabulary and to the commendation and recognition they deserve.

Exploring this notion further, it is important to recognise the clear differences in 'time served' between a paid officer, to that of a Special Constable, and how this will naturally relate to proficiency, expertise, and experience in operational policing. Using the common metric of a minimum expectation of sixteen voluntary hours per month (Cheshire Constabulary, 2025; British Transport Police, 2025; Sussex Police, 2025), or approximately two shifts, compared to an average working week of 37-40 hours (National Careers Service, 2025) of a paid police officer, it is understandable that even a very committed Special Constable, will take years to become as skilled and proficient as those in full-time employment.

Due to the feelings of inadequacy in the role, Plimley and Krahenbuhl (2019) explore how Specials themselves, report on using the negativity from regular officers as a motivating factor to become better officers and therefore gain more respect from their salaried peers. This aligns with the thoughts of Millie (2019) who explores how voluntary roles are naturally supportive in nature, but also seen as subordinate to paid staff, both civilian and officers, adding additional depth to the challenges faced by SCs. Previous research by Gaston and Alexander (2001) explored a number of factors that underpinned the relationship between the volunteer and paid elements of frontline policing, driving home the value of the aforementioned works. Motives to work as a Special Constable were called into question, alongside levels of capability and effectiveness (Gill and Mawby, 1990), highlighting that some 35 years later, many of the same opinions still ring true.

Linking these concepts together, Pepper (2022) speaks of the importance in the development of a ‘role identity’ (seen as the self-perception and behaviours an individual adopts, based on their perceived role as a law enforcer) which serves two main functions here, particularly from a voluntary capacity. First, the feeling of alignment, belongingness and satisfaction with an organisation, will likely increase the chances of continued volunteering (Tidwell, 2005) and second, role identity takes time to develop, however once established, can again be a critical element in maintaining a long-term commitment to volunteer activity (Penner and Finkelstein, 1998). Applying this to the desired PEEL characteristics, there is evidence to suggest that a greater understanding of role identity, combined with an improved respect for voluntary activities, should assist forces with their retention issues, and foster an environment that ensures all staff feel welcomed and included.

RECOMMENDATIONS

The purpose of this chapter was to highlight some of the fundamental challenges faced by Special Constables at the earliest stages of their journey into their voluntary careers, with the argument being put forward that this happens at the very beginning - that being the application and assessment part of the recruitment process. If this argument is to be accepted, then it should naturally follow that for police forces to meet the 'good' rating and strive for outstanding as per the HMICFRS PEEL framework, then steps need to be taken to work with the Special Constabulary on enhancing their recruitment provision.

Work from Wadley (2024) proposes a key set of recommendations directly tied to improving the application and assessment experiences of Special Constables and must be considered of value as it is the first involvement a candidate has with its potential force of the future. In order to achieve an outstanding service level as per the targets set by HMICFRS, adopting a joined-up approach, which is future focused, is a necessity for all forces as they move forwards. Fundamentally, some of the more time-critical recommendations include:

- *Expediting notification to applicants of the outcomes of their various assessments* – the processing times for most elements (excluding vetting) should be measured in days and not months, improving applicant experience.
- *Improved communication between recruiting teams and applicants* – if there are unexpected delays at any point, then the recruiting team should notify applicants to keep them 'warm' and ensure they are still motivated to join the Special Constabulary.
- *Greater access to support for all elements of the recruitment process* – comprehensive and supportive guidance documentation to be shared by the College of Policing and implemented at force level.
- *Embedding serving (or former) Special Constables within the recruitment teams* – ensures that their lived experience, support, and guidance will prove invaluable to candidates.
- *Sharing of good practice by forces such as Humberside and Cumbria Police* – strong outcomes in the building, supporting, and protecting the workforce aspect of their respective PEEL assessments, are evidence of proactive thinking and implementation of easily replicable strategies to minimise staff exit rates.
- *Reducing attrition rates by removing the specials/regulars divide* – adopting a culture that is welcoming, respectful, that acknowledges skills and expertise and encourages development and longevity as a Special.

In closing this section, it is pertinent to acknowledge one of Marshall and Britton's (2024) drivers for change that fully aligns with Q9 of the PEEL framework – they state that organisations must:

> *"Embed consistently a culture within police forces to treat volunteers with respect, to support them to have the impact they and members of the public would want, and to empower them. Wearing the same uniform, having the same*

powers and responsibilities, and performing the same challenging role should mean something."
(Marshall and Britton, 2024: pg1)

CONCLUSION

For forces seeking an outstanding grading, the correct emphasis needs to be placed upon improving the application and assessment processes for its Special Constable recruits as a first port of call, which in turn should have a significant impact to the retention challenges suffered by forces. In many instances, working as a Special Constable is seen as a stepping stone (Gaston and Alexander, 2001) to becoming a full-time officer and as such, numbers will always fluctuate, and change based on this.

As expressed by Callendar et al., (2022) senior strategic leaders in policing need to be engaged more closely into the debate surrounding the future landscape of the Special Constabulary, with a focus on roles and contribution and must break down the barrier that Special Constables, by their very nature, are of less value or less competent than their regular peers. Recognition of role competence is often attributed to length of service in a role, so a volunteer working a handful of shifts per month, may well take significantly longer to achieve the same level of operational proficiency as a full-time officer, but their commitment to the organisation never needs to come into question.

In order to support, nurture and grow the Special Constabulary and develop officers for future positions within the force, the management structure need to acknowledge and appreciate the value of each SC by their own individual merit. It is easy to understand how regular officers may simply see a new Special Constable on the force as someone who is inexperienced from a policing perspective, but work needs to be carried out to fully explore each participant's background and expertise, and where they can be used to strengthen and enhance frontline policing. The ability to allow Special Constables to specialise in a greater range of roles within policing is testament to how this can be applied – the challenges come from forces who are either resistant to change or who are slow on the uptake.

The opportunity exists to significantly improve the recruitment process moving forwards, with relatively minor steps. The development of a standardised set of comprehensive guidance documentation and associated material, which can be issued to all forces could be the first easy win, in the driver to enhance recruitment, increase volunteer numbers, whittling down negative experiences felt by Special Constable applicants. Recruitment teams should identify Special Constables who can work directly with candidates undertaking the recruitment and selection process – their knowledge and lived experience will not only support during the assessment phase but should help with transitioning to operational policing once they have passed all phases of recruitment and training.

Ultimately, the Special Constabulary is made up of men and women who offer their own time freely and selflessly to the betterment of the force they volunteer for and come with experience and expertise in a plethora of roles, experiences and sectors - all of which have scope to positively impact the community they serve and the organisation they sit within. It would be remiss of forces across the UK to not take the steps necessary to enhance Special Constable experiences (starting from the application and assessment process), especially in a climate where resources are finite and willing volunteers are there to offer their help.

REFERENCES

British Transport Police (2025) [Online] Special Constables. Available at: Special Constables | British Transport Police

Britton, I. (2020). Analysis of Special Constable statistics for England and Wales, Association of Special Constabulary Officers *Policing*, *15*(4), 2053–2069.

Britton, I., Callender, M., & Farquharson, L. (2022). Special beginnings: An explorative study of the early career experiences of volunteer special constables. *The Police Journal*, *96*(4), 611–625.

Britton, I., & Knight, L. (2016). *2030 Vision: Specials and Police Support Volunteers - At the Heart of Policing Reform*. Institute for Public Safety, Crime and Justice, University of Northampton.

Britton, I., Knight, L., & Lugli, V. (2018). *Citizens in Policing 2018 Benchmarking Exercise*. Institute for Public Safety, Crime and Justice.

Caless, B., Bownas, J., Simpson, M., Spruce, B., & Underwood, R. (2010). *Blackstone's Handbook for the Special Constabulary*. Oxford University Press.

Callender, M., Britton, I., & Knight, L. (2022). Exploring strategic perspectives on the Special Constabulary, *Police Journal: Theory. Practice and Principles*, *94*(4), 691–712.

Callender, M., Cahalin, K., Cole, S., Hubbard, L., & Britton, I. (2018). Understanding the Motivations, Morale, and Retention of Special Constables: Findings from a National Survey. *Policing*, *14*(3), 670–685.

Cambridgeshire Constabulary (2025) [Online] A brief history of the special constabulary. Available at: A brief history of the special constabulary | Cambridgeshire Constabulary

Cheshire Constabulary (2025) [Online] The role of a Special Constable. Available at: The role of a special constable | Cheshire Constabulary

College of Policing (2020) [Online] Special Constables. Available at: Special constables | College of Policing

College of Policing (2022) [Online] Joining as a special constable. Available at: Joining as a special constable | College of Policing

College of Policing (2023) [Online] Online assessment process candidate guide. Available at: Online assessment process candidate guide | College of Policing

College of Policing (2025) [Online] Special constable. Available at: Special constable | College of Policing

Colley, H. (2012). Not learning in the workplace: Austerity and the shattering of illusion in public service work. *Journal of Workplace Learning*, *24*, 317–337.

Devon and Cornwall Police (2019) [Online] *Freedom of Information Act Request No: 5694/18.* Available at: 0001 RECORD 1.DOC.doc

Gaston, K., & Alexander, J. (2001). Effective organisation and management of public sector volunteer workers Police Special Constables. *International Journal of Public Sector Management*, *14*(1), 59–74.

Gill, M., & Mawby, R. (1990). *Special Constables: A Study of the Police Reserve.* Gower.

Glenny, L. (2016). Being a special constable and a medic. *BMJ (Clinical Research Ed.)*, *354*, 1–2. PMID: 31055483

HM Government (2019) [Online] Becoming a Special Constable. A Guide for Employees. Available at: Becoming a Special Constable - Employee Guide

Hesketh, I., & Stubbs, G. (2023). Positive action paradox in UK police recruitment: a critical perspective, *Police Journal: Theory. Practice and Principles*, *97*(2), 1–21.

His Majesty's Inspectorate of Constabularies, Fire and Rescue Services (2023) [Online] Cumbria PEEL Assessment 2023-2025. Available at: Cumbria PEEL Assessment 2023–2025 - His Majesty's Inspectorate of Constabulary and Fire & Rescue Services

His Majesty's Inspectorate of Constabularies, Fire and Rescue Services (2023a) [Online] Humberside PEEL Assessment 2023-2025. Available at: Humberside PEEL Assessment 2023–2025 - His Majesty's Inspectorate of Constabulary and Fire & Rescue Services

His Majesty's Inspectorate of Constabularies, Fire and Rescue Services (2023b) [Online] PEEL Assessment Framework (PAF) 2023-2025. Available at: PEEL Assessment Framework (PAF) 2023–2025 - His Majesty's Inspectorate of Constabulary and Fire & Rescue Services

Home Office (1967) Police Manpower, Equipment, and Efficiency: Reports of Three Working Parties, HMSO, London.

Home Office. (2025) [Online] Police workforce, England and Wales: 30 September 2024. Available at: Police workforce, England and Wales: 30 September 2024 - GOV.UK

Leicestershire Police (2019) [Online] *Freedom of Information Request 000009/19.* Available at: Special Constable Ranks - Leicestershire Constabulary - a Freedom of Information request to Leicestershire Constabulary - WhatDoTheyKnow

Marshall, C. and Britton, I. (2024) *The Police Foundation.* Where have all the Special Constables gone and what can we do about it? (long read). Available at: Where have all the Special Constables gone, and what can we do about it? (long read) - The Police Foundation

Metropolitan Police (2023) [Online] Special Constables by Patrol Status. Available at: Special Constables By Patrol Status | Metropolitan Police

Millie, A. (2019). Citizens in policing: The lived reality of being a Police Support Volunteer. *Policing and Society, 29*(4), 407–419.

Millie, A., & Wells, H. (2019). Introduction: Contemporary policing and non-warranted volunteering. *Policing and Society, 29*(4), 371–375.

Mirrlees-Black, C., & Byron, C. (1994) Special Consideration: Issues for the Management and Organisation of the Volunteer Police, Home Office Research and Planning Unit, London National Careers Service (2025) [Online] Police officer. Available at: Police officer | Explore Careers | National Careers Service

National Police Chiefs' Council. (2018) [Online] Special constabulary national strategy, 2018-2023. Available at: https://www.npcc.police.uk/SysSiteAssets/media/downloads/publications/publications-log/2019/npcc-national-special-constabulary-strategy.pdf

Nesbit, R., & Brudney, J. (2010). At your service? Volunteering and national service in 2020. *Public Administration Review, 70*, 107–113.

Newburn, T. (2008). *Handbook of Policing* (2nd ed.). Willan Press.

Nottinghamshire Police (2024) [Online] Force's volunteer officers hit 10,000 hours milestone. Available at: Force's volunteer officers hit 10,000 hours milestone | Nottinghamshire Police

Penner, L., & Finkelstein, M. (1998). Dispositional and structural determinants of volunteerism. *Journal of Personality and Social Psychology, 74*(2), 525–537.

Pepper, I., & Wolf, R. (2015). Volunteering to serve: an international comparison of volunteer police officers in a UK North East Police Force and a US Florida Sheriff's Office, *Police Journal: Theory. Practice and Principles, 88*(3), 209–219.

Pepper, M. (2022). Theorising the police support volunteer experience in an English constabulary: A role identity perspective. *Policing and Society, 32*(8), 1031–1047.

Plimley, S., & Krahenbuhl, S. (2019). *"Proud to be a Special": a qualitative study exploring the experiences of Special Constables in the UK.* Safer Communities.

HM Prison & Probation Service (2024) [Online] Become a probation officer, Available at: How to apply – Prison and Probation Jobs

Ramshaw, P., & Cosgrove, F. (2020). Changing motivations of the special constable: A qualitative analysis of the role of the organisational experience in retaining satisfaction and commitment. *Policing and Society, 33*(8), 933–949.

Rogers, C. (2025) Fact 10: The number of volunteer 'special' constables has reduced from 67,000 in the 1950s to under 10,000 in the last decade. In Lamb, J., Hart, M., Treadwell, J., Lynes, A. and Kelly, C. (Eds) *50 Facts Everyone Should Know About the Police.* Bristol: Bristol University Press, pp 51-56

Singapore Police Force (2025) [Online] Volunteer Special Constabulary VSC. Available at: SPF I Volunteer Special Constabulary

Statista (2024) [Online] Number of police officers in the United Kingdom in 2024, by police force. Available at: UK largest police forces 2024I Statista

Stubbs, G., Elkaroui, E., & Harny, I. (2023). *Understanding the nature of social embeddedness in police recruitment in England and Wales, Police Journal: Theory.* Practice and Principles.

Sussex Police (2025) [Online] Special constables. Available at: Find out how you can volunteer as a Special Constable I Sussex Police

The Police Foundation (2024) [Online] Where have all the Special Constables gone and what can we do about it? Available at: Where have all the Special Constables gone, and what can we do about it? (long read) - The Police Foundation

Thompson, H. (2022) [Online] French police launch recruitment of 30,000 reserve officers, The Connexion, 6th March 2022. Available at: French police launch recruitment of 30,000 reserve officers

Tidwell, M. (2005). A social identity model of prosocial behaviours within nonprofit organisations. *Nonprofit Management & Leadership, 15*(4), 449–467.

Wadley, S. (2024). Improving the application and assessment experiences of special constable candidates in England and Wales. *Policing, 47*(5), 817–830.

Warwickshire Police (2023) [Online] FOI 459-2023/MAY 2023/Special Constables. Available at: FOI 459-2023 / MAY 2023 / Special Constables I Warwickshire Police

West Midlands Police (2023) [Online] Special Constables (728A/23). Available at: Special Constables (728A/23) - Freedom of Information - West Midlands Police

Wolf, R., Pepper, I., & Dobrin, A. (2017). An exploratory international comparison of professional confidence in volunteer policing. *Police Journal (Chichester)*, *90*(2), 91–106.

Chapter 4
Police Education

Denise Martin
http://orcid.org/0000-0002-9890-8011
Northumbria University, UK

ABSTRACT

Introducing higher education routes into policing has raised controversy in recent years (Brown, 2018, Simmel-Binning and Tower 2017). Many argue that having educated officers particularly given the complexity of the role they now engage in is a necessity (NPCC 2016). Research also suggests in can increase public satisfaction and reduce complaints, increase cultural diversity, reduce the use of force and enhance legitimacy (Brown, 2018; Paoline and Terrill, 2015; Paterson, 2011). This chapter will discuss the role of education and development in ensuring police officers have the relevant skills to do their job, including initial training routes and continuous professional development. It will outline what 'good' looks like and why forces need to adapt their approaches and invest more in their people.

INTRODUCTION

Pillar Four of the recent National Police Chiefs Council Policing Vision 2030 is 'to develop and inspire our workforce and evolve our culture'. The proposed outcome is 'to develop a talented, representative and inclusive workforce that feels supported and has the capabilities to meet future policing challenges' (NPCC 2030). The increased emphasis on ensuring a workforce is fully developed and supported has also been incorporated into recent PEEL inspections framework for Her Majesty's Inspectorate of Constabularies and the Fire and Rescue Service (HMICFRS). In both the 2023 to 2025 assessment phase and the current phase 2025 to 2027 one of the core questions that police forces are measured against relates to the workforce and how good they are at building and developing their staff and encouraging an

DOI: 10.4018/979-8-3373-2757-0.ch004

ethical, lawful and inclusive workplace. In the 2023 to 2025 assessment phase this included how those entering the service were developed and retained (HMICFRS 2023). A key framework for developing staff was proposed through the Police Education Qualifications Framework (PEQF) by the College of Policing (2016). The original PEQF model proposed new graduate routes into policing and further suggested that opportunities to gain qualifications should be embedded throughout someone's policing career. This was viewed as critical if forces wanted to successfully continue to build the capabilities and knowledge of staff particularly in the increasingly complex environment in which policing operates (Shohel et al., 2020). While not directly assessed with the HMICFRS PEEL inspections process, retaining new recruits and providing them with the right level of skills is viewed as essential for the organisation. Research suggests that at present the police are struggling to retain police staff even at early stages of someone's career, even though many officers originally intend to stay in the career for 10 years plus, data suggests this is not occurring (Watkinson-Miley et al., 2022; Stanislas 2025). Outstanding forces would aim to support develop and retain their staff. When staff feel that they are invested in there are more likely to experience job satisfaction and remain in post (Smith 2025). This chapter discusses how ensuring effective delivery of routes into policing are essential to a sense of belonging that new recruits have towards the force and how they can potentially improve on their approaches to learning and development to meet broader service requirements. It will also be suggested that this should be assessed as a core part of the PEEL inspection process in the future and that there have been missed opportunities to examine the effectiveness and benefits of police education and skills development in the existing PEEL assessments.

INTRODUCING POLICE EDUCATION

A key strategy for professionalising the police in the UK in recent years has been a shift towards stronger links with Higher Education Institutions (HEI's) and adopting higher degree level qualifications for officers (Tong and Hallenberg 2018, Shohel et al., 2020, Martin 2022). Many argue that having better educated officers is necessary particularly given the complexity of the role they now engage in (NPCC 2016, College of Policing, 2020). Some research suggests that having degree educated officers can increase public satisfaction and reduce complaints, increase cultural diversity, reduce the use of force and enhance legitimacy (Paoline and Terrill, 2015; Paterson, 2011; Brown, 2018). Peter Neyroud (2011) a former Chief Constable, strongly believed that the police required a national regulatory body that was responsible for overseeing the development of a learning culture into policing. He recommended the creation of the College of Policing (COP) who would be responsible for developing a framework of accredited qualifications across the organisation, adopting a code of ethics, and developing a strong knowledge base dictated by scientific evidence. Established in 2012, the COP have proceeded to oversee changes to the delivery of training within policing, including adopting graduate entry through the introduction of the Police Qualifications Education Framework (PEQF), developing a code of ethics, a strong emphasis on the need to adopt evidence-based policing (Sherman, 2013) and the strengthening of police/academic partnerships. The HMICFRS in their annual assessment of police forces similarly argued that extended training as introduced via the PEQF framework will provide officers with the correct levels of skills and knowledge required to do the role. This would suggest that they see this as a critical aspect of improving police services.

THE DEVELOPMENT OF POLICE EDUCATION

The idea of education in policing is not new and even in the early part of the 20th century it was deemed essential for police officers to receive an education (Vollmer & Iwata, 1992). However, the process of embedding higher education into policing has been slow and challenging at times, and influenced by a broader set of political and external dynamics (Ramshaw & Soppitt, 2018; Tong & Hallenberg, 2018, Martin, 2022, Engelmann and Tatnell, 2023). Prior to the introduction of the PEQF, there had been previous attempts to consolidate and improve initial police training through the introduction of the Initial Police Learning and Development Programme (IPLDP) at the start of the 2000s. This was driven by one of the only reports to review police training by the Her Majesty's Inspectorate of Constabulary (HMIC) in their thematic Inspection 'Training Matters' (HMIC 2002). One of the primary concerns raised was that the way police training was structured could make it more difficult to resolve issues regarding the police occupational culture being reinforced through socialisation at training colleges (Heslop, 2011; Ramshaw & Soppitt, 2018). Further concerns were raised around inconsistencies in quality assurance, lack of clear management structure and commitment to training, overall, the current offer was seen no longer fit for purpose (HMIC 2002, Heath 2011). At this time, it was suggested that one solution was for the police to improve its relationship with higher education establishments and look to accredit some of the learning that recruits did. This report was followed by subsequent government policies to further 'professionalise the police' (Flannigan 2008; Neyroud 2011) and introduce enhanced learning and accreditation into policing. Although forces could choose how to deliver the programme, they were encouraged to develop partnerships with universities so as they could undertake some of the classroom delivery. Despite attempts to improve police education through these measures, the outcomes have not necessarily been as intended (Ramshaw & Soppitt, 2018). Heslop (2016) argued that what developed was a mixed economy of police education where there was a variety of different types of approach where police academic partnerships were only one style of delivery, police training also continued to be delivered in house and by private companies. The downside to these arrangements continued to be over quality, content of delivery and a varied approach to education and training across the 43 forces in England and Wales. As Heath (2011) states only 14 constabularies established relationships with HEI's following the initial recommendations by the HMIC report in 2002.

One challenge to the progress of implementing police education has been the resistance to fully embedding educational pathways (Martin 2024, Andrews 2025). Critics argue that policing is a more practical occupation based on developing craft knowledge and experiential learning rather than classroom-based learning (Engelmannn and Tatnell 2025). Internally the perceived value of higher education qualifications has also been questioned (Norman and Williams 2017, Cockcroft & Hallenberg, 2022). Several commentators found officers who had undertaken qualifications while in service often faced scepticism and dismissal of their ideas from colleagues and supervisors (Hallenberg & Cockcroft, 2017; Norman and Williams, 2017). In their research on emerging police studies programmes situated in HEIs, Heslop and White (2011) observed resistance from student officers to engage fully with their course because they perceived it as irrelevant to professional development. This is explained by the disconnect between theory and practice, where students find it difficult to see the relevance of social and police science to their role. In addition, police recruits in some university settings did not necessarily feel that academic staff viewed them as real students because they had not entered academia through traditional routes, creating further tensions between lecturing staff and police students (Heslop, 2011). Research also suggests that officers can face role conflict in relation to being a student and an officer at the same time where expectations and ways of doing things might differ (Heath 2011). The problems identified through attempts to change police recruit training by introducing the IPLDP led to the eventual development of the PEQF framework introduced to formalise educational routes and reinforce the notion that education was critical in shaping the future police workforce.

IMPLEMENTING THE PEQF SUCCESS OR FAILURE

Andrews (2025) argued that some influential Chief Constables have used the cloak of operational independence to suggest that the imposition of a national educational framework limits their ability to fulfil the demands of front-line policing. Other Chief Officers were much more supportive of the PEQF and embraced its expansion and development. This varied response might have had an impact on the success of educational routes success within policing and ultimately whether police forces have invested in these fully.

SUCCESS INDICATORS

Student experience

There is quite substantial support to suggest that engaging with academic programmes is both beneficial and rewarding to police officers whether they have pursued this individually or as part of a graduate entry programme. For example, early evidence of the experience of officers engaging with degree programmes appeared to be positive (College of Policing 2020). However, there has been limited evaluations and any that have been completed show that how students feel about the degree routes can vary according to a range of different factors (Birdsall et al., 2022, Watkinson-Miley 2022, Andrews 2022).

Watkinson-Miley et al (2022) suggested that the success of the new police entry programmes depends on student satisfaction with the learning experience, furthermore it relies on their ability to put that learning into practice and make a connection between theory and practice (Hough and Stanko 2019). Research on police cohorts in Lancashire Constabulary at the early stages of the implementation of the new programmes compared the experiences of IPLTP, PCDA and PEQF found overall that students wanted more protected time to learn, more scenario-based teaching, better lecturing, less online provision and more time for critical reflection (Birdsall 2022). While students studying on the PCDA are provided with protected study leave to enable them to complete their studies away from work stresses there has been mixed reviews on whether students are always afforded the opportunity to fully participate in their protected study times (College of Policing 2022).

Student Success and support

One of the critical indicators of success is the progression and retention of students on these policing programmes is student support. For example, the COP survey (College of Policing 2022) on new PCDA recruits' satisfaction with university education and training was most strongly correlated with satisfaction with support from university staff, online learning, and the amount of study being clearly explained during recruitment.

On all routes assessed by the College of Policing survey, worse mental wellbeing and work-life balance were strongly correlated with dissatisfaction with support from tutor constables, force trainers and line managers. This demonstrates the importance not just on the delivery of the programmes but the surrounding infrastructure organisationally to support initial entry programmes be successful. For instance, Cockcroft et al's (2025) research suggested that as new recruits were viewed as a much-needed resource by their organisations their learning and development were viewed as secondary, this was reinforced by tutor constables who felt that there was little space for supporting reflective practice for those under their supervision.

Providing students with the support they need to manage their studies while working in a highly pressured profession can be difficult to get right. In assessing the ability of police forces to ensure students success only 2 forces were identified as outstanding in the Peel Inspection Process in the 2023 to 2025 Framework. For example, Cumbria were praised for focusing on the development needs of individual officers by tracking their progression and putting systems in place to identify any welfare or well-being needs (HMICFRS 2024a).

Similarly, Humberside also rated outstanding for the supporting students in their progress looking after their welfare needs and supporting their learning and practice by assessing all students for neurodivergence including dyslexia. The force ensures a record was kept on students so the correct adaptations could be put in place to ensure their needs were met (HMICFRS 2024b). Other forces although not rated outstanding in the broader question of supporting the workforce they were also praised by the HMICFRS in supporting new recruits when they provided examples of supporting them to manage challenges to learning (providing dyslexia support), systems to support and identify recruits that may consider leaving, for example retention ambassadors (HMICFRS 2025) and supporting the well being of recruits after experiencing challenging incidents (HMICFRS 2024C).

BARRIERS TO SUCCESS

One of the biggest challenges to the introduction of the new constable entry routes has been strengthening the link between academia and policing (Martin and Wooff 2020, Bacon 2021). Effective and success collaboration was viewed as a critical element to delivering these new programmes but also to enhance the evidence-based practice into policing. Where research by academics can be useful in providing police services with evidence of what works best in preventing and reducing crime. This has proved a continued barrier with the world of academic and police often being seen as at odds with each other or as Bradly and Nixon (2009) suggested a dialogue of the deaf where the two worlds of academia and policing collide and have different perspectives on the value of research and what is can offer as well as generally working in different ways that are not always compatible

(Hallenberg, 2012) . While police academic partnerships have improved over time, these alliances are still fragile and difficult to manage (Bacon et al., 2021).

Strong collaboration can overcome this in relation to police and academic relationships. However, negotiating partnerships can be complex and rely on individual relationships between the academic institution and individual police services (Martin and Wooff 2019). In could also depend on the delivery model, Andrews (2023) suggests that sole delivery models which tend to separate police and academic training are not conducive to creating sustainable partnerships. Collaborative approaches are much more effective. There have been successful partnerships that are proving strong relationships can help to develop police officers and help them gain good results in relation to embedding evidence-based policing (Rogers et al., 2022, Richards & Hammond, 2025). Establishing strong educational partnerships is also important for officer success and there are now many examples where police forces and their educational partners are working effectively to produce positive outcomes on the new police constable degree programmes across England and Wales (Leek 2020, Honess and Clarke 2023, Norman et al., 2025; Richards & Hammond, 2025). These positive partnerships should be reported in the PEEL Inspections as they reflect an encouraging change in creating and supporting police officers to gain accreditation for their role but also because it demonstrates a strong relationship with partners to improve police education and develop the profession. Often relationships build through education partnerships can stimulate opportunities for collaborative research or knowledge exchange to support police innovation and work toward creating the police as a learning environment.

CONTINUING PROFESSION DEVELOPMENT (CPD)

The professionalisation of policing is not just about supporting initial recruits but like other recognised professions should have a dedication to life-long learning which is view as critically important to ensure that police within the organisation retain the skills. It can also support professionals' commitment and sense of organisational connection (Williams et al., 2022). The HMICFRS PEEL Assessment framework does to some extent assess a force's ability to develop staff, but the assessments tend to focus on where forces are supporting diversity initiatives or have clear systems in place to support staff well-being. Also, some assessments examine programmes in place to support first line leaders. Reference to CPD appears to be limited in this framework and it is difficult to ascertain how this is assessed through the inspection process. However, according to the PEEL framework outcomes table only 2 forces (already named) achieved an Outstanding grade for the question on building and development their workforce.

The College of the Policing have a role to play in supporting professional development, setting standards for professional practice particularly in operational aspects of the role. It has created an infrastructure where there is a body to co-ordinate and support professional development around policing. Creating such as national body to oversee the continued development of the profession is positive and it provides an opportunity to implement key standards and skills development opportunities (College of Policing 2013).

Despite the changing landscape and the setting up of a national body to support CPD the picture on how forces prioritise staff development is mixed. Research found that between the period of 2011/12 and 2017/18, 33 of the 43 forces reduced their budgeted spending on training in real terms by a greater percentage than their overall reduction in spending (Martin et al., 2019a). There was a real lack of investment in monetary terms but also in strategic direction and valuing the skills and capabilities of existing members of staff (Martin et al., 2019a; Martin et al., 2019b; Engelmann & Tatnell, 2025). Certain elements of training are prioritised, for example operational aspects of police services are well developed in relation to CPD but this is not consistent across police forces or across roles. For example, recent work on police investigations on rape and serious sexual offences (RASSO) identified that there were several gaps in opportunities for formal learning and CPD opportunities for investigators (Williams et al., 2022) This is supported in work by Honess (2020) who suggested that most officers were dissatisfied with the level of ongoing training they received feeling they were not offered to opportunity to update their learning. Prospects for development and training are still not being felt across the whole service. The pay and morale survey issues by the Police Federation (2024) provides a picture of dissatisfaction with the opportunities available for staff with approximately 40% of staff responding to the survey reporting that they were either very dissatisfied or dissatisfied with the CPD opportunities available. While officers were aware of the availability of Personal Development Reviews (PDR's), nearly half (48%) of respondents were not satisfied with their experience of this process. Martin et al., (2019b) found that there were discrepancies in practice across forces in relation to the PDR systems with some forces demonstrating clear structures in place where in other forces PDR processes had been neglected or were insufficient. This is also reflected in the HMICFRS PEEL assessments.

CONCLUSIONS

The emphasis on Police Education has increased in recent years particularly with the introduction of the PEQF, subsumed by the Police Constable Entry Routes. This has led to an increased number of officers entering the police with the opportunity to gain a qualification whilst working. The introduction of this framework has not been without its issues including a lack of broad acceptance by the police service itself (Honess and Clark 2023, Andrews, 2025). This has meant embedding the new routes into policing has been difficult. Despite these challenges the growth and improving relationships between police and higher educational institutions has helped to strengthen these partnerships and the delivery of the police curriculum. Those who are successful in this space have managed to work through the issues to deliver strong programmes that provide students with the support and knowledge they need to do their roles. This still needs to become even more embedded and spread more widely. Recently a new journal to showcase the work of students' officers has also been developed again demonstrating the desire by dedicated colleagues to enhance the educational experience of officers and support better engagement with evidence-based policing (LJMU 2024). Officers realising the value of educational experience and qualifications still needs to be measured and evaluated over the longer term, but we know that there is evidence to suggest those that gain accredited qualifications personally benefit from their engagement with higher education (Norman and Fleming 2022). Research (Andrews 2024) also suggests that higher levels of qualification are more desirable to the public strengthening the argument that education is also important for enhancing police trust and legitimacy a critical issues given recent declines in support for policing (Casey 2023).

Further opportunities for embedding of life-long learning into policing still needs to be developed further. In the Strategic Policing Review by the Police Foundation (Police Foundation 2022) it was suggested that there needs to be increased investment in CPD and that high quality learning opportunities should be developed. A further suggestion is to embed learning at every level of the organisation, support is required to develop individual, group and organisational skills and abilities, which in turn will contribute to the creation of new knowledge and confidence within and across the organisation (Martin et al., 2019a) Putting in appropriate systems and processes to enable learning and to share good practice within, across and from outside the organisations is also critical (Williams et al., 2016) . This means improving performance review processes and creating better opportunities for staff to engage in appropriately designed and structured CPD that aims to enhance and support their role.

While some forces are taking steps to improve the opportunities available to police staff and officers (Martin 2019b HMICFS 2024), the development of CPD could still be better across the board. Only a small number of forces rated good or outstanding in the HMICFRS PEEL assessments 2023 to 2025 in relation to building, supporting and protecting the workforce. As the work by Williams et al (2022) demonstrates this is not just about providing CPD but ensuring it is relevant to the role and is designed to enable police personnel to do their job effectively with sufficient investment and support from the organisation. Evidence suggests that this is also what police personnel also want. There is a desire there for more opportunities to develop and strengthen skills and knowledge that staff have and to ensure that the service has the capabilities required for the complex roles and responsibilities they now face. The advantages of embedding opportunities for staff are likely to also support retention and recruitment.

As a result, it is important that the HMICFRS continue to assess forces on their ability to build and support the workforce as this is critical for effective delivery of police services. They could also build upon this further by expanding their assessment further by asking more in-depth questions about what forces offer to staff in relation to education and CPD and the extent to which this supports their development in the workforce. Overall, there is still a lack of evidence on the impact that education and. other learning opportunities provided to police officers and staff. At present the Inspections do not go far enough to make clear judgements about whether forces are sufficiently addressing the skills requirements of their workforce and whether they have developing the capabilities and capacity to meet future police demands. A most robust systems to identify those forces doing this well is required.

REFERENCES

Andrews, T. (2023). Perceptions of student officers of the police constable degree apprenticeship. *The Police Journal, 97*(4), 634–657. DOI: 10.1177/0032258X231208904

Andrews, T. (2024). Public expectations of police education in England and Wales. *Policing. Journal of Policy Practice, 18*, paad101.

Andrews, T. (2025). Education or indoctrination? An exploration of the resistance towards making policing a degree-level profession. *The Police Journal, 98*(1), 234–248.

Bacon, M., Shapland, J., Skinns, L., & White, A. (2021). Fragile alliances: Culture, funding and sustainability in police–academic partnerships. *Evidence & Policy, 17*(1), 93–109.

Brown, J. (2018). Do Graduate Police Officers Make a Difference to Policing? Results of an Integrative Literature Review. *Policing I, 14*(1), 9–30.

Cockcroft, T., & Hallenberg, K. M. (2022). Unpacking the Blue Box: Structure, control and education in policing. *Policing and Society, 32*(9), 1146–1165.

College of Policing. (2013) About us. Available at: https:// www.app.college.police .uk/about-app/ Accessed 20/01/2026).

College of Policing. (2016). *Developing and Delivering an Education Qualification Framework for Policing: The College of Policing Response to the Consultation. Ryton-On-Dunsmore.* College of Policing.

College of Policing. (2020). Evaluation of the Police Constable Degree Apprenticeship (PCDA): First Interim Report. https://whatworks.college.police.uk/Research/Docu ments/PCDA_evaluation.pdf. Accessed 28 June 2025).

Engelmann, L., & Tatnell, A. (2023). Researching police professionalisation in Scotland, Sweden, and Finland. In *Introduction to Policing Research* (pp. 77-93). Routledge.

Engelmann, L., & Tatnell, A. A. (2025). Blending the 'craft'and 'science' of policing: Challenges and opportunities for police as professional learning organizations. *Policing. Journal of Policy Practice, 19*, paaf036.

Hallenberg, K. (2012). Scholarly detectives: Police professionalisation via academic education (Doctoral thesis, The University of Manchester).

Hallenberg, K. & Cockcroft, T. (2017). From indifference to hostility: Police officers, organizational responses and the symbolic value of 'in-service' higher education in policing. *Policing: a journal of policy and practice, 11*(3), 273-288.

Heslop, R. (2011). 'The British Police Service: Professionalization or 'McDonaldization'?'. *International Journal of Police Science & Management, 13*(4), 312–321.

Heslop, R. (2016). A comparison of police pre-employment training and education in the UK and USA. In *4th Annual Conference of the Higher Education Forum for Learning and Development in Policing (POLCON 4).*

HMIC. (2002). *Training Matters*. HMSO.

HMICFRS. (2024C) PEEL 2023–25 Police effectiveness, efficiency and legitimacy An inspection of Cambridgeshire Constabulary. https://s3-eu-west-2.amazonaws.com/assets-hmicfrs.justiceinspectorates.gov.uk/uploads/peel-assessment-2023-25-cambridgeshire.pdf. Accessed 12/01/2025.

HMICFRS. (2024a) PEEL 2023–2025: An inspection of Cumbria Constabulary https://hmicfrs.justiceinspectorates.gov.uk/publications/peel-assessment-2023-25-cumbria. Accessed 24/04/25.

HMICFRS. (2024b) PEEL 2023–2025: An inspection of Humberside Police, https://hmicfrs.justiceinspectorates.gov.uk/publications/peel-assessment-2023-25-humberside. Accessed 23/05/2025

HMICFS. (2025) PEEL 2023–25 Police effectiveness, efficiency and legitimacy An inspection of Essex Police. https://s3-eu-west-2.amazonaws.com/assets-hmicfrs.justiceinspectorates.gov.uk/uploads/peel-assessment-2023-25-essex.pdf. Accessed 12/01/2026.

Honess, R., & Clarke, S. (2023). 'It's Not "Uni" Work, it's Essential Learning to be a Police Officer': Examining the Higher Education Elements of Police Education Qualifications Framework Programmes, *Policing. Journal of Policy Practice, 17*, paad023. Advance online publication. DOI: 10.1093/police/paad023

Hough, M., & Stanko, E. A. (2019). 'Designing Degree-Level Courses for Police Recruits in England and Wales: Some Issues and Challenges.' Policing. *Journal of Policy Practice*, *14*(1), 31–42.

Hough, M., & Stanko, E. A. (2019). 'Designing Degree-Level Courses for Police Recruits in England and Wales: Some Issues and Challenges.' Policing. *Journal of Policy Practice*, *14*(1), 31–42.

Leek, A. F. (2020). Police forces as learning organisations: learning through apprenticeships. *Higher education, skills and work-based learning, 10*(5), 741-750.

LJMU. (2024) Policing Journal, https://www.ljmu.ac.uk/about-us/news/articles/2024/8/13/policing-journal. Accessed 3 July 2025.

Martin, D. (2022). Understanding the reconstruction of police professionalism in the UK. *Policing and Society, 32*(7), 931–946.

Martin, D. (2024). The re-emergence of police education. *International Journal of Police Science & Management, 26*(4), 452–459.

Martin, D., Hartley, J., Khalil, L., & Harding, R. (2019a). *Strategic Narrative for Learning and Development. MOPAC and The Open University. Available at: Martin, D., Khalil, L., Harding, R. (2019b) Collaborative Deep Dive Summary Report.* MOPAC and The Open University., https://university.open.ac.uk/centres/policing/sites/www.open.ac.uk.centres.policing/files/files/MOPAC/Strategic%20Narrative%20Final%20Version%20Final%20V1_2

Martin, D., & Wooff, A. (2020, June). Treading the Front-Line: Tartanization and Police–Academic Partnerships, *Policing. Journal of Policy Practice, 14*(2), 325–336.

Neyroud, P. (2011). *Review of Police Leadership and Training*. Home Office.

Norman, J., & Fleming, J. (2022). Utilising police knowledge and skills: Experiences from police practitioners studying a police specific degree. *International Journal of Police Science & Management, 24*(2), 162-174. https://doi.org/ (Original work published 2022)DOI: 10.1177/14613557211064051

Norman, J., Lambert, J., & Partridge, L. (2025). Police-Academic Partnerships: Delivering the Police Constable Degree Apprenticeship. In *Creativity and Critique in Digital Learning and Teaching: Insights for Learning Design in Business and Law* (pp. 151–177). Springer Nature Switzerland.

Norman, J., & Williams, E. (2017) 'Putting Learning into Practice: Self-Reflections from Cops', European Law Enforcement Research Bulletin – Special Conference Edition, no. 3, pp. 197-203.

Paoline, E. A., Terrill, W., & Rossler, M. T. (2015). Higher Education, College Degree Major, and Police Occupational Attitudes. *Journal of Criminal Justice Education, 26*(1), 49–73.

Paterson, C. (2011). Adding Value? A Review of the International Literature on the Role of Higher Education in Police Training and Education. *Police Practice and Research, 12*(4), 286–297.

Police Federation. (2024) Pay and Morale Survey https://www.polfed.org/resources/pay-and-morale-survey. Accessed 25/06/25.

Ramshaw, P., & Soppitt, S. (2018). Educating the recruited and recruiting the educated: Can the new Police Education Qualifications Framework in England and Wales succeed where others have faltered. *International Journal of Police Science & Management, 20*(4), 243-250. https://doi.org/ (Original work published 2018) DOI: 10.1177/1461355718814850

Richards, J., & Hammond, L. (2025). Innovative approaches to embedding evidence-based policing, supporting police learning and continuing professional development: Reflections from a police–academic partnership. *International Journal of Police Science & Management*, •••, 14613557251395972.

Rogers, C., Pepper, I., & Skilling, L. (2022). Evidence-based policing for crime prevention in England and Wales: Perception and use by new police recruits. *Crime Prevention and Community Safety*, *24*, 328–341. DOI: 10.1057/s41300-022-00158-w

Sherman, L. W. (2013). The rise of evidence-based policing: Targeting, testing, and tracking. *Crime and Justice*, *42*(1), 377–451.

Shohel, M. M. C., Uddin, G., Parker-McLeod, J., & Silverstone, D. (2020). 'Police Education in the United Kingdom: Challenges and Future Directions. In Nugmanova, M. (Ed.), *Education.* Human Rights and Peace in Sustainable Development, IntechOpen.

Simmill-Binning, C. A., & Towers, J. S. (2017) 'Education, Training and Learning in Policing in England and Wales', Policing Research Partnership. https://eprints.lancs.ac.uk/88307/1/N8_PRP_TL_Report_FINAL.pdf [Accessed: 28/06/2025].

Smith, R. (2025). Lifelong Learning: Exploring Inclusive Adult Education Amongst Police Officers in England and Wales. In *Inclusive Adult Education: Embedding Diversity and Supporting Alternative Learning Environments in UK Higher Education* (pp. 101–117). Springer Nature Switzerland.

Stanislas, P. (2025). The Negative Consequences of the Recruitment and Retention Crisis on Policing in the United Kingdom. In *Special Topics in Policing: Critical Issues and Global Perspectives* (Vol. 3, pp. 3–12). Springer Nature Switzerland.

Terpstra, J., & Schaap, D. (2021). The politics of higher police education: An international comparative perspective. *Policing: a journal of policy and practice, 15*(4), 2407-2418.

Tong, S., & Hallenberg, K. (2018). Education and the police professionalisation agenda: a perspective from England and Wales. In Rogers, C., & Frevel, B. (Eds.), *Higher Education and Police: An International View* (pp. 17–34). Springer International.

Vollmer, T. R., & Iwata, B. A. (1992). Differential reinforcement as treatment for behavior disorders: Procedural and functional variations. *Research in Developmental Disabilities, 13*(4), 393–417. DOI: 10.1016/0891-4222(92)90013-v PMID: 1509180

Watkinson-Miley, C., Cox, C., & Deshpande, M. (2022). A New Generation of Police Officers: Experiences of Student Officers Undertaking the Police Constable Degree Apprenticeship in One UK Police Force, *Policing. Journal of Policy Practice, 16*(1), 122–134. DOI: 10.1093/police/paab062

Williams, B. N., Brower, R. S., & Klay, W. E. (2016). Community-centred police professionalism: A template for reflective professionals and learning organisations with implications for the co-production of public safety and public order. *The Police Journal, 89*(2), 151–173.

Williams, E., Norman, J., Ward, R., & Harding, R. (2022). Linking professionalism, learning and wellbeing in the context of rape investigation: Early findings from Project Bluestone. *International Criminology, 2*(3), 262–275.

Winsor, T. (2011) The Independent Review of Police Officer and Staff Remunerations and Conditions, Part 1 (Cmmd Paper 8024). London: HMSO.

Chapter 5
Sustainability of the Police Education Qualification Framework and Associated Potential

Kate Benson
http://orcid.org/0009-0006-9190-0769
Brunel University of London, UK

ABSTRACT

This chapter presents a case study examining the sustainability of the Police Education Qualifications Framework (PEQF) by exploring its origins and assessing the future potential of a more highly educated police workforce. It analyses the College of Policing's professionalisation agenda and the introduction of a standardised national curriculum, considering concerns around creating an increasingly educated and potentially perceived as 'elitist' police service. The chapter evaluates the operational implications of the rapid influx of young and inexperienced officers and identifies key barriers to embedding evidence-based policing within current organisational cultures. Finally, it highlights opportunities to reduce police–academic bureaucracy and strengthen long-term collaborative partnerships essential for meaningful and enduring reform.

INTRODUCTION

Public confidence in the police has become increasingly strained, with police professionalism frequently scrutinised in the global media (Bartkowiak-Théron, 2019). Sir Michael Barber, author of the *Strategic Review of Policing,* argued that

DOI: 10.4018/979-8-3373-2757-0.ch005

the perpetual high-profile cases of police misconduct have contributed to a deterioration in public confidence (Barber, 2022). Barber acknowledges that there has been some evidence of police reform; however, the recent well-documented independent review into policing culture found racism and misogyny have had a lasting effect (Casey, 2023). Forces must therefore regain public trust and confidence, which is central to the concept of policing by consent in England and Wales (Hyde, 2022). One proposal to achieve cultural change has been to establish policing as an academic discipline (Martin, 2024).

In a dynamically changing world, the appetite for becoming a police officer as a lifelong career profession has lessened. Robust leadership is essential for shaping organisational culture, supporting workforce wellbeing, and fostering an environment in which officers feel valued and motivated to remain in service. Whilst the Police Education Qualifications Framework (PEQF) is not an isolated PEEL inspection criterion, the delivery of effective and professional policing increasingly relies on policing leadership that recognises that officers need to possess both comprehensive training and a strong educational foundation to meet the demands of contemporary police work (Pepper et al, 2025).

The evolving challenges facing policing and the need to strengthen the credibility of police education have brought police training and professional development back to the forefront of policy and academic debate. In England and Wales, this has prompted a shift from traditional craft-based vocational training towards a higher-education model (McDowall and Brown, 2019). This case study chapter therefore examines the development and prospective trajectory of the Police Education Qualifications Framework to illustrate what a highly educated police workforce may look like.

CONTEXTUALISING THE POLICE EDUCATION QUALIFICATIONS FRAMEWORK

A modern-day police officer is required to balance numerous political and societal pressures, in addition to an increasingly complex caseload and a variety of crime types. Former police training was labelled as insufficient to prepare officers for the changes in demand (Ramshaw and Soppitt, 2018; Martin, 2024), and a shift towards police education was born. The College of Policing, established in 2012 as the central body for determining police standards in England and Wales, embarked on a professionalism agenda to reform police education (Williams et al, 2019). Current reforms to re-professionalise policing have been shaped by the introduction of the

PEQF and the rise of evidence-based approaches, rooted in professional autonomy and practitioner-led trust.

In 2010, Neyroud's *Review of Police Leadership and Training* encouraged forces to develop a stronger police-academic partnership, more closely linking operational practice to academic research and training (Home Office, 2010). The PEQF was subsequently designed as a concept in 2016 by the College of Policing together with the UK Government to support the delivery of the Policing Vision 2025 (National Police Chiefs' Council, 2016), with the first degree recruits enrolled in 2018. The Policing Vision 2025, which predates the two subsequent iterations, was a 10-year strategy to identify key priority themes such as shaping resource allocation and a more representative workforce. This strategy hoped to attract and recruit diverse applicants (College of Policing, 2020) where police officers and staff would better align both in their skillset and the communities which the police represent.

The PEQF brought opportunity for three new Level 6 pathways for police recruits: a pre-joiner degree in Professional Policing, a fee-free (for the learner) three-year Police Constable Degree Apprenticeship (PCDA) and a two-year Degree-Holder Entry Programme (DHEP) diploma (College of Policing, 2020). The momentum of academic accreditation of police education quickly grew, and 42 of the 43 England and Wales police forces had transitioned to deliver one or more of the initial learning programmes by March 2022 (College of Policing, 2022a).

Predating the PEQF was the Initial Police Learning and Development Programme (IPLDP), a shorter, localised police training delivered to all new probationary recruits. The IPLDP and PEQF represent markedly different approaches to probationer training, with the methods of instruction, curriculum content, and assessment strategies varying substantially (College of Policing, 2020). Under the PEQF, all recruits graduate with a Level 6 qualification, whereas accreditation of the IPLDP remained optional and inconsistently implemented across forces. Operating since 2006, the IPLDP was characterised as redundant and insufficiently aligned with the complexities of contemporary frontline policing (College of Policing, 2020), with 28 forces discontinuing the outdated IPLDP by 2021 (College of Policing, 2021). Of note, PCDA students expressed higher overall satisfaction than those on the IPLDP pathway, yet many found the academic demands challenging and stressful, particularly given that the completion of the degree was required to secure their continued employment (College of Policing, 2022b).

The launch of the PEQF coincided with the Police Uplift Programme, a Conservative Government initiative requiring the recruitment of 20,000 new police officers in England and Wales to be in post by 2023 (College of Policing, 2021). An expansion of police capacity was broadly welcomed, particularly given that "*England and Wales have fewer police officers per head of population than any comparable European nation*" (Jacques, 2022). Nonetheless, the commitment to recruit 20,000 additional officers was insufficient to meet the European average of 357 officers per 100,000 people. Research suggests that forces would need to recruit approximately 70,000 further officers to achieve parity, in addition to the 20,000 already pledged (Jacques, 2022).

The rapid recruitment of over 20,000 new officers under the Police Uplift Programme was not without challenges (Pepper et al, 2025). The accelerated recruitment resulted in an inexperienced frontline, with officers stretched beyond their limits managing their own workload and that of their new recruit counterparts. His Majesty's Inspectorate of Constabulary and Fire & Rescue Services 2018/2019 PEEL inspections warned that a vast increase in workforce numbers inspections risked masking underperformance, as larger personnel structures can cover gaps in capability and overall effectiveness (HMICFRS, 2020).

Between March 2020 and January 2021, the Conservative Government implemented three national lockdowns in response to the COVID-19 pandemic (HM Government, 2021). The immediate closure of schools, retail, and non-essential hospitality sectors resulted in an unprecedented number of workers across multiple industries seeking alternative employment. Despite the wider market disruption, police recruitment under the Police Uplift Programme continued largely unaffected, drawing consistently high application volumes from individuals across a range of professional backgrounds. This influx broadened the diversity of experience, skills, and occupational histories represented within the new policing cohorts, enriching the workforce in ways not typically seen under previous recruitment conditions.

PERCEIVED ELITISM OF A DEGREE-EDUCATED WORKFORCE

Good policing and the qualities of a good police officer are intertwined (McDowell and Brown, 2019). The PEQF aims to professionalise policing by recognising the complexity and diversity of the role (Police Federation, 2019), whilst bringing officer education in line with other public sector organisations such as nursing, midwifery and teaching. Compulsory degree police education seeks to raise professional standards by producing a more academically trained workforce, which in turn may help challenge entrenched negative occupational cultures within the organisation (Martin, 2024). This is supported by evidence from other sectors, such as healthcare, where degree-qualified nurses have been associated with improved patient outcomes, suggesting that an educated workforce can positively influence operational effectiveness (Williams, 2023).

The PEQF is developed through formal, contracted partnerships between police forces and higher education providers across England and Wales. The collaboratively designed programme content must align with the College of Policing's National

Policing Curriculum (Pepper et al, 2025). The nationally standardised framework for police education was intended to promote equity in training quality across forces and provider consortia, supporting greater consistency for probationers. In its formative years, governance of the PEQF largely centred on the implementation support given by the College of Policing and governmental oversight (Martin, 2024), reinforced by the rigorous quality assurance processes implemented by the accrediting academic provider.

The PEQF aimed to bring inclusivity, open-mindedness and opportunity, with the College of Policing (2020) stating the degree route is "*an enabler to join, not a barrier*". However, limiting police recruitment solely through the PEQF pathways excludes a cross-section of society, risks reinforcing perceptions of elitism, and misses opportunities to fulfil a representative workforce. Critics argue the compulsory degree model exploits the fragility of police legitimacy, concerned that graduate education "*could make police elitist leading to a disconnect with communities*" (Martin, 2024, p.454). However, Neyroud disagrees, claiming that historical concerns connecting educational requirements with social elitism have lessened over time, as a substantial proportion of working-age adults in England now hold high-level qualifications (Home Office, 2010).

The duration of the PEQF (a two-year diploma or a three-year degree) was a deterrent for some applicants and forces alike. Forces such as Hampshire and Isle of Wight Constabulary (2024) withdrew from higher education routes and closed their degree apprenticeship programmes, only to reinstate the PCDA shortly after when losing student officers to neighbouring forces. This suggests, at least in part, that there is a sustained demand for higher-education pathways into policing.

In 2022, the IPLDP was reinstated by the Conservative Government to run alongside the PEQF to increase operational resilience. Scrapping compulsory degrees was seen as a backwards step by many academics (Williams, 2023), undermining the broader professionalisation agenda that sought to embed higher-level academic learning within police education. The IPLDP formally ended following amendments to the Police Regulations in April 2023 (College of Policing, 2022a), though not before creating the conditions for a potential two-tier entry system (see *Police Constable Entry Programme*, College of Policing, 2025).

BARRIERS TO THE IMPLEMENTATION OF THE PEQF

Central to the wider professionalisation agenda was the notion that PEQF recruits would have the prospect to embed their academic learning in operational practice (Williams and Sondhi, 2022). Unlike traditional police training, contemporary police education emphasises understanding research, contextualising the Evidence-Based

Policing (EBP) agenda, and integrating evidence into decision-making (Williams et al., 2019). EBP offers the potential to adopt a targeted approach to address rising demands with limited resources.

The limited capacity for evidence-based policing in an environment saturated by change is evident. Opportunities for practical application of EBP have often been discouraged in operational contexts, with police graduates reporting a lack of support from peers and line managers when seeking to apply their newfound policing knowledge to the organisation (Williams et al, 2019). Findings from a qualitative study of police Bachelor of Science graduates (predating the PEQF) concluded that "*officers need to be trusted and encouraged to use their learning in a way that develops their own personal sense of professionalism*" (Williams et al, 2019, p.259).

A great emphasis is placed on soft skills and effective communication within academic environments (Martin, 2024) to prepare students with the "*knowledge, skills, attitudes and behaviour to meet the increasingly complex demand of contemporary policing*" (Ramshaw and Soppitt, 2018, p.245). These soft skills cultivated through the PEQF are readily transferable to operational practice (Williams, 2023). Degree students are required to learn critical thinking, research skills, reflective practice and leadership, in addition to law, legislation, policy and procedures (Williams, 2023). Through carefully constructed assessment design, interpersonal skills such as teamwork, public speaking and active listening are developed through presentations, reflective journals and briefing orders. Given the increasing complexity of contemporary policing, officers must engage with a broad evidence base to inform real-time decision-making.

PEQF students find it challenging to balance their academic studies and operational demands. The College of Policing, in collaboration with the Home Office, periodically conducted qualitative interviews with student officers to assess both the PEQF and the Police Uplift Programme (College of Policing, 2022b). Students reported feeling better prepared with concepts such as EBP, critical thinking and problem-solving approaches as a PEQF learner (College of Policing, 2023). In contrast, recruits undertaking the early iteration of the PEQF placed little importance on the academic component, perceiving it to be disconnected from the practical realities of frontline policing and questioned the relevance of a degree-level qualification to operational practice (College of Policing, 2022). In a pilot study of four police forces analysing the perception and implementation potential of EBP, one participant stated "*We have a treadmill existence. There is no time to step aside and work out more efficient ways to do it. We can barely stay up to date with the constant changes in policy and law, let alone research*" (Fleming and Wingrove, 2017, p.211).

Professionalising policing through mandatory degree education was set to create the 'leaders of tomorrow', however, many forces appear to lack the organisational culture and infrastructure necessary to embed EBP into everyday policing practice

(Williams, 2019). Reducing barriers to EBP requires forces to cultivate officer autonomy, encourage innovation, and rebalance the emphasis on narrowly defined performance metrics (Fleming & Wingrove, 2017). Ultimately, the impact of EBP will remain limited unless the organisation itself recognises the value of meaningful change.

It is recommended therefore, that forces view the current PEQF probationers as an opportunity to shape the future leaders of the organisation. Senior officers pursuing academic qualifications tend to be viewed more favourably than early-career officers, who are often questioned about the relevance or necessity of obtaining additional qualifications at the outset of their service (Martin, 2024). In this context, strong future leaders should be nurtured to develop the capability of meeting the complex demands of policing through high-level critical and creative thinking (Roberts et al, 2016).

SUSTAINING THE PEQF THROUGH DIVERSITY OF RECRUITMENT STRATEGIES

In the wake of professionalisation reform, the policing landscape has shifted. Forces are managing an inexperienced workforce, both in service and experience. The higher education policing model has created a junior workforce, with over a third of officers having less than five years' service and resignation rates increasing year on year (Pepper et al, 2025).

Prior to the Police Uplift Programme (College of Policing, 2021), Home Office figures from 2017 to 2019 indicate a 131% increase in police officers under 26 years of age (Williams and Sondhi, 2022). Williams and Sondhi (2022) predicted that approximately 80 per cent of the 20,000-recruitment target would be under 26 years old, doubling the proportion of young officers in this short period. There was a noticeable shift in personal priorities following the COVID-19 pandemic, with younger officers favouring a work-life balance ahead of their operational policing role (Williams and Sondhi, 2022). Young officers require a contemporary style of leadership and expect additional support through transparent and linear management structures. This may cause friction with some longer-serving officers, who have only known a ‘top-down’ hierarchical command (Williams and Sondhi, 2022).

One strand of The Policing Vision 2025 (National Police Chiefs' Council, 2016) sought to shape a more diverse workforce through academic accountability, and the PEQF may have encouraged applicants who would have otherwise been deterred from a career in policing (College of Policing, 2020). Police recruitment models often prioritise meeting recruitment targets over retaining experienced personnel. The demand on police services and the complexity of investigations have risen, yet there are fewer officers and staff to investigate (HMICFRS, 2020). Certain nuances of policing cannot be conveyed through classroom-based, didactic instruction, including professional curiosity and intuition that arise when a situation does not align with the information presented. Recruitment strategies that emphasise high volumes of entry-level recruits at lower cost undervalue the craft expertise developed through years of service, ultimately weakening the depth of experience within the workforce.

The 2019 HMICFRS *PEEL Spotlight Report* highlighted that only seven per cent of police officers in England and Wales identified as being from an ethnic minority background. Whilst this was the highest percentage on record, proportionally, officers from diverse backgrounds are still underrepresented relative to the wider population (HMICFRS, 2020). By 2024, Home Office data indicated that white officers account for 91.6% of the police workforce, while officers from minority ethnic backgrounds (excluding white minority groups) comprise the remaining 8.4% (Home Office, 2025). The HMICFRS *Race and Policing review* reported encouraging signs of leadership within the Police Uplift Programme, noting a clear emphasis on recruiting and retaining a more diverse workforce (HMICFRS, 2023). However, consulted stakeholders indicated that meaningful progress would require stronger strategic direction and sustained commitment from the Home Office.

To enhance workforce diversity, several police forces have introduced tailored entry pathways specifically designed for military veterans. Forces have recognised the closely shared qualities, transferable skills and proven resilience gained through military service, enabling ex-military personnel to join the police without the listed entry requirement qualifications in some areas (Devon and Cornwall Police, 2025). In 2023, Nottinghamshire Police, in collaboration with the University of Derby, developed the *Military Service Leavers Pathway into Policing*. This pioneering initiative was designed as a Level 4 qualification to support individuals in their military resettlement period, accelerating participants into frontline policing roles. The 12-week pilot enabled ex-military personnel to fast-track through the first year of the PCDA, joining their police counterparts for a two-year probation period (Nottinghamshire Police, 2023). The combination of on and off-the-job learning was delivered in partnership with the University of Derby, the Ministry of Defence, and the Career Transition Partnership. This programme has been widely regarded by forces as an effective mechanism for strengthening police–academic collaboration and facilitating the transition of veterans and service leavers into policing.

While the PEQF expands opportunities for diverse entry into policing, recruitment alone cannot achieve a representative workforce (Casey, 2023). Effective retention strategies are essential if the diversity growth facilitated by the PEQF is to be maintained and translated into long-term organisational change. Taking the UK's largest Metropolitan Police Service as an example, female officers are leaving at a slightly higher rate than their male counterparts, with this trend particularly evident among new recruits. Although overall probationer attrition remains relatively low at around 10 per cent, female recruits are resigning at four times the rate of probationers (Casey, 2023). Forces should focus on retaining recruits and encouraging those with experienced careers to remain.

CONCLUSION

There is an increased awareness of the value higher education can bring to policing, and yet, the resistance to the academisation of policing persists (Martin, 2024). The credibility of police education lies in the ability to balance craft skills and academic rigour. There is a long-held notion that recruits should actively participate in operational, practical policing as their primary knowledge. Police education programmes should strive to achieve a balanced integration of academic study and operational training to ensure recruits are both intellectually equipped and professionally prepared for the complex demands of modern policing. Organisations should welcome knowledge contributions from their staff, encourage innovation, openness and strategic foresight.

Successful partnerships between police forces and academic institutions are long overdue, and many previous attempts have failed. The PEQF style of compulsory education was initially perceived as a hindrance. Rising operational demands coincided with lengthy periods of university abstraction, while frontline capability was further weakened by a largely inexperienced workforce. Long-term sustainability requires ongoing investment, strong relationships and a genuine collaboration between academic and police institutions for multi-stakeholder success (Martin, 2024). Embedding long-lasting academic and police collaborations is imperative to improve the organisational culture and infrastructure to support the College of Policing professionalisation agenda (Ramshaw and Soppitt, 2018).

There remains limited empirical research comparing the operational performance of graduate and non-graduate officers, making it difficult to determine the impact of degree-level education versus traditional craft-based training (McDowell and Brown, 2019). More research is needed to assess the impact of higher education on policing (Martin, 2024) and the integral relationships which this can bring to the professionalism agenda. The long-term viability of the PEQF depends on its ability to evolve with societal expectations, embed continuous professional development, and uphold rigorous educational standards. Through the integration of ethical training, cultural competence, and evidence-based practice, the framework has the potential to cultivate a more professional and outstanding policing workforce. If these elements are upheld, the PEQF can serve as a resilient model for professional policing that meets the contemporary challenges, while reinforcing public trust and legitimacy.

REFERENCES

Barber, M. (2022). The final report of the Strategic review of Policing in England and Wales. Accessed online. Available at: https://police-foundation.org.uk/policingreview2022/wp-content/uploads/srpew_final_report_summary.pdf

Bartkowiak-Théron, I. (2019). Research in police education: Current trends. *Police Practice and Research, 20*(3), 220–224. DOI: 10.1080/15614263.2019.1598064

Casey, L. (2023). BARONESS CASEY REVIEW Final Report. https://www.met.police.uk/SysSiteAssets/media/downloads/met/about-us/baroness-casey-review/update-march-2023/baroness-casey-review-march-2023a.pdf

College of Policing. (2020). Policing Education Qualifications Framework Initial entry routes. Learning to date: development and implementation, 2016 to 2019. https://assets.college.police.uk/s3fs-public/2021-02/peqf-learning-to-date.pdf

College of Policing. (2021). College of Policing Limited Annual Report and Accounts for the year ended 31 March 2021. https://assets.college.police.uk/s3fs-public/2021-12/Annual-Report-and-Accounts-2021.pdf

College of Policing. (2022a). College of Policing Limited Annual Report and Accounts for the year ended 31 March 2022. https://assets.college.police.uk/s3fs-public/2022-12/College-of-Policing-annual-report-and-accounts-2022-web.pdf

College of Policing. (2022b). New recruits survey 2022: Views of student officers. https://assets.college.police.uk/s3fs-public/2022-12/New-recruits-survey-December-2022.pdf

College of Policing. (2023). College of Policing New recruits survey 2023: View of student officers. https://assets.college.police.uk/s3fs-public/2024-07/New-recruits-survey.pdf

College of Policing. (2025) Joining the police as a new police constable (PC) | College of Policing. https://www.college.police.uk/career-learning/joining-police/joining-new-pc

Devon and Cornwall Police. (2025) Veteran recruitment - Dorset Police and Devon & Cornwall Police working in Partnership https://recruitment.devon-cornwall.police.uk/devon-cornwall-police-careers/veteran-recruitment/

Fleming, J., & Wingrove, J. (2017, June). 'We Would If We Could … but Not Sure If We Can': Implementing Evidence-Based Practice: The Evidence-Based Practice Agenda in the UK, Policing. *Journal of Policy Practice*, *11*(2), 202–213. DOI: 10.1093/police/pax006

Government, H. M. (2021). Government News. Accessed online. Available at: https://www.gov.uk/government/news/prime-minister-announces-national-lockdown

Hampshire and Isle of Wight Constabulary. (2024). Apprenticeships: Hampshire and Isle of Wight Constabulary. Accessed online. Available at: https://www.hampshire.police.uk/police-forces/hampshire-constabulary/areas/careers/careers/apprenticeships/

His Majesty's Inspectorate of Constabulary and Fire & Rescue Services. (2020). PEEL spotlight report: Diverging under pressure - An overview of 2018/19 PEEL inspections. https://assets-hmicfrs.justiceinspectorates.gov.uk/uploads/peel-spotlight-report-diverging-under-pressure-2018-19-overview.pdf

His Majesty's Inspectorate of Constabulary and Fire & Rescue Services. (2023). Race and Policing: A review of the police service's leadership and governance arrangements for race-related matters - His Majesty's Inspectorate of Constabulary and Fire & Rescue Services https://hmicfrs.justiceinspectorates.gov.uk/publication-html/review-of-the-police-services-leadership-and-governance-arrangements-for-race-related-matters/

Home Office. (2010). Police Leadership and Training report: review. https://assets.publishing.service.gov.uk/media/5a7ae186ed915d71db8b3247/report.pdf

Home Office. (2025). Police workforce, England and Wales: 31 March 2024 - GOV.UK. https://www.gov.uk/government/statistics/police-workforce-england-and-wales-31-march-2024/police-workforce-england-and-wales-31-march-2024

Hyde, R. (2022). The thin(ning) blue line: Police numbers and the impact on crime in society https://policinginsight.com/feature/analysis/the-thinning-blue-line-police-numbers-and-the-impact-on-crime-in-society/

Jacques, P. (2022). Police Professional | England and Wales have fewer police officers than any major European nation https://policeprofessional.com/news/england-and-wales-have-fewer-police-officers-than-any-major-european-nation/

Martin, D. (2024). The re-emergence of police education. *International Journal of Police Science & Management*, *26*(4), 452–459. DOI: 10.1177/14613557241298821

McDowall, A., Brown, J. (2019). Do Good Cops Need a Degree? Introduction to the Special Issue on Developing and Evaluating Graduate Policing Training, *Policing: A Journal of Policy and Practice*, Volume 14, Issue 1, March 2020, Pages 1–8, https://doi.org/DOI: 10.1093/police/paz072

National Police Chiefs' Council. (2016). Policing Vision 2025. https://www.npcc.police.uk/SysSiteAssets/media/downloads/publications/policing-vision/policing-vision-2025.pdf

Nottinghamshire Police. (2023). Pioneering military recruitment scheme showcased to UK police forces | Nottinghamshire Police https://www.nottinghamshire.police.uk/news/nottinghamshire/news/news/2023/december/pioneering-military-recruitment-scheme-showcased-to-uk-police-forces/

Pepper, I., Gardiner, C., Dwyer, J., Bartkowiak-Théron, I., & O'Connor, C. D. (2025). Incorporating Higher Education into Initial Police Training: An International Comparison of Practices and Challenges. *Journal of Criminal Justice Education*, •••, 1–23. DOI: 10.1080/10511253.2025.2460812

Police Federation. (2019). Police Federation Research & Policy Support Briefing Paper: Policing Education Qualifications Framework (PEQF) implementation Frequently Asked Questions (2019). https://www.polfed.org/Wilts/media/1580/policing-eductation-qualifications-framework-faqs.pdf

Ramshaw, P., & Soppitt, S. (2018). Educating the recruited and recruiting the educated: Can the new Police Education Qualifications Framework in England and Wales succeed where others have faltered. *International Journal of Police Science & Management*, *20*(4), 243–250. DOI: 10.1177/1461355718814850

Roberts, K., Herrington, V., Jones, W., White, J., & Day, D. (2016, March). Police Leadership in 2045: The Value of Education in Developing Leadership, Policing. *Journal of Policy Practice*, *10*(1), 26–33. DOI: 10.1093/police/pav045

Williams, E., Norman, J., & Rowe, M. (2019). The police education qualification framework: A professional agenda or building professionals? *Police Practice and Research*, *20*(3), 259–272. DOI: 10.1080/15614263.2019.1598070

Williams, E., & Sondhi, A. (2022). A Narrative Review of the Literature on the Recruitment of Younger Police Officers in Age and in Service: What Are the Implications for the Police in England and Wales? Policing. *Journal of Policy Practice*, *16*(4), 648–662. DOI: 10.1093/police/paac001

Williams, T. (2023) Axing police degree rule 'backward step' | Times Higher Education (THE) https://www.timeshighereducation.com/news/braverman-axing-compulsory-degrees-police-starts-backwards-step

Chapter 6
Mental Health and Wellbeing in Policing:
Occupational Mental Health in Policing – Findings From the UK and Ireland

Paul Gavin
http://orcid.org/0000-0002-6216-0144
University of the West of England, UK

Finley MacDonald
University of the West of England, UK

Cody Porter
University of the West of England, UK

ABSTRACT

Policing is an increasingly complex occupation, shaped by evolving crime, public attitudes, resource constraints, and policy shifts. This chapter explores occupational stressors affecting police officers' mental health and morale, examining both organizational and operational pressures. Key stressors include trauma exposure, workplace bullying, heavy workloads, and limited managerial support, all intensified by policing culture. Drawing on data from 152 officers in the UK and Ireland, it highlights barriers to seeking mental health support and the urgent need for systemic change.

DOI: 10.4018/979-8-3373-2757-0.ch006

INTRODUCTION

Policing is a challenging and complex job, even under the best of circumstances. Police officers are expected to balance a wide range of responsibilities. These include responding to emergencies, crime prevention, victim support and community engagement. On any given day they might encounter incidents of child abuse, domestic violence, substance misuse, sexual offending or murder. All these incidents require a different emotional response and a different set of skills, and all can place a significant strain on the mental wellbeing of police officers. The stress associated with police work is now widely recognised and typically falls into two categories: operational stress, which is linked with the frontline nature of the job, and organisational stress, which relates to internal structures and workplace culture (Gavin & Porter, 2024; Porter & Gavin, 2024; Purbu & Demou, 2019).

The PEEL assessment framework (2023-2025) (His Majesty's Inspectorate of Constabulary and Fire & Rescue Services, 2023) identifies as a topic area that "The force understands the main factors that influence its workforce's well-being and takes effective action to address any related problems." The characteristics of good which would demonstrate and satisfy this are set out as follows: "1. The force clearly understands what factors have positive and negative effects on its workforce's well-being, as well as any related stress, in all areas. It uses this understanding to inform resourcing decisions and aims to strike a balance between operational needs and looking after its people. 2. The force is taking effective action to address any well-being challenges it has identified. It provides a good range of preventative and supportive measures, including enhanced support to those in high-risk roles or those experiencing potentially traumatic incidents. 3. The force's occupational health service provides support and interventions that improve officer and staff well-being." These were expanded on in the PEEL assessment framework (2025-2027) (His Majesty's Inspectorate of Constabulary and Fire & Rescue Services, 2025) which clearly set out the importance of the police forces ability to attract, develop and retain its workforce. It states that that the police force should support its workforce by making good efforts to retain officers and staff through understanding the well-being challenges that its workforce faces. It does this through leadership and management at all levels, who "prioritise and promote the physical and mental health of all officers and staff".

In 2023 two of the authors (Gavin and Porter) published an online survey which considered the impact of the policing role on the mental health of police officers in the UK and in Ireland. These jurisdictions were chosen as they are both English speaking, follow common law systems and have very close social, historical and cultural ties. The findings presented in this chapter are based on analysis of the following research questions which were posed to participants:

1. How would you rate your mental health? - Before starting your job and now
2. How has your job impacted upon your mental health?
3. How does your organisation support mental health?
4. What do you feel are the main barriers to accessing mental health support in your organisation?

OPERATIONAL AND ORGANISATIONAL STRESSORS IN POLICING

Operational stressors, associated with the frontline, day-to-day nature of police work, often include exposure to traumatic events, violence, crimes involving children, and the handling of sexual offences (Brewin et al., 2022; Miller et al., 2022). While some view such exposure as simply being a part of the policing role (Foley et al., 2023; Porter & Lee, 2023), it can evoke emotions such as fear, rejection, humiliation, and abandonment (Mind, n.d.). Police officers are also subject to organisational stressors like those in other professions. These stressors include shift work, long hours, inadequate pay, insufficient support from senior management, excessive workloads, increasing administrative responsibilities, and the impact of austerity measures on staffing levels (Solar & Smith, 2022). It has been argued that organisational stressors may be more significant sources of stress for police officers than operational stressors, as officers often perceive them as oppressive, unnecessary, unavoidable, and beyond their control (Purba & Demou, 2019).

Exposure to organisational and operational stressors can lead to Emergency Responder Exhaustion Syndrome (Kirschman et al., 2014; Edwards & Wilkerson, 2020), symptoms of which include anger, depression, isolation, and exhaustion, with more severe manifestations such as insomnia, hypervigilance, chronic fear, panic attacks, emotional constriction, depersonalization, memory disturbances, and agoraphobia (Kirschman et al., 2014). Both are closely associated with a decline in organisational commitment, increased absenteeism and presenteeism, and concerns regarding staff retention and voluntary resignations from the police force (Stevelink et al., 2020; Charman & Bennett, 2022). Exposure may also lead to a range of mental health issues, including Post-Traumatic Stress Disorder (PTSD) and Complex Post-Traumatic Stress Disorder (CPTSD) (Stevelink et al., 2020; Brewin et al., 2022), depression, anxiety (Jetelina et al., 2020; Stevelink et al., 2020), and burnout. The prevalence of PTSD and depression among police officers is more than twice that of the general population (Kessler et al., 2005; Syed et al., 2020), and these conditions are linked to substance abuse (Menard & Arter, 2014), absenteeism, aggression (Rajaratnam et al., 2011), self-harm and suicide (McCafferty et al., 1992; Hem et al., 2001). PTSD has also been shown to impair cognitive functioning in police officers, with those affected exhibiting lower performance in executive function, verbal learning, memory, and lexical access compared to their peers without PTSD (Bisson Desrochers et al., 2021).

Support is made available to police officers after a critical or traumatic incident. This is typically through a welfare led process known as Trauma Risk Management 'TRiM', through the 'Emergency Services Trauma Intervention Programme 'ESTIP' or through Critical Incident Stress Management 'CISM'. Trauma Risk Management (TRiM) is a UK-based peer-support programme developed to reduce stigma surrounding mental health within the armed forces and police services (Frappell-Cooke et al., 2010; Greenberg et al., 2008). Typically implemented following exposure to critical or traumatic incidents, TRiM recognises that such experiences can lead to long-term psychological difficulties. Evidence supporting TRiM is encouraging. Watson and Andrews (2018) found that police officers who engaged with TRiM reported fewer symptoms of PTSD, reduced stigma around mental health, and more positive help-seeking behaviours than those in a control group. However, research suggests that support should be embedded within everyday organisational practice rather than provided solely in response to traumatic events (Van der Velden et al., 2010). The Emergency Services Trauma Intervention Programme (ESTIP) is a specialised initiative supporting emergency personnel, including police officers, firefighters, and paramedics. It provides peer-support networks, immediate and ongoing trauma support, and training to help staff recognise signs of stress and maintain resilience. ESTIP also equips managers and colleagues with knowledge to support affected staff, with the aim of enhancing wellbeing and sustaining operational effectiveness. Critical Incident Stress Management (CISM) has also been widely adopted by police organisations internationally. As a comprehensive crisis intervention framework, CISM seeks to reduce acute psychological distress and prevent long-term trauma-related harm, promoting coping strategies and overall mental wellbeing (Everly et al., 2002). Given that the PEEL assessment framework (2023-2025) (His Majesty's Inspectorate of Constabulary and Fire & Rescue Services, 2023) states that "The force understands the main factors that influence its workforce's well-being and takes effective action to address any related problems", the availability of these support measures show that this is in fact being met. In terms of the characteristics of good which are outlined, the availability of such support measures shows that the force understands on its workforce's well-being, as well as any related stress, that it provides a range of preventative and supportive measures, including support to those in high-risk roles or those experiencing potentially traumatic incidents, and, that the force's occupational health service provides support and interventions that improve officer and staff well-being.

THE MENTAL HEALTH OF POLICE OFFICERS IN THE UK AND IRELAND

54 police officers (30 male, 24 females) from the UK took part in this study. This equated to a response rate of 56% male and 44% female. This compares to a police force, which in 2024, was 65% males and 35% female. Despite our UK based sample being somewhat less representative than our Irish sample, it is consistent with other UK based research (Charman & Bennett, 2022). The age of participants ranged from 20 – 59 years of age and the length of service ranged from 1 to 25 years. Participants ranged in rank from Police Constable 'PC' to Detective Inspector, and had experience in various roles including intelligence, response, sex worker liaison, TRiM (Trauma Risk Management) leader, terrorism, domestic violence and hate crime. Participants rated their mental health more positively before joining the police ($M = 5.41$, $SD = 1.31$), compared to how they felt currently ($M = 3.93$, $SD = 1.56$), $t(45) = 5.29$, $p < .001$, $d_{\text{RM, pooled}} = -0.60$, 95% CI [-1.00, –0.21].

98 members of An Garda Síochána (Irish police force) (67 male; 31 female) completed the survey. The gender split in our dataset (male: 68%; female: 32%) is representative of that of An Garda Síochána (male: 72%; female: 28%) (An Garda Síochána HR Directorate webpage, 2024). The age of participants ranged from 26–63 and the length of service ranged from 2–40 years. Participants ranged in rank from Garda to Chief Superintendent. Irish based participants also rated their mental health more positively before joining the police ($M = 6.07$, $SD = 0.93$), compared to how they felt currently ($M = 4.29$, $SD = 1.85$), $t(93) = 9.01$, $p < .001$, $d_{\text{RM, pooled}} = -0.72$, 95% CI [–1.05–0.40].

There are, however, some limitations on the findings in this study. It should be noted that most responses from the UK based sample came from England and Wales. Findings are, therefore, unlikely to be representative of all police officers in the UK but rather skewed towards those from England and Wales. The relatively small sample size needs to be considered as should the potential for bias in the responses. By this we mean that the sample may be skewed towards the proportion of police officers in the UK and in Ireland who are happy to discuss issues related to mental health.

Operational And Organisational Stressors

Analysis of responses to the question 'How has your job impacted upon your mental health?' revealed that participants suffered from being exposed to a range of operational and organisational stressors. Operational stressors included dealing with scenes of murder, rapes, suicide, and road traffic accidents. Participants spoke at length about being victims of violence, where they were assaulted by members of the public in the course of their duty. Such exposure resulted in several participants suffering from PTSD and CPTSD, as well as suffering from panic attacks, anxiety and depression. These issues were highlighted by participants in the UK and in Ireland, regardless of gender, age or length of service. Participants from both jurisdictions noted that their PTSD and depression were a result of 'trauma experienced in the workplace' (*Male, Garda, Ireland, 27 years old, 4 years of service*) and attending 'serious and highly emotive incidents' (*Female, Police Constable, UK, 24 years old, 3 years of service*). Participants who responded to road traffic accidents noted that 'Attending serious incidents can be distressing and traumatising... As a traffic officer I attend collisions where bodies are seriously deformed. I find that the job has blunted my emotions and sometimes leaves me treating friends and family differently' (*Male, Police Constable, UK, 26 years old, 4 years of service*).

Participants also cited a wide range of organisational stressors related to bullying and excessive and unmanageable workloads. Participants from both the UK and Ireland claimed that there was a culture of bullying and harassment in the police which generally went unchecked by management when reported. Bullying from management was also highlighted as a concern. These issues cut across rank, age, gender and length of service. For example, one participant wrote that after being bullied and harassed in the job, they eventually stood up for themselves. They found this to be isolating and they 'became the target of group bullying, harassment, and had opportunities taken away from me' (*Female, Special Constable, UK, 26 years old, 3 years of service*), while another participant stated that 'bullying is all too common' throughout the organisation. (*Male, Inspector, UK, 49 years old, 25 years of service*). Irish participants also highlighted bulling as a major cause of concern, with one writing that 'bullying is commonplace by supervisors who are promoted beyond their capabilities (the Peter Principle - unable to go further)' (*Male, Detective Sergeant, Ireland, 43 years old, 16 years of service*).

Participants highlighted the negative impact of excessive workloads, citing increasing levels of bureaucracy, paperwork and administrative duties, as being damaging to their mental health. Again, these issues were raised by participants across both jurisdictions, regardless of age, rank, gender or length of service. Irish participants stated that excessive workload, especially administrative duties 'are becoming an overwhelming aspect especially for supervisors' (*Male, Sergeant, Ireland, 57 years old, 33 years of service*). One participant stated that 'stress relating to court cases, paperwork and general workload has invaded my personal life regularly' (*Male, Detective Sergeant, Ireland, 53 years old, 27 years of service*). This increase in workload, especially that associated with an increase in administrative related work, has led to 'feelings of frustration in people who joined to make a positive impact in their community by contributing to public safety and enjoying an exciting career' (*Male, Sergeant, Ireland, 57 years old, 33 years of service*).

In the UK workload was also cited as a contributing factor to poor mental health. One participant wrote that they ended up suffering from stress, burnout and anxiety due to 'massive workloads and intense pressures in a heavily negative environment.' (*Male, Inspector, UK, 37 years old, 14 years of service*) while another stated that excessive workload was one of the biggest impacts there is on the mental health of police officers. They claimed that a lack of resources and an increasing workload of, with 'more and more work being demanded for less has an incredibly detrimental effect on the mental health of myself and colleagues' (*Male, Police Constable, UK, 32 years old, 9 years of service*).

Support Available

Analysis of responses to the question 'How does your organisation support mental health?' revealed that while participants were aware of support mechanisms, they were also very critical of the support that was offered. Peer support and support from management was seen to be of vital importance.

Irish participants wrote about a new mobile phone app, as well as counselling and welfare services which are made available through an Employee Assistance Programme. One participant wrote that 'There are systems in place to help me from wellbeing to mental illness. It is a matter of self-responsibility to look out for oneself and colleagues' (*Male, Garda, Ireland, 43 years old, 22 years of service*). This suggests that at the very least, there is an awareness of the support options available. Some felt that mental health support was as good as it has ever been in the organisation and while there were no barriers to accessing such support a greater culture of openness was needed when discussing mental health within the organisation. However, others were very critical of the mental health support that was offered. One participant wrote that 'It has a token counselling service in place for anyone looking for it but our own management have little to no regard for the mental health of their staff...we are expected to suck it up (or worse, bottle it up) and get on with things. Our management don't care and don't want to know about anyone struggling to deal with the stresses of the job.' (*Male, Detective Garda, Ireland, 45 years old, 17 years of service*).

Participants from the UK wrote of similar experiences. There was an awareness of the support that was in place for mental health and wellbeing, but there was also a lot of criticism of those supports. One participant wrote that 'There is a wellbeing service but that is for when you're well and truly broken...you're pushed to the absolute limit every second of every day. Only after you brake [sic] do they care' (*Male, Sergeant, UK, 34 years old, 16 years of service*). Another wrote 'They have schemes and groups on offer but a lot of supervision don't seem to take it seriously. There is still a lot of taboo and a lot of officers I know feel they wouldn't dare take time off because they won't receive support' (*Female, Police Constable, UK, 21 years old, 1 year of service*). Many participants were of the view that the most important support came from their work colleagues and their supervisors – in the view of many participants, peer support could make a significant difference to their mental wellbeing. One participant wrote about a time when their sergeant and inspector were supportive and contacted them regularly to check on their wellbeing. They went on to describe how 'colleagues on my team stepped up and were good at providing some of the support needed' (*Female, Police Constable, UK, 33 years old, 6 years of service*). However, others were of the view that relying on colleague of such support was not sufficient and that more was needed. They wrote 'We rely on each other as colleagues to get that support but that isn't good enough' (*Female, Police Constable, UK, 29 years old, 3.5 years of service*).

Barriers to Support

Analysis of responses to the question 'What do you feel are the main barriers to accessing mental health support in your organisation?' found there to be several barriers to accessing mental health support. Many wrote about the ongoing stigma around mental health, which makes it hard to ask for help without fear of being judged. Others worried that speaking up might harm their chances of promotion or affect how they're seen at work. There was also a clear lack of trust—both in the support services available and in management. All these barriers can be related back to a more pervasive issue: a policing culture that promotes bravado, stoicism and suspicion of weakness. For example, participants from the UK wrote 'Firstly, the culture of Policing. Showing any signs of weakness has an effect on how your team view you' (*Female, Police Constable, UK, 33 years old, 6 years of service*) and 'Your [sic] more than likely to be told to "get on with it" and let us know how you feel tomorrow if you raised an issue with your mental health' (*Male, Police Constable, UK, 38 years old, 10 years of service*).

Similarly, participants from Ireland were critical of the culture within the organisation when it came to seeking help for one's mental health. Comments included 'It's a taboo subject due to the nature of the job a sense of "that's what you signed up for so get on with it" due to years of this way being the norm' (*Female, Garda, Ireland, 36 years old, 16 years of service*) and 'Stigma. Removal from role. Exclusion from potential future roles. Lack of training of managers and supervisors. Macho culture' (*Male, Sergeant, Ireland, 52 years old, 27 years of service*).

DISCUSSION

While support mechanisms like TRiM, ESTIP and CISM all demonstrate that the police do work to support the mental health and wellbeing of its members, the experiences of police officers in this research do not seem to reflect this. While these support measures are welcome, the police should also be supporting those officers whose mental health and wellbeing has suffered because of the police itself as an institution. By this we mean that while support is available for those who have experienced a traumatic event, where is the support for those who are bullied at work, or for those who are emotionally overwhelmed with their workload? It seems to us that until the police support its members whose mental health and wellbeing have been negatively impacted from within the police force, as opposed to those who have experienced or witnessed traumatic events, they will not be satisfying the PEEL Assessment marker of clearly understanding what factors have positive and negative effects on its workforce's well-being, as well as any related stress, in all areas. It uses this understanding to inform resourcing decisions and aims to strike a balance between operational needs and looking after its people.

Furthermore, the role of police culture must also be considered as a significant barrier to help seeking for mental health and wellbeing. Police culture has been characterised by several core features, including a strong sense of mission shaped by action, cynicism and pessimism; suspicion of the public; solidarity with colleagues alongside social isolation from outsiders; a conservative outlook; machismo or bravado; institutional racism; and pragmatism (Reiner, 2010). Although these elements often relate to how police officers engage with the public, they also shape internal dynamics and can create barriers to help-seeking, particularly around mental health.

Expectations of machismo and emotional toughness may discourage officers from openly discussing psychological difficulties. Those who do disclose mental health concerns risk being perceived as weak or unreliable, potentially reinforcing pessimistic attitudes and suspicion within the occupational culture. While police officers are frequently described as cynical and distrustful of the public, these attitudes can also be directed towards colleagues who speak openly about mental health. As a result, officers who seek support may experience stigma, scepticism, or reduced confidence from peers. Such reactions can undermine solidarity, a central feature of police culture that typically fosters strong bonds between colleagues. When solidarity is disrupted, officers who disclose mental health struggles may become socially isolated within their teams. This isolation can further discourage help-seeking and reinforce a culture in which emotional vulnerability is suppressed rather than supported (Gavin & Porter, 2025).

CONCLUSION

The findings in this chapter are generally consistent with existing research examining the relationship between policing and mental health and wellbeing (Fallon, 2018; Jetelina et al., 2020; Purba & Demou, 2019; Soomro & Yanos, 2018). Operational stressors, such as exposure to traumatic incidents, remain an unavoidable aspect of policing (Foley et al., 2023), and officers whose mental health is affected by such experiences must receive appropriate and sustained support from their organisations. By contrast, organisational stressors—including bullying, inadequate supervision, and excessive workloads—are preventable and therefore demand urgent attention. Addressing police wellbeing requires systemic and cultural change that moves beyond rhetorical commitment to meaningful action.

Police organisations should implement comprehensive, preventative wellbeing strategies that integrate mental health support into everyday working practices. This includes ensuring adequate staffing levels, manageable workloads, and access to confidential psychological services that are routinely promoted and normalised. Embedding wellbeing within organisational structures signals that mental health is a core operational concern rather than an individual responsibility. Leadership and management practices must prioritise supportive and inclusive workplace cultures. Training supervisors to recognise signs of distress, challenge bullying behaviours, and actively listen to frontline concerns can foster trust and reduce stigma. By addressing organisational stressors and strengthening supportive leadership, policing institutions can better protect the mental health and wellbeing of their workforce.

REFERENCES

Bisson Desrochers, A., Rouleau, I., Angehrn, A., Vasiliadis, H. M., Saumier, D., & Brunet, A. (2021). Trauma on duty: Cognitive functioning in police officers with and without posttraumatic stress disorder (PTSD). *European Journal of Psychotraumatology, 12*(1). Advance online publication. DOI: 10.1080/20008198.2021.1959117 PMID: 34721819

Brewin, C. R., Miller, J. K., Soffia, M., Peart, A., & Burchell, B. (2022). Posttraumatic stress disorder and complex posttraumatic stress disorder in UK police officers. *Psychological Medicine, 52*(7), 1287–1295. DOI: 10.1017/S0033291720003025 PMID: 32892759

Charman, S., & Bennett, S. (2022). Voluntary resignations from the police service: The impact of organisational and occupational stressors on organisational commitment. *Policing and Society, 32*(2), 159–178. DOI: 10.1080/10439463.2021.1891234

Edwards, D., & Wilkerson, N. (2020). Emotional exhaustion and its relationship with suicide risk in emergency responders. *Psychiatry Research, 293*, 113379. DOI: 10.1016/j.psychres.2020.113379 PMID: 32841890

Everly, G. S., Flannery, R. B., & Eyler, V. A. (2002). Critical incident stress management (CISM): A statistical review of the literature. *The Psychiatric Quarterly, 73*(3), 171–182. PMID: 12143079

Fallon, F. (2018). *Garda Representative Association Wellbeing Survey 2018*. Garda Representative Association.

Foley, J., Jones, F., Hassett, A., & Williams, E. (2023). 'Holding onto trauma?' the prevalence and predictors of PTSD, anxiety and depression in police officers working with child abuse, rape and sexual exploitation victims. *The Police Journal, 97*(2), 1–24. DOI: 10.1177/0032258X231183638

Frappell-Cooke, W., Gulina, M., & Green, K.. (2010). Does trauma risk management reduce psychological distress in deployed troops? *Occupational Medicine, 60*, 645–650. PMID: 20889815

Gavin, P., & Porter, C. N. (2024). Understanding the impact of organisational and operational stressors on the mental health of police officers in Ireland. *Police Practice and Research, 26*(1), 90–100. DOI: 10.1080/15614263.2024.2364247

Gavin, P., & Porter, C. N. (2025). Barriers to engaging with mental health support services for police officers in Ireland. The Police Journal: Theory. *Practice and Principles, 98*(4), 724–739. DOI: 10.1177/0032258X251333621

Hem, E., Berg, A. M., & Ekeberg, Ø. (2001). Suicide in police - a critical review. *Suicide & Life-Threatening Behavior, 31*, 224–233. PMID: 11459255

His Majesty's Inspectorate of Constabulary and Fire & Rescue Services. (2023). PEEL assessment framework 2023-2025. Available at https://hmicfrs.justiceinspectorates.gov.uk/publications/peel-assessment-framework-2023-2025/

His Majesty's Inspectorate of Constabulary and Fire & Rescue Services. (2025). PEEL assessment framework 2025-2027. Available at https://hmicfrs.justiceinspectorates.gov.uk/publications/peel-assessment-framework-2025-2027/

Jetelina, K. K., Molsberry, R. J., Gonzalez, J. R., Beauchamp, A. M., & Hall, T. (2020). Prevalence of mental illness and mental health care use among police officers. *JAMA Network Open, 3*(10), e2019658. DOI: 10.1001/jamanetworkopen.2020.19658 PMID: 33026452

Kessler, R. C., Berglund, P., Demler, O., Jin, R., Merikangas, K. R., & Walters, E. E. (2005). Lifetime Prevalence and Age-of-Onset Distributions of DSM-IV Disorders in the National Comorbidity Survey Replication Erratum. *Archives of General Psychiatry, 62*(6), 768. DOI: 10.1001/archpsyc.62.7.768

Kirschman, E., Kamena, M., & Fay, J. (2014). *Counseling Cops: What Clinicians Need to Know*. The Guilford Press.

McCafferty, F. L., McCafferty, E., & McCafferty, M. A. (1992). Stress and suicide in police officers: Paradigm of occupational stress. *Southern Medical Journal, 85*(3), 233–243. PMID: 1546346

Menard, K. S., & Arter, M. L. (2014). Stress, coping, alcohol use, and posttraumatic stress disorder among an international sample of police officers: Does gender matter? *Police Quarterly, 17*(4), 307–327. DOI: 10.1177/1098611114548097

Miller, J., Brewin, C., Soffia, M., Elliott-Davies, M., Burchell, B., & Peart, A. (2022). The development of a UK police traumatic events checklist. *The Police Journal, 95*(1), 207–223. DOI: 10.1177/0032258X211002597

Mind. (No date). Vicarious Trauma. Available at https://www.mind.org.uk/media/4tybnie0/headlines-guide-to-vicarious-trauma.pdf

Porter, C., & Lee, R. (2023). The policing culture: An exploration into the mental health of former British police officers. *Current Psychology (New Brunswick, N.J.), 43*, 2214–2228. DOI: 10.1007/s12144-023-04365-y

Porter, C. N., & Gavin, P. (2024). 'Constant pressures from all angles': Understanding the mental health of UK police officers. The Police Journal: Theory. *Practice and Principles*, *98*(2), 306–323. DOI: 10.1177/0032258X241280217

Purba, A., & Demou, E. (2019). The relationship between organisational stressors and mental wellbeing within police officers: A systematic review. *BMC Public Health*, *19*, 1286. DOI: 10.1186/s12889-019-7609-0 PMID: 31615479

Rajaratnam, S. M. W., Barger, L. K., Lockley, S. W., Shea, S. A., Wang, W., Landrigan, C. P., O'Brien, C. S., Qadri, S., Sullivan, J. P., Cade, B. E., Epstein, L. J., White, D. P., & Czeisler, C. A. (2011). Sleep disorders, health, and safety in police officers. *Journal of the American Medical Association*, *306*(23), 2567–2578. PMID: 22187276

Reiner, R. (2010). *The Politics of the Police*. Oxford University Press.

Solar, C., & Smith, M. (2022). Austerity and governance: Coordinating policing and mental health policy in the UK. *Policy Studies*, *43*(2), 352–369. DOI: 10.1080/01442872.2020.1711876

Soomro, S., & Yanos, P. T. (2018). Predictors of mental health stigma among police officers: The role of trauma and PTSD. *Journal of Police and Criminal Psychology*, *34*, 1–9.

Stevelink, S., Opie, E., Pernet, D., Gao, H., Elliott, P., Wessely, S., Fear, N. T., Hotopf, M., & Greenberg, N. (2020). Probable PTSD, depression and anxiety in 40,299 UK police officers and staff: Prevalence, risk factors and associations with blood pressure. *PLoS One*, *15*(11), e0240902. PMID: 33180769

Syed, S., Ashwick, R., Schlosser, M., Jones, R., Rowe, S., & Billings, J. (2020). Global prevalence and risk factors for mental health problems in police personnel: A systematic review and meta-analysis. *Occupational and Environmental Medicine*, *77*(11), 737–747. PMID: 32439827

Van der Velden, P. G., Kleber, R. J., & Grievink, L.. (2010). Confrontations with aggression and mental health problems in police officers: The role of organizational stressors, life-events and previous mental health problems. *Psychological Trauma: Theory, Research, Practice, and Policy*, *2*(2), 135–144.

Chapter 7
Capacity and Capability Building to Support and Protect the Workforce

Eric Halford
http://orcid.org/0000-0002-3913-1679
Rabdan Academy, UAE

ABSTRACT

Capacity and capability building are essential for ensuring UK police services can effectively meet evolving demands. This chapter explores how these concepts are integrated into the Force Management Statement (FMS) process, enabling forces to identify workforce challenges and implement strategic planning. Capacity building focuses on resource allocation and operational resilience, while capability building enhances individual skills and expertise. Examining Cumbria Constabulary and Humberside Police—both recognized for excellence—this chapter highlights key enablers, including leadership, innovation, human resource management, technology, and knowledge management. By adopting evidence-based strategies, police services can enhance workforce resilience, retention, and operational effectiveness.

INTRODUCTION

Capacity and capability building are critical concepts in organisational development, strategic planning, and public sector management (Massingham & Tam, 2015). These are each highly relevant to policing, and, like the chapter on demand-based strategic planning, within the HMICFRS inspection framework they are intricately linked to and driven by the Force Management Statement (FMS) process. In this context, the FMS enables police forces to identify threats to capacity and implement

DOI: 10.4018/979-8-3373-2757-0.ch007

strategic workforce planning to ensure they have the right people and infrastructure to meet the evolving challenges they prioritise. Furthermore, the FMS supports capability development by highlighting training needs, driving technological investments, and ensuring forces are well-equipped to tackle emerging threats such as cybercrime and safeguarding vulnerable communities. The FMS empowers police services to make informed, evidence-based decisions that enhance the effectiveness and sustainability of their strategic workforce development programs.

In this chapter, we will explore this issue by first defining both capacity and capability, as these terms are often used interchangeably without a true understanding of their distinctions. We will outline several evidence-based theories that underpin capacity and capability building, along with the key drivers that enable organisations to do so effectively. To contextualise the discussion, we will case study both Cumbria Constabulary and Humberside Police who are both recognised as outstanding in their approach to "building, supporting and protecting the workforce," which is the inspection category most closely aligned with capacity and capability building. This combined overview of evidence-based practice and case study analysis will provide readers with the foundational components necessary to develop an outstanding capacity and capability building workforce development plan to support their FMS.

CAPACITY AND CAPABILITY BUILDING

Capacity and capability building are fundamental to enhancing the effectiveness and sustainability of police services. Capacity building refers to the strategic development of an organisation's overall ability, systems, and personnel to effectively perform its functions, address challenges, and achieve its stated objectives (Saputra et al., 2024; Simmons et al., 2011). It focuses on strengthening resources, infrastructure, and processes to ensure long-term operational resilience and continuous improvement (Saputra et al., 2024; Simmons et al., 2011). In policing, capacity building encompasses initiatives related to recruiting and retaining officers, developing specialised units to address emerging issues like cybercrime, and optimising operational processes to enhance service delivery. A critical aspect of capacity building is the strategic allocation of financial, physical, and human resources that are used to underpin development in a manner that ensures sustainability and adaptability, both of which are vital for operating in a complex and evolving landscape like that experienced in policing (Saputra et al., 2024; Simmons et al., 2011).

Capability building, in contrast, is more targeted towards developing the specific skills, competence, and expertise required for individuals and teams to effectively conduct their roles (Gill and Delahaye, 2004; Gill, 2006). Unlike capacity building, which takes a broader organisational perspective, capability building focuses on performance-oriented objectives, such as the organisation's strategic intent and individual knowledge (Gill and Delahaye, 2004) by ensuring that personnel are equipped to conduct their functions. In modern policing, this would include specialised training programs in areas such as digital forensics, cybercrime, violence against women and girls, community engagement, and crisis response, to name a few, all of which are essential for tackling the ever-increasing list of challenges faced by police services. Capability building is often achieved through structured training programs, knowledge transfer initiatives, and professional development efforts aimed at enhancing operational effectiveness (Gill and Delahaye, 2004; Gill, 2006). Failure to do so effectively can leave an organisation at a disadvantage, potentially making them ill equipped or unable to adequately perform their core functions, negatively affecting public confidence, and even risking the legitimacy of a police service being called into question.

While capacity and capability building are distinct, they are deeply interdependent and must be strategically integrated to achieve optimal organisational performance, and resilience. Capacity building provides the foundational structure by ensuring the availability of adequate resources and personnel, while capability building ensures that individuals possess the necessary expertise to perform their roles effectively. In policing, this interplay is particularly evident in the development of specialised units. While the recruitment and deployment of officers represent the capacity building, their capability is ensured by equipping them with the technical, legal, procedural, and even emotional and psychological skills to manage the challenges within their specific environment.

The Force Management Statement (FMS) process plays a pivotal role in facilitating this integration by providing the structured framework that enables police forces to continuously assess, plan, and adjust their workforce development strategies. The FMS, if used correctly, should support forces in aligning their capacity and capability needs with present, evolving, and future demand, thereby ensuring they are well-positioned to make informed decisions regarding workforce planning, resource allocation, and operational improvements.

THEORIES UNDERPINNING CAPACITY AND CAPABILITY BUILDING

Capacity and capability building have been widely discussed in academic and professional literature, with systematic reviews (Bergeron et al., 2017) identifying distinct theories, models, and frameworks that underpin these concepts. These include the Resource Based Theory of the Firm (RBTF) (Barney 2000; Grant 1991), Diffusion of Innovations Theory (Rogers et al., 2014), the Ecological Model

(Bronfenbrenner, 1977), the Interactive Systems Framework for Dissemination and Implementation (Wandersman et al., 2008), and Implementation Theory (May, 2013). Outlining these is important as it provides readers with signposts for further exploration that will mature their breadth of knowledge in this area. In this regard, this section provides the initial overview.

Resource Based Theory

It has been argued there are three domains within which capacity and capability building operate. First, 'strategic intent' relates to the direction the organisation is heading and is heavily built upon what is referred to as the Resource Based Theory of the Firm (RBTF) (Barney 2000; Grant 1991), or what is sometimes called the resource-based view theory (RBV) (Cooke et al 2005). At their core, both consider the organisation's human capital as the foundation for strategy and as the key asset of the workforce, recognising the importance of the organisation's intangible resources, not least the knowledge, skills and unique characteristics and qualities of their employees (Barney 2000; Cooke et al 2005; Grant 1991). Second, the domain of 'organisational structure', encapsulates the function of modern human resource strategies and processes used to ensure there are sufficient employees who can respond to demand, emergent change, and enable the organisation to remain flexible and capable of functioning at a high level, sustainably (Gill and Delahaye, 2004), thereby ensuring the organisations strategic intent can be achieved. Third, the individual knowledge domain relates to the unique knowledge, skills, and abilities that everyone contributes to the organisation (Gill and Delahaye, 2004). These encompass much more than just their work roles, and reflect the broader qualities, capabilities and attributes each employee brings to the organisation (Gill and Delahaye, 2004).

The Ecological Model

Underpinning the delivery of these three domains—strategic intent, organisational structure, and individual knowledge—there are several important theories that enable effective capacity and capability building. The Ecological Model focuses on how individual behaviours are influenced by levels within an environment (Bronfenbrenner, 1977). The model outlines the microsystem (family) mesosystem (workplace and peers), exosystem (social networks and community), and macrosystem (law and policies) (Bronfenbrenner, 1977). Modem police services encapsulate all these system levels, each of which provide distinct influences upon employees and the organisation. When applied to capacity and capability building this model ensures that police services consider the full range of systemic factors affecting workforce well-being, habits, and policy adherence, thereby fostering a more holistic understanding of their employees' needs and influencing factors (Besboruah, 2021) so that they can maximise the volume and impact of both capacity and capability.

Diffusion of Innovation and Interactive Systems

The diffusion of innovation theory explains how new ideas, practices, or technologies spread within a social system, such as a police service. It identifies key factors influencing adoption, including whether the innovations provide a relative advantage and alignment with the vision, mission, and role of the organisation (Rogers et al., 2014). In the context of capacity and capability building, this theory helps organisations, including police services, introduce and scale new interventions across their workforce effectively (Bergeron et al., 2017). This is vital for tackling emergent issues for which the evidence-base is not yet established, such as the policing response to artificial intelligence.

The interactive systems framework provides a structured approach for translating evidence-based practices into operational delivery. In today's world where evidence-based policing (EBP) is becoming increasingly ingrained, it provides utility for services to transfer theory into practice. It focuses on three key systems: the delivery system, which refers to the organisation's implementation plan; the support system, which provides training and assistance; and the synthesis system, which consists of evidence-based guidelines and processes (Wandersman et al., 2008). In the context of capacity and capability building, it helps structure the dissemination and implementation of workforce development programs more effectively and can help avoid so called 'implementation failure.'

Implementation Theory

Finally, implementation theory offers a more comprehensive framework that considers the full array of processes, challenges, and factors influencing the successful adoption and integration of workforce development practices, policies, or interventions within organisations. It outlines several key stages, beginning with exploration, where receptivity to change is assessed and potential barriers are identified. This is followed by preparation, which focuses on establishing the necessary infrastructure and resources. The next stage, initial implementation, involves pilot testing and early adoption, and if successful, leads to full implementation, where the intervention is scaled up across the organisation (May, 2013). Invaluable for the context of capacity and capability building is the key components that implementation theory suggests as contributing to success, such as leadership, organisational culture, employee motivation, resource availability, and stakeholder engagement. In implementation theory it is argued all of these play a critical role in ensuring sustainable change (May, 2013) and delivery of successful workforce development strategies.

Kirby (2013) offers a valuable contribution to understanding how these theoretical principles of implementation are operationalised within policing. In his book, he illustrates how successful implementation in law enforcement depends on the interplay between organisational structures, leadership commitment, and the interpretive discretion of officers. Kirby highlights that while theoretical models, such as those proposed by May (2013), emphasise staged and systematised processes, effective delivery in policing also requires adaptability to cultural, operational, and environmental contingencies. This practical acknowledgement is particularly relevant to capacity and capability building, as it underscores that implementation is not merely a procedural exercise but an adaptive, context-dependent process.

DRIVERS OF CAPACITY AND CAPABILITY BUILDING

By examining the underpinning theories, frameworks, and systematic reviews (Bergeron et al., 2017; Gill and Delahaye, 2004; Gill, 2006; Saputra et al., 2024) related to capacity and capability building, it is possible to identify key drivers that facilitate the effective workforce development programs required to establish an outstanding police service, and tackle the threats and risks highlighted with the FMS. While these drivers may necessitate strengthening institutional structures through financial investment, governance adjustments, or logistical changes, the primary features can be distilled into leadership, human resource management, innovation, technology, and knowledge management.

Leadership and Human Resource Management

Effective leadership helps align the police services strategic goals with its workforce development initiatives. It is also vital in fostering the right organisational culture, ensuring receptivity to change, and encouraging a learning environment that supports continuous improvement (Shafait & Huang, 2024). Human Resource Management (HRM) plays a crucial role in building, supporting, and protecting the workforce, not least because most of a police services assets are in human capital (National Police Chiefs Council, 2017). In this context, HRM facilitates recruitment, talent development, and diversity management, key components required to build a capable and inclusive workforce (Soost & Moog, 2021). Effective HRM also ensures that police services retain their experienced and talented employees, either by supporting them to overcome personal, emotional, and psychological issues that may cause them to leave policing, or by aiding in their career progression, and addressing skill gaps through professional development.

Innovation and Technology

Innovation, often perceived within policing as a 'nice to do' rather than an essential consideration, is fundamental to building, supporting, and protecting the workforce as it fosters organisational growth and improvement. In this regard it should encompass new approaches to processes, people, technology, and service delivery. Process innovations focus on streamlining operational procedures, reducing bureaucracy, and increasing efficiency. Service innovations introduce tailored solutions to meet community needs, enhancing public satisfaction and trust (Ibrahim et al., 2022). Innovation can also be embedded by developing a mature culture of continuous improvement through acceptance of evidence-based policing, and a commitment to research and development, philosophies that are not routinely accepted within policing (Lumsden, 2017).

Technology is a key enabler of workforce development, particularly service delivery and capability building, where it can dramatically improve employee productivity through automation, thereby reducing the burden of manual, time-consuming tasks and the workplace stress associated with high caseloads (Ibrahim et al., 2022). It is also essential for responding to emerging challenges, such as those posed by the proliferation of smart devices, the Internet of Things (IoT), the rapid evolution of artificial intelligence, the increasing use of cryptocurrency, and the complexity of blockchain investigations. All these areas are increasingly encroaching into policing and require innovative workforce development and capability building to ensure employees possess the skills required to face the operational and investigative challenges they generate. Failure to do so will further contribute to significant stress for employees as staff will feel increasingly ill equipped to conduct their roles effectively (Domingues and Machado, 2017).

Knowledge Management

Knowledge Management involves the collection, storage, sharing, and application of knowledge within the police service (Putri et al., 2023; Tran et al., 2022). Traditionally provided through internal training departments, workforce knowledge is now increasingly supported by higher education institutions before officers join the service. Training within UK policing is heavily underpinned by authorised professional practice (APP) from the College of Policing and is delivered via a mix of face-to-face learning and digital platforms, with varying degrees of success (Honess, 2020; Halford and Yousanamouth, 2024). In this regard, repeated inspections and case reviews have highlighted that many police employees lack the requisite skills and knowledge to perform their duties effectively due to inadequate training provision, which often leads to significant service failures, frequently with fatal outcomes (Allnock, et al, 2020). Outstanding police services recognise this challenge and invest heavily in both accredited and in-house training programs to ensure their workforce is fully equipped to meet operational demands. The most effective knowledge management programs introduced as part of a capability building program not only provide mandatory industry knowledge but identify gaps in learning and take pro-active steps to address these, so all employees are equipped with the necessary skills to meet the service's strategic goals (Umer et al., 2023).

An increasingly significant mechanism for enhancing workforce capability through knowledge management within policing is the variety of police constable education routes, which includes the Degree in Professional Policing (DPP), the Police Constable Degree Apprenticeship (PCDA), and the Degree Holder Entry Programme (DHEP). Introduced by the College of Policing, these routes aim to professionalise the entry pathways into the profession, ensuring that new recruits possess a high level of academic, practical, and ethical competence aligned with the demands of contemporary policing (College of Policing, 2020). This ensures that officers should arrive in police services with a high degree of capability and knowledge. Emerging evidence supports this and suggests that graduates entering through these routes often demonstrate stronger theoretical knowledge, analytical skills, and ethical decision-making capability than those entering via the apprenticeship pathway (for a detailed outline of these programs and their effectiveness see the chapter on the Police Education Qualifications Framework [PEQF]).

In summary, leadership, HRM, innovation, technology, and knowledge management are critical drivers of capacity and capability building in police services. Services that embrace and integrate these drivers within their strategic planning frameworks are better positioned to achieve and sustain operational excellence while effectively responding to evolving policing challenges that are identified during the FMS process.

CASE STUDIES OF OUTSTANDING SERVICES

Cumbria Constabulary and Humberside Police have both received outstanding recognition in the 2023-2025 HMICFRS inspection rounds for their efforts in "building, supporting, and protecting their workforce," demonstrating their ability to effectively implement capacity and capability-building strategies. To achieve this status, both services have focused heavily on their largest assets, their people, and fostered an environment that promotes resilience and well-being through targeted initiatives designed to address the needs of key personnel groups, a fundamental principle in workforce development (Chakraborty & Biswas, 2020). Their success lies in the innovative and holistic nature of their approaches, which systematically capture all groups within their organisations. This includes recruiting and retaining new officers while also ensuring the well-being and sustained performance of their existing workforce. In addition, both forces prioritise retaining experienced personnel, ensuring they continue to contribute effectively. These efforts are underpinned by a strong commitment to diversity, equity, and inclusion (DEI), with targeted support provided to those who need it most.

For example, a key initiative in Cumbria Constabulary's success is the 'Student Officer Progression Framework,' which systematically tracks and supports the development and welfare needs of new recruits (HMICFRS, 2024a). This initiative ensures tailored support throughout officers' early careers and helps prevent capacity gaps caused by high resignation rates, an issue faced by many forces across the UK. In parallel, Cumbria's 'Wiser Mind' training programme, designed to enhance resilience through evidence-based psychological principles, provides officers with essential coping skills to manage occupational stress more effectively (HMICFRS, 2024a). Recognised by the Oscar Kilo Awards (the UKs national police wellbeing lead), this initiative highlights Cumbria's commitment to embedding resilience, which is a core feature of workforce capability (Do et al., 2022), and vital for maintaining high-capacity levels. Similarly, Humberside Police introduced the 'Strength in Being Blue' initiative, a video campaign featuring real-life stories of officers dealing with mental health challenges (HMICFRS, 2024b). By incorporating well-being support teams during screenings, Humberside ensure officers receive immediate assistance when needed, providing an opportunity to foster a culture of openness, whilst providing support.

To further enhance workforce well-being, Cumbria has also introduced the 'Fair Passport' system, which provides continuity for officers moving between roles by ensuring they do not have to repeatedly disclose and relive traumatic experiences (HMICFRS, 2024a). Additionally, their 'Heads Up' online reporting tool offers a confidential platform for officers to raise workplace concerns and seek support anonymously (HMICFRS, 2024a). These initiatives contribute to sustaining organisational resilience by reducing absenteeism, improving retention, and maintaining operational capacity (Jackman et al, 2021; Moustaghfir et al., 2020).

Both forces also recognise the heightened risks faced by certain personnel based on their roles, age, gender, and other factors. Humberside Police, for instance, implemented a health check campaign for officers aged 40 and above, which achieved an 80% participation rate within three months (HMICFRS, 2024b). For officers in high-risk roles, such as those handling child sexual abuse and exploitation cases, the 'Pause Point' programme allows structured breaks from these roles, recognising the need for recovery from the psychological toll associated with such work (HMICFRS, 2024b). Similarly, the 'Watch My Six' referral process provides dedicated mental health support for armed response officers (HMICFRS, 2024b), ensuring they are equipped to manage occupational stress more effectively, which helps maintain workforce capacity within a highly specialist capability (Baek et al., 2021; Santa Maria et al, 2018).

Retaining experienced personnel is also crucial for sustaining operational capacity, as well as knowledge, experience, and ergo, capability. Police forces have conducted exit interviews for many years, but their goal is rarely to retain employees. Instead, they are often reactive with a view of learning lessons. In contrast, Cumbria's 'Stay Conversation' initiative offers opportunity for pro-active dialogue between senior officers and those considering leaving, enabling leaders to consider solutions such as flexible working, relocation, and mentorship opportunities (HMICFRS, 2024a). Likewise, Humberside Police's 'Say and Stay' initiative has been successful in addressing officers' concerns and retaining valuable knowledge and experience within the organisation (HMICFRS, 2024b).

A strong emphasis on diversity, equity, and inclusion (DEI) is another key driver of capacity and capability building (Mary et al., 2023), which is at the forefront in both outstanding services examined. In this regard, Cumbria Constabulary offers targeted mentoring and development programs for underrepresented groups (HMICFRS, 2024a), addressing barriers to career progression and ensuring equal opportunities for growth and advancement. Similarly, Humberside Police's 'Women's Integrated Network' is a dedicated development program provide that provides mentoring, leadership training, and confidence-building sessions to promote career progression and improve representation within specialist roles (HMICFRS, 2024b). Also in Humberside, the 'Top 30 Under 30' Young Leadership Excellence Acceleration Programme (LEAP) provides development opportunities for young officers who might otherwise be overlooked due to their age or length of service (HMICFRS, 2024b). Each of these programs help improve the knowledge and skills of those involved and therefore improve the capability within potentially underrepresented groups.

In addition to the wide range of wellbeing and knowledge development initiatives, these forces have also found ways to leverage technology and data to optimise workforce management in a way that also provides resilient levels of capacity and capability. For example, Cumbria Constabulary uses the Cambridge Harm Index to ensure workload distribution and management is based not just on volume but also on the impact of cases (HMICFRS, 2024a). This offers a more integrated approach to workload management that takes account of multiple measures of demand that cases can place on employees, thereby fostering better identification of the need for additional capacity or capability. This serves to further reduce workplace stress and associated capacity and capability issues, most notably sickness and absenteeism (Baek et al., 2021; Santa Maria et al, 2018).

DELIVERING EFFECTIVE CAPACITY AND CAPABILITY BUILDING

The previous section outlined how police services have applied the information provided in this chapter in practice to implement workforce development plans that help maintain or improve capacity and capability. In this section, we offer further advise to help do this effectively. This is vital to ensure that workforce development plans stand the greatest chance of success. To begin with, the use of methodologies such as one-to-one meetings, focus groups, surveys, anonymous reporting lines, and other initiatives—such as those implemented by Cumbria and Humberside Police—can all help police services identify organisational issues, internal behaviours, and habits that negatively affect employees, undermine resilience, and ultimately hinder workforce development plans or even reduce capacity and capability. To address these challenges, police services should focus on the primary drivers outlined—leadership, human resource management, innovation, technology, and knowledge management—which can all be leveraged to bring about meaningful change. In doing so they should concentrate on key areas in policing that have the greatest impact on capacity and capability, such as employee recruitment, retention, and well-being initiatives, all of which will help maximise productivity and effectiveness, particularly by reducing sickness and absenteeism.

When implementing workforce development programs, police services must follow tried and tested methods. First, they should establish a robust theoretical and methodological evidence base for their initiatives. This is particularly important for programs aimed at improving capacity and capability by addressing emotional, physical, or psychological well-being. Establishing such a foundation not only ensures the effectiveness of the program but also provides reassurance to the inspectorate that the proposed changes are well-considered, empirically sound, and pose a low risk of unintended negative consequences. It is also vital that police services adopt a tailored approach specific to the unique operational, cultural, and community needs of their organisation. Simply replicating best practices from other forces without adaptation may yield short-term success but could also lead to unforeseen challenges. Although a culture of "copy-paste" solutions may be tempting, police services must develop bespoke strategies that ensure workforce development initiatives remain relevant, effective, and sustainable in the long term for their organisation. The FMS is designed to help services do this if used correctly.

Once the theory and method of workforce development are established, police services must follow well-established implementation methods to create the strong delivery systems required for success (Wandersman et al., 2008). This involves establishing the necessary infrastructure and resources to deliver the change, tracking, and measuring its effectiveness through pilot testing, and, if proven successful, proceeding with full implementation (May, 2013). To support these efforts, police services must also build a robust support system that includes comprehensive training and knowledge transfer. It is crucial that all affected employees understand and align with the vision of the implementation, ensuring they are well-equipped to execute associated policies and processes effectively (Wandersman et al., 2008). This is especially relevant for leaders in supervisory and management positions, who play a critical role in ensuring the success and sustainability of the changes.

CONCLUSION

Capacity and capability building are essential for achieving an outstanding grading in the HMICFRS inspection area related to "building, supporting, and protecting the workforce." The FMS plays a key role in identifying areas where such measures are required. In this chapter, we have outlined the distinctions between capacity and capability building and discussed the primary evidence-based theories that underpin workforce development programs. By integrating these elements, police services can develop an effective strategy that enables them to achieve outstanding results in their efforts to build, support, and protect the workforce.

Exemplar services, such as Cumbria Constabulary and Humberside Police, have demonstrated that when capacity and capability building programs are inspired by innovation driven by strong leadership, with a commitment to employee well-being, outstanding results can be achieved. However, successful implementation requires a comprehensive and pro-active approach that leverages the key capacity and capability drivers—leadership, innovation, human resource management, technology, and knowledge management. Through resilience programs, mental health support, retention strategies, diversity initiatives, and more effective workload monitoring practices, police services can significantly enhance both capacity and capability ensuring they improve employee well-being and foster a culture of continuous development that contributes to long-term organisational resilience that can meet demands effectively.

REFERENCES

Allnock, D., Dawson, J., & Rawden, H. (2020). *The role of police in responding to child and adult vulnerability: A meta-analysis of 126 reviews of death and serious harm*. Vulnerability Knowledge and Practice Programme.

Baek, H., Han, S., & Seepersad, R. (2021). The impact of social support and occupational stress on burnout in the Trinidad and Tobago Police Service. *Police Quarterly*.

Barney, J. B. (2000). Firm resources and sustained competitive advantage. In *Economics meets sociology in strategic management* (pp. 203–227). Emerald Group Publishing Limited.

Bergeron, K., Abdi, S., DeCorby, K., Mensah, G., Rempel, B., & Manson, H. (2017). Theories, models, and frameworks used in capacity building interventions relevant to public health: A systematic review. *BMC Public Health*, *17*(1), 1–12. PMID: 29183296

Besboruah, K. (2021). Building and strengthening communities: What works? What doesn't? In *Building Community and Family Resilience* (pp. 1–17). Research, Policy, and Programs.

Bronfenbrenner, U. (1977). Toward an experimental ecology of human development. *The American Psychologist*, *32*(7), 513–531. DOI: 10.1037/0003-066X.32.7.513

Chakraborty, D., & Biswas, W. (2020). Articulating the value of human resource planning (HRP) activities in augmenting organisational performance toward a sustained competitive firm. *Journal of Asia Business Studies*, *14*(1), 62–90. DOI: 10.1108/JABS-01-2019-0025

Cooke, F. L., Shen, J., & McBride, A. (2005). Outsourcing human resource as a competitive strategy. *Human Resource Management Journal*, *44*(4), 413–432.

Do, H., Budhwar, P., Shipton, H., Nguyen, H.-D., & Nguyen, B. (2022). Building organisational resilience, innovation through resource-based management initiatives, organisational learning, and environmental dynamism. *Journal of Business Research*, *141*, 808–821. DOI: 10.1016/j.jbusres.2021.11.090

Domingues, I. P., & Machado, J. C. (2017). The loosely coupled factors of organisational stress in police forces. *Policing*, *40*(4), 657–671.

Gill, L., & Delahaye, B. (2004). Building organisational capability: Your future, your business. In *Proceedings of the 18th Annual Conference of the Australian and New Sealand Academy of Management*, Dunedin, NS.

Gill, L. M. (2006). *Building organisational capability* (Doctoral dissertation, Queensland University of Technology).

Grant, R. M. (1991). The resource-based theory of competitive advantage: Implications for strategy formulation. *California Management Review*, *33*(3), 114–135.

Halford, E., & Youansamouth, L. (2024). Emerging results on the impact of COVID-19 on police training in the United Kingdom. *The Police Journal*, *97*(1), 105–130.

His Majesty's Inspectorate of Constabularies, Fire and Rescue Services. (2024a). PEEL 2023–25: Police effectiveness, efficiency, and legitimacy: An inspection of Cumbria Constabulary. *His Majesty's Inspectorate of Constabularies, Fire and Rescue Services*. Retrieved from https://hmicfrs.justiceinspectorates.gov.uk/peel-reports/cumbria-2023-25/

His Majesty's Inspectorate of Constabularies, Fire and Rescue Services. (2024b). PEEL 2023–25: Police effectiveness, efficiency, and legitimacy: An inspection of Humberside Police. *His Majesty's Inspectorate of Constabularies, Fire and Rescue Services*. Retrieved from https://hmicfrs.justiceinspectorates.gov.uk/peel-reports/humberside-2023-25/

Honess, R. (2020). Mandatory police training: The epitome of dissatisfaction and demotivation? *Policing. Journal of Policy Practice*, *14*(1), 191–201.

Ibrahim, M., Yusheng, K., & Adam, D. R. (2022). Linking service innovation to organisational performance: Mediating role of employee productivity and job satisfaction. *International Journal of Service Science, Management, Engineering, and Technology*, *13*(1), 1–16. DOI: 10.4018/IJSSMET.295558

Jackman, P. C., Clay, G., Coussens, A. H., Bird, M. D., & Henderson, H. (2021). 'We are fighting a tide that keeps coming against us': A mixed method exploration of stressors in an English county police force. *Police Practice and Research*, *22*(4), 370–388.

Kirby, S. (2013). *Effective policing?: Implementation in theory and practice*. Palgrave Macmillan.

Lumsden, K. (2017). Police officer and civilian staff receptivity to research and evidence-based policing in the UK: Providing a contextual understanding through qualitative interviews. *Policing. Journal of Policy Practice*, *11*(2), 157–167.

Mary, S. R. S., Malhotra, L., Goswami, I., Kumari, P. A., & Priya, U. (2023). A study on the effect of employee diversity on organisational performance. *International Journal of Professional Business Review*, *8*(4), e01239. DOI: 10.26668/businessreview/2023.v8i4.1239

Massingham, P. R., & Tam, L. (2015). The relationship between human capital, value creation, and employee reward. *Journal of Intellectual Capital, 16*(2), 390–418. DOI: 10.1108/JIC-06-2014-0075

May, C. (2013). Towards a general theory of implementation. *Implementation Science : IS*, *8*(1), 1–14. PMID: 23406398

Moustaghfir, K., El Fatihi, S., & Benouarrek, M. (2020). Human resource management practices, entrepreneurial orientation, and firm performance: What is the link? *Measuring Business Excellence*, *24*(2), 267–283. DOI: 10.1108/MBE-12-2019-0119

National Police Chiefs Council. (2017). Better understanding demand–Policing the future. *Performance Management Coordination Committee*. Retrieved from https://www.npcc.police.uk/2017%20FOI/CO/078

Putri, N. K. S., Permatasari, D., Susanto, R., Lee, C. K., & Kurniawan, Y. (2023). Knowledge management evaluation using digital capability maturity model in higher education institution. *Electronic Journal of Knowledge Management, 21*(2), 140–157. DOI: 10.34190/ejkm.21.2.3009

Rogers, E. M., Singhal, A., & Quinlan, M. M. (2014). Diffusion of innovations. In *An integrated approach to communication theory and research* (pp. 432–448). Routledge.

Santa Maria, A., Wörfel, F., Wolter, C., Gusy, B., Rotter, M., Stark, S., Kleiber, D., & Renneberg, B. (2018). The role of job demands and job resources in the development of emotional exhaustion, depression, and anxiety among police officers. *Police Quarterly*, *21*(1), 109–134.

Saputra, N., Putera, R. E., & Setra, A., Aswar, Valentina, T. R., & Mulia, R. A. (2024). Capacity building for organisational performance: A systematic review, conceptual framework, and future research directions. *Cogent Business & Management*, *11*(1), 2434966.

Shafait, S., & Huang, J. (2024). Examining the impact of sustainable leadership on green knowledge sharing and green learning: Understanding the roles of green innovation and green organisational performance. *Journal of Cleaner Production*, *457*, 142402. DOI: 10.1016/j.jclepro.2024.142402

Simmons, A., Reynolds, R. C., & Swinburn, B. (2011). Defining community capacity building: Is it possible? *Preventive Medicine*, *52*(3–4), 193–199. PMID: 21320524

Soost, C., & Moog, P. (2021). Gender and organisational performance in business succession. *Journal of Small Business and Entrepreneurship*, *33*(1), 93–122. DOI: 10.1080/08276331.2019.1692765

Tran, H. T., Santarelli, E., & Wei, W. X. (2022). Open innovation knowledge management in transition to market economy: Integrating dynamic capability and institutional theory. *Economics of Innovation and New Technology*, *31*(7), 575–603. DOI: 10.1080/10438599.2020.1841942

Wandersman, A., Duffy, J., Flaspohler, P., Noonan, R., Lubell, K., Stillman, L., & Saul, J. (2008). Bridging the gap between prevention research and practice: The interactive systems framework for dissemination and implementation. *American Journal of Community Psychology*, *41*(1–2), 171–181. PMID: 18302018

Chapter 8
Police Values, Ethics, Diversity, and Inclusion:
How Good Is the Force at Building, Developing, and Looking After Its Workforce

Ross Campbell
http://orcid.org/0009-0002-2283-6063
Independent Researcher, UK

ABSTRACT

This chapter examines how police forces build, develop, and look after their workforce to create an ethical, lawful, and inclusive workplace. It evaluates the role of leadership development, workforce wellbeing, and diversity and inclusion initiatives in shaping internal culture. Drawing on national inspections, workforce surveys, and inquiry reports, the chapter highlights the importance of psychological safety, representation, and professional development as foundations for public trust and legitimacy. Key issues such as first line leadership capability, the experience gap in policing demographics, and the risk of tokenistic development are explored. The chapter emphasises that fostering a culture of fairness and support from recruitment through progression is essential for sustaining public confidence and upholding the Peelian principles of policing.

INTRODUCTION

> *How good is the force at building, developing and looking after its workforce, and encouraging an ethical, lawful and inclusive workplace?*

DOI: 10.4018/979-8-3373-2757-0.ch008

Effective policing begins with its most valuable asset, people. The officers, staff and volunteers who make up a police force, and the service as a whole, are critical to effective service delivery, and in turn, maintaining public trust, confidence and legitimacy in policing. How they are led, developed, supported and treated directly shapes operational delivery and internal morale and well-being. In the 2023-2025 His Majesty's Inspectorate of Constabulary and Fire and Rescue Services (HMICFRS) PEEL inspection framework, Question 9 focuses on how well a police force builds, develops and invests in their workforce, and to what extent they foster an ethical, lawful and inclusive workplace. This is central to the concepts of policing legitimacy, organisational performance, and professional standards and its importance is fundamental to the institutional integrity upon which policing is based. A force which demonstrates its true value, invests in well-being, develops capable leaders, creates a psychologically safe space for its workforce to challenge and act upon behaviour and culture, promotes inclusion, builds trust from within and in turn, earns it from the public it serves.

The recent impact of high profile national reviews and inquiries; particularly The Angiolini Inquiry, Baroness Casey Review and the HMICFRS thematic inspection on Vetting, Misconduct and Misogyny in the Police Service have exposed failings in workplace culture, supervision and inclusion. These failings have had an unwavering effect on public trust and confidence and have highlighted the critical need for policing to prioritise its people. Forces which are graded as outstanding in this area are those who embed ethical values in leadership, take tangible steps to support wellbeing which go beyond superficial, short term measures and initiatives and create development opportunities which are fair, inclusive and transparent.

This chapter examines how forces can excel in this area, drawing upon practice from across the police service, HMICFRS findings and national learning. It focuses on how new recruits are supported from day one, the development of first line and mid line leaders courses, support for underrepresented groups and initiatives such as Fast Track promotion routes, ASPIRE and Senior Leadership Programmes alongside cultural reform linked to the Peelian principles of consent and legitimacy.

SUPPORTING NEW RECRUITS AND INCLUSION FROM DAY ONE

The initial experience of a new policing recruit, and staff member can determine their long-term commitment, confidence and professional identity. Whilst an individual's core values and morals are shaped by many different factors, such as upbringing, education and prior experiences, research shows that workplace environments and culture significantly influence whether those pre-established values are reinforced or eroded (Ashford & Anand, 2003). Forces who support their new joiners most effectively through structured training, inclusive supervision and identifying early and proactive wellbeing interventions and support are more likely to develop, and importantly retain a capable, motivated, diverse and capable workforce. The PEEL framework closely scrutinises how new recruits are welcomed, supervised and supported, especially those from underrepresented backgrounds.

The College of Policing's evaluation of the Police Uplift Programme (PUP) identified that a significant proportion of recruits, particularly those from ethnic minority backgrounds struggled to gain a sense of belonging in the early stages of their career (College of Policing, 2023). Forces that give consideration to this when designing and delivering new recruit programmes and allocate more experienced tutors, create inclusive cohorts and engage recruits in developing internal culture, build stronger links and improve retention. However, it is recognised that the police service is now younger and less experienced than at any point in recent history, with 37% of officers having less than five years of service (Home Office, 2024). This shift means that the available pool of experienced tutors is limited, particularly in front line roles so this will cause challenges in some police forces. As Loftus (2009) highlighted, workplace culture is shaped heavily in early service and without values based tutoring or mentoring, there is a risk of informal socialisation which can reinforce outdated or exclusionary behaviours. Police Forces must therefore prioritise tutor development and diversity to ensure new recruits understand the expectations which are being placed upon their standards and behaviours from the outset and equally, the expectations of tutors and mentors. Cumbria Police's approach for example in respect of new recruits, includes a personal welcome from the Chief Constable, structured welfare check-ins throughout the initial training and tailored support for those officers who are experiencing difficulties and challenges. This approach has been associated with improved retention rates, particularly where support has been sustained, and creates a sense that the organisation cares about the progression and wellbeing of their staff, in a new and pressured environment (HMICFRS, 2023a).

In contrast, the Baroness Casey review illustrates what happens when these positive experiences, and processes do not happen. She identified that in particular female and ethnic minority officers in the Metropolitan Police Service frequently reported feeling targeted and unwelcome during training and operational postings (Casey, 2023). One particular example cited in the report was from a female officer who faced sexualised comments from tutors with no challenge or intervention, and the behaviour was accepted and normalised. Others recall racist comments being seen as 'banter' that again, went unchallenged. Baroness Casey also observed an absence of consistent formal mentoring or visible role models. She concluded that the early experiences of underrepresented recruits often reinforced exclusion, and suggested that discriminatory behaviours and practices were, in the absence of challenge, tolerated. This in turn meant that trust in the organisation, and the wider police service as a whole was eroded.

Angiolini (2024) also highlighted this theme in her Inquiry, commenting that organisational culture is 'absorbed rapidly' by new recruits. Drawing on Baroness Caseys observations, Lady Angiolini described that where inappropriate language, behaviour, discrimination or exclusion is tolerated, even at a low level, that these behaviours become accepted as the norm. Police forces must therefore see the importance of the early stages of training and supervision as the critical stage for cultural immersion, and those cultures must be the right ones. Supervisors, tutors and training leads all carry the responsibility for setting the tone. A number of forces have implemented schemes for peer support and mentoring for new joiners from and throughout their careers. Greater Manchester Police for example has outlined its commitment to supporting minority recruits and building trust and confidence in its Achieving Race Equality Report 2024 (Greater Manchester Police, 2024). Workplace adjustment passports are also increasingly used across the police service supporting officers and staff with disabilities or long term health conditions, with formal schemes in place in Warwickshire, Gloucestershire, West Midlands and the Metropolitan Police Service, supported by national guidance from the College of Policing (College of Policing, n.d; Gloucestershire Constabulary, n.d; Police Federation, n.d; Warwickshire Police, n.d). These practices reflect the growing recognition of the requirements for supporting and retaining a diverse workforce and can be used to determine if a police force is proactively inclusive.

Attrition data also supports the importance of this focus. The Home Office (2024) reported that officers from ethnic minority backgrounds are still more likely to leave policing within their first three years of service and this trend has persisted despite recent recruitment efforts. This supports the viewpoint that internal toxic cultures, which are sometimes unseen and unchallenged, have long term and wide-reaching consequences and also reinforces the need to set, communicate and reinforce expectations to the workforce as a whole. Forces that do not adapt their inclusion approaches, wellbeing strategies and internal cultures, which includes the lived experiences of diverse recruits in order to understand the real barriers that exist, risk losing them which, not only wastes large investments made in the recruitment and training of officers but also misses vital opportunities to build representative workforces.

DEVELOPING CAPABLE FIRST LINE AND MID LINE LEADERS

As well as Senior Leadership, where there have been structured national programmes in place for many years, including the Executive Leadership Programme (formerly the Senior Police National Assessment Centre and the Strategic Command

Course) and Senior Leadership Development Course (SLDP), strong first and mid line leadership is essential to creating a lawful, inclusive and high performing workforce. Sergeants and Inspectors (as well as police staff equivalent roles) shape team culture from the front and in some of the most challenging operational environments, uphold standards, support wellbeing and significantly influence whether officer and staff feel supported. Poor supervision is consistently cited as a key contributory factor in low morale, wellbeing issues and decisions to leave the service (HMICFRS, 2022).

Effective leadership at this level requires more than operational competence and experience, it demands emotional awareness and intelligence, good ethical judgement and the confidence to call out and challenge poor behaviour, and support and advocate for inclusion. Many forces have invested in structured first line leadership programmes. This is in line with College of Policing's commitment to structurally reform its approach to leadership, through the National Centre for Police Leadership (College of Policing 2023). These programmes equip new, current and aspiring leaders with tools to lead fairly and competently. Areas of focus include managing conduct and performance, the development of people, wellbeing and mental health awareness and inclusive leadership. The best performing forces go further, embedding leadership development at all ranks and promoting broad coaching cultures within their organisations. Cumbria Police, rated outstanding in this area by HMICFRS has built a leadership framework that extends from the initial promotion to long term and ongoing development. Supervisors receive regular training refreshers and are held accountable for how they lead their teams (HMICFRS, 2023a). Warwickshire Police has introduced a first line and mid line leadership programmes that includes cultural competence training using lived experience, demonstrating a commitment to equipping supervisors with awareness and skills to lead inclusively (Warwickshire Police, 2024).

Mid line leadership programmes, which are for Inspectors, Chief Inspectors and police staff equivalent managers aim to bridge the gap between operational and strategic leadership, but at a rank or grade that very much sits between the two. These can be some of the most challenging positions in policing. Needing to be close to, and understand the challenges of the front line, and foster trust with their teams, but equally display sufficient strategic insight in order that key priorities can be delivered effectively. These programmes focus more on change leadership, professional standards and working more broadly across the force and more collaboratively. Whilst a more recent introduction to first line leaders programmes, nationally there has been increased emphasis and scrutiny on supporting leaders at all levels to more robustly uphold ethical and professional standards. There has been little, national investment on first and mid line leadership over the years, which is where toxic cultures breed and can flourish if not challenged, where leaders can become part of the problem and not the solution to it. Therefore, the focus in this area is welcome and overdue. This is supported by the findings of the 2022 HMICFRS thematic inspection on Vetting, Misconduct and Misogyny in the Police Service, which highlighted that too many supervisors were unaware of, or unwilling to act on concerning behaviour in the workplace. Angiolini (2024) echoed this, calling for stronger, values driven leadership, and a more emphasis on supervisors to prevent and respond to inappropriate behaviours and misconduct. Casey (2023) similarly found that leadership in the Metropolitan Police Service was often failed to challenge toxic behaviour that were passed off as 'banter'. Forces that perform best in this area, such as Humberside and Cumbria, have invested in leadership training, visibility and accountability.

WORKFORCE WELLBEING AND MORALE

Workforce wellbeing should be regarded as essential to operational resilience, strategic workforce planning, and institutional legitimacy. It goes without saying that forces that are proactive and that understand, and support staff wellbeing are better positioned to retain skilled personnel, minimise sickness-related absences, and ensure more reliable service delivery. The PEEL framework evaluates how well forces assess and address workplace stressors, how proactive their occupational health and wellbeing provisions are and importantly, how the workforce feels about their working environment and the support measures which are in place. The relationship between workforce wellbeing and operational performance has been well documented, although implementation remains variable across forces. Low morale, unmanaged stress, fatigue and burnout weakens professionalism, increases errors, erodes judgement and can contribute to misconduct (Wolfe & Nix, 2017).

The College of Policing's work with Oscar Kilo, the National Police Wellbeing Service has significantly raised the profile of wellbeing as a strategic issue across policing. The Blue Light Wellbeing Framework offers forces a self-assessment tool and many forces now have dedicated wellbeing leads, peer support networks and access to counselling and trauma support, whether it be in house or outsourced. However, the picture is not even or consistent nationally. In forces which are graded 'requires improvement', HMICFRS have noted fragmented provision, lack of meaningful staff engagement and poor provision or visibility of occupational health. The best performing forces use data insights such as stress related absence, exit interviews and pulse surveys to understand where pressure points exist, and importantly, positively and proactively act on them. Humberside Police provides an example of excellence. Graded 'outstanding' for workforce support, they embedded wellbeing as a core leadership responsibility. The Chief Officer team personally championed the initiative, with a 'Well Together' board, driving improvements from equipment to counselling access (HMICFRS, 2023b). Following a major incident in 2023, they developed an on-site wellbeing hub for all staff, which included TRiM (Trauma Risk Management) practitioners, refreshments and chaplaincy; a model now seen as best practice nationally.

In contrast, the Police Federation of England and Wales's (PFEW) Pay and Morale Survey (2023) painted a bleak picture of the service nationally. Over 94% of officers said morale in the service was low. 1 in 5 were planning on leaving within two years, citing poor workplace treatment, lack of recognition and high (unsafe) workloads, with nearly half stating that they were rarely, or never supported after a traumatic incident (PFEW, 2023). The disconnect, between strategic wellbeing strategies and frontline reality in forces where policies and initiatives are not embedded, undermines trust within the workforce and therefore, public service. This underlines the importance of the investment in, and training for first line leaders.

Wellbeing is particularly important in the context misconduct and organisational trust. Angiolini (2024) highlighted how toxic workplace cultures, where abuse is normalised and whistleblowers alienated, destroys psychological safety. Casey (2023) similarly found that the Metropolitan Police Services grievance and misconduct processes were so poorly trusted that officer and staff often suffered in silence. Police forces which do not protect their people, as described at the beginning of this chapter, their most valuable asset from harm, they not only lose talent but breed cynicism, silence, mistrust and disengagement. Quite simply, the wider impact is that those who are causing the most harm to the service and the public, are able to remain in it unchallenged.

Good and effective supervision is critical. Officers frequently cite their sergeant or inspector as the biggest factor when they feel supported. Forces that equip leaders to have welfare conversations, despite how difficult they can be, spot early warning signs, quickly build trust and and put rapid support measures in place. In Cumbria, new recruits and long serving staff alike reported high levels of confidence in their supervisors. This cultural normalisation of wellbeing, as everyone's business and not just a tick box or a bolt on, was key to their 'outstanding' grading.

DISPROPORTIONALITY, INCLUSION AND INTERNAL LEGITIMACY

The hardest places to reach in a police forces culture are those experienced by people who are underrepresented, more exposed to bias, or disconnected from traditional lines of influence. How they are treated reveals far more about an organisations values than any policy that might exist. Disproportionality in career progression, disciplinary outcomes and lived experience is a clear indicator of whether a workplace is genuinely inclusive and ethical. The HMICFRS thematic inspection (2022) identified that ethnic minority officers were disproportionately subject to complaints and misconduct proceedings, and that women in policing continued to face harassment and exclusion. Casey (2023) reported that, within the Metropolitan Police Service, Asian women were four times more likely to lodge an employment tribunal claim than white women, and that Black officers were more likely to face disciplinary sanctions. Angiolini (2024) linked these patterns to systemic failures in culture and leadership. Where low level misconduct was ignored and predatory behaviour allowed to continue unchecked.

Disproportionality damages internal legitimacy, which is the belief amongst officers and staff that their organisation is fair. As Myhill and Quinton (2011) argue, procedural justice inside policing shapes how fairly officers act towards the public. Tyler (2005) notes that public legitimacy – how they view an organisation from the outside, is similarly affected. When the public sees discrimination or abuse inside of policing, trust erodes. Recent reports and inquiries as described in this chapter, have made this a real and tangible problem across the police service. Some forces are taking steps to address disparities in progression and misconduct outcomes. West Midlands Police for example has been recognised for monitoring and publishing workforce data related to diversity and inclusion (HMICFRS, 2023b). Nationally, the College of Policing offers development programmes such as ASPIRE for underrepresented groups and encourage applications for fast track promotion routes (to Inspector and Superintendent), as well as the Executive Leadership Programme to support the progression of diverse talent (College of Policing, 2025). However, HMICFRS has cautioned that without a supportive and inclusive organisational culture, these schemes have limited impact. Development initiatives that are not underpinned by a sense of belonging may serve more as preventive measures than agents of genuine transformation. Forces must create environments where difference is genuinely embedded in daily practice, not simply acknowledged in strategy documents (HMICFRS, 2023c).

CONCLUSION

How a police force builds, develops and looks after its workforce goes beyond internal management, it defines public legitimacy of the service. The PEEL assessment rightly recognises that workplace culture, leadership standards and ethical behaviour are not peripheral issues, they are central to public trust and confidence. A force that fails its people, will, in time, fail its public, and at the same time risk developing toxic cultures which run through its core. At the heart of this lies a fundamental principle: You cannot deliver ethical policing to the public if unethical behaviour is tolerated within the organisation. The Peelian principle that the police and the public are the police depends fundamentally on mutual respect, fairness and consent. All of these, mean legitimacy. That trust and consent must begin inside of the organisation with how officers and staff are treated, valued and held accountable. Internal legitimacy underpins external legitimacy.

Police forces which are graded as outstanding in this area do more than just tick boxes. They invest in values-based leadership, inclusive progression and meaningful wellbeing support characterised by visible and engaged Chief Officer leadership. They equip first and mid line leaders to lead with integrity, call out harmful behaviours early and create cultures where people can speak up and where psychological safety is embedded. They use data to understand and address disproportionality, with purpose.

National programmes through the College of Policing such as ASPIRE, Fast Track promotion schemes and the Executive Leadership Programme offer opportunities, but without an inclusive culture across the service they risk reinforcing inequality rather than breaking it down. Development with belonging is key. The national picture, highlighted by Casey, Angiolini and HMICFRS, indicates that many forces have permitted damaging cultural patterns to persist despite sustained scrutiny an over many years have allowed harmful cultures to develop, exist and thrive. Trust has been lost, but the opportunity now and into the future is to rebuild it; force by force and leader by leader. This starts with how forces treat the people who wear the uniform and those who work for and within policing, whatever their role. This is central to restoring public trust, confidence and legitimacy.

This is a critical juncture for policing, and it has a choice. Transform from within or be transformed by public pressure and external scrutiny. The choices made today will define its future tomorrow and for generations to come.

REFERENCES

Angiolini, E. (2024). *Report of the independent inquiry into the abduction, rape and murder of Sarah Everard (Part 1)*. Home Office.

Baroness Casey. (2023). *The Baroness Casey review*. Metropolitan Police Service.

College of Policing. (2023). *Police uplift programme: Insights into the experience of new recruits*. College of Policing.

College of Policing. (2025). *Enhancing leadership capability: Our leadership development offer for policing*. https://assets.college.police.uk/s3fs-public/2025-01/Our-leadership-development-offer-for-policing.pdf

College of Policing. (n.d.). *Workplace adjustments passports*. https://www.college.police.uk/support-forces/diversity-and-inclusion/workplace-adjustments-passports

Gloucestershire Constabulary. (n.d.). *Disability policy*. https://www.gloucestershire.police.uk/SysSiteAssets/foi-media/gloucestershire/policies/disability-policy

Greater Manchester Police. (2024). *Achieving race equality report 2024*. https://www.gmp.police.uk/SysSiteAssets/media/downloads/greater-manchester/about-us/achieving-race-equality-report/achieving-race-equality-report-2024.pdf

HMICFRS. (2022). *An inspection of vetting, misconduct, and misogyny in the police service*. HMICFRS.

HMICFRS. (2023a). *PEEL inspection: Cumbria Constabulary*. HMICFRS.

HMICFRS. (2023b). *West Midlands PEEL assessment 2023–2025*. HMICFRS.

HMICFRS. (2023c). *State of policing: The annual assessment of policing in England and Wales 2023*. HMICFRS.

Home Office. (2024). *Police workforce statistics, England and Wales: 2023/24*. Home Office.

Loftus, B. (2009). *Police culture in a changing world*. Oxford University Press.

London Assembly. (n.d.). *Met workforce – disabilities*. https://www.london.gov.uk/who-we-are/what-london-assembly-does/questions-mayor/find-an-answer/met-workforce-disabilities

Myhill, A., & Quinton, P. (2011). *It's a fair cop? Police legitimacy, public cooperation, and crime reduction*. National Policing Improvement Agency.

Police Federation. (2023). *Pay and morale survey*. Police Federation of England and Wales.

Police Federation. (n.d.). *Reasonable adjustments passports*. https://www.polfed.org/westmids/our-work/equality/equality-faqs/reasonable-adjustments-passports

Tyler, T. R. (2005). Policing in Black and White. *Police Quarterly*, *8*(3), 322–342.

Warwickshire Police. (2024). *Race and equality plan update – September 2024*. https://www.warwickshire.police.uk/SysSiteAssets/media/downloads/warwickshire/about-us/equality-and-diversity/warwickshire-police-race-and-equality-plan-update-september-2024.pdf

Warwickshire Police. (n.d.). *HR and occupational health unit privacy notice*. https://www.warwickshire.police.uk/police-forces/warwickshire-police/areas/warwickshire-police/about-us/about-us/hr-and-occupational-health-unit-privacy-notice

Wolfe, S. E., & Nix, J. (2017). The consequences of low self-control and poor supervision on police misconduct. *Criminal Justice and Behavior*, *44*(5), 635–657.

Chapter 9
Achieving and Maintaining Workforce Integrity:
Rebuilding Trust – Police Ethics and Integrity

Jeremy Pearson
http://orcid.org/0000-0003-1941-6439
University of Sunderland, UK

ABSTRACT

This chapter critically explores how UK police forces can build and sustain an ethical workforce. It examines the erosion of public trust following high-profile cases, such as the 2021 murder of Sarah Everard by a serving officer, and the systemic failures these cases exposed in vetting, leadership, and culture. It highlights the role of ethical leadership in the HMICFRS PEEL inspection regime and the central importance of the College of Policing's Code of Ethics, updated in 2024. Case studies illustrate that positive leadership and clear standards support ethical policing, while misconduct, misogyny, and racism can flourish under an ineffective leadership regime. Key areas covered include vetting, misconduct management, and counter-corruption, with discussion of AI innovations, confidential reporting, and reforms in forces like Cleveland and South Yorkshire. Drawing on the Angiolini Inquiry and Casey Review, the chapter concludes that meaningful reform relies on ethical, consistent leadership and a proactive, values-driven culture across all levels of policing.

DOI: 10.4018/979-8-3373-2757-0.ch009

INTRODUCTION

The public rightly expects the highest standards of integrity from police officers who serve their communities and similarly expect the police to operate within the rules of law. Failure to adhere to these standards can result in a loss of both trust and legitimacy within those communities (Hough, 2021). This may, in turn, manifest itself in simmering resentment of the police and occasionally lead to large-scale outbreaks of civil disorder of the kind most famously seen during the 1980s in London and Manchester (Wain & Joyce, 2012) and in several other locations since then. Sadly, within the United Kingdom, several high-profile cases of police criminality have further eroded that trust in recent years, none more so than the murder of Sarah Everard at the hands of former police officer Wayne Couzins in 2021 (Herbert et al, 2025, Pickering et al, 2024, Hohl et al, 2022).

The loss of experienced officers and an influx of younger inexperienced officers due to the recent surge in recruitment causes further difficulties for forces. This issue is not without precedent and was highlighted as far back as 1981 as being a potential driver for community tension (Scarman, 1981). Therefore, given that the link between police malpractice and criminality is so clearly linked to community dissatisfaction and a loss of legitimacy (Low & Owen-Evans, 2024), police forces must do all that they can to ensure the integrity of their workforce. As part of the PEEL inspection regime, HMICFRS specifically inspect the effectiveness of forces in achieving this aim and how forces might create and maintain an outstanding culture of integrity within their organisations.

The characteristics of an outstanding force include significant evidence of innovation and effectiveness beyond that exhibited by forces that are performing well. Within the PEEL inspection regime, HMICFRS inspects forces to determine how well they develop and maintain an ethical culture, as well as tackling potential corruption (HMICFRS, 2018). A further feature of the PEEL framework is an examination of how well forces conduct vetting checks for both new recruits and existing staff; as well as managing organisational corruption. This chapter will seek to explore these areas in greater detail so that readers might better understand the characteristics of a force that is truly outstanding in delivering and maintaining workforce integrity.

CODE OF ETHICS

At the heart of any attempt to establish an ethical culture within a force, lies the Code of Ethics. First launched by the College of Policing in 2014, the code aimed to provide policing with a clearly defined set of ethical standards, similar to those already long established within the medical and legal professions. The code was given a significant update in 2024 when it was relaunched consisting of a set of Ethical Policing Principles and Guide for ethical and professional behaviour in policing (College of Policing, 2024). A codified set of standards allows senior officers to address allegations of wrongdoing within their force, while removing much of the ambiguity and subjectivity that existed within the misconduct system prior to its introduction. The Code and its accompanying set of Ethical Principles provide explicit guidance to officers regarding behaviours and attitudes that are unacceptable, preventing them from claiming ignorance of the rules, as was often the case before its introduction (Westmarland & Rowe, 2018). Consequently, the job of Professional Standards Department (PSD) investigators has to some extent, become easier since the code's introduction. A further imperative for the police service to embrace the Code of Ethics and the prescriptive standards it brings is the clear link between ethical police behaviour, procedural fairness, and legitimacy in the eyes of the public (Ramshaw et al., 2019, p25). However, application of new models within policing can be difficult due to the ambiguous nature of the role (Ramshaw et al., 2019, p31).

For the code to be truly effective in moving forces towards an ethical culture, it needs to be properly promoted and supported within forces. That requires strong leadership from chief officers with a determination to embed an ethical culture within their forces. HMICFRS has previously highlighted examples of this style of leadership, noting that within South Yorkshire, force leaders developed an ethical culture by setting standards within the force and acting as role models (HMICFRS, 2018). Sadly, examples of good practice are not seen frequently enough and the need to establish and maintain ethical cultures within forces has remained a challenge for many Chief Constables.

ETHICAL CULTURE

HMICFRS rightly seeks to identify whether force leaders promote ethical standards within their organisations and lead by example, providing strong role models for junior ranks. Unfortunately, there is no doubt that in recent years, the large number of high-profile examples of chief officers being disciplined or dismissed (Jacques, 2023; Heywood, 2024) for unethical behaviour has the ability to erode public confidence in the police. The sense that the police are not themselves adhering to those rules and laws that the public are held to, will almost certainly result in a loss of legitimacy in the eyes of the community (Hough, 2021). When chief officers lie, break the rules or otherwise indulge in corrupt behaviour, they additionally send a clear message to the rest of the force, that ethical behaviour is not a priority. Conversely, those police officers who believe their managers to be ethical are more likely to behave properly themselves (Sheldon et al, 2022, p80). Therefore, chief officers should ethically, be beyond reproach themselves, while being focussed upon rooting out corruption and misconduct. Those that are truly effective in promoting and creating an ethical culture, will also show a determination to lead from the front in confronting wrongdoing within their forces, while holding other senior officers to account for their actions (Punch, 2013, p193).

Consequently, outstanding police leaders are both focussed and innovative in their efforts to embed an expectation of ethical behaviour in all staff; and previously failing forces such as Cleveland Police have been able to significantly improve their performance through strong leadership. Graded as 'inadequate' by HMICFRS with a number of 'causes for concern' including some related to ethical conduct (HMICFRS, 2018), the force made subsequent improvements by maintaining a clear focus on ethical standards. The force a series of internal measures including messaging from chief officers, internal and external ethics committees and the appointment of an operational ethics lead. The Code of Ethics was embedded within all recruitment and promotion processes and internal prevent leads engage regularly with the workforce with one taking responsibility for standards and ethics and the other managing counter-corruption efforts (Cooke, 2021). These measures demonstrate what can be achieved when police leaders afford time, energy and resources to promoting ethical standards.

A great deal has been written about the negative effects of police culture and its ability to derail efforts to change police officers' attitudes and behaviour (Bowling, 2019, p168). While much of the writing describing the negative effects of police 'canteen culture' is somewhat overblown (Waddington, 1993), there is no doubt that some particularly problematic behaviours are consistently found to be exhibited by serving police officers with misogyny chief amongst them (Casey, 2023, Hohl et al, 2022, Selby, 2021). This issue was highlighted within the Angiolini Report (Part 1) which is discussed in greater detail later within this chapter, and it is clear that forces need to urgently change organisational cultures that allow misogynistic and other unethical attitudes to flourish. One potential solution might be to ensure that enhanced selection arrangements and vetting are required before the appointment of officers to the role of Tutor Constable. This might serve to minimise the potential for new recruits to be exposed to negative cultures immediately upon entering the service. However, given that racist, misogynistic and other unsavoury attitudes exist within some members of the general public and not exclusively within police forces, it could also be argued that the issue is a problem that society as well as police leaders must address.

Given that police forces recruit from the general population, until such attitudes no longer survive within society, the potential exists for the police service to import them with each batch of new recruits. Therefore, measures such as effective vetting must be taken by forces to ensure that improper persons are prevented from becoming constables (Sheldon et al, 2022, p89).

VETTING

Vetting is perhaps the single most effective means that the police service has of preventing corruption and future misconduct by attempting to ensure that unsuitable persons are prevented from joining the police in the first instance (Cubitt, 2023). The first line of defence in these efforts are force vetting units (HMICFRS, 2019) which should properly be part of each force's Professional Standards Department (College of Policing, 2019). The link between those individuals with previous convictions or a history of misconduct in other occupations and corruption or misconduct after joining the police, is already well established (Donner, 2019).

Efforts to regulate and raise vetting standards across UK policing have been ongoing since the early 2000s with a series of recommended operating procedures being provided to forces (ACPO, 2010). The College of Policing subsequently issued a Vetting Code of Practice and accompanying guidance to forces as detailed initially within Section 39A (5) of the Police Act 1996, as amended by Section 124(5) of the Anti-social Behaviour, Crime and Policing Act 2014 (College of Policing, 2023). In recent years, some forces have flirted with the idea of shifting responsibility for vetting into Human Resources (HR) departments. This universally poor idea had the potential to take decision making on matters of a police applicant's suitability for the role, away from seasoned PSD officers with an enhanced understanding of risk, and award it to HR professionals. However, the recent rash of high-profile cases of police criminality and corruption has served to focus the minds of chief officers, the public and HMICFRS to the importance of vetting to ethical policing. Consequently, vetting units now sit almost exclusively within force PSDs. However, vetting is not foolproof and some individuals with malign intentions can still slip through the net. Additionally, as acknowledged by the College of Policing (2019), vetting is '*not effective if used in isolation. It must be part of a wider protective security regime*'.

As well as an adequately resourced Vetting Unit whose staff are themselves vetted to a high standard, forces must ensure that all staff are kept up to date on the latest vetting obligations incumbent upon them (College of Policing, 2025). New technologies offer an opportunity for chief officers, operating within limited resources, to manage the administrative burden associated with more frequent vetting of both new entrants and existing staff. Such technologies may include automated data-matching systems, workforce analytics and open-source intelligence tools, which together could enable forces to move towards more continuous and risk-based integrity checking of serving officers (Dathan, 2024). Background checks of social media are another important yet time consuming part of the vetting process. Some commercial companies are offering products designed to fully automate this process and these systems, if proven to be reliable, offer some hope of forces being able to continuously monitor staff social media activity in a resource friendly manner. Artificial Intelligence (AI) offers further opportunities for enhanced monitoring of staff who might represent risk. Forces such as Avon and Somerset and West Mercia Police have already trialled new systems that use AI to scan huge amounts of internet material, emails and social media posts (Sylvester, 2025). These systems will only improve and develop over time, and they present forces with the opportunity to improve vetting processes and to conduct continuously updated risk assessments of officers.

MISCONDUCT

'The way police officers behave can have a huge impact on how the public feels about the police and therefore it can be argued that how complaints about police actions are dealt with can either damage or restore public trust in policing'. (Sheldon et al, 2022, p78). It therefore goes without saying that forces must properly investigate and manage complaints and reports of misconduct. While a robust regime of appropriate sanctions must exist for those officers who have been found to have committed misconduct, a great many more officers simply require advice or further training to address their conduct. This fact was acknowledged within the Police (Conduct) Regulations 2020 when the Reflective Practice Review Process was formally adopted as a potential outcome to a complaint designed to encourage learning and improvement (IOPC, 2022). The College of Policing has acknowledged that a 'blame culture' in policing will inhibit openness and learning; while reflection will assist staff development (College of Policing, 2024). Consequently, a balance between disciplinary approaches to police misconduct and a 'no blame' learning environment, needs to be found by forces.

Innovative work can be seen around the UK where forces have embraced this concept. The Metropolitan Police service (MPS), working with academic partners developed a 'Praise to Blame' model which sought to identify potential reasons why officers fail in their duties while acknowledging that things can and occasionally do go wrong. The model was subsequently used to inform a new MPS Complaint and Conduct Reflection Scheme (Tomkins & Hartley, 2021). In South Yorkshire Police, an organisational justice model has been developed which uses a model to determine whether officers have deliberately committed misconduct or whether their actions were due to decisions made with good intentions but unintended consequences.

This approach has allowed the force to ensure proportionality in the disciplinary sanctions applied to officers (HMICFRS, 2019).

COUNTER-CORRUPTION

Most police forces have a Counter-Corruption Unit (CCU) located within their Professional Standards Department that is tasked with exposing and acting against police corruption (Hagger Johnson, 2013). A number of practical steps can be taken by CCU to reduce the risk of corruption, and these include maintaining and policing a register of officers' business interests together with a robust policy that is well understood by staff on the declaration of inappropriate associations. Confidential reporting lines are also useful in allowing concerned police officers the opportunity to pass on information about the activities of colleagues (Rajakaruna et al, 2015). Given the considerable publicity and resultant public disquiet that has resulted from a number of high-profile cases involving misogynistic behaviour by police officers, this is a clear area of focus for CCUs. The suspicion that a great many officers display misogynistic attitudes and behaviours (Lloyd-Rose, 2023), together with the findings of the Angiolini Inquiry, mean that a range of interventions must be considered by forces. Expanding the use of confidential reporting lines to specifically include anonymous reporting for misogyny and discrimination is one potential avenue for forces to explore.

Gifts and hospitality are a further potential area for corrupt activity and one that many chief officers have fallen foul of over the years (BBC, 2010). Given that receipt of high value gifts or offers of hospitality place a degree of reciprocal obligation on police officers to provide favours back to the giver, it is essential that all officers are aware of force policies and that they fully understand when and how to declare items. CCUs should maintain and robustly scrutinise Gifts and Hospitality registers to ensure that any practices that might potentially lead to misconduct or corruption are nipped in the bud. As with vetting, AI systems might yet prove to be valuable in allowing CCUs to conduct proactive monitoring of staff to identify integrity risks. CCUs already possess a range of intelligence led covert tactics to monitor officers' behaviour, but background data analysis conducted by AI raises the future possibility of corrupt officers otherwise unknown to the CCU, being identified promptly before their activity escalates.

THE ANGIOLINI INQUIRY

The Angiolini Inquiry was established in 2023 to examine how serving police officer Wayne Couzins was able to abduct, rape and murder Sarah Everard, a member of the public (Angiolini Inquiry, 2025). Part 1 of the inquiry focussed on Couzins' offending while Part 2 will take a broader view of women's safety including an examination of prevailing police culture. Following the conviction in 2023 of Metropolitan Police officer David Carrick for multiple offences of rape, Part 3 of the inquiry was established to examine his offending behaviour. Thus far, only the first strand of the inquiry concerning the actions of Couzins has published a finalised report; with a total of 16 recommendations being made *'which are designed to help prevent a situation where anyone entrusted with the powers of a serving police officer abuses that trust in such a heinous way again'* (Angiolini, 2024). The report highlights a number of serious failings by police forces which should have prevented Couzins from gaining employment as a police officer and could have addressed his offending behaviour before it was allowed to escalate to the point that he committed murder. Inadequate vetting of Couzins' financial and offending history, as well as his overall character, allowed him to serve as a constable in three separate police forces. Poor police investigation of earlier offences of indecent exposure committed by Couzins was a further area of concern highlighted by the report.

THE CASEY REVIEW

Also commissioned in the aftermath of Sarah Everard's murder, the Casey Review examined the wider culture within the Metropolitan Police Service examining key issues such as misogyny, racism, abuse of power and the failure of vetting systems. The final review report was damning in its criticism of the Metropolitan Police Service, describing it as badly managed with poor recruitment and vetting processes that fail to *'guard against those who seek power in order to abuse it'* (Casey, 2023). To a large extent, mirroring the Angiolini Report, Casey found that ethical standards were not clear within the MPS and that opportunities to identify and act against predatory and unacceptable behaviour displayed by officers, were frequently not taken. Among a raft of recommendations for improvement were calls for a completely new and more effective vetting regime together with force reorganisation to address problematic internal cultures, behaviours and practices that were especially prevalent among some officers within specialist areas of policing.

CONCLUSION

Both the Angiolini Inquiry Report (Part 1) and the Casey Review Report make sobering reading for any police leader. They detail in the starkest possible terms the challenges that exist within the Metropolitan Police and the wider police service. There are clear and obvious areas of concern within these documents, and they provide a roadmap for chief officers to address priority areas within their own forces. The abuse of the office of constable, particularly in cases involving sexual misconduct, represents a real and previously under-recognised threat to public trust in policing. This problem together with other forms of corruption and misconduct must be fought with bold and consistent leadership, robust systems and a dogged commitment to integrity. It is not enough for chief officers to simply reassure themselves that systems and processes are in place to address these issues. To be an outstanding force, systems and processes must be frequently revisited and tested to ensure that they remain fit for purpose and are being followed by staff. Doing what has always been done is not an option and innovative practices are needed to ensure that all staff understand and adhere to ethical standards at all times. This will require a proactive, preventative approach which may involve PSD-led targeted campaigns, training, or other change initiatives. Ultimately, the culture within an organisation is set by its leaders and chief officers should be ethically beyond reproach themselves and be tireless in their efforts to ensure that ethical standards are in place within their forces. As we look to the future, the police service can do much to regain the trust of the public and restore the reputation of British policing. This process will be assisted with the acknowledgement that ethical standards need to improve and chief officers ensuring with absolute certainty that they do.

REFERENCES

ACPO. (2010). *ACPO & ACPOS National Vetting Policy for the Police Community*. Association of Chief Police Officers. https://discoverleveson.co.uk/evidence/Exhibit_KW_NIPA11/9496/media

Angiolini, E. (2024). *Angiolini Inquiry Part 1 Report Statement to Press Conference*. The Angiolini Report. https://iipcv-prod.s3.eu-west-2.amazonaws.com/STATEMENT-FOR-PRESS-PACKS-FINAL-1.pdf

BBC. (2010). Met chief Sir Paul Stephenson questioned over gifts. *BBC News*. https://www.bbc.com/news/10329062

Bowling, B. (2019). *The politics of the police* (5th ed.). University Press.

Casey, B. (2023). *An independent review into the standards of behaviour and internal culture of the Metropolitan Police Service*. https://www.met.police.uk/SysSiteAssets/media/downloads/met/about-us/baroness-casey-review/update-march-2023/baroness-casey-review-march-2023a.pdf

College of Policing. (2019). *Vetting Code of Practice*. https://library.college.police.uk/docs/appref/C553I0117-Vetting-Code-of-Practice-online-04.10.17.pdf

College of Policing. (2023). *Vetting Code of Practice*. College of Policing. https://www.college.police.uk/guidance/vetting-code-practice

College of Policing. (2024a). *Code of Ethics | College of Policing*. https://www.college.police.uk/ethics/code-of-ethics

College of Policing. (2024b). *Guidance for ethical and professional behaviour in policing |*. https://www.college.police.uk/ethics/code-of-ethics/guidance

College of Policing. (2025a). *Professional standards | College of Policing*. https://www.college.police.uk/app/professional-standards

College of Policing. (2025b). *Vetting - Authorised Professional Practice*. https://assets.college.police.uk/s3fs-public/2024-12/Vetting-authorised-professional-practice.pdf?VersionId=lvkOlukt26I3eQsjhOpkPlXGcGIvI4LV

Cooke, S. A. (2021). *Cleveland Police cause of concern revisit – Ethics and culture*. https://hmicfrs.justiceinspectorates.gov.uk/publication-html/cleveland-police-cause-of-concern-revisit-ethics-and-culture/

Cubitt, T. I. C. (2023). The value of criminal history and police intelligence in vetting and selection of police. *Crime Science*, *12*(1), 8–12. DOI: 10.1186/s40163-023-00186-3

Dathan, M. (2024). *New police vetting system aims to avoid repeat of Couzens failures.* The Times. https://www.thetimes.com/uk/article/new-digital-vetting-system-to-monitor-integrity-of-police-officers-fj9vz5cx7

Donner, C. M. (2019). "The best predictor of future behavior is…": Examining the impact of past police misconduct on the likelihood of future misconduct. *Journal of Crime and Justice*, *42*(3), 300–315. DOI: 10.1080/0735648X.2018.1537882

Hagger Johnson, H., Smith, G., & Roberts, C. (2013). Disproportionality in Internal Misconduct and Counter-Corruption Proceedings in Three English Police Services. *Policing. Journal of Policy Practice*, *7*(4), 359–369. DOI: 10.1093/police/pat030

Herbert, S. R. J., Ioannou, M., Tzani, C., Fletcher, R., & Williams, T. J. V. (2025). How the Sarah Everard Case has Changed Public Perceptions of Police Officers. *Violence Against Women*, *0*(0). Advance online publication. DOI: 10.1177/10778012251366237 PMID: 40785494

Heywood, H. (2024). *Northamptonshire chief constable who lied about naval rank dismissed.* BBC News. https://www.bbc.com/news/articles/ceqq74pg1evo

HMICFRS. (2018a). *Cleveland PEEL.* https://hmicfrs.justiceinspectorates.gov.uk/peel-assessments/peel-2018/cleveland/legitimacy/

HMICFRS. (2018b). *HMICFRS Judgment Criteria.* His Majesty's Inspectorate of Constabulary and Fire and Rescue Services. https://assets-hmicfrs.justiceinspectorates.gov.uk/uploads/PEEL-2018-judgment-criteria.pdf

HMICFRS. (2018c). *South Yorkshire PEEL.* https://hmicfrs.justiceinspectorates.gov.uk/peel-assessments/peel-2018/south-yorkshire/legitimacy/detailed-findings/

HMICFRS. (2019). *Detailed Findings.* His Majesty's Inspectorate of Constabulary and Fire & Rescue Services. https://hmicfrs.justiceinspectorates.gov.uk/peel-assessments/peel-2018/south-yorkshire/legitimacy/detailed-findings/

Hohl, K.. (2022). *A Procedural Justice Theory Approach to Police Engagement with Victim-Survivors of Rape and Sexual Assault: Initial Findings of the "Project Bluestone" Pilot Study* (Vol. 2). International Criminology., https://link.springer.com/content/pdf/10.1007/s43576-022-00056-z.pdf

Hough, M. (2021). *Good policing: trust, legitimacy and authority.* Policy Press.

Inquiry, A. (2025). *The Angiolini Inquiry*. The Angiolini Inquiry. https://www.angiolini.independent-inquiry.uk/

IOPC. (2022). *Reflective practice review process summary report*. Independent Office for Police Complaints. https://www.policeconduct.gov.uk/sites/default/files/documents/RPRP_summary_report.pdf

Jacques, P. (2023). *Gross misconduct of former chief constable 'so serious' he would have been dismissed, says PCC* [Police Professional |]. https://policeprofessional.com/news/gross-misconduct-of-former-chief-constable-so-serious-he-would-have-been-dismissed-says-pcc/

Lloyd-Rose, M. (2023). *'The sexism was so blatant, as if officers felt irreproachable': my year on the streets with the Met police*. The Guardian. https://www.theguardian.com/uk-news/2023/may/06/metropolitan-police-sexism-misogyny-year-special-constable

Low, N., & Owen-Evans, R. (2024). *Public trust and confidence in the police*. UK Parliament. https://post.parliament.uk/public-trust-and-confidence-in-the-police/

Pickering, S.. (2024). London, you have a problem with women: Trust towards the police in England. *Policing and Society*, *34*(8), 747–762. DOI: 10.1080/10439463.2024.2334009

Punch, M. (2013). *Police Corruption: Exploring Police Deviance and Crime* (1st ed.). Taylor and Francis.

Rajakaruna, N., Henry, P. J., & Scott, A. J. (2015). A necessary safety net: Use of a confidential internal telephone line to report unethical behaviour. *Police Practice and Research*, *16*(5), 431–443. DOI: 10.1080/15614263.2014.932695

Ramshaw, P., Silvestri, M., & Simpson, M. (2019). *Police leadership: changing landscapes*. Palgrave Macmillan.

Scarman, L. (1981). *The Scarman Report: The Brixton Disorders 10-12 April 1981*. HMSO.

Selby, J. (2021). *Opinion: The government gaslights women by pretending police misogyny doesn't exist*. Independent Digital News & Media. https://search.proquest.com/docview/2582274362?pq-origsite=primo&accountid=14154

Sheldon, B., Williams, P., & Blockley, T. (2022). *Understanding Policing and Professional Practice*. Taylor & Francis Group. https://ebookcentral.proquest.com/lib/sunderland/detail.action?docID=6961859

Sylvester, R. (2025). *AI there, you're nicked! Tech is reshaping how we fight crime*. https://www.thetimes.com/comment/columnists/article/ai-there-youre-nicked-tech-is-reshaping-how-we-fight-crime-jb9bv7qh3

Tomkins, L., & Hartley, J. (2021). *Organizational learning in action: 2020-2021*. The Open University. https://university.open.ac.uk/centres/policing/research/leadership-management-and-organisation/322-organizational-learning-action-2020-2021

Waddington, P. A. J. (1993). Police (canteen) sub-culture. An appreciation. *British Journal of Criminology*, *39*(2), 287–309. DOI: 10.1093/bjc/39.2.287

Wain, N., & Joyce, P. (2012). Disaffected communities, riots and policing: Manchester 1981 and 2011. *Safer Communities*, *11*(3), 125–134. DOI: 10.1108/17578041211244030

Westmarland, L., & Conway, S. (2020). Police ethics and integrity: Keeping the 'blue code' of silence. *International Journal of Police Science & Management*, *22*(4), 378–392. DOI: 10.1177/1461355720947762

Westmarland, L., & Rowe, M. (2018). Police ethics and integrity: Can a new code overturn the blue code? *Policing and Society*, *28*(7), 854–870. DOI: 10.1080/10439463.2016.1262365

Section 2
Efficiency

Chapter 10
Demand Based Strategic Planning

Sophie Curtis-Ham
http://orcid.org/0000-0001-8093-4804
University of Waikato, New Zealand

Eric Halford
http://orcid.org/0000-0002-3913-1679
Research and Innovation, Rabdan Academy, UAE

ABSTRACT

This chapter explores how UK police services use demand-based strategic planning through the Force Management Statement (FMS) process to ensure efficiency, effectiveness, and sustainability under the HMICFRS inspection framework. Achieving an "outstanding" rating requires a strong commitment to understanding and managing demand. Historically, police services employed forecasting, technology, and prioritization strategies (Walley & Adams, 2019). However, recent analysis highlights new enablers: data-driven insights, demand visualization, systematic use of technology, and evidence-based methodologies. Effective management relies on prioritization, resource alignment, agile performance structures, and workforce development. This chapter examines these enablers, detailing how outstanding services optimize strategic planning to meet evolving demands.

INTRODUCTION

"*How good is the force at leading and managing its services to make sure they are efficient, effective and sustainable*?" is a primary question posed to UK services under the HMICFRS inspection framework (HMICFRS, 2025). Answering

DOI: 10.4018/979-8-3373-2757-0.ch010

this question requires considering how police services strategically respond to and manage both present and future demand. This chapter explored this by conducting an analysis of services graded outstanding. Methodologically, this was achieved by conducting what is best described as a 'scoping review' of HIMCFRS PEEL inspections of all services graded outstanding in any of their past two official reports. This enabled us to identify how police services conduct and utilise demand based strategic planning to help lead and manage their services, through the Force Management Statement (FMS) process, which is the police's annual self-assessment submitted to HMICFRS.

For services to achieve outstanding requires them to be highly competent in a multitude of areas. This includes preventing and deterring crime and antisocial behaviour, reducing vulnerability, efficiently responding to the public, effectively investigating crime, and building a highly skilled, motivated and healthy workforce. Examining all these areas is beyond this chapter, and they are covered elsewhere in this book. Instead, this chapter focuses on the key enablers for achieving such a grading in these areas, each of which, outstanding services already use in their strategic FMS planning process.

Understanding and managing demand is foundational to the FMS process. This not only relates to external demand driven by crime, anti-social behaviour and calls for service, but also harm and vulnerability. Internal demand is equally important as this can detract resources from key frontline functions. All forms of demand must be considered in relation to their spatial and temporal impact on the service's capacity and capability. Research on historical methods of understanding and managing such demand employed by UK police services, has categorized them into a few key approaches (Walley and Adams, 2019). These include use of forecasting models to identify peaks in demand; adoption of new and emerging technologies to manage demand more efficiently; prioritization and grading of incoming demand; implementation of policies and protocols to manage demand deemed inappropriate for police response; and methods to reduce unnecessary deployment, such as telephone resolution or investigation; (Walley and Adams, 2019).

Our review and subsequent analysis of the reports identified that demand management practices have changed in the past half decade. Enablers for *understanding* demand can now be categorized as: developing a data-driven awareness of demand; visualizing demand; harnessing technological innovations systematically; and using evidence-based approaches to understand demand. Enablers of *managing* demand can be categorized as: using prioritization methodologies; aligning resources and activities to demand through culture, capability and collaboration; implementing a robust performance management and accountability structure that enables agile and flexible resource allocation; and adopting a workforce development and training mindset aligned to existing and future demand orientated priorities. Outstanding police forces use the full array of these enablers to demonstrate a strong commitment to understanding and managing demand in fine grain detail. In this chapter, after first introducing the overarching FMS process in more detail, we discuss each of these steps and enablers in turn.

FORCE MANAGEMENT STATEMENTS

The FMS plays a vital role in the strategic, financial, and workforce planning of all UK police services. Its intention is to help services achieve an outstanding grade by creating an operating model that is effective at managing demand by ensuring they have the right systems, processes, people and skills to tackle priorities related to current and future demand. The concept of the FMS was introduced to UK policing in 2015 in a letter to all chief constables from the then inspectorate of constabularies, Sir Thomas Winsor WS (Her Majesty's Inspectorate of Constabulary, 2015). The concept was piloted and refined by several police services, leading it to its current format. The existing FMS requires services to follow four key steps: assess current and projected demand, evaluate workforce performance and well-being, outline improvements to meet future demand, and identify risks related to unmet (hidden) demand, and mitigation strategies (HMICFRS, 2022a). The FMS is used to inform HMICFRS inspections on efficiency and effectiveness and supports thematic inspections and performance monitoring visits.

The FMS's goal is to force police services to consider their strategic planning more effectively by requiring each to provide a clear analysis of key concerns, supported by data and evidence, and to demonstrate how technology, evidence-based research, and innovation are incorporated to enhance their policing response. Structured into two parts, the FMS provides a summary that highlights key findings, strategic risk assessments, and decisions. It is supported by a detailed analysis across 12 sections covering finance, workforce well-being, public engagement, crime prevention, investigations, safeguarding vulnerable people, offender management, serious and organized crime, major events, IT systems, force-wide functions, and partnerships (HMICFRS, 2022a). Each section is expected to use data to identify projected trends over a four-year period and to evaluate workforce capacity and resilience to meet predicted demand and risks effectively, and, where necessary and relevant, to outline strategic improvements to enable them to do so.

UNDERSTANDING DEMAND

Data Driven Demand Understanding

Outstanding forces achieve deeper situational awareness through practices that leverage big data using advanced forecasting tools and predictive analytics. For example, Lancashire Constabulary uses algorithmic software to predict call volumes and crime trends up to four years ahead (HMICFRS, 2024a). Similarly, Avon and Somerset have developed a 'demand status plan' to provide an accurate, real-time overview of demand across the constabulary's entire jurisdiction and enable identification of trends over a 12-month period (HMICFRS, 2020b). This is used to consider both resource availability and anticipated calls for service and to adjust resource levels accordingly using four demand levels ranging from level 1 (normal operations) to level 4 (exceptional demand) (HMICFRS, 2022b). This has enabled their supervisors and managers to follow specific protocols for each demand level that outline procedures for mobilizing resources to manage operational pressures when needed.

The best police services also integrate internal demand in their strategic planning. Specifically, outstanding services understand who does what, and how long each function takes. They also use external data from partner organizations such as children's and adult social services, to aid their knowledge acquisition processes, providing a broader understanding of demand.

Although developing such a detailed awareness of demand provides obvious benefits, Avon and Somerset constabulary should act as a cautionary tale of unintended consequences. Lauded for their approach to understanding demand in 2020, their subsequent inspection was far less complimentary. It highlighted how the resources used to address peaks in demand were met using officers from vital roles, such as neighbourhood teams, leaving gaps in community policing that allowed problems to emerge or remain unresolved, negatively impacting longer term issues, and subsequent inspection ratings (HMICFRS, 2023a). This highlights the careful balance required to address sudden rises in demand, whilst maintaining core functions, such as problem solving, crime prevention and deterrence.

Similarly, Norfolk Constabulary was graded as outstanding for their strategic planning in 2021/22 and praised for their development of a combined partnership data warehouse to strengthen the police service's demand awareness and management potential (HMICFRS, 2023b). However, the following inspection highlighted how despite their initial ambitions, the constabulary was frequently hamstrung in leveraging technology to improve day to day functions to increase productivity and efficiency by insufficient capacity and capability within their IT departments (HMICFRS, 2023b). This demonstrates that simply possessing or having access to data is insufficient to drive outstanding services alone. To achieve this, the service must be able to capitalise on the capabilities presented by the available technology.

Demand Visualization

Combining predictive modelling and data visualization tools, outstanding organizations consistently find new ways to improve resource decision-making using data visualization technology. To help improve interpretability, visualization tools such as Power BI are commonplace in outstanding services, where they provide dashboards to enhance the service's agility by visualising spikes and trends in ways that are accessible for supervisors and managers. To support these, some services also supply additional performance analysis to frontline roles. For example, since 2022, West Yorkshire have used district-level performance researchers and a scorecard system to generate real-time data for monitoring demand and improving response performance (HMICFRS, 2023b).

Dashboards and tactical use of performance analysts both serve as ways police services can create an agile ability to identify emerging threats to capacity and capability, thereby enabling them to better prioritize risks and deploy resources accordingly. Arguably, a pre-requisite for any service to achieve an outstanding rating is to invest in hardware, software and people that enable them to effectively leverage data to analyse, visualize, and most importantly, use this information to drive strategic, operational and tactical responses at a daily, weekly, monthly and annual level.

Technological Innovation

Outstanding services do not simply possess and visualize data; they also leverage technology to improve productivity of their employees. Innovation in technology to underpin strategic demand planning and management is a recurring theme across outstanding services. They automate repetitive functions and replace manual and time-consuming tasks wherever technology enables. Above all, when doing so they take great care to ensure that IT driven digital solutions do not create additional demand for employees or jeopardize other key requirements, such as crime data and integrity. This was infamously exemplified by the Integrated Operational Policing System (iOPS) within Greater Manchester Police (GMP). Intended to modernize investigative record management for GMP, iOPS instead became a source of considerable turmoil, resulting in the force failing to properly record 80,000 crimes, leading to it being abandoned in 2022 after a £27 million investment (Scheerhout, 2022).

Moving forward, services looking to achieve or retain an outstanding grading will find ways to embrace emergent technology such as Artificial Intelligence, specifically machine learning, natural language processing and generative large language models. These technologies can be applied for a wide range of use cases that can improve the productivity and efficiency of services in responding to present and predicted demand (Halford, 2024). Specifically, studies are beginning to emerge that highlight its potential to aid report writing (Adams, 2025; Potts, 2024), conduct threat and risk assessments (Halford and Webster, 2024), and assist digital forensics investigators (Scanlon et al., 2023). A recent policing productivity review produced by the UK Home Office (2023) indicated that one service saved over 600,000 staff hours when they used generative AI to redact sensitive documents, producing real cost savings. However, caution has been advised, as promise and potential are not always realised (Boehme et al, 2025). Furthermore, as police services begin to consider automation and augmentation of policing functions using AI it is likely to have considerable effects on the workforce, both positive and negative. Therefore, the most forward-thinking police services will effectively balance the potential efficiency and effectiveness of embracing such technologies, with fairness and equitability in the redeployment and reskilling of their workforce (Halford, 2025). Services that do this best, will evidence this within the FMS and use this to articulate their reasoning, thereby ensuring they are best placed to achieve an outstanding grading.

Evidence-Based Approaches to Understanding Demand

Commonly referred to as the '*Pareto Principle*', or 80/20 rule, it is argued that 80% of any issue is caused by just 20% of the problem (Corsaro, 2018). Recent literature exploring this ratio for crime suggests it may be even higher: *"half of all crime events are concentrated within 3% of all street segments… harm is even more heavily concentrated, with half of all harm located in just 1%...*" (Weinborn et al., 2017, p1). Such concentrations in crime and demand relate to repeat victims, offenders and places (Clarke, 1983; Lee et al., 2017; Martinez et al., 2017a; Martinez et al., 2017b). Outstanding police services understand this and recognize that crime and demand concentrate spatially, temporally, and around certain individuals and groups (Lee et al., 2017; Martinez et al., 2017a; Martinez et al., 2017b; Weisburd, 2015), and they systematically seek to identify and address high demand generators. They do this across key areas of the FMS, such as calls for service, crime rates, vulnerable people, dangerous offenders, and serious and organized crime, to help focus their investigative, prevention and deterrence efforts for the greatest impact.

Traditionally, the police have used limited methods to identify whom, where and when crime and demand is concentrated. Think 'hotspot' and 'problem orientated' policing, which are overwhelmingly evidenced to reduce and prevent crime when applied in response to issues related to repeat victims, offenders and places (Braga et al., 2019; Weisburd et al., 2010). Historically, these approaches rely on volume counts (i.e., number) of crimes or incidents where each crime/incident is counted equally. More recent approaches consider a tripartite of demand forms that includes volume but also harm and effort (defined by time). All three should be considered by police services with ambitions of being graded outstanding, as doing so enables them to generate the most comprehensive understanding of demand, and to demonstrate this within the FMS.

Crime harm indices (CHIs) and Crime Severity Scores (CSSs) offer frameworks for understanding crime-related demand by accounting for the harm different crimes cause (Bangs, 2016; Sherman et al., 2016). To do this, police services can use either the Cambridge Crime Harm Index (Lewis et al., 2024; Sherman et al., 2017), or the Crime Severity Score, provided by the Office of National Statistics (Bangs, 2016). Both have their individual strengths and weaknesses, and for a detailed comparison of these, see the work of Ashby (2018). However, both ultimately have the same objective, to assign weights to different offenses based on the harm they (typically) inflict, as reflected in the sentences offenders receive for committing them, or the score they are assigned (Ashby, 2018; Bangs, 2016; Sherman et al., 2016). Crimes that incur more severe penalties have higher weights to reflect their relative harm (Sherman et al., 2016). Operationally, these values can then be applied to crime data, allowing the aggregated harm to be analysed across victims, offenders, times and places (Bangs, 2016), thereby helping pinpoint high harm /score problems that might not otherwise be identified (see Curtis-Ham, 2022). Police can then target resources and strategies to manage and reduce harm, not just crime volume (e.g., Walton et al., 2020; Weissofner et al., 2017).

A comprehensive strategic response to demand also considers the effort required from the police in responding to different types of demand. In the context of the FMS, examining effort also demonstrates that the police service has considered all aspects of demand in their strategic planning. Research has typically measured police effort in response to demand as response travel time (from dispatch to arrival at an incident) and/or time spent on scene (from arrival to 'closure' of the call) (Ratcliffe, 2021; Lum et al., 2021). A notable study that combined control room data with officer self-reported time logs found that crime-related incidents made up 24% of volume but 55% of officers' time, including subsequent investigation activity (Chartrand and Verret, 2023). Understanding what, where, when and on whom police effort is spent is vital strategically, operationally, and tactically, but also for the FMS.

Complementary to crime harm and score indices, a 'police response effort index' (PREI) offers a framework for understanding both crime and non-crime related demand by accounting for the effort involved in responding to different types of demand (Curtis-Ham et al., 2024). PREIs assign weights to different demand types based on the time typically taken during initial police attendance. Incidents that take more time to resolve have higher weights to reflect their relative effort. These values can then be applied to demand data, allowing the aggregate effort to be analysed across people, places or times to pinpoint high effort problems that might not otherwise have been identified. For example, Curtis-Ham et al. (2024) found that some low-volume demand categories account for disproportionately high levels of effort/time, whereas certain high-volume categories represent relatively lower volumes of effort/time. Further, some high-harm offenses, such as murder, contribute minimally to both volume and initial response effort/time indicating harm, volume and police time/effort are not always concentrated in the same areas. Using a PREI, resources and strategies can be targeted to time-consuming demand alongside high volume demand and high harm demand. PREIs are easily developed using Computer Aided Dispatch data following the method set out by Curtis-Ham et al. (2024).

Crime harm, scoring and effort indices are useful tools for understanding demand from different perspectives, but they do not tell the full demand story. As proxy estimates for the relative harm or effort involved in different types of demand, they do not capture all aspects of harm to victims (or society) or police effort. Where possible, therefore, police services should use additional data to understand harm and effort more fully. For example, violent offences can be analysed by the extent of injury and property offences can be analysed by the value of loss. If time on investigating and resolving crime/demand beyond the initial response phase is captured, this could supplement PREI based analysis[1]. Examining the actual time spent during initial response is also important, to identify changes in demand or police practice (Curtis-Ham et al., 2024). Accordingly, outstanding services use multiple methods of analysis to understand and address issues driving all three forms of demand. They use the FMS to articulate this and in doing so, reassure the inspectorate that the service is being lead efficiently and effectively.

MANAGING DEMAND

Prioritization

Analysing and responding to demand alone is not sufficient. Due to the increased scale and complexity of issues that police services face it is not possible to address all identified demand. Prioritization is paramount and it thus forms a key emphasis of the FMS, and of outstanding services. As the saying goes '*if everything is a priority, nothing is*'. Therefore, the priorities of outstanding police services are clear and linked to the vision and mission of the organization, complementing the police and crime plans of their commissioner's office. To help prioritize, they also rigorously engage with communities through multiple mediums to understand what is important to them. This information—combined with insights on volume, harm and police time/effort related to crime, incidents and vulnerability—provides services with a holistic backdrop to enable effective prioritization, which should be reflected in the FMS.

To conduct this function, outstanding services incorporate this information into the application of response models and risk management tools to better assess threat, harm and risk, enabling evidence-based prioritization. The Threat, Harm, Risk, Investigation, Vulnerability, and Engagement (THRIVE) model is one example. This model helps determine the appropriate response to a service call by evaluating the potential risks and focusing on the specific needs of the victim (College of Policing, 2021), thereby enabling more effective response prioritization. In high-performing services, the THRIVE philosophy is ingrained not only in control rooms, but the broader organization (Keningale et al., 2024).

Many organizations have also adopted The Management of Risk in Law Enforcement (MoRiLE) model, especially in areas reliant on intelligence analysis. The structured methodology within MoRiLE aids in prioritization and offers a consistent approach to identifying tactical and strategic priorities (College of Policing, 2020). If done well, this ensures that police services are effectively conducting the risk management step of the FMS process by identifying risks related to identified and unmet demand.

Outstanding services also take a culturally proactive approach to partnership information sharing, embracing a '*responsibility to share*' mindset, which is crucial for effective risk assessments underpinning Multi-Agency Risk Assessment Conferences (MARAC), and Multi-Agency Public Protection Arrangements (MAPPA). These multi-agency forums bring together statutory and voluntary agencies to share information about high-risk individuals and enable police services to work with partners to better prioritize vulnerable or dangerous people and develop coordinated action plans to respond or manage them. Although conducted in every police service in the UK, the best police services position such partnership working as a foundational component across all areas of business, including managing all forms of vulnerable people and dangerous offenders—including those linked to missing persons, all types of exploitation, violence against women and girls, serious and organized crime and terrorism.

Alignment of Resources and Activities

A deep understanding of demand enables outstanding services to excel in meeting it by aligning their culture, capacity, and capabilities, including those related to finance, IT, prevention, investigation, safeguarding, offender management, serious and organized crime, and partnerships. This approach optimises their use of resources and enhances the overall effectiveness of their response to all demand forms. For instance, Humberside and South Yorkshire have implemented practices that alleviate the burden on frontline officers by systematically shifting non-police duties to support staff (HMICFRS, 2024b; and 2023d). This reallocation allows warranted officers to focus on priority functions that require their specific powers and expertise. Additionally, beyond the impact of COVID-19, many outstanding services now encourage and enable remote working for tasks that can be done off-site, increasing productivity and supporting employee well-being.

South Yorkshire stands out as a strong example in the context of problem-solving through the way they have cultivated a culture where every part of the organization is dedicated to this philosophy (HMICFRS, 2023d). Similarly, within neighbourhood policing Lancashire Constabulary achieves effective alignment of resources and activities by employing a two-tier approach to Problem-Oriented Policing (POP), creating comprehensive POP plans for medium- to long-term solutions to local issues, while using a simplified version, 'POP-lite', for more immediate, short-term resolutions (HMICFRS, 2024a). This approach ensures officers are deployed to address the most pressing problems.

Collaboration with partner organizations is another key method used by outstanding services to leverage others' resources in responding to demand. Outstanding services have matured their partnership relationships to the extent that they can call on multi-agency resources when required. For example, Humberside Police actively collaborate with health and social services to manage high-intensity service users, helping to reduce repeat demand through their "Right Care, Right Person" initiative. It ensures vulnerable individuals are directed at the earliest opportunity to the appropriate agency, significantly saving police time (HMICFRS, 2024b). All the aforementioned activity should be identified as a requirement, with actions highlighted within the FMS process.

Governance and Accountability Frameworks

Mature performance frameworks are essential for driving effective alignment of capacity and capabilities but are not always given the attention they deserve. Outstanding services use well-designed frameworks to establish clear accountability and ensure organizational priorities are aligned with police activity. This ensures that what they say they are doing in their mission and vision statements, and reported in their FMS, is taking place. They do this by defining clear key performance indicators (KPIs) and establishing mechanisms for regular monitoring and review. Responsibility and accountability are enabled by ensuring that decision-makers have access to timely, accurate data about demand, capacity and capabilities, allowing leaders to use their skills to effectively allocate resources and proactively manage police activity. Outstanding forces have in place regular performance meetings where data on demand pressures are examined, and tactical and strategic responses adjusted accordingly. Governance structures also facilitate multi-agency oversight, allowing senior leaders to have a clear view of performance metrics across different agencies that influence their demand.

If done well, such performance and governance frameworks, often conducted daily, weekly, monthly and annually, help identify emerging issues and enable leaders to allocate resources to address present or projected gaps in capacity or capabilities (National Police Chiefs Council, 2017). This facilitates adaptability and responsiveness to changing demands, and ensures corrective actions are taken swiftly when necessary, ensuring that police and partnership capacity and capabilities are consistently aligned to meet demand (National Police Chiefs Council, 2017).

Workforce Assessment and Development

Workforce assessment and development also plays a critical role in the FMS process and enables police services to meet both current and future challenges, whether related to capacity and capabilities of their hard assets, such as vehicles and technology, or of their employees. Outstanding services' workforce development strategies place great emphasis on continuous learning and upskilling in the face of shifting demands. They do not stand still but take an innovative and proactive approach to ensure that the workforce, including its technology, is not only reactive to current issues but also anticipates future needs, positioning them to be more agile and responsive to the evolving landscape. As the threat posed by AI technologies grows—with expected rises in cyber-enabled crime, including fraud and offences involving deepfakes such as stalking and harassment (Europol, 2022)—services with this growth mindset will ensure they are prepared for the forthcoming challenges. Those who do not adapt their workforce will struggle to provide adequate services to their communities.

In this regard, West Yorkshire have been complimented for investing heavily in comprehensive training programs to ensure personnel are prepared for evolving challenges like those experienced in cybercrime (HMICFRS, 2023b). Norfolk and South Yorkshire have taken similar strategic steps to address skills gaps in cybercrime and digital forensics, which are becoming increasingly crucial in modern policing (HMICFRS, 2023c and 2023d). These forces have aligned not just their training, but also their skills and technological investments with their broader strategic goals to build expertise in technical areas required to stay ahead of criminal activities that increasingly involve digital elements. This alignment naturally ensures their workforces are equipped to tackle the present and forthcoming challenges and is one of the primary motivations of development of the FMS.

RECOMMENDATIONS FOR POLICE SERVICES

Drawing from the practices identified from our review of services graded outstanding under the HMICFRS PEEL inspection framework, we are able to outline a set of key recommendations that police forces can follow to enhance efficiency, and effectiveness, through demand-based strategic planning, in an effort to support an outstanding grading:

1. Embed the Force Management Statement (FMS) at the Core of Strategic Planning

Treat the FMS not as an annual, administrative requirement, but as a living framework that continuously informs strategic, operational, and workforce planning. Ensure it captures quantitative evidence of current and future demand, workforce capability, and identified risks.

2. Develop a Comprehensive Understanding of Demand

Build integrated data systems that combine external and internal workload metrics with data from partners to map all sources of demand including crime, vulnerability, and service calls. Use predictive analytics to forecast emerging trends and anticipate dynamic resource pressures.

3. Invest in Data Visualisation and Real-Time Decision Support Tools

To realise understanding, deploy platforms such as Power BI dashboards and geospatial visualisations to provide supervisors with dynamic, accessible insights into patterns of demand, capacity, and harm. Then, empower them to act on these insights.

4. Leverage Technology and Artificial Intelligence Responsibly

Adopt automation and augmentation using generative AI to streamline administrative, analytical, and process related functions, while ensuring safeguards for data integrity, ethics, and fairness. Deploy savings in time and resources into frontline delivery. Use the FMS to evidence how technology adoption drives productivity, improves risk management, and workforce upskilling.

5. Apply Evidence-Based Frameworks to Understand and Manage Demand

Integrate Crime Harm Indices, Crime Severity Scores, and Police Response Effort Indices (PREI) to measure demand across three dimensions: volume, harm, and effort. Use these tools to enable prioritised, proportionate responses to demand.

6. Institutionalise Prioritisation and Risk Assessment Models

Embed models such as THRIVE and MoRiLE organisation-wide to ensure consistent assessment of threat, harm, and risk across a variety of roles and functions. Use these models to inform both resource allocation and community engagement priorities.

7. Align Resources, Culture, and Collaboration to Demand

Streamline internal structures by systematically reallocating non-essential duties to core functions, foster multi-agency collaboration, and embed a culture of problem-solving across all departments. Use initiatives like *Right Care, Right Person* to redirect inappropriate demand and maximise police capacity.

8. Strengthen Governance, Accountability, and Performance Frameworks

Establish robust KPI systems with transparent oversight at tactical, operational and strategic levels. Use regular data-driven reviews to monitor capacity, identify performance gaps, and adapt resourcing dynamically.

9. Prioritise Workforce Development and Technological Literacy

Adopt a proactive learning culture by investing in continuous upskilling, particularly in digital forensics, cybercrime, and emerging issues, such as Generative AI applications. Align training and recruitment with the service's strategic forecast of future crime trends and demand areas.

10. Foster a Forward-Thinking and Adaptive Organisational Mindset

View demand-based planning as a continual process of reflection and innovation. Encourage leadership behaviours that support experimentation, use of the best available data and evidence, and learn from failure.

CONCLUSION

Demand-based strategic planning, underpinned by the Force Management Statement (FMS), is critical for ensuring that police services are efficient, effective, and sustainable in responding to both current and future challenges. As illustrated in this chapter, outstanding services use the FMS practically and demonstrate a commitment to a data-driven understanding of demand, leveraging technology and evidence-based approaches to inform decision-making and resource allocation. Through robust prioritization frameworks, effective partnerships, and governance structures, these services systematically align their resources, investments and operational action with strategic priorities, both present and projected, ensuring effectiveness and resilience in the face of evolving policing issues. Moreover, the alignment of their workforce development and technological innovation is central to their success, enabling them to meet their identified challenges. Ultimately, services that excel in demand-based strategic planning are those that embrace a proactive and forward-thinking approach, using the insights provided by the FMS to continuously improve and deliver better services for their existing and future communities.

REFERENCES

Adams, I. T. (2025). Automation and artificial intelligence in police body-worn cameras: Experimental evidence of impact on perceptions of fairness among officers. *Journal of Criminal Justice*, *97*, 102373.

Ashby, M. P. (2018). Comparing methods for measuring crime harm/severity. *Policing. Journal of Policy Practice*, *12*(4), 439–454.

Bangs, M. (2016). *Research outputs: developing a Crime Severity Score for England and Wales using data on crimes recorded by the police*. Office for National Statistics.

Boehme, H., Adams, I. T., & Barter, M., Jr. I. A. G., & McLean, K. (2025). Writing at the Speed of Hype: Officers' Post-Experimental Perceptions of AI Report Writing. CrimRxiv. https://doi.org/DOI: 10.21428/cb6ab371.bfbd0534

Braga, A. A., Turchan, B., Papachristos, A. V., & Hureau, D. M. (2019). Hot spots policing of small geographic areas effects on crime. *Campbell Systematic Reviews*, *15*(3), e1046. PMID: 37133274

Chartrand, E., & Verret, E. (2023). Beyond the scene: The importance of time consumed on incident report task components in workload-based patrol allocation and deployment assessments. *The Police Journal*. Advance online publication. DOI: 10.1177/0032258X231192009

Clarke, R. V. (1983). Situational crime prevention: Its theoretical basis and practical scope. *Crime and Justice*, *4*, 225–256.

College of Policing (2020) Evaluation and review. MoRILE. Accessed Online. Available at: Evaluation and review | College of Policing

College of Policing (2021) Introduction to vulnerability-related risk. Accessed Online. Available at: Introduction to vulnerability-related risk | College of Policing

Corsaro, N. (2018). More than lightning in a bottle and far from ready-made. Criminology & Pub. *Pol'y*, *17*, 251.

Curtis-Ham, S. (2022). Measuring harm with crime harm indices. In Bland, M., Ariel, B., & Ridgeon, N. (Eds.), *The crime analyst's companion* (pp. 177–192). Springer International Publishing., DOI: 10.1007/978-3-030-94364-6_1

Curtis-Ham, S., Jones, R., Dunstan, E., Looc, R., & Jordan, C. (2024). A Police Response Effort Index to complement counts and harm indices in understanding crime and policing demand. *Crime Science*, *13*(1), 1–12.

Europol (2022), Facing reality? Law enforcement and the challenge of deepfakes, an observatory report from the Europol Innovation Lab, Publications Office of the European Union, Luxembourg.

Halford, E. (2025). Policing in the age of artificial intelligence: A simulation study modelling workforce automation scenarios. *Police Practice and Research*, •••, 1–24.

Halford, E., & Webster, A. (2024). Using chat GPT to evaluate police threats, risk and harm. *International Journal of Law, Crime and Justice*, *78*, 100686.

Her Majesty's Inspectorate of Constabulary. (2015) Letter to chief constables and police and crime commissioners introducing FMSs. Accessed online. Available at: https://assets-hmicfrs.justiceinspectorates.gov.uk/uploads/2015-07-10-letter-to-CCs-PCCs-re-FMS.pdf

His Majesty's Inspectorate of Constabularies, Fire and Rescue Services. (2020b) PEEL Police effectiveness, efficiency and legitimacy 2018/19 An inspection of Avon and Somerset Constabulary. Accessed online. Available at: https://hmicfrs.justiceinspectorates.gov.uk/publications/peel-assessment-2018-19-avon-and-somerset/

His Majesty's Inspectorate of Constabularies, Fire and Rescue Services. (2022a) Force management statement template and guidance. Accessed online. Available at: https://hmicfrs.justiceinspectorates.gov.uk/publication-html/force-management-statement-guidance-for-forces/

His Majesty's Inspectorate of Constabularies, Fire and Rescue Services. (2023a) PEEL 2021/22 Police effectiveness, efficiency and legitimacy an inspection of Avon and Somerset Constabulary. Accessed online. Available at: https://hmicfrs.justiceinspectorates.gov.uk/peel-reports/avon-and-somerset-2021-22/

His Majesty's Inspectorate of Constabularies, Fire and Rescue Services. (2023b) PEEL 2021/22 Police effectiveness, efficiency and legitimacy an inspection of West Yorkshire Police. Accessed online. Available at: https://hmicfrs.justiceinspectorates.gov.uk/peel-reports/west-yorkshire-2021-22/

His Majesty's Inspectorate of Constabularies, Fire and Rescue Services. (2023c) PEEL 2021/22 Police effectiveness, efficiency and legitimacy an inspection of Norfolk Constabulary. Accessed online. Available at: https://hmicfrs.justiceinspectorates.gov.uk/peel-reports/norfolk-2021-22/

His Majesty's Inspectorate of Constabularies, Fire and Rescue Services. (2023d) PEEL 2021/22 Police effectiveness, efficiency and legitimacy an inspection of South Yorkshire Police. Accessed online. Available at: https://hmicfrs.justiceinspectorates.gov.uk/peel-reports/south-yorkshire-2021-22/

His Majesty's Inspectorate of Constabularies, Fire and Rescue Services. (2024a) PEEL 2023–25 Police effectiveness, efficiency and legitimacy an inspection of Lancashire Constabulary. Accessed online. Available at: https://hmicfrs.justiceinspectorates.gov.uk/peel-reports/lancashire-2023-25/

His Majesty's Inspectorate of Constabularies, Fire and Rescue Services. (2024b) PEEL 2023–25 Police effectiveness, efficiency and legitimacy an inspection of Humberside Police. Accessed online. Available at: https://hmicfrs.justiceinspectorates.gov.uk/peel-reports/humberside-2023-25/

Home Office. (2023). Independent report. Policing Productivity Review. Independent review into productivity in policing, with recommendations on how to improve it. https://www.gov.uk/government/publications/policing-productivity-review

Keningale, P., Halford, E., Bullock, K., & Garland, J. (2024). Optimising intelligence operations for international law enforcement: harnessing THRIVE for national intelligence model advancement. *Journal of Policing, Intelligence and Counter Terrorism*, 1-21.

Lee, Y., & Eck, J. E., O, S., & Martinez, N. N. (2017). How concentrated is crime at places? A systematic review from 1970 to 2015. *Crime Science*, *6*, 1–16.

Lewis, S., Pina-Sánchez, J., & Birks, D. (2024). The risk of negative feedback loops in some weighted measures of crime harm. *Crime Science*, *13*(1), 18.

Lum, C., Koper, C., & Wu, X. (2021). Can we really defund the police? A nine agency study of police response to calls for service. *Police Quarterly*, *25*, 109861112110350. DOI: 10.1177/10986111211035002

Martinez, N. N., Lee, Y., & Eck, J. E. (2017a). How concentrated is crime among victims? A systematic review from 1977 to 2014. *Crime Science*, *6*(1), 1–16.

Martinez, N. N., Lee, Y., & Eck, J. E., & O, S. (2017b). Ravenous wolves revisited: A systematic review of offending concentration. *Crime Science*, *6*, 1–16.

National Police Chiefs Council. (2017). Better understanding demand–Policing the future. Performance Management Coordination Committee. *Retrieved from NPCC:* https://www. npcc. police. uk/2017% *20FOI/CO/078*.

Potts, J. (2024). The impact of large language models on police report writing and beyond. Police1. Retrieved from https://www.police1.com/tech-pulse/the-impact-of-large-language-models-on-police-report-writing-and-beyond

Scanlon, M., Breitinger, F., Hargreaves, C., Hilgert, J. N., & Sheppard, J. (2023). ChatGPT for digital forensic investigation: The good, the bad, and the unknown. *Forensic Science International Digital Investigation*, *46*, 301609.

Scheerhout, J. (2022). Key part of GMP's troubled iOPS computer system FINALLY set to be scrapped: Greater Manchester News. Accessed online. Available at: https://www.manchestereveningnews.co.uk

Sherman, L. W., Neyroud, P. W., & Neyroud, E. (2016). The Cambridge crime harm index: Measuring total harm from crime based on sentencing guidelines. Policing. *Journal of Policy Practice*, *10*(3), 171–183.

Walley, P., & Adams, M. M. (2019). *An evaluation of demand management practices in UK police forces*. Centre for Policing Research and Learning.

Walton, D., Martin, S., & Li, J. (2020). Iwi community justice panels reduce harm from re-offending. *Kotuitui*, *15*(1), 75–92. DOI: 10.1080/1177083X.2019.1642921

Weinborn, C., Ariel, B., Sherman, L. W., & O'Dwyer, E. (2017). Hotspots vs. harm-spots: Shifting the focus from counts to harm in the criminology of place. *Applied Geography (Sevenoaks, England)*, *86*, 226–244.

Weisburd, D. (2015). The law of crime concentration and the criminology of place. *Criminology*, *53*(2), 133–157.

Weisburd, D., Telep, C. W., Hinkle, J. C., & Eck, J. E. (2010). Is problem-oriented policing effective in reducing crime and disorder? Findings from a Campbell systematic review. *Criminology & Public Policy*, *9*(1), 139–172.

Weissofner, N. M., Henry, P. J., & Scott, A. J. (2017). A preliminary examination of the effect of Operation Turning Point Western Australia: An evidence-based policing strategy. *Australia and New Zealand Journal of Evidence Based Policing*, *2*(1), 30–35.

ENDNOTE

1 In the authors' experience, this information is not usually recorded against specific crimes/incidents to be able to include when creating a PREI, but it may be captured in HR systems in a way that can otherwise help identify high investigative effort demands. Further, given high harm crimes tend to require more investigative effort, CHI-based analysis somewhat 'plugs the gap' of investigative effort not captured in a PREI.

Chapter 11

Achieving Maximal Efficiency Using Systems Thinking:

Creating a Systems of Effectiveness – Criminal Investigation

Robert David Ewin
http://orcid.org/0000-0003-0611-5207
South Wales Police, UK

ABSTRACT

The author in this chapter situates the development of systems thinking within policing as a model to achieve outstanding outcomes. An analysis is presented of the necessary elements of systems thinking to develop criminal investigation with an example from Cumbria Constabulary. Critical to this is leadership, and a commitment to understanding elements of the system at a deep level before taking steps to initiate change. This approach had the potential to secure justice for victims and enhance investigative reliability which is critical to the legitimacy of modern policing.

INTRODUCTION

This chapter explores the application of systems thinking to the practice of criminal investigation, situating policing within a broader tradition of systemic approaches that have long been established in sectors such as aviation, manufacturing, and public-sector reform. Systems thinking emphasises the optimisation of whole

DOI: 10.4018/979-8-3373-2757-0.ch011

systems rather than isolated components, challenging reductionist, command-and-control models that dominate many organisational environments. Drawing on Seddon's Vanguard Method, the chapter examines how leaders' understanding of system purpose, demand, flow, and capability can shape investigative performance and organisational learning. This perspective is contrasted with traditional approaches that rely on technological solutions, outsourcing, or increased specialisation, which often fail to address the underlying causes of failure demand or the complexity of investigative work.

Using Cumbria Constabulary's 'Principles of Investigation' (POI) as a case study, the chapter demonstrates how a clearly defined and consistently applied investigative system can enhance investigative quality, reduce avoidable demand, and support more coherent supervisory oversight. The POI provide a structured framework for initial investigative planning, supervisory review, handover, victim updates, and case closure, offering a shared language and set of expectations for officers, supervisors, and reviewers. Through comparative analysis with other forces' PEEL assessments, the chapter highlights how inconsistent systems, weak supervisory capability, and fragmented handover processes contribute to investigative failure and undermine public confidence.

The chapter also draws parallels with established systems-thinking disciplines, particularly aviation, where checklists, structured decision-making, and post-event learning have been central to improving safety and reliability. These comparisons illustrate how policing can benefit from adopting similar principles of system design, continuous learning, and organisational reflection. The discussion emphasises that systems thinking is not solely a technical exercise but a cultural and leadership endeavour. Effective implementation requires leaders at all levels to model reflective practice, support learning rather than blame, and engage practitioners in the design and refinement of investigative systems.

Overall, the chapter argues that forces seeking to improve investigative effectiveness must prioritise system design, cultural adoption, and leadership engagement over isolated procedural fixes. By embedding systems thinking into investigative practice, policing can develop more resilient, consistent, and purpose-driven investigative models capable of delivering justice with integrity. The chapter contributes to the growing body of literature advocating for systemic approaches in policing and provides a practical example of how such approaches can be operationalised within a UK force.

INTRODUCING A SYSTEMS APPROACH IN JUSTICE.

Introducing a systems approach to justice requires looking beyond the final outcome of a court process and examining the integrity of the investigation that precedes it. Justice is not solely defined by conviction or disposal; it is shaped by the quality, consistency, and fairness of the investigative journey. For an investigation to support justice, it must operate with a high degree of system integrity, ensuring that each stage of the process is purposeful, coherent, and aligned with the needs of victims and the public.

Modern police forces increasingly rely on technology to support investigative frameworks (Prince et al., 2021). While such tools can assist with structure and workflow, they cannot replace the human and organisational elements that determine investigative quality. What remains essential is a system that focuses investigative effort, enables effective review, and ensures that outcomes are appropriate and defensible. Achieving this depends on investigators and leaders adopting a systems-thinking mindset rather than relying solely on procedural or technological solutions.

The PEEL Assessment Framework (PEEL) 2023–2025 (HMICFRS, 2023a) evaluates how effectively forces investigate crime. Its judgments are shaped by factors such as supervisory oversight, the competence and capacity of investigative teams, and the consistency with which forces apply investigative standards. A content analysis of PEEL assessments across 30 forces graded as 'inadequate', 'adequate', or 'requiring improvement' shows that most commentary focuses on resources, skills, and supervisory capability. While these elements are important, they do not fully explain investigative effectiveness. It is equally necessary to consider the system within which investigators operate; particularly, in forces where new IT solutions coexist with legacy systems, creating complexity, fragmentation, and interoperability challenges.

Seddon's systems-thinking principles offer a useful lens for understanding investigative performance. From this perspective, the victim becomes the primary customer of the investigative system, and the aim is to design processes that reliably meet their needs. Reducing failure demand, such as repeated victim contact due to delays or poor updates, creates time savings and improves investigative flow. Leadership plays a critical role in embedding a mindset where failure is not associated with blame but is instead viewed as an opportunity to refine and strengthen the system. This aligns with HMICFRS findings from the 2023–2025 PEEL cycle, which noted that the 'Principles of Investigation' were "consistently applied and were welcomed by officers and staff across the organisation," providing a clear and trusted quality framework for investigations (HMICFRS, 2024).

Cumbria Constabulary was the only force graded 'Good' for investigating crime during the 2023–25 PEEL cycle (HMICFRS, 2024). This achievement reflects sustained investment in a consistent investigative process, supported by regular oversight and a commitment to continuous improvement. With further refinement and wider application across the investigative system, the force has the potential to progress from 'Good' to 'Outstanding'. However, such progress depends on maintaining stability and resisting abrupt shifts toward untested or poorly developed models. A systems approach emphasises learning, consistency, and purposeful design; these qualities that can be undermined by sudden organisational change.

CREATING SYSTEMS OF EFFECTIVENESS – CRIMINAL INVESTIGATION.

The purpose of this discussion is to demonstrate the applicability of systems thinking in policing and to contrast this with other sectors where systems thinking is more established. As Seddon's Vanguard Method emphasises, systems thinking requires organisations to move beyond attributing blame for failure demand and instead understand the underlying conditions that shape performance. A similar perspective is evident in air accident investigation, where Bennett (2015) describes systems thinking as a means of understanding pilot cognition, system behaviour, and ultimately aircraft performance. In aviation, pilots are presented with complex information that must be interpreted using inflight manuals and checklists (Zieja et al., 2015). These checklists are the product of extensive research and learning from previous failures, designed to provide reliable solutions when followed correctly (Bennett, 2015; Afrazeh & Bartsch, 2007).

This checklist concept ensures that an aircraft departs, flies, and lands safely in a consistent and repeatable way. The same principle should guide systems of effectiveness around investigation, such as the Principles of Investigation (POI). A systems-based approach can also be applied to other areas of policing, from missing-person enquiries to digital-evidence handling. The essential requirement is that the system is adopted consistently across the organisation, preventing failures in one part of the system from undermining others (Bennett, 2015; Seddon & O'Donovan, 2023). When the investigative system fails, there should be an effective post-event review that identifies how the system can be refined, rather than a search for individual blame.

Ultimately, passenger confidence in aviation is strengthened through continuous learning and the systematic removal of ineffective practices (Zieja et al., 2015). In policing, public confidence similarly depends on the reliability and consistency of investigative systems. The Nottinghamshire PEEL Assessment (2023–2025), graded 'inadequate' for investigating crime, highlighted that case-handover templates were often incomplete or unchecked, resulting in subsequent investigators having to redo tasks such as obtaining statements or seizing evidence (HMICFRS, 2023b). This reflects a system that has not been fully understood or embedded, aligning more closely with command-and-control thinking than with systems thinking. Templates and checklists alone cannot create an effective system unless they are supported by leadership, training, and a culture that values learning and consistency.

A critical component of developing a systems-thinking approach is the deliberate effort to embed a mindset that supports it. Cumbria's experience demonstrates that systems thinking cannot be sustained through process design alone; it requires cultural adoption. Leaders must model the behaviours expected of investigators: curiosity, reflection, and a focus on purpose rather than compliance. Supervisors need to understand demand, system conditions, and investigative flow, enabling them to guide officers through problem-solving rather than simply enforcing activity targets. Training, reflective practice, and shared learning opportunities help investigators internalise the principles of systems thinking. Over time, this creates a culture where system failures are viewed as opportunities for refinement rather than triggers for blame, and where the investigative process becomes a shared organisational responsibility rather than a series of isolated tasks.

To develop a systems-thinking approach around investigation, organisations must first recognise the repeated events and patterns that occur, using these to develop tools that guide or reshape future behaviour (Monet & Gannon, 2015). Complex and volume investigations are often treated as distinct categories, with complex cases attracting more resources. However, the increasing complexity of volume crime means investigative labour is spread more thinly, increasing the risk of ineffective practice. Techniques traditionally associated with complex crime are now frequently required in volume investigations (Home Office, 2023).

If policing systems focus on developing specialist resources without considering the system those resources operate within, the investment is likely to be wasted. This reflects a command-and-control mindset. Investigations do not happen by chance; yet in practice they are often reduced to routinisation, categorisation, and bureaucratic crime management (Newburn et al., 2012). At the outset of a case, investigators and supervisors should have a clear understanding of the minimum requirements for success. Defining success early helps focus attention on the system of effectiveness required for a high-quality investigation.

The West Yorkshire PEEL Assessment (2023–2025), graded 'requires improvement', highlighted the use of Quality Assurance Thematic Testing (QATT) as a means of dip-sampling investigations. While useful, this is a post-event approach: the investigation has already occurred, and the system has already been applied. QATT can identify training needs or supervisory issues, but it does not provide investigators with a clear system for recording, sequencing, or structuring their work. A systems-thinking approach requires defining the system first, then applying quality assurance to ensure it is used consistently. This avoids reductionist approaches that oversimplify complex investigative work.

The POI provides one such system for managing investigative effectiveness, but its success depends heavily on first-line leadership. Supervisory capability and capacity remain significant challenges: "Supervisors are busy and frequently have high workloads, particularly in specialist teams. And they are often inexperienced (and managing inexperienced teams)" (HMICFRS, 2023). Research into unsolved homicide investigations shows that supervisory experience significantly influences the early direction of cases (Hill & O'Neill, 2019). Forces with high workloads and limited supervisory oversight experience reduced investigative effectiveness.

This pattern is reflected in the Staffordshire PEEL Assessment (2023–2025), which identified weaknesses in early supervisory reviews, and in Bedfordshire, where poor-quality handovers and insufficient supervisory checks were highlighted (HMICFRS, 2023d; 2023e). Early review and handover are critical components of an effective investigative system, yet they are often weak points. This may reflect a limited understanding of what a good handover system looks like.

The challenge of effective handover is not unique to policing. In healthcare, particularly nursing, the transfer of critical patient information has been widely studied, with emphasis on safety scans to ensure vital systems have not been compromised (Chaboyer et al., 2010). The POI incorporates similar principles, requiring safeguarding checks and resource identification at the point of handover. In policing, where specialist teams often take over from frontline officers, the clarity and consistency of handover processes are essential. Effective handover ensures that investigative systems function as intended and that investigators and supervisors can maintain the integrity of the investigative process.

THE PRINCIPLES OF INVESTIGATION – A BLUEPRINT SYSTEM OF MINIMUM INVESTIGATIVE INFORMATION.

This section describes the POI which is a means by which the investigation is structured systematically to provide information to key parties to the investigation at both the initial and review stages. This system is used by Cumbria Constabulary and underpins their achievement of a 'Good' rating, alongside an oversight and governance framework to ensure the system is working – like QATT. The system uses six investigative quality principles: PLANS, OPENS, HANDOVERS, REVIEWS, CLOSED and FILE. These act as a minimum standard 'checklist' for the presentation of information within an investigation.

Principle 1 – PLANS

Within the initial Officers Report the OIC should inform supervisors, and those reviewing the crime, about their PLANS to investigate the case. This should provide a direction for the case by making clear any key points the OIC may want a supervisor to consider, for example: an early decision to close the case, a summary indicating people who might be at risk, and which actions they will complete by way of a priority to bring some conclusion to the case. In practice the PLANS Principle is designed to occur at the beginning of the case, or whenever a case is returned to an OIC having been investigated elsewhere, for example within the custody investigation team – here PLANS would show what has been done with the case and give clarity to the officer continuing the investigation and an action should be raised for them to review this information. Table 1. Below outlines the elements of the PLANS principles:

Table 1. PLANS Principles

P – People and Property.	You should indicate if people and property are protected appropriately from the risk of further harm, re-victimisation, or intimidation. This should include your actions concerning any safeguarding you have applied or considered and a review of any risk assessment within safeguarding reports.
L – Location of Evidence is identified.	Provide a clear summary on where the evidence you have gained can be found and where it is currently stored (BWV, Statements, PNB's). This should include any system passwords for digitally stored material which might need to be accessed by other investigators.
A – Actions are raised and completed.	Develop your lines of enquiry clearly within the case by way of actions and comments. These should be individually separated where further actions are needed or added and concluded as a comment. These should be clear and concise especially around victims, witnesses, interviews with suspects, forensic evidence, CCTV, telecoms.
N – Next Review Action set.	Set an action for the supervisor in the case to complete their review and add any actions for dedicated reviewing officers or specialist review functions within the organisation.
S – Summary of the case.	Provide a clear and accurate summary as your first action and include a clear and concise summary of the incident giving rise to Police involvement and the investigation detailing key victims, witnesses, or those suspected of offences and any key locations.

Principle 2 – OPENS

Once the OIC's PLANS have been added to the case, and any actions raised updated and completed have been added, the next key element within the investigation is the first supervisor's review. At this point the supervisor OPENS the scheduled process of any subsequent REVIEWS. This is a critical opportunity to identify resources needed to investigate the case and set the priorities for the OIC. This first review is often critical to determining the success of the case. This success might not mean a positively recorded crime outcome. Moreover, this is an opportunity to recommended that the officer should instigate the CLOSED Principle or update the case with further actions. The OPENS assessment should be completed as soon is reasonably practical, and in any case within four days. The Principle of OPENS is outlined in Table 2.

Table 2. OPENS Principles

O – Officer Investigating.	An indication about the resources needed to investigate, who will be the OIC, and any application of the force resource allocation matrix.
P – People and Property.	A review of **PLANS** made by the OIC to protect people & property from the risk of further harm, re-victimisation, or the loss of evidence.
E – Early Supervisory Assessment.	Early clarity on appropriate offences from a review of the information initially recorded (Log/Call to Police etc.,) with an early decision on the need to investigate further or direct the application of the **CLOSED** principles to the OIC to finalise the case or consider further enquiries. Identifying and raising any lines of investigation not raised by the OIC.
N – Next Review Action.	Ensure a review action is set for 30 days as necessary, or ensure the case is immediately brought to the attention of any Dedicated Reviewing Officer before closure.
S – Specific Offences.	Indicate to the investigating officer what offences they will be investigating or provide a rationale as to why they will not be.

Principle 3 – HANDOVERS

Handovers between investigators, and departments, present a distinct risk to an investigation. This is often because information, and the location of evidence, or material, is lost or forgotten between investigators. Where a person is wanted, or their arrest outstanding, then a HANDOVERS update should be added to the case. The whole purpose of this principal is clarity between investigators who handover cases between functions and departments. The principles of HANDOVERS are outlined in Table 3.

Table 3. HANDOVERS Principles

H – Handover Details – a clear and concise summary.	A clear and concise summary of the incident giving rise to Police involvement and the investigation prior to the point of handover, detailing key victims, witnesses, or those suspected of offences and any key locations.
A – Assessment of risk to people, property and evidence.	A clear indication of any identified risks to people, property, and evidence. Reference any safeguarding reports submitted, the risks that have been identified and if the grade has been reviewed by the supervisor overseeing the handover. You should also clearly highlight any risks to evidence have been considered (i.e. loss of CCTV/limited witness availability/intelligence).
N – Notify reviewing officers or dedicated review officer.	Provide an indication of anyone contacted about the investigation in order to bring the details to the attention of any relevant specialist reviewing officers (Hate crime, RASSO)
D – Detained Persons (or those wanted)	The details of any detained persons, those who maybe additionally wanted or outstanding with associated custody references wanted person details.
O – Offences under Investigation.	A clear and accurate summary of the offences, or further offences, along with those where further offences need to be considered by someone on any further enquiry team.
V – Victims and Witnesses.	The details of any victims and witnesses, their contact details and willingness to provide evidence if not already submitted within the handover.
E – Evidence Location.	Provide a clear summary on where the evidence you have gained can be found and where it is currently stored (BWV, Statements, PNB's, property). This should include any system passwords for digitally stored material.
R – Raise and complete outstanding enquiries and actions.	Provide a clear and concise summary of the outstanding actions, in order of priority, as seen by the officer handing over the case. Detail any contact details for witnesses and what evidence is needed for the case to be further investigated.
S – Supervisor Certification.	A clearly visible action or comment made by a supervisor to certify that the principles of **HANDOVERS** has been applied correctly in preparation for the case to be further investigated.

Principle 4 – REVIEWS

Reviews are of critical importance to the process of managing investigations, it is an opportunity to provide direction and make decisions about the progress of an investigation. The Principle of REVIEWS should be completed at 30-day intervals by persons of a relevant rank and role, these are:

Every 30 Days – (Detective) Sergeant shut up what do you want is bindi

Every 60 Days – (Detective) Inspector

Every 90 Days – (Detective) Chief Inspector

The Principle of REVIEWS is designed to provide a consistent structure to supervisory reviews, so that investigators understand the review, and Inspecting ranks or specialist review officers can interpret previous reviews clearly. Auxiliary departments may also quality assure the information which may be shared to other organisations, civil or criminal courts, and in quality assurance processes. The REVIEWS Principle is shown in Table 4.

Table 4. REVIEWS Principles

R – Reasonable Lines of Enquiry.	Assess the current and future investigative options, when these are expected to be concluded, and make clear what the reasonable lines of enquiry are for those investigating the case. These may include those originating from suspect enquiries such as interviews, other statements in the case, and CCTV.
E – Evidence Assessment.	Provide clear direction on the merits of continued investigation, applying any necessary public interest (Seriousness, culpability, harm, cost) or evidential decision making and consider the case for any early referral to CPS for investigative advice, or an early charging decision. In every case, ensure any additional offences identified during the investigation are recorded/negated in line with NCRS. Your evidence assessment is key and should be made in line with the Code for Crown Prosecutors 2018 (admissibility, reliability and credibility of witnesses, undermining material) or offence specific guidance.
V – Vulnerability.	Assess the status of any people and property who might be vulnerable to further harm and victimisation. Instigate any actions to mitigate the risks them. This may mean referrals to community safety, Child Centred Policing, Victim Support, or by the making of further arrests and investigative actions.
I – identified Suspects.	Assess any outstanding or current suspects and provide a rationale for continued RUI or bail. If people are no longer suspects, then ensure records are closed and they are updated. The pole map should be current and feature those involved in the case.
E – Evaluate Resources.	Provide direction to the OIC on prioritisation of the case within their overall workload. Decide if the current OIC is still the best person to investigate the case. This is an opportunity for supervisors to assess the case against other priorities the investigating officer has.
W – Working Together.	Assess if any partnerships are needed to work together on the investigation. This could mean to gather third party material, provide investigative support, or provide protection to those are risk (Child Centred Policing Teams, Social Services, Youth Offending, Probation, HMP, forensic services etc.). Cases may also be subject to parallel proceedings and disclosure; these must be prioritised in working together.
S – Set an action for the next review.	Set an action for the next review (Sgt 30 days, Insp 60 Days, Ch Insp 90 days), or a review by any dedicated reviewing officer.

Principle 5 – CLOSED

Wherever a case is to be finalised, the OIC should apply the principles of CLOSED. This ensures that information is provided in an orderly way for the reviewing and finalising supervisors. The CLOSED Principle is closely associated with Principle six – the Inspectors FILE. An OIC, prior to finalisation, must ensure that CLOSED is applied as a single action or comment which is endorsed as being completed by a reviewing sergeant, the principle is as illustrated in Table 5.

Table 5. CLOSED Principles

C – Correct Classification and Crimes – recorded or additional?	Recorded or Additional? Recorded Crime Outcome - OIC to provide the outcome for the recorded crimes using the outcome numbers (1-21). Apply alternative outcome when the recorded crime if different from the offence used in the positive outcome. Example, recorded crime of Assault ABH, offender charged with Common Assault - ABH crime would then have an outcome of OC 1a Charged with Alternative Offence. Additional Crimes Investigated - Check the positive outcome, or NFA decision, on all additional offences investigated as part of the investigation. If any unrecorded crime has a positive outcome consider if the crime should be recorded. Example: recorded crime for assault with an outcome of NFA but secondary crime of criminal damage with the same victim, is charged. The damage crime would then be recorded separately.
L – Legally Appropriate.	The victim's code is applied and updated and for relevant cases the Victim's Right to Review (VRR) is explained and the victim record closed. Endorse and ensure that all reasonable lines of enquires are completed and any requests for disclosures to the family court or other proceedings have been made, if requested before closure.
O – Outstanding Records and Property.	Ensure that RUI/Bail has been cancelled on force and national systems and assess and return any property and mark property records appropriately.
S – Safeguarding Review.	A final review and comment on what safeguarding has been put in place during the investigation and what might continue to be relevant or need to be reviewed in the future. This might include a comment on the outcome of civil orders or other diversionary action.
E – Evidence Location.	Record any reference numbers where the evidence which has been subject to the investigation can be found. This will ensure any audit can be effective and any future location of the evidence discovered easily.
D – Decision.	Ensure any reviewing decision or finalisation closure by a supervisor is evidenced, clear, and made at an appropriate rank/role.

Principle 6 – FILE

Ensuring crimes are CLOSED means a sergeant's certification before an inspectors FILE. This final principle puts the finalisation of cases at the hands of inspectors who are challenged with agreeing that all the processes' have been applied correctly. If this is undertaken effectively, the task of quality assurance and dip sampling is reduced as the principals drive the effectiveness and consistency of the process during the final stages of all investigations and is shown in table 6.

Table 6. FILE Principles

F – finalised correctly.	Acknowledgement of the CLOSED principals and a check on crime finalising.
I – Investigation.	The investigation has been completed to a satisfactory level with clear supervisory oversight. Any minimum standards applied, or locally instigated trigger plan/community profile/problem profile is completed.
L – legally relevant	Final certification that the victims code has been completed and complied with and that the investigation has been proportionately carried out.
E – Evidential review officer.	There is clear oversight of any dedicated reviewing officer.

It should be recognised when reading these POI, that the design considered the repeated and consistent events which Monet and Gannon (2015) describe as being essential to developing a systems thinking approach. A significant study was undertaken to understand themes and trends within both error and addressing failure demand. This interrelates to Seddon's Vanguard Method of building on normative experiences by a series of studies of the system. Within the early development of the POI, there were a series of Deliberative Inquiry (DI) phases. DI is a research method used for examining complex issues and drawing consensus (Kanuka, 2010). This approach significantly enhances the changes of any approaches to system change being adopted, it is essential to systems thinking to fully understand the problem before embarking on significant change.

CONCLUSION

This chapter has demonstrated how Cumbria Constabulary's adoption of a systems-thinking approach contributed to its 'Good' rating for investigating crime, highlighting the value of a coherent, evidence-based investigative system. The experience of Cumbria shows that systems thinking is not an abstract concept but a practical method for improving investigative quality, reducing failure demand, and strengthening public confidence. For any force aspiring to move from 'Good' to 'Outstanding', the essential task is to undertake a comprehensive examination of the investigative system itself demand, flow, conditions, measures, and culture, rather than relying on isolated procedural fixes.

While the Vanguard Method provides a robust framework for understanding and redesigning investigative systems, its effectiveness depends on more than the identification of failure demand. A narrow focus on post-event problems risks replicating the aviation model of learning only after a collision. True systems thinking requires proactive design, continuous learning, and a commitment to understanding how the system shapes behaviour long before failure occurs.

Leadership is central to this endeavour. Crucially, leadership in a systems context is not confined to rank or hierarchy. It is expressed through the behaviours of supervisors, investigators, analysts, and senior officers who collectively shape the investigative environment. Systems-based leadership is participatory, reflective, and grounded in evidence. It encourages curiosity rather than compliance, learning rather than blame, and collaboration rather than siloed working. When leaders at all levels engage in the design, implementation, and ongoing refinement of investigative systems, the organisation becomes aligned with its core purpose: delivering justice.

Forces seeking to achieve outstanding investigative performance must therefore invest not only in tools and processes but in the mindset and culture that sustain them. A systems approach offers a pathway to this transformation and one that prioritises understanding over assumption, design over reaction, and collective responsibility over individual fault. By embedding these principles, policing can build investigative systems that are consistently effective, trusted by practitioners, and capable of delivering justice.

REFERENCES

Afrazeh, A., & Bartsch, H. (2007). Human reliabitiy and flight safety. *International Journal of Reliability Quality and Safety Engineering*, *14*(05), 501–516.

Bennett, S. A. (2015). The benefits of a systems-thinking approach to accident investigation. In *Applications of Systems Thinking and Soft Operations Research in Managing Complexity: From Problem Framing to Problem Solving* (pp. 203–226). Springer International Publishing.

Chaboyer, W., McMurray, A., & Wallis, M. (2010). Bedside nursing handover: A case study. *International Journal of Nursing Practice*, *16*(1), 27–34. PMID: 20158545

Hill, S., & O'Neill, M. (2019). Reviewing the situation: practitioner perspectives on the use and effectiveness of 28-day homicide reviews. *Journal of Criminological Research, Policy and Practice*.

HMICFRS. (2023a) Police performance: Getting a grip. Accessed online. Available at: https://hmicfrs.justiceinspectorates.gov.uk/publication-html/police-performance-getting-a-grip/

HMICFRS (2023b) Nottinghamshire PEEL Assessment 2023–2025. Accessed online. Available at: Nottinghamshire PEEL Assessment 2023–2025 - His Majesty's Inspectorate of Constabulary and Fire & Rescue Services

HMICFRS. (2023c) Staffordshire PEEL Assessment 2023–2025. Accessed online. Available at: https://hmicfrs.justiceinspectorates.gov.uk/peel-reports/staffordshire-2023-25/

HMICFRS. (2023d) West Yorkshire PEEL Assessment 2023–2025. Accessed online. Available at: https://hmicfrs.justiceinspectorates.gov.uk/peel-reports/west-yorkshire-2023-25/

HMICFRS. (2023e) Bedfordshire PEEL Assessment 2023–2025. Accessed online. Available at: https://hmicfrs.justiceinspectorates.gov.uk/peel-reports/bedfordshire-2023-25/

HMICFRS. (2024) Cumbria PEEL Assessment 2023–2025. Accessed online. Available at: https://hmicfrs.justiceinspectorates.gov.uk/peel-reports/cumbria-2023-25/

Home Office. (2023) Official Statistics - Crime outcomes in England and Wales 2022 to 2023 Published 20 July 2023. Accessed online. Available at: https://www.gov.uk/government/statistics/crime-outcomes-in-england-and-wales-2022-to-2023/crime-outcomes-in-england-and-wales-2022-to-2023

Kanuka, H. (2010). Deliberative inquiry. In *New Approaches to Qualitative Research* (pp. 116–123). Routledge.

Newburn, T., Williamson, T., & Wright, A. (Eds.). (2012). *Handbook of criminal investigation*. Routledge.

Prince, H., Lum, C., & Koper, C. S. (2021). Effective police investigative practices: An evidence-assessment of the research. *Policing*, *44*(4), 683–707.

Seddon, J., & O'Donovan, B. (2023). The Vanguard Method: Beyond Command and Control. *Journal of Systems Thinking.*, *3*. Advance online publication. DOI: 10.54120/jost.000006

Zieja, M., Smoliński, H., & Gołda, P. (2015). Information systems as a tool for supporting the management of aircraft flight safety. *Archives of Transport*, *36*(4), 67–76.

Chapter 12
Artificial Intelligence and Machine Learning

Robert David Ewin
http://orcid.org/0000-0003-0611-5207
South Wales Police, UK

Rob David Ewin
South Wales Police, UK

ABSTRACT

This chapter explores the evolving role of Artificial Intelligence (AI) and Machine Learning (ML) in UK policing through an analysis of application in investigations, predictive analytics, and workforce development. The chapter highlights the challenges of fragmented adoption, ethical oversight, and data governance, while proposing a strategic "Pathway to Excellence" for integrating AI and ML. The emphasis throughout is around transparency, collaboration, and digital capability. These technologies can enhance operational effectiveness and public trust in law enforcement but there is a need for strategic leadership, inter-force collaboration, and public engagement.

INTRODUCTION

Artificial intelligence (AI) refers to the simulation of human intelligence by machines, encompassing processes such as reasoning, problem-solving, and decision-making. Within this field, machine learning (ML) enables systems to learn from data and improve performance over time without explicit programming, while natural language processing (NLP) allows computers to interpret and analyse human lan-

DOI: 10.4018/979-8-3373-2757-0.ch012

guage, facilitating applications such as speech recognition, automated transcription, and text analysis (Shoenbill et al., 2023).

To date, no UK police service has been graded as *outstanding* in its use of these technologies under the HMICFRS PEEL inspection framework. This chapter therefore examines the growing investment in AI and ML for investigative purposes, workforce development, and analytics, each representing key areas of emerging innovation within policing. Current applications include predictive analytics, facial recognition, NLP-based intelligence processing, AI-assisted mobile forensics, network pattern analysis, automated video and audio analysis, and document redaction (Raji and Sholademi, 2024).

The integration of AI and ML into policing has advanced alongside wider digital transformation, offering significant potential to reshape how data is processed and how officers interact with the public. Yet policing as a sector has struggled to keep pace, often adopting these technologies inconsistently and without coherent strategy (HMICFRS, 2023a; 2025). Achieving an *outstanding* standard requires demonstrable evidence of innovation, measurable performance improvements, and sustainable outcomes. While AI and ML can enhance the speed and accuracy of investigations, thereby improving victim satisfaction, these benefits must be systematically validated before national adoption can occur.

Ethical challenges remain central to this evolution. Concerns around privacy, surveillance, algorithmic bias, and the opacity of proprietary systems risk eroding public trust if such technologies are not transparently and responsibly managed. Moreover, large-scale data systems and predictive models can be susceptible to data manipulation or "poisoning," potentially compromising both fairness and operational integrity. This chapter critically explores these opportunities and challenges in the context of how AI and ML can responsibly transform policing.

ARTIFICIAL INTELLIGENCE IN POLICING INVESTIGATIONS: DATA AND PRIVACY

AI and ML possess the potential to transform policing in ways that are both profound and unprecedented, particularly in human-centred areas such as investigation and data processing (NPCC, 2024). As Shoenbill et al. (2023) explain, AI refers to systems that simulate human intelligence, ML enables those systems to learn from data, and natural language processing (NLP) allows machines to interpret and analyse human language. These capabilities closely mirror the analytical and interpretive skills traditionally performed by police investigators. Their integration into investigative processes could therefore redefine the nature and scope of human labour within policing, especially in domains directly related to public safety.

At the same time, policing organisations are overwhelmed by the sheer volume of data generated through modern technology (McDaniel and Pease, 2021), ranging from behavioural data and digital communications to mobile-phone extractions and CCTV footage. ML offers opportunities to process and interpret this information, revealing patterns and insights that can inform future investigations. The exponential growth of such data underscores the urgency for policing to not only adopt AI and ML but to sustain their strategic integration in order to remain effective and responsive (Partridge and Zaghloul, 2023).

To be recognised as *outstanding*, police services must demonstrate leadership, foresight, and an evidence-based rationale showing that AI and ML adoption delivers measurable value. This extends beyond operational efficiency to encompass alignment with ethical and rehabilitative objectives, particularly those centred on harm reduction and social reintegration. Certain human-driven areas of policing, such as rehabilitation, offender management, and victim support, require careful consideration before automation. Strength-based approaches in desistance and rehabilitation research highlight more than 150 protective factors that rely on human empathy, reasoning, and judgement (Garant and Ouellet, 2024). Similarly, Lenkens et al. (2024) emphasise the importance of peer-led support in fostering desistance through mechanisms such as empathy, hope, and trust.

AI-enabled systems must therefore be designed to complement, not replace, these inherently human dimensions of policing. Within investigative contexts such as family liaison, interviewing, and rehabilitation-focused policing, empathy and ethical reasoning remain irreplaceable. Desistance research consistently shows that meaningful behavioural change arises from relational and experiential support. While AI can enhance efficiency and insight, it is ultimately human consciousness and compassion that drive transformation and sustain legitimacy in policing practice

Data and Policing Investigations

In its 2021–2025 strategy, HMICFRS, under the leadership of Sir Tom Winsor, warned that policing risks falling behind if it fails to realise the benefits of emerging technologies—particularly artificial intelligence (AI) and machine learning (ML) in investigations (HMICFRS, 2021). The inspectorate noted that these technologies had already produced promising practices, particularly in automating the examination of digital media such as CCTV footage, mobile phone data, and other evidential imagery.

However, the NPCC Science and Technology Strategy (NPCC, 2024) suggests that earlier technological advances, such as automatic number plate recognition (ANPR) and body-worn video, now represent only a primitive stage in the digital evolution of policing. The strategy therefore identifies the advancement of AI in criminal investigations as a national priority. One key opportunity lies in the disclosure of evidence, where investigators face overwhelming volumes of documentation. Companies such as Adobe are emerging as leaders in developing AI-driven redaction and text analysis tools. Yet, despite significant progress, research highlights that many current AI and ML systems continue to operate with limited accuracy and efficiency, reinforcing the need for robust evaluation and oversight (Chen and Kirkham, 2024).

Some forces are already taking proactive steps. Cumbria Constabulary, for example, has invested in AI tools to assist with CCTV analysis, leading to enhanced investigative capability and significant time savings for officers (HMICFRS, 2025). At the national level, projects such as the Police National Database (PND), which replaces the legacy Police National Computer (PNC), represent major advances in real-time information sharing and provide a platform for wider use of AI technologies such as facial recognition. Similarly, the National Data and Analytics Office (NDAO) is exploring the centralisation of data capabilities across forces, potentially enabling shared access, reducing duplication, enhancing interoperability, and accelerating innovation in AI-driven policing (NPCC, 2025).

While many forces recognise the potential of such technologies, realising their full benefit requires sustained investment, both financial and organisational. This begins with a systematic analysis of internal processes to identify where AI can add value, and where existing developments by other forces could be adopted or shared. Only through this strategic approach can policing ensure that technological innovation translates into measurable efficiency, improved investigations, and public value.

Privacy and Investigations

Policing is not immune from the ethical and legal concerns surrounding artificial intelligence, particularly regarding privacy and human rights (Ünver, 2024). One of the primary issues lies in how AI systems store and process data, often retaining information that can later be accessed or repurposed without the knowledge of the individuals concerned (Akhtar, 2019). Public acceptance of AI in policing therefore depends on maintaining a careful balance between technological advancement and the legitimacy of its use.

For instance, police forces such as Humberside employ near-real-time dashboards to monitor operational performance, including tracking outstanding suspects and assessing case file quality. Such applications, focused on internal performance management, are unlikely to generate public concern (HMICFRS, 2023). In contrast, systems designed to predict public behaviour or analyse extensive CCTV and mobile phone data raise significant questions about surveillance, proportionality, and privacy (UK Parliament Joint Committee on Human Rights, 2025).

Transparency in how AI systems are deployed is key to maintaining public trust. Studies show that openly communicating the design, scope, and oversight of AI applications can reduce suspicion and foster legitimacy. For example, Raj et al. (2021) evaluated the use of machine learning in detecting cyberbullying through natural language processing techniques that mapped language patterns on social media. By documenting each stage of the process and incorporating human validation to correct inaccuracies, the study demonstrated how transparency can mitigate privacy concerns. A similar approach—clearly explaining how investigative AI systems function and how outcomes are derived—could enhance accountability in law enforcement contexts.

Collaborations between policing organisations and academic partners are crucial for achieving this level of transparency and ethical oversight (HMICFRS, 2023). Such partnerships provide independent validation of methods, strengthen governance structures, and ensure compliance with legal and ethical standards. Moreover, transparent evaluation can demonstrate tangible benefits, such as quantifiable time savings or efficiency gains, while identifying integration challenges. Some AI tools may streamline individual processes but remain underutilised if poorly aligned with communication systems or reporting workflows.

Ultimately, achieving *outstanding* performance in this area requires strategic leadership at the chief officer level, strong data governance, and operational accessibility at the tactical level. Above all, transparency must be embedded across all stages—from system design to courtroom disclosure—to build public confidence that AI-enabled policing is conducted ethically, efficiently, and openly. Having addressed the role of AI and ML in investigations, the next section turns to their application in crime prediction, a precursor to investigative work where analytical leverage has particular promise.

LEVERAGE ANALYTICS AND GEOSPATIAL INTELLIGENCE

Leverage Analytics (LA) refers to the application of data-driven AI and ML to support decision-making in areas such as crime prevention, organisational performance, and resource allocation (NPCC, 2024). The proliferation of web-based data has dramatically increased the volume and complexity of information available to police organisations, necessitating advanced analytical capabilities. This has given rise to what is now commonly termed Big Data Analysis (BDA), the process of extracting meaningful insights from vast and complex datasets (Mathrani and Lai, 2021).Through daily interactions with the public, police services collect substantial amounts of passive data. When structured and analysed appropriately, this information can help guide resource deployment and inform decision-making processes traditionally managed by analytical teams and human supervisors (Syed and Albalawi, 2024).

Merseyside Police exemplifies promising practice in this area. The force has been recognised for its use of AI-driven geospatial analytics to map crime hotspots and identify vulnerable individuals involved in county lines activity (HMICFRS, 2023). This represents one of the most forward-looking uses of leverage analytics in UK policing. Similarly, the UK Home Office has funded multiple hotspot policing trials, each evaluated with an emphasis on ensuring that hotspot identification and analysis are continually updated through near real-time data monitoring (Home Office, 2025). Although this process remains resource-intensive, it is vital for addressing public concerns and ensuring operational responsiveness to emerging patterns of crime and disorder.

Legitimacy in policing is strengthened when data-driven decisions visibly align with community concerns. Outstanding services demonstrate this alignment by clearly communicating how they identify and prioritise patrol hotspots, and by explaining the difference between locations with high *perceived* crime and those with high *actual* crime. Transparent communication of these distinctions not only supports public understanding but also reinforces trust in data-informed policing. For forces seeking an *outstanding* grade, this form of openness and analytical accountability represents a defining feature of modern, intelligence-led practice.

Geospatial Intelligence

The use of geospatial intelligence to inform decisions on police deployment has expanded significantly in recent years, both in scope and application (Jefferson, 2018). However, its development across UK policing remains fragmented and inconsistent. While some forces have achieved *outstanding* outcomes through geospatial mapping of crime patterns, the wider adoption of such tools must be carefully safeguarded against bias—particularly in areas where policing activity is already concentrated. There is a well-established relationship between police presence, community confidence, and crime reporting; therefore, modelling areas with high patrol activity risks reinforcing existing biases while overlooking communities where crime remains under-reported. Although artificial intelligence (AI) can assist in identifying heavily policed areas, it is often less effective in detecting patterns of unreported or hidden crime, limiting its utility for equitable deployment.

Two major factors continue to constrain the productive use of leverage analytics in policing: poor data recording and inconsistent accuracy across datasets. A third and equally significant issue is the failure to fully harness and interpret geospatial intelligence (Home Office, 2024). Without coherent leadership and standardised approaches, these issues will continue to hinder the development and integration of advanced analytical tools.

A key challenge lies in the fragmented technological landscape of policing. Many forces operate incompatible ICT systems and lack shared cloud-based environments capable of supporting large-scale data processing across multiple jurisdictions (HMICFRS, 2022). This fragmentation limits the potential for big data analytics and cross-force collaboration. To overcome these barriers, police services must adopt a consistent national strategy for the development and procurement of analytical technologies. Strategic leadership should prioritise the reduction of data silos, ensure compliance with legal and ethical standards in data processing, and promote collaborative procurement models that enhance interoperability and public transparency.

Ultimately, claims that leverage analytics can "put officers back on the beat" will remain superficial unless underpinned by meaningful, system-wide integration. Only when data systems, analytical tools, and geospatial intelligence are coherently aligned across organisational boundaries will the technology yield substantial and sustainable improvements in police productivity and community outcomes.

Infrastructures for Leverage Analytics and Geospatial Intelligence

HMICFRS has repeatedly criticised police forces for developing and purchasing ICT solutions in isolation, with little or no coordination between them, despite facing similar operational challenges and requiring near-identical technological tools (HMICFRS, 2023). While a unified commercial framework could partially address this issue, studies suggest that the establishment of shared data lakes, with configurable 'plug-in' systems—offers a more flexible and sustainable approach. Such models allow multiple organisations to work within common data governance structures while tailoring outputs to their specific operational needs (Schuilenburg and Soudijn, 2023; Karimah, 2023).

The use of algorithms in policing is expected to grow substantially as larger, cross-organisational initiatives attract commercial investment and attention (Bunnik, 2024). This makes collaboration with the private sector both necessary and potentially advantageous, particularly when approached through multi-force partnerships. However, reliance on proprietary algorithms introduces risks related to intellectual property ownership and transparency. If police services cannot fully account for how algorithmic tools produce outcomes, this lack of explainability may undermine accountability and public confidence. Moreover, disputes over intellectual property could require legal intervention at force or even government level, offsetting any cost efficiencies achieved through commercial collaboration.

Weak ethical oversight and fragmented "tech-spending" further compound these challenges. Without coordinated governance, the very legitimacy gained through commercial partnerships can be eroded. The UK Government's AI Playbook (Government Digital Service, 2025) provides guidance on managing the AI lifecycle, from deployment and maintenance to evaluating limitations and risks. These principles underscore the importance of structured governance in ensuring responsible and sustainable adoption.

AI and ML should not be treated as a panacea for policing challenges. Without rigorous oversight, lifecycle management, and strategic alignment, they risk becoming resource-intensive distractions rather than enablers of efficiency. For a force to achieve *outstanding* performance in leverage analytics and geospatial intelligence, HMICFRS expects robust governance across every stage of the analytical process, including data acquisition, preparation, processing, evaluation, version control, and lifecycle management.

Equally essential is the development of a technical workforce capable of sustaining these innovations. Building internal capability ensures that forces remain informed consumers of technology, able to critically evaluate, adapt, and transparently manage the analytical tools they employ. Only through such integration of governance, collaboration, and expertise can leverage analytics and geospatial intelligence fulfil their potential as transformative assets for modern policing.

BUILDING, AND RETENTION, OF AN OUTSTANDING TECHNICAL WORKFORCE

Strategies for developing a technically capable policing workforce traditionally focus on specialist departments such as digital forensics, communications data, network architecture, and analytical units (NPCC, 2020). However, the integration of machine learning (ML) and artificial intelligence (AI) demands that digital literacy extends across all roles, not just technical specialists. To become truly digitally capable, every member of a police organisation must possess a baseline understanding of how digital technologies operate, their benefits, and their limitations. This includes the ability to interpret patterns and trends derived from routine data sources, such as mobile phone downloads or crime-mapped hotspots, and to make informed judgements about their operational value.

The UK Home Office has emphasised that the future investigative workforce must adapt rapidly to evolving patterns of public technology use to maintain an operational advantage over increasingly sophisticated criminal networks (Home Office, 2024). Strategic workforce planning must therefore anticipate this future operating environment and integrate technological adaptability into recruitment, training, and professional development from the outset. However, in addition to building new skills, forces must also offer competitive incentives and meaningful career progression to retain these highly skilled employees within policing.

Recruitment strategies will require significant reform if police services are to attract and prepare a workforce capable of operating in digitally dynamic environments (Kadhim, 2024). Digital literacy alone is insufficient; what is needed is digital agility, the ability to interpret, manage, and apply data insights effectively across multiple operational contexts. This challenges traditional models of police deployment and demands a more sophisticated understanding of how technology supports frontline and investigative work. International examples illustrate these challenges. In Australia, where police recruitment numbers are in decline, agencies face difficulty attracting candidates who can balance community engagement with advanced technological competencies, such as operating drones and remote tracking devices used in monitoring suspects in vast, rural areas (Miles-Johnson, 2024). Addressing similar workforce challenges in the UK will require enhancing the police service's reputation as an attractive, digitally invested employer, particularly in the application of AI and ML to contemporary policing problems.

Retention presents an equally pressing challenge. High levels of burnout are reported among digital forensic practitioners who are routinely exposed to distressing material and pressured to process large volumes of digital evidence (Kelty et al., 2021). This highlights the intersection between workforce capability development and the strategic use of ML to augment productivity while minimising human exposure to harmful content. Allowing practitioners to automate certain repetitive or emotionally taxing aspects of their work, while maintaining evidential integrity, offers a sustainable pathway to improved wellbeing and performance.

Bridging the current knowledge and skills gap in the supervision and management of digital teams is also critical. Effective leadership in these environments requires understanding both the technical complexities of ML-assisted investigation and the human factors that influence cognitive load, stress, and decision-making. At the organisational level, police services must develop mechanisms to assess and monitor workforce stress associated with digital workloads, particularly where personnel are required to interpret machine-generated outputs alongside human reasoning.

Building and retaining an *outstanding* technical workforce will therefore depend on more than technological investment alone. It requires a strategic, human-centred approach that combines recruitment reform, skills development, ethical technology use, and proactive support for wellbeing. Only through this balance can policing sustain a digital workforce that is resilient, adaptive, and equipped to lead in an era defined by AI and data-driven innovation.

A Workforce Facing Future AI Criminality

Temporary Chief Constable Alex Murray has warned that criminals are already embracing and exploiting artificial intelligence (AI) tools, stressing that policing must act swiftly to avoid falling behind (NPCC, 2024). The future trajectory of criminal behaviour is likely to intensify this challenge, as automation and AI increasingly underpin illicit markets, facilitating the trading of drugs, cash, and other illegal commodities. Investigators will not only need to identify the offenders behind these activities but also navigate complex, automated systems involving sophisticated algorithms, adaptive performance, and deliberate obfuscation.

The Essex Police "Analytics for Everyone" programme represents a promising model for improving digital agility and analytical capability. By embedding a culture of creativity and data-informed responsiveness, the initiative has enhanced organisational understanding of leverage analytics (HMICFRS, 2023). However, while such programmes advance internal capability, they may not fully prepare police services to counter the next generation of AI-enabled criminality. Forces aspiring to *outstanding* status must therefore recognise and address this gap through sustained investment in advanced technical expertise, strategic workforce development, and collaboration with academic and private sector partners.

HMICFRS has also observed that many forces continue to equate digital investment with the acquisition of traditional hardware, such as laptops and desktop computers, while neglecting the infrastructure required to obtain, preserve, and analyse complex cloud-based or encrypted data (HMICFRS, 2023). For example, a new recruit tasked with investigating online crime may quickly discover that their organisation lacks the technical capacity to recover digital evidence stored in sophisticated cloud environments, capabilities that are commonplace in other sectors. Such experiences can lead to professional frustration, diminished engagement, and ultimately higher rates of organisational turnover, undermining efforts to build a resilient and skilled workforce.

Building an *outstanding* police service around a technically competent workforce will depend on embedding digital inclusivity as a foundational principle. This requires ensuring that all personnel, from frontline officers to specialist investigators, have access to the knowledge, tools, and systems necessary to operate effectively within an increasingly digital landscape. Beyond this baseline, forces must invest in cutting-edge technologies that enhance both public engagement and operational effectiveness. Initiatives such as digital academies, research hubs, and embedded learning programmes should equip investigators to recognise, access, and preserve diverse forms of digital evidence, while enabling frontline officers to interpret AI-informed insights in real time.

A truly *outstanding* workforce will be characterised by consistent leadership, technical agility, and future-oriented adaptability. Without these qualities, even the most promising AI and ML solutions risk remaining underdeveloped and underutilised, resulting in organisational stagnation, workforce dissatisfaction, and a widening gap between policing capability and the pace of technological change.

CONCLUSION

This chapter has critically examined the evolving role of machine learning (ML) and artificial intelligence (AI) in policing across three interrelated domains: investigative enhancement, workforce development, and leverage analytics. Although no UK police service has yet achieved an *outstanding* grade in the use of these technologies (HMICFRS, 2025), the potential for transformative change is clear when supported by strong leadership, ethical governance, and strategic workforce planning. Excellence in this field must be grounded in robust data readiness, consistent infrastructure, and transparent decision-making.

McDaniel and Pease (2021) note that policing continues to suffer from a surplus of unstructured digital information. ML offers a way to convert such data into actionable insights that can improve investigations and prevent future harm. However, these benefits can only be realised through rigorous attention to data reliability, governance, and ethical oversight, ensuring public confidence in how information is collected and used (Ünver, 2024; Akhtar, 2019). Building legitimacy will depend on early engagement with stakeholders, including Police and Crime Commissioners, and maintaining transparency about both system capabilities and limitations (IOPC, 2025). The National Policing Digital Strategy (2020–2023) acknowledges that there are still no definitive answers for creating a fully AI-empowered policing sector (NPCC, 2020), but the foundations for progress are now well defined.

A Digitally Capable Workforce

Sustainable excellence in AI and ML depends first on a digitally capable and resilient workforce. Organisational learning must remain at the centre of development strategies. As Garant and Ouellet (2024) and Lenkens et al. (2024) demonstrate, empathy and experiential understanding remain critical to human-centred policing and must complement, not compete with, technological advancement. Similarly, Kelty et al. (2021) highlight the psychological toll of digital forensic work, reinforcing the need for ML to automate repetitive or distressing tasks while retaining human oversight and ethical reasoning.

Strong partnerships with academia and industry will be essential to build future skills pipelines, conduct applied research, and cultivate innovation within the police service. Co-developed learning initiatives should integrate AI and ML literacy into every layer of police work—from investigative practice and neighbourhood policing to communications and contact management. A mature research and development culture will not only enhance technical capacity but also embed the evaluative mindset required for responsible technology adoption. The Government Digital Service (2025) AI Playbook provides practical guidance for managing algorithmic lifecycles, ensuring accountability, and preventing resource inefficiency.

Seamless Integration

Operational success requires the seamless integration of AI and ML tools into everyday policing. HMICFRS (2023) has repeatedly criticised fragmented ICT procurement and duplication of effort across forces, while Schuilenburg and Soudijn (2023) advocate for shared *data lake* environments with configurable plug-ins to enhance interoperability. The Essex Police "Analytics for Everyone" programme (HMICFRS, 2023) illustrates how digital agility can be fostered locally, yet broader strategic alignment is still needed to counter AI-enabled criminality (NPCC, 2024).

Forces should collaborate nationally to harmonise data standards, align infrastructure, and reduce duplication in cloud and data-centre investment. Integration also depends on cultivating synergy between human and digital systems. AI should augment—not replace—human interaction, particularly in frontline and investigative contexts where trust, empathy, and discretion are vital. A truly integrated model will merge machine-driven efficiency with the uniquely human qualities that underpin legitimate and ethical policing.

Cultural Acceptance and AI as Everyday Practice

Culture often determines whether strategy succeeds or fails. Achieving excellence in AI and ML adoption therefore requires more than technological investment; it demands a cultural shift towards innovation, ethical governance, and continuous adaptation. Strategic intent must align with operational reality, ensuring that AI and ML strengthen public safety, enhance investigative integrity, and support a digitally fluent workforce.

The move from fragmented experimentation to unified excellence will depend on collaboration across forces, transparent data practices, and consistent adherence to quality frameworks. Excellence in this area is as much cultural as it is technical—it is rooted in openness, learning, and the willingness to evolve. While these ambitions may once have seemed speculative or “sci-fi,” they now represent essential steps toward a policing service that is innovative, resilient, and future-ready.

REFERENCES:

Akhtar, M. (2019). Police use of facial recognition technology and the right to privacy and data protection in Europe. *NAVEIÑ REET: Nordic Journal of Law and Social Research*, (9), 324–344.

Bunnik, A., 2024. *Policing the future?: Assessing the mobilisation of big data by UK law enforcement.*

Chen, Y., & Kirkham, R. (2024). Exploring how UK public authorities use redaction to protect personal information. *ACM Transactions on Management Information Systems*, *15*(3), 1–23.

Garant, E., & Ouellet, F. (2024). Protective factors related to desistance in sexual offending: A scoping review. *SAGE Open*, *14*(4), 21582440241281606. DOI: 10.1177/21582440241281606

Government Digital Service. (2025). *Artificial intelligence playbook for the UK government* [online]. HM Government. Available at: https://www.gov.uk/government/publications/ai-playbook-for-the-uk-government/artificial-intelligence-playbook-for-the-uk-government-html [Accessed 23 May 2025].

HMICFRS. (2021). *HMICFRS strategy 2021–25* [online]. Available at: https://hmicfrs.justiceinspectorates.gov.uk/publication-html/hmicfrs-strategy-2021-25/ [Accessed 5 May 2025].

HMICFRS. (2022). *Digital forensics: An inspection into how well the police and other agencies use digital forensics in their investigations.* His Majesty's Inspectorate of Constabulary and Fire & Rescue Services. Available at: https://hmicfrs.justiceinspectorates.gov.uk/news/news-feed/police-forces-overwhelmed-and-ineffective-when-it-comes-to-digital-forensics/ [Accessed 31 Oct. 2025].

HMICFRS. (2023). *Police performance: Getting a grip* [online]. Available at: https://hmicfrs.justiceinspectorates.gov.uk/publications/police-performance-getting-a-grip/ [Accessed 22 April 2025].

HMICFRS. (2023a). *State of policing: The annual assessment of policing in England and Wales 2022* [online]. Available at: https://hmicfrs.justiceinspectorates.gov.uk/publication-html/state-of-policing-the-annual-assessment-of-policing-in-england-and-wales-2022/ [Accessed 10 May 2025].

HMICFRS. (2025). *An inspection into how effectively the police investigate crime* [online]. Available at: https://hmicfrs.justiceinspectorates.gov.uk/publications/how-effectively-police-investigate-crime/ [Accessed 2 May 2025].

Home Office. (2024). *Policing productivity review* [online]. Available at: https://www.gov.uk/government/publications/policing-productivity-review/policing-productivity-review-accessible [Accessed 23 May 2025].

Independent Office for Police Conduct (IOPC). (2025). *Public confidence and engagement.* [online] Available at: https://www.policeconduct.gov.uk/our-work/research-and-statistics/public-confidence [Accessed 31 Oct. 2025].

Jefferson, B. J. (2018). Predictable policing: Predictive crime mapping and geographies of policing and race. *Annals of the Association of American Geographers, 108*(1), 1–16.

Kadhim, M. J. (2024). Digital literacy and its importance in the modern workforce. *International Journal of Social Trends, 2*(2), 44–50.

Karimah, F., 2023. *Leveraging open data with machine learning algorithms.* Jurnal Sistem Informasi dan Teknik Informatika (JAFOTIK), 1(2), pp.62–69.

Kelty, S. F., McQueen, E., Pymont, C., & Green, N. (2021). Avoiding burnout at the digital forensics coalface: Targeted strategies for forensic agencies in the management of job-related stress. *Forensic Science International Digital Investigation, 38*, 301127.

Lenkens, M., van Lenthe, F. J., Schenk, L., Sentse, M., Severiens, S., Engbersen, G., & Nagelhout, G. E. (2024). Experiential peer support and desistance from crime: A systematic realist literature review. *Psychology, Crime & Law, 30*(10), 1421–1451. DOI: 10.1080/1068316X.2023.2203925

Mathrani, S., & Lai, X. (2021). Big data analytic framework for organizational leverage. *Applied Sciences (Basel, Switzerland), 11*(5), 2340.

McDaniel, J. L., & Pease, K. (Eds.). (2021). *Predictive policing and artificial intelligence*. Routledge.

Miles-Johnson, T. (2024). *To train or educate? or train and educate?: The Australian police recruit training versus tertiary education dilemma*. Policing. *Journal of Policy Practice, 18*, paae067.

National Police Chiefs' Council (NPCC). (2024). *Policing will always use Artificial Intelligence responsibly.* [online] Available at: https://news.npcc.police.uk/releases/policing-will-always-use-artificial-intelligence-responsibly [Accessed 31 Oct. 2025].

National Police Chiefs' Council (NPCC). (2025). *National Data and Analytics Office (NDAO).* [online] Available at: https://www.npcc.police.uk/our-work/modernising-policing/national-data-and-analytics-office/ [Accessed 31 Oct. 2025].

NPCC. (2020). *National policing digital strategy (2020–2023)* [online]. NPCC AoP-CC. Available at: https://www.npcc.police.uk/SysSiteAssets/media/downloads/our-work/digital-policing/national-policing-digital-strategy-2020-2030.pdf [Accessed 23 May 2025].

NPCC. (2024). *NPCC science and technology strategy* [online]. Available at: https://science.police.uk/site/assets/files/1253/npcc_science_and_technology_strategy.pdf [Accessed 23 May 2025].

Partridge, J. and Zaghloul, F., (2023). *Policing the data: Can data analytics help law enforcement?*. Journal of Information Technology Teaching Cases, p.20438869231212214.

Raj, C., Agarwal, A., Bharathy, G., Narayan, B., & Prasad, M. (2021). Cyberbullying detection: Hybrid models based on machine learning and natural language processing techniques. *Electronics (Basel)*, *10*(22), 2810.

Raji, I., & Sholademi, D. B. (2024). Predictive Policing: The Role of AI in Crime Prevention. *International Journal of Computer Applications Technology and Research*, *13*(10), 66–78. Retrieved October 31, 2025, from https://ijcat.com/archieve/volume13/issue10/ijcatr13101006.pdf

Schuilenburg, M., & Soudijn, M. (2023). *Big data policing: The use of big data and algorithms by the Netherlands Police*. Policing. *Journal of Policy Practice*, *17*, paad061.

Shoenbill, K. A., Kasturi, S. N., & Mendonca, E. A. (2023). Artificial Intelligence, Machine Learning, and Natural Language Processing. In Daaleman, T. P., & Helton, M. R. (Eds.), *Chronic Illness Care* (pp. 469–479). Springer Nature Switzerland AG., DOI: 10.1007/978-3-031-29171-5_36

Syed, S., & Albalawi, E. M. 2024. *Transforming law enforcement: Exploiting big data science and data analytics for precision decision-making and crime pattern anticipation in police operations*. [Online] https://doi.org/ [Accessed 23 May 2025]. DOI: 10.21203/rs.3.rs-4677394/v1

UK Parliament Joint Committee on Human Rights. 2025. *New inquiry: Human Rights and the Regulation of Artificial Intelligence*. [online] Available at: https://committees.parliament.uk/committee/93/human-rights-joint-committee/news/208676/new-inquiry-human-rights-and-the-regulation-of-artificial-intelligence/ [Accessed 31 Oct. 2025].

Ünver, H.A., (2024). *Artificial intelligence (AI) and human rights: Using AI as a weapon of repression and its impact on human rights*. Policy Department for External Relations Directorate General for External Policies of the Union. PE 754.450. European Parliament.

Chapter 13
Innovation in Policing

Naomi Davis-Crane
http://orcid.org/0009-0009-0956-7269
Liverpool John Moores University, UK

ABSTRACT

Innovation in organisations is the coordinated and concerted practice of conceiving, developing and implementation new products and services to benefit both customers and the organisation itself. Innovation thus requires new ways of thinking, communicating, and acting, an openness to potential failure, and flexibility in structures, processes, and resourcing. This chapter examines the nature of innovation in policing, including the relationship between innovative practice and PEEL outcomes. Before progressing to examine cultural, situational and organisational factors which may influence the innovation capability and capacity of a policing organisation as a precursor to providing police leaders with advice to catalyse innovation within their force. The chapter closes with a case study from a UK police force recognised for its innovative practice in the most recent series of PEEL inspections, demonstrating the potential of novel approaches to police business.

INTRODUCTION

Innovation in organisations is the coordinated and concerted practice of conceiving, developing and implementing new products and services to benefit both customers and the organisation itself. Innovation thus requires new ways of thinking, communicating, and acting, an openness to potential failure, and flexibility in structures, processes, and resourcing. In addition to embracing principles of continuous organisational learning. In contrast, organisational systems are often subconsciously orientated toward maintaining the status quo. This chapter provides an exploration of innovation within law enforcement, drawing upon an analysis of

DOI: 10.4018/979-8-3373-2757-0.ch013

PEEL inspection outcomes to emphasise the role of innovative practice in achieving outstanding policing performance. Before progressing to examine barriers to, and enablers of, innovation in law enforcement and the role of leaders in fostering an innovation culture in which new ideas flourish.

DEFINING INNOVATION IN POLICING

Multiple definitions of innovation exist across various business sectors, each representing the types of innovation and contexts unique to that environment. Given the particular circumstances in which police forces operate and the need for conceptual clarity at the outset of this chapter, it is necessary to define what is meant by innovation in policing in the mid-to-late 2020s. Using Varadarajan's (2024) framework we therefore propose the following definition:

Innovation in policing is the conception, development, implementation and evaluation of novel approaches to police business, resulting in the creation of value for stakeholders.

This definition therefore comprises five specific elements:

- The need for a novel concept (product, process or practice) which differs to those previously developed within or outside of the policing body.
- The requirement for the continued development, testing and refinement of the novel concept based upon iterative feedback and evaluation.
- The focus upon policing business as unique to this sector, but which may capture the broad swathe of activities involved in the operation of a modern police force.
- The derivation of value, whether tangible or intangible.
- Which is to the benefit of internal and/or external stakeholders such as police personnel, partner agencies, the public, or HM Government.

Innovation is commonly conceived to involve the development of a new technological product, such as an app or device, yet it has the potential to be so much more. Particularly in a multi-dimensional context such as policing where there exists the opportunity to innovate across numerous areas such as the types of service provided, processes and ways of working, preventative and investigative activity, the rationalisation of administration and bureaucracy, internal and external communications, and the use of data to inform decision making. This is recognised in PEEL inspections.

WHAT DOES PEEL SAY ABOUT INNOVATION?

Innovation is not scored in its own right in PEEL inspections and thus there are no set criteria for forces to attain. Instead, innovation is recognised as individual case studies within PEEL reports aligned to the individual inspection areas. In preparing this chapter the author conducted a review of the 2023-2025 PEEL inspections conducted at the time of writing[1] with a view to identifying any pattern in the types of innovation featured in inspection reports and potential relationships between innovative practice and inspection outcomes. In doing so it was ascertained that there is no clear relationship between the recognition of innovation within a PEEL inspection and the overall outcomes for the force. However, a weak relationship was identified between the number of innovation case studies featured in a report and the extent to which that force achieved gradings of GOOD or above. This is perhaps to be expected given the wealth of research which points to the positive association between flourishing innovation within an organisation upon areas such as performance (Oumlil, Faouzi and Juiz, 2020).

Clearer trends were apparent in terms of the areas in which forces were conducting innovation with a substantial number of the included case studies relating to the area of *preventing and deterring crime and antisocial behaviour and reducing vulnerability*. The second most common domain of innovation being *building, supporting and protecting the workforce*, with lower but still notable recognition of innovation in the fields of:

- *Leadership and force management*
- *Protecting vulnerable people*
- *Responding to the public*
- *Police powers and treating the public fairly and respectfully.*

Notably the least innovation was seen in the fields of *Investigating crime* and *Managing offenders and suspects*, both of which are areas of significant regulation, high demand, and substantial multi-agency engagement. Which, as we shall see in the next section, may serve to impede the potential for innovation.

BARRIERS TO AND ENABLERS OF INNOVATION

Research into innovation thwarting factors identifies bureaucracy, financial constraints, change resistance and the absence of time as key influences. In contrast, key enablers include collaboration, culture, education, knowledge, leadership, structure, strategy, and diversity (Johnsson, 2017). Yet it is important to recognise that these factors do not exist in isolation and may be mutually influential, and that innovation catalysts and inhibitors may be specific to individual organisations, teams, or employees. Thus, here we will deal with the major influences upon innovation capability which may be experienced in policing.

The nature of police, organisational and occupational culture has been substantially debated for decades across professional and academic publications. Particular facets of which may have an inhibiting or enabling influence upon organisational innovation. For example, a strong in-group mentality and suspicion of outsiders may serve to limit receptivity to new ideas from other teams, organisations or sectors, and increase resistance to collaborative working (Loftus, 2009), which is itself an innovation enabler (Johnsson, 2017). Further, police culture is inherently competitive (Buhrig, 2024), which, when coupled with suspicion of outsiders, may exacerbate siloed working and impede the exchange of ideas and knowledge with each party seeking to retain sole credit. Elsewhere, resistance to change identified in multiple policing commentaries (Skogan, 2008; Duxbury et al., 2017) may prevent new ideas being conceived, hinder their development and or act to thwart their wider proliferation. Though this phenomenon may potentially be limited through engaging practitioners in innovation from the outset, including giving life to their ideas such that they have a vested interest in the particular change progressing.

Innovation in policing may further be impeded by risk averse culture manifesting in heightened bureaucracy relating to resource allocation and the need for rapid evidence of success. This aversion, stemming from intense internal and external scrutiny of policing organisations, including a fear of individual and/or collective reputational damage. In this vein, PEEL itself and the desire to perform well in force management and leadership may impede innovation. The fear of failure and criticism resulting in an unwillingness to allocate scarce resource to untested initiatives. Whilst at an individual employee level, the need to demonstrate success to achieve promotion criteria in a hierarchical and competitive environment may impede willingness to take the risk of innovation.

Yet whilst this section has so far interpreted police culture as a negative for innovation. There are aspects which may catalyse novel forms of working, including an action orientation and pragmatic outlook which facilitate creative approaches to solving problems, particularly at the operational level (Reiner, 2010). Likewise intra-team solidarity may be associated with the psychological safety to experiment and share ideas.

From a leadership perspective, an innovation strategy, vision and values are integral to establishing clear direction for the innovation effort and demonstrating a commitment to innovation principles (Pisano, 2018), provided that these are subsequently reflected in decisions and actions. Whilst leaders also play a key role in establishing and maintaining innovation culture as facilitative or thwarting and possess the power and authority to allocate or withhold many of the resources necessary for innovation to thrive. Yet a review of the force strategies conducted in the course of writing this chapter identified innovation as an expressed priority for a negligible number of forces. Painting a picture of a lack of leader interest in novel means of organisational development, despite the potential for innovation to assist in the achievement of other police strategic objectives, such as increasing public trust and reducing vulnerability.

Even where innovation supportive strategic intent exists, the nature of police leadership may suppress innovation, particularly where strict adherence to notions of hierarchy endures. For example, new ideas conceived at the operational level will typically be fed up through the hierarchy for authorisation, risking their distortion, blockage or simply being lost in a miasma of police business. Despite the best efforts of all those involved. Whilst hierarchy may also induce a reluctance to give honest upward feedback (Riegel, 2022). Leader approach is also associated with the attainment of innovation potential. Requiring an open, authentic, transparent approach which encourages autonomy and individual development within a supportive environment (Alblooshi, Shamsuzzaman, and Haridy, 2021). In contrast, authoritarian, transactional and micromanagement approaches will likely inhibit innovation via a detrimental impact upon motivation and organisational commitment, amongst other factors.

More practically, bureaucracy is an anathema to innovation through its impact upon slowing processes down considerably or even bringing them to a complete stop through the existence of layers of red tape which impede flexible experimentation and result in a loss of project momentum (Turner, 2018). Whilst a degree of governance is necessary in a publicly funded police organisation, the proliferation of bureaucracy in modern forces is immense (Sweetland, 2024) and the extent to which it is actually serving to assist with risk management is debatable. Bureaucracy may also serve to limit the viability of collaborations and/or the availability of resource for innovative initiatives. Resourcing being a further key determinant of an organisation's innovation potential (Kedia, 2016). To be creative, individuals and teams need time and space to come up with, discuss, and adjust ideas, alongside physical and financial resources to develop ideas. Yet, a substantial number of police employees are working at or above capacity. Resulting in a detrimental impact upon well-being (Oscar Kilo, 2023) and thus likely limiting their ability to be creative (Lim, Williams and Bullock, 2023). In other words, police employees are simply too exhausted to innovate. Which, when coupled with low morale and motivation in many quarters (Police Federation, 2024), further undermines law enforcement's innovation potential. The financial picture is similarly challenging, with many forces still required to make substantial savings despite increased government funding for the service overall (Wiggett, 2025). In this climate, allocating money and/or people to innovation initiatives where success is not guaranteed likely appears a risky prospect for police leaders.

From a human resource angle teams and organisations which excel in innovating are typically those where there is a broad range of backgrounds, skills, knowledge, and experience, and where everyone's perspective is valued (Hewlett, Marshall and Sherbin, 2013). This requires not only a commitment to recruiting a diverse employee group, but to also ensuring the equitable availability and time for all to engage in continual learning. Alongside a willingness to engage with insight drawn from outside the law enforcement sector (West and Bogers, 2013). Further, innovative teams require more than the presence of subject matter experts. Research has shown that the most successfully innovative teams are those which marry specialist knowledge with a willingness to collaborate, open mindedness to new ideas, an action focus, understanding of the internal and external environment, and a degree of tenacity (Johnsson, 2017b). Thus, the development of innovative team requires a considered approach to talent management not just at the recruitment and promotion stage, but in the crafting of team composition.

Furthermore, in respect of governance, public sector organisations, including policing, face considerable pressure to deliver innovative service transformation, yet are unable to exert radical change due to stasis in internal and external governance. For example, the strategic direction of forces is considerably influenced by and accountable to local and national political representatives, which may act as a brake in terms of endorsing necessary investment in technological infrastructure, and/or require prioritisation of politically motivated initiatives over and above innovation projects. Further, inflexible governance of areas such as procurement may impede the experimentation and collaboration necessary for innovative development through emphasising cost as the most influential determinant as opposed to wider determinants of value. Whilst the complex multi-agency policing environment, with considerable interdependencies may impede innovation where partners are either unwilling and/or unable to collaborate in open innovation projects.

Likewise, the wider operational context of policing may also serve to limit innovation. Policing is inherently reactive in nature, requiring responses to emerging threat and risk. But also, culturally reactive by way of a short-term focus on solving immediate problems, which acts as a barrier to more strategic, innovative development and maintains focus upon previous and present challenges. This is particularly the case where resources are limited and thus necessarily focused upon firefighting in the present rather than preparing for the future.

Finally, innovation in policing may be impeded by the extensive range of innovative technologies and practices available, presenting challenges with identifying the most effective option for the particular force context. A further complication in this respect stemming from public sector procurement rules which place a significant weighting upon cost. Further, whilst police-higher education collaborations present significant opportunities for both parties in furthering innovative practices, these too may be limited by bureaucracy on both sides. Whilst innovations proposed by groups external to policing face the additional barrier of lacking understanding of operational reality, thereby emphasising the necessity of collaboration and knowledge sharing in innovation development.

L imitations upon innovation in policing are therefore organisationally and culturally derived, with many of them being deeply entrenched in practice, norms and values which have perpetuated for a considerable period of time. However, history has also shown that innovation may prosper in policing, and the establishment of an innovation culture is one means by which this may be achieved.

FOSTERING AN INNOVATION CULTURE

An innovation culture is an organisational environment in which creative thinking is encouraged by organisational leadership, processes and practices such that everyone in the organisation is empowered to innovate to the benefit of the organisation and its stakeholders. A positive innovation culture promotes communication within and between organisations, including the sharing of knowledge, experiences and ideas, enabling progression and learning. A positive innovation culture further serves to embed and perpetuate the values which catalyse innovation, including a learning mindset, tolerance of failure and willingness to take risks. Thus, enabling organisations to progress and avoid stasis (Li and Lui, 2022). Whilst from a workforce perspective, a positive innovation culture is one in which employees perceive greater autonomy in their roles and experience competency through skills development and learning. Together, these factors having a positive influence upon motivation and organisational commitment.

For leaders seeking to develop and nurture an innovation culture within their forces we therefore offer the following practical advice.

i. *Establish a collective strategic vision for innovation* and embed this into the force strategy and values. Doing so requires consultation across the hierarchy and business areas to understand others' perceptions and needs when it comes to innovation, building a coalition of support for the resultant strategic objectives. In addition to the development of an associated implementation plan with specific measurable objectives each assigned to a named owner with a defined timeline for delivery. This step also requires the active demonstration of the vision, values and strategy in the actions and decisions of leadership, including addressing and amending contradictory existing policy and procedure, and setting an example as to the nature of innovation supportive leadership the organisation aspires to.

ii. *Promote communication.* A thriving innovation culture is fuelled by transparent two-way communication across and between all levels of the organisation which enables the sharing of knowledge, facilitates access to resources, and enables the actioning of ideas. Such communication can be a particular challenge in hierarchical semi-disciplined contexts such as policing and therefore requires leaders to actively and demonstrably nurture its achievement. Including through acting on feedback received, providing constructive feedback to others, and making greater use of open engagement sessions with senior leaders where attendees have both the option to submit anonymous questions in advance and spontaneous questions during the event. In addition to supporting employees with developing active listening skills and seeking feedback from across the force as to the most effective communication channels for developing engagement.

iii. *Promote collaboration.* Coupled with accelerating communication is the requirement to enhance collaboration within and across teams, and with organisations outside of the individual force. This requires cultivating a mindset in which external insight is regarded as enhancing rather than replacing internal capabilities and challenging the 'us and them' mindset often seen in policing organisations. In practice emphasising the benefits of partnership working for all involved may assist with achieving this, including encouraging those involved in collaborative projects to speak out about their experiences and learning, and emphasising the wider benefit to the force in terms of effective resource management, and the alignment between the strategic objectives of the participating bodies. Whilst also ensuring the collaborative initiatives are led by relationship focused individuals with a clear terms of reference for the overall project and the respective participants.

iv. *Recognise and reward learning.* Characteristics of a learning organisation include a culture of continuous collaborative learning in which employees share experiences, cohesive systems exist to facilitate knowledge sharing, learning is integrated into daily operations, and leaders champion learning through communications, decisions and role-modelling behaviours (Senge, 1990). However, policing operational debriefs and commendation processes are invariably focused upon outcomes and the successes achieved. With much less value placed on the learning which can be built upon for the future. Particularly in cases where the operation/initiative did not deliver the initial objectives. Developing an innovation culture requires demonstrable recognition and reward of learning in spite of the outcome. This could take the form of flipping debrief and appraisal formats to consider learning ahead of successes. Alongside introduction of reflective questions into promotion processes to encourage applicants to focus on what they gained by way of knowledge and how this can be applied in the future, rather than simply what was achieved. And giving consideration as to how learning may be recognised and rewarded in official commendation processes.

v. *Look outside of the immediate force, or even policing, for inspiration and encourage others to do the same.* The potential sources of ideation are endless, and it pays to take the time to explore these including reflecting on how they could be adapted to the specific force concept. Key examples may include the Office of the Police Chief Scientific Adviser, Police Digital Service, conferences, police research partnerships, or the Research Map and 'What Works' repositories managed by the College of Policing. Innovation does not have to entail coming up with a brand-new technology, process or policy. It may lie in applying a concept from outside policing in a novel way to the context of a particular force or using tooling in new ways. Keeping abreast of emerging ideas is potentially time consuming but identifying and subscribing to the social media feeds of innovation thought leaders, business publications, and research organisations can reduce some of the demand. Whilst sharing these with others within your force will not only catalyse discussion on innovation, but it will also be a clear demonstration of your commitment to the organisational innovation vision, strategy and values as a senior leader.

vi. *Enabling autonomy.* Individuals who feel empowered to make decisions in their role, including in the ways in which tasks are fulfilled, and in the management of their working lives show a greater propensity toward innovative behaviour. Achieving autonomy in this manner requires leaders to avoid the temptation to micromanage and to trust in their employees' expertise, whilst also being sufficiently present to set objectives, offer support, feedback and unblock barriers. It may also incorporate allowing greater flexibility in working arrangements and encouraging individuals to take control of their professional development through the setting of individual appraisal objectives in addition to, or instead of, those prescribed by their role or the force.

vii. *Embrace experimentation.* In addition to recognising learning and giving employees the autonomy to experiment, it is essential to energise experimentation through emphasising its role in creating data on which subsequent improvements and decisions may be made. This may include running small experiments in a contained (sandbox) environment to explore initial viability prior to a decision upon wider roll out to test the initial assumptions on which the idea was predicated. Thus, increasing confidence in investing further and ensuring that the future development is grounded in evidence. However, the need for an objective analysis of resulting data is also pivotal to prevent limit bias in the decision-making process.

viii. *Enhance psychological safety.* Experimentation will only happen if the participants feel psychologically safe in doing so. The fear of being judged in the event of failure can have a powerful effect on an individual's decision to try, particularly in a hierarchical and competitive culture such as policing. In this vein, leaders may cultivate psychological safety through promoting compassionate, empathetic and authentic communication, demonstrating this in their own engagement with others and not being afraid to appear vulnerable or humble. In addition to establishing clear norms for how problems, mistakes or failure are handled (which incorporate an emphasis on learning) to reduce uncertainty induced anxiety and assure individuals that they will be supported by the organisation.

ix. *Ensure innovation in resourced.* Through resource management strategies which place value on time, financial and other resource expenditure on new initiatives. This has the potential to be challenging in a public sector climate where resources are limited. However, strategic recognition of the necessity of innovation to deliver long term sustainability of the organisation may go some way to alleviate concerns, particularly where strategic messaging places value on innovations which enable greater efficiency in resource use. Whilst embedding innovation as a core competency within individual role appraisals may assist with enhancing recognition of its place as an essential skill to be developed and nurtured by employees.

x. *Foster diversity of perspective.* Finally, innovation requires a diversity of thought, experience and skills, which may be facilitated through talent management, recruitment, and training. But also giving consideration to greater flexibility of employment structures such as the use of secondments into and out of the organisation or teams to promote the proliferation of new perspectives.

Leadership plays a key role in shaping the (innovation) culture of an organisation through their ability to establish strategy, allocate resource and influence the behaviour of employees. Thus, a concerted innovation strategy which is consistently supported by the actions and decisions of an organisation's leaders has the potential to go a long way toward energising creativity, experiment and continuous organisational learning to the benefit of all involved.

CASE STUDIES

Key enablers of innovation within police forces are therefore derived from the culture, leadership, and context in which it operates. The following case studies illustrate some of the wide range of innovative practices in UK policing today, as enabled by the concepts discussed in this chapter.

Cambridgeshire Constabulary demonstrate innovation in both practice and technology in addressing contemporary policing challenges (HMICFRS, 2024). For example, the Force uses technology to enable effective scrutiny of the use of stop and search powers through community participation. When an individual is subject to a stop and search, they are provided with a QR code to enable access to information explaining the associated process and powers. In addition to an invitation to participate in the community scrutiny panel who are responsible for reviewing the use of stop and search and providing feedback to the force. Thereby seeking to facilitate the establishment of a panel representative of the community and enhancing the relationship between the Force and local populace.

Other forces have also adopted innovative approaches to engaging with local communities. For example, Gloucester Constabulary (HMICFRS, 2024b) engaged a well-known social media influencer in hosting a podcast, during their campaign to raise awareness of stalking. Thereby widening the scope of the potential audience for the initiative beyond those who typically interact with law enforcement social media. Likewise, as part of the response to the Police Race Action Plan, West Midlands Police have worked with social media influencers in developing their understanding of perceptions of policing amongst young members of the Black community. Including through the use of videos and engagement events which enabled feedback that was subsequently used to inform officer training (HMICFRS, 2023). These examples demonstrating the ability of forces to think differently about community engagement and experiment with new ways of working.

Elsewhere forces are innovating in the use of data analytics in more effective management of threat, risk and resources. West Midlands Police, for example, have used data analytics to develop a tool to predict likely locations of knife crime (HMICFRS, 2023), enabling the introduction of mitigating measures to minimise risk. Whilst multiple forces are demonstrating innovativeness in workforce management, including in the fields of recruitment, wellbeing and retention. For example, Hertfordshire Police (HMICFRS, 2024c) have recruited data scientists via a collaboration with a local university, recruitment provider and social media platform to enable greater exploitation of performance data. The programme including opportunities for internships within teams involved in the strategic development of the policing response. Allowing the Force the deeper insight, skills and diverse perspectives provided by the graduates, some of whom may go on to longer term careers within the organisation. In relation to wellbeing, Merseyside Police are working with higher education to explore the benefits of wearable technology in empowering employees to manage their health and assist with developing more bespoke solutions to wellbeing needs (Cox et al., 2024; LJMU, 2025). Whilst finally, Greater Manchester

Police have introduced a Stay Team, to explore the causes of voluntary resignation within the force and work with individuals considering leaving to understand and address barriers to their remaining (HMICFRS, 2023b). Collectively these examples demonstrating the value of collaboration in fostering innovation whether within a force, or between policing and other organisations. As enabled by through strategic vision, resourcing and a culture which emphasises continual learning.

CONCLUSION

Innovation in tooling, process and policy is increasingly essential to delivering effective, efficient and sustainable policing organisations for the future. And whilst innovation is not a key direct determinant of outstanding performance in PEEL, it is almost certain that innovative initiatives across the PEEL domains are demonstrative of a well-run, effective, and efficiently functioning force. For example, innovation thrives in a climate of effective *leadership and management*, where *employees are supported*, two of the key PEEL dimensions. Whilst in turn, innovation will enable a force to be more successful in delivering upon the other domains such as *investigating crime*, *managing offenders*, and *protecting vulnerable people*, amongst others.

Yet, as this chapter has shown, many of the practices, cultural norms, policies and processes in modern day policing have the potential to suffocate innovation at the outset. Thus, placing a responsibility upon leaders to address these aspects through a clear vision, strategy and values which empower employee innovation within a collaborative, flexible, and supportive environment which rewards learning and facilitates the expression of diverse perspectives. This will not be easy, but is achievable when consistently, transparently, and authentically aspired toward as part of a holistic approach to sustainable organisational learning and development.

REFERENCES

Alblooshi, M., Shamsuzzaman, M., & Haridy, S. (2021). The relationship between leadership styles and organisational innovation: A systematic literature review and narrative synthesis. *European Journal of Innovation Management, 24*(2), 338–370.

Buhrig, R. (2024). Masculinity contest cultures and organizational outcomes in police organizations, *Policing. Journal of Policy Practice, 18*. Advance online publication. DOI: 10.1093/police/paae100

Cox, C., Yates, J., O'Brien, F., Pajon Moreno, L., Farrell, A., Ward, M., McCabe, P., James, A., & McNamara-Catalano, I. (2024). Wearable technology: A wellbeing option for serving police officers and staff? A comparison of results of a pilot study with firearms officers and a group of mixed officers and staff. *International Journal of Environmental Research and Public Health, 21*(2), 1–17. DOI: 10.3390/ijerph21020001 PMID: 38397677

Duxbury, L., Bennell, C., Halinski, M., & Murphy, S. (2017). Change or be changed: Diagnosing the readiness to change in the Canadian police sector. *The Police Journal: Theory. Practice and Principles, 91*(4), 316–338. DOI: 10.1177/0032258X17740317

Hewlett, S. A., Marshall, M., & Sherbin, L. (2013, December). How diversity can drive innovation. *Harvard Business Review*.

His Majesty's Inspectorate of Constabulary and Fire & Rescue Services (HMICFRS). (2023). *West Midlands PEEL assessment 2023–2025.* https://hmicfrs.justiceinspectorates.gov.uk/peel-reports/west-midlands-2023-25/

His Majesty's Inspectorate of Constabulary and Fire & Rescue Services (HMICFRS). (2023b). *Greater Manchester PEEL assessment 2023–2025.* https://hmicfrs.justiceinspectorates.gov.uk/peel-reports/greater-manchester-2023-25/

His Majesty's Inspectorate of Constabulary and Fire & Rescue Services (HMICFRS). (2024). *Cambridgeshire PEEL assessment 2023–2025.* https://hmicfrs.justiceinspectorates.gov.uk/peel-reports/cambridgeshire-2023-25/

His Majesty's Inspectorate of Constabulary and Fire & Rescue Services (HMICFRS). (2024b). *Gloucestershire PEEL assessment 2023–2025.* https://hmicfrs.justiceinspectorates.gov.uk/peel-reports/gloucestershire-2023-25/

His Majesty's Inspectorate of Constabulary and Fire & Rescue Services (HMICFRS). (2024c). *Hertfordshire PEEL assessment 2023–2025.* https://hmicfrs.justiceinspectorates.gov.uk/peel-reports/hertfordshire-2023-25/

Johnsson, M. (2017). Innovation Enablers for Innovation Teams – A Review. *Journal of Innovation Management.*, *5*(3), 75–121.

Johnsson, M. (2017b). Creating high-performing innovation teams. *Journal of Innovation Management*, *5*(4), 23–47.

Kedia, A. (2016). Resourcing – Integral to systemic innovation. In Garrison Darrin, M. A., & Krill, J. A. (Eds.), *Infusing Innovation into Organisations*. CRC Press.

Li, Z., & Liu, L. (2022). The impact of organizational innovation culture on employees' innovation behavior. *Social Behavior and Personality*, *50*(12), 1–10.

Liverpool John Moores University (LJMU). (2025, March 18). *Police turn to wearable tech to improve sleep and fitness.* https://www.ljmu.ac.uk/about-us/news/articles/2025/3/18/police-turn-to-wearable-tech

Loftus, B. (2009). Police occupational culture: Classic themes, altered times. *Policing and Society*, *20*(1), 1–20.

Oscar Kilo. (2023) National Police Wellbeing Survey 2023 Results. https://www.oscarkilo.org.uk/news/national-police-wellbeing-survey-2023-results

Oumlil, R., Faouzi, H., & Juiz, C. (2020). Uncovering Two Decades of Open Innovation Benefits: A Qualitative Meta-Analysis. *International Journal of Innovation and Technology Management.*, *17*(8), 2030006. DOI: 10.1142/S0219877020300062

Pisano, G.P. (2018) You Need an Innovation Strategy. *Harvard Business Review*. June 2015

Police Federation. (2024) Pay and Morale Survey 2023 – Headline Report February 2024. https://www.polfed.org/media/19164/pay-and-morale-survey-report-2023.pdf

Reiner, R. (2010). *The Politics of the Police*. Oxford University Press.

Senge, P. M. (1990). *The fifth discipline: The art and practice of the learning organization*. Doubleday.

Skogan, W. G. (2008). Why reforms fail. *Policing and Society*, *18*(1), 23–34. DOI: 10.1080/10439460701718534

Sweetland, J. (2024) HMCIC Andy Cooke: 'The CJS is now the most bureaucratic and the slowest that I've ever seen it'. *Police Insight*. https://policinginsight.com/feature/interview/hmcic-andy-cooke-the-cjs-is-now-the-most-bureaucratic-and-the-slowest-that-ive-ever-seen-it/

Turner, E. (2018). *Be Less Zombie: How great companies create dynamic innovation, fearless leadership and passionate people*. Wiley.

Varadarajan, R. (2024). Mitigating the definitional quagmire in innovation research: An inclusive definition of innovation as a template for defining various types of innovations uniformly. *Journal of Product Innovation Management*, *41*(4), 703–723. DOI: 10.1111/jpim.12729

West, J., & Bogers, M. (2013). Leveraging external sources of innovation: A review of research on open innovation. *Product Innovation Management*, *31*(4), 814–831.

Wiggett, I. (2025) England and Wales police budgets for 2025-2026: Despite significant increases, forces will still need to make savings. *Police Insight.* https://policinginsight.com/feature/analysis/england-and-wales-police-budgets-for-2025-26-despite-significant-increases-forces-will-still-need-to-make-savings/

ENDNOTE

1 February 2025

Chapter 14
Delivering and Assessing High Performance

Eric Halford
http://orcid.org/0000-0002-3913-1679
Rabdan Academy, UAE

ABSTRACT

This chapter examines the evolution of police performance management in the UK, highlighting the challenges posed by shifting oversight models and the limitations of traditional performance metrics. It explores the distinction between targets and measures, emphasizing the need for ethical performance assessment to prevent distortions caused by target-driven policing. The chapter outlines evidence-based methodologies such as Data Envelopment Analysis (DEA), Crime Harm Indexes, and Proactive Policing Indexes to provide a more nuanced understanding of police effectiveness. A performance management model is proposed, integrating strategic objectives, accountability, and ethical oversight to enhance transparency, efficiency, and public trust in policing.

INTRODUCTION

Within policing in the United Kingdom (UK), the past several decades have seen significant shifts in oversight models occurring in response to political and societal pressures. Each individual transformation has led to periods of incremental change and refinement, but arguably, the overall pattern reflects a cycle of centralization, decentralization, and re-centralization (Perkins and Davies, 2024). This constant movement in oversight has caused significant confusion in the management of police performance, particularly in how to assess it. In this chapter, the issue of consistently delivering and assessing high performance within police services is examined. To

DOI: 10.4018/979-8-3373-2757-0.ch014

begin, an overview of the historical backdrop provides the foundation for sections that consider the traditional method of assessing policing performance, an overview of the methodology used by the inspectorate to assess police services, and the metrics used, with particular emphasis on understanding the distinction between targets and measures. The chapter will then consider the components required to deliver ethical performance, before outlining several evidence-based methods of assessment that can be used in policing. Finally, the chapter concludes by outlining a model for delivering police performance that effectively captures all the outlined features.

THE EVOLUTION OF POLICE PERFORMANCE MANAGEMENT IN THE UK

The development of police performance management in the UK over the past 40 years has been shaped by broader public sector reforms. In particular, the 1980s witnessed the emergence of a New Public Management (NPM) philosophy, which aimed to enhance efficiency and accountability across all government services, not just the police (de Maillard & Savage, 2012). As a result, a drive emerged to instil performance-driven accountability across the whole public sector (Ranson & Stewart, 1994; Pollitt, 2002). By the early 1990s, increasing concerns over police effectiveness led to the introduction of formal performance measurement frameworks, including the establishment of league tables that compared police forces based on crime rates, detection rates, and public satisfaction levels (Home Office, 1993; de Maillard & Savage, 2012). In these nascent stages of police performance, the Audit Commission (1995) played a crucial role in defining statutory national performance indicators for police services, which primarily focused on raw data available from crime and response time statistics.

The election of the Labour government in 1997 accelerated the drive toward performance-driven policing, integrating it into the Best Value framework, which required police forces to demonstrate continuous improvement (Boyne, 2000). During this period, the then Her Majesty's Inspectorate of Constabulary (HMIC) introduced the Police Performance Assessment Framework (PPAF), which later evolved into the Assessments of Policing and Community Safety (APCS) framework. This framework assessed police effectiveness in key areas, including crime prevention, public trust, and resource management (Home Office, 2007).

The transition to intelligence-led policing (ILP) (See Ratcliffe, 2016) and problem-oriented policing (POP) (See seminal work by Goldstein, 1991) arguably emerged because of the drive for models to deliver performance-based policing. Both ILP and POP and emphasised strategic resource allocation and intelligence-driven police activity. However, the implementation of both encountered several significant challenges. One of the primary issues lay in technological and data management limitations. Both ILP and POP relied heavily on data analysis, yet at their inception, many police forces lacked standardised IT infrastructure or data-sharing mechanisms, making information processing inefficient (Ratcliffe, 2008). This early problem was articulated by Ellingworth et al. (1995) who suggested police services were information rich but knowledge poor, describing how they possessed large volumes of data, but they failed to produce meaningful assessments of intervention outcomes, thereby hindering performance improvements (Ratcliffe, 2016).

Another major barrier to their implementation was cultural resistance within policing. Many officers viewed these new models as a departure from traditional policing methods and resisted the shift (Chan, 1996; Ericson and Heggarty, 1997). This cultural resistance hindered their adoption at both the operational and leadership levels, slowing the transition toward evidence-based decision-making that was required to deliver effective police performance (Maguire & John, 1995). Parallel to these newly emerged models, the National Intelligence Model (NIM) was introduced as a performance framework designed to standardize intelligence-led policing practices across UK policing, yet its implementation also faced resistance from senior police leaders, many of whom viewed it as an attempt to centralize policing authority (Stelfox, 1998).

CHALLENGES AND CRITICISM OF PERFORMANCE MANAGEMENT IN POLICING

Even after efforts to standardize police performance measurement and implement new models to improve police effectiveness and efficiency had been embedded, criticisms persisted. One of the main issues for leaders was the centralization of policing targets. Many argued that the rigid numerical benchmarks placed upon them distorted policing priorities, pressuring them to focus on achieving statistical targets rather than delivering meaningful outcomes (Golding and Savage, 2012).

Operationally, others cited the challenge of measuring the policing of organized crime within a performance-driven framework, arguing that traditional performance measures relied on clear, measurable data, such as crime figures, clearance rates and response times. These measures were considered inadequate for organized crime investigations which required long-term intelligence operations, the results of which did not align with easily quantifiable targets (Gill, 2000; Porter, 1996). Some even suggest that as performance management became more embedded, it reshaped police priorities, often at the expense of community-focused policing (Loveday, 2006).

Despite these concerns, the Police Reform Act of 2002 further expanded central government oversight, embedding performance management as a mandatory process for all forces (Jones, 2003). However, growing concerns over the limitations of target-driven policing led to the 2008 Green Paper on Policing, which proposed shifting the emphasis away from quantitative metrics and toward public confidence as the primary measure of success (Home Office, 2008).

DECENTRALIZATION AND THE ROLE OF POLICE AND CRIME COMMISSIONERS

The introduction of Police and Crime Commissioners (PCCs) in 2012 was intended to improve performance by decentralising police governance and enhancing local accountability in performance management (Home Office, 2010). The changes gave local leaders greater control over performance assessment, monitoring and resource allocation and marked a fundamental shift from national oversight to localized decision-making (Perkins & Davies, 2024). However, this naturally led to significant differences in how policing services were delivered, resulting in inconsistent and fragmented approaches to police performance management. Forces were no longer required to meet national KPIs, and instead, performance expectations were set locally, depending on PCC priorities (Perkins & Davies, 2024).

However, this lack of centralized oversight did not persist for long. Emerging crime trends, such as those caused by knife crime and exploitation, highlighted high-profile policing failures, prompting calls for a return to stronger national oversight. As a result, the National Policing Board (NPB) and the Crime and Policing Performance Board (CPPB) were created to coordinate national policing priorities, while agencies like His Majesty's Inspectorate of Constabulary and Fire & Rescue Services (HMICFRS) began to play an increasingly influential role in shaping police performance standards through their inspection framework (Perkins & Davies, 2024).

TRADITIONAL POLICE PERFORMANCE MANAGEMENT

Despite the tumultuous twists and turns in centralization and decentralization of police performance, how it was assessed has remained relatively consistent for the past two decades. Traditionally, the performance of police organisations has been assessed and measured in two ways. At the strategic and operational level, police services place great emphasis on assessing and measuring quantifiable activities such as arrests, stop-and-search activity, warrants executed, and convictions (Cascio, 1977; Fabricatore et al., 1978; Guilfoyle, 2016; Ratcliffe, 2018). In terms of human resources, performance measurement focuses on capacity and capability factors such as absence levels and the number of employees on performance plans. At the tactical level, it is argued that police services focus more on assessing performance traits (Shane, 2010). These refer to individual-level behaviours that are deemed to reflect high performance. As these traits are typically observed by first- and second-line managers, they are more subjective and include characteristics such as appearance, professionalism, communication, decisiveness, and leadership (Iannone, 1987; Landy, 1977).

Although these measures provide some insight into police performance, they do not accurately measure performance itself. More importantly, they fail to reflect the true nature of police effectiveness, which, according to the Peelian Principles, is to "*recognise always that the test of police efficiency is the absence of crime and disorder, and not the visible evidence of police action in dealing with them*" (Lentz, 2007, p71). In this context, many traditional and existing metrics used to assess and measure performance reflect political, financial, or subjective priorities, rather than actual policing effectiveness. Instead, a more accurate measure of performance is the actions taken by officers, their associated outcomes, and how these relate to the objectives of the police service—not just statistical evidence of police activity (Ratcliffe, 2022). To be an outstanding police service, all three components must align (objectives, activity, and outcome) to maximise efficiency and effectiveness.

HOW PERFORMANCE IS ASSESSED BY HMICFRS

Arguably, the disconnect between traditional perspectives on performance measurement in policing and the criteria used by HMICFRS has resulted in many police services receiving lower-than-expected inspection gradings. This occurs because existing police performance management structures fail to effectively connect the three primary components—organisational objectives, officer activity, and measurable outcomes (Shane, 2010). HMICFRS recognises the interdependent nature of these three features, and for police services to achieve an outstanding grading they must employ a comprehensive approach to performance assessment, measurement and management that integrates all three, as HMICFRS employs a thorough holistic inspection process to assess whether they do so effectively.

To first ensure that police forces establish appropriate objectives, HMICFRS regularly engages with governmental bodies and technical advisory groups, which help define and confirm policing priorities. These priorities are then assessed against detailed data from sources such as the Home Office, the Office for National Statistics (ONS), and the British Crime Survey (BCS). These datasets provide comprehensive insights into crime trends, demographic information, and financial data specific to each police service. Using this information, the analytical team at HMICFRS assesses strategic-level data against key policing objectives, identifying potential performance concerns in individual services, which can then be subjected to 'intelligence-led' inspections. To ensure these inspections are targeted and effective, HMICFRS compiles detailed data briefing packs, which align with inspection questions for each police force. These packs help inspectors focus on underperforming areas and ensure that resources are directed to the areas of greatest import, or those requiring improvement.

The inspection process itself is carried out by specialists from relevant policing areas, such as child protection, often including serving and retired experts. These experts conduct inspections through interviews, focus groups with officers, and reviews of internal policies and procedures. However, the most important and revealing aspect of inspections is often case audits, which have become a critical component of inspections over the past decade. These audits, often involving hundreds of cases, examine each in fine detail, ensuring that best practices are adhered to, police service policies and procedures are followed, and most importantly, the outcomes are appropriate.

Through this multi-faceted approach, HMICFRS ensures that its assessments are rigorous, and evidence based. Any weaknesses in the alignment between objectives, activities, and outcomes is likely to result in downgrading of efficiency and effectiveness. Ensuring this alignment is maintained is essential for police services aiming to achieve and sustain an outstanding performance rating. The remainder of this chapter will outline how this can be accomplished.

METRICS OF POLICE PERFORMANCE - TARGETS VS MEASURES

As outlined, the interplay between objectives, activity, and outcomes drives police performance. Setting objectives and police activity are both covered in other chapters of this book, therefore, in this chapter the focus is on how they can be assessed and measured to understand police performance. To do this, it is vital to consider the metrics of measurement as these underpin each component (objectives, activity, and outcomes). In 2015 the home secretary commissioned a report that examined the police target culture that had emerged as a direct result of the emphasis on performance and a primary finding was that there is a key distinction between measures and targets (Curtis, 2015; Guilfoyle, 2016). It was outlined that 'Measures provide information that supports decision-making, whereas targets set specific numeric goals that must be achieved' (Curtis, 2015). At the time of writing (2015), the report indicated that although many police services had moved away from numerical targets, they were still applying target-based thinking, and performance metrics remained focused on easily quantifiable crime data rather than holistic indicators of policing success (Curtis, 2015; Guilfoyle, 2016). This is not to say targets have no place, the truth is that both (targets and measures) are vital for assessing and measuring performance. Outstanding police services recognise this and take a mature approach that leverages the strengths of both and balances them accordingly.

Targets

Targets refer to specific numeric goals that must be achieved (Guilfoyle, 2016). These are often used as benchmarks to aim for and evaluate against police performance. Common targets include crime reduction and detection rates (Ratcliffe, 2018). Response time targets are also prevalent and are used to ensure that emergency calls are attended within a specified timeframe, such as answering 90% of 999 calls within ten seconds. Although inadvisable, historically, arrest quotas, frequency of intelligence entries and stop and search targets have all been used in UK policing to dictate the frequency of activity that should be conducted within a given timeframe (Guilfoyle, 2016). Conviction rate targets are also frequently used to focus police services on achieving a higher percentage of cases resulting in successful prosecutions, particularly in areas like domestic abuse.

Measures

In contrast, measures provide information to support decision-making without setting explicit goals that must be met. This allows police forces to assess performance trends without the unintended consequences that rigid targets can sometimes create, which are outlined shortly. In this context, data such as recorded crime rates should be measured to tracks trends in offense types and provide a broader understanding of crime patterns (Ratcliffe, 2018). More innovative metrics like crime harm and severity scores provide an alternative to simply counting offenses. Case outcome tracking provides insight into fluctuations in volumes of cases leading to formal charges or resolutions. Similarly, stop and search demographic analysis examines disparities in police activity based on race or age. Public confidence can be measured to offer insights into how safe communities feel and their level of trust in the police. Victim satisfaction rates can be used to measure how well victims perceive police respond to incidents. Workforce well-being measures often focus on causes of officer sickness, stress, and job satisfaction to assess the overall health of the policing workforce.

Integrating Targets and Measures

While targets and measures serve different purposes, both play a role in policing performance management. Targets set clear objectives that can help drive ambition and provide accountability, while measures provide the broader information that enables the context needed to understand the effectiveness, or otherwise, of policing strategies. A balanced approach, integrating both, ensures that police forces can set high standards while also making informed, data-driven decisions that can help strategic, operational and tactical activity.

The problem for police services, and especially leaders, is identifying the appropriate targets and measures (Guilfoyle, 2016). For example, when considering targets, the distinctions between them mean that some are valid, while others can drive unethical practices (Guilfoyle, 2016). For instance, few would argue against the target to answer 90% of 999 calls within ten seconds, or targets to raise the detection or conviction rate for rape and serious sexual offences, or violence against women and girls. They key issue is how they are used. In this regard, there is extensive evidence to suggest that, historically, the excessive pursuit of targets in policing has placed undue emphasis on quantitative data at the expense of qualitative aspects, such as the quality of service (Guilfoyle, 2016; Hood, 1995; Loveday, 2006). Furthermore, frontline employees often perceive targets as restrictive and counterproductive (Cockcroft & Beattie, 2009), most likely as they can significantly reduce an officers' decision-making discretion (Evetts, 2009). In addition to limiting discretion, target-driven policing frequently results in unnecessary bureaucracy, requiring officers to conduct excessive reporting, with officers suggesting they create a box-ticking mentality, where administrative compliance takes precedence over meaningful police work (Curtis, 2015; Guilfoyle, 2016). Together, the reduction in discretion and increase in bureaucracy, has a negative impact on officer morale, reducing their discretionary effort, which ultimately reduces their overall performance (Hesketh et al, 2017). This is a frequent unintended consequence when applying targets in policing.

At their worst, targets can lead to the manipulation of statistics to meet performance expectations rather than genuinely improving outcomes (Eterno & Silverman, 2017; Guilfoyle, 2016; Hough, 2010). This, in turn, fosters dysfunctional behaviours such as manipulating crime data, downgrading serious crimes to lesser offenses, such as recording a burglary as theft, pressuring suspects to admit to additional offenses, and prioritizing easily resolvable quick wins over more complex crime investigations (Curtis, 2015; Eterno & Silverman, 2017; de Maillard & Savage, 2021). This gaming of the performance system creates a distortion in perceptions of effectiveness and helps understand why there is often a disconnect between what the police report, and how communities feel. For example, the gaming of burglary statistics to meet reduction and detection targets was prevalent in the early 2000s. Many victims saw attempts to burgle their homes downgraded to criminal damage to a dwelling in official statistics to massage official burglary data. This behaviour not only affected subsequent criminal intelligence analysis, proactive policing responses, and investigative resources, but also undermined public trust (Curtis, 2015; Eterno & Guilfoyle, 2016; Silverman, 2017; de Maillard & Savage, 2021). Victims and communities felt overlooked and unhappy with the policing response. Such feelings are often manifested in negative community feedback and victim satisfaction surveys, despite the fact that 'on paper' the police may be doing a good job at tackling burglary.

Due to these issues, it is essential that any framework to assess and measure police performance has safeguards to ensure ethical practice. It must also include community feedback, victim satisfaction, and other measures of public legitimacy as ensuring these are captured and embedded in performance frameworks provides a more holistic understanding of whether objectives, activity, and outcomes are aligned. The next sections will outline how this can be achieved.

COMPONENTS OF ETHICAL PERFORMANCE MANAGEMENT

Ethical performance management is essential not only to maintain public trust and confidence but also to prevent the dysfunctional behaviours historically associated with target-driven policing. Achieving this requires several key considerations. One of the most critical components is ethical crime recording, which ensures that performance data accurately reflects real levels of crime and reported incidents. Without high-integrity data, police services risk eroding public confidence, compromising effective response strategies, and ultimately diminishing their ability to achieve outstanding performance ratings.

Equally important is balancing crime and non-crime measures. Police services that achieve outstanding performance use a broad range of targets and measures that align with their organisational vision and mission. Rather than relying solely on recorded crime figures, these forces incorporate measures that reflect both crime trends and quality of service, community feedback, victim satisfaction, and other measures of public legitimacy, ensuring a more holistic assessment of performance.

Beyond simple monitoring, performance data should be leveraged to improve decision-making and problem-solving, rather than merely tracking statistics or being used as a tool for evaluating individual employee performance (Ratcliffe, 2018). Effective performance management identifies strategic issues, trends, emerging threats, and risks, allowing resources to be allocated proactively and effectively (Guilfoyle, 2016; Ratcliffe, 2018). A policing approach that prioritises problem-solving and proactivity will naturally yield positive results without the need for rigid numerical targets, or unethical practices.

Another crucial element is ensuring that performance management supports officers in making the right decisions for victims, rather than just burdening them with excessive reporting requirements (Guilfoyle, 2016; Ratcliffe, 2018). Reducing unnecessary bureaucracy is essential to maintaining operational efficiency. While accountability remains important in this regard, officers must retain the ability to exercise judgment without fear of repercussions for deviating from actions whose sole purpose is to improve performance metrics. Doing so puts what is being measured, above what is right for the victim.

The success of any performance management framework is ultimately dependent on leadership and culture (Ratcliffe, 2018). Senior officers must cultivate an environment that promotes the values and ethics of UK policing, whilst enabling professional discretion and problem-solving, rather than fixating on target-chasing behaviours (Ratcliffe, 2018). As outlined, the latter can have a detrimental impact on officer morale and motivation, which in turn negatively affects overall organisational performance. Leaders who encourage an ethical culture of critical thinking, innovation, and continuous improvement will see better long-term results than those who enforce a rigid, numbers-driven approach, often in pursuit of short-term success. In essence, if you create the right culture, the numbers look after themselves.

Finally, improving communication and transparency is fundamental to ethical performance management. Both targets and measures should be clearly presented to employees and used as tools for learning and improvement, rather than as punitive mechanisms (Curtis, 2015; Guilfoyle, 2016). Police forces should foster two-way communication, ensuring that officers not only understand performance expectations but also feel empowered to provide feedback without fear of reprisal. Open communication and transparency contribute significantly to positive leadership and a strong performance culture, both of which are essential for achieving outstanding performance ratings.

By embracing these principles, police services can establish an ethical, effective, and sustainable performance management framework that enhances both accountability and operational effectiveness while maintaining public trust and officer morale.

EVIDENCE-BASED METHODS OF PERFORMANCE MEASUREMENT

As already outlined in detail in this chapter, the assessment and measurement of police performance have traditionally relied on crime counting metrics. This conventional approach, while providing a good foundation, does not offer the nuanced assessment of service delivery required to achieve an outstanding grading (Ratcliffe, 2018; Sherman et al., 2020). To refine performance assessments and measurements, precisely what is analyzed is vital. In this section a range of evidence-based methods of performance measurement are therefore outlined to provide police services with an increased variety of methods and metrics for assessing and measuring their performance. This includes those outlined by policing scholars that are yet to be fully embraced by policing.

Measuring Police Efficiency - Data Envelopment Analysis

First, measuring police efficiency is considered the most complex. Traditional metrics fail to assess whether resources are allocated effectively or if policing activity contributes to tangible improvements in outcomes. To achieve this, methods such as Data Envelopment Analysis (DEA) (Asif et al., 2018) and Multicriteria Decision Analysis (MCDA) (Nepomuceno et al., 2020) are required to create a balanced performance assessment and measurement system that considers both efficiency and effectiveness. These methodologies may be beyond police analysts alone, and necessitate external assistance to conduct or implement, but can provide considerable value.

DEA is a recognized methodology for measuring the efficiency of units (Asif et al., 2018). When used in the policing context, it can measure police efficiency by comparing resource inputs, such as personnel, vehicles, and operational budgets, to policing outputs, such as crime clearance rates, response times, and arrests (Asif et al., 2018). The method constructs an efficiency measure by identifying high-performing police 'units', often defined as police stations or divisions, and flags underperforming ones (Asif et al., 2018). This enables police services to model their efficiency more productively and allows more informed decision-making regarding resource allocation (Asif et al., 2018).

Measuring Police Effectiveness - Multicriteria Decision Analysis

Efficiency alone does not equate to effective policing. Methods such as Multicriteria Decision Analysis (MCDA), particularly Preference Ranking Organization Methods for Enrichment Evaluations (known as the PROMETHEE II methodology), is a decision-support method that ranks alternative responses based on multiple, often conflicting criteria (Brans and Vincke, 1985). Using this method to assess and measure police performance allows services to systematically compare different intervention strategies, operational priorities, and their relative resource allocation levels, by assigning weights to various data indicators accessible within police data systems (Nepomuceno et al., 2020). Unlike DEA, which focuses only on the relationships between resource-output, MCDA also considers external influences, such as crime trends, socio-economic conditions, and the complexity, time or effort involved in responding to or investigating incidents (Nepomuceno et al., 2020). In addition, the method also enables decision-makers to evaluate trade-offs between competing priorities, ensures that efficiency-driven measurements and their associated decision-making do not overshadow indicators of effectiveness (Nepomuceno et al., 2020). By integrating both DEA and MCDA, police services can develop a comprehensive assessment of their performance that moves well beyond simplistic numerical targets, demonstrating to HMICFRS outstanding awareness and decision-making capabilities.

Crime Harm and Severity Indexes

One of the most significant advancements in evidence-based policing measurement that has emerged in the past decade is the introduction of the Crime Harm Index (CHI), and Crime Severity Scoring (Bangs, 2016) (for a detailed insight to these approaches see the chapter on *Demand Based Strategic Planning).* Both methods quantify crimes based on their holistic impact rather than simply counting incidents (Sherman et al., 2016). By assigning weights to different crime types, such methods ensure that crimes with greater impact are given higher significance in performance evaluations (Ashby, 2018; Bangs, 2016; Sherman et al., 2020). Incorporating this into a police services assessment and measurement of performance enables them to understand how much harm and impact they are preventing or reducing in their service area.

A variation of this model, the Historic Offences Crime Harm Index (HOCHI) (see Sherman et al., 2020), accounts for crimes reported in the current year but committed in previous years (Sherman et al., 2020). Separating indexes in this manner helps prevent distortions in crime harm and score assessments and measurements by enabling police services to acknowledge the delayed workload impact of historic crime reporting (Sherman et al., 2020), thereby enabling them to present current 'real time' performance.

Company-Detected Crime Harm Index

If police services wish to provide additional layers of performance assessment and measurement they can also consider the Company-Detected Crime Harm Index (CDCHI) (see Sherman et al., 2020), which captures crimes identified and reported by private organizations. This includes offences such as shoplifting and fuel drive offs, which are highly influenced by individual entities' corporate reporting practices, and not necessarily the performance of the police service in question. Measuring such crimes in this way prevents distortions in performance measurements beyond that which the police service can heavily influence (Sherman et al., 2020).

Harm Detection Fraction (HDF) and Detection Ratios

To assess police effectiveness in resolving serious crimes, the Harm Detection Fraction (HDF) evaluates the proportion of total crime harm that police successfully detect and bring to justice. Unlike raw detection rates, this measure prioritizes solving serious 'high harm' crimes over minor offences, ensuring that police performance assessments reflect meaningful impact (Sherman et al., 2020). Such a measure may be useful for providing community reassurance and enhancing public confidence in areas where serious crime is an issue.

Proactive Policing Index

Similarly, the Proactive Policing Index (PPI) (see Sherman et al., 2020) distinguishes between crimes detected through proactive policing efforts and those reported by victims. This includes offenses uncovered through organized crime investigations, surveillance operations, stop and search activity, drug or knife crime enforcement action, to name a few sources, ensuring that proactive police work is measured separately from reactive crime statistics (Sherman et al., 2020). This distinction further enables a police service to understand how it is performing in distinct dimensions i.e. generalized crime reduction and prevention impact, and proactivity.

As a cover all metric, detection rates per 100 reported crimes across all categories provide a standardized measure of police effectiveness, enabling comparisons across the full range of different crime types. This measure is used by some police services and helps highlight variations in detection success and ensures that police forces are assessed based on their ability to investigate and solve crimes rather than merely responding to incidents (Sherman et al., 2020). Ultimately, what this section highlights is that by incorporating a more varied approach to assessment and measurement of police performance, services can develop a more holistic understanding of their strategic, operational, and tactical effectiveness. Such an informed position allows for a more informed policing performance framework, and one that demonstrates considerable awareness.

A MODEL FOR DELIVERING PERFORMANCE MANAGEMENT

Simply measuring and assessing performance is not enough, it must also be delivered. This section therefore consolidates the key areas discussed in this chapter into a comprehensive model of police performance. To do this the, the police performance measurement framework developed by Jon Shane from the John Jay College of Criminal Justice, New York, in 2010, is used. The original framework outlines how organisational objectives, officer activity, and measurable outcomes are brought together to deliver police performance and is outlined in Figure 1.

Figure 1. Shane's performance measurement framework (2010).

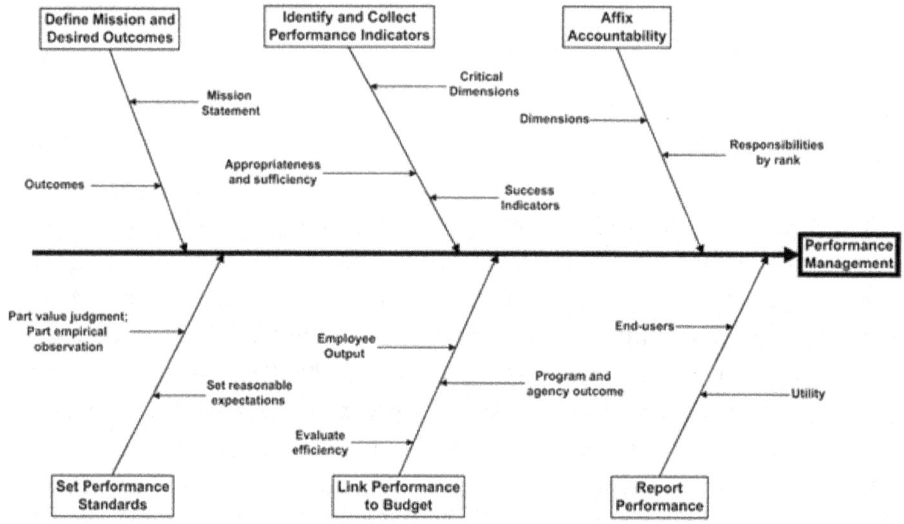

In this section the framework is updated by outlining how police leaders can incorporate more recent innovations in police performance to enable police services to effectively integrate objectives, activities, and outcomes, ethically, while balancing the use of both traditional and evidence-based targets and measures. In this regard, the section outlines 'what' needs to be done. What this section does not do is outline how this can be achieved. The 'how' is an equally complex question that has to take into consideration a multitude of challenges that police services face in delivering high performance such as leadership, workforce development, change management, workforce resistance, political interference, institutional inertia, budgetary and resource constraints, to name a few. Insight into how to address some of these challenges is covered in greater detail other chapters in this book.

1. Defining the Mission

The foundation of effective police performance management begins with a clearly defined mission statement. As discussed in Chapter 1, mission statements are essential for delivering and assessing high performance, enabling police services to articulate their core objectives and priorities. A well-defined mission ensures that all policies, programs, and resource allocations align with the organisation's broader vision, enhancing both accountability and public trust (Shane, 2010; Curtis, 2015).

2. Defining Desired Outcomes

Once objectives are established using the mission statement, clearly defined desired outcomes must be outlined. These are a crucial aspect of performance management and ensure transparency in what the police service aims to achieve. While traditional targets such as crime reduction, improving detection rates, and reducing emergency response times remain relevant, they should be supplemented with qualitative indicators that provide a more comprehensive view of policing success. Positive desired outcomes could include crime harm/score reduction, improved victim satisfaction, and procedural fairness, to name a few. Moving beyond simplistic target outcomes allows police forces to demonstrate their impact in a more meaningful way (Sherman et al., 2020; Curtis, 2015).

3. Setting Ethical Performance Standards and Behaviours

To ensure performance management is conducted in an ethical, fair, and objective manner, checks and balances must be in place to prevent the negative consequences of target-driven policing that this chapter has outlined. Establishing an Ethical Performance Oversight Panel is recommended to review performance management practices, policies and processes. Such a panel would ensure that crime recording practices are accurate and free from manipulation, preventing statistical distortion for the sake of meeting targets (Sherman et al., 2020). It should also assess how performance management may impact officer discretion in decision-making to prevent rigid enforcement actions that undermine this vital aspect of policing, and may unintentionally erode community trust (Evetts, 2009). Additionally, the panel should monitor staff well-being and engagement to understand if excessive performance pressures are leading to workplace stress, lower morale, and ultimately reducing organisational performance (Curtis, 2015).

4. Identifying and Collecting Evidence Based Performance Indicators

Performance indicators should extend beyond traditional metrics alone to incorporate measures that assess the full range of potential outcomes. This could include Efficiency measurement tools, such as Data Envelopment Analysis (DEA) or Multi-criteria Decision Analysis (MCDA), as well as the Crime Harm Index (CHI), Crime Severity Scoring (CCS), Historic Offences Crime Harm Index (HOCHI), Proactive Policing Index (PPI), victim satisfaction surveys, procedural fairness assessments, community engagement data, evaluations of neighbourhood policing effectiveness, and workforce well-being measures. Together, this framework will provide a deep understanding of performance against a multitude of strategic areas.

5. Linking Performance to Budgetary Decision Making

Financial planning should include budgets to both improve efficiency metrics and focus on strategic investments that have been proven to reduce harm and enhance long-term public safety (Loveday, 2006). Specifically, rather than funding interventions that solely increase enforcement activity, which may not always lead to positive outcomes, police forces should use data-driven decision-making to determine which areas of policing require increased investment (Ratcliffe, 2018). Evaluations of crime reduction strategies, anti-social behaviour interventions, and vulnerability prevention initiatives should inform where resources are allocated (Ratcliffe, 2018). This should not just include personnel, but also investment in digital transformation and tools e.g., dashboards, live-data systems, AI, that underpin and enable performance improvement, and enable real-time oversight. By doing so, the police service will demonstrate that they prioritise evidence of success and long-term positive impact, reinforcing the link between policing activity and meaningful outcomes (Curtis, 2015; Ratcliffe, 2018).

6. Affixing Accountability

Effective performance management also requires clear mechanisms for accountability. Police services must have systems of responsibility that ensure both leaders and frontline officers are aware of and held accountable for meeting performance standards. However, rather than emphasizing punitive measures, accountability should focus on progress evaluation, learning, and constructive feedback and training to enable professional development that, at a collective level, will lead to continuous organisational performance improvement (Shane, 2010). To achieve this, performance accountability should be structured around ensuring alignment between vision, mission, objectives, activity, and outcomes. This helps employees understand their contribution to the organisation's broader goals, fostering a culture of collaboration and shared responsibility. By focusing on continuous improvement rather than blame and punitive compliance, accountability frameworks will then motivate staff to engage more effectively with performance expectations, increasing discretionary effort.

7. Reporting Performance

Finally, transparent reporting is critical to building trust and ensuring continuous performance improvements. Performance data should be systematically collected, regularly reviewed, and openly communicated to ensure that employees and external stakeholders can track progress and understand the impact of policing efforts. Effective reporting should reflect the wide range of performance measures outlined, ensuring that all employees can see and appreciate the progress being made. This creates a positive feedback loop, where visible improvements enhance engagement, job satisfaction, and motivation. Furthermore, making performance reports accessible to internal leadership, government agencies, and the public ensures complete transparency and accountability, strengthening public confidence in the police service in question.

CONCLUSION

Delivering and assessing high performance within UK policing requires a strategic, evidence-based, and ethically sound approach. Over the past several decades, shifts between centralization and decentralization have resulted in evolving oversight structures, with varying degrees of government intervention and local autonomy shaping police performance management. Despite these changes, the persistent reliance on numerical targets and crime statistics has often led to perverse incentives, and an overemphasis on enforcement activity at the expense of public trust and problem-solving. The traditional metrics of police performance, while offering some insight, have failed to accurately measure effectiveness, often prioritizing crime volume over harm reduction and procedural fairness. In response, HMICFRS have increasingly moved toward holistic, evidence-based assessments that balance efficiency, effectiveness, and ethical considerations.

This chapter has outlined the necessity of moving beyond rigid numerical targets, embracing a blend of quantitative and qualitative measures that align with crime harm indices, public confidence metrics, and ethical crime recording practices. The proposed police performance management model outlined how services can improve their assessment and measurement of performance and ensure that they can effectively link activity and outcomes. This is achieved by incorporating methodologies such as Data Envelopment Analysis (DEA) and Multicriteria Decision Analysis (MCDA) to ensure that police efficiency and effectiveness are measured in a balanced manner, preventing a singular focus on crime volume. Furthermore, embedding an ethical oversight panel, transparent reporting structures, and community engagement measures safeguard against unethical practice and reinforce public trust in policing. The integration of performance-linked budgeting ensures that proactive crime reduction strategies are prioritized and ultimately enables police services to demonstrate accountability, reduce harm, and build public trust, through ethical, effective, and sustainable performance management practices.

REFERENCES

Ashby, M. P. (2018). Comparing methods for measuring crime harm/severity. *Policing. Journal of Policy Practice*, *12*(4), 439–454.

Asif, M., Shahzad, M., Awan, M. U., & Akdogan, H. (2018). Developing a structured framework for measuring police efficiency. *International Journal of Quality & Reliability Management*, *35*(10), 2119–2135.

Audit Commission. (1995). *Helping With Enquiries: Tackling Crime Effectively*. HMSO.

Bangs, M. (2016). *Research outputs: developing a Crime Severity Score for England and Wales using data on crimes recorded by the police*. Office for National Statistics.

Boyne, G. A. (2000). External Regulation and Best Value in Local Government. *Public Money & Management*, *20*(3), 7–12.

Brans, J. P., & Vincke, P. (1985). Note—A Preference Ranking Organisation Method: (The PROMETHEE Method for Multiple Criteria Decision-Making). *Management Science*, *31*(6), 647–656.

Cascio, W. F. (1977). Formal education and police officer performance. *Journal of Police Science and Administration*, *5*(1), 89–96.

Chan, J. (1996). Changing police culture. *British Journal of Criminology*, *36*(1), 109–134.

Cockcroft, T., & Beattie, I. (2009). Shifting Cultures: Managerialism and the Rise of "Performance" in Policing. *Policing*, *32*(3), 526–540.

Curtis, I. (2015). Review of Targets in Policing. An independent review of the use of targets in policing by Chief Superintendent Irene Curtis. Home Office.

de Maillard, J., & Savage, S. P. (2012). Comparing Performance: The Development of Police Performance Management in France and Britain. *Policing and Society*, *22*(4), 363–383.

Ellingworth, D., Farrell, G., & Pease, K. (1995). A victim is a Victim is a Victim? *British Journal of Criminology*, *35*, 360–365.

Ericson, R. V., & Heggarty, K. D. (1997). *Policing the Risk Society*. Clarendon Press.

Eterno, J. A., & Silverman, E. B. (2017). The crime numbers game: Management by manipulation. crc Press.

Evetts, J. (2009). New professionalism and new public management: Changes, continuities and consequences. *Comparative Sociology*, *8*(2), 247–266.

Fabricatore, J., Azen, S., Schoentgen, S., & Snibbe, H. (1978). Predicting performance of police officers using the 16 personality factor questionnaire. *American Journal of Community Psychology*, *6*(1), 63–69.

Gill, P. (2000). *Rounding Up the Usual Suspects? Developments in Contemporary Law Enforcement Intelligence*. Ashgate.

Golding, B., & Savage, S. P. (2012). Leadership and performance management. In *Handbook of policing* (pp. 753–787). Willan.

Goldstein, H. (1991). *Problem-Oriented Policing*. McGraw Hill.

Guilfoyle, S. (2016). Getting police performance measurement under control. Policing. *Journal of Policy Practice*, *10*(1), 71–87.

Hesketh, I., Cooper, C. L., & Ivy, J. (2017). Wellbeing and engagement in policing: The key to unlocking discretionary effort? *Policing. Journal of Policy Practice*, *11*(1), 62–73.

Home Office. (1993). *Police reform: a police service for the 21st century the Governments proposals for the police service in England and Wales*. Home Office.

Home Office. (2007). *Delivering Safer Communities: A guide to effective partnership working*. Home Office.

Home Office. (2008). *From the Neighbourhood to the National: Policing Our Communities Together*. Policing Green Paper.

Home Office. (2010). *Policing in the 21st Century: Reconnecting Police and the Public*. Home Office.

Hood, C. (1995). The "new public management" in the 1980s: Variations on a theme. *Accounting, Organizations and Society*, *20*(2-3), 93–109.

Hough, M. (2010). Policing, new public management and legitimacy. In *The new public leadership challenge* (pp. 70–84). Palgrave Macmillan UK.

Iannone, N. F. (1987). *The Supervision of Police Personnel* (4th ed.). Prentice-Hall.

Jones, T. (2003). The Governance and Accountability of Policing. In Newburn, T. (Ed.), *Handbook of Policing* (pp. 603–627). Willan Publishing.

Landy, F. (1977). *Performance Appraisal in Police Departments*. Police Foundation.

Lentz, S. A. (2007). Revisiting the Peelian Principles. *Law Enforcement Executive Forum*, *7*(4), 75–88.

Loveday, B. (2006). Policing performance: The impact of performance measures and targets on police forces in England and Wales. *International Journal of Police Science & Management*, *8*(4), 282–293.

Maguire, M., & John, T. (1995). *Intelligence, Surveillance and Informants: Integrated Approaches*. Police Research Group: Crime Detection and Prevention Series, Paper 64, 1-58.

Nepomuceno, T. C. C., Daraio, C., & Costa, A. P. C. S. (2020). Multicriteria Ranking for Police Efficient and Effective Analysis. *Preprints*. https://doi.org/DOI: 10.20944/preprints202012.0014.v1

Perkins, M., & Davies, M. (2024). Shifting Oversight: The Evolution of Modern Police Performance Management in England and Wales. *Policing and Society*, *34*(1), 101–120. PMID: 39691914

Pollitt, C. (2002). Clarifying Convergence: Striking Similarities and Durable Differences in Public Management Reform. *Public Management Review*, *4*(1), 1–22.

Porter, M. (1996). *Tackling Cross Border Crime: Crime Detection and Prevention Series Paper 79*. Home Office.

Ranson, S., & Stewart, J. (1994). *Management for the Public Domain: Enabling the Learning Society*. Macmillan.

Ratcliffe, J. H. (2008). *Intelligence-Led Policing*. Willan Publishing.

Ratcliffe, J. H. (2016). *Intelligence-led policing* (2nd ed.). Routledge.

Ratcliffe, J. H. (2018). *Reducing crime: A companion for police leaders*. Routledge.

Ratcliffe, J. H. (2022). *Evidence-based policing: The basics*. Routledge.

Shane, J. M. (2010). Performance management in police agencies: A conceptual framework. *Policing*, *33*(1), 6–29.

Sherman, L. W., & Cambridge University associates. (2020). How to count crime: The Cambridge harm index consensus. *Cambridge Journal of Evidence-Based Policing*, *4*(1), 1–14.

Sherman, L. W., Neyroud, P. W., & Neyroud, E. (2016). *The Cambridge Crime Harm Index: Measuring Total Harm from Crime Based on Sentencing Guidelines*. Policing. *Journal of Policy Practice*, *10*(3), 171–183.

Stelfox, P. (1998). Policing Lower Levels of Organised Crime in England and Wales. *Howard Journal of Criminal Justice*, *37*(4), 393–406.

Chapter 15
Turning Evidence Into Practice

Larissa Engelmann
http://orcid.org/0000-0002-6639-0684
University of Leeds, UK

ABSTRACT

This chapter provides an overview of the ways in which police services can translate evidence into practice. It explores the emergence of the evidence-based policing agenda, its influence, challenges, and opportunities. Based on this exploration, the chapter presents a different model, evidence-informed practice, to highlight other important ways in which police could and should engage in knowledge creation, translation and evaluation. It is suggested that police services would benefit from reflecting on adult and organisational learning theories to develop as learning organisations which can help police services to more naturally and sustainably translate evidence into practice in partnership with others. By further developing as learning organisations, it is hoped that a learning sector emerges supporting the holistic whole-system responses required to address the challenges police, partners and communities are facing.

INTRODUCTION

Turning research into evidence-based practice is an essential task to address most, if not all assessment criteria for His Majesty's Inspectorate of Constabulary and Fire & Rescue Services (HMICFRS) Police Effectiveness, Efficiency, and Legitimacy (PEEL) assessments of police forces in England and Wales. It involves the effective translation of different forms of 'evidence' into individual and organisational practice to further improve policing, increase public trust and confidence,

DOI: 10.4018/979-8-3373-2757-0.ch015

and address new, emerging and persistent challenges such as cybercrime, Violence against Women and Girls, or terrorist threats. As the chapter in this book on Capacity and Capability Building highlights, knowledge management through meaningful delivery and support can enable innovation and improve police officer wellbeing and retention. To address the HMICFRS core areas of Effectiveness, Efficiency and Legitimacy, police forces require a good understanding of 'what works' to address certain crimes, to support more efficient response mechanisms, ensuring fair and trustworthy services for the public, whilst looking inwards to support staff. In recent years, this translation process has been dominated by an evidence-based policing (EBP) agenda as a driving force in encouraging police services to use the most up-to-date research and knowledge to inform their policies and practices.

EBP has been the topic of much debate amongst practitioners and academics (Betts, 2024; E. L. Piza et al., 2022; Staller & Koerner, 2021). The increased availability of, and access to, robust research evidence, makes this an exciting time for police services to identify ways in which to use scientific knowledge for their benefit. There will be some focus within this chapter on PEEL assessment questions eleven (how to manage and lead police forces to be efficient, effective and sustainable), and twelve (how to inform effective vetting of officers and staff suitable for modern police forces), whilst also reflecting on the wider benefits for police forces to commit to learning values and practices. Discussions will support police leaders and other stakeholders to better understand the role of EBP and how police services might use it in practice to achieve an HMICFRS 'outstanding' rating.

This chapter will also provide a structured overview of what the literature tells us about translating evidence into practice, by discussing what is meant by 'evidence', a brief history of EBP, what theories and frameworks support its application, and highlighting best practice examples. Presented in this chapter is empirical research and practice which has proven the importance of reflecting on translational activities, and more importantly, on how organisational structures, leadership, and support mechanisms impact evidence-based practice. Readers will not be provided with all the theories available in this space but rather will be introduced to a select few to better understand the process behind translating evidence into practice. They will also learn about critical appraisal and reflection to build stronger more resilient police services which withstand the test of time.

THE EVOLUTION OF EBP

The introduction of emergency phone numbers accelerated policing's focus on reactive response policing, i.e. something happens, the police attend, does something to address the problem, and then leaves as quickly as possible to go to the next call.

Policing became understood as the three 'R's: random patrol; rapid response; and reactive investigation (Sherman, 2013). There was little focus on patterns of criminal behaviour, prediction of crimes, systematically testing the effectiveness of crime control mechanisms, or the ability to create, use and apply learning from research to improve practice. It took some time before the EBP movement emerged to drive more coordinated, measured, and sometimes more effective responses to policing problems. This was influenced by the comparably recent (1960s) development of police research as a body of knowledge within academic circles, separate from Criminology (Jaschke et al., 2007).

The growing neoliberalist ideology of EBP led to an increased focus on police performance and public trust in policing, particularly in the United States and the United Kingdom (UK). Sherman (2013), who is considered the 'godfather' of EBP, argues there has been a significant shift within policing from the three 'R's to what he calls the three 'T's: targeting, testing and tracking, which has increased extensively since the early 2000s. There has also been an associated shift in the value attached to scientific research-based evaluation of policing practice.

Hence, "evidence-based policing means that research, evaluation, analysis, and scientific process should have 'a seat at the table' in law enforcement decision making about tactics, strategies, and policies" (Lum & Koper, 2017, pp. 3–4). Lum and Koper (2017) further highlight the importance of the translation process and the way in which appraised knowledge should then be institutionalised into practice for long term impact. Recent research through the European Society of Criminology Working Group on Policing highlighted, however, that EBP has not developed equally across European countries and manifests in different ways and across a continuum of more or less academic influence. This may be explained by different alignments between the worlds of politics, academia and policing in each country (Engelmann & Tatnell, 2023). However, police forces in many countries (including Canada, US, India, Australia and New Zealand) have reaped the benefits of some of the evidence-based driven policing initiatives, such as police-led diversion schemes or community policing programmes (Neyroud, 2022).

EBP has been heavily intertwined with debates about ongoing professionalisation efforts in the UK, particularly in relation to increased engagement with Higher Education. This is exemplified by the establishment of the College of Policing in 2012. In the review driving this change, (Neyroud, 2011) it was argued that there was a need within policing in England and Wales for a professional body to set policing standards and further expand research-informed practice. UK police services will be aware of EBP and the development of the 'what works' Centre within the College of Policing, which has had a significant influence on all UK police services promoting EBP. Nevertheless, the way in which College of Policing resources are used and applied in practice can vary significantly between police services.

To enable honest reflections and learning about how to turn evidence into practice within an EBP model, it is important to consider what 'evidence' in the context of policing means, what some of the challenges of this approach have been, and how police leaders and other stakeholders may approach turning evidence into practice in the future.

EBP - CONTROVERSIES AND CHALLENGES

EBP has been criticised for its narrow conceptualisation of knowledge, its often-complex relationship with politics, and its hierarchy of what knowledge is preferred in the context of policing (e.g. the positioning of quantitative randomised-controlled trials as the methodological 'gold standard' compared with other more qualitative-based approaches) (Wood et al., 2018). When reflecting on adult and organisational learning theories, creating hierarchies of knowledge can create power dynamics which rather than encourage innovation and effective practice, can hamper it through blinkered views of 'what works', and a lack of wider engagement with contrasting and sometimes equally important viewpoints. Therefore, although this chapter is entitled 'Turning Research into Evidence Based Practice', it is important to discuss what 'evidence' we are talking about here and how police officers, political leaders and other stakeholders may decide on the most relevant, useful and effective evidence.

Critical scholars have warned against the politicization of knowledge and the use of evidence-based policing agendas. In particular, studies have uncovered the different ways in which evidence can be used to frame problems in ways that produce or re-produce significant harm rather than solve or reduce the causes of criminal behaviour, particularly for people from ethnic minorities (Hall et al., 2013). In the same vein, it is important to recognize how political and ideological influence can lead to social policy making and policing interventions seemingly based on evidence with significant adverse effects on those it should help (Brown et al., 2025; Koch et al., 2024; Squires, 2006). There is also a growing argument even within criminology, that the body of knowledge often providing the evidence for evidence-based policing, is limited in its criticality and depth requiring more critical reflective viewpoints to avoid reproducing inequality (Mokhtari, 2025). For police forces, this means that whilst evidence-based policy may be imposed from above, such evidence should still be held accountable through critical reflective practice.

Furthermore, there is a fear amongst some police officers and scholars that the focus on EBP, as presented within current dominant discourses in the UK and US, constrain "the knowledge, skill, and judgement, patrol officers acquire through their daily experience" (Willis & Mastrofski, 2018, p. 27), or what some might refer to as 'Practical Wisdom' (Schwartz & Sharpe, 2006). As mentioned above, evidence can also draw attention away from the granular experiences of officers and communities, particularly those traditionally structurally marginalized and not visible in the data.

Nevertheless, there is general agreement that evidence-based practice, despite its limitations, can have several benefits, such as improved accountability, trust, and legitimacy through improved practice (Mitchell & Lewis, 2017). Recent examples include the implementation of an evidence-based scenario-based training programme in Avon and Sommerset which reduced police use of force without increasing injury to officers (Sanders et al., 2025). These benefits however are heavily curtailed by the abovementioned limitations and without critical reflection, evaluation and accountability mechanisms, EBP could exacerbate or create new policing problems.

The central tenant underpinning EBP is that evidence can be translated into practice, which for many is still considered a central challenge within the constraints of strong police cultures holding on to traditional ways of doing things (Lum et al., 2010), resource limitations, and the way in which knowledge is currently valued within organsiations (Engelmann & Tatnell, 2025). One of the main barriers to turning evidence into practice is the perceived theory-practice divide. Academics have often been accused of creating evidence or knowledge which does not reflect the complexities of policing practice thereby hampering its translation into practice (Easton & De Vlieger, 2018). In the same vein, there has been frustration amongst academics that they are not listened to by policing practitioners and their research-based recommendations are not adopted into practice (Bradley & Nixon, 2011).

In line with other scholars in the UK, I tend to prefer the term evidence-informed practice (Aston et al., 2021; Fyfe & Wilson, 2012; Hunter et al., 2019), highlighting a more nuanced understanding of how 'evidence' may be used in practice and how it is translated. Indeed, the translation of 'evidence' into practice is a process by which whatever 'evidence' has been deemed relevant to a particular problem is critically assessed by practitioners with relevant skill and training, who can adapt findings to inform their practice based on their own experiences and context. Hence, evidence-informed practice is less conducive to a hierarchy of knowledge and its possible (sometimes unintended) consequences but suggests that "empirical evidence is better regarded as one component in the mutual and constantly changing journey of client and practitioner" (Nevo & Slonim-Nevo, 2011, p. 1178). In that way, evidence-informed policing promotes a more symbiotic relationship between the practitioner or organisation and the knowledge creator, thereby narrowing the perceived theory-practice divide. Whilst evidence-informed practice may not be able to address all the abovementioned limitations by itself, through a more interactive use of knowledge it is hoped that evidence-informed practice is more able to question limitations of knowledge and encourage critical engagement through reflective practice and the use of experience and 'craft' knowledge (Engelmann & Tatnell, 2025).

To summarise, Klose (2024, p.5) has redefined EBP as "a decision-making process which integrates the best available evidence, professional judgement, and community values, preferences and circumstances… as a research-informed, practitioner-centred, and community-oriented approach to policing practice". With increased recognition of the value of officer voices, focus on co-production of knowledge with practitioners and the public, and a focus on multi-agency, whole system responses to further improve service provision for those most vulnerable, this definition provides a useful starting point from which to think through the ways in which research evidence may be assessed and translated into practice.

HOW TO TURN EVIDENCE INTO PRACTICE

The development of the Police Education Qualifications Framework (PEQF) in the UK, as part of wider ongoing professionalisation efforts, outwardly claims to ensure that officers (and staff) have access to ongoing professional development and education to support the skills, attitudes and behaviours needed in modern policing. This highlights the link, previously made in this book, between police officer education, skill, the ability to think critically, and the ability to translate evidence into practice. The thinking behind the PEQF closely aligns with that of Senge's model of the learning organisation which seeks to embed and distribute learning across the organisation (Senge, 1997). The model suggests the implementation of *concrete learning processes, supportive leadership and a supportive learning environment* to instigate positive sustainable change and innovation within policing (Garvin et al., 2008). Taking this concept further, it has been argued that a *learning sector* (Engelmann & Tatnell, 2025), rather than organisation, is required to address the wicked problems (Grint, 2022) police forces in the UK and elsewhere are facing.

The focus on police services as learning organisations would also address the National Police Chief's Council (NPCC) 2030 vision 'to embed a culture of continuous improvement and innovation in policing' (Strategic Policing Partnership Board, 2023). Harding et al. (2019) have co-developed with police forces in the UK, a 'Destination Map' which can support police services to rethink learning and development within policing, by reflecting on how staff are empowered and supported to learn and apply such learning; how what is being applied is adding value to the public, organisations and individuals; maximising the benefits of technology; strong values, ethics and mission which drive learning, development and evidence-informed practice. This map provides an insight into some of the characteristics and tools which can support police services to naturally, continuously and meaningfully translate evidence into practice.

More broadly, vision and mission statements can provide a powerful tool to instigate, support and create change or reform, whilst recognising the constraints on police resources (Dario et al., 2022). Mission statements set out the purpose of an organisation and can therefore help to provide direction and motivation for employees and assure members of the public, partners and policy makers as to what the police intend to do and what it should be measured against. The Metropolitan Police Service's mission statement for example encompasses a broad focus on both internal (employee wellbeing and ethical behaviour of officers and the organisation) and external (listening to community voices, working with partners and seizing new opportunities) factors whilst focusing on innovation and new opportunities (learning, striving to improve and seizing opportunities in data and tech). This mission statement demonstrates a comprehensive approach, relevant to 2025-2027 PEEL inspection criteria, and in line with key findings from a report on Police Reform in England and Wales by the Police Foundation (2025).

Another example presented as innovative in the 2023-25 PEEL Inspection for Cumbria Police is their child-centred policing strategy using stop and search data to review communication and support offers for children and their families, with early referrals to partners and educational and support interventions in place to create more holistic responses (HMICFRS, 2025). Similarly, as part of their outstanding rating, Cumbria shows promising practice in providing a supportive environment to improve retention, integrating evidence-based solutions, such as 'buddy' systems and 'stay conversations' followed by action.

Where police services (and partners) have developed such learning structures, evidence-informed practice has therefore thrived because the organisation is able to assess the strength and weaknesses of the 'evidence' they encounter, the compromises required to implement it, and to identify gaps which need more research or attention (Lum & Koper, 2017). The College of Policing provides an extensive library of further examples which can help police services to solve problems or improve practice. This library includes crime reduction toolkits, operational policing guidance, a practice bank, problem solving guides, practical tools and research maps. Additionally, it links to external resources such as George Mason University's EBP Matrix.

However, and this is important to remember, whilst resources through established sites such as the College of Policing, or certain research centres such as the Centre for Policing Research and Learning within the Open University, provide useful starting points to search for 'evidence', they are not complete libraries of everything that is available or what is most up-to-date relevant evidence for the problem you are facing. The 'evidence' you are seeking might for example already be within your organisation, and engagement with the relevant teams, officers or staff may enable a solution to the problem at hand. Other times, the solutions may still have to be developed and require collaboration with relevant stakeholders (officers, academics, communities) to identify appropriate responses. Reflecting on what is not in the libraries you access, is as important as assessing the evidence that is there.

The College of Policing uses what is called the EMMIE framework (Effect, Mechanism, Moderators, Implementation and Economic cost) to assess evidence and in particular systematic reviews of evidence. This framework considers for example how many people have been impacted and how; any moderating or contextual factors; key sources of success and failure for implementation; and the economic costs and benefits. EMMIE therefore enables a systematic and clear analysis of certain types of evidence. However, when it comes to, for example, people experiencing vulnerability, such as through online child sexual abuse or exploitation, a more flexible and adaptable tool may be required. The impact of such abuse may not be easily quantifiable and police responses being reduced to their economic costs is not sufficiently nuanced, particularly in the required holistic and multi-agency partnerships to address this complex growing problem (Engelmann et al., 2025). Whilst identifying the impact interventions have on resources, particularly with ongoing financial instability for many public services, including the police, is important, impacts on the prevention of current and future social harm may result in more significant savings in the longer term, to say nothing of the human costs to victims and their families.

Police vision and mission statements and strategies can play an important part in driving such work forward, however there is widespread recognition that what the stated intentions of police are and how these are implemented can differ widely. Interpretation and implementation gaps can manifest where the impact of police culture and the realities of the job conflict with what the organisation intends to achieve or is measured against (Dario et al., 2022). Where mission statements are outward-facing communications of policing goals, they need to be followed by internal support mechanisms to ensure their implementation into practice, and where possible should be informed by evidence that includes officer and community voices. As stated in a recent Police Foundation report to create organisational and system reform it is important to utilise "local knowledge and nuance, encourage innovation, learn from evaluation, articulate purpose, build pace and momentum, and – above all – engage the workforce in the process of change" (Police Foundation, 2025, p. 5).

Critical appraisal of sources of evidence, no matter where they are from is important. Such an appraisal should question why this evidence is being used to inform decision-making and what other evidence may add to this process. Such critical appraisal should include an assessment of who has come up with the evidence, the methods used, where it was done and how ethically sound it is, to name a few. Research groups and centres in the UK and elsewhere can play an important part in helping police forces assess evidence and explore best practice, for example through systematic reviews and evaluations[1]. The next and last section will highlight a few examples, including some from the most recent PEEL inspection, to show how evidence into practice has manifested.

PROMISING AND OUTSTANDING PRACTICE EXAMPLES

One way to promote evidence-informed practice is by supporting police officers and staff to gain critical thinking and research skills so that they can better understand different kinds of evidence. A recent study highlights that new recruit final year projects within the Police Constable Degree Apprenticeship (PCDA) as part of the PEQF "can embed evidence-based practices, support the career paths of new police officers and assist the development of the workforce" (Skilling & Thomas, 2024, p. 13). For example, one project developed a cost-benefit analysis creating an evidence-base to develop a Drone Unit within one UK police force. Another project provided critical analysis of Stop and Search data which had previously raised concerns about disproportionality within one police force. Both PCDA student projects enabled police forces to develop locally contextualised evidence informing local practice, easing the translation process through engagement in evidence creation with academic support. To further enable such work, early identification of Subject Matter Experts to support the identification of valuable and relevant projects to address current policing challenges and discuss impact strategies early on are recommended (Skilling & Thomas, 2024). With increasing numbers of policing students coming into policing through higher education routes where final year research projects are a requirement, UK police services are presented with unique opportunities to collaborate to empower their staff and organisation to be part of the process.

Another example of translating evidence into practice is that of Lancashire Police and their development of a county wide Anti-social Behaviour (ASB) response, Operation Centurion, following extensive consultation of the available evidence and key stakeholders (Office of the Lancashire Police and Crime Commissioner, 2024, p. 12). This evidence-informed response has led to an increase in arrest rates but also involved increased police officer presence in neighbourhoods. Undoubtedly, this will be a positive development in the wake of the Governments renewed focus on neighbourhood policing. Lancashire Constabulary's ability to engage in reflection and identifying ways to address problems in this way, highlights elements of a learning organisation well placed to address and anticipate changes in governmental priorities.

A final example from the British Transport Police (BTP) may provide police services with ideas on how to improve their vetting systems. Whilst BTP's vetting efforts have previously been measured as 'inadequate', BTP has significantly invested time, resources and effort to improve their practice. To do this they have worked closely with HMICFRS to respond to their recommendations. After a review of its current vetting systems and available evidence on 'what works', new counter-corruption e-learning and Lawful Business Monitoring Policy supports staff to report and raise concerns, and the NPCC 'Historic Data Wash' exercise ensures that data in the new vetting system is up-to-date (British Transport Police Authority, 2024). BTP is one of two forces in the UK to have the 'ISO9001 Quality Management System accreditation' which has recently been reaccredited (British Transport Police Authority, 2025). Whilst it is not yet clear if BTP's efforts will lead to a better grading, their efforts highlight different ways in which vetting challenges may be approached. Indeed, a first point of call could be the new College of Policing Vetting Code of Practice and Authorised Professional Practice.

The recently awarded National Police Chiefs' Council's Policing Academic Centres of Excellence (P-ACE's), introduce collaborations with a strong track record of working in tandem with police forces to create evidence that can and is translated into practice. Police services have access to centres such as these within their local, regional and national structures. Where problems are identified, tapping into these may provide a first point of call to better understand what evidence is available and discuss how this evidence could be applied in a new context. Nevertheless, it will be important to remember that these centres and other partnerships have their own agendas and goals and they work within their own funding, culture and knowledge constraints which may impact the evidence they create. Hence, accountability and critical reflection will be key to assess the created evidence-base and avoid unintended consequences for local communities or police staff.

CONCLUSION

Turning evidence into practice is not an easy feat, but it is possible and where police services, and in particular police leaders, and partners, are open to listening to different viewpoints and willing to critically reflect on where 'evidence' comes from and what the benefit of its application would be, there is immense potential to solve even the most complex policing problems in ways which lead to positive outcomes.

There are many factors influencing the translation of evidence into practice. I will focus here on three of these. Firstly, the need for a structured approach to engaging with evidence through ongoing partnerships which are built on trust and understanding. Secondly, upskilling officers and staff in critically creating and appraising evidence, for example through engagement with higher education. Lastly, ensuring continued evaluation and monitoring of the application of evidence into practice, either in-house or preferably independently. This can then provide further evidence of what works or identify gaps which need more elaboration. The continued development of police as learning organisations and the law enforcement and public health sector as a learning sector, could provide the framework to address the above-mentioned enduring challenges more effectively.

REFERENCES

Aston, E., Murray, K., & O'Neill, M. (2021). Achieving cultural change through organizational justice: The case of stop and search in Scotland. *Criminology & Criminal Justice*, *21*(1), 40–56. DOI: 10.1177/1748895819839751/ASSET/AA62DB80-D0D6-4E4F-A430-FB51BD7E07DF/ASSETS/IMAGES/LARGE/10.1177_1748895819839751-FIG1.JPG

Betts, P. (2024). *Critiquing Evidence-Based Policing in Britain: A Genealogy - Paul Betts*. Palgrave Macmillan.

Bradley, D., & Nixon, C. (2011). Ending the 'dialogue of the deaf'': evidence and policing policies and practices. An Australian case study. In Johnston, L., & Shearing, C. (Eds.), *Innovative Possibilities: Global Policing Research and Practice* (pp. 13–25). Routledge., DOI: 10.4324/9781315873466-3

British Transport Police Authority. (2024). *British Transport Police Fund - Annual Report and Accounts for the year ending 31 March 2024*.

British Transport Police Authority. (2025). *BTPA response to HMICFRS's PEEL and Vetting reports*. https://btpa.police.uk/?news-article=btpa-response-to-hmicfrss-peel-and-vetting-reports

Brown, K., Grace, S., & Redman, S. (2025). Policing Vulnerability: The Care and Control of Sex Workers Through Designated Police Officers. *British Journal of Criminology*, *65*(1), 17–36. DOI: 10.1093/BJC/AZAE026

Dario, L. M., Cesar, G. T., & Crichlow, V. J. (2022). Reappreciating the varieties of police behavior: A national examination of contemporary police mission statements. *Policing*, *45*(6), 893–907. DOI: 10.1108/PIJPSM-02-2022-0026

Easton, M., & De Vlieger, S. (2018). Belgian reflections on the dialogue of the deaf. *European Journal of Policing Studies*, *5*(3), 36–54. DOI: 10.5553/EJPS/2034760X2018005003004

Engelmann, L., & Tatnell, A. (2023). Researching police professionalisation in Scotland, Sweden, and Finland. *Introduction to Policing Research: Taking Lessons from Practice, Second Edition*, 77–93. https://doi.org/DOI: 10.4324/9781003276456-9/RESEARCHING-POLICE-PROFESSIONALISATION-SCOTLAND-SWEDEN-FINLAND-LARISSA-ENGELMANN-ANDREW-TATNELL

Engelmann, L., & Tatnell, A. (2025). Blending the 'craft' and 'science' of policing: Challenges and opportunities for police as professional learning organisations. *Policing. Journal of Policy Practice*, •••, 19.

Engelmann, L., Weirich, C. A., & May-Chahal, C. (2025). Developing quality standards for community-based online child sexual exploitation and abuse interventions. *Child Abuse & Neglect, 164*. Advance online publication. DOI: 10.1016/J.CHIABU.2025.107444 PMID: 40215894

Fyfe, N. R., & Wilson, P. (2012). Knowledge exchange and police practice: Broadening and deepening the debate around researcher–practitioner collaborations. *Police Practice and Research, 13*(4), 306–314. DOI: 10.1080/15614263.2012.671596

Garvin, D. A., Edmondson, A. C., & Gino, F. (2008). Is Yours a Learning Organization? *Harvard Business Review*. https://www.researchgate.net/publication/5440662

Grint, K. (2022). Critical Essay: Wicked problems in the Age of Uncertainty. *Human Relations, 75*(8). Advance online publication. DOI: 10.1177/00187267211070770

Hall, S., Critcher, C., Jefferson, T., Clarke, J., & Roberts, B. (2013). Policing the Crisis: Mugging, the state and law and order. In *Policing the Crisis*. Red Globe Press., DOI: 10.1007/978-1-137-00721-6

Harding, R., Hartley, J., Khalil, L., & Martin, D. (2019). *Police Learning & Development 2025: Destination Map - Equipping Professionals for Better Policing.*

HMICFRS. (2025). *PEEL 2023–25: Police effectiveness, efficiency and legitimacy – An inspection of Cumbria Constabulary.*

Hunter, G., May, T., & Hough, M. (2019). Are the police embracing evidence-informed practice? A view from England and Wales. *Policing and Society, 29*(3), 251–265. DOI: 10.1080/10439463.2018.1557180

Jaschke, H.-G., Bjørgo, T., Romero, F. del B., Kwanten, C., Mawby, R., & Pagon, M. (2007). *Perspectives of police science in Europe - Final Report.*

Klose, S. (2024). Re-defining evidence-based policing. *Policing. Journal of Policy Practice, 18*, 1–7. DOI: 10.1093/POLICE/PAAD095

Koch, I., Williams, P., & Wroe, L. (2024). 'County lines': Racism, safeguarding and statecraft in Britain. *Race & Class, 65*(3), 3–26. DOI: 10.1177/03063968231201325/FORMAT/EPUB

Lum, C., Koper, C. S., Telep, C. W., Lum, C., Telep, C. W., & Koper, C. S. (2010). The Evidence-Based Policing Matrix. *Journal of Experimental Criminology 2010 7:1, 7*(1), 3–26. https://doi.org/DOI: 10.1007/S11292-010-9108-2

Lum, C. M., & Koper, C. S. (2017). *Evidence-based policing : translating research into practice*. Oxford University Press.

Mitchell, R. J., & Lewis, S. (2017). Intention is not method, belief is not evidence, rank is not proof: Ethical policing needs evidence-based decision making. *International Journal of Emergency Services*, *6*(3), 188–199. DOI: 10.1108/IJES-04-2017-0018/FULL/PDF

Mokhtari, M. (2025). 'Who better to be training them?!': Renewed Moments of Liberal Carceral Expansion and the Role of Higher Education. *British Journal of Criminology*, *65*(6), 1298–1314. DOI: 10.1093/BJC/AZAF020

Nevo, I., & Slonim-Nevo, V. (2011). The Myth of Evidence-Based Practice: Towards Evidence-Informed Practice. *British Journal of Social Work*, *41*(6), 1176–1197. DOI: 10.1093/BJSW/BCQ149

Neyroud, P. (2011). *Review of Police Leadership and Training*.

Neyroud, P. (2022). Globalizing evidence-based policing. Case studies of community policing, reform, and diversion. In Piza, E., & Welsh, B. (Eds.), *THE GLOBALIZATION OF EVIDENCE-BASED POLICING. Innovation in Bridging the Research-Practice Divide* (pp. 23–38). Routledge., https://www.researchgate.net/profile/Peter-Neyroud/publication/356757484_The_Globalization_of_Evidence-Based_Policing_Innovations_in_Bridging_the_Research-Practice_Divide/links/61aa48f4ca2d401f27c06897/The-Globalization-of-Evidence-Based-Policing-Innovations-in-Bridging-the-Research-Practice-Divide.pdf

Office of the Lancashire Police and Crime Commissioner. (2024). *Annual Report 2023-2024*. https://www.lancashire-pcc.gov.uk/wp-content/uploads/2024/08/OPCC-Annual-Report-2023-24-FINAL.pdf

Piza, E. L., Brandon, ·, & Welsh, C. (2022). Evidence-Based Policing Is Here to Stay: Innovative Research, Meaningful Practice, and Global Reach. *Cambridge Journal of Evidence-Based Policing*, *6*, 42–53. DOI: 10.1007/s41887-022-00074-x

Police Foundation. (2025). *Delivering Police Reform – Mission, People, Technology - The Police Foundation*. https://www.police-foundation.org.uk/publication/delivering-police-reform-mission-people-technology/

Sanders, M., Bancroft, K., Hume, S., Chetwynd, O., & Quinton, P. (2025). The Impact of Training on Use of Force by Police in an English Police Force; Evidence from a Pragmatic Stepped Wedge Randomized Controlled Trial. *Justice Evaluation Journal*, *8*(1), 20–39. DOI: 10.1080/24751979.2024.2412333

Schwartz, B., & Sharpe, K. E. (2006). Practical wisdom: Aristotle meets positive psychology. *Journal of Happiness Studies*, *7*, 377–395. DOI: 10.1007/S10902-005-3651-Y

Senge, P. m. (1997). The fifth discipline. *Measuring Business Excellence, 1*(3), 46–51. DOI: 10.1108/EB025496/FULL/XML

Sherman, L. W. (2013). The rise of evidence-Based policing: Targeting, testing, and tracking. *Crime and Justice, 42*(1), 377–451. DOI: 10.1086/670819

Skilling, L., & Thomas, L. (2024). Student officer research projects: Evidence-based knowledge embedded into policing practice? *The Police Journal*, •••, 1–15. DOI: 10.1177/0032258X241299741/FORMAT/EPUB

Squires, P. (2006). New Labour and the politics of antisocial behaviour. *Critical Social Policy, 26*(1), 144–168. DOI: 10.1177/0261018306059769

Staller, M. S., & Koerner, S. (2021). Evidence-based policing or reflexive policing: A commentary on Koziarski and Huey. *International Journal of Comparative and Applied Criminal Justice, 45*(4), 423–426. DOI: 10.1080/01924036.2021.1949619

Strategic Policing Partnership Board. (2023). *Policing Vision 2030.*

Willis, J. J., & Mastrofski, S. D. (2018). Improving policing by integrating craft and science: What can patrol officers teach us about good police work? *Policing and Society, 28*(1), 27–44. DOI: 10.1080/10439463.2015.1135921;PAGE:STRING:ARTICLE/CHAPTER

Wood, D., Cockcroft, T., Tong, S., & Bryant, R. (2018). The importance of context and cognitive agency in developing police knowledge: Going beyond the police science discourse. *The Police Journal: Theory, Practice and Principles, 91*(2), 173–187. DOI: 10.1177/0032258X17696101

ENDNOTE

1 Examples of research centres and partnerships in the UK: N8 Policing Research Partnership, ESRC Vulnerability and Policing Futures Research Centre, The Open University Centre for Policing Research and Learning, Anglia Ruskin University International Policing and Public Protection Research Institute, University of Portsmouth Policing Research Group, Canterbury Centre for Policing Research.

Section 3
Effectiveness

Chapter 16
Effectiveness Within Policing

Jacob Thandi
http://orcid.org/0009-0003-1922-926X
Leeds Trinity University, UK

ABSTRACT

This chapter provides an overview of effectiveness within policing, considering the roles of various agencies and how specific metrics are utilised to provide insight. It explores the limitations of certain frameworks and highlights how these could be advanced and considers the role in which effectiveness holds in our understanding of policing. Considering public perceptions of policing and how the model of policing by consent informs our interpretation of effectiveness. This introduction to effectiveness within policing consider the framework utilised by His Majesty's Inspectorate of Police and Fire & Rescue Services (HMICFRS), PEEL assessments.

INTRODUCTION

Effectiveness within policing is a measure of how well policing organisations achieve their primary objectives and obligations. At the inception of the metropolitan police force in 1829, Sir Robert Peel emphasised that 'the measure of police efficiency is the absence of crime and disorder, not the visible evidence of police actions in dealing with them'. This near 200-year-old statement, rings true today in how the public, senior police officers and key stakeholders, view the measure of effectiveness for contemporary policing (Andrews, 2025). Effectiveness within policing in England and Wales is measured through a multitude of mechanisms and extends to examine the variety of areas and roles within policing organisations. Generally, effectiveness within policing is associated with how well policing organ-

DOI: 10.4018/979-8-3373-2757-0.ch016

isations achieve their intended goals, whilst these goals may differ depending on leadership and locality, the broad aims for most policing organisations are reducing crime, protecting the public, improving public safety, and maintaining public trust and legitimacy (HMICFRS, 2024). Importantly, effectiveness within policing differentiates to efficiency. As effectiveness refers to the results and impacts of police organisations and whether they are achieving their desired outcomes, for example reducing crime. Whereas efficiency is primarily concerned with whether the mechanisms of effectiveness are being implemented appropriately, considering resources and productivity. Therefore, this chapter will focus primarily on how we measure police effectiveness and what factors are behind these measurements.

In England and Wales, policing organisations are primarily assessed for their effectiveness by His Majesties' Inspectorate of Constabularies and Fire & Rescue Services (HMICFRS), who utilise the PEEL framework to assess organisations (HMICFRS, 2023). The PEEL framework, standing for Police Efficiency, Effectiveness and Legitimacy assessment highlights the three key areas that policing organisations are assessed against. Effectiveness is one of these three pillars with the criteria being evaluation for effectiveness which considers 'how well' or 'how effective' certain aspects of policing organisations are. The PEEL framework is designed to assess as much as possible within policing organisations to offer a fair assessment of an organisations effectiveness against reducing crime and protecting the public. As the PEEL assessments are a metric utilised across all territorial policing organisations in England and Wales it allows for comparing the strengths and weaknesses of how effective each force is (Sheldon, 2025). Whilst this is considered helpful and allows organisations to share best practice, it has also highlighted the vast differences between how each police organisation operates across the country. The assessments have also drawn criticism for how valid, accurate and useful the outcomes and findings may be. Police organisations can utilise these assessments, and other measures of effectiveness derived from statistical data or reviews, to highlight their performance compared with neighbouring police forces. This also highlights the role that police effectiveness, or perceived effectiveness, may have in securing public trust, building relationships with the community and establishing legitimacy. This chapter introduces the concept of effectiveness, what effectiveness is and how it may be measured. Whilst also considering the implications of effectiveness within policing and how it may develop in the future. In doing so, it sets the foundations for the forthcoming chapters in this section which provide greater detail on how police services can deliver effectiveness at a strategic, operational and tactical level.

DEFINING EFFECTIVENESS

Generally, effectiveness within policing has been tied to how well organisations can reduce and prevent crime. Effectiveness therefore being universally measured through quantitative metrics such as crime statistics and data linked explicitly to crime reduction and prevention (Bayley 1994; Loveday, 2000). One key criticism to measuring police effectiveness through quantitative measures is that there is little consideration for the wider role of the police function within society, such as building trust with communities they serve and establishing legitimacy (Skogan, 2006; Ludwig et al, 2017). However, these metrics can be helpful for us to understand what reported crimes are most prevalent in specific policing areas, and by extension, how the police organisation responsible is responding with these crimes. Despite the usefulness of these statistics, they are a crude insight that focusses specifically on crime reduction and prevention. This presents an issue in that utilising crime statistics and arrest rates as the primary measure for effectiveness within policing we accept that the role of police is to reduce and prevent crime. However, as Bayley (1994) describes this is the 'myth of the police', that whilst the public see the police as crime preventers, police professionals, academics and stakeholders recognise that the police do not prevent crime. If there is this indication that the police do not prevent crime, then measuring effectiveness through these metrics solely, seem out of place (Shilston, 2008). This does recognise the difference between public expectations and realities of operational policing and highlights that effectiveness cannot be solely measured through the police's role within crime reduction and prevention. Additionally, prevention and reduction are seen as the primary drivers of operational frontline policing and don't necessarily recognise the broader roles that modern policing encompasses such as investigating crime, supporting victims and witnesses, supporting the community and responding to non-crime occurrences.

WHY IS EFFECTIVENESS IMPORTANT?

Importantly, we must also consider *why* effectiveness within policing is important and who the key stakeholders are. Firstly, effectiveness within policing is a necessary mechanism for organisations to self-analyse to establish how well it is achieving its primary objectives of providing safety and security for the public, preventing and reducing crime and supporting victims and witnesses. Measuring and understanding effectiveness within policing allows for stakeholders to hold organisations to account. For example, the roles of police and crime commissioners (PCC) across England and Wales are designed to hold the Chief Constable accountable in achieving their priorities, which can vary across the territorial police organisations.

PCCs are elected by the public and provide a voice for members of the community directly to the leadership of policing organisations (Roberts et al, 2025). Moreover, the greater the public perceive the police to be effective the more likely they are to hold positive attitudes towards the police and engage with them (Sargeant, 2017), ultimately supporting policing objectives.

Ultimately, whilst effectiveness within policing is important for police leaders to inform their practice and for stakeholders such as PCCs, HMICFRS and the College of Policing to advance and promote developments in policing, the public also have a key role in underscoring effectiveness. The importance of the polices' relationship with the public in England and Wales come from its founding principles and the model of policing by consent. Therefore, the police must be perceived to be effective in order for the model of policing by consent to remain, without which contemporary policing across England and Wales would have to dramatically change.

EFFECTIVENESS WITHIN THE PEEL ASSESSMENT FRAMEWORK

The PEEL assessment framework, the standardised measure of effectiveness within the police across England and Wales (HMICFRS, 2023), is a tool that encompasses both quantitative data and qualitative, considering the police role in reducing and preventing crime but also treatment of victims and witness. However, the PEEL assessment considers legitimacy as separate to effectiveness rather than a component to it. The assessment utilises feedback from the community, performance data including crime statistics to comprehensively understand how effectively an organisation prevents crime, investigates crime and protects the vulnerable. The assessment grades 9 areas of police organisations on a 5-point scale from inadequate through to outstanding, asking how good the force is at each area; for each police organisation the findings are publicly available. These 9 areas include leadership and management; diversity and inclusivity in the workforce; fair and appropriate use of powers; effectiveness in crime prevention; responding to the public; investigating crime; safeguarding children and adults at risk; managing fraud and providing a safe and lawful custody environment (HMICFRS, 2024).

The advantages of this framework are that is allows for transparency; publicly available findings online, standardisation; all organisations are compared on the same metrics, and a drive to improve policing provisions across England and Wales as all organisations should provide actions plans and strategic oversight for improving in areas in which they are falling short. The 'Policing Performance' born out of the collect PEEL assessments provides an overview and insight into the general state of policing and where improvements are needed, such as how organisations are run by senior leaders and developing the culture within policing (HMICFRS, 2023). There are also criticisms that measuring effectiveness and performance could drive senior leaders to focus on single issues rather than general across the board changes within organisations, in order to demonstrate success (Cheng, 2023).

Despite the strengths of the PEEL assessment framework for assessing effectiveness within policing, there are limitations and criticisms regarding its accuracy. For example, one of the more recent, and more damning, PEEL assessments of Lincolnshire Police highlight that assessments often do not emphasise contextual factors in which policing organisations can be differentiated. Lincolnshire Police argue unique circumstances regarding their funding, reintegration of functions from a private company and their ratio of officers per 1000 of the population (HMICFRS, 2025). These arguments highlight that the PEEL framework, whilst offering standardisation of a measure of effectiveness, neglect the important factor that each of England and Wales 43 territorial police organisations are unique; based on leadership, force demographic and geographic differences which lead to variation in funding and resource allocation (Mawby & Wright, 2012). This leads practioners to the belief that the PEEL assessments are nothing more than a box-ticking exercise that scrutinises how the organisation is run without offering meaningful suggestions for improvement. The framework does allow for modernisation and improvements, and continuous adaptation is expected to align with the broader objectives of improving policing, and effectiveness within organisations. Nevertheless, the PEEL assessment framework remains the primary tool for assessing effectiveness within policing in England and Wales.

BEYOND PEEL ASSESSMENTS

Whilst PEEL assessments are the primary measure for police effectiveness, they do not capture the entire picture. Therefore, when considering effectiveness within policing we may need to look at other datasets, metrics or frameworks to establish a well-informed view. Within British policing the data sets utilised to scrutinise police effectiveness come from the Office of National Statistics (2024) and the crime survey for England and Wales (CSEW) which has been recording crime since 1981 and surveys members of the public on their experiences of crime in the previous year. The feedback from these surveys is utilised alongside crime statistics to establish an overview of both police effectiveness in responding to crimes practically and public perceptions of police effectiveness. For policing in England and Wales the public play a vital role in policing through the model of policing by consent.

However, heavy reliance on utilising crime statistics for measuring effectiveness has come under scrutiny in the past. Whilst these quantitative measures offer us a reasonable insight to the scale of certain issues, historically there has been recognition that crime statistics have been manipulated by the police (Maguire, 1997; Loveday, 2000). Whilst the metrics are useful to understand crime problems, caution should be taken when considering that police are effectively responding to these problems. One of the reasons for this is crime statistics are often pulled directly from police recorded data, meaning they are only as valid as the entries made by officers. This means that officer's discretion can influence what is recorded and contributes to the crime statistics for a given area, which could lead to under, or mis, reporting of crime problems (Myhill & Johnson, 2016). Two problems arise from this, firstly the crime data is skewed and shows an inaccurate image of crime problems and whether the police are being effective in responding to it (Buil-Gil et al, 2022). Secondly, the impact on public trust in the police which can impact an organisations legitimacy and consequently their perceived effectiveness. The relationship between legitimacy and effectiveness indicates that when a policing organisation is perceived with less legitimacy from the public, they are also deemed to be less effective (Kochel et al, 2013). Beyond police misreporting there has also been a reported decrease in the proportion of crimes that are reported to police (Brunton-Smith et al, 2024) which further skews the reliability of crime statistics. Therefore, it is difficult to confidently utilise crime statistics to review effectiveness within police. As such, effectiveness cannot be just about metrics and measurements but also how the roles of the police intersect with the broader objectives of society, maintaining safety, ensuring fairness and general societal wellbeing. This highlights another advantage of PEEL assessments as a measurement of effectiveness; they are an inspection of specific organisations and thus can identify challenges and strengths within them.

One consideration to make is that PEEL assessments, and other metrics or measurements that examine police effectiveness don't necessarily consider how effective police organisations respond and adapt to new threats and crime types. Take for example Fraud and Cyber Crime representing such a significant proportion of crime in England and Wales, and the one in which most people are likely to be victims of (ONS, 2022). Yet considering the scale of the crime type the policing response is not equitable when compared to more traditional crime types, such as robberies and burglaries. This is not to say that policing responses to fraud are ineffective, but instead to argue that a police force cannot be effective if it is not able to respond to new and emerging crime types. Extending on this point, when considering the ability of the police to investigate a multitude of factors, including the underreporting of crime, contribute to a knowledge gap existing, with the polices response to cybercrime and cyber-enabled frauds lacking the skills of other sectors (Cockcroft et al, 2021). Therefore, meaning the police response to these new and emerging crime types is inherently limited in its effectiveness. Moreover, that an effective police organisation should be capable of adapting to new and emerging threats through specialist training.

WHAT DOES AN EFFECTIVE POLICE ORGANISATION LOOK LIKE?

Addressing the previous points and wider context of effectiveness within policing it leads us to consider what specifically effectiveness within policing is, and how an organisation can operate effectively. Whilst measuring effectiveness within policing through crime rates, statistics and ability to reduce crime is a common tool internationally used (Baradaran Baughman, 2020), it arguably skims the surface of effective policing. However, when considering crime reduction and prevention utilising these statistics to measure organisations influence on them can be seen as justified. Extending this further, effectiveness within policing should be examining the relationship between their strategies and policies and whether it is influencing crime rates: employing evidence-based policing strategies. Effectiveness of specific policing strategies can therefore be monitored and mapped to establish 'what works', the moniker that the College of Policing utilise to promote evidence-based policing strategies. The utilisation of evidence-based practices has increased and continues to do so as not only a tool for improving police effectiveness but also police efficiency (Sherman, 2013). The implementation of these strategies is encouraged through the College of Policing though how police leaders and organisations employ them differ. Hence a drive to promote a culture which embeds evidence-based practices and a leadership that recognises the strengths of understanding the relationship between crime reduction and police intervention (Pepper et al, 2024). This can be monitored as effective leadership through the PEEL assessment framework.

An effective police force must also consider the specific needs of the local jurisdiction, despite policing in England and Wales often being aggregated as one entity the areas and demographics in which they police vary greatly. This is reflected in the different sizes, budgets and departments that make up each individual organisation. Therefore, to be effective an organisation must consider the unique expectations placed upon beyond that of its primary expectations of crime reduction and prevention by the local community they serve.

In addition, for a police organisation to be effective it must surely consider the culture and standards of the officers and staff working within it. The Equality and Human Rights Commission (2024) makes this argument that the PEEL assessment framework must include considerations of how the workforce are treated internally. Particularly given the findings of the Casey Review (2023) of the Metropolitan Police Service in which misogyny was highlighted as a toxic component of the organisations culture. In addition, HMICFRS' own report into the vetting, misconduct and misogyny in the police service (2022) also identified issues associated with how officers and staff were treated in service. Therefore, one can argue that for a police organisation be effective it must consider the treatment and welfare of its own workforce, which will likely directly influence their effectiveness at achieving the organisations primary objectives (Dubord et al, 2021). Furthermore, studies indicate that the quality of the service they receive and being treated with fairness and respect is the top priority of the public, and that this can improve confidence (Myhill & Bradford, 2012). Arguably this means that for the public, effectiveness through crime reduction and prevention, whilst important is not their priority. However, this may suggest that the goal of policing organisations is to provide a quality service and treat people fairly, and therefore this can be a measure of how effective a policing organisation is.

CONCLUSION

This chapter offers an insight into effectiveness within policing but doesn't encompass every factor that could be included as effectiveness. For example, an effective police force would be expected to handle and treat data with integrity and ensure they maintain effective and secure data records. Whilst this is something that many would not consider as a proponent of effectiveness within policing, the consequences of poor data handling can impact public trust and legitimacy; influencing the perceptions of how effective and organisation may be.

Additionally, effectiveness within policing is a difficult concept for the public to comprehend in England and Wales but also across the world, due to the police functioning as one proponent of the criminal justice system. Implying that the police are seen as a part of a wider system and if that wider system is faltering, whether that be a backlog in the court system or overcrowding in prisons, then the entire criminal justice system is deemed ineffective. In essence effectiveness can exist within policing however perceived effectiveness from the public, which can directly impact operational policing, is arguably equally as important yet arguably less efforts are prescribed to remedy this.

In conclusion, effectiveness within policing must be understood as an intersection between operational competency, efficient utilisation of resources and maintenance of legitimacy. There is a need for the police to adapt to modern and technologically enabled crimes, and this should be considered in our contemporary understanding of effectiveness. As a tool for measuring effectiveness the PEEL framework provides a fair mechanism of evaluation across policing organisations, it must however adapt and evolve to ensure it recognises innovative evidence-based practices. It is clear from the literature that effective policing must include adaptability to new and emerging threats, employing evidenced based strategies and placing a greater role on legitimacy and public trust in the police.

REFERENCES

Andrews, T. (2025). The 'Peelian Principles': Their historical and contemporary veracity. *Policing and Society, 35*(5), 584-602.Baradaran Baughman, S. (2020). How effective are police? The problem of clearance rates and criminal accountability. *Alabama Law Review*, *72*, 47.

Bayley, D. H. (1994). *Police for the Future*. Oxford University Press.

Brunton-Smith, I., Cernat, A., Pina-Sánchez, J., & Buil-Gil, D. (2024). Estimating the reliability of crime data in geographic areas. *British Journal of Criminology, 64*(6), 1347–1361.

Buil-Gil, D., Moretti, A., & Langton, S. H. (2022). The accuracy of crime statistics: Assessing the impact of police data bias on geographic crime analysis. *Journal of Experimental Criminology, 18*(3), 515–541.

Casey, L. (2023, March 21). *An independent review into the standards of behaviour and internal culture of the Metropolitan Police Service*. Metropolitan Police Service. https://www.met.police.uk/SysSiteAssets/media/downloads/met/about-us/baroness-casey-review/update-march-2023/baroness-casey-review-march-2023a.pdf:contentReference[oaicite:2]index=2https://hmicfrs.justiceinspectorates.gov.uk/publications/an-inspection-of-vetting-misconduct-and-misogyny-in-the-police-service/

Cheng, X. (2023). *Efficiency, effectiveness and public trust in policing in the era of austerity: a study of police forces in England and Wales, 2011-2017* (Doctoral dissertation, University of Bath).

Cockcroft, T., Shan-A-Khuda, M., Schreuders, Z. C., & Trevorrow, P. (2021). Police cybercrime training: Perceptions, pedagogy, and policy. *Policing. Journal of Policy Practice, 15*(1), 15–33.

Dubord, N., & Griffiths, C. T. (2021). Creating a change culture in a police service: The role of police leadership. *Policing. Journal of Policy Practice, 15*(1), 168–180.

Equality and Human Rights Commission. (2024, November 1). *Response to HMICFRS proposed policing inspection framework and programme 2025–2029*. https://www.equalityhumanrights.com/response-hmicfrs-proposed-policing-inspection-framework-and-programme-2025-2029

His Majesty's Inspectorate of Constabulary and Fire & Rescue Services. (2022, November 2). *An inspection of vetting, misconduct, and misogyny in the police service.*

His Majesty's Inspectorate of Constabulary and Fire & Rescue Services. (2023). *PEEL assessment framework 2023–2025*. https://www.justiceinspectorates.gov.uk/hmicfrs/publication-html/peel-assessment-framework-2023-25/

His Majesty's Inspectorate of Constabulary and Fire & Rescue Services. (2025, May 14). Serious concerns over Lincolnshire Police's performance. https://hmicfrs.justiceinspectorates.gov.uk/news/news-feed/serious-concerns-over-lincolnshire-police-performance/ hmicfrs

HMICFRS. (2023). *Police performance: Getting a grip*. https://hmicfrs.justiceinspectorates.gov.uk/publication-html/police-performance-getting-a-grip/

HMICFRS. (2024). State of Policing: The Annual Assessment of Policing in England and Wales 2023.

Kochel, T. R., Parks, R., & Mastrofski, S. D. (2013). Examining police effectiveness as a precursor to legitimacy and cooperation with police. *Justice Quarterly*, *30*(5), 895–925.

Loveday, B. (2000). Managing crime: Police use of crime data as an indicator of effectiveness. *International Journal of the Sociology of Law*, *28*(3), 215–237.

Ludwig, A., McLean, I., & Norton, M. (2017). *Measuring police effectiveness*. Chartered Institute of Public Finance & Accountancy.

Maguire, M. (1997). Crime statistics, patterns and trends: changing perceptions and their implications. *The Oxford handbook of criminology, 2*, 135-219.

Mawby, R. C., & Wright, A. (2012). The police organisation. In *Handbook of policing* (pp. 224–252). Willan.

Myhill, A., & Bradford, B. (2012). Can police enhance public confidence by improving quality of service? Results from two surveys in England and Wales. *Policing and Society*, *22*(4), 397–425.

Myhill, A., & Johnson, K. (2016). Police use of discretion in response to domestic violence. *Criminology & Criminal Justice*, *16*(1), 3–20.

Office for National Statistics. (2022, September 26). *Nature of fraud and computer misuse in England and Wales: Year ending March 2022*. https://www.ons.gov.uk/peoplepopulationandcommunity/crimeandjustice/articles/natureoffraudandcomputermisuseinenglandandwales/yearendingmarch2022

Office for National Statistics. (2024). *Crime in England and Wales: year ending December 2023*. https://www.ons.gov.uk/releases/crimeinenglandandwalesyearendingdecember2023

Roberts, M., Lakhani, U., & Noorbakhsh, N. (2025). Supporting PCCs and Their Offices to Engage with Data: The Role of the Association of Police and Crime Commissioners. In *Applied Policing Policy Research: Improving Evidence Based Oversight of the Police* (pp. 31–43). Springer Nature Switzerland.

Sargeant, E. (2017). Policing and collective efficacy: The relative importance of police effectiveness, procedural justice and the obligation to obey police. *Policing and Society*, *27*(8), 927–940.

Sheldon, B. (2025). Police Governance and Accountability. In *Understanding Policing and Professional Practice* (pp. 61–79). Routledge.

Sherman, L. W. (2013). The rise of evidence-based policing: Targeting, testing, and tracking. *Crime and Justice*, *42*(1), 377–451.

Shilston, T. G. (2008). One, two, three, what are we still counting for? Police performance regimes, public perceptions of service delivery and the failure of quantitative measurement. *Policing: a journal of policy and practice, 2*(3), 359-366.

Skogan, W. G. (2006). *Police and Community in Chicago: A Tale of Three Cities*. Oxford University Press.

Chapter 17
Police Responding

Tony Blockley
Leeds Trinity University, UK

ABSTRACT

This chapter examines the effectiveness of police response to public calls for service, drawing on national PEEL (Police Effectiveness, Efficiency, and Legitimacy) assessments, procedural justice theory, and empirical research. It explores how the timeliness, fairness, and professionalism of police responses shape public perceptions of legitimacy, trust, and operational competence. Through a structured analysis of call handling, response capability, public engagement, and case studies, the chapter identifies key operational and cultural factors that enable effective response policing. Emphasis is placed on triage systems like THRIVE, officer communication, technological infrastructure, and the growing complexity of non-crime demand such as mental health and safeguarding incidents. The chapter highlights examples of promising practice from forces and contrasts them with underperforming services to illuminate barriers such as staffing shortfalls, inconsistent supervision, and outdated systems.

INTRODUCTION

Police response to calls for service remains one of the most visible and impactful aspects of policing. Whether the public contacts the police through 999, 101, or online reporting, the timeliness, professionalism, and fairness of that interaction often shape broader perceptions of legitimacy, public trust, and operational competence (Bradford, 2014; Sindall et al., 2017). An effective initial response can prevent harm, secure evidence, and provide reassurance, while a delayed or poorly managed

DOI: 10.4018/979-8-3373-2757-0.ch017

response can lead to frustration, disengagement, and diminished confidence in the justice system (HMICFRS, 2023a).

PEEL assessments provide an important lens for understanding how well police forces meet public expectations in this area. These inspections focus on several key aspects of the police response: how effectively calls are handled, how risk and vulnerability are assessed, how quickly officers are deployed, and how fairly and professionally they interact with the public once on scene. While response speed remains a critical performance indicator, the quality of engagement and the use of discretion, empathy, and communication are equally important (Myhill & Bradford, 2013; Tyler, 2006).

Response policing is not limited to the immediate containment of crime. Officers are increasingly responding to complex situations involving mental health crises, missing persons, safeguarding concerns, and public order events. These pressures have created a challenging landscape in which response teams must balance volume, complexity, and public expectations, often with limited resources (College of Policing, 2022). Forces that perform well under PEEL scrutiny tend to have adequate governance arrangements, consistent triage systems, trained call handlers, and mechanisms to ensure timely officer deployment informed by threat, harm, and risk assessments (HMICFRS, 2023b).

chapter explores the principles and practices that underpin effective police response, drawing on theoretical frameworks such as procedural justice, operational evidence from inspections, and real-world examples of promising practice. It also considers the challenges facing response policing and recommends improving public-facing services to enhance trust and effectiveness.

Beyond the immediate outcome of individual incidents, police response plays a critical role in shaping wider public confidence and perceptions of legitimacy. Public judgements about policing are rarely formed solely through personal experience; rather, they emerge cumulatively through repeated encounters, shared community narratives, media reporting, and perceptions of how consistently and fairly the police respond to members of the public (Bradford, Jackson & Stanko, 2009; Bottoms & Tankebe, 2012). As such, each response interaction contributes not only to the satisfaction of the individual caller but to broader collective beliefs about whether the police can be relied upon to act competently, proportionately, and in the public interest. Where response policing is perceived as slow, inconsistent, or dismissive, this can undermine public buy-in and willingness to engage with policing more generally. Conversely, professional, respectful, and transparent responses, even where outcomes are limited, can reinforce legitimacy and support ongoing cooperation with police services. (Tyler, 2006; Bradford, 2014).

THEORETICAL AND OPERATIONAL CONTEXT

Effective police response cannot be understood solely in operational terms. (O'Brien et al, 2020; Lauf et al, 2021) Amuya and Kahuthu (2025) argue that it is also shaped by public expectations, legal obligations, and theoretical frameworks that define acting fairly, proportionately, and professionally. One of the most influential frameworks is procedural justice theory, which emphasises how authority is exercised rather than whether it is effective. According to Tyler (2006), the perceived fairness of police decision-making, the quality of interpersonal treatment, and individuals' ability to voice their concerns all contribute significantly to public trust and compliance. In response policing, how officers engage with people during initial encounters, whether they are respectful, explain their actions, and listen, is just as important as how quickly they arrive on the scene.

Operational guidance from the College of Policing reinforces this emphasis on fairness and professionalism. Authorised Professional Practice (APP) outlines how forces should manage initial contact and deploy officers based on a structured threat, harm, and risk assessment. The "THRIVE" model, widely adopted across England and Wales, provides a framework for triaging calls and allocating resources to prioritise vulnerability and safeguarding rather than relying solely on crime type or urgency (College of Policing, 2022). Research has shown that forces using consistent triage systems are more likely to deploy resources appropriately and ensure that vulnerable individuals receive a timely and proportionate response (HMICFRS, 2022).

However, the relationship between procedural justice and response efficiency is not always linear. (Moges & Amentie, 2022) As Hill et al (2020) note, there is a tension between public demands for immediate action and the operational reality of stretched resources, complex calls, and increasing mental health-related demand. Studies have highlighted that forces are increasingly responding to non-crime incidents involving vulnerability, risk of self-harm, missing persons, or public welfare issues, tasks that often require extended time on scene and inter-agency coordination (Millie, 2016; Enang et al, 2021; College of Policing, 2022). In these situations, a procedurally just approach remains critical, particularly when officers cannot deliver the outcome that callers expect.

High-performing forces balance response speed, decision-making quality, and interpersonal fairness. This involves not only the deployment of officers but also how control room staff handle calls, how supervisors manage response workloads, and how technology supports timely and informed decisions. PEEL assessments consistently highlight that where forces invest in supervision, training, and clear response protocols, the quality of service improves across both emergency and non-emergency interactions (HMICFRS, 2023).

Bevan et al (2022) suggest that the effectiveness of police response depends not just on the logistics of attending incidents but also on the quality of interactions throughout the process, from call handling and triage to officer conduct and follow-up. As Croci (2024) contends, procedural justice and operational competence must work in tandem to meet public expectations and deliver fair, effective policing.

CALL HANDLING AND INITIAL RESPONSE

When someone contacts the police, how their call is handled often shapes their view of the entire police service. (Bennell et al, 2022) Most people interact with the police through emergency (999) or non-emergency (101) lines. As Mackay et al (2022) contend, how control room staff speak to callers, their decisions, and how quickly help arrives all influence public confidence.

Call handlers must remain calm under pressure and ask the right questions to assess risk. If they fail to identify signs of danger or vulnerability, the police response may be delayed or inappropriate. Forces that perform well in PEEL assessments tend to use clear triage protocols, maintain good supervision, and provide regular training to their staff (HMICFRS, 2023).

THRIVE assessments help call handlers make decisions based on risk and vulnerability, not just incident type. This approach supports fair and consistent decisions about when and how to respond. A non-urgent crime may still need a fast response if the caller is vulnerable or in danger. When forces apply this approach well, victims are more likely to receive timely and appropriate support (College of Policing, 2022).

Response time still matters, especially in emergencies. (Balfour et al, 2022) However, how officers interact with the public upon arrival is equally important. As Peters et al (2022) point out, officers who listen, explain what they are doing, and treat people with respect build trust, even when outcomes are disappointing. Studies show that victims care about fairness and being taken seriously, not just how fast police arrive (Myhill & Bradford, 2013).

Some forces have struggled with long wait times for non-emergency calls or limited officer availability in rural areas. These challenges often relate to staffing, shift planning, or managing demand. Forces that perform well tend to use mobile technology, clear standards, and regular reviews to match resources to public need (HMICFRS, 2022). From a broader perspective, access to the police through call-handling functions is a key point at which collective public expectations are formed. Long waiting times, difficulties accessing non-emergency services, or inconsistent responses to similar incidents can quickly become shared community concerns, particularly in areas experiencing sustained demand or limited visible policing

(HMICFRS, 2023). These experiences often circulate beyond the original caller, shaping neighbourhood-level perceptions of police availability and responsiveness, including among those who have not had direct contact with the police themselves (Sindall, McCarthy & Brunton-Smith, 2017). In this sense, call handling and triage systems do not simply manage demand, they also act as visible indicators of organisational reliability and fairness. Forces that communicate clearly about response standards, manage expectations transparently, and apply triage consistently are better placed to maintain public confidence, even where resources are constrained (College of Policing, 2022).

In short, effective call handling is about making the right decisions, responding with care, and focusing on the caller's needs. When this works well, the public feels heard and protected. When it fails, confidence in the police quickly declines.

RESPONSE CAPABILITY AND CAPACITY

A police force's ability to respond quickly and effectively depends on its staffing levels, resource management, and infrastructure. (Samanta et al, 2022) As Verlaan and Ruiter (2023) point out, even the best triage systems will fail if there are not enough officers available to attend incidents. PEEL assessments regularly highlight concerns about response capacity, especially in forces facing high demand, officer shortages, or inconsistent deployment across different areas (HMICFRS, 2023).

Some forces operate with fewer response officers than needed. This can result in long waits for non-emergency incidents and slower responses to priority calls. In rural areas or during peak times, response units are often several miles away when an incident is reported. This affects how safe people feel and may discourage them from calling the police in future (College of Policing, 2022).

As Samanta et al (2022) argue, effective shift planning and resource allocation can reduce these problems. Forces that perform well often use real-time data to match officer availability to likely demand. (Dewinter et al, 2020). Berk (2021) also notes this includes deploying officers based on patterns from previous incidents, using predictive mapping tools, and adjusting staffing during high-risk periods such as weekends or holidays. Forces with mobile data terminals and vehicle tracking are better able to respond flexibly and update plans as demand changes throughout the day.

Davies et al (2024) note that response capability also depends on the quality of supervision. Supervisors play a key role in managing workloads, supporting new officers, and ensuring that calls are dealt with promptly. (Dau et al, 2023) In some underperforming forces, a lack of supervision has led to response delays, poor communication with control rooms, and errors in recording or follow-up.

Another challenge is increased demand from non-crime incidents. As Seo et al (2021) note, police are often called to deal with mental health crises, welfare checks, or missing persons. As Balfour et al. (2022) recognise, these incidents take hours and often involve coordination with other services. Feuer (2021) suggests officers may feel overwhelmed without proper support. As Laufs et al (2021) posit, response teams may become tied up with non-urgent cases, reducing their ability to attend new calls.

Improving response capacity is not just about numbers. It also requires technology, supervision, planning, and clear priorities. Where these elements work together, the police can better respond to the public quickly and fairly.

Public Satisfaction and Engagement

In their research, Nägel and Nivette (2023) identify that public satisfaction with the police is shaped by factors beyond response times. They further point out that how officers behave when they attend incidents plays a significant role in building or damaging trust. People often care as much about how they are treated as they do about the outcome. If officers listen, explain their actions, and show respect, callers are more likely to feel satisfied, even when the incident cannot be resolved in their favour (Bradford, 2014; Tyler, 2006).

While public satisfaction is often measured through individual encounters, its implications extend well beyond those interactions. Repeated patterns of response policing, particularly in relation to repeat callers, vulnerable individuals, or communities experiencing sustained demand, contribute to shared understandings of police priorities, competence, and fairness (Jackson et al., 2012). Where people observe consistent, respectful, and communicative responses, confidence in policing is more likely to extend beyond personal experience to a broader sense of institutional trust and legitimacy (Bradford, 2014). Conversely, perceived inconsistency, lack of follow-up, or poor communication can generate collective scepticism, even among those who have not directly engaged with the police. In this way, response policing operates as a key mechanism through which individual encounters are translated into wider public trust or disengagement (Nägel & Nivette, 2023).

Balog-Way et al (2020) argue that good communication during initial contact and follow-up after an incident improves public confidence. When officers take time to update victims, explain what will happen next, and provide reassurance, people are more likely to view the police as fair and effective (Sindall et al., 2017; Myhill & Bradford, 2013). In contrast, when officers appear rushed, dismissive, or fail to provide information, trust often declines.

Frontline officers and the quality of call handling influence satisfaction levels. If people struggle to get through on 101 or their concerns are not taken seriously, they may lose faith in the police. Forces with better communication protocols tend to perform more strongly in public confidence measures (HMICFRS, 2022).

PEEL inspections increasingly consider public feedback as part of their assessment. Forces that regularly monitor satisfaction, including through surveys and complaints data, can better identify problems and respond quickly. Some have introduced follow-up teams or victim care units to maintain contact after a response. These approaches help close the gap between initial action and long-term engagement. Public satisfaction depends on many factors: speed, communication, fairness, and follow-up. Forces that recognise this complexity are more likely to build long-term relationships with the communities they serve.

CASE STUDIES FROM PEEL REPORTS

Comparing how different forces perform under PEEL inspections helps identify promising practices and areas where services fall short. These assessments, discussed earlier in this chapter (see HMICFRS, 2022; 2023a), consistently show that well-performing forces tend to combine good governance, responsive deployment models, and effective use of triage and risk assessments—key elements described in the theoretical and operational context and call handling sections.

For example, Durham Constabulary has been recognised for its strong response function. The force uses real-time intelligence and a well-structured deployment model, aligning with the earlier discussion on predictive resourcing and demand mapping (see Samanta et al., 2022; College of Policing, 2022). Its call handlers are trained to conduct thorough risk assessments, and officers are deployed with relevant background information. These practices reflect the importance of combining operational capability with interpersonal fairness, as discussed in the procedural justice framework section. As a result, the force has received positive public feedback and improved outcomes for victims (HMICFRS, 2022).

In contrast, some forces have struggled to meet public expectations. These challenges echo issues explored earlier in the chapter, including limited officer availability (Verlaan & Ruiter, 2023), high demand (Laufs et al., 2021), and weak triage or supervision (Dau et al., 2023). PEEL reports describe how, in some forces, delays in responding, particularly in rural or under-resourced areas, have led to missed safeguarding opportunities and lower public satisfaction. In one example, priority incidents experienced increased response times, and victims often received no follow-up, reflecting points raised in the public satisfaction and challenges sections.

Learning from such case studies allows other forces to review and refine their practices. Initiatives such as introducing mobile technology (see also Dewinter et al., 2020), redesigning shift patterns, and creating dedicated response supervision teams align with earlier recommendations in the chapter on future directions.

High-performing forces also avoid working in silos. They integrate response functions with safeguarding, investigations, and victim care services, supporting the whole-system policing model outlined in the final recommendations section. This ensures continuity of service, avoids duplication, and provides a consistent point of contact for victims, an issue raised earlier with poor communication and disengagement (see Balog-Way et al., 2020; Myhill & Bradford, 2013).

CHALLENGES AND BARRIERS

While many forces have improved their response functions, several persistent challenges affect performance and public satisfaction. These barriers are often interconnected with the themes explored earlier in this chapter, particularly concerning capacity, communication, and procedural fairness. One of the most significant issues is the rising demand. Forces increasingly respond to a mix of crime and non-crime incidents, including mental health crises, missing persons, and welfare concerns, an issue also discussed under "Response Capability and Capacity" (see Feuer, 2021; Laufs et al., 2021; Seo et al., 2021). These incidents are often time-consuming and require collaboration with external agencies. Officers may spend several hours managing a single non-crime case, reducing their availability for other calls (College of Policing, 2022).

Staffing pressures also remain widespread. Many forces report difficulties maintaining adequate officer numbers, especially during evenings and weekends or in large, rural areas—factors noted earlier in the operational context and the case study examples (see HMICFRS, 2023; Verlaan & Ruiter, 2023). This can lead to backlogs in attending non-urgent calls and contribute to officer fatigue. As noted by Samanta et al. (2022), overworked teams may experience reduced decision-making capacity and strained interactions with the public.

Inconsistent triage and call grading systems further compound the problem. Earlier sections highlighted how the structured use of THRIVE improves risk assessment (College of Policing, 2022). However, urgent cases may not be prioritised correctly when these systems are inconsistently applied or when staff diverge from established protocols. This creates operational confusion and increases risk to vulnerable individuals (HMICFRS, 2023).

Technology, while helpful, is not always reliable. Some forces rely on outdated mobile systems or lack integrated incident tracking platforms. As highlighted in the "Response Capability" section, these technological gaps undermine real-time coordination and can delay deployment and decision-making (Dewinter et al., 2020; Dau et al., 2023).

Communication breakdowns also continue to damage trust. This links closely with the findings under "Public Satisfaction and Engagement," which showed that unclear updates, poor explanations, or a lack of follow-up after incidents contribute to public dissatisfaction (Balog-Way et al., 2020; Myhill & Bradford, 2013). Forces that do not systematically collect feedback or review complaints are slower to detect and resolve these communication issues (HMICFRS, 2022).

Finally, there is an underlying cultural challenge. In some response teams, informal expectations favour speed over quality. Officers may feel under pressure to close jobs quickly rather than fully understand the circumstances, especially in high-demand environments. As discussed earlier in this chapter, this tendency risks undermining procedural justice, particularly for vulnerable or repeat callers who require more time, explanation, and care (Tyler, 2006; Nägel & Nivette, 2023).

To address these challenges, forces must adopt a joined-up approach. This includes effective workforce planning, consistent triage systems, investment in reliable technology, and a focus on officer wellbeing. Building on earlier recommendations, enhanced communication training and stronger supervision will help ensure that the public always receives fair, proportionate, and responsive service.

FUTURE DIRECTIONS AND RECOMMENDATIONS

Improving the police response to the public requires more than reducing attendance times. It demands a shift toward more intelligent systems, better training, and transparent communication. As discussed earlier in this chapter, high-performing forces do not rely solely on speed but focus on combining operational effectiveness with fairness, consistency, and public engagement (Myhill & Bradford, 2013; Tyler, 2006).

A growing number of forces are now using data analytics to anticipate demand. Supervisors can deploy officers more effectively before incidents by analysing where and when calls are most likely to occur. This predictive approach, already evident in forces highlighted in PEEL inspections, has reduced pressure on control rooms and allowed units to respond faster and more precisely (College of Policing, 2022; Samanta et al., 2022).

Mobile technology plays a vital role in this shift. Officers equipped with live updates, maps, and access to case data are better able to make informed decisions at the scene. Combined with effective supervision and real-time intelligence support, officers can respond more confidently and accurately to diverse and evolving situations (Dewinter et al., 2020; HMICFRS, 2022). As noted in the "Response

Capability" section, this is particularly valuable during high-demand periods or in geographically dispersed areas.

Training also remains central to improving response effectiveness. Forces should prioritise development in three key areas: decision-making, communication, and vulnerability awareness. Many calls involve individuals in crisis who need safeguarding or support rather than enforcement. Officers trained to assess risk and respond appropriately are more likely to prevent harm and build trust, particularly in high-stakes, non-crime encounters (Laufs et al., 2021). Including trauma-informed practice in some forces' training programmes reflects this evolving understanding of what professional response policing entails (HMICFRS, 2022).

Aftercare is another area with significant potential for impact. The policing experience should not end when the officer leaves the scene. Forces that offer follow-up contact, victim care services, and clear information about the next steps are more likely to retain public confidence and support continued engagement with the justice process. This echoes earlier findings in the "Public Satisfaction and Engagement" section, where communication and follow-up were identified as key drivers of trust (Balog-Way et al., 2020; Bradford, 2014).

Importantly, response policing must be understood not in isolation, but as part of a wider, interconnected system. How an incident is handled at the point of contact directly influences subsequent safeguarding, investigation, and neighbourhood engagement. Forces that integrate these functions, rather than operating in silos, are more likely to deliver continuity of care and reduce duplication or delay, as seen in the case study of Durham Constabulary and others within *PEEL assessments (HMICFRS, 2022; 2023).*

To advance further, forces need to align five strategic priorities, each supported by evidence from academic research and PEEL inspections. First, they must use local knowledge and demand data to anticipate and allocate resources effectively, a practice shown to improve response efficiency in forces adopting predictive deployment models (Samanta et al., 2022; College of Policing, 2022). Second, communication training should be a core element for both call handlers and frontline officers, as clear and respectful interactions are consistently linked to increased public trust and satisfaction (Bradford, 2014; Balog-Way et al., 2020). Third, supervision must be strengthened to support decision-making and resilience under pressure. Research and inspection reports highlight the importance of frontline leadership in managing demand and ensuring service consistency (Davies et al., 2024; HMICFRS, 2022). Fourth, forces must systematically monitor public satisfaction and follow up with individuals after incidents, practices associated with stronger community relationships and accountability (Sindall et al., 2017; Myhill & Bradford, 2013). Finally, forces must treat response policing not as a standalone function but as a central component of whole-system policing. Integration with safeguarding, investigation, and neighbourhood functions is essential to deliver seamless, fair, and effective services (HMICFRS, 2023; Verlaan & Ruiter, 2023). When these principles are applied together, forces are more likely to deliver a responsive, fair, and trusted service that reflects the complex realities of modern policing.

CONCLUSION

Police response is one of the public service's most visible and influential aspects. How quickly officers arrive, how they interact with the public, and whether they handle situations fairly all shape perceptions of legitimacy and trust. As discussed throughout this chapter, an effective response is not only about speed, it also depends on professional decision-making, clear communication, and care for those involved (Tyler, 2006; Bradford, 2014).

Forces performing well in PEEL assessments tend to have structured triage systems, trained call handlers, and officers supported by real-time intelligence and effective supervision (HMICFRS, 2022; College of Policing, 2022). These forces also demonstrate a willingness to listen to public feedback and use that information to review and improve practice, reflecting principles of procedural justice and accountability (Myhill & Bradford, 2013).

Importantly, the impact of response policing should be understood not only at the level of individual service delivery but in terms of its cumulative effect on public trust and consent. Patterns of police response, particularly consistency in decision-making, clarity of communication, and fairness in treatment, contribute to collective judgements about legitimacy and organisational competence (Bottoms & Tankebe, 2012; Bradford et al., 2009). In an environment of heightened scrutiny and constrained resources, these cumulative judgements play a significant role in shaping public willingness to cooperate with the police, comply with the law, and engage constructively with policing institutions over time (Tyler, 2006).

Despite these strengths, challenges remain. Response teams continue to face growing demand, limited resources, and increasingly complex calls, often involving mental health or vulnerability. Delays, inconsistent communication, and a lack of follow-up can all weaken public confidence, even when frontline staff do their best under pressure (Laufs et al., 2021; HMICFRS, 2023).

To move forward, forces must invest in both people and infrastructure. This includes upgrading mobile technology, strengthening supervision, and embedding trauma-informed training across response roles. As highlighted in the final sections of this chapter, response policing should not be seen as an isolated function but as an integrated part of a wider system that connects to safeguarding, neighbourhood teams, and investigations (Samanta et al., 2022; Verlaan & Ruiter, 2023). A strong, fair, responsive police service is essential to public confidence. When forces get this right, through clear strategy, competent frontline delivery, and ongoing engagement with communities, they build lasting trust and improve outcomes for all those they serve.

REFERENCES

Amuya, L. O., & Kahuthu, J. N. (2025). Police bureaucratization and 'selectivity' of law enforcement: Digging deeper into senior officers' occupational attitudes. *Police Practice and Research, 1*(1), 1–20. DOI: 10.1080/15614263.2025.2497267

Balfour, M. E., Hahn Stephenson, A., Delany-Brumsey, A., Winsky, J., & Goldman, M. L. (2022). Cops, clinicians, or both? Collaborative approaches to responding to behavioral health emergencies. *Psychiatric Services (Washington, D.C.), 73*(6), 658–669. PMID: 34666512

Balog-Way, D., McComas, K., & Besley, J. (2020). The evolving field of risk communication. *Risk Analysis, 40*(S1), 2240–2262. PMID: 33084114

Bennell, C., Jenkins, B., Blaskovits, B., Semple, T., Khanizadeh, A. J., Brown, A. S., & Jones, N. J. (2022). Knowledge, skills, and abilities for managing potentially volatile police–public interactions: A narrative review. *Frontiers in Psychology, 13*, 818009. PMID: 35330722

Berk, R. A. (2021). Artificial intelligence, predictive policing, and risk assessment for law enforcement. *Annual Review of Criminology, 4*(1), 209–237.

Bevan, M. P., Priest, S. J., Plume, R. C., & Wilson, E. E. (2022). Emergency first responders and professional wellbeing: A qualitative systematic review. *International Journal of Environmental Research and Public Health, 19*(22), 14649. PMID: 36429361

Bottoms, A., & Tankebe, J. (2012). Beyond procedural justice: A dialogic approach to legitimacy in criminal justice. *The Journal of Criminal Law & Criminology, 102*(1), 119–170.

Bradford, B. (2014). Policing and social identity: Procedural justice, inclusion and cooperation between police and public. *Policing and Society, 24*(1), 22–43. DOI: 10.1080/10439463.2012.724068

Bradford, B., Jackson, J., & Stanko, E. A. (2009). Contact and confidence: Revisiting the impact of public encounters with the police. *Policing and Society, 19*(1), 20–46. DOI: 10.1080/10439460802457594

College of Policing. (2022). *Response Policing: Evidence Briefing*. College of Policing. Available at: https://www.college.police.uk/research

Croci, G. (2024). *The Complex Landscape of Police Culture: Challenges and Opportunities for Reform*. Social Justice Center, 3.

Dau, P. M., Vandeviver, C., Dewinter, M., & Witlox, F. (2023). Policing directions: A systematic review on the effectiveness of police presence. *European Journal on Criminal Policy and Research, 10*(1), 1–20. https://link.springer.com/article/10.1007/s10610-021-09500-8 PMID: 34177120

Davies, A. J., Stephenson, A., & Briggs, B. (2024). What do we know about key influences on police attrition and retention rates? A literature review 2019–2023. *Policing*. Advance online publication. DOI: 10.1108/pijpsm-11-2023-0149

Dewinter, M., Vandeviver, C., & Vander Beken, T. (2020). Analysing the police patrol routing problem: A review. *ISPRS International Journal of Geo-Information*, *9*(3), 157. https://www.mdpi.com/2220-9964/9/3/157

Enang, I., Murray, J., Dougall, N., Aston, E., Wooff, A., Heyman, I., & Grandison, G. (2021). Vulnerability assessment across the frontline of law enforcement and public health: A systematic review. *Policing and Society*, *32*(4), 540–559. DOI: 10.1080/10439463.2021.1927025

Hill, R., Guest, D., Pickford, R., Hopkinson, A., Daszkiewicz, T., Whitton, S. & Towler, A. (2020). *Covid-19 pandemic second interim operational review*. C19 National Foresight Group.

HMICFRS. (2022). *PEEL 2021/22: An inspection of the effectiveness, efficiency and legitimacy of police forces in England and Wales*. London: HMICFRS. Available at: https://www.justiceinspectorates.gov.uk/hmicfrs/publications

HMICFRS. (2023a). *State of Policing: The Annual Assessment of Policing in England and Wales 2022*. London: HMICFRS. Available at: https://www.justiceinspectorates.gov.uk/hmicfrs/publications/state-of-policing-the-annual-assessment-2022/

HMICFRS. (2023b). *PEEL Inspection Reports: Force Summaries*. London: HMICFRS. Available at: https://www.justiceinspectorates.gov.uk/hmicfrs/peel-assessments/

Jackson, J., Bradford, B., Hough, M., Myhill, A., Quinton, P., & Tyler, T. R. (2012). Why do people comply with the law? Legitimacy and the influence of legal institutions. *British Journal of Criminology*, *52*(6), 1051–1071. DOI: 10.1093/bjc/azs032

Laufs, J., Bowers, K., Birks, D., & Johnson, S. D. (2021). Understanding the concept of 'demand' in policing: A scoping review and resulting implications for demand management. *Policing and Society*, *31*(8), 895–918.

MacKay, M., Colangeli, T., & Thaivalappil, A. (2022). A review and analysis of the literature on public health emergency communication practices. *Journal of Community Health*, *10*(2), 1–20. https://link.springer.com/article/10.1007/s10900-021-01032-w PMID: 34515962

Millie, A. (2016). What is policing for? Examining the ends of the police. *British Journal of Criminology*, *56*(5), 859–876. DOI: 10.1093/bjc/azv078

Moges, A., & Amentie, C. (2022). *Effect of organizational justice on organizational performance with mediating variables of job satisfaction and organizational commitment: A systematic article review*. Journal of Economics, nokspublishing.com. https://nokspublishing.com/index.php/AJMSS/article/view/58

Myhill, A., & Bradford, B. (2013). Overcoming cop culture? Organisational justice and police officers' attitudes toward the public. *Policing*, *36*(2), 338–356. DOI: 10.1108/13639511311329732

Nägel, C., & Nivette, A. E. (2023). Unexpected events during survey design and trust in the police: A systematic review. *Journal of Experimental Criminology*, *19*(4), 891–917. PMID: 35729978

O'Brien, A., Read, G. J., & Salmon, P. M. (2020). Situation Awareness in multi-agency emergency response: Models, methods and applications. *International Journal of Disaster Risk Reduction*, *48*, 101634.

Peters, L., Hobson, C. W., & Samuel, V. (2022). A systematic review and meta-synthesis of qualitative studies that investigate the emotional experiences of staff working in homeless settings. *Health & Social Care in the Community*, *30*(1), 58–72. PMID: 34255385

Samanta, S., Sen, G., & Ghosh, S. K. (2022). A literature review on police patrolling problems. *Annals of Operations Research*, *329*(1), 1–28. https://link.springer.com/article/10.1007/s10479-021-04167-0

Seo, C., Kim, B., & Kruis, N. E. (2021). A meta-analysis of police response models for handling people with mental illnesses: Cross-country evidence on the effectiveness. *International Criminal Justice Review*, *31*(2), 182–202.

Sindall, K., McCarthy, D. J., & Brunton-Smith, I. (2017). Young people and the formation of attitudes towards the police. *British Journal of Criminology*, *57*(6), 1271–1288. DOI: 10.1093/bjc/azw087

Tyler, T. R. (2006). *Why People Obey the Law* (2nd ed.). Princeton University Press.

Verlaan, T., & Ruiter, S. (2023). Predictors of police response time: A scoping review. *Crime Science*, *12*(1), 19.

Chapter 18
Delivering Outstanding Custody Services

Hannah Jane Simpson
http://orcid.org/0009-0005-9375-7161
Police Scotland, UK

ABSTRACT

This chapter explores the critical role of custody services in policing, highlighting their influence on police legitimacy, public trust, and detainee welfare. It examines how outstanding custody practices - aligned with the PEEL assessment framework - can enhance operational efficiency, transparency, and ethical standards. Key components such as staff training, safeguarding, facility management, and technology integration are discussed alongside best practices from UK police forces. The chapter also addresses recurring challenges, such as disproportionate use of force and inadequate healthcare, offering forward-looking recommendations to support continuous improvement and excellence in custody service delivery.

INTRODUCTION

Custody services play a pivotal role in the broader framework of policing, bridging the gap between frontline policing and criminal justice systems. Effective custody services not only ensure the humane treatment of persons in custody, but also significantly influence public perceptions of police legitimacy and trust (Tyler & Jackson, 2013). Custody practices directly impact the perceived fairness and ethical conduct of police forces, thereby affecting the willingness of communities to cooperate and comply voluntarily with the law (Tyler & Huo, 2002).

The Police Effectiveness, Efficiency, and Legitimacy (PEEL) assessment framework, developed by His Majesty's Inspectorate of Constabulary and Fire & Rescue

DOI: 10.4018/979-8-3373-2757-0.ch018

Services (HMICFRS), underscores the importance of delivering outstanding custody services as part of the overall evaluation of police performance. Aligning custody services with PEEL standards involves ensuring transparency, accountability, safeguarding vulnerable individuals, and maintaining high ethical and professional standards (HMICFRS, 2023).

Research consistently highlights the critical relationship between high-quality custody management and overall police legitimacy. Tyler (2004) emphasises that the legitimacy of policing institutions is heavily influenced by perceptions of fairness and ethical treatment of suspects. Similarly, Bradford, Milani, and Jackson (2020) argue that procedural justice within custody environments - characterised by impartiality, respect, and transparency - directly affects public perceptions of police legitimacy. Outstanding custody services contribute to reducing the risk of conflict and abuse, maintaining the dignity of arrested persons, and ultimately strengthening public trust in policing institutions.

This chapter explores key practices, benchmarks from exemplary police forces, and offers practical guidance for police leaders aiming to achieve outstanding custody service ratings. It integrates academic research, best practices from leading UK police forces, and actionable strategies that align custody services with HMICFRS expectations of efficiency.

CUSTODY SERVICES AND THE PEEL FRAMEWORK: IMPLICATIONS FOR EXCELLENCE

The integration of custody services within the proposed 2025–2027 PEEL framework highlights their essential role in ensuring that those held in police custody are treated lawfully, humanely, and ethically. This inclusion demonstrates an explicit recognition by HMICFRS of the need to assess police forces comprehensively; particularly regarding detention practices, to maintain public trust and uphold legal and human rights standards. For the proposed 2025-2027 PEEL framework, custody services will be explicitly assessed through updated judgement criteria emphasising fairness, detainee welfare, transparency, and ethical practices (HMICFRS, 2023).

Several key judgement criteria are already identified within the HMICFRS framework, specifically for inspection of custody services. Firstly, treatment and conditions within custody environments are examined to ensure detainees are consistently managed with dignity and provided facilities that meet defined standards. Secondly, rigorous assessments of risk management and safety procedures are carried out to ascertain the effectiveness of identifying and mitigating potential harms to detainees and custody staff alike. Thirdly, healthcare provisions, including mental health support, are scrutinised to guarantee timely and adequate medical assistance to detainees. Fourthly, detainees' legal rights and entitlements, including access to legal representation and family communication, are evaluated to ensure compliance with statutory obligations. Finally, the proportionality and appropriateness of force and restraint used in custody environments are carefully reviewed to ensure ethical practices (HMICFRS, 2022).

Going forward, the evaluation of custody services will be integrated into the PEEL assessment framework. Topic areas and characteristics of 'outstanding' custody services are yet to be developed, but it is expected they will be largely based on the current rolling programme of custody inspection (HMICFRS, 2024). The current proposed areas of inspection are: leadership, accountability and working with partners; pre-custody, officers and staff should consider alternatives to detention at first point of contact; in the custody suite, people are treated respectfully and with dignity; in the custody cell, detainees are held in clean and safe conditions with access to healthcare and safeguarding; and any release or transfer from custody is both safe and prompt (HMICFRS, 2024).

Striving for excellence within the enhanced PEEL framework presents a range of important considerations for police forces. Ongoing professional development, strong internal oversight, collaboration with external partners, and the use of innovative technologies are all central to delivering high-quality, ethical custody services. The next section explores these key components in more detail, whilst also acknowledging that they represent just part of a broader set of interrelated elements essential to achieving and sustaining policing excellence.

KEY COMPONENTS OF AN 'OUTSTANDING' CUSTODY SERVICE

Outstanding custody services encompass several critical elements that contribute significantly to their effectiveness and the dignity with which detainees are treated. These include comprehensive staff training, rigorous safeguarding practices, and meticulous facility management.

Staff Training and Professionalism

Effective custody services hinge upon the quality and professionalism of their staff. Regular training and continuous professional development are essential for ensuring that staff and officers are well-equipped to handle complex and dynamic situations within custodial environments (Johnston & Shearing, 2018). Such training must be comprehensive and frequent to reinforce best practices and update staff on evolving standards and policies. Research indicates that continuous professional development enhances employee confidence, reduces workplace stress, and improves overall service quality (Fisher & Fisher, 2020).

Integral to staff training is education in ethics, diversity awareness, mental health awareness, and conflict resolution skills. Ethics training ensures that custody staff act with integrity, upholding the human rights of detainees and minimising instances of abuse or misconduct (Smith et al., 2021). Additionally, diversity training fosters cultural competence and sensitivity, significantly reducing discriminatory practices and promoting fairness in treatment (Hall & Cooper, 2019). Mental health awareness training is especially crucial in custody settings, as many detainees present with underlying psychological conditions. Equipping staff with the ability to recognise and appropriately respond to mental health concerns can mitigate crises and improve detainee outcomes (Greenberg & Jennings, 2019). Lastly, conflict resolution training enables staff and officers to effectively de-escalate potentially volatile situations, maintaining a safer environment for both detainees and staff.

Safeguarding and Vulnerability

Safeguarding vulnerable detainees is paramount in custody services, demanding proactive identification and management of risks. Vulnerability may stem from mental health conditions, substance abuse issues, or physical disabilities, and services must implement thorough assessment protocols upon entry to custody (Walker & Bryant, 2020). Effective safeguarding involves clear guidelines for staff to identify signs of vulnerability early and to respond promptly and appropriately.

Protocols for managing mental health crises, substance abuse situations, and medical emergencies must be clearly established and rigorously enforced. These protocols should include timely access to healthcare professionals, ongoing monitoring and observation procedures, and clear guidelines for escalation to specialised care when necessary (World Health Organization, 2021). Proper management of such crises significantly reduces incidents of self-harm, violence, and fatalities in custody settings, thus protecting detainee well-being and reducing legal liability for institutions (Harris & Brown, 2022).

Facility Management and Environment

Maintaining custody facilities to high standards is vital for ensuring safety, dignity, and security. Facilities must comply with national and international standards, ensuring appropriate physical conditions, including adequate space, hygiene, ventilation, lighting, and privacy considerations (UNODC, 2019). Research highlights the positive impacts of well-maintained custodial environments, noting reductions in detainee distress and improved overall behavioural outcomes (Andrews & Bonta, 2020).

Moreover, incorporating feedback from both detainees and staff is crucial for ongoing improvement of custody facilities. Soliciting and actively responding to feedback can highlight practical issues overlooked by management and help in developing a more humane, respectful environment (Jones et al., 2021). Engagement with detainees in the feedback process also contributes positively to their sense of agency and dignity, aligning custodial practices with broader rehabilitative goals.

Use of Technology

The integration of Closed-Circuit Television (CCTV), body-worn cameras (BWCs), and digital record-keeping systems has significantly enhanced transparency in police operations. CCTV surveillance within custody suites provides continuous monitoring, supporting detainee safety and staff compliance with protocols. However, challenges such as poor image quality can impede the effectiveness of digital visual technologies more broadly. For instance, reporting highlighted that between 2019 and 2024, Police Scotland's custody photographs were of insufficient quality for facial recognition purposes, necessitating improvements in resolution standards (The Times, 2025), an issue that aligns with broader HMICFRS concerns regarding digital infrastructure, data quality, and evidential integrity within custody environments (HMICFRS, 2022).

BWCs have become instrumental in documenting interactions between officers and detainees, promoting accountability and serving as valuable evidence in investigations. They have been shown to improve evidence collection, strengthen officer performance, and enhance agency transparency (U.S. Department of Justice, 2014; College of Policing, 2021). Additionally, digital record-keeping facilitates accurate documentation of custody procedures, ensuring that records are tamper-proof and readily accessible for review (Bureau of Justice Assistance, 2015).

Independent Custody Visitor Schemes and External Oversight

Independent Custody Visitor (ICV) schemes involve trained volunteers conducting unannounced visits to police custody facilities to assess detainee treatment and welfare. Established following concerns about custody conditions and subsequently embedded through the Police and Criminal Evidence Act 1984 (PACE), Independent Custody Visitor schemes provide an impartial evaluation of custody conditions, reinforcing public confidence in policing practices (Home Office, 2016).

ICVs have unrestricted access to detainees and custody areas, enabling them to report on issues such as detainee rights, facility conditions, and staff conduct.

Their findings are communicated to police authorities and the public, fostering transparency and accountability.

Regular Internal Audits and Inspections

Conducting regular internal audits and inspections is essential for maintaining high standards in custody services. These processes involve systematic reviews of procedures, compliance with legal and ethical standards, and the identification of areas for improvement. HMICFRS inspections have highlighted that several forces have implemented internal oversight mechanisms to ensure adherence to custody protocols and address deficiencies promptly (HMICFRS, 2008). Such proactive measures not only enhance operational efficiency but also demonstrate a commitment to self-regulation and continuous improvement.

In summary, the integration of these aforementioned key components collectively ensures custody environments that are not only secure and respectful, but also highly efficient. Each element plays a critical role in streamlining processes, reducing operational delays, and enabling staff to respond swiftly and appropriately to challenges. This increased efficiency directly contributes to more consistent and positive outcomes for both detainees and staff. Moreover, by fostering transparency, accountability, and high professional standards, such environments help build and sustain public trust - an essential pillar of effective, modern policing.

BEST PRACTICE, EMERGING TRENDS, AND INNOVATIONS IN CUSTODY SERVICES

UK police forces have increasingly adopted innovative approaches and advanced technologies to enhance custody services, improve detainee welfare, and strengthen public trust, with several forces having already demonstrated excellence in custody services through the implementation of these practices.

Norfolk and Suffolk Police provide an outstanding example of innovation in detainee care and rights management through their introduction of digital information guides within custody cells. This initiative leverages video technology to communicate detainees' legal rights and entitlements in a clear, user-friendly format. By replacing traditional, paper-based approaches that can be inaccessible or confusing, detainees achieve better comprehension of their rights, leading to increased autonomy and procedural fairness (University of Sheffield, 2024).

In Scotland, the application of trauma-informed training programs for custody officers illustrates another pioneering approach. Recent research found that such training significantly improved officers' attitudes and behaviours towards detainees, emphasising empathetic interaction and heightened sensitivity towards detainees' psychological needs. This approach advocates for ongoing, specialised training and multi-agency collaboration to better address detainees' vulnerabilities, ultimately leading to improved detainee welfare and reduced incidents of distress or conflict within custody settings (Goodall et al., 2023). Whilst this force is not monitored by HMICFRS, it is still an exemplary practice which can be easily adopted by neighbouring forces in England and Wales.

The effective use of data analytics is further exemplified by the College of Policing's initiative examining procedural justice practices within custody suites. This study utilised coded CCTV footage to analyse interactions between custody sergeants and detainees. Insights from this analysis directly informed targeted improvements in staff training and procedural policy, demonstrating the practical benefits of evidence-based decision making and enhancing perceived fairness and transparency of custody operations (College of Policing, 2023).

Emerging technological advancements further support improvements in custody management. Body-worn cameras and biometric identification systems, such as live facial recognition, have streamlined detainee processing and enhanced security. Predictive analytics is increasingly employed to anticipate risks such as self-harm or violence among detainees. These analytics optimise resource allocation and facilitate proactive interventions, thereby enhancing detainee safety and operational efficiency (Perry, 2024).

Nevertheless, the use of predictive tools necessitates robust governance frameworks to address ethical considerations, potential biases, and privacy concerns (Babuta & Oswald, 2019). Collectively, these best practices and innovations reflect a broader evolution in custody services in which technological and analytical advancements enhance efficiency and safety, but must remain firmly anchored in human rights compliance, ethical oversight, and public accountability.

CHALLENGES AND AREAS FOR IMPROVEMENT

Whilst many forces are already beginning to display excellence in best practice, ensuring the safety and dignity of detainees within police custody remains a critical responsibility; and previous inspections have consistently revealed challenges that police forces must address to enhance custody service quality and maintain public trust. Notably, HMICFRS has identified recurring issues concerning the appropriate use of force, inconsistent healthcare provision, and inadequate oversight and governance within custody environments (HMICFRS, 2017; HMICFRS, 2022).

These challenges are frequently compounded by broader structural and operational pressures faced by police forces, including persistent staffing shortages, high levels of sickness and attrition, and ageing or unsuitable custody estates. Many custody suites operate within buildings that were not designed to meet contemporary standards of dignity, privacy, and accessibility, placing an additional strain on staff attempting to deliver person-centred care. Resource constraints can also limit access to specialist training, healthcare provision, and technological upgrades, creating variability in service quality both within and between forces. Acknowledging these systemic pressures is essential to ensuring that expectations of excellence remain realistic, evidence-informed, and grounded in operational reality (HMICFRS, 2022; National Police Chiefs' Council, 2023).

HMICFRS (2022) highlighted instances where force used by officers appeared disproportionate relative to the threats presented by detainees. Further exacerbating this issue was incomplete or inaccurate documentation, resulting in poor transparency and accountability. For instance, an inspection of Nottinghamshire Police revealed that data on the use of force were unreliable, and not all staff completed the necessary documentation. Some instances of force appeared disproportionate to the risk posed, indicating a need for improved recording and justification of such actions (HMICFRS, 2013). Although this inspection is not recent, the issues identified remain consistent with recurring themes highlighted in subsequent national custody inspections and independent oversight activity, illustrating the enduring importance of robust governance, supervision, and learning in this area (HMICFRS, 2022).

Another significant concern pertains to healthcare provision, where inspections have found systemic inadequacies in delivering timely and effective medical services to detainees, including delays in mental health assessments and inconsistent access to healthcare professionals across custody suites (HMICFRS, 2017). Weak oversight mechanisms have been flagged as a significant contribution to such inconsistent healthcare quality, affecting detainees' rights and welfare negatively (HMICFRS, 2017).

In addition, learning drawn from Independent Office for Police Conduct (IOPC) 'lessons learned' publications provide further insight into recurring custody-related risks, particularly around early risk identification, supervision, information sharing, and learning cultures following adverse incidents. Although such publications are often reactive in nature, they offer valuable system-level learning that can be used proactively to strengthen preventative practice and embed continuous improvement within custody governance frameworks (IOPC, 2022; IOPC, 2023).

To effectively tackle these ongoing problems, police forces should prioritise comprehensive training programs emphasising appropriate use of force, accurate documentation, and ethical standards. Establishing clear accountability mechanisms - such as regular supervisory reviews and performance evaluations - can significantly improve adherence to procedural guidelines (College of Policing, 2022). Additionally, developing robust governance structures for healthcare provision, including standardised protocols and consistent performance monitoring, is critical for enhancing detainee outcomes (HMICFRS, 2017).

According to Lyons (2014), regular performance feedback to custody officers substantially impacts their professional development and operational consistency. Likewise, frameworks such as the Continuous Improvement Self-Assessment Matrix (CI SAM) provided by the College of Policing facilitates self-assessment and drives improvements through structured, reflective practices (College of Policing, 2022). Addressing these identified pitfalls through targeted training, improved oversight, and comprehensive feedback mechanisms will significantly enhance transparency, accountability, and overall service quality within police custody environments (College of Policing, 2022; HMICFRS, 2022).

FORWARD-LOOKING RECOMMENDATIONS

As police forces prepare for the forthcoming 2025–2027 PEEL assessments, strategic planning is essential to meet evolving standards and expectations. The upcoming PEEL framework emphasises a more frequent and in-depth evaluation of custody services, with inspections increasing from every six years to every four years. Custody will now be a graded area of inspection, aligning it with other critical policing functions (National Police Chiefs' Council, 2024). To excel in these assessments, forces must proactively align their custody operations with the updated Performance Assessment Framework (PAF), ensuring that policies and practices reflect current best practices and legal standards.

To enhance custody services in line with future PEEL assessments, police forces should strategically prioritise policy development, training, partnerships, and technological adoption, all while maintaining adaptability to legislative and societal changes. Clear and comprehensive policies are essential for promoting consistency and adherence to best practices, particularly regarding detainee welfare, appropriate use of force, and healthcare provision (HMICFRS, 2022).

Continuous training programs focusing on de-escalation strategies, mental health awareness, and ethical decision making equip officers to manage complex custody scenarios effectively and humanely, reducing risks and improving outcomes for detainees (Goodall et al., 2023). Additionally, securing and maintaining collaborative partnerships with healthcare professionals, mental health services, and community organisations significantly enhances detainee care, facilitates appropriate referrals, and improves community-police relations (College of Policing, 2022).

Using advanced technology, such as fingerprint or facial recognition systems, electronic record-keeping, and data analysis, can help manage detainees more accurately, allocate resources efficiently, and identify potential risks early. However, it is important to closely monitor the use of these technologies to protect individuals' privacy, avoid biases or unfair treatment, and ensure compliance with changing laws and public expectations (Babuta & Oswald, 2019; The Guardian, 2024).

Moreover, the policing landscape is continually influenced by legislative reforms and societal expectations. For instance, increasing regulatory and public scrutiny of facial recognition technologies and data retention practices underscores the need for police forces to remain adaptable and responsive to legal mandates and public concerns (Information Commissioner's Office, 2021; The Guardian, 2024). Establishing mechanisms for regular policy reviews, stakeholder engagement, and community feedback is vital to ensure that custody services remain lawful, ethical, and aligned with societal values. By implementing these forward-looking strategies, police forces can enhance the quality and integrity of their custody services, thereby fostering public trust and achieving excellence in future PEEL assessments.

CONCLUSION

Delivering outstanding custody services is fundamental to upholding the legitimacy, integrity, and effectiveness of modern policing. As evidenced throughout this chapter, the humane and ethical treatment of detainees not only reflects an organisation's commitment to human rights but also directly influences public trust and confidence in policing institutions. The integration of the PEEL framework reinforces the necessity of placing custody services at the heart of performance evaluation, accountability, and professional practice.

To meet the expectations of the evolving 2025–2027 PEEL framework, police forces must embrace a multi-faceted approach that includes comprehensive staff training, robust safeguarding mechanisms, and facility environments that promote dignity and safety. Technology and data-driven innovation offer promising avenues to enhance transparency and efficiency, yet these advancements must be balanced with ethical oversight and privacy protections.

Learning from best practice examples across the UK, and drawing on academic and policy research, it is clear that continuous improvement - through self-assessment, external scrutiny, and community feedback - is essential for service excellence. Ultimately, embedding a culture of accountability, respect, and procedural justice across all aspects of custody operations will be pivotal to achieving and sustaining 'outstanding' ratings under the PEEL framework and, more importantly, fostering stronger, more efficient policing.

REFERENCES

Andrews, D. A., & Bonta, J. (2020). *The psychology of criminal conduct* (6th ed.). Routledge.

Babuta, A., & Oswald, M. (2019). *Data-driven policing and privacy: An assessment of UK practices*. Royal United Services Institute.

Bradford, B., Milani, J., & Jackson, J. (2020). Procedural justice in policing: Theoretical and empirical developments. *Policing. Journal of Policy Practice, 14*(3), 305–317. DOI: 10.1093/police/paz014

Bureau of Justice Assistance. (2015). *Digital recording of custodial interrogations: A guide for law enforcement agencies*. https://bja.ojp.gov

College of Policing. (2021). *Body-worn video: Authorised professional practice*. https://www.college.police.uk

College of Policing. (2022). *Performance assessment framework and continuous improvement tools*. https://www.college.police.uk

College of Policing. (2023). *CCTV analysis and procedural justice in custody suites*. https://www.college.police.uk

Fisher, R., & Fisher, D. (2020). Professional development in high-stress environments. *Journal of Police Leadership, 12*(1), 34–49.

Goodall, M., Barclay, A., & MacLeod, K. (2023). Trauma-informed custody: A review of implementation in Scottish police services. *Journal of Policing and Society, 8*(2), 156–172.

Greenberg, N., & Jennings, P. (2019). Addressing mental health in custody: Strategies for staff and detainees. *Occupational Medicine, 69*(3), 186–192. DOI: 10.1093/occmed/kqz010

Hall, M., & Cooper, R. (2019). Diversity awareness in law enforcement: Challenges and progress. *Equality, Diversity and Inclusion, 38*(5), 567–581.

Harris, J., & Brown, A. (2022). Crisis management and detainee welfare in custody settings. *British Journal of Criminology, 62*(4), 712–730.

His Majesty's Inspectorate of Constabulary and Fire & Rescue Services. (2008). *Review of custody practices: Metropolitan Police Service*. https://www.justiceinspectorates.gov.uk

His Majesty's Inspectorate of Constabulary and Fire & Rescue Services. (2013). *Custody inspection: Nottinghamshire Police*. https://www.justiceinspectorates.gov.uk

His Majesty's Inspectorate of Constabulary and Fire & Rescue Services. (2017). *Police custody inspections: National thematic report*. https://www.justiceinspectorates.gov.uk

His Majesty's Inspectorate of Constabulary and Fire & Rescue Services. (2022). *Custody services: National overview*. https://www.justiceinspectorates.gov.uk

His Majesty's Inspectorate of Constabulary and Fire & Rescue Services. (2023). *PEEL 2023/25 assessment criteria*. https://www.justiceinspectorates.gov.uk

His Majesty's Inspectorate of Constabulary and Fire & Rescue Services. (2024). *PEEL framework and custody assessment*. https://www.justiceinspectorates.gov.uk

Home Office. (2016). *Independent custody visiting: Code of practice*. https://www.gov.uk

Independent Office for Police Conduct. (2022). *Learning the lessons: Preventing deaths and serious harm in police custody*. IOPC. https://www.policeconduct.gov.uk

Independent Office for Police Conduct. (2023). *Learning from adverse incidents: thematic findings and recommendations*. IOPC. https://www.policeconduct.gov.uk

Information Commissioner's Office. (2021). *The use of live facial recognition technology in public places*. https://ico.org.uk

Johnston, L., & Shearing, C. (2018). *Governing security: Explorations in policing and justice*. Routledge.

Jones, A., Patel, R., & McCormack, T. (2021). Improving feedback mechanisms in police custody. *International Journal of Police Science & Management*, *23*(3), 203–219.

Lyons, J. (2014). Performance feedback and professional development in custody settings. *Policy Review*, *9*(1), 44–58.

National Police Chiefs' Council. (2023). *Policing workforce strategy 2023–2028*. NPCC. https://www.npcc.police.uk

National Police Chiefs' Council. (2024). *Preparing for PEEL 2025–27: Strategic briefing paper*. https://www.npcc.police.uk

Perry, M. (2024). Predictive policing in UK custody: Benefits and risks. *Policing and Technology Review*, *6*(1), 45–60.

Smith, K., Williams, T., & Carter, R. (2021). Ethics education in police custody services. *Journal of Criminal Justice Education*, *32*(2), 145–160.

The Guardian. (2024, February 10). *Facial recognition technology and privacy: A legal crossroads*. https://www.theguardian.com

The Times. (2025, January 15). *Police Scotland's custody photos fail facial recognition test*. https://www.thetimes.co.uk

Tyler, T. R. (2004). Enhancing police legitimacy. *The Annals of the American Academy of Political and Social Science*, *593*(1), 84–99. DOI: 10.1177/0002716203262627

Tyler, T. R., & Huo, Y. J. (2002). *Trust in the law: Encouraging public cooperation with the police and courts*. Russell Sage Foundation.

Tyler, T. R., & Jackson, J. (2013). Future challenges in police legitimacy. In Tankebe, J., & Liebling, A. (Eds.), *Legitimacy and criminal justice: An international exploration* (pp. 83–102). Oxford University Press.

United Nations Office on Drugs and Crime. (2019). *Handbook on prison conditions and detainee rights*. https://www.unodc.org

University of Sheffield. (2024). *Digital rights communication in custody: An evaluation report*. https://www.sheffield.ac.uk

U.S. Department of Justice. (2014). *Implementing a body-worn camera program: Recommendations and lessons learned*. https://bja.ojp.gov

Walker, J., & Bryant, H. (2020). Safeguarding in custody: A framework for risk identification. *British Journal of Community Justice*, *18*(2), 33–47.

World Health Organization. (2021). *Guidelines on mental health and human rights in detention*. https://www.who.int

Chapter 19
Conducting Quality Investigations

Kate Benson
http://orcid.org/0009-0006-9190-0769
Brunel University of London, UK

ABSTRACT

Effective criminal investigation is fundamental to public confidence and the legitimacy of policing. This chapter examines the principles, structures, and practices that underpin high-quality investigations within police forces in England and Wales, drawing upon recent HMICFRS PEEL inspection findings. It explores how robust investigative governance is achieved through clear accountability and experienced supervision, to drive consistency and quality across all levels of investigation. Key themes include maximising investigative opportunities, embedding an investigative mindset across the workforce, and advancing victim-focused, evidence-led prosecutions. Short-term reforms focus on improving oversight, documentation, and compliance with the Victims' Code of Practice, while long-term reforms call for leadership development, workforce planning, and a learning culture centred on reflective practice. The chapter argues that forces achieving investigative excellence are those that balance procedural fairness, victim engagement, and organisational learning.

INTRODUCTION

Investigating crime effectively is fundamental to public confidence and the legitimacy of policing. As summarised by Stelfox (2009), "*It is difficult to overstate the importance that criminal investigation has assumed in contemporary society.*" Society has an ever-increasing expectation of the police to demonstrate investigative

DOI: 10.4018/979-8-3373-2757-0.ch019

competence at all levels and across all categories of offending, ranging from minor infractions to the most serious crimes.

The probability of offenders being brought to justice in England and Wales has continued to decline, as reflected in the decreasing proportion of recorded crimes resulting in a charge. This downward trend has contributed to diminishing public confidence in the criminal justice system, creating a self-perpetuating cycle in which victims are increasingly reluctant to report offences or support prosecutions. The quality, quantity, and integrity of evidential material obtained during the early stages of a criminal investigation have a direct bearing on the effectiveness of the wider criminal justice system and the confidence of those who depend on successful prosecution outcomes. Research indicates that forces which emphasise procedural fairness enhance both crime control effectiveness and perceptions of police legitimacy (Tyler, 2006).

The quality of service afforded to a victim of crime will directly impact public trust and confidence, both the individuals involved, their families and the wider community. Victims who feel at the outset that their complaint will not be treated seriously, or that the investigation will be handled unprofessionally, are less likely to come forward and report a crime. His Majesty's Inspectorate of Constabulary and Fire & Rescue Service (HMICFRS) warn that this distrust can manifest throughout the criminal justice system, reducing the likelihood that justice will ultimately be achieved (2020). The 2018-19 PEEL inspection cycle identified a disparity in victim experience between police forces and a lack of faith in criminal justice outcomes. As a result, HMICFRS revised the criteria for future inspections, gathering data through a victim service assessment to monitor a victim's involvement with the police from initial call to conclusion of the investigation (HMICFRS, 2020).

This chapter examines how police forces can deliver high-quality investigations by effectively assessing risk and vulnerability by adhering to investigative procedures in a timely and methodical manner. Achieving an 'Outstanding' HMICFRS grading in the Investigating Crime category reflects a force's commitment to deliver high-quality, victim-centred investigations, supported by effective governance, innovative practices, and adherence to legal standards. This requires the strategic allocation of resources, supported by experienced supervision, within an organisational culture united by a shared commitment to delivering outcomes that align with public expectations.

CRIMINAL INVESTIGATIONS AS A METHOD TO CONTROL CRIME

Over the past decade, policing has faced a significant increase in both the volume and complexity of demand, driven in part by the emergence of new crime types stemming from advances in technology. Over the same time period, Home Office data indicate that the number of crimes recorded per police constable has increased by 32.6 per cent (HMICFRS, 2025b). Forces undoubtedly need more resources across all departments. HMICFRS have acknowledged that a shortfall of officers will constrain the police's ability to detect crime, however, it argues that more should be done with the resources that police forces currently have at their disposal to improve the effectiveness of investigations and the service given to victims and witnesses (HMICFRS, 2025b).

Criminal investigations serve as a central mechanism through which the police seek to control crime. Research demonstrates that individuals who have previously been victimised face a higher risk of future victimisation, underscoring a key objective of investigative practice: reducing the likelihood of repeat offending against specific victims (Stelfox, 2009). It is recognised that only a limited proportion of offenders are apprehended relative to the total number of reported offences. While the police's influence over broader prevention and diversion strategies remains constrained, investigators nonetheless retain the capability to implement targeted actions within individual cases that contribute meaningfully to crime reduction and prevention. As a recent HMICFRS inspection report discusses, *"...there is little in policing that is more important to the public than investigating crime"* (HMICFRS, 2025, pg. 2).

During the 2021-22 HMICFRS PEEL inspection programme, all 43 police forces were inspected. Nine police forces were graded 'good' at effective criminal investigations, with 12 graded 'adequate' and the remaining 22 deemed to 'require improvement' or 'inadequate' at effectively investigating crime (HMICFRS, 2021). In the subsequent 2023-25 inspections, Cumbria Constabulary were the only force to be graded 'good' at Investigating Crime out of the 37 police forces inspected. Cumbria Constabulary has been consistently awarded 'good' at criminal investigations as far back as their 2018-19 PEEL inspections. However, no police force in England and Wales has achieved the highest ranking of 'outstanding' crime investigation in either the 2021-22 or 2023-25 PEEL inspections. In fact, of the 37 forces inspected under the 2023-25 framework, 16 forces performed worse than the previous inspection year (HMICFRS, 2025a).

It should be noted that the grades awarded in the 2023-25 PEEL inspection and those from the previous cycle are not directly comparable due to a revised methodological focus and changes to the specific domains being assessed. Later inspections place a greater emphasis on evaluating the extent to which police forces are achieving appropriate outcomes for the public, reflecting the evolving priorities in contemporary policing.

MAXIMISING INVESTIGATIVE OPPORTUNITIES

Given that many forces are struggling to meet essential governance standards, with officer workloads continuing to rise and an influx of new staff resulting in a decline in overall experience, there is a compelling case for forces to return to fundamental policing principles.

All police personnel involved in crime reporting, from call handlers to first responders, should adopt an investigative mindset (HMICFRS, 2025b) to ensure evidence is not otherwise lost, damaged, concealed or altered as required under the Police and Criminal Evidence Act (1984; HM Government). Identifying investigative opportunities at the outset of a crime report will maximise the likelihood of promptly identifying and arresting offenders. Investigators should assess evidential opportunities which are most available immediately after a crime or incident has occurred. The 'golden hour' is the critical period closely after a crime or incident has been committed (which is not specifically an hour), when key evidence is most effectively collected (College of Policing, 2025a). Preservation of evidence during the golden hour should be prioritised, as investigative possibilities steadily decline as time elapses.

The Criminal Procedure and Investigations Act (CPIA, 1996) provides the governance for fair and transparent criminal investigations. CPIA states that all reasonable lines of inquiry should be pursued, and if the material collected through the course of an investigation may be relevant, it should be recorded, retained and revealed. The 2023–25 HMICFRS inspections found that officers and staff generally exhibited confidence in formulating 'reasonable' lines of enquiry (HMICFRS, 2025a). However, those who were uncertain often relied solely on personal judgement, which in some cases may have been shaped by limited experience or insufficient guidance. It is recommended that forces should provide officers and staff with clear guidance on the definition of 'reasonable', including a detailed explanation and practical examples, to support sound decision-making when prioritising lines of enquiry (HMICFRS, 2025b).

Another recurring theme that may result in missed opportunities to preserve and secure vital evidence is the absence of a clear sense of investigative ownership. A recent PEEL inspection report offers that *"many response and neighbourhood officers don't think their primary role is to investigate crime"*, generating a cycle of missed opportunities (HMICFRS 2025b, pg. 6). Qualitative interviews conducted with response officers in five forces identified that they often fail to commence the initial investigation at scene because they are "*slaves to the radio*", under constant pressure from supervisors and the control room to deploy to the next high-priority call (HMICFRS, 2025b). Inexperienced officers often refrain from challenging radio demands due to a lack of confidence and the necessary experience to advocate for the time required to conduct an effective investigation. Enhanced autonomy is essential for officers to effectively manage their workload and to ensure compliance with their obligation to pursue all reasonable lines of enquiry during investigations.

Neighbourhood officers generally operate with greater autonomy and institutional support, recognising the importance of crime prevention and problem-solving as a mechanism to identify the underlying causes of crime and vulnerability. Response officers, by contrast, face continued pressures to meet the force's target response times for crimes and incidents. As an illustrative case study, crime prevention is highlighted as a key priority in the Metropolitan Police Service (MPS) strategic policing plan, *A New Met for London*. However, the 2023–25 HMICFRS inspection found that the MPS remains heavily focused on responding to immediate demands, with officers and staff outside of neighbourhood policing often disregarding crime prevention and community engagement as part of their responsibilities (HMICFRS, 2024b).

To maximise investigative opportunities, it is recommended that police forces reaffirm fundamental policing principles and provide explicit, practical guidance on what constitutes a 'reasonable' line of enquiry to support sound investigative decision-making. All personnel involved in crime reporting, from call handlers to first responders, should cultivate an investigative mindset. Moreover, strengthening officer autonomy and fostering a clear sense of investigative ownership are critical to managing workloads effectively and ensuring compliance with the duty to pursue all reasonable lines of enquiry.

CORE COMPETENCIES FOR POLICE INVESTIGATORS

Developing an investigative mindset is a skill refined through continual practice and repeated exposure to investigative processes, and yet, as of 2025 many responders, investigators and supervisors have fewer than five years of service. This has resulted in inexperienced supervisors lacking the confidence and the ability to direct investigations (HMICFRS, 2025b). Forces should review their policies to ensure supervisory reviews support the delivery of effective investigations, aligning with the standards set out in the College of Policing's Authorised Professional Practice (College of Policing, 2025a). The Authorised Professional Practice (APP) is a central, trusted resource of national guidance, supporting officers with operational best practice and the latest legislative changes, to deliver consistent and ethical policing.

Unsurprisingly, forces that closely adhere to the College of Policing's APP guidance perform highly in Investigating Crime (College of Policing, 2025a).

All police investigators in England and Wales operate in accordance with the nationally recognised standards of the Professionalising Investigations Programme (PIP), with PIP Level 1 established as the minimum training requirement to achieve operational competence. The PIP provides a structured framework comprising four tiers of criminal investigation, each distinguished by the level of complexity and seriousness of the offence (College of Policing, 2025a). PIP Level 1 investigations focus on priority and high-volume crimes and are generally handled by frontline officers. Officers and staff investigating PIP Level 1 crimes must have basic investigative skills, be proficient in evidence collection, scene preservation, and the effective interviewing of victims, witnesses, and suspects. In most forces, PIP Level 1 investigators will retain responsibility for the respective category one crimes, as defined by the National Crime Recording Standards (HMICFRS, 2025b). This supports continuity of evidence and consistency of victim contact.

Sequentially, serious and complex crime investigations are undertaken by PIP Level 2–accredited officers, typically detectives. The complexity and scope of serious investigations necessitate that investigators possess a range of knowledge and skills distinct from those in other police fields. Despite this, there is a growing reliance on frontline officers and staff to investigate serious offences, driven by the limited capability and resources available within specialist departments.

Although investigating officers demonstrate a strong commitment to delivering the high-quality service that victims are entitled to, they report being constrained by the persistent pressures of frontline policing, which impede their ability to meet this standard (HMICFRS, 2025b). The 2023–25 HMICFRS inspection cycle highlighted cases in which inexperienced officers were tasked with complex investigations or managing high vulnerability. Individual officers frequently managed caseloads exceeding twenty crime reports, often within teams lacking the requisite skills to conduct thorough investigations and receiving limited supervision (HMICFRS, 2024b). These conditions, characterised by overstretched, inexperienced staff operating without adequate support, are strongly linked to diminished victim satisfaction.

To enhance investigative quality, forces should prioritise staff development through ongoing practice and strengthen supervisory oversight. Investigative strategies should align with the College of Policing's Authorised Professional Practice (APP) and PIP-based training, with Level 1 investigators managing priority crimes and Level 2 officers handling complex cases. Reducing reliance on inexperienced frontline staff, managing caseloads effectively, and providing sufficient supervision are essential to supporting thorough, victim-focused investigations.

VICTIM-FOCUSED AND EVIDENCE-LED PROSECUTIONS

Victims too often cite delays in the criminal justice process as a major reason for withdrawing their support for prosecution, with such delays linked to high officer workloads, postponed charging decisions, or adjourned court proceedings (HMICFRS, 2025b). Multiple police forces have been criticised for not documenting the reason victims withdraw their support for prosecution, which is particularly relevant in cases involving vulnerability or coercion (HMICFRS 2025b). Some forces bypass a written victim withdrawal statement, opting instead to record the victim's intention using Body Worn Video. HMICFRS (2022a) recommends creating an auditable record through a signed statement to ensure that the victim's wishes are formally documented and considered before a case outcome is determined. Such records also allow forces to identify patterns and enhance the quality of service provided.

In some criminal investigations, cases may be in the public interest to prosecute even in the absence of victim support. Known as 'evidence-led prosecutions', the prosecution case can rely on other investigative opportunities, such as digital evidence (body-worn video, CCTV footage or mobile phone downloads), initial emergency call recordings and witness testimonies. Encouraging evidence-led prosecutions on behalf of victims who are unwilling or unable to support prosecution is especially pertinent in domestic abuse investigations, where the close personal relationship between the victim and the perpetrator can heavily influence the victim's willingness to support prosecution. Cumbria Constabulary implemented a strategy to strengthen oversight, mandating that an Inspector conduct supervisory reviews for all cases in which a victim had withdrawn (HMICFRS, 2024a).

More than 60 per cent of serious sexual assault victims withdraw from prosecution (End Violence Against Women, 2024). It is essential to believe and support victims at every stage to maintain their engagement throughout the often-lengthy legal process (HM Government, 2024). The critical role of PIP Level 1 officers to recognise the early indicators of criminal activity, even before offences are formally reported, is frequently underestimated. Forces are encouraged to hold domestic abuse surgeries, where specialist domestic abuse officers can offer case management guidance to support response officers (HMICFRS, 2024a).

Scientific and technological developments have expanded the scope of knowledge investigators must possess, requiring expertise in a wider range of investigative techniques (Stelfox, 2009). There is a pressing need for forces to anticipate and plan for the growing demand for advanced digital forensic capabilities (HMICFRS, 2022f). The process of downloading and reviewing digital evidence undoubtedly causes delays in investigations, potentially hindering the ability to meet prosecution time limits and deterring initial disclosures (HMICFRS, 2025b). This issue has been particularly prominent in investigations involving serious sexual assault and rape, which are national priorities within the Violence Against Women and Girls agenda (Home Office, 2021).

The introduction of legislation such as the Police, Crime, Sentencing and Courts Act (Home Office, 2022) was introduced, in part, to combat the 'digital strip search' experienced by victims. Under this legislation, the police must only request a victim's phone if deemed necessary and proportionate to the investigative strategy. This is reinforced by policy in all 43 police forces requiring a device for rape and serious sexual assault victims to be downloaded within 24 hours. Regrettably, the HMICFRS thematic inspection reviewing the use of digital forensics found that few forces met this obligation (HMICFRS, 2022e). Humberside Police, who were awarded 'good' in Investigating Crime in their 2021-22 inspection, adopted a triage capability for early evidential searches on electronic devices. This two-tier process allowed officers to prioritise workloads to assess whether a full examination is necessary (HMICFRS, 2022c).

The *End-to-End Rape Review* outlines the government's action plan for improving the criminal justice response to rape in England and Wales. The review stipulated compulsory training for all officers involved in the initial reporting of rape and sexual offences and concluded that frontline police training had improved (HM Government, 2024). However, the charity organisation *End Violence Against Women* argued that despite the legislative and policy changes, mobile phone downloads continue to be misused, highlighting the concerning frequency of police requests for open-ended third-party material, primarily authorised to assess the 'credibility' of rape survivors (End Violence Against Women, 2024).

To enhance victim-focused and evidence-led prosecutions, forces should ensure victims are believed throughout the legal process. Forces should provide consistent support to victims, and withdrawals should be formally documented through auditable, signed statements. Effective evidence-led prosecutions require a clear understanding across the workforce. Senior leaders must uphold their duty of care to promote a reflective learning culture and ensure investigators are competent in applying legal, procedural, scientific, and technical frameworks effectively (Stelfox, 2009). Investigative efficiency can be improved through early triage of electronic devices, whilst domestic abuse surgeries can provide specialist case management guidance to response officers.

SUSTAINABLE GOVERNANCE

Robust supervisory oversight of investigations is essential to ensure that all reasonable investigative opportunities are thoroughly pursued. While some forces are more successful than others in overseeing investigations, excessive workloads often undermine the quality of supervision (HMICFRS, 2025b). Investigative quality is strengthened when officers and staff perceive their workload as manageable, an outcome achieved by consistent supervision (HMICFRS, 2025). The initial supervisory review of a crime investigation is especially important for less experienced investigators. In some cases, this review occurs too late in the investigation to effectively engage victims or preserve critical evidence.

There is a common, yet erroneous assumption that supervisors automatically possess the requisite skills to effectively oversee the workload of others because they have previously served as investigators and demonstrated competence in managing their own caseloads. Forces frequently fail to recognise that investigation supervisors may have insufficient or no formal training in crime management (HMICFRS, 2024b). A pilot Professionalising Investigations Programme (PIP) Level 1 for supervisors has been implemented across 13 police forces (College of Policing, 2025b). This initiative adopts an evidence-based framework in response to the HMICFRS report on *How Effectively the Police Investigate Crime* (HMICFRS, 2025b), with an objective to increase the quality of investigation management, improve outcomes for victims, and strengthen public confidence in the police's ability to administer justice.

United States law enforcement officers typically receive minimal leadership training until after they have been appointed to a supervisory role, a pattern similar to that seen in England and Wales. In contrast, the military model of leadership development provides personnel with extensive proactive training, often lasting weeks or months before assuming supervisory responsibilities. This philosophy is deeply embedded within military culture, where supervisors are evaluated based on the performance and development of those they lead, rather than on their individual accomplishments (Fritsvold, n.d.). Several forces have revised their promotion processes to incorporate supervisory ability, coaching, and mentoring as key assessment criteria to identify candidates who demonstrate strong leadership qualities.

Inadequate supervision of crime investigation has been defended in some forces, with supervisors being required to *teach* staff the principles of investigation, rather than supervising them (HMICFRS 2022a; HMICFRS 2024c). To address this challenge, forces such as Hampshire Constabulary and Greater Manchester Police retained a cadre of experienced investigators (such as retired detectives) for ongoing guidance and investigative advice, strengthening the capabilities of less experienced staff while alleviating supervisory pressures (HMICFRS, 2025b).

Investigator workload and the working environment have been closely linked to wellbeing, with the sustained occupational and societal demand of policing making officers more susceptible to burnout. Studies have suggested that the high-stress nature of policing is amplified among Chinese policing due to the distinct cultural and operational contexts. Whilst there is disparity amongst the research on occupational burnout (with Western studies dominating the field), Zhou et al (2024) identified a positive correlation between work pressure and occupational burnout among Chinese police officers. Fostering positive coping strategies appears to be an essential tool for officers to mitigate occupational burnout.

In the formative 2021-22 PEEL inspection grading of 'good' at Investigating Crime, Nottinghamshire Police were recognised for their commitment to continuous improvement in workforce wellbeing (HMICFRS, 2022b). Investigators commented feeling satisfied with their workload when receiving consistent support from line managers. Similarly, Merseyside Police took innovative steps to construct wellbeing at the core of investigative success (HMICFRS, 2022d). Supervisors at Merseyside Constabulary actively promote a healthy work-life balance by encouraging physical and reflective activities, as well as 'no-email Fridays' initiatives to help reduce staff demand. These alternative coping strategies appeared effective, with the workforce reporting that their workloads were generally manageable (HMICFRS, 2022d).

The principles of managing effective investigations should be deeply integrated into the policing culture, with forces performing optimally when a consistent approach is adopted. The principles of investigation should be led by the senior leadership team, monitored through the daily management meetings and best practice techniques should be mirrored across all management levels. Forces that exhibit effective supervision are backed by an organisational framework distinguished by clear policies and procedures.

It is recommended that sustainable governance of crime investigations is best achieved through the integration of continuous professional development within officer and staff training at all levels. Supervisors should be provided with enhanced guidance and training to equip them with the leadership competencies and investigative expertise necessary for effective oversight. Senior officers must uphold the organisation's duty of care to both the public and its workforce by fostering a positive, reflective learning culture that promotes the continual development of investigative capability.

FORCE OPERATING MODELS AND INTEGRATED INVESTIGATION STRATEGY

Over the past decade, many forces have adopted operating models in which only a portion of the workforce is tasked with responding to calls, while separate teams are responsible for conducting investigations (HMICFRS, 2025b). This disjointed approach is hindered by inefficient cross-departmental handovers and prolonged delays in reallocating crime reports, resulting in missed opportunities for evidence collection and impacting victims as they navigate an already complex criminal justice system. Forces which have adopted such operating models have seen a cumulative effect of investigative inhibitors across the workforce, resulting in a generation of investigators and supervisors with limited investigative experience (HMICFRS, 2025b). Research by Robinson and Tilley (2009) identified that prompt deployment to a crime scene and the timely completion of initial enquiries were critical determinants in the quality of the initial police response and successful detection of crime.

Forces with supervisory structures that prioritise consistent oversight, detailed guidance, and a sustained focus on investigative quality demonstrate more embedded and effective performance cultures across all ranks (HMICFRS, 2024a). However, under current performance pressures, many officers prioritise responding to calls over maintaining high standards in initial investigations, as the latter is not routinely measured. Performance management frameworks should evaluate officers based on the quality and effectiveness of their investigations rather than on minimum compliance standards or the volume of cases completed (HMICFRS, 2025a).

Forces that implement overly complex crime allocation processes can significantly undermine the willingness of victims to engage with and support prosecution (HMICFRS, 2025b). In addition to the contact agreement, investigators should complete an initial victim needs assessment to determine if a victim requires enhanced support, which may be self-activating if the victim is vulnerable or intimidated by the nature of the crime committed. Supervisors can maximise compliance with the victim service assessment by routinely reviewing cases as part of the supervisory review.

Not all forces share clear guidance on investigation plans, what they should document or by whom. High-quality investigations are characterised by strong victim support, as evidenced through victim service assessments and the completion of comprehensive investigation plans (HMICFRS, 2024a). In the 2021-22 HMICFRS PEEL inspection for Cumbria Constabulary (HMICFRS, 2022e), officers and staff welcomed the implemented 'Principles of Investigation' standards documents, which sets out clear expectations for the workforce regarding investigative standards. Key elements covered by these principles include initial investigation templates, effective handovers to other staff, the completion of initial and subsequent supervisory reviews, timely investigation updates and appropriate disposals.

Police forces that adopt investigative principles for both staff and officers tend to demonstrate strong performance; however, the effectiveness of such approaches is contingent upon the implementation of appropriate governance structures to ensure that investigations are carried out expeditiously. In a recent inspection of Nottinghamshire Police, HMICFRS concluded that despite a mandated force direction on the compulsory initial investigative principles at a crime scene, officers were failing to comply, and supervisors did not challenge poor performance (HMICFRS, 2024c). Another area of concern was the lack of continuity in investigations, with handovers frequently incomplete or absent. This often required the receiving investigator to repeat initial enquiries, leading to delays and the avoidable loss of evidence.

The Code of Practice for Victims of Crime (Ministry of Justice, 2025) is a statutory framework which denotes the minimum service standards that victims should receive throughout the criminal justice process in England and Wales. One of the twelve overarching rights states that victims of crime have the right to be informed about the police investigation and subsequent prosecution (Ministry of Justice, 2025). While all forces implement various levels of victim contact monitoring, many performance management systems typically rely on quantitative, checklist-style evaluations rather than assessing the *quality* of the service delivered to victims (HMICFRS, 2025b). HMICFRS emphasised that police forces should place greater priority on enhancing their compliance with the Victims' Code of Practice (HMICFRS, 2025b).

Some forces have introduced victim-focused desks in response to the challenges victims encounter when attempting to contact the officer responsible for their case (HMICFRS, 2024b). These dedicated units enable victims to make direct contact with the police for updates on their cases, regardless of officer shift patterns or abstractions, thereby improving communication and support. This system was limited by its reliance on investigators accurately and promptly updating the crime report. HMICFRS argue that if investigators are complying with the requirements of the Victim Codes of Practice (Ministry of Justice, 2025) by providing timely updates to victims at set intervals, the enhanced layer of a victim focus desk is obsolete (HMICFRS, 2024b).

CONCLUSIONS AND RECOMMENDATIONS

A commitment to consistently delivering high-quality investigations is a defining feature of an outstanding police force. This chapter highlights that achieving this level of performance requires robust investigative governance, achieved through strong leadership, clear accountability and consistent oversight of investigations, to drive quality and ensure continuous improvement. Achieving an 'Outstanding' grading in HMICFRS PEEL inspections necessitates a comprehensive approach to investigative excellence.

In the short term, police forces should prioritise strengthening investigative governance through improved supervision, clearer accountability, and enhanced quality assurance mechanisms. Immediate reforms should focus on ensuring that investigation plans are clearly documented, regularly reviewed, and guided by supervisors who provide active oversight from the outset of each case. Supervisory reviews must be timely and meaningful, ensuring that all reasonable lines of enquiry are pursued and evidence-led prosecutions are considered where appropriate. Forces should also embed structured risk assessment frameworks such as THRIVE+ across all operational levels to ensure early and consistent identification of vulnerability, particularly among repeat victims and those at heightened risk. Compliance with the Victims' Code of Practice (Ministry of Justice, 2025) must be reinforced by guaranteeing that victims are provided with personal statement opportunities, needs assessments, and consistent case updates. Collectively, these short-term measures aim to stabilise investigative quality, enhance victim confidence, and reduce inconsistencies in frontline investigative practice.

Over the longer term, forces should embed a culture of sustainable investigative excellence through leadership development, resource planning, and continuous professional learning. Building capacity and capability within supervisory ranks will be crucial to maintaining oversight quality and developing a learning organisation focused on reflective practice. Long-term reforms should also include strategic workforce planning to mitigate abstractions and strengthen specialist investigative functions through targeted training, mentorship, and peer review systems. To maintain public trust and achieve sustained improvement, forces must institutionalise victim-centred governance frameworks that systematically monitor satisfaction and outcomes linked to investigative quality rather than output quantity. Embedding these principles within organisational policy and performance management will ensure that high-quality investigations become a defining and enduring feature of policing excellence, aligning with HMICFRS PEEL standards and public expectations.

REFERENCES

College of Policing. (2025a). College of Policing APP (authorised professional practice). Accessed online. Available at: https://www.college.police.uk/app

College of Policing. (2025b). Transforming leadership of police investigations | College of Policing. Accessed online. Available at:https://www.college.police.uk/article/transforming-leadership-police-investigations

Criminal Procedure and Investigations Act. (1996). Accessed online. Available at: https://www.legislation.gov.uk/ukpga/1996/25/contents

End Violence Against Women. (2024). Accessed online. Available at:https://www.endviolenceagainstwomen.org.uk/review-shows-scale-of-police-requests-for-rape-survivors-counselling-notes/

Fritsvold, E. (no date). The Case for More Effective Police Leadership Training. Blog accessed online. Available at: https://onlinedegrees.sandiego.edu/police-management-training/#:~:text=In%20a%20PoliceOne.com%20articleexamining

Government, H. M. (2024). Rape Review progress update: End-to-end Rape Review. Accessed online. Available at: https://assets.publishing.service.gov.uk/media/65cb5cc2103de2000eb8f375/rape-review-progress-update.pdf

His Majesty's Inspectorate of Constabulary and Fire & Rescue Services. (2020). PEEL spotlight report: Diverging under pressure – Overview of themes from PEEL inspections 2018/19 - His Majesty's Inspectorate of Constabulary and Fire & Rescue Services: https://hmicfrs.justiceinspectorates.gov.uk/publications/peel-spotlight-report-overview-of-themes-2018-19/

His Majesty's Inspectorate of Constabulary and Fire & Rescue Services. (2021). PEEL Assessments 2021/22 - His Majesty's Inspectorate of Constabulary and Fire & Rescue Services. Accessed online. Available at:https://hmicfrs.justiceinspectorates.gov.uk/peel-reports-year/2021-22/

His Majesty's Inspectorate of Constabulary and Fire & Rescue Services (2022a).

His Majesty's Inspectorate of Constabulary and Fire & Rescue Services (2022b).

His Majesty's Inspectorate of Constabulary and Fire & Rescue Services (2022c).

His Majesty's Inspectorate of Constabulary and Fire & Rescue Services (2022d).

His Majesty's Inspectorate of Constabulary and Fire & Rescue Services. (2022e). PEEL 2021/22: Police effectiveness, efficiency and legitimacy – An inspection of Cumbria Constabulary. Accessed online. Available at:https://hmicfrs.justiceinspectorates.gov.uk/peel-reports/cumbria-2021-22/

His Majesty's Inspectorate of Constabulary and Fire & Rescue Services. (2022f). An inspection into how well the police and other agencies use digital forensics in their investigations. Accessed online. Available at:https://hmicfrs.justiceinspectorates.gov.uk/publications/how-well-the-police-and-other-agencies-use-digital-forensics-in-their-investigations/

His Majesty's Inspectorate of Constabulary and Fire & Rescue Services. (2024a) PEEL Assessments 2023–2025 - An inspection of Cumbria Constabulary. Accessed online. Available at: https://hmicfrs.justiceinspectorates.gov.uk/peel-reports/cumbria-2023-25/

His Majesty's Inspectorate of Constabulary and Fire & Rescue Services. (2024b). PEEL Assessments 2023–2025 - An inspection of the Metropolitan Police Service. Accessed online. Available at: https://hmicfrs.justiceinspectorates.gov.uk/peel-reports/metropolitan-2023-25/peel-assessment-2023-25-metropolitan.pdf

His Majesty's Inspectorate of Constabulary and Fire & Rescue Services. (2024c). PEEL 2023/25: Police effectiveness, efficiency and legitimacy – An inspection of Nottinghamshire Police. Accessed online. Available at:https://hmicfrs.justiceinspectorates.gov.uk/peel-reports/nottinghamshire-2023-25/

His Majesty's Inspectorate of Constabulary and Fire & Rescue Services. (2025a). PEEL Assessments 2023–25. Accessed online. Available at: https://hmicfrs.justiceinspectorates.gov.uk/peel-reports-year/2023-25/

His Majesty's Inspectorate of Constabulary and Fire & Rescue Services. (2025b). Crime investigations: An inspection into how effectively the police investigate crime. Accessed online. Available at: https://s3-eu-west-2.amazonaws.com/assets-hmicfrs.justiceinspectorates.gov.uk/uploads/inspection-into-how-effectively-the-police-investigate-crime.pdf

Home Office. (2021). Tackling violence against women and girls strategy. Accessed online. Available at: https://www.gov.uk/government/publications/tackling-violence-against-women-and-girls-strategy

Home Office. (2022). Police, Crime, Sentencing and Courts Act. Accessed online. Available at: https://www.gov.uk/government/collections/the-police-crime-sentencing-and-courts-bill

Ministry of Justice. (2025). Code of Practice for Victims of Crime in England and Wales. Accessed online. Available at:https://www.gov.uk/government/publications/the-code-of-practice-for-victims-of-crime/code-of-practice-for-victims-of-crime-in-england-and-wales-victims-code

PEEL. (2021/22). Police effectiveness, efficiency and legitimacy – An inspection of the Metropolitan Police Service. Accessed online. Available at: https://hmicfrs.justiceinspectorates.gov.uk/peel-reports/metropolitan-2021-22/

PEEL. (2021/22). Police effectiveness, efficiency and legitimacy – An inspection of Nottinghamshire Police. Accessed online. Available at: https://s3-eu-west-2.amazonaws.com/assets-hmicfrs.justiceinspectorates.gov.uk/uploads/peel-assessment-2021-22-nottinghamshire.pdf

PEEL. (2021/22). Police effectiveness, efficiency and legitimacy – An inspection of Humberside Police. Accessed online. Available at:https://hmicfrs.justiceinspectorates.gov.uk/peel-reports/humberside-2021-22/

PEEL. (2021/22). Police effectiveness, efficiency and legitimacy – An inspection of Merseyside Police. Accessed online. Available at:https://hmicfrs.justiceinspectorates.gov.uk/peel-reports/merseyside-2021-22/

Robinson, A., & Tilley, N. (2009). Factors influencing police performance in the investigation of volume crimes in England and Wales. *Police Practice and Research, 10*(3), 209–223. DOI: 10.1080/15614260802381091

Stelfox, P. (2009). Criminal Investigation: An Introduction to Principles and Practice (1st ed.). Willan. Accessed online. Available at: DOI: 10.4324/9781315880730

Tyler, T. R. (2006). Psychological perspectives on legitimacy and legitimation. *Annual Review of Psychology, 57*(1), 375-400. Accessed online. Available at: DOI: 10.1146/annurev.psych.57.102904.190038

Zhou, S., Li, M., Chen, S. et al. (2024) Work pressure, coping styles and occupational burnout among Chinese police officers: a meta-analytic review. BMC Psychol 12, 275. Accessed online. Available at: DOI: 10.1186/s40359-024-01779-6

Chapter 20
Reducing and Preventing Crime and Anti-social Behavior

Eric Halford
http://orcid.org/0000-0002-3913-1679
Rabdan Academy, UAE

ABSTRACT

Crime prevention is a fundamental principle of UK policing, embedded in the HMICFRS inspection framework. To achieve an "outstanding" rating, police services must demonstrate leadership in prioritising crime and anti-social behaviour (ASB) prevention at local, regional, and national levels. This chapter presents a strategic framework for achieving excellence through five key themes: prioritisation, preparation, understanding, response, and evaluation. Drawing on case studies of outstanding police services, it explores how proactive leadership, structured problem-solving, community engagement, and data-driven evaluation enhance effectiveness. By embedding crime prevention into strategic and operational priorities, police services can drive sustainable reductions in crime and ASB.

INTRODUCTION

Attributed to Sir Robert Peel, the Peelian Principles consist of nine guiding tenets that define the delivery of policing services. The first principle is crime prevention, which emphasises that the primary objective of policing is to prevent crime and disorder, rather than merely reacting to and punishing offenders (Lentz et al., 2007). Embracing this principle has meant that crime prevention has been a fundamental policing function that has been embedded in the ethos of police services in the

DOI: 10.4018/979-8-3373-2757-0.ch020

United Kingdom (UK) for nearly a century. Recognising the importance of this principle, His Majesty's Inspectorate of Constabulary and Fire & Rescue Services (HMICFRS) has placed crime prevention at the core of its inspection framework. A dedicated section in the inspection framework evaluates how UK police services work to prevent and deter crime, anti-social behaviour (ASB), and vulnerability (HMICFRS, 2023a). In this chapter, vulnerability is excluded, as it represents a more complex area of policing that is examined in detail elsewhere. Instead, the focus is on the key components required to deliver effective crime prevention and reduction, rather than the many well-established, proven, and documented tactical interventions.

In this context, HMICFRS stipulates that for a police service to be considered "good," it must demonstrate a clear understanding of and commitment to crime prevention. This includes identifying and prioritising threats facing its communities, protecting the public from crime and ASB, deploying effective tactics and interventions, and using evidence to continuously strengthen its approach. To achieve an outstanding grade, police services must go beyond these standards, distinguishing themselves at local, regional, and national levels through exemplary leadership in developing, sharing, and influencing crime prevention strategies (HMICFRS, 2023a). Achieving this level of excellence is no easy task. However, it can be accomplished by distilling this broad area of policing into five essential themes: understanding, prioritisation, preparation, response, and evaluation. In this chapter it is outlined how each of these themes can be strategically delivered and is supported with case studies of existing outstanding police services who have achieved this.

DEFINING KEY CONCEPTS AND EXISTING THEORIES

Before exploring the five core themes (understanding, prioritisation, preparation, response, and evaluation) it is important to distinguish between the related but conceptually distinct terms used by HMICFRS: crime prevention, crime reduction, anti-social behaviour (ASB), and intervention. It is also necessary to provide an overview of the existing criminological theories related to these areas so as to provide a grounding for what is to come.

Key Concepts

Crime prevention refers to proactive measures designed to stop crime before it occurs by addressing the underlying causes, situational opportunities, or social conditions that enable offending (Clarke, 2017). It is inherently anticipatory, encompassing both social prevention (targeting root causes) and situational prevention (reducing opportunities through design, surveillance, or guardianship). Crime reduction, by contrast, refers to strategies aimed at lowering the frequency or impact of offences that are already occurring. It typically involves operational or tactical approaches, such as hotspot policing, targeted enforcement, or rehabilitation initiatives. While prevention seeks to avert incidents from ever occurring, reduction seeks to diminish their volume, frequency, scale or severity.

Anti-Social Behaviour (ASB) occupies a distinct but related domain. Defined under the Anti-social Behaviour, Crime and Policing Act 2014, ASB involves conduct that causes harassment, alarm, or distress to individuals or communities. It often bridges the boundary between non-criminal nuisance and criminality, making it a central focus of community safety partnerships and local authority-led prevention initiatives. Finally, intervention encompasses the spectrum of actions taken by the police or partner agencies once a problem has been identified and includes law enforcement, diversion, support, or treatment. Such interventions may be preventive or corrective, but their defining feature is responsiveness to an identified pattern.

Theoretical Frameworks

Understanding crime and antisocial behaviour through multiple theoretical lenses allows for a more comprehensive and preventative approach to reduction. Over the past five decades. traditional enforcement-based responses have gradually evolved into strategies informed by criminological, sociological, and public health frameworks, each offering their own respective, and often complementary insights into why crime occurs and how it can be reduced. From a criminological standpoint, Clarke's (2017) Situational Crime Prevention (SCP) offers a foundational philosophy that proposes that crime can be reduced by manipulating immediate environmental factors to increase the effort and risk for offenders while reducing rewards and provocations. This approach underpins many environmental design initiatives such as Crime Prevention Through Environmental Design (CPTED) and modern problem-solving frameworks used by police partnerships.

Underpinning such problem-solving frameworks is the work of Goldstein, who in 1979 outlined his theory of Problem-Oriented Policing (POP), which helps operationalise the principles of SCP and CPTED by shifting focus from incidents to underlying causes. POP requires police services to analyse patterns, and contributing conditions, using systematic frameworks such as the SARA model (Scanning, Analysis, Response, Assessment). When effectively implemented, it can transform policing from reactive enforcement to proactive problem-solving rooted in analysis and evidence. Complementing these models, Hotspot Policing is now established as a primary response and multiple studies on its effectiveness (Braga et al, 2019). Hotspot policing works by addressing the principle that the concentration of crime occurs in small geographic areas and as such, strategic resource deployment to high-intensity "hotspots," combined with situational and problem-oriented measures, yields significant reductions in crime without widespread displacement (Braga et al, 2019).

Beyond criminology, sociological and public health perspectives view crime and ASB as socially produced phenomena influenced by deprivation, inequality, and community cohesion. The public health model of violence prevention, developed by the World Health Organisation (WHO, 2002) and later adopted by UK policing strategies such as the Violence Reduction Unit (VRU) model, conceptualises crime as preventable through early intervention, education, and partnership collaboration. This approach reframes offending as a symptom of social harm, best addressed through interagency coordination and by developing community resilience, rather than enforcement alone. Integrating each of these frameworks together can provide a highly robust foundation for modern police services to develop outstanding prevention and reduction capabilities.

ESSENTIAL COMPONENTS FOR CRIME AND ASB PREVENTION AND REDUCTION

As outlined earlier, outstanding police services have mastered the integration of five essential component themes that underpin all of their Crime and ASB Prevention and Reduction efforts: understanding, prioritisation, preparation, response, and evaluation.

Understanding

Naturally, understanding the issues at hand is the first stage. For police services to effectively prevent and reduce crime and ASB, it is essential that they understand how, where, and when problems exist or emerge. While this has been discussed in the broader context in other chapters, it is particularly critical for crime prevention and reduction. In this context, HMICFRS asserts that police services must have a comprehensive understanding of the threats facing communities and must proactively identify and assess these threats, including those that are hidden (HMICFRS, 2023a). Achieving such an informed position is not possible without systematically and continuously working in close collaboration with communities, partner organisations, and other stakeholders. Outstanding police services do this by embracing data-driven strategies that leverage structured engagement, two-way communication, and localised planning. This enables them to develop a deep understanding of community problems and threats which enables them to anticipate, prevent, and respond effectively to emerging crime and ASB issues, ensuring a proactive rather than reactive policing model.

This begins with a fundamental level of situational awareness and understanding that is established using multiple data streams. For example, Lancashire Constabulary utilises data from traditional and innovative sources, including Police and Communities Together (PACT) meetings, police surgeries, and informal engagement opportunities such as the innovative 'Coffee with a Cop' program, conducted in the heart of the local community (HMICFRS, 2024b). All of these serve as data sources to help the police service, and particularly their NHPTs, to better understand the needs of the communities they serve. The constabulary tracks this activity through an engagement planning tool, so they understand the frequency of such events, and recording the results ensures that the community insights gathered inform its crime prevention strategies (HMICFRS, 2024b).

Similarly, Humberside Police leverages data from multiple sources to enhance its understanding of community problems by including information from the 'Acorn dataset', which provides socioeconomic insights across the UK, and information from community safety partner organisations, such as homeless support services (HMICFRS, 2024a). As a result, the force has been successful in developing a highly detailed understanding of areas requiring problem solving initiatives, allowing it to target its policing interventions efforts more effectively.

However, information sharing must be a two-way process, ensuring that communities and partners have opportunities to contribute their insights as well as receive information. Many outstanding services use innovative systems to help foster this two-way engagement with the public, enabling them to both gather valuable intelligence on community concerns, and share updates and other information their communities and partners may find informative. For instance, Lancashire employs 'Lancashire Talking', a two-way communication system that uses surveys to understand public concerns (HMICFRS, 2024b). Humberside Police operates the 'My Community Alert' service, allowing them to share important news and information directly with people via their smartphones and other devices. Additionally, as seen in Lancashire, 'Humber Talking' is a further community survey example that also encourages residents to voice their concerns and priorities (HMICFRS, 2024a). Neighbourhood officers then update the public on the policing activities being undertaken to address these concerns. Importantly, Humber Talking also offers multilingual functionality, ensuring accessibility for diverse communities so that all community members feel informed, included and empowered in the problem-solving taking place. In Surrey, the police have implemented the Home Office 'Street Safe' tool, which allows the public to report locations where they feel unsafe. Officers analyse data from this tool to identify hotspots of concern and investigate underlying causes, helping to direct problem-solving resources more effectively.

Such engagement must also be frequent and systematic. To ensure this, outstanding services have structured processes for tracking and managing community engagement. For example, Humberside monitors the number of public meetings held and the extent of engagement with different community groups (HMICFRS, 2024a). Each area also has a local Independent Advisory Group (IAG), which is common among all services, but has been evolved to include themed subgroups to ensure that specific communities, such as young people, women and girls, and those impacted by the Israel–Palestine conflict, have a voice in shaping policing priorities (HMICFRS, 2024a).

It is also vital that understanding of local issues is retained at the BCU level, rather than being confined to strategic oversight, and delivered in a top-down approach. In Lancashire, this is achieved by ensuring all local Neighbourhood Policing Teams (NHPTs) operate under individual local engagement plans, managed by the local inspector, which details how officers and police community support officers (PCSOs) interact with residents and engage with communities (HMICFRS, 2024b). This ensures that engagement is structured, transparent, and locally driven. Likewise, Humberside has developed individual ward profiles to assess and identify the specific policing skills and personnel required at the local level (HMICFRS, 2024a). These profiles ensure that police resources are aligned with the needs of different communities, enhancing both effectiveness and public confidence.

Prioritisation

In the context of reducing and preventing crime and ASB, prioritisation does not carry the same broad connotations as it does in areas such as completion of the force management statements (FMS) or demand based strategic planning cycles. Instead, in this context, prioritisation is demonstrated at a far more conceptual level. Specifically, outstanding services must show that their entire leadership structure prioritises crime prevention, ensuring that it remains a key focus at every level of the force (HMICFRS, 2023a). The problem for leaders, therefore, is achieving this in practice.

From an organisational perspective, there are only a limited number of business areas where leadership can visibly demonstrate what they stand for. As outlined in Chapter 1, this begins with the vision and mission of the organisation. Therefore, any police service aiming to demonstrate a genuine commitment to reducing and preventing crime and ASB should explicitly embed these objectives within their vision and mission statements.

Since the majority of a police service's assets relate to its workforce, all human capital functions, including recruitment and selection, talent management, promotion, training, education, professional development, performance management, and reward and recognition, should also align with the goal of reducing and preventing crime and ASB. Each of these areas must demonstrate a considered and relevant focus on crime prevention.

However, as will be outlined in subsequent sections of this chapter, ensuring this alignment does not need to be overly complex or burdensome. For example, recruitment and selection criteria can incorporate requirements for candidates to demonstrate problem-solving capabilities. Similarly, lateral applications and promotion processes can be enhanced by including assessment criteria related to crime prevention and ASB reduction. This ensures that all employees seeking career progression or supervisory roles place an emphasis on this area. Additionally, reward and recognition programs play a vital role in reinforcing prioritisation, which is why many outstanding police services have introduced Problem-Oriented Policing (POP) awards, which recognise officers and staff who excel in crime prevention. Implementing such formal reward structures provides a clear signal that reducing and preventing crime and ASB is a core organisational priority.

Furthermore, training, education, and professional development can all be strategically aligned with crime prevention by delivering specialist training, individual mentoring and tuition, providing dedicated support, or developing advocates within teams, departments, and Borough Command Units (BCUs). As the coming sections will demonstrate, the examination of police services graded as outstanding in this area reveals a common theme: they have achieved excellence by executing the fundamentals exceptionally well. As a result, these services have positioned themselves at the forefront regionally and nationally in developing, sharing, and influencing best practices for reducing and preventing crime and ASB, which is a key HMICFRS requirement in this domain.

Preparation

As indicated, preparing to effectively reduce and prevent crime and ASB should be a strategic focus of any outstanding police service. If it is not, they risk becoming or remaining a reactive service, only capable of responding to emerging problems rather than preventing them. To ensure they are adequately prepared, a mature, well-established, and safeguarded network of NHPTs is essential. These units should be primarily responsible for proactive, problem-solving, and community-based prevention activities. Although this may seem obvious, history has shown that some forces, such as Avon and Somerset Constabulary, have previously lost sight of this principle in their efforts to manage surges in demand. This has often led to the diversion of NHPT resources into response policing (HMICFRS, 2023b), ultimately resulting in a decline in their performance in crime prevention.

While occasional redeployment may be unavoidable, particularly in response to major incidents, the habitual reliance on NHPTs to bolster frontline resourcing risks undermining long-term efforts to prevent and reduce crime and ASB. This, in turn, allows problems to emerge, persist, or escalate, potentially generating even greater demand and creating a self-perpetuating cycle of reactionary policing. To avoid this pitfall, outstanding police services place strong emphasis on protecting NHPTs operationally, ensuring they remain focused on prevention activities except in exceptional circumstances. Notable examples of this approach can be found in Surrey and Humberside, where both forces have been commended for introducing policies that restrict the diversion of NHPTs to emergency incidents. In Humberside, NHPT officers can only be reassigned when there is an immediate threat to life (HMICFRS, 2024a).

Beyond the specific roles of NHPT officers, outstanding services prepare their entire workforce for problem-solving, recognising that opportunities to prevent and reduce crime and ASB can arise at any time, in any department. To facilitate this, they equip a wide range of employees with the necessary knowledge and skills to engage in problem-solving. For example, Lancashire Constabulary has implemented advanced problem-solving courses and accredited crime prevention training for officers, ensuring a deeply ingrained and high-level understanding of both College of Policing recommendations, and best practices for engaging communities to identify and address local issues (HMICFRS, 2024b).

In services graded as outstanding, the culture of prevention evidently permeates all corners of policing, even Criminal Investigation Departments (CID). A leading example of this can be found in South Yorkshire, where the force has made significant efforts to embed a problem-solving culture throughout the organisation (HMICFRS, 2023c). This was achieved by training approximately 2,000 employees, including officers, staff, and partner agencies, in problem-solving techniques. This level of investment in transformative capability building, not only served as an act of knowledge exchange but as a tool for cultural change, and as a demonstration of leadership and commitment to prevention, both of which are key to achieving an outstanding rating. As a result of such investment, services can expect to see sustained improvements in service delivery, and measurable reductions in crime and ASB through well-designed, medium- and long-term prevention strategies.

In addition to training, outstanding services implement structural solutions to enhance their capacity to prevent and reduce crime and ASB. In Leicestershire, for example, response officers, local intelligence officers, and detectives have all been co-located in local police stations alongside NHPTs (HMICFRS, 2022a). This approach has reportedly increased shared responsibility for problem-solving, thereby improving the force's overall capacity and capability in tackling local issues (HMICFRS, 2022a).

Other services have embedded technology-driven systems and processes to support their crime prevention efforts. One of the most notable developments in the 2025 inspection cycle is the system used by Lancashire Constabulary, where they have successfully implemented a two-tier Problem-Oriented Policing (POP) system. This system provides employees with a database to input, document, and manage their POP plans for medium- and long-term crime prevention strategies while also supporting "POP-lite" for short-term interventions (HMICFRS, 2024b). Similarly, in Leicestershire, the force has implemented a Problem Management Plan (PMP) process to enhance the focus on problem-solving (HMICFRS, 2022a). Reports indicate that the widespread adoption of PMP has improved the identification of root causes, generated more targeted action, and ultimately led to better crime and disorder prevention outcomes. Surrey, on the other hand, has customised the well-established SARA (Scanning, Analysis, Response, and Assessment) model, introducing its own variation known as OSARA (Objective, Scanning, Analysis, Review, and Assess) to underpin their prevention initiatives.

Beyond structural, technological and process changes, Humberside and Lancashire have further encouraged problem-solving through reward and recognition programs, including annual local and force-wide POP awards. These initiatives reinforce the value of proactive crime prevention within the organisation, significantly motivating employees to adopt innovative and evidence-based approaches to policing prevention. Regardless of the approach used, these examples demonstrate that outstanding services have taken extensive preparatory steps to develop well-established and mature frameworks and cultures capable of reducing and preventing crime and ASB within their communities.

Responding

Understanding and preparing to respond to crime and ASB problems are only the first steps for police services; they must also effectively implement interventions to address them. To be graded as outstanding, a service must demonstrate that it proactively tackles crime and ASB through both local and cross-organisational activities, employing appropriate tactics and interventions (HMICFRS, 2023a). This chapter does not aim to detail every type of intervention but instead highlights exemplary practices that have been successfully implemented. In this regard, as the theoretical foundations of effective crime reduction and prevention strategies are well established, to begin with, many police services could make significant progress simply by firmly embedding existing tactical philosophies in the psyche of their staff. For example, the 'What Works Centre for Crime Reduction', a collaboration between the

College of Policing and University College London, provides police services with the resources and tools necessary to select the most effective interventions (College of Policing, 2025). The resources, available online and open source, include the Crime Reduction Toolkit to help select an appropriate intervention, access to early research on crime prevention via the Research Map, operational policing guidance on translating evidence into practice, a 'Practice Bank' showcasing successful crime reduction initiatives, and practical tools for evaluating policing projects, interventions, and tactics (College of Policing, 2025).

While such resources may not provide solutions to every crime or ASB issue, they offer a wealth of knowledge that can prevent police services from reinventing the wheel. Given that policing often has a short institutional memory, embedding these resources within a service's culture and operational decision-making significantly improves the likelihood of successful crime and ASB reduction efforts. These efforts are most effective when they are targeted at community needs and coordinated with other agencies to maximise impact.

Strong examples of services these tools have been embraced include Lancashire and Leicestershire Constabulary, and Humberside Police, each graded outstanding in this area. For example, in Lancashire they have taken a partnership-based approach to implementing traditional hotspot policing to reduce ASB's impact on communities. Their method includes the use of youth referrals and civil orders, alongside efforts to identify and support vulnerable individuals who are either committing ASB or being affected by it. Following its success, the same approach has been expanded to address shoplifting hotspots.

Humberside Police has also demonstrated an innovative crime prevention approach by adopting the Clear, Hold, Build (CHB) framework. CHB is a multi-agency strategy traditionally used to combat organised crime, integrating police, statutory partners, and local communities into a cohesive and sustainable approach to long-term problem-solving. The framework consists of three distinct phases: the Clear phase, where police disrupt and dismantle the groups responsible for community harm; the Hold phase, which stabilises the area to prevent exploitation by other offenders; and the Build phase, where local communities are empowered to address root causes and create lasting resilience. While CHB has been primarily used to combat serious organised crime, the Home Office evaluation indicates it is also effective in tackling broader issues, including high crime rates, ASB, and social deprivation. In Humberside for example, they effectively applied CHB to locations experiencing heightened levels of harm and developed a systematic, long-term program to enhance community safety. This example highlights how data-driven, partnership-based approaches focus on key drivers of harm, particularly offenders and locations, while utilising evidence-based situational crime prevention tactics, enable services to pinpoint priority areas, target offenders, and not only solve immediate problems but create long-term improvements in community safety.

A similar holistic approach to crime and ASB reduction has been adopted by Leicestershire Police, which has partnered with charitable and statutory organisations to shift from a traditional policing model to a public health approach. This model ensures that all agencies, including police, work together on shared priorities. The World Health Organisation endorses this approach to tackle community problems by identifying common risk factors and strengthening protective factors to prevent crime from occurring in the first place.

In addition to innovative operational interventions, these outstanding services also make full use of the available legal powers, both criminal and civil, to prevent and reduce crime and ASB. For example, Humberside Police has developed a civil enforcement system that applies to a traffic light model to determine the appropriate response to repeat offenders. This system categorises offenders into green, amber, or red tiers based on their level of risk and helps officers decide the most appropriate and effective interventions. By providing multiple opportunities for rehabilitation, including referrals to partner agencies for individuals with underlying causal issues such as addiction, the model ensures that enforcement efforts are both effective and proportionate.

Lancashire Constabulary has taken a different approach by establishing a dedicated centralised civil powers team to provide guidance and support to officers applying for civil orders. Each Borough Command Unit (BCU) also has a dedicated civil orders intelligence officer who plays a crucial role in identifying breaches of orders in real time, maximising the use of protection orders such as Domestic Violence Protection Notices (DVPNs), Domestic Violence Protection Orders (DVPOs), Sexual Harm Prevention Orders (SHPOs), Sexual Risk Orders (SROs), and injunctions, by ensuring frontline officers are supported in obtaining orders that prevent reoffending. This approach enhances the volume and effectiveness of civil intervention applications by ensuring officers have specialist expertise to help them navigate legal complexities of obtaining them.

To further strengthen their responses, outstanding services also leverage the capacity of volunteers, such as special constables, cadets, and volunteer groups, to supplement intervention efforts. This approach has been successfully implemented in Lancashire and Leicestershire, where volunteer mobilisation has helped to expand police capacity in specific areas. In Leicestershire, the force also collaborates with local universities to enhance problem solving by hosting a quarterly multi-agency 'What Works' meeting to provide a platform to record and promote the effectiveness of joint working initiatives, ensuring that police, partners, and community groups generate and share successful practices and apply evidence-based learning to crime and ASB reduction efforts.

Evaluating

The ninth and final Peelian principle states that the true test of policing is the absence of crime and disorder, rather than the visible enforcement activities carried out by officers (Lentz et al., 2007). In this context, for a police service to be graded as outstanding in its efforts to reduce and prevent crime and ASB, it must not only demonstrate that interventions have been implemented but also provide evidence that they have been effective, most notably, through reductions in both.

To achieve this, police services must incorporate objective evaluations into their response interventions, ensuring that their efforts create meaningful impact and, more importantly, that this impact aligns with their vision and mission, and needs of the community (HMICFRS, 2023a). To achieve this HMICFRS requires evaluations to be embedded as a core element of all interventions, rather than being reserved for major initiatives (HMICFRS, 2023a). Evaluations must also be continuous to ensure that the effects of interventions are long-lasting and not merely short-term successes. A longer-term analysis also helps police services identify and mitigate unintended consequences, whether negative or positive, allowing them to refine their approaches accordingly.

Ensuring that interventions are rigorously evaluated does not require complex new processes. Modern police services already have access to a wealth of data that can be used to assess effectiveness by measuring reductions in crime and ASB. Performance analysts are highly trained in statistical techniques, making the task of accessing data, analysing trends, and presenting findings relatively straightforward. However, the biggest challenge is often not the ability to conduct evaluations but rather the failure to prioritise them. Some services treat evaluation as an afterthought, while others lack objectivity and fall into the trap of being 'doomed to succeed', a term used to describe the practice of reporting interventions as successful, regardless of their actual impact.

This phenomenon is common in policing, where the sheer volume of data available often allows forces to cherry-pick variables that appear to tell a positive story. However, modern HMICFRS inspections no longer rely on leader-delivered presentations featuring carefully selected data. The inspectorate now has full access to internal police data and can request additional information at any time. They also cross-reference open-source datasets, such as the Crime Survey for England and Wales, which not only measure crime and ASB levels but also assess public confidence. As a result, attempting to manipulate performance data to demonstrate artificial success is unlikely to be effective, not to mention questionable.

As such, it is important services prioritise evaluations, and a truly robust process must begin with the establishment of clear success metrics at the outset of any intervention. These may naturally include crime and ASB rates, response times, victim satisfaction scores, or public confidence levels. In Humberside, for example, increases in public confidence within intervention areas were used as a key success metric in evaluating their Clear, Hold, Build (CHB) programme (HMICFRS, 2024a), and demonstrated significant improvements.

It is a well-recognised truism that 'not everything that can be counted counts, and not everything that counts can be counted.' Outstanding services recognise this and take care to ensure that their metrics are evidence-based, clearly defined, and effectively measured. To ensure this, evaluations should also consider hidden metrics, those that may not be immediately obvious or readily available to police services. These could include data held by partner agencies, insights gained from qualitative research, or findings from focus groups and interviews. .

Outstanding evaluations also incorporate pre- and post-intervention comparisons. Where baseline data is not easily available, services must make efforts to source it prior to implementation to ensure meaningful comparisons can subsequently be made. Without this, it is difficult to attribute reductions in crime and ASB to the intervention itself, rather than external factors such as changes in weather patterns, which are known to influence crime trends. Ideally, when safe and feasible, evaluations should include randomised control trials, which make efforts to account for and eliminate all contributory factors and are the so called 'gold standard' of intervention evaluation (Campbell et al., 2000). However, for a variety of reasons, these are not always possible to achieve in the policing context, as such, simple comparisons with areas that did not receive the intervention can be used to further strengthen the findings (Scantlebury et al., 2017). This is best achieved when an initiative is first piloted in a test location before being rolled out force wide. However, when an intervention is introduced simultaneously across an entire organisation, such comparisons become more difficult.

To enhance objectivity, the best police services engage external partners, particularly higher education institutions, to support their evaluation capacity and capability. In Leicestershire, for instance, academic evaluations are regularly used as a standard approach to assessing policing interventions (HMICFRS, 2022a). Some forces have gone a step further by establishing strategic research partnerships. A notable example is the N8 Policing Research Partnership, which brings together eight research-intensive universities and eleven police forces across Northern England to promote evidence-based policing and ensure that interventions undergo rigorous academic scrutiny (May et al., 2020). Similarly, the Centre for Policing Research and Learning at The Open University provides an avenue for academic collaboration on evaluation and analysis (The Open University, 2023). Other services leverage internal expertise by encouraging officers and staff to conduct evidence-based policing projects as part of postgraduate studies. Many forces support officers undertaking master's and PhD dissertations focused on evaluating police interventions. Regardless of the approach, outstanding police services excel at tapping into the evaluation resources available to them to ensure that their interventions are measured, assessed, and continuously improved (Huey and Mitchell, 2016).

Fundamentally, a data-driven and evidence-based approach to evaluation ensures that police services do not simply implement interventions for the sake of acting without due consideration for their effects, but instead focus on delivering genuine, long-term reductions in crime and ASB. By embedding evaluation as a core component of policing practice, outstanding services demonstrate transparency, accountability, enhance public trust, and practically refine their approaches based on what works—a fundamental principle of modern, professional policing.

BARRIERS TO CRIME AND ASB PREVENTION AND REDUCTION

While the model for achieving the strategic benefits of prevention and partnership approaches can be established, its practical implementation often encounters significant systemic, operational, and cultural obstacles. As such, it is important that police services understand and acknowledge these to maximise their chance of success. At the systemic level, fluctuating political priorities and funding constraints can undermine long-term prevention efforts. Short-term performance targets frequently prioritise enforcement outputs over preventive outcomes, creating a disincentive for innovation and collaboration. Financial pressures, particularly under austerity conditions, limit the ability of police services and partner agencies to sustain proactive programmes or invest in analytical and community-focused capacities.

At the operational level, partnership work is resource-intensive and requires dedicated resources and sustained coordination across agencies, often with differing mandates, data systems, and performance cultures. Information-sharing also remains a persistent challenge, and is constrained by privacy legislation, and incompatible IT infrastructures. These issues reduce efficiency and can lead to duplication or fragmented delivery of services. At the cultural level, mistrust between partners and a deep-rooted emphasis on reactive enforcement within policing can inhibit the shift toward prevention and early intervention. Many officers continue to perceive proactive or community-based initiatives as secondary to 'core policing,', or a role for other agencies, reflecting the enduring 'crime-fighting' identity that undervalues problem-solving.

In addition, as policing becomes increasingly reliant on technology, such as artificial intelligence, data analytics, and predictive algorithms, new ethical and operational dilemmas arise. Although this book advocates for a data-driven policing, which in this context offers significant potential for improving efficiency and effectiveness by targeting high-risk locations, repeat offenders, or vulnerable victims, it also risks reinforcing existing inequalities if not carefully governed. Concerns include algorithmic bias, over-policing of marginalised communities, and the erosion of privacy through pervasive surveillance. Studies in this area caution that predictive systems trained on historical data can replicate structural biases, perpetuating disproportionate scrutiny of specific demographics or areas (Ferguson, 2017; Oswald et al, 2018).

Overcoming these barriers requires not only structural reform but also cultural realignment, embedding prevention and partnership as measures of success in their own right. In addition, ethically sound data-driven policing requires transparency, accountability, and human oversight, underpinned by ethical impact assessments, independent audits, and public engagement within technological adoption processes ensures legitimacy and public confidence (Halford, 2025). Achieving this transformation demands sustained leadership commitment, transparent cross-agency governance, and workforce development that equips practitioners to operate confidently within collaborative, problem-solving frameworks.

CONCLUSION

This chapter has explored the essential components of an outstanding approach to reducing and preventing crime and ASB, drawing on five core themes of prioritisation, preparation, understanding, response, and evaluation. We suggest that these elements provide a strategic framework for police services aiming to move beyond reactive enforcement towards proactive, evidence-based crime prevention. At the heart of this model lies strong leadership, ensuring that crime prevention is embedded across all levels of the service. Outstanding services achieve this by prioritising prevention through clear strategic vision, structured human resource policies, and dedicated reward and recognition mechanisms that reinforce problem-solving. Their preparation includes the development of robust Neighbourhood Policing Teams (NHPTs), investments in training and technology, and the creation of collaborative problem-solving cultures that extend across departments.

A fundamental requirement for success is deep situational awareness and understanding of crime and ASB issues within communities. Outstanding police services systematically gather, analyse, and share information using data-driven engagement and innovative community feedback mechanisms. They embrace structured problem-solving approaches, leveraging models such as hotspot policing, Clear, Hold, Build (CHB), and public health approaches, which integrate partnerships, enforcement, and community empowerment to create long-term safety improvements.

Crucially, the effectiveness of these interventions is not measured by demonstrable impact, with evaluation a cornerstone of outstanding initiatives. By embedding evaluation as a continuous, systematic process, police services can identify successful interventions, mitigate unintended consequences, and engage in transparent, evidence-based assessments, often in partnership with academic institutions and external evaluators. Ultimately, the police services that stand out in this area are those that excel at doing the fundamentals exceptionally well. They ensure that crime prevention is not an afterthought, but a core operational priority, shaping decision-making at every level.

REFERENCES

Braga, A. A., Turchan, B. S., Papachristos, A. V., & Hureau, D. M. (2019). Hot spots policing and crime reduction: An update of an ongoing systematic review and meta-analysis. *Journal of Experimental Criminology*, *15*(3), 289–311.

Campbell, M., Fitzpatrick, R., Haines, A., Kinmonth, A. L., Sandercock, P., Spiegelhalter, D., & Tyrer, P. (2000). Framework for design and evaluation of complex interventions to improve health. *BMJ (Clinical Research Ed.)*, *321*(7262), 694–696. PMID: 10987780

Clarke, R. V. (2017). "Situational" crime prevention: Theory and practice. In *Crime Opportunity Theories* (pp. 471-482). Routledge.

College of Policing. (2025). *What Works Centre for Crime Reduction*. Retrieved from https://www.college.police.uk/research/what-works-centre-crime-reduction

Ferguson, A. G. (2017). The rise of big data policing: Surveillance, race, and the future of law enforcement. In *The rise of big data policing*. New York University Press.

Goldstein, H. (1979). Improving policing: A problem-oriented approach. *Crime and Delinquency*, *25*(2), 236–258.

Halford, E. (2025). The Transformer Led Policing model: A framework for applying generative artificial intelligence in policing. *Policing. Journal of Policy Practice*, *19*, paaf027.

His Majesty's Inspectorate of Constabulary and Fire & Rescue Services. (2022a). *Leicestershire PEEL Assessments 2021/2022*. Retrieved from https://hmicfrs.justiceinspectorates.gov.uk/peel-reports/leicestershire-2021-22/

His Majesty's Inspectorate of Constabulary and Fire & Rescue Services. (2022b). *Surrey PEEL Assessments 2021/2022*. Retrieved from https://hmicfrs.justiceinspectorates.gov.uk/peel-reports/surrey-2021-22/

His Majesty's Inspectorate of Constabulary and Fire & Rescue Services. (2023a). *PEEL Assessment Framework (PAF) 2023–2025*. Retrieved from https://hmicfrs.justiceinspectorates.gov.uk/publication-html/peel-assessment-framework-2023-25/

His Majesty's Inspectorate of Constabulary and Fire & Rescue Services. (2023b). *PEEL 2021/22 Police effectiveness, efficiency and legitimacy: An inspection of Avon and Somerset Constabulary*. Retrieved from https://hmicfrs.justiceinspectorates.gov.uk/peel-reports/avon-and-somerset-2021-22/

His Majesty's Inspectorate of Constabulary and Fire & Rescue Services. (2023c). *PEEL 2021/22 Police effectiveness, efficiency and legitimacy: An inspection of South Yorkshire Police*. Retrieved from https://hmicfrs.justiceinspectorates.gov.uk/peel-reports/south-yorkshire-2021-22/

His Majesty's Inspectorate of Constabulary and Fire & Rescue Services. (2024a). *Humberside PEEL Assessment 2023–2025*. Retrieved from https://hmicfrs.justiceinspectorates.gov.uk/peel-reports/lancashire-2023-25/

His Majesty's Inspectorate of Constabulary and Fire & Rescue Services. (2024b). *Lancashire PEEL Assessment 2023–2025*. Retrieved from https://hmicfrs.justiceinspectorates.gov.uk/peel-reports/lancashire-2023-25/

Huey, L., & Mitchell, R. J. (2016). Unearthing hidden keys: Why pracademics are an invaluable (if underutilized) resource in policing research. *Policing. Journal of Policy Practice*, *10*(3), 300–307.

Lentz, S. A., & Chaires, R. H. (2007). The invention of Peel's principles: A study of policing "textbook" history. *Journal of Criminal Justice*, *35*(1), 69–79. DOI: 10.1016/j.jcrimjus.2006.11.016

May, T., Sen, R., & Hough, M. (2020, May). *The N8 Policing Research Partnership: Examining the first four years*. ICPR.

Oswald, M., Grace, J., Urwin, S., & Barnes, G. C. (2018). Algorithmic risk assessment policing models: Lessons from the Durham HART model and 'Experimental' proportionality. *Information & Communications Technology Law*, *27*(2), 223–250.

Scantlebury, A., McDaid, C., Booth, A., Fairhurst, C., Parker, A., Payne, R., & Hewitt, C. (2017). Undertaking a randomised controlled trial in the police setting: Methodological and practical challenges. *Trials*, *18*, 1–7. PMID: 29273077

The Open University. (2023). *Centre for Policing Research and Learning Annual Report 2023*. Retrieved from https://university.open.ac.uk/centres/policing/sites/www.open.ac.uk.centres.policing/files/files/CPRL_AnnualReport2023_DIGITAL.pdf

World Health Organization. (2002). [*reducing risks, promoting healthy life*. World Health Organization.]. *World Health Report*, •••, 2002.

Chapter 21
Effectively Managing Offenders and Suspects:
An Analysis of Effective Current Practice

Christopher Thomas Scott
http://orcid.org/0009-0001-3176-6565
Brunel University of London, UK

ABSTRACT

This chapter examines how UK police forces manage offenders and suspects, based on findings from the 2022–2025 HMICFRS PEEL inspection reports. No force achieved an "Outstanding" grade in this area, despite high public concern over violent and sexual crime. Focusing on seven forces rated "Good," the chapter identifies five shared strengths: use of technology, consistent risk assessment, proactive enforcement, resource management, and application of ancillary orders. It explores emerging tools such as AI, polygraph testing, and digital monitoring, alongside new operational models like peer-reviewed casework and dynamic arrest teams. Structural and demographic factors—such as being smaller, rural, and more affluent—may also contribute to success. A composite model of best practice is proposed to help raise national standards.

INTRODUCTION

As of 2025, one striking feature of the current PEEL inspection reports is the absence of any police force receiving an "Outstanding" grade in Managing Offenders and Suspects. Given the high level of public concern and scrutiny around violent and sexual offending (Police Foundation, 2023), this area might be expected to be a

DOI: 10.4018/979-8-3373-2757-0.ch021

primary focus for police forces. The inspections during this period clearly concentrate on the management of individuals who pose the greatest risk to public safety. Even a brief review of recent inspections reveals a national shortfall in exemplary practice within this crucial area.

While the definition of this inspectorate review area is somewhat open to interpretation, it appears from the inspections carried out that the Inspectorate's focus is heavily weighted towards the management of serious and violent offenders (MoSOVO), offenders and suspects linked to domestic abuse, and perpetrators of violent crime related to gang activity. Indeed, 74% of Areas for Improvement (AFI) under "Managing suspects and offenders" are directly linked to serious/violent offender frameworks including (MOSOVO) and Organised Crime and Acquisitive and Illicit Trade (OCAIT) (NPCC / HMICFRS, 2024).

There are, however, seven forces that achieved a rating of "Good." This indicates evidence of practice which, if considered collectively, might amount to an outstanding service. With that in mind, this chapter will assess by thematic analysis those forces who achieved a "Good" rating identifying what these forces are doing right and identify areas of compatibility among their processes to suggest ways in which all forces can elevate their performance in managing those posing the greatest risk to the public.

The seven forces exhibiting the best practice in the 2023–2025 PEEL reports, released up to the commencement of writing this chapter in January 2025, are as follows:

- *Wiltshire*
- *Cumbria*
- *North Yorkshire*
- *Leicestershire*
- *Surrey*
- *Humberside*
- *Lancashire*

A thematic review identified the following areas of effective practice present in all of the seven:

1. The Use of Technology
2. Effective and Consistent Risk Assessment
3. Proactive Criminal Enforcement Operations
4. The Management of Resources
5. Maximising the Use of Ancillary Orders

It is notable that none of the forces included are "Metropolitan". Wiltshire, the smallest police force in the United Kingdom by officer establishment, features among them. Each of these seven forces has a substantial rural component, with four (57%) located in the North of England and only Surrey positioned within commuting distance of London. This geographical spread reflects a blend of rural, semi-rural and small urban policing environments. Socio-economically, these forces operate in areas that are generally more affluent relative to their respective regions. While all seven fall within the national average range for disposable household income, Surrey, Wiltshire and North Yorkshire are considered above average or affluent (ONS, 2021). Such socio-economic conditions are typically associated with lower levels of acquisitive and volume crime, potentially affording these forces greater capacity to focus on proactive, neighbourhood, and safeguarding work.

As illustrated in Table 1, all seven forces rated "Good" demonstrate a higher proportion of residents living in rural communities than the national average (Department for Environment, Food and Rural Affairs [Defra], 2024). The national employment rate for adults aged 16–64 was 75.2 per cent between May and July 2025 (Office for National Statistics, 2025), with only Leicestershire and Humberside falling marginally below this figure. The remaining five forces can be characterised as enjoying higher employment and, by extension, relative social stability. Cumbria stands out as the most rural of the seven and maintains the most favourable officer-to-population ratio, at 275 officers per 100,000 residents. This combination of strong community context and higher police visibility may help explain its positive inspection outcomes and capacity to sustain performance across dispersed geographic areas.

Table 1. Police Force Size, Population and Employment Context across Selected English Counties (2020–2025)

Police Area	Force size (officers, FTE)	Population (approx.)	Employment rate (16–64)	% living in rural areas (approx.)
Wiltshire	1,240	751,500	80.4%	~38%
Cumbria	1,383	502,900	~80%	~55%
North Yorkshire	1,681	828,100	~79%	~45%
Leicestershire	2,248	1,135,400	~75%	~28%
Surrey	2,312	1,216,800	~80%	~20%
Humberside	2,330	943,300	~74%	~33%
Lancashire	3,578	1,548,900	~79%	~21%
England	**147,430**	**56,489,800**	**75.2%**	**~17%**

Sources: Home Office (2024); House of Commons Library (2024); Office for National Statistics (ONS) (2023); ONS/Nomis (2024); Department for Environment, Food and Rural Affairs (Defra) and ONS (2023).

THE USE OF TECHNOLOGY

Online Child Sexual Abuse remains a policing priority and with the highest level of recidivism of any sexual offence the deployment of AI tools could help disrupt and deter a significant and dangerous offending group (Wakeling et al, 2019).

The meteoric rate at which Artificial Intelligence (AI), specifically Generative AI represents an opportunity for police forces to enhance efficiency and accuracy. When considering the management of sexual and violent offenders its potential uses are perhaps most attractive. However, Halford's (2025) observations that the assessment of risk by Generative AI may return an accurate risk rating in only 62% of cases suggests that this option for the management of those posing the most significant risk is not currently viable.

The examination of digital devices during visits to registered sex offenders' residences constitutes a central component of intelligence collection, safeguarding and dynamic risk assessment. Frontline triage solutions such as Magnet AXIOM Examine (Scout), Cellebrite Frontline and MSAB XRY/XAMN are increasingly deployed by police forces to expedite on-scene assessment and to prioritise subsequent forensic processing. Cloud-enabled triage workflows can produce faster and more comprehensive initial assessments, improving investigators' ability to identify immediate risks and allocate safeguarding resources effectively (McManus and Halford, 2023).

In Leicestershire, the introduction of digital Indecent Images of Children (IIOC) triage software that categorises and grades imagery supports more rapid identification of offending and reduces the volume of material that officers must view. This both accelerates investigative and prosecutorial processes for offenders who reoffend and mitigates officers' exposure to distressing content, with attendant benefits for staff wellbeing and resilience (HMICFRS, 2024d).

The deployment of remote monitoring platforms, exemplified by Surrey Police's investment in 300 eSafe licences, enables continuous, targeted oversight of high-risk individuals' personal electronic devices (HMICFRS, 2023a). When integrated with welfare-centred practice, such capabilities permit timely interventions that prioritise victim safety and offender engagement with support services, while ensuring intrusive scrutiny is proportionate, governed and focused on reducing harm.

AI appears to be an area untouched by even the better performing forces in this area. Whilst nationally there are examples of forces using AI in limited measure (Christie, 2021) it has not yet become embedded practice or yielding a meaningful benefit. The use of this technology is not without controversy but represents the chance to increase both efficiency and effectiveness if properly and safely harnessed.

Amongst the seven forces achieving a Good rating only Cumbria (HMICFRS, 2024a) and North Yorkshires Constabulary's (HMICFRS, 2024d) inspection reports make mention of the effective use of Polygraph testing, (commonly referred to as lie detector tests). This is an instrument-assisted interrogation method that records physiological responses during a structured question sequence and uses deviations from control responses to infer deception, in this case for offender supervision rather than as proof of guilt (National Research Council, 2003). The fact that polygraph is not reliable enough to be considered evidential in criminal proceedings remains a limitation. Polygraphs have however been used there to assist in the assessment of the risk of registered sex offenders. Nationally, forces have been able to overcome initial reluctance from the courts (Northumbria University Law School (2025) and in Cumbria inspectors found that the product returned by polygraph testing not only better informs the forces risk assessment of sex offenders but allows for Sexual Harm Prevention Order (SHPO) applications and variations to carry additional weight (HMICFRS, 2024a) giving extra powers to their police offender managers. This too, within the evidentiary limitations of the polygraph as a tool provides intelligence that allows resources to be deployed to areas of greater risk. Whilst this testing is still outsourced in many areas including Cumbria. Multi Agency Public Protection Arrangements (MAPPA) and effective partnership working with HMPPS who have their own polygraph capacity means that increasingly forces are able to access polygraph testing more readily and at lower cost.

Wiltshire Police's approach to risk assessment and offender management, as reflected in recent HMICFRS PEEL findings, demonstrates an evolving emphasis on collaboration, flexibility, and early intervention. Rather than maintaining discrete technological and analytical resources within individual departments, the force adopts a shared-systems model (HMICFRS, 2024f), enabling data integration and organisational agility. This model is mirrored in workforce deployment, where officers and staff receive broad-based training that facilitates transition between specialist roles most notably between the Management of Sexual or Violent Offenders (MOSOVO) team and the Child Internet Exploitation Team. Such an approach enhances operational resilience and promotes a shared understanding of offender risk across investigative functions; however, it also introduces potential vulnerabilities, particularly in the preservation of specialist expertise and the continuity of complex risk management processes.

The same ideas underpin Wiltshire's proactive management of online offending. The constabulary has adopted a strategy that prioritises early arrest and rapid safeguarding actions, viewing these as integral components of risk reduction rather than mere precursors to prosecution. While this approach reflects a progressive alignment with harm-reduction principles, it also presents a tension between immediate safeguarding outcomes and the procedural justice. HMICFRS's report (2024f) highlights this balance as a critical aspect of effective offender management acknowledging that risk-focused intervention can reduce harm but must be supported by consistent review and a robust evidential framework to ensure long-term legitimacy.

The Violent and Sexual Offender Register (ViSOR) computer system satisfies a statutory requirement for the police to maintain records documenting the status of violent and sexual offenders living in the community (HM Prison and Probation Service, 2021). Its use nationally is inconsistent in terms of data quality despite both national and regional user groups being established to facilitate consistency and share best practice (McCartan and Kemshall, 2015). In Leicestershire HMICFRS Inspectors found that the system was used in a way consistent with best practice and because home visits were documented and reports uploaded on to the system in a timely way. The data held was suitably accurate for other users to react to any event or change in risk more effectively and more efficiently (HMICFRS, 2024d). Whilst this finding reinforces the effectiveness of several policies at play regarding the handling of data and the use of ViSOR (National Police Chiefs' Council, 2010) it is also worthy of note that this practice is simply the adherence to expected standards and does not amount to innovation.

EFFECTIVE AND CONSISTENT RISK ASSESSMENT

For Registered Sex Offenders managed in the community, the Active Risk Management System (ARMS) has been the approved dynamic assessment model for police forces since 2016. While the underpinning risk factors demonstrate reasonable validity and reliability (Kewley, 2017; Kewley et al, 2019; McNaughton Nicholls and Webster, 2014; Mann and Lundrigan, 2021), inspection findings indicate that its application remains inconsistent. Issues with the completion of recorded information, quality assurance and the accurate coding of risk indicators undermine the reliability of overall risk gradings. Despite standardised training provided by the College of Policing, there remains variation between forces and regions in how ARMS is applied and interpreted.

HMICFRS has previously observed that the joint use of ARMS by police and probation services has not always promoted cohesive offender management. Differing professional priorities and differing thresholds for risk have, at times, contributed to fragmented assessments and inconsistent recording practice (Mann & Lundrigan, 2021). As a result, while ARMS remains a credible and conceptually sound framework, its effectiveness is dependent on practitioner competence, robust supervision, and consistent local oversight. These findings suggest the need for renewed focus on data integrity and inter-agency alignment in risk assessment practice. In this context, it may be timely to reconsider the potential role of structured actuarial models such as Thornton's Risk Matrix 2000 (Thornton et al, 2003), which, while less sensitive to dynamic variables, offer greater consistency and mitigate the influence of human subjectivity in grading risk. The use of this tool is, of course, fraught with risk itself. The lack of dynamic factors can lead to a blindness to shifting risk irrespective of it is increasing or decreasing.

In relation to persons considered "wanted" or "outstanding" for all offences Lancashire Constabulary use a peer review system to ensure their records, case files, risk assessments and actions are defensible (HMICFRS, 2024c). This approach reduces the potential for subjective error including risk aversion but also has efficiency implications with an element of repetition or "double keying" likely. With finite resources this is an effective but perhaps less sustainable method. Meanwhile, Surrey police have used a risk assessment tool, of their own design for all outstanding suspects allowing them to prioritise high risk individuals for action and arrest. The force then uses dedicated arrest teams to locate and bring suspects into custody promptly (HMICFRS, 2023a). This is a clear example of how assessing the risk of those committing violent offences can minimise ongoing risk of harm to the public across a spectrum of offending categories. Whilst Surrey and Lancashire's approaches differ, they both appear effective indicating that there is scope for individual forces to identify what will work best for them with consideration to their own policing priorities and capacities.

PROACTIVE CRIMINAL ENFORCEMENT OPERATIONS

Proactive operations for the purposes of this section will mean intelligence-led, pre-emptive activities designed to identify, monitor, and disrupt individuals who pose a high risk of serious harm before offences are committed or can escalate.

Reductions in resource capacity, specifically staffing levels have seen a lesser capacity to conduct proactive operations targeting the most dangerous offenders. (Police Foundation, 2024). This is seen most acutely in gang related crime and domestic abuse whilst advances in technology have seen a rise charges for both sexual offences against the child and sexual offences against women over the age of 16. The cost of running covert surveillance teams and associated parallel investigative strategies has led to a decrease in their use in recent years (Le Core, 2024). This may have had a significant impact on the targeting management of the most serious of offenders, particularly violent and sexual offenders.

Humberside Police hold the second highest arrest rate of any of the 42 home office forces (HMICFRS, 2024b). This is achieved through a strong governance structure. Daily meetings are used to identify high risk individuals and crimes at a senior level with taskings then given locally for officers to action. HMICFRS found that in 33 of 34 cases they reviewed arrests were made in appropriate time. Where identification is an issue Humberside's Vision On portal has made it easier for police officers to made identifications. Just under 1 in 5 images uploaded to this system resulted in a positive identification. HMICFRS were impressed by this but there is no published data presently available to compare. IT may well be that this system provides a positive outcome as see in other forces rather than offering extra value.

When investigating online sexual offences Humberside uses a "Digi Dog" (HMICFRS, 2024b). This trained Canine animal can search and help to locate digital devices hidden by those who are looking to hide their offending from the police both pre- and post-conviction when under Multi-Agency Public Protection Arrangements (MAPPA) supervision. This offers an option for police to gather material pertinent to risk more easily and reducer the potential for indicators or risk or evidence of offending to be lost. In a question to the Mayor of London in 2019 it was disclosed that the Metropolitan Police had deployed a Digi Dog on 10 occasions and 9 of those deployments resulted in the recovery of a concealed or hidden device (London Assembly, 2019).

MANAGEMENT OF RESOURCES

Focusing resources on those who cause the most harm and who target vulnerability has been shown to be both effective and popular with the community (Vulnerability Policing Futures Research Centre, 2024). With only 37% of Britons currently having confidence in the Police to deal with violent crime the allocation of resources to this area is key. Not only is it relevant in keeping people safe from harm but to maintain public confidence in a climate where only 31% believe the standard of policing to be "Good" (Shrimpton and Jones, 2023).

Whilst the College of Policing were unable to provide a response to the authors request for details of the recommended ratio for Sex Offenders to Police Managers (College of Policing: FOIA-2025-055) evidence across the 2022-2025 PEEL reports completed saw a range from 30/1 in Wiltshire to 80/1 in other forces (HMICFRS, 2023a). Forces with lower ratios consistently perform better when inspected and rated under PEEL. Fundamentally, the more time a manager must dedicate to each case the more effective the management will be. Whilst this is not unexpected it is also only fair to consider the wider financial limitations and strains on policing in the UK. Forces and Police and Crime Commissioners need to manage resources and preventative spending on initiatives that involve education or schools' involvement. This may be seen, as politically less valuable than more visible and tangible results as HMICFRS have found themselves in some previous cases (HMICFRS, 2024a). This may be an area worthy of further scrutiny and research.

When considering the other five areas of opportunity for excellence allocation of resources is a significant part of each. The balancing act is difficult, and it can reasonably be argued that the seven forces who have achieved a rating of "Good" may have done so at a cost of a less favourable grade in other areas by funnelling resources to this area. Leicestershire, for example achieved a "Good" rating in Managing Offenders but were found to "Require Improvement" in both Investigating Crime and in Responding to the Public (HMICFRS, 2024d).

North Yorkshire Police have used a Dashboard (a Microsoft Excel spreadsheet-based tool) to control offender/manager ratios more equitably in MoSOVO (HMICFRS, 2024e). Not only does the dashboard help manage resources effectively it also safeguards against overburdening of officers leading to mental health issues and absence. The Dashboard (at a raw data level) is available to all in the department so colleagues can be reassured of fairness. This is used to more accurately assess risk but has a benefit in terms of resource management. When an offender's risk level can be lowered the resources allocated to them decrease, this can happen more quickly and with more confidence after a satisfactory polygraph test. Whilst the report makes no mention of other factors contributing to a holistic understanding of risk other factors should be considered by forces looking to replicate this success, rather than reliance on one form of information: the polygraph and following the application of a decision-making tool such as the National Decision-Making Model (NDM). These measures have seen the force achieve a 45/1 ration for offenders to managers and whilst comparisons are unreliable between forces this ratio as reported by HMICFRS (2024d) would appear adequate.

When addressing outstanding violent offenders, including domestic abuse of all categories, North Yorkshire have an initiative called Operation Ankle in place. This permits the authorisation of overtime for all cases where a suspect has been wanted for 28 days or more. This ensures resources are always available to arrest and proactively safeguard victims (HMICFRS, 2024e).

Fundamentally, as with all policing areas there is a cry for more. It is not an unreasonable assertion that funds and resources are allocated more readily to other policing activities in Metropolitan areas leaving offender management as a more secondary consideration. Recent analysis indicates that the police service remains under-resourced relative to the breadth and complexity of modern policing demand. The College of Policing (2021) found themselves that reductions in officer numbers and funding had coincided with a significant increase in non-crime demand, including vulnerability, mental health, and safeguarding incidents, leaving many forces unable to meet all operational expectations. The true concern here is that the aspiration of achieving an outstanding police service may be unachievable because of financial and resource constrains.

MAXIMISING THE USE OF ANCILLARY ORDERS

Sexual Harm Prevention Orders (SHPOs) and Sexual Risk Orders (SROs) are civil orders issued by UK courts to manage individuals who pose a risk of sexual harm, imposing specific prohibitions or requirements to prevent offending or reoffending.

The effectiveness of SHPOs in reducing sexual offending is limited by the challenges associated with enforcement and operational consistency. Practical monitoring of SHPOs is uneven across police forces, with variations in resourcing and prioritisation leading to inconsistent enforcement and follow-up (Kelly and Picton, 2020). MoSOVO Units frequently report that staffing shortages and competing demands inhibit their capacity to conduct proactive compliance checks or digital device examinations, leaving many conditions under-supervised (HMICFRS, 2023). Without specialist digital forensics capacity or structured inspection regimes, enforcement often depends on opportunistic discovery rather than systematic supervision (Kelly and Picton, 2020). Even when breaches are detected, these do not always correspond with heightened risk, a fact that often sits uncomfortably with police offender managers. Empirical and qualitative studies suggest that many recorded breaches involve administrative or low-level non-compliance, which may divert resources away from high-risk monitoring without delivering measurable improvements in public protection (Rodgers, Harris and Harrison, 2023). Collectively, these issues reveal a significant implementation gap between the intended preventive purpose of SHPOs and their practical enforcement in the community.

Cumbria Constabulary holds monthly meetings with CPS at which a member of the MoSOVO team attends to contribute to a standing item on the agenda concerning the use of Sexual Harm Prevention Orders (SHPOs). This prioritises their use and ensures focus on the utilisation of the tool across the criminal justice system by allowing prosecutors to advise on case progress at the earliest point possible. It is claimed that these meetings have also allowed for charging to be consistently appropriate and to lead to conviction more frequently. However, HMICFRS, Cumbria Constabulary and the CPS have not published evidence that supports this. The group also review declined SHPO applications and look to identify learning that will help future applications to be successful (HMICFRS, 2024a).

Whitten (2025) argues the SROs are underused but have the potential to be an extremely effective safeguarding tool against sexual offenders. To this point there is little evidence to suggest they are being implemented in a meaningful way amongst any of the 42 forces.

When considering the use of Domestic Violence Protection Orders (DVPOs) we can see in Figure 1 that of the seven forces considered "Good" by HMICFRS two fall in the "Significantly higher than average" bracket of breaches of DVPO's. This can be interpreted in several ways, but it is likely that it is viewed by HMICFRS as forces being proactive in monitoring orders and responding quickly when breaches are seen.

Figure 1. Domestic Violence Protection Orders breached per 100,000 population across forces in England and Wales in the year ending 30 September 2023

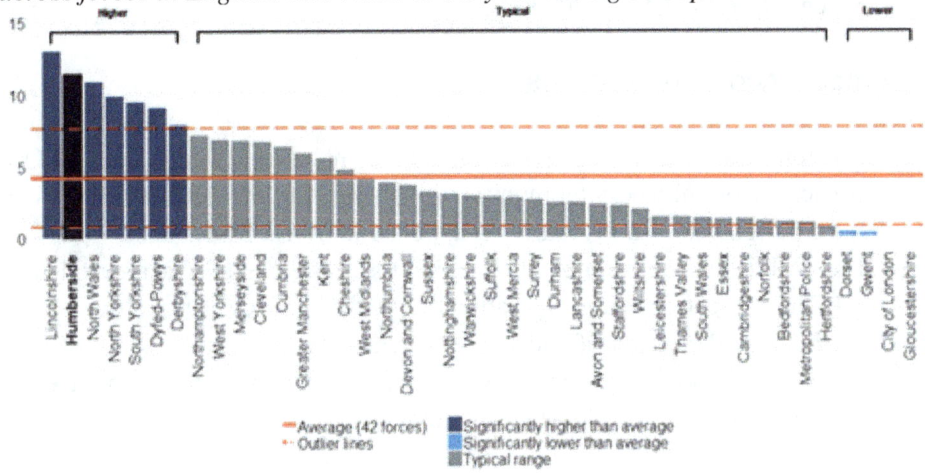

Source: HMICFRS, 2024b..

CONCLUSION

Smaller (in terms of police officer establishment, not geographical size) forces located in more affluent areas where the community has a higher level of disposable income seem to deliver the more effective offender management (See Table 1). The rural makeup of the performing forces and the absence of a Metropolitan force being rated above adequate in this area indicates there may also be environmental factors that contribute to this success. Further research may be valuable in this area.

Policy Recommendations

- Strong governance over risk. Specifically, with regards to all outstanding arrestable violent offenders as well as those suspected of sexual offending.
- Use Ancillary Orders more readily. Both as a safeguarding and preventative measure but also as an enforcement tool. This will require trained and dedicated staff.

- Maintenance of best practice when deploying the ARMS tool and DA risk assessment tools used. Monitoring and refresher training.
- Commitment of designated and resources to this area of business, specifically domestic abuse and sex offender management. These areas have a significant impact on public confidence with DA alone accounting for 25-35% of all police time (HMICFRS, 2023).

Practice Recommendations

- The routine use of Polygraph testing by all home office forces on RSO's, greater use of online digital monitoring software for internet enabled devices and a designated lead for future AI application in risk assessment.
- The establishment or strengthening of high-risk arrest teams that are evidence-led. The replication and proliferation of *Operation Ankle* nationally.
- Establish evidence led offender/manager ratio based on that seen in forces achieving a "good" rating in MoSOVO. 45/1 with consideration to the equitable breakdown of risk level within that.

Future Research Possibilities

- Development of an understanding of enforcement consistency regarding SHPOs and SROs across forces.
- Research into the links between performance in the management of risk by police forces and the socio-economic makeup of the community.
- To what extent is ARMS APP compliance linked to performance in MoSOVO teams.
- What is the real offender/offender manager ration in MoSOVO teams in the UK and what can variation tell us about performance?

REFERENCES

An inspection into activism and impartiality in policing. (2024). *Her Majesty's Inspectorate of Constabulary and Fire & Rescue Services (HMICFRS).* https://hmicfrs.justiceinspectorates.gov.uk/publication-html/activism-and-impartiality-in-policing/ (Accessed: 9 May 2025).

Cellebrite. (2025). *UFED (Universal Forensic Extraction Device)/Frontline.* https://cellebrite.com/en/ufed/ (Accessed: 9 October 2025).

Christie, L. (2021). *AI in policing and security.* Parliamentary Office of Science and Technology. https://post.parliament.uk/ai-in-policing-and-security/ (Accessed: 3 June 2025).

College of Policing. (2025). *FOIA-2025-055.* Correspondence retained by author.

Department for Environment. Food & Rural Affairs (Defra) and Office for National Statistics (ONS). (2023). *Rural-Urban classification 2021 of local authority districts and unitary authorities in England: Methodological guide and lookup tables.* London: Defra/ONS.

Department for Environment. Food and Rural Affairs (Defra). (2024). *Statistical digest of rural England: Population April 2024.* London: Defra. https://assets.publishing.service.gov.uk/media/661d3b95ac3dae9a53bd3dd3/16_04_2024_-_1_-_Population.pdf (Accessed: 9 October 2025).

Forensics, M. (2025). *Magnet AXIOM Scout/AXIOM.* https://www.magnetforensics.com (Accessed: 9 October 2025).

Halford, E. (2025). Transformer led policing model: A framework for applying generative artificial intelligence in policing. *Policing. Journal of Policy Practice,* •••, 19.

Her Majesty's Inspectorate of Constabulary and Fire & Rescue Services (HMICFRS). (2023). *PEEL assessment 2022/23: Protecting vulnerable people and managing offenders.* HMICFRS.

Her Majesty's Inspectorate of Constabulary and Fire & Rescue Services (HMICFRS). (2023a). *PEEL assessment 2023/24 – Surrey Police: An inspection of police performance.* https://hmicfrs.justiceinspectorates.gov.uk/peel-reports/surrey-2023-25/

Her Majesty's Inspectorate of Constabulary and Fire & Rescue Services (HMICFRS). (2024a). *PEEL assessment 2023/24 – Cumbria Constabulary: An inspection of police performance.* https://hmicfrs.justiceinspectorates.gov.uk/peel-reports/cumbria-2023-25/ (Accessed: 9 May 2025).

Her Majesty's Inspectorate of Constabulary and Fire & Rescue Services (HMICFRS). (2024b). *PEEL assessment 2023/24 – Humberside Police: An inspection of police performance.* https://hmicfrs.justiceinspectorates.gov.uk/peel-reports/humberside-2023-25/ (Accessed: 3 June 2025).

Her Majesty's Inspectorate of Constabulary and Fire & Rescue Services (HMICFRS). (2024c). *PEEL assessment 2023/24 – Lancashire Constabulary: An inspection of police performance.* https://hmicfrs.justiceinspectorates.gov.uk/publications/peel-assessment-2023-25-lancashire/ (Accessed: 9 May 2025).

Her Majesty's Inspectorate of Constabulary and Fire & Rescue Services (HMICFRS). (2024d). *PEEL assessment 2023/24 – Leicestershire Constabulary: An inspection of police performance.* https://hmicfrs.justiceinspectorates.gov.uk/publications/peel-assessment-2023-25-leicestershire/ (Accessed: 9 May 2025).

Her Majesty's Inspectorate of Constabulary and Fire & Rescue Services (HMICFRS). (2024e). *PEEL assessment 2023/24 – North Yorkshire Police: An inspection of police performance.* https://hmicfrs.justiceinspectorates.gov.uk/publications/peel-assessment-2023-25-north-yorkshire/ (Accessed: 9 May 2025).

Her Majesty's Inspectorate of Constabulary and Fire & Rescue Services (HMICFRS). (2024f). *PEEL assessment 2023/24 – Wiltshire Constabulary: An inspection of police performance.* https://hmicfrs.justiceinspectorates.gov.uk/peel-reports/wiltshire-2023-25/ (Accessed: 9 May 2025).

HM Prison and Probation Service (HMPPS). (2021). *ViSOR policy framework.* London: Ministry of Justice. https://www.gov.uk/government/publications/hmpps-visor-policy-framework (Accessed: 9 October 2025).

Home Office. (2024). *Police workforce, England and Wales, 31 March 2024.* Home Office.

House of Commons Library. (2024). *Police service strength (England and Wales).* UK Parliament.

Kelly, L., & Picton, H. (2020). Sexual harm prevention orders and the test of necessity: Protecting the public or placing civil liberties at risk? UCL Faculty of Laws., https://discovery.ucl.ac.uk/id/eprint/10091813/, Retrieved October 10, 2025, from.

Le Core, R. (2024). Elephant in the room: Declining use of covert tactics in UK policing. *Royal United Services Institute (RUSI),* 7 March. https://www.rusi.org/networks/shoc/informer/elephant-room-declining-use-covert-tactics-uk-policing (Accessed: 9 May 2025).

London Assembly. (2019). *Electronic device sniffer dogs.* London: Greater London Authority. https://www.london.gov.uk/who-we-are/what-london-assembly-does/questions-mayor/find-an-answer/electronic-device-sniffer-dogs (Accessed: 10 October 2025).

London Polygraph Ltd. (n.d.). *FAQ.* https://liedetectortest.london/faq/ (Accessed: 9 May 2025).

Mann, N., & Lundrigan, S. (2021). Dynamic assessment of registered sexual offenders: The national practitioner perspective on the use of the 'Active Risk Management System' (ARMS). *Anglia Ruskin Research Online (ARRO).* https://hdl.handle.net/10779/aru.23765835.v1

McCartan, K., & Kemshall, H. (2015). Police officer attitudes to the practicalities of the sex offenders' register (ViSOR). University of the West of England., https://uwe-repository.worktribe.com/output/875102, Retrieved October 9, 2025, from.

McManus, M., & Halford, E. (2023). 40: Policing serious, violent and sexual offending. In *Forensic psychology, crime and policing*. Policy Press.

MSAB. (2025). *XRY / XAMN.* https://www.msab.com (Accessed: 9 October 2025).

National Police Chiefs' Council (NPCC). (2010). *ViSOR standards v2.0.* London: NPCC. https://www.npcc.police.uk/documents/crime/2011/20110404%20ViSOR%20Standards%20v2%200_Nov%202010.pdf (Accessed: 10 October 2025).

NPCC / HMICFRS. (2024). *PEEL inspection programme.* Presentation, 4 December.

Office for National Statistics (ONS). (2021). *Mapping inequality in the UK.* https://www.ons.gov.uk/visualisations/dvc1370/index.html (Accessed: 9 May 2025).

Office for National Statistics (ONS). (2023). *Population estimates for the UK, England and Wales, Scotland and Northern Ireland: Mid-2022.* ONS.

Office for National Statistics (ONS). (2025). *Employment in the UK: May to July 2025.* Newport: ONS. https://www.ons.gov.uk/employmentandlabourmarket/peopleinwork/employmentandemployeetypes (Accessed: 9 October 2025).

ONS / Nomis. (2024). *Annual population survey: Employment rate (aged 16 to 64), local authority series (year ending 2023–2024).* Nomis/ONS.

Police Foundation. (2023). The public want the police to be more visible and to focus on core tasks, according to new research. https://www.police-foundation.org.uk/news/the-public-want-the-police-to-be-more-visible-and-to-focus-on-core-tasks-according-to-new-research/ (Accessed: 9 May 2025).

Police Foundation. (2024). *Evidence on policing for the future: Changing demands and resources (written evidence).* https://committees.parliament.uk/writtenevidence/77936/html/ (Accessed: 10 October 2025).

Rodgers, K., Harris, N., & Harrison, J. (2023). Civil preventive orders and the policing of risk: The case of Sexual Harm Prevention Orders. *Policing: A Journal of Policy and Practice.* Advance online publication. https://academic.oup.com/policing/article/doi/10.1093/police/paad033/7210191 (Accessed: 10 October 2025).

Shrimpton, H., & Jones, H. (2023). Globally, Britons among the least confident in law enforcement's ability to stop crime. *Ipsos.* https://www.ipsos.com/en-uk/globally-britons-among-least-confident-law-enforcements-ability-stop-crime (Accessed: 3 June 2025).

Thornton, D., Mann, R., Webster, S., Blud, L., Travers, R., Friendship, C., & Erikson, M. (2003). Distinguishing and combining risks for sexual and violent recidivism. In R. A. Prentky, E. S. Janus, & M. C. Seto (Eds.), *Sexually coercive behavior: Understanding and management* (pp. 225–235). *Annals of the New York Academy of Sciences, 989.* https://doi.org/ (Accessed: 3 June 2025).DOI: 10.1111/j.1749-6632.2003.tb07315.x

Vulnerability Policing Futures Research Centre / Vulnerability Policing. (2024). *What do the public want from police? Towards a minimum policing standard.* https://vulnerabilitypolicing.org.uk/what-do-the-public-want-from-police-towards-a-minimum-policing-standard/ (Accessed: 10 October 2025).

Wakeling, H. C., Howard, P., & Barnett, G. (2019). Reoffending rates in a U.K. community sample of individuals with convictions for indecent images of children. *Sexual Abuse*, *31*(3), 294–313.

Whitten, D. (2025). Sexual risk orders: A tactic of early intervention, or a last resort? *Policing Insight.* https://policinginsight.com/feature/analysis/sexual-risk-orders-a-tactic-of-early-intervention-or-a-last-resort/ (Accessed: 3 June 2025).

Chapter 22
Outlining the Co-Development of Twelve Desistance Principles to Reduce Sexual Reoffending:
A Case Study

Stephanie Cain
http://orcid.org/0000-0001-6841-5577
Liverpool John Moores University, UK

Sarah Pemberton
Birmingham City University, UK

Leona Mydlowski
University of Central Lancashire, UK

Paul Burnside
Centre of Expertise on Child Sexual Abuse, UK

Andy Horne
Lancashire Constabulary, UK

ABSTRACT

The number of people managed under MAPPA in England and Wales has risen significantly, creating new challenges for police supervising individuals with sexual convictions. Responding to calls for desistance-focused practices, this case study

DOI: 10.4018/979-8-3373-2757-0.ch022

explores a co-produced project designed to support MOSOVO officers in adopting desistance-oriented approaches. Through participatory action research, police officers, people with lived experience, and academics collaborated to create three practical tools: a Desistance Practice Framework, a Desistance Management Plan, and Twelve Principles for Assisting Desistance. These were refined through stakeholder input and aim to help police support individual change, reduce reoffending, and manage growing caseloads more effectively. The principles provide a foundation for embedding desistance into policing, aligning risk management with rehabilitation and human rights.

INTRODUCTION

Over the last decade the number of people managed by Multi-Agency Public Protection Arrangements (MAPPA) and subject to sexual offender notification requirements, in England and Wales, has risen by 52% (Kewley & Karsna, 2025). This growth is likely a result of improved recording of sexual offences (Office for National Statistics, 2023), the introduction of several new sexual offences (Voyeurism Act, 2019; Serious Crime Act, 2015; Online Safety Act 2023), changes to sentence lengths (UK Parliament, Sentencing Bill, 2023) and updates to the provision of civil orders (Anti-social Behaviour, Crime and Policing Act 2014; Police, Crime, Sentencing and Courts Act 2022). The trajectory of this growth is set to continue, meaning more people subject to sexual offender notification requirements will be managed in the community by the police for longer periods of time. With over 73% of this population already managed by the police (Cain et al., 2026), this is a concern.

The increase in demand brings with it significant challenges to police professionals responsible for the risk assessment and management of this population. Across England and Wales public protection officers or Management of Sexual and Violence Offender (MOSOVO)[1] officers have a unique role, that requires them to supervise people subject to sexual offender notification requirements (by developing risk management plans that both restrict and prevent the person from causing harm to others), whilst balancing their needs by applying constructive interventions into the risk management plan. It is vital that public protection strategies do not compromise the human rights of any individual, including the people MOSOVO officers manage as well as the rights of the victims and general public ('College of Policing', 2025). However, in a predominantly risk averse criminal justice system, this tension is difficult for MOSOVO officers to address in practice - particularly when working with individuals known to the system who may present a risk of reoffending (Pemberton et al., 2023).

In addition, the context in which MOSOVOs operate consists of multiple interlocking challenges, including, workforce pressures and recruitment (Hesketh & Stubbs, 2025), the systemic problems of detecting and investigating serious sexual offences (Dalton et al., 2022), under-resourcing of multi-agency teams (e.g. probation, health, housing) that impact the quality of supervision and opportunity to treatment support (Kirton & Guillaume, 2019) along with poor inter-agency information sharing, that further complicates efforts to balance public protection with rehabilitation (Mann et al., 2018). Any further sexual re-offending is unacceptable but, the re-conviction rate of people with sexual convictions, when compared to other offender types are relatively low. Research finds recidivism rates of between 5% to 15% (after five years in the community) and 10% to 20% after a 10 year follow up period (Hanson & Bussiere, 1998; A. J. R. Harris & Hanson, 2004; Helmus et al., 2012). This is in keeping with a recent proactive online investigation (between April 2020 and September 2022), whereby the National Crime Agency detected one in 10 people of committing child sexual abuse to be 'actively' managed by either probation or police services (National Crime Agency, 2024). To assist MOSOVO officers in supervising people subject to notification requirements and determine the level of intervention required, robust risk assessments must be undertaken.

The Active Risk Management System (ARMS) is a structured professional judgment risk assessment tool, it guides MOSOVO officers to identify both dynamic risk and protective factors related to sexual offending and desistance that should inform a subsequent risk management plan (Mydlowski & Turner-Moore, 2023; Mydlowski, Turner-Moore & Kewley, 2024; Kewley & Blandford, 2017). The quality of these assessments has been found to be problematic, in recent studies risk management plans were inconsistent and poor (Kewley, Osman, et al., 2020) problems around the utilisation of plans (Mann & Lundrigan, 2021) were found to be, in part, due to the insufficient police public protection resources (Mann et al., 2019). Thus, with this increasing population, and scarce public agency resources, an alternative approach to managing this population is needed.

In a recent independent review of police-led management of people with sexual offences Creedon (2023) made several recommendations, one of which called for MOSOVOs to engage a greater focus on supporting the desistance process and promoting protective factors with people with sexual offences. This, he argued would not only help reduce the risk a person may present in the community but would help to alleviate the burden of large caseloads, allowing MOSOVOs to invest greater resources to those with the greatest risk and need. This approach algins with the PEEL 2025-27 assessment framework, that will measure the extent to which forces effectively engage with "prevention orders and schemes to safeguard vulnerable people and manage the risk that offenders pose" (PEEL assessment framework 2025–27. p.18).

THE CASE STUDY

This case study briefly outlines and introduces work produced following a co-developed research project[2]. The work was undertaken in response to Creedon's (2023) call for the police to have a greater focus on desistance practice when supervising people subjected to sexual notification requirements. A small internal 'seedcorn' grant was awarded by Liverpool John Moores University Forensic Research Institute and in-kind resources from Lancashire Constabulary to help fund the work. We co-developed three outputs from this project which includes a *Desistance Practice-Framework*, *Twelve Desistance Principles*, and a *Desistance Management Plan*. We do not intend to discuss all outputs; details of the Desistance Practice Framework and Desistance Management Plan can be accessed in Cain et al (2026). Here we summarise the Twelve Desistance Principles needed for police constabularies to embed desistance focussed practice.

A NOTE ON DESISTANCE

Desistance is the cessation of criminal behavior. It requires both cognitive and behavioural change, through increased pro-social and structural support (Maruna, 2001; Laws & Ward, 2011). Positive informal (e.g. family and friends) and formal (e.g. police supervisors) relationships are crucial in fostering successful desistance outcomes (Weaver, 2015). As are But because desistance combines several psycho-social theories, applying these into the everyday police supervision of people subject to sexual notification requirements is complex and requires guidance (Fox, 2022). To support police constabularies and MOSOVO teams in the process of embedding desistance into practice, we developed these resources to help MOSOVOs encourage people with sexual convictions towards the process of change and long-term desistance. That said, we recognise there are some people, who despite criminal sanctions and opportunities of support, remain intent and motivated to sexually offend. Strategies for people motivated in this way, will always require monitoring, control and containment approaches. While we believe, with appropriate support, all people can make positive changes in their life, we recognise if there is ever a conflict between a desistance and risk management approach, public protection will always take precedence.

METHOD

All work was approved by the Liverpool John Moores University Research Ethics Committee (Ref No: 24/PSY/049). We used participatory action research to undertake this work (Seal, 2018). This provided an inclusive approach which enabled us to draw on the knowledge of key stakeholders, as well as help to work *with*, rather than *gaze into* this space (Telep et al., 2020). Stakeholders included MOSOVO officers, police management and people with sexual convictions. By working with people most impacted by the MOSOVO teams, especially people with lived experiences of sexual offending, we were able to learn from their 'real world' insights; and our collaborative approach allowed them to share with us how they might best be supported in their process of desistance (Brierley, 2023). We experienced some of the expected challenges reported by fellow criminological academics (see Lane et al., 2004) when undertaking participatory action research in a correctional context (i.e. needing to build trust fast, navigating the limitations of a secure setting, and working with vulnerable participants) however, these challenges were mitigated through clear and regular communication across the research team. To support the process, a Theory of Change (ToC) was developed by the research team. The ToC method is a valuable collaborative tool to help visualise and formalise concepts being examined while also helping to advance changes needed (Doherty et al., 2022). From this point, we facilitated three stages of consultation (see blue boxes in Fig 1) to gain feedback from key stakeholders to refine the resources.

Figure 1. Process chart

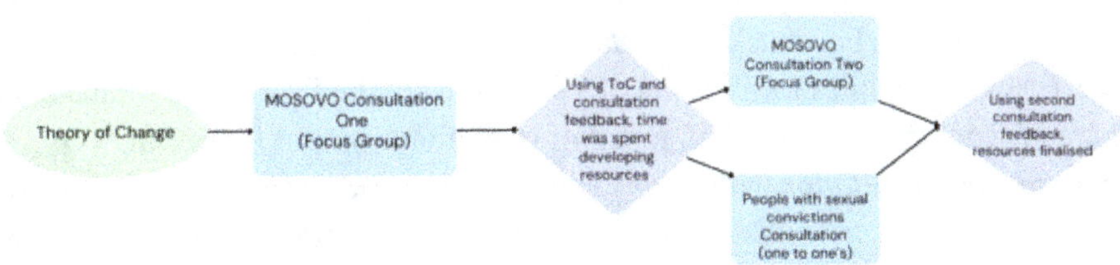

Focus group one: We invited MOSOVOs from each of the three Lancashire Constabulary units to attend a hybrid consultation session with the research team. Sessions were held during working hours, in a meeting room at police headquarters. Use of a hybrid format helped facilitate attendance. In the two-hour session with 13 MOSOVOs we introduced the project, summarised what desistance is, gave a summary of the ToC and then facilitated a discussion. We asked MOSOVOs to think about what they might need to help them work in a more desistance focussed way. After some discussion, MOSOVOs highlighted the need for desistance training and opportunities to develop their supervisory skills; and a resource that might help them focus on desistance factors to track the progress of people they were supervising.

Resource development: The research team held three face-to-face development days and several online sessions to draft the resources ahead of the second consultation event. By drawing on the desistance literature and our previous work and experiences in this space see (Kewley et al., 2020; Kewley and Brereton, 2022; Kewley and Burke, 2023; Pemberton et al., 2023; Mydlowski & Turner Moore 2023; Mydlowski et al., 2024; Pemberton and Kewley, 2025) we developed the following resources:

- Twelve Principles for Assisting Desistance
- Desistance Management Plan
- Desistance Practice Framework

Focus group two: We again invited MOSOVOs from each of the three units to attend this second consultation session. Ideally, we would have preferred the same participants from group one but due to operational commitments, rest days etc. it was not possible to coordinate this; six people attended. In this session, we went over the research project and ToC again, as some participants were not at the first session, and then presented the drafted documents ahead of a group discussion. Prior to the discussion we sent a copy of the resources, as pre-reading, to support a richer discussion. We prepared some prompts and open-ended discussion questions to generate discussion. Feedback again was positive. No major changes were requested to the Twelve Principles for Assisting Desistance, but the Desistance Management Plan required some extra work in terms of operationalising it for MOSOVOs.

One to one consultation with people with sexual convictions: We undertook seven one-to-one discussions with adults convicted of a sexual offence and living in Lancashire. Six were male and one female, average age was 44 (SD = 17.96) they had been managed by Lancashire Constabulary on average for 9 years (SD = 5.4) and had convictions for rape (of an adult female); making, possession and distribution of indecent images of a child; Causing/inciting a male child under 13 to engage in sexual activity; Causing/inciting/prostitution of/pornography involving a child under 13; and voyeurism. In terms of their risk levels as determined by their ARMS assessment, three were assessed as Low Risk; two Medium Risk; and two High Risk.

Participants were recruited via the MOSOVOs who spoke with potential participants about the project and provided those interested with a Participant Information Sheet and Consent Form. Potential participants were given over a week to consider if they wished to take part, the first authors' contact details was also provided for those wishing to discuss the project prior to agreeing to take part; one person telephoned the first author with questions but then subsequently agreed to be interviewed. Discussions were held in a private room at their local police station, travel arrangements to and from the venue were arranged between the MOSOVO and the participant, travel costs were covered by Lancashire Constabulary. The interviewers (authors one and three) went over the information sheet allowing time for further questions, collected verbal and signed consent from participants. Discussions were undertaken without the presence of any MOSOVO. No incentives were given for participation and with consent each discussion was audio recorded.

Interviewers followed a semi-structured schedule which included an introduction of the concept of desistance, followed by a discussion centered on the drafted Twelve Principles for Assisting Desistance and the Desistance Management Plan. Participants were not asked about their own experiences of being managed by the police (or any other criminal justice agency) this was made clear in the Participant Information Sheet and Consent Form, instead participants were invited to express their views and perceptions of the resources presented to them. Despite this several people still volunteered their own lived experiences to highlight points they were making, these included times when offender managers practice was both positive and 'desistance focussed' as well as those times when they were not. Indeed, as was to be expected, participants had mixed experiences of the criminal justice system and gave plenty of examples of practice that would not be recognised as conducive to promoting desistance. Participants were de-briefed at the end of the discussion with two being signposted to services that provide support for adult survivors of child sexual abuse. Again, information about childhood experiences was not sought, but through discussion, reports of childhood sexual abuse were made.

Following these consultations and feedback from participants, a final process was undertaken to update and refine resources. These were then presented to Lancashire Constabulary. Prior to outlining the Twelve Principles for Assisting Desistance, it is important to note that the consultation process described here underpins the development of a set of resources that will be piloted across four constabularies in England and Wales. Accordingly, this case study captures the formative phase of this ongoing work.

DESISTANCE PRINCIPLES

The desistance principles should be deployed in conjunction with the implementation of the Desistance Practice Framework (for a full description of the framework and underpinning theory (see Cain et al. 2026). The framework aims to support police policy and practice in the prevention of sexual reoffending. Indeed, it complements the work undertaken by MOSOVOs helping them carry out robust, comprehensive and balanced risk assessment. The Framework aligns various police strategies including the National Policing Prevention Strategy (CD3 Secondary prevention and CD4 Tertiary Prevention) and Policing Violence Against Women and Girls – The National Framework for Delivery: 2024 – 2027 and engage actively in professional curiosity and strategic investigative thinking (Gehl & Plecas, 2017). Drawing on our knowledge of the desistance literature and the consultation process with key stakeholders, we agreed the following twelve principles should be adopted by police constabularies committed to embedding desistance approaches in the work of MOSOVO supervisors. The principles are not hierarchical, but instead mutually support each other. Figure 2 provides a summary of each principle.

Figure 2. Twelve Principles for Assisting Desistance

PRINCIPLES

Recognise desistance approaches reduce risk: To engage in desistance practice MOSOVO officers and other police professionals supporting their work must recognise the value of adopting desistance approaches. It is essential they subscribe to a value base that recognises the role desistance approaches can play in reducing risk and reoffending. While traditional rehabilitation models like the Risk-Need-Responsivity (RNR) model (Andrews & Bonta, 2016) are effective, these models primarily aim to reduce and manage the risk of sexual recidivism, rather than enhance the individual's quality of life (Chu & Ward, 2015). Solely focusing on criminogenic risk factors—though important—is unlikely, on its own, to motivate or sustain desistance.

Recognise all as members of society, with rights, responsibilities: MOSOVOs should recognise people convicted of sexual offending as equal members of society, with rights, responsibilities. They have agency and self-determination; however, they require support to achieve goals and contribute to society (Ward & Connolly, 2008).

Promote meaningful relationships and access to purposeful activity: MOSOVOs must understand people do not exist in the world in a vacuum; meaningful, and positive social relationships and purposeful activities are essential to promote connection and help people create new social roles, strengthen new identities (Healy, 2012) and increase social capital potential. Promoting and advocating for meaningful relationships and support access to purposeful activity can make positive changes that will reduce risk and increase desistance from offending.

Promote the reconstruction of positive social identities: Desistance involves identity transformation; people need to shift from seeing themselves as an "offender" to a non-offending self. This is reinforced by others' acceptance (Maruna, 2001). Support from formal agents, like MOSOVOs, can strengthen self-efficacy and promote lasting change (de Vel-Palumbo et al., 2023). MOSOVOs should therefore promote the reconstruction of positive social identities and provide people convicted of sexual offending opportunities to showcase change.

Recognise impact of adverse life experiences: People with sexual convictions often experience poor mental health (Lussier et al., 2024) and have had several adverse life experiences (Kahn et al., 2021), much of which goes undiagnosed and untreated. MOSOVOs should adopt a welfare-focused approach (Mann et al., 2019) to help the person address/manage these through advocacy, signposting, and/or coaching.

Work collaboratively: MOSOVOs should work collaboratively with people convicted of sexual offending; the commitment to the desistance process should be a shared activity. Embracing a sense of collectivism, will foster a sense of 'we'; a collaborative relationship, works 'with' the person rather than doing things 'to' them (Ward & Maruna, 2007).

Adopt desistance approaches regardless of risk/offence type: Desistance approaches should be adopted by the MOSOVO with all people convicted of sexual offending, regardless of risk/offence type and stages of the desistance process. Working motivationally and supporting strengths, even pre-desistance, can increase the likelihood of change (Ward & Stewart, 2003).

Recognise the impact of intersectionality and power differences: Feelings of powerlessness to achieve positive personal goals will reinforce a belief of being *doomed to deviance* (Maruna, 2001) and impede the desistance process. MOSOVOs must be sensitive to the diversity and protective characteristics of people they supervise.

The explicit and implicit power differences within their relationship will impact how they can assist desistance.

Engage in appropriate training and supervision: To support Creedons' (2023) call for desistance focused practice far greater training and support in this space is needed. MOSOVOs must engage and receive appropriate desistance training and regular clinical supervision to help improve outcomes for the people they supervise.

Work with transparency and hope: Hope is essential to the desistance process. People must believe their life goals are achievable and that a path to success exists (Snyder et al., 2000). But, past offending or criminal justice sanctions often hinder access to core life domains (Levins & Mjåland, 2021); MOSOVOs should work transparently and in response to changes in risk and need by adopting an individualised and collaborative approach when working with people convicted of sexual offending.

Use person centred, de-stigmatising language: MOSOVOs should use person-centred language when working with people attempting to desist from crime, as this supports all stages of the desistance process (D. A. Harris, 2021). Avoiding stigmatising labels (e.g., "sex offender") and instead focusing on describing behaviors (e.g., "sexual abuse") helps shift the narrative towards positive change (Willis, 2018).

Embedded desistance force wide: Building trust to help promote desistance takes time, therefore, desistance approaches should be recognised, understood and embedded force wide. This will help colleagues unintentionally undermining the work of MOSOVOs.

In presenting our work in this case study, we outline the *Twelve Principles for Assisting Desistance.* We note however, this work is preliminary in nature. We have commenced piloting these principles, along with our Desistance Practice Framework (Cain et al., 2026) across four police constabularies. Further work will be undertaken to empirically examine the utility and effectiveness of these resources. We also make several recommendations in support of the findings of the Creedon (2023) review. In particular, we call on the College of Policing to review current training guidance to local areas for police professionals working with people with sexual convictions. Specifically, we recommend that desistance-focussed content be incorporated into the *Introduction to managing sexual offenders and violent offenders* training package and offered as a continuing professional development module for staff who have already completed this course. Finally, we suggest that the College of Policing update the *Authorised Professional Practice* resource to reflect and integrate our Desistance Practice Framework.

CONCLUSION

The recidivism rate of people with sexual convictions is low compared to other offence types, and desistance appears to be the norm (Hanson, 2018). Even people assessed as high risk of reconviction, can go on to desist and lead offence free lives (Hanson et al, 2014; Hanson et al., 2018), although the risk of recidivism may increase over time (Lussier et al., 2025). With more people with sexual convictions under extended police supervision (Kewley & Karsna, 2025), MOSOVOs play a critical role in supporting desistance, reducing risk and protecting the public. Focusing on strengths is as important as focussing on risk (Thornton, 2024), since reinforcing protective factors and developing personal capacities, reduces reoffending; goal-oriented interventions are generally more engaging and motivational than purely risk-reduction activities (Mann et al., 2004). One example of a successful desistance-focused intervention is Circles of Support and Accountability (CoSA) as illustrated by Richards (2021). This community-based intervention fosters accountability, reintegration, and identity transformation. CoSA professionals are integrated into broader criminal justice and community systems, but critically they provide people with sexual convictions consistent opportunities for personal growth and social reintegration.

That said, the desistance process is complex and can be easily derailed, often being impeded by criminal justice systems, which as observed across many international contexts (including England and Wales) are not always conducive to desistance (Farrall, 2021). The literature underpinning our theoretical understanding of this process equally requires further development. In particular, drawing on international comparisons would strengthen our knowledge base. For example greater clarity is needed regarding the mechanisms that mediate support (Lenkens et al., 2024), the validity of protective factors (Garant & Ouellet, 2024), the cultural challenges individuals face (Farrall et al., 2025), the differences between those with heightened risk profiles (Netten & Wakeling, 2025) and crucially, the role of formal agents in the process of desistance (Villeneuve et al., 2021).

Thus, in an effort to help contribute to this growing body of work and to support MOSOVOs and police constabularies better exploit opportunities in current practice to assist people into a process of desistance, we have presented here twelve principles that, in conjunction with our Desistance Practice Framework, should guide MOSOVO practice. Despite resource challenges, MOSOVOs are extremely well positioned to serve as formal agents of change and promote desistance with people with sexual convictions. Indeed, by adopting desistance-focused approaches and interventions they can target the underlying drivers of sexual violence which in turn, will help to prevent future sexual reoffending.

REFERENCES

Andrews, D. A., & Bonta, J. (2016). *The psychology of criminal conduct* (5th ed.). Routledge.

Anti-social, B. (2014). [UK]. *Crime and Policing Act, c*, 12.

Brierley, A. (2023). Desistance and practice: Where does the experience stop and practice begin? *Probation Quarterly, 28*. https://www.probation-institute.org/news/desistance-and-practice

Chu, C. M., & Ward, T. (2015). The good lives model of offender rehabilitation: Working positively with sexual offenders. In *Positive criminology* (pp. 140–161). Routledge.

College of Policing. (2025). [Authorised Professional Practice]. *Multi-Agency Public Protection Arrangements (MAPPA)*. https://www.college.police.uk/app/major-investigation-and-public-protection/managing-sexual-offenders-and-violent-offenders/multi-agency-public-protection-arrangements-mappa

Creedon, M. (2023). *Independent Review into the Police-led Management of Registered Sex Offenders in the Community: Executive Summary*. Home Office. https://www.gov.uk/government/publications/independent-review-of-police-led-sex-offender-management

Dalton, C. T., Barrett, S., Horvath, M. A. H., & Davies, K. (2022). A Systematic Literature Review of Specialist Policing of Rape and Serious Sexual Offences. *International Criminology*, *2*(3), 230–252. DOI: 10.1007/s43576-022-00062-1

de Vel-Palumbo, M., Halsey, M., & Day, A. (2023). Assisted Desistance in Correctional Centers: From Theory to Practice. *Criminal Justice and Behavior, 50*(11), 1623–1642. DOI: 10.1177/00938548231193313

Doherty, R., Quinn, N., Colson, A., Tucker, A., & Cameron, J. (2022). Developing a theory of change methodology to support the evaluation of place-based systems change interventions to support child and adolescent mental health and well-being. *Evaluation*, *28*(4), 466–483. DOI: 10.1177/13563890221110257

Farrall, S. (2021). International Perspectives and Lessons Learned on Desistance. In *Desistance From Crime: Implications for Research, Policy, and Practice*. National Institure of Justice. https://www.ojp.gov/pdffiles1/nij/301502.pdf

Farrall, S., Warr, J., Shaw, A., & Sharma, K. (2025). What Do We Know About How Processes of Desistance Vary by Ethnicity? *The Howard Journal of Crime and Justice*, *64*(3), 279–294. DOI: 10.1111/hojo.12606

Fox, K. J. (2022). Desistance frameworks. *Practice Frameworks in the Criminal Justice System*, *63*, 101684. DOI: 10.1016/j.avb.2021.101684

Garant, E., & Ouellet, F. (2024). Protective Factors Related to Desistance in Sexual Offending: A Scoping Review. *SAGE Open*, *14*(4), 21582440241281606. DOI: 10.1177/21582440241281606

Gehl, R., & Plecas, D. (2017). *Introduction to criminal investigation: Processes, practices and thinking*. Justice Institute of British Columbia. https://pressbooks.bccampus.ca/criminalinvestigation/chapter/chapter-1-introduction/

Hanson, R. K. (2018). Long-Term Recidivism Studies Show That Desistance Is the Norm. *Criminal Justice and Behavior*, *45*(9), 1340–1346. DOI: 10.1177/0093854818793382

Hanson, R. K., & Bussiere, M. T. (1998). Predicting relapse: A meta-analysis of sexual offender recidivism studies. *Journal of Consulting and Clinical Psychology*, *66*(2), 348–362. DOI: 10.1037/0022-006X.66.2.348 PMID: 9583338

Hanson, R. K., Harris, A. J., Letourneau, E., Helmus, L. M., & Thornton, D. (2018). Reductions in risk based on time offense-free in the community: Once a sexual offender, not always a sexual offender. *Psychology, Public Policy, and Law*, *24*(1), 48. DOI: 10.1037/law0000135

Hanson, R. K., Harris, A. J. R., Helmus, L., & Thornton, D. (2014). High-Risk Sex Offenders May Not Be High Risk Forever. *Journal of Interpersonal Violence*. Advance online publication. DOI: 10.1177/0886260514526062 PMID: 24664250

Harris, A. J. R., & Hanson, R. K. (2004). Sex offender recidivism: A simple question 2004-03. *Public Safety and Emergency Preparedness Canada*. https://www.publicsafety.gc.ca/cnt/rsrcs/pblctns/sx-ffndr-rcdvsm/index-en.aspx?wbdisable=true

Harris, D. A. (2021). Desistance From Sexual Offending. *Current Psychiatry Reports*, *23*(2), 7. DOI: 10.1007/s11920-020-01219-3 PMID: 33404825

Healy, D. (2012). Advise, assist and befriend: Can probation supervision support desistance? *Social Policy and Administration*, *46*(4), 377–394.

Helmus, L., Hanson, R. K., Thornton, D., Babchishin, K. M., & Harris, A. J. (2012). Absolute recidivism rates predicted by Static-99R and Static-2002R sex offender risk assessment tools vary across samples: A meta-analysis. *Criminal Justice and Behavior, 39*(9), 1148–1171. DOI: 10.1177/0093854812443648

Hesketh, I., & Stubbs, G. (2025). Police recruitment and positive action: The social building blocks of service. *International Journal of Police Science & Management, 27*(1), 31–42. DOI: 10.1177/14613557241248312

His Majesty's Inspectorate of Constabulary and Fire & Rescue Services. (2025) PEEL assessment framework (PAF) 2025–2027 https://hmicfrs.justiceinspectorates.gov.uk/publications/peel-assessment-framework-2025-027/#:~:text=This%20is%20the%20assessment%20framework%20for%20our%20police,several%20core%20questions%20set%20out%20in%20this%20framework

Kahn, R. E., Jackson, K., Keiser, K., Ambroziak, G., & Levenson, J. S. (2021). Adverse Childhood Experiences Among Sexual Offenders: Associations With Sexual Recidivism Risk and Psychopathology. *Sexual Abuse, 33*(7), 839–866. DOI: 10.1177/1079063220970031 PMID: 33158402

Kewley, S., & Blandford, M. (2017). The development of the active risk management system. *Journal of Criminal Psychology, 7*(3), 155–167. DOI: 10.1108/JCP-10-2016-0034

Kewley, S., & Brereton, S. (2022). Public Protection: Examining the impact of strengthened public protection policy on probation practice. In *Reimagining Probation Practice* (pp. 112–131). Routledge.

Kewley, S., & Burke, L. (2023). *9: Forensic psychology and desistance.* Policy Press., DOI: 10.51952/9781447359418.ch009

Kewley, S., & Karsna, K. (2025). *Child sexual abuse in 2023/24: Trends in official data.* Centre of Expertise on Child Sexual Abuse., DOI: 10.47117/IZAK2457

Kewley, S., Osman, S., & McGuinness, Á. (2020). How well do police specialists risk assess Registered Sexual Offenders? *Journal of Sexual Aggression, 26*(3), 302–315. DOI: 10.1080/13552600.2019.1628315

Cain, S., Pemberton, S., Mydlowski, L., Burnside, P., & Horne, A. (2026). A desistance practice framework to support police professionals working with people with sexual convictions. *International Journal of Law, Crime and Justice, 84*, 100826.

Kewley, S., Pemberton, S., & Rahman, M. (2020). *Preventing Sexual Harm: Positive Criminology and Sexual Abuse*. Routledge.

Kirton, G., & Guillaume, C. (2019). When Welfare Professionals Encounter Restructuring and Privatization: The Inside Story of the Probation Service of England and Wales. *Work, Employment and Society, 33*(6), 929–947. DOI: 10.1177/0950017019855229

Lane, J., Turner, S., & Flores, C. (2004). Researcher-Practitioner Collaboration in Community Corrections: Overcoming Hurdles for Successful Partnerships. *Criminal Justice Review, 29*(1), 97–114. DOI: 10.1177/073401680402900107

Laws, D. R., & Ward, T. (2011). *Desistance from sex offending: Alternatives to throwing away the keys*. Guilford Press.

Lenkens, M., van Lenthe, F. J., Schenk, L., Sentse, M., Severiens, S., Engbersen, G., & Nagelhout, G. E. (2024). Experiential peer support and desistance from crime: A systematic realist literature review. *Psychology, Crime & Law, 30*(10), 1421–1451. DOI: 10.1080/1068316X.2023.2203925

Levins, A., & Mjåland, K. (2021). Authoritarian exclusion and laissez-faire inclusion: Comparing the punishment of men convicted of sex offenses in England & Wales and Norway*. *Criminology, 59*(3), 454–479. DOI: 10.1111/1745-9125.12276

Lussier, P., Chouinard Thivierge, S., Fréchette, J., & Proulx, J. (2024). Sex Offender Recidivism: Some Lessons Learned From Over 70 Years of Research. *Criminal Justice Review, 49*(4), 413–452. DOI: 10.1177/07340168231157385 PMID: 39494044

Lussier, P., McCuish, E., St-Pierre, E., & Baguet, A.-L. (2025). Examining Benchmarks of Sexual Recidivism Rates for Short, Moderate, and Long-Term Follow-Up Periods: A Meta-Analysis of Canadian and American Studies. *Trauma, Violence & Abuse, 15248380251338791*. Advance online publication. DOI: 10.1177/15248380251338791 PMID: 40462275

Mann, N., Devendran, P., & Lundrigan, S. (2018). Policing in a Time of Austerity: Understanding the Public Protection Paradox through Qualitative Interviews with Police Monitoring Officers. *Policing. Journal of Policy Practice, 14*(3), 630–642. DOI: 10.1093/police/pay047

Mann, N., Devendran, P. N., & Lundrigan, S. (2019). 'You're never really free': Understanding the barriers to desistance for registered sexual offenders in the community. *Criminology & Criminal Justice, 1748895819853861*. Advance online publication. DOI: 10.1177/1748895819853861

Mann, N., & Lundrigan, S. (2021). Dynamic assessment of registered sexual offenders: The national practitioner perspective on the use of the 'Active risk management System'. *Policing and Society*, •••, 1–18. DOI: 10.1080/10439463.2021.1873324

Mann, R. E., Webster, S. D., Schofield, C., & Marshall, W. L. (2004). Approach Versus Avoidance Goals in Relapse Prevention with Sexual Offenders. *Sexual Abuse*, *16*(1), 65–75. DOI: 10.1023/B:SEBU.0000006285.73534.57 PMID: 15017827

Maruna, S. (2001). *Defining desistance*. American Psychological Association.

Mydlowski, L., & Turner-Moore, R. (2023). Tensions between police training and practice for the risk assessment of registered sex offenders in England and Wales. *Journal of Sexual Aggression*, •••, 1–14.

Mydlowski, L., Turner-Moore, R., & Kewley, S. (2024). Can we expect the police to integrate 'risk' and 'desistance' practice during home visits of those convicted of sexual offences? *Journal of Criminal Psychology*.

National Crime Agency. (2024). National Strategic Assessment 2024 of Serious and Organised Crime. *Annex-CSA Scale Methodology 2023*. https://www.nationalcrimeagency.gov.uk/images/campaign/CSA_Scale_Methodology_2023.pdf

National Police Chiefs' Council. (2022). *National policing prevention strategy*. https://www.npcc.police.uk/SysSiteAssets/media/downloads/publications/publications-log/2022/npcc-prevention-strategy-1.pdf

National Police Chiefs' Council. (2024). *Policing violence against women and girls – The national framework for delivery: 2024–2027*. https://www.npcc.police.uk/SysSiteAssets/media/downloads/our-work/vawg/vawg-framework-for-delivery.pdf

Netten, K., & Wakeling, H. (2025). Men subject to supervision who sexually reoffend. A narrative literature review to identify factors which raise risk, and support desistance. *Journal of Criminal Psychology*. Advance online publication. DOI: 10.1108/JCP-11-2024-0103

Office for National Statistics. (2023). *Sexual offences prevalence and trends, England and Wales: Year ending March 2022*. https://www.ons.gov.uk/peoplepopulationandcommunity/crimeandjustice/articles/sexualoffencesprevalenceandtrendsenglandandwales/yearendingmarch2022#:~:text=The%20increases%20in%20police%20recorded,to%20come%20forward%20and%20report

Online Safety Act. 2023, c. 50. (UK).

Parliament, U. K. (2023). *Sentencing Bill 2023*. Retrieved from. [parliament.uk]

Pemberton, S., & Kewley, S. (2025). *Contrary to popular belief, at the end of Registered Sexual Offenders' prison and community sentences they are managed solely by specialist police officers. In 50 Facts Everyone Should Know about the Police*. Policy Press.

Pemberton, S., Kewley, S., & Mydlowski, L. (2023). The Police as Formal Agents of Change: Assisting Desistance in Individuals Convicted of Sexual Offences. *Journal of Community Safety & Well-being*, *8*(4), 191–196. DOI: 10.35502/jcswb.332

Police, C. (2022). [UK]. *Sentencing and Courts Act, c*, 32.

Richards, K. (2021). *Desistance from Sexual Offending The Role of Circles of Support and Accountability*. Routledge New York. https://www.taylorfrancis.com/books/mono/10.4324/9781003125532/desistance-sexual-offending-kelly-richards

Seal, M. (2018). *Participatory pedagogic impact research: Co-production with community partners in action*. Routledge.

Serious Crime Act. (2015). c. 9. (UK).

Snyder, C. R., Ilardi, S., Michael, S. T., & Cheavens, J. (2000). Hope theory: Updating a common process for psychological change. In *Handbook of psychological change: Psychotherapy processes & practices for the 21st century* (pp. 128–153). John Wiley & Sons, Inc.

Telep, C. W., Wright, K. A., Haverkate, D. L., & Meyers, T. J. (2020). The Value of Participatory Action Research in Corrections: Introduction to the Special Issue. *Corrections : Policy, Practice and Research*, *5*(1), 1–5. DOI: 10.1080/23774657.2020.1713636

Thornton, D. (2024). What Works in Assessing Recidivism Risk in Men Convicted of Contact Sexual Offenses. In *The Wiley Handbook of What Works in Correctional Rehabilitation* (pp. 93–104). https://doi.org/DOI: 10.1002/9781119893073.ch8

Villeneuve, M.-P., F. -Dufour, I., & Farrall, S. (2021). Assisted desistance in formal settings: A scoping review. *The Howard Journal of Crime and Justice*, *60*(1), 75–100.

Voyeurism (Offences) Act. (2019). c. 2. (UK).

Ward, T., & Connolly, M. (2008). A human rights-based practice framework for sexual offenders. *Journal of Sexual Aggression*, *14*(2), 87–98. DOI: 10.1080/13552600802007874

Ward, T., & Maruna, S. (2007). *Rehabilitation: Beyond the risk paradigm*. Routledge.

Ward, T., & Stewart, C. A. (2003). The treatment of sex offenders: Risk management and good lives. *Professional Psychology, Research and Practice*, *34*(4), 353–360.

Weaver, B. (2015). *Offending and desistance: The importance of social relations*. Routledge.

Willis, G. M. (2018). Why call someone by what we don't want them to be? The ethics of labeling in forensic/correctional psychology. *Psychology, Crime & Law, 24*(7), 727–743. DOI: 10.1080/1068316X.2017.1421640

ENDNOTES

1 Within police constabularies in England and Wales, the term MOSOVO is used to denote both individual officers and the specialist public protection units to which they are assigned.

2 A collaboration between Liverpool John Moores University, Lancashire Constabulary, Birmingham City University, University of Central Lancashire and the Centre of expertise on child sexual abuse

Chapter 23
Getting Business-Like About Organised Crime:
Adopting an Organised Crime Business (OCB) Mindset for Intelligence, Investigation, and Disruption

John Coxhead
http://orcid.org/0009-0009-5864-5016
De Montfort University, UK

Chris Allen
De Montfort University, UK

Ian Davidson
De Montfort University, UK

Michael Harrison
University of East London, UK

ABSTRACT

Arresting our way out of organised crime is not working, so new ways of thinking are needed. Many business processes within organised crime have been uncharted because law enforcement has been asking the wrong questions about how things work. Now is an opportunity to supplement existing capabilities for state agencies to better protect the public by understanding the often-sophisticated business of crime, not just to arrest it but destroy it from the inside out. At a time of restructures for increased efficiency and productivity, policing aspires to work smarter. It is only

DOI: 10.4018/979-8-3373-2757-0.ch023

by exploring bold thinking about the adoption of an OCB mindset, and by investing in additional skillsets, that a new performance growth can be unleashed. Such new ways of thinking about the business of crime offer a transformational opportunity to turn policing funding and performance crises into a generational opportunity.

INTRODUCTION

This conceptual chapter is intended to contribute to this book by highlighting a new way of industrialising policing capability to be both more intrusive and proactive. The opportunity for such growth is based upon the entrepreneurial nature of Organised Crime (Gottschalk, 2010, 2010) and, more importantly, how entrepreneurial business skills can be used by policing and partners. 'Think OCB' builds upon the existing and established model of Organised Crime Groups (OCGs) Keane and Bell (2013), De León (2014), Murray (2016). The contribution in this chapter is to be explicit that some OCGs have evolved to become OCBs, hence why OCG tactics have become blunted in effecting real impact. Operational tactics against OCGs have a limited impact because they too often focus upon nominal prosecution, rather than the business of crime, which very often continues uninterrupted.

Exploring the concept 'Think OCB' requires better understanding business practices and business modelling (Osterwalder & Pigneur, 2010) because many contemporary criminals utilise business models and practices in the execution of their criminal enterprises (Wainwright, 2016). Think OCB complements, yet extends the existing OCG model by offering additional, alternative tools and modes of analysis that are currently limited amongst traditional capabilities of policing strategies and tactics.

Conventional thinking in relation to organised criminality treats it operationally in a form of singularity as a gang or group hence the term OCG. In the UK the police generally investigate crimes committed by individuals and gangs – not businesses per-se Marks (1996), Thompson (2007), Glenny (2008), Harvey & Hornsby (2016).

We argue such labelling has held us back in recognising that many criminal enterprises operate as Organised Crime Businesses (Allen et al, 2025). There are 4, 500 mapped OCGs in the UK (Coxhead, 2022; Allen et al., 2025). In reality, this is the tip of the iceberg. No mapping exercise has been conducted in relation to OCBs because even though they exist, conventional approaches have not been looking for them (Pearson and Hobbs, 2004; Escobar, 2010).

RIGHT RESOURCES IN RIGHT PLACES AT RIGHT TIME

We recommend 'Think OCB' for improved additionality in intelligence assessments and to broaden investigative, and disruption, opportunities, for example improving the quality and interrogation of Suspicious Activity Reports (SARs). Current policing restructures offer an ideal time to consider where business and financial tracking expertise could be located to enable sharing of resource from national to local. Further, expanded capabilities could be achieved through more multi-agency integration, for example specialist CPS staff with enhanced business understanding, supporting intelligence development and investigative direction for restraint orders and asset confiscation.

'Think OCB' offers new skillsets and mindsets to expand the conventional policing orthodoxy, enabling a more entrepreneurial and dynamic capability. Initiating an OCB methodology creates an organisation which uses resources more effectively to meet demand effectively and maintain sustainability. Moreover, OCB principles and practices aid operational effectiveness in relation to an enhanced and proactive level of intelligence development, investigations, crime prevention, and organised crime disruption.

Think OCB asserts crime is a big business and not being able to get on top of it can affect public trust and confidence. Even experienced professionals trying to combat SOC can become disillusioned by a lack of any transformational change in tackling such criminality, so the opportunity presented here is to get more strategically upstream, beyond simply continually reacting to criminal acts using often outdated tools.

UNDERSTANDING ENTREPRENEURIAL BEHAVIOUR IN ORGANISED CRIMINALS

In this section we consider the current professional landscape of OCG practices and compare these to the transformational potential of 'Think OCB'. It is widely accepted that Organised Crime (OC) is entrepreneurial in nature (Hobbs, 1987; Smith, 2021). Likewise, although the terms *Criminal Entrepreneurship* and *Criminal Entrepreneur* are now ubiquitous, they have no utility in relation to the investigation of Organised Crime (Allen et al, 2025).

Our research indicates that many Senior Officers and SIOs are aware of the entrepreneurial proclivities of Organised Criminals yet the inability of the police as an organisation to tackle this fact. This points to a capabilities gap; yet there is a solution. We argue that *Entrepreneurial Criminals* (ECs) have identifiable profiles and that the police need to be able to understand *Entrepreneurial Behaviour* in Organised Criminals (Smith, 2009).

Indeed, Smith (2009) argued that OCs who are entrepreneurial have a different *Modus Operandi* (Method of Operating) to traditional OCs and that they also have differing styles in relation to their unique *Modus Essendi* (state of being/intelligence) and *Modus Vivendi* (a communicational relationship) which are related to their MO's (Smith, 2021).

Nuanced within OCBs will be a spectrum straddling criminals with an entrepreneurial flair or businessmen with a criminal propensity. The former may see their profession through the lens of *Criminal Nous* and the latter *Business Nous*. This may influence their propensity to commit violence but there may be hybrid cases where a criminal possesses both sets of nous. In most cases, greed and financial gain lie behind their criminal enterprises but other drives may be in play. Even where motivations are not primarily financial, however (such as Internet illegal porn) is more often the case that a (dark) industry has been built around product provision, and that enabling business is profit based.

Irrespective of whether one is dealing with an OCG or OCB one must profile what type of criminal enterprise one is dealing with e.g., are they craft criminals engaged in one type of crime such as theft, robbery, people smuggling / trafficking, drug trafficking, gun running, fraud, forgery, smuggling contraband etc. This is important because although they may share similar structures and criminal strategies, they will have different *Criminal Profiles*, *Skill Sets* and *Playbooks*. The latter element of Playbooks is important because just like conventional MOs each OCG will have identifiable actions and responses it undertakes in committing its crimes but some of these will be unique to OCG acting as a signature. It is also helpful to map Law Enforcement Playbooks to compare them with the play-booked responses of criminal enterprises to identify organisational, communicational and skills-based mismatches. See Table 1 for a brief discussion of profiling criminal enterprises.

Table 1. Profiling – Criminal Enterprises. Individual nominals and collectives

	**OCG** – Organised along traditional criminal hierarchal structures with stereotypical criminal roles from boss, underboss to foot soldiers all of which self-identify as criminals ideologically and semiotically. The leader may may or may not adopt a criminal identity and may present as a Businessman Gangster or Legitimate Businessman and may operate legitimate and illegal income streams simultaneously. OCGs have identifiable Modus Operandi's and Modus Vivendi's. Most OCG members will have criminal convictions and be known to the police. There will not be a recognisable business model. Although, an OCG may not appear to fit the criteria for being considered an OCB/HCG it is still useful to anlayse their activities using a knowledge of business, business models and business theories.
	**OCB** – Organised along non-traditional criminal lines as a business with a CEO and business functions and may take on the appearance of a legitimate company. Containing a confusing mixture of legitimate and illegal elements. Those that lean towards the legitimate may not even be recognisable as a criminal enterprises per se. To effectively and efficiently investigate an OCB one must adopt aa sophisticated mapping strategy because investigators may not initially see, nor understand the hidden structures, as OCG categorisation mapping works in a strictly deductive fashion. If it is headed up by an apparently legitimate businessman, it may not even be considered to be an OCG. There will be criminal facilitators and deniable associates. Some OCB staff may or may not be fully aware they are a front for organized crime. Staff may self-identify with business roles, ideology and semiotics. The structure is fluid and may include legitimate and illegal shadow infrastructures. There will be an identifiable manager even if they are a figurehead only. Some OCB members will have no criminal convictions and be unknown to the police. They will have an identifiable Modus Operandi's and Modus Vivendi's and have a recognisable business model. One must also consider the existence of Illegal/Illicit shadow infrastructure (Smith and McElwee, 2024). To investigate an OCB using traditional policing strategies is not efficient, nor effective practice because one will miss the business elements that could lead to new lines of inquiry.

THE BUSINESS OF CRIME

The aim of business is to maximise return, whilst retailing goods and services: to make profit. OCBs tend to operate in monopolistic or oligopolistic forms, which is seen less rarely in pure legitimate businesses (Schelling, 1971; Arlaachi, 1988; Cockayne, 2016; Catino, 2019). Yet business principles otherwise apply across all legitimate and illegitimate business in how they operate, and how they think (Wainwright, 2016).

Given the reality that most income from retailing will take the form of money (rather than barter), this will flow toward paying suppliers and staff. Existent research (Levitt and Venkatesh, 1998) indicates that drug dealing gangs operate a franchise model, in which workers are paid a compensating differential. This factors the risk of arrest and legal sanction and maintains the incentive for drug 'runners' to engage in the work.

Levitt and Venkatesh (1998) were able to determine that the business structure of a drug dealing gang often placed the handling of money, into the hands of a more senior, and out the way, gang member, who may have more specialist knowledge. McLean (2018) makes a similar finding more recently in Scotland, where youth gang members can be seen to mature their gang organization to incorporate business like practices. Also, distinct roles develop such as importers, distributors, and sellers.

However, in engaging with OCGs the police and other law enforcement agencies tend to approach anchor their investigations around nominal investigation from arrest to conviction. Resources and tactics are seldom able or allowed to consider any *Business Model and Business Strategy* of the OCG or criminal enterprise, either as widened investigation or for intelligence purposes. Such an observation builds upon existing capacities but offer an additionality to do more for better impact.

Even if an OCG is mapped and profiled as a traditional one it may still have a hidden business model underpinning its activities, both illegal and legal. Developing an understanding of 'Think OCB' offers exposing the relevance of operational supply chains, financial records, matrix structures, logistics, and communication tactics.

OCG investigations rely more on traditional policing skills whereas OCB investigations require business related knowledge and skills adopting an 'all systems' of cross agency work, skilled investigators (including financial), lawyers and business analysts (rather than just crime analysts) to enable proactive business intelligence development, investigation and disruption.

WHY IS INVESTIGATING CRIMINAL BUSINESSES IMPORTANT?

According to ex-Chief Constable John Alderson (2000) the traditional purpose of the police *per se* was to protect the middle and upper classes from criminal elements within the working class. Similarly, Alderson argued that the police also treat the business community with deference because often the business community is the victim of predatory crime. The 'haloed' societal view of businessmen feeds into this as businessmen did not fit into the *Sociological Stereotype* of the Organised Criminal (Chapman, 1968). Consequentially, traditional illegal activity by rogue businessmen was not investigated as rigorously as crimes committed by Organised Criminals.

The possession of a previous conviction legitimises the recording of intelligence and as many businessmen do not have convictions any intelligence about them was held locally as *oral intelligence* (Smith, 2009). When businessmen were involved in a crime they were often used as witnesses against those perceived to be *real criminals*. This led to a situation where crimes committed by members of the business community were under investigated (Smith, 2016). This is despite the fact that the economist William Baumol (1996) has argued that many entrepreneurs and criminals emerge from the same social strata and remain networked to each other and went to school together.

These are amongst the reasons the police as a service did not develop a capability of investigating them as a category of OCs in their own right and did not develop intelligence sources within it. Indeed, many police officers do not know how to begin investigating businesses or how to search Companies House and similar repositories for details of company directors and owners. There is no training manual for SIOs on how to investigate such crimes. As an example, at a practical level, even though there has been a recent focus on nail shops and barbers on the High Street as covers for OC, the intelligence profiles of who owns what spaces (and facilitates their use) on our High Streets is surprisingly scant. Where one business front is closed because some nominals are arrested, the business itself reappears quickly, so the OCB nature of High Street spaces is just one example of why traditional law enforcement fails to make any lasting impact.

WHAT IS THE OCB APPROACH?

Think OCB is a new, practice based investigative ethos for targeting and disrupting SOC (Coxhead, 2022). It is an investigative process of gathering intelligence and evidence, which utilises business skills to both uncover OC and use them against OC infrastructures. Its main aim is to encourage police and other investigative authorities to target criminal enterprises and associated businesses – knowing that businesses can carry many vulnerabilities and weaknesses and criminal justice outcomes are not the only way to proceed.

The role of sabotage is key. Small marketplace interventions can cause a business to spiral into a crisis which loses money, not makes it. Whilst prosecutions are always appreciated for their disruptive qualities – nominals are easily replaced (akin to the game of *Whac A Mole*) and some even direct business from within jail in any case. Yet, business market and infrastructure crises are not so easily recoverable.

Interdicting criminal enterprises is a core role for the police but complex investigation is time consuming and costly and it is both efficient and effective to consider developing other strategies for disrupting OCGs and criminal activity. The aim of the approach is to disrupt the operations of the criminal businesses, their supply chains and fiscal flows to bring about a more disruptive and permanent change.

Ultimately, the aim is to prove what constitutes business activities from a HMRC perspective to reveal OCBs have been illegally earning over a period of time so that they can be held legally and financially accountable. As well as Asset Confiscation exercises - hitting an OCB with a Tax Bill will hurt them more in the long run and send a clear message. To do this entails establishing evidence of money laundering, tax evasion, bribery, corruption and the flouting of business regulations pertinent to their business niche, thus requiring a multi-agency approach.

SUGGESTIONS FOR OPERATIONALISING ORGANISED CRIMINAL BUSINESS METHODOLOGIES

We envisage a stage-based model of Mapping; Profiling; Teaming; and Implementation:

Figure 1.

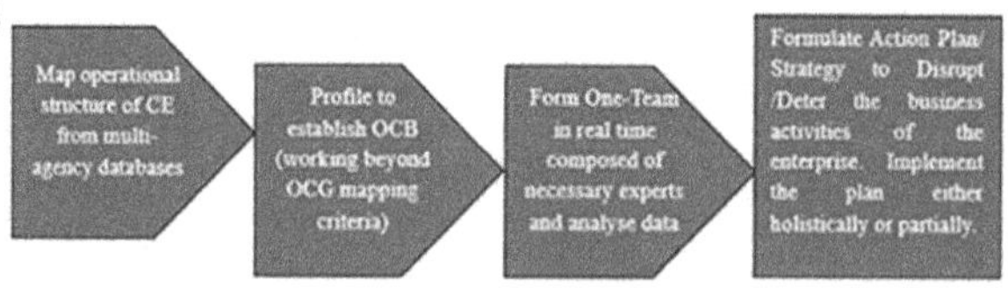

The veracity of the OCB premise has been outlined from an academic perspective in the earlier phase of this chapter; the key question is what these findings can do from a practical policing standpoint. Stakeholder experts could include academics; experienced entrepreneurs who can advise on how to disrupt the business cycles; HMRC agents or forensic accountants; experts in business legislation; as well as officers of any rank who have a working knowledge of the targets. The focus should be on the evidence, not the process and concentrating upon on identifying business structures and assets for future asset confiscation exercises. The aim is to confirm that the OCB is running an illegal business with the potential to tax earned revenues.

Such an inductive enquiry can be conducted overtly or covertly and in tandem with other diversionary tactics to blind the targets to the real purpose of the operations, hence hiding OCB approach from the (OCB) targets. For the sake of efficiency and effectiveness it is important to analyse the operational learning to refine future operational iterations and ensure continual agility by instilling more of sense of business guile to supplement a traditional enforcement mindset. We advocate utilising business and entrepreneurship theories (particularly supply chain theories) to develop a more nuanced understanding of how to better disrupt OCBs. The beauty of the methodology is that it utilises known policing models such as the 4/7D's (Deny, Detect, Disrupt, Deter etc) and also *Clear, Hold, Build*, consequently by dovetailing existing efforts there is an eclectic morphing of each skill sets any expert brings to this new (business) war room approach.

Additionally, one could utilise an adapted Business Modelling approach (Pinguer, et al, 2010) based on the successful Business Model Canvass to develop a more nuanced intelligence picture of the enterprise, the players and its supply chain. Allen (2025b) explains the origins and concept of the Organised Crime Applicability factor; a sorting tool designed as a mechanism to assess the suitability of business analysis techniques to be transposed to organised crime investigation.

Only a portion of business analysis techniques are suitable for application to an OCG. A major reason for this is while there are huge similarities between the operations of both groups, by dint of the illicit nature of their products and the corresponding lack of regulation that accompanies this, OCGs need not concern themselves with some elements that legitimate enterprises have to contend with, such as human resources, legal or ethical constraints and therefore elements of business analysis that refer to these factors are not relevant.

BUSINESS ANALYSIS OF BUSINESS CRIME

Business analysis, as defined by the International Institute of Business Analysis (2021), is the practice of defining needs and recommending solutions within an organisation to facilitate change. However, in the case of organised crime, the objective isn't to enhance operations but to disrupt and dismantle criminal entities. Allen (Centre for the Study of Organised Crime: 2025a, 2025b) highlights that through reverse-engineering criminal organisations, law enforcement can use business analysis techniques to identify weaknesses, exploit vulnerabilities, and impede the criminal activities that sustain OCGs.

Business analysis is not just about improving efficiency but rather understanding an organisation's strengths, weaknesses, and operational vulnerabilities (in this case to best sabotage them). Through techniques such as strategic analysis and change management, law enforcement can identify the weaknesses in an OCG's structure, operations, and illicit strategies. For example, by understanding how an OCG generates profit, such as through drug trafficking or fraud, law enforcement can identify weaknesses and target critical points in their operations, causing major damage to the criminal ecosystem, and potentially at less cost to agencies than using traditional law enforcement methods.

Profit (money) is a key factor in OCB business models and can reflect a weakness in the OCB in terms of the evidence trail it may create, but also its irreplaceability when disrupted. Therefore, activity which closes off the ability of an OCB member who handles financial matters to do their work, is perhaps more detrimental to the enterprise, compared to the arrest of a drug runner or small-time or mercenary member who may be, in terms of the *business*, highly visible but also highly expendable.

DIRTY MONEY

Money in any business model must be capable of movement, otherwise it has no real-world value. Indeed, business continuation depends upon business liquidity, which is the ability to settle short term debts in cash (Atrill and McLaney, 2024). This settlement may move upon multiple rails including, cash, the established banking system and the cryptocurrency system.

The established banking system, in the UK, is subject to the Money Laundering Regulations (2017) which operationalise elements of the Proceeds of Crime Act (2002). In addition, the Financial Services and Markets Act (2000), has powers to investigate approved and registered firms which show poor application of Anti-Money Laundering regulations (Blair et al, 2009).

This raises the possibility that cryptocurrencies will be used as a means of settlement instead. It is important to note that not all cryptocurrency use is illicit, some use it in a genuine search for yield (Harrison, 2024). Indeed, research indicates that cryptocurrencies are a conduit for illicit transactions. Of all illicit activity, 33% of transactions seek to evade sanctions, 29% seeks to reach blocked recipients or circumvent Anti-Money Laundering processes, and 24% are transactions as a result of scams & fraud (Mondoh, 2025). A key initial indicator of crypto misuse is the way in which the system is accessed: use of non-custodial wallets, cold storage wallets, and crypto ATMs. All of these could be attempts to avoid using regulated crypto exchanges which undertake Anti-Money Laundering Precautions in a similar way to banks (FCA, 2024).

The Proceeds of Crime Act (2002) had an excellent basis not least because it did not focus on 'money or 'laundering' but rather the movement and use of 'criminal property', which carries a far greater opportunity for law enforcement. has a far broader meaning. Sadly, these offences are not used enough. Firstly, because they do not show in crime data unless detected (thereby attracting less attention). Secondly, they are misunderstood with many practitioners lacking confidence to pursue them. Lastly, the criminal justice system, including prosecutors and the judiciary, tend to only regard these should only be used for complex matters, which is not what the legislators envisaged. Overall, more could be done with the Act combined with a 'Think OCB' mindset.

UPSKILLING THE WORKFORCE

Part of any change in the future would require better training and education of policing professionals, including managers and chief officers. This would not need to financial investigator training as such, but more to open their eyes to what is available to them if they thought more laterally. Legal interpretation help was crafted in the Professional Practice Financial Investigation (2014), but this now need both refreshing to integrate 'Think OCB' and then writing into more training interventions, to widen the proactive toolkit of policing professionals.

There are more resources available to further upskill investigators, such as the tactical suite U BATTLE toolkit (Utilising Business Analysis Towards Targeted Law Enforcement) (Allen 2023, Allen 2025a). This comprises a spectrum set of tools that merge business analysis techniques with policing strategies. Trialled on live and historic law enforcement cases (Allen, 2023) the toolkit's self-diagnosis questions allow users to explore key vulnerabilities across the three main areas of *Business Operations* (understanding functions and logistics), *Financial Vulnerabilities* (assessing the generation and use of financial resources, both legitimate and illicit) and *Market Vulnerabilities* (mapping interaction and interdependencies with other criminal groups, suppliers, buyers, and competitors).

The derived answers to these questions aid users to think differently about how to best understand, and sabotage, a criminal enterprise. In turn this also complements the development of a targeted investigative strategy, by adding additional capabilities. Pinpointing where critical intelligence is missing, and such omissions only tend to become apparent by asking these different sorts of questions. By answering business analysis questions investigators and intelligence analysts can identify and uncover previously hidden patterns, weaknesses, and opportunities within and around any criminal organisation.

CONCLUSION

Policing already does a lot and in most instances with scan resource or funding. However, the risk and threat from organised crime is such that the drive to constantly improve must be relentless. Think OCB offers an additionality in a focused mindset with additional skills, opening up wider investigation, greater intelligence returns and creative disruption tactics.

'Think OCB' does not reject OCG workstreams, but rather builds upon them in a dynamic way. 'Think OCB' offers entrepreneurial and lateral creativity compared to an investigation process which tends to be rigidly linear. Such a step change could reap untold rewards and could well cause some surprise and market uncertainty amongst criminal business networks who have perhaps become used to being able to assess how policing tactics have traditionally worked.

Such change would require some investment for return. It would be worthwhile to develop a training manual and playbooks relating to different OCB scenarios – this would require investment for collaborative action research to ensure all eclectic expert insights viewpoints were integrated. A similar exercise to capture the most useful elements of the proposed *Criminal Business Model Canvass* would be helpful – but again this would require pump-prime investment (Verhoeven, et al, 2024).

Overall, although the approach we advocate is simple it should not be misinterpreted as being easy to do as it is nuanced and not easily portrayed via one single transactional schematic. Nor should the paradigm shift of the necessary cultural mindset change needed to think beyond just traditional law be underestimated. Policy and practice can be wedded to the old ways and changing to a different way of looking at things can be slow. However, the speed and depth to which 'Think OCB' could seize the initiative away from traditional OCG operations may well appeal to many practitioners, once they see the possibilities and are allowed to experiment. To operationalise OCB interventions training materials will need to be developed to ensure the smooth running of any pilots, and agile learning from such pilots must be collated to inform continual improvement.

However, if law enforcement only does what it did before it will likely get the same, or worsening, results as organised crime business continue to adapt often thrive. To be more business-like about criminal profit offers not only a way for traditional law enforcement to restructure and better use existing – and new - resources but also a bold way to seize more criminal assets and reinvest them for the public good to help put crime out of business.

REFERENCES

Alderson, J. (2000). Principled Policing, *The Police Journal: Theory, Practice and Principles*, 73(1)

Allen, C. (2023). *Investigating organised crime - perspectives from within the police: A case study on business techniques and how can they be applied to analysing OCGs in a police setting*. Doctoral thesis, Liverpool John Moores University.

Allen, C. (2025a). Centre for the Study of Organised Crime 2025 https://centresoc.com/wp-content/uploads/2025/02/Introducing-the-U-BATTLE-Toolkit-1.pdf

Allen, C. (2025b). (Centre for the Study of Organised Crime 2025 b) https://centresoc.com/wp-content/uploads/2025/03/The-Organised-Crime-Applicability-Index.pdf

Allen, C., Coxhead, J., Harrison, M., & Smith, R. (2025). *Understanding Organised Crime Businesses (OCBs) from a practical and theoretical perspective*. Springer.

Arlaachi, P. (1988). *Mafia business: The Mafia ethic and the spirit of capitalism Oxford*. Oxford University Press.

Atrill, P., & McLaney, E. (2024). *Accounting and Finance for Non-Specialists* (12th ed.). Pearson Higher Education.

Baumol, W. J. (1996). Entrepreneurship: Productive, Unproductive and Destructive. *Journal of Business Venturing*, *11*, 3–22.

Blair, Q. C. (2009). *Blackstone's guide to the Financial Services and Markets Act 2000*. Oxford University Press.

Catino, M. (2019). *Mafia Organizations: the visible hand of criminal enterprise*. Cambridge University Press.

Chapman, (1968). *Sociology and the Stereotype of the Criminal*. London, Tavistock.

Cockayne, J. (2016). *Hidden Power: the strategic Logic of organised crime*. Hurst and Company.

Coxhead, J. (2022). *Organised Crime Businesses* – Presentation, Institute of Policing, University of Staffordshire.

De León, L. (2014). Organised Crime from a business perspective the case of the Mexican Meth Mafia. *International Journal of Asian Social Science*, *4*(9), 977–990.

Escobar (2010): Drugs, Guns, Money, Power. Great Britain: Hodder and Stoughton

Glenny, M. (2008). *McMafia: Crime without Frontiers*. Bodley Head.

Gottschalk, P. (2010). 'Entrepreneurship in organised crime'. *International Journal of Entrepreneurship and Small Business, 9*(3), 295.

Harrison, M. (2024). The role of FinTech in driving sustainability and inclusive practices in banking. In *International Banking in Global Perspective* (pp. 158–176). Routledge.

Harvey, J., & Hornsby, R. (2016). The Criminal Entrepreneur: a case study of an organised criminal family. In van Duyne, P., Scheinost, M., Antonopoulos, G., & Harvey, J. (Eds.), *Narratives on organised crime in Europe: criminals, corrupters & policy* (pp. 167–192). Wolf Legal.

Hobbs, D. (1987). *Doing The Business: Entrepreneurship, the Working Class, and Detectives in the East End of London.* Clarendon Press.

Italian Organised Crime Threat Assessment. *The Hague Financial Conduct Authority (2024). Cryptoassets: AML/CTF regime. Available at:* https://www.fca.org.uk/firms/financial-crime/cryptoassets-aml-ctf-regime

Keane, J., & Bell, P. (2013). A case study analysis of Israeli Organised Crime (IOC) (1990-2005): Applying the Crime Business Analysis Matrix (CBAM). *Mustang Journal of Law and Legal Studies, 5*, 79–96.

Levitt, S. D., & Venkatesh, S. A. (2000). An economic analysis of a drug-selling gang's finances. *The Quarterly Journal of Economics, 115*(3), 755–789.

McLean, R. (2018). An Evolving Gang Model in Contemporary Scotland. *Deviant Behavior, 39*(3), 309–321.

Mondoh, B. S. (2025). *Decoding Crypto Crime.* Available at: https://thebarristergroup.co.uk/blog/insights-from-trm-labs-2025-crypto-crime-report

Murray, K. (2016). 'Filling black holes – using business process analysis in criminal intelligence'. *Journal of Financial Crime, 24*(3), 412–424.

Osterwalder, A., & Pinguer, Y. (2010). *The Business Model Canvass.* Self-published.

Pearson G & Hobbs D (2004) ''E' is for enterprise: Middle level drug markets in ecstasy and stimulants'. *Addiction Research & Theory*, 12:6, 565-576, 181

Schelling, T. C. (1971). What is the Business of Organised Crime? *The American Scholar, 40*(4), 643–652.

Smith, R. (2009). Understanding Entrepreneurial Behaviour in Organised Criminals. *Journal of Enterprising Communities: People and Places, 3*(3), 256–268.

Smith, R. (2016). Of bad-seed, black-sheep and prodigal-sons: Profiling crime and enterprise in a small-business-community. *International Journal of Entrepreneurial Behaviour & Research*, *22*(1), 39–62.

Smith, R. (2021). *Entrepreneurship in Policing and Criminal Contexts*. Emerald Publishing.

Verhoeven, S., van Bergen, K., & Snaphaan, T. (2024). Criminal Business Model Canvas : inzicht in criminele verdienmodellen. *Congres Ondermijning & Georganiseerde Criminaliteit, Abstracts*. Presented at the Congres Ondermijning & Georganiseerde Criminaliteit, Spoorwegmuseum, Utrecht.

Wainwright, T. (2016). *Narconomics: How to run a drug cartel*. Ebury press.

Chapter 24
Responding to Fraud

Ann Stevens
http://orcid.org/0009-0006-7658-7372
Liverpool John Moores University, UK

ABSTRACT

Given that Fraud accounts for more than 40% of reported crime in the UK, which is rising year over year, this chapter will provide an overview of fraud. The focus will be on understanding the current landscape, offender type, fraud type, key organisations and government agencies and their strategic response to this growing problem. This topic has been added to the HMICFRS PEEL inspections from 2025 and the chapter aims to provide the reader with a better understanding of the problem and the part they play as a member of a police service that will be subject to an HMICFRS Fraud inspection at some point during which they hope to achieve an 'outstanding' rating. The author has extensive experience in this complex crime from both public and private sector organisations and brings that experience to the chapter by drawing upon a combination of key literature and range of industry and government reports. Education is a key theme throughout the chapter as knowledge gaps exist and impact the reporting process.

INTRODUCTION

Economic crime is one of the fastest-growing crime problems in the United Kingdom, facilitated in part by globalisation and the digital age (Economic Crime Plan, 2023). Within this category, fraud is the most commonly reported crime type in England and Wales (NCA, 2025), accounting for 43% of all crime reported (ONS, 2024). Official estimates indicate that annual fraud losses in the UK were £2.46 billion in 2021, representing a 17% increase on the previous year (ONS, 2022). However, these figures are widely regarded as conservative. For example, the Crowe

DOI: 10.4018/979-8-3373-2757-0.ch024

(2023) report estimates total fraud losses at up to £219 billion. Taken together, these indicators suggest that economic crime represents a significant threat to national security and UK prosperity (Economic Crime Plan 2023–2026), with an estimated one in 15 adults experiencing fraud victimisation in 2022 (ONS, 2022).

Fraud is increasingly enabled by serious organised crime (SOC), and its scale and pace of growth present substantial challenges for policing and wider law enforcement in detecting, disrupting, and deterring offenders. Over the past decade, organised criminality has become more complex to investigate and remains a continuing priority for those leading and conducting investigations. Technological innovation has enabled offenders to operate within virtual environments, expand reach across jurisdictions, and scale offending in unprecedented ways. The Government's Fraud Strategy (2023) emphasises pursuing and blocking fraudsters as a central mechanism for reducing fraud. Operation Russian Coms provides a recent example, with the National Crime Agency (NCA) reporting the disruption of a fraud platform believed to have generated 1.8 million scam calls to victims (NCA, 2024).

Operation Russian Coms exemplifies a defining feature of the contemporary threat, which is that the majority of fraud is no longer geographically bounded. The NCA estimates that 67% of fraud is cyber-enabled (NCA, 2025), meaning offenders can target victims without being physically present in the location of the crime, or even in the same country. This increases both investigative complexity and criminal opportunity, allowing offenders to exploit a global victim pool. In response, collaborative partnerships sit at the core of the UK Government's approach to combating fraud, alongside a consistent emphasis on intelligence, joint working, and innovation through improved technology use. Reflecting the specialised skills required, the UK Government has also introduced the Government Counter Fraud Profession (GCFP) to develop and recognise the skills of staff working in counter-fraud roles across government departments and to support a more consistent approach to investigations.

This chapter explains what these national developments mean for policing at force level and, in particular, how police forces can evidence a credible, inspection-ready response to fraud. It first situates fraud within the PEEL (police efficiency, effectiveness and legitimacy) framework and outlines why HMICFRS scrutiny of fraud is likely to intensify. It then describes the current architecture of the UK fraud response, including the roles of national reporting and intelligence functions, and clarifies what local forces are expected to own and deliver within this system.

From this foundation, the chapter uses identity fraud to illustrate how improved knowledge and scenario-based learning can strengthen frontline triage, investigative decision-making, and victim safeguarding, thereby supporting a more consistent and effective police contribution to the national response. Finally, the chapter draws together the key lessons emerging from HMICFRS's published reporting and translates them into practical expectations for forces. It sets out the core requirements associated with local ownership, investigation where viable lines of enquiry exist, demand analysis, effective use of intelligence products, workforce capability, and prevention and public protection.

POLICING FRAUD AND PEEL PRINCIPLES

The PEEL (police efficiency, effectiveness and legitimacy) principles were introduced in 2014 by His Majesty's Inspectorate of Constabulary and Fire & Rescue Services (HMICFRS). The PEEL Assessment Framework (PAF) is used to assess each police force in England and Wales. Given the prevalence of fraud, and its recent inclusion in key government strategy reports, it is unsurprising that fraud will feature on the HMICFRS inspection agenda from 2025. Notably, HMICFRS has previously made critical observations in its thematic reviews of fraud reporting by police forces in 2019 and 2022. It reported that the police response to fraud was "disjointed and ineffective", that "roles and responsibilities were not clear", and that "resources allocated to fraud don't match the scale of the problem" (HMICFRS, 2019; HMICFRS, 2022).

The Police Fraud Response

Figure 1 outlines the current structure of the UK's law enforcement response to fraud. While the breadth and scope of this response are extensive, and underpinned by defined processes, further improvement is required.

Figure 1. The Strategic Policing Model - National Policing Fraud Strategy, 2022

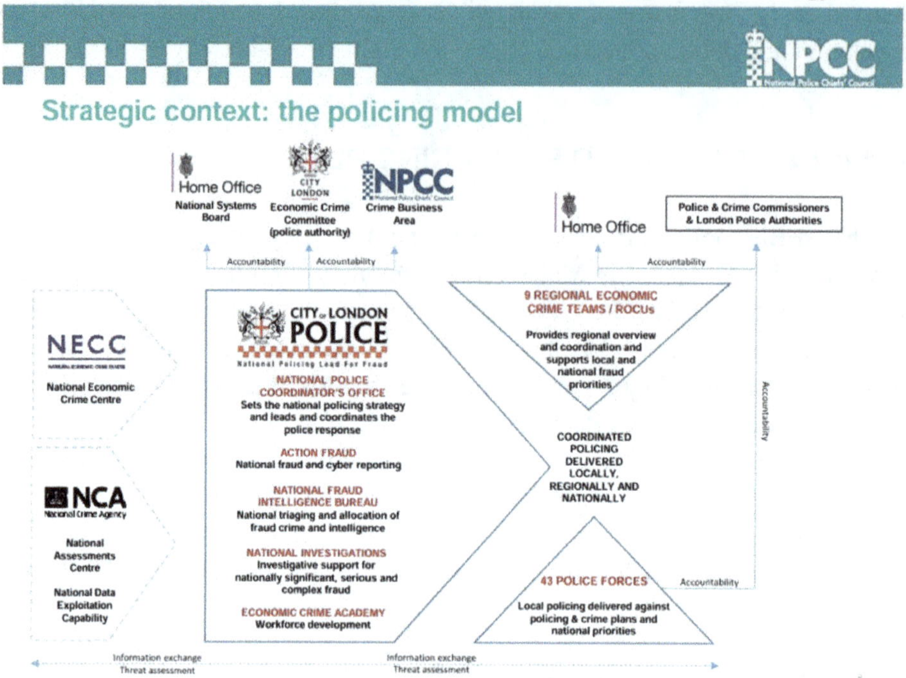

This need is illustrated by a 33% year-on-year increase in reported fraud incidents between 2023 and 2024 (ONS, 2024). In response, Action Fraud is undergoing changes, including rebranding as a national fraud and cybercrime reporting service, alongside anticipated improvements in technology and in intelligence and analysis outputs. However, at the time of writing, these changes had not been finalised.

Regardless of proposed national reforms, individual police forces will be expected to demonstrate a response to fraud that is consistent, comprehensive, and contributes meaningfully to the overall system. A fundamental expectation is that forces investigate reports where viable lines of enquiry exist. HMICFRS has previously stated that "some forces seek reasons not to investigate allegations of fraud", citing one force that closed as many as 96% of cases received from the National Fraud Intelligence Bureau without further action (HMICFRS, 2023). HMICFRS noted that many of these cases contained potential lines of enquiry, including identified suspects (HMICFRS, 2023). This finding should put all forces on notice that future fraud inspections are likely to expect, as a minimum, that forces pursue investigations where opportunities exist. Failure to do so is likely to result in an inadequate grade in this area.

Roles and Responsibilities

Formulating an adequate response involves not only dealing with fraud reports received from national law enforcement partners but also responding to reports made directly by the public. There is evidence that officers at local level respond to allegations of fraud by referring victims to Action Fraud, with no further local action. This approach is circular. It increases demand on Action Fraud, and, in many cases, reports are subsequently returned to local forces for investigation. Earlier acceptance of investigative responsibility could therefore save time and reduce avoidable duplication. Moreover, where HMICFRS can evidence that officers understand the need to take ownership of offences they encounter, and can demonstrate an appropriate local response, this is likely to contribute positively to future HMICFRS fraud inspection findings.

Capacity and Capability

Several explanations are offered for why officers do not assume responsibility for fraud offences they encounter. A Police Foundation study (2018) found that fraud is not prioritised by policing. However, it can also be argued that the volume of reported fraud is not currently manageable within existing resources. In practice, this may lead officers to redirect cases to other agencies as a means of workload management. A further possibility is that some personnel lack the specialist skills and confidence to respond effectively.

This latter issue was highlighted in HMICFRS's 2023 report, which found substantial evidence of "a lack of awareness among investigators and supervisors of important resources such as authorised professional practice and the fraud investigation model" (HMICFRS, 2023). Consequently, as with many contemporary policing challenges, staff knowledge, awareness, and the time invested in training are likely to be scrutinised in future inspections. Forces that can demonstrate sustained investment in fraud capability—through training, supervision, access to guidance, and clear operating models—are therefore likely to receive more favourable inspection findings.

In this context, Figure 2 outlines the key tenets for structuring capacity and capability for an effective fraud response. The model's core aim is to "protect the public by preventing and disrupting fraud through capable, coordinated and effective policing at all levels". In turn, forces will be expected to demonstrate tangible contributions to fraud prevention. This need not be onerous. Communications channels such as social media can be used to amplify national messaging while also delivering targeted preventative advice to communities within the force area that are particularly vulnerable to fraud.

Figure 2. Key components of an effective fraud response, taken from the National Policing Fraud Strategy, 2022.

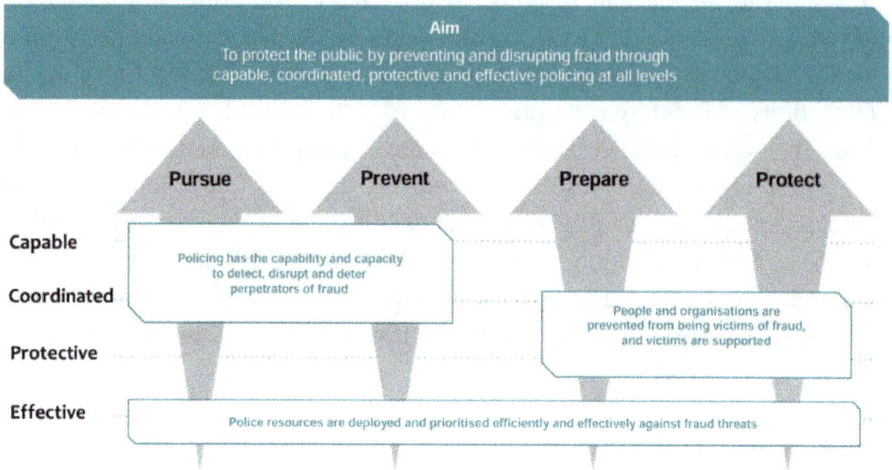

In the case of investigations, the City of London Police (COLP) have the role as the National Lead Force for Fraud. Serious and Complex Fraud investigations are conducted on behalf of policing by COLP. As such, except in exceptional circumstances, police services need not necessarily invest large resources into complex fraud cases and instead may be best served focusing time and effort on those that most frequently affect the public in their area. As well as taking responsibility for owning these, each should begin with a clearly defined investigation plan that aligns with the College of Policing Authorised Professional Practice, that follows the Fraud Investigation Model (FIM) (COLP, 2022).

Intelligence and Analysis

A further area that HMICFRS has highlighted as underutilised is the intelligence and analysis undertaken by police forces in response to fraud. Central government has increasingly emphasised the need to make better use of intelligence to combat fraud, to the extent that intelligence and analysis features within proposals to rebrand Action Fraud. Despite these developments, intelligence analysis is still less routinely applied to fraud within many local policing environments, even though it could materially enhance organisational learning and improve operational responses.

Forces will be expected not only to develop local fraud intelligence products, but also to make effective use of those provided by national partners. HMICFRS has specifically identified "the ineffectual use of intelligence products (such as monthly victim lists) given to forces by the National Fraud Intelligence Bureau" (HMICFRS, 2023). In one force area, HMICFRS found that these products were used only to count the number of victims in the force area, rather than to identify safeguarding needs or take action to support victims (HMICFRS, 2023). This is indicative of a wider lack of ownership and a failure to translate intelligence into practical activity.

HMICFRS also identified forces that were unable to provide basic data on fraud demand, including the volume of reports received and how many resulted in an active police response (HMICFRS, 2023). This lack of demand analysis undermines other critical aspects of an effective fraud response, particularly decisions about capacity, capability, and resource allocation. Reflecting this, HMICFRS (2022) recommended that the Economic Crime Strategic Board ensure that demand analysis includes all fraud, not solely serious and complex offending.

There are, however, examples of more effective practice. King and Doig (2016), for instance, reviewed Greater Manchester Police's introduction of a Volume Fraud Team (VFT), operating alongside its specialist economic crime capability. The VFT supported the identification of patterns and trends linked to fraud types and offender behaviours. It also enabled the identification of recurring vulnerabilities and service gaps that could be addressed to improve victim support, thereby strengthening police legitimacy. In this regard, GMP demonstrated improved effectiveness through the systematic analysis of fraud reports.

Future HMICFRS inspections are therefore likely to expect forces to demonstrate a mature understanding of local fraud dynamics. This includes a clear picture of fraud demand, typologies, trends, patterns, repeat victims, and repeat offenders. Investment in analytical capability, and, critically, in the operational use of analytical products, should consequently be treated as a contributor to improved HMICFRS grading in respect of the threat presented by fraud.

Increasing Knowledge and Awareness

Greater use of intelligence and analysis can also strengthen force capability. One of the most plausible contributors to inconsistent frontline responses is that some officers lack a clear understanding of the nature of fraud and the harms it creates, which in turn shapes decision-making at the point of report. Although fraud is covered in initial training, the emphasis is often placed on offence definitions and points to prove. There is therefore scope to enhance training through scenario-based case studies that reinforce the threat, harm and risk that fraud poses to victims, the economy and national security (NFI, 2025). To illustrate this, the section below uses identity fraud as a single fraud type and provides hypothetical and real world case studies to exemplify differences in scale, breadth and complexity.

Identity fraud

A key challenge for officers dealing with fraud reports is recognising and accurately classifying identity-related fraud. CIFAS (2025) reports that identity fraud is the most common fraud type, with 86% committed via online channels, which aligns with the wider rise in cyber-enabled crime. At the point of reporting, understanding the different way's identity fraud can be committed supports more efficient and effective decision-making. Gordon et al. (2007) emphasise the importance of identifying patterns and trends in identity fraud so that policing can better understand the problem and adopt a more proactive approach. Without sufficient training and confidence, however, it may be difficult for staff to determine what type of fraud has occurred at first contact. For example, many practitioners would struggle to explain, under pressure, the distinction between first-, second- and third-party fraud.

First-party fraud is when an individual uses their own identity to commit fraud for personal gain. During periods of economic pressure, this form of fraud may increase as individuals attempt to generate income or relieve financial strain (Experian, 2023).

Second-party fraud occurs when an individual knowingly allows another person to use their identity to commit fraud. A common example is "money mule" activity, where a person allows their bank account to be used to move criminal proceeds, often linked to money laundering.

Third-party fraud, which often presents the greatest risk, involves a stolen identity or the creation of a false identity using stolen or manufactured data (Experian, 2023).

The case studies below are designed to illustrate that, while each example can be categorised as identity-related fraud, they vary materially in scale, complexity and the level at which a police response is likely to be effective.

Case study 1 – UK individual localised offender

A number of credit cards are stolen from vehicles in a local area and then used at retail premises in the city centre to make fraudulent purchases. The investigation identifies a single offender responsible for both the thefts and the subsequent fraudulent transactions. This illustrates a localised pattern of offending for which a local investigative response is both expected and proportionate.

Case study 2 – UK organised crime

Five members of a criminal group are arrested for a complex identity fraud offence. Over four and a half years, the group submits thousands of false credit applications, causing an estimated financial loss of £53 million. Although markedly more complex, this remains consistent with third-party fraud because the identities used include both real and fabricated identities. With appropriate resourcing and partnership support, such an investigation could still be owned locally, potentially led by a single force with cross-agency collaboration.

Case study 3– global cybercrime

In 2024, Interpol published an update on Operation First Light, reporting the arrest of 3,950 individuals and the identification of a further 14,643 suspected offenders across 61 countries. The operation focused on online fraud, including the creation of fake websites designed to trick users into providing personal information and making payments for items that did not exist. The reported scale included 6,745 bank accounts, with many frozen, and approximately US$257 million in assets seized. Such activity requires substantial international coordination, complex legal authorities, and specialist economic crime capability to identify offences, trace assets, and pursue restraint and recovery. It is therefore unsuitable for local ownership and would typically require national or international leadership and coordination, for example through a national agency such as the NCA.

These case studies demonstrate the practical challenge faced by the officer or staff member who is the first point of contact for recording fraud. In this context, understanding behavioural indicators, potential complexity, and the likely investigative and partnership requirements (including technology, specialist skills and legal powers) is essential to recognising what can be owned locally and what should be escalated. This knowledge needs to be formalised, consistently understood, and embedded through training and supervision.

KEY RECOMMENDATIONS

Bringing together the themes across this chapter, I can now outline a clear set of expectations that I believe will underpin what "good" looks like in a force response to fraud. HMICFRS will require forces to demonstrate ownership, competence, and operational grip over the fraud demand that manifests locally. In practice, scrutiny is likely to focus less on whether a force can investigate every fraud report end-to-end, and more on whether it can evidence a coherent system that allocates responsibility appropriately, investigates where opportunities exist, safeguards victims, uses intelligence effectively, and can account for demand and outcomes. To support this, I set out seven recommendations for forces to ensure they are inspection ready.

1. HMICFRS will expect forces to demonstrate clear ownership of fraud, rather than treating it as an issue displaced to national or regional partners. The in-

spection focus is likely to examine whether frontline and supervisory practice reflects an understanding that referral to Action Fraud is a reporting route, not a substitute for police responsibility. Forces will therefore need to evidence that officers and staff recognise when local action is required, and that they do not use referral pathways to avoid investigative decision-making. Where a force can show that it takes responsibility for offences encountered and that this is reinforced through supervision and clear policy, it is likely to be viewed more positively.

2. HMICFRS is likely to treat investigation where viable lines of enquiry exist as a baseline expectation. The practical standard is not that every case is fully resourced, but that a force can demonstrate a consistent approach to pursuing investigative opportunities, particularly where suspects are identifiable, evidence is accessible, or safeguarding needs are apparent. In this context, inspectors are likely to look for consistent application of recognised professional frameworks, including alignment to the College of Policing's Authorised Professional Practice and the Fraud Investigation Model. HMICFRS is also likely to test whether cases are screened out appropriately and ethically, or whether decisions are shaped by convenience and workload pressure. Put simply, as with other crime types, where opportunities exist a force will be expected to act, document decisions properly, and justify any decision not to investigate.
3. Forces will be expected to evidence defined roles, responsibilities, and governance for fraud. A recurring criticism in HMICFRS reporting is a lack of clarity over who does what. Future inspections are therefore likely to examine whether fraud has clear ownership at leadership level, whether responsibilities are understood across the operating model (frontline, CID/economic crime, safeguarding, analysts, supervisors), and whether there is an accountable structure that connects local activity to the wider national system. This includes evidence that processes are not merely written but understood and enacted consistently.
4. HMICFRS will expect forces to show a credible understanding and management of fraud demand. A force that cannot describe the volume and nature of fraud affecting its communities and cannot explain how many reports receive a local police response, will struggle to evidence efficiency, effectiveness, or legitimacy. Demand analysis is therefore likely to be a core inspection theme. Forces should be able to articulate what fraud looks like locally, how it is changing, where harm concentrates (including repeat victims), and how this informs resourcing and prevention priorities. Critically, this analysis should underpin defensible decisions about capacity, capability, and service delivery.
5. HIMCFRS inspectors are likely to assess whether forces make effective use of intelligence and analysis, both locally produced and provided by national partners. HMICFRS criticism of the underuse of intelligence products is likely to translate

into inspection scrutiny of whether forces can demonstrate that they convert intelligence into activity. It will not be sufficient to hold or count intelligence outputs; forces will need to show how products drive investigation, safeguarding, targeting, disruption activity, and organisational learning. In inspection terms, this becomes a question of whether intelligence is operationalised.

6. HMICFRS will expect forces to demonstrate capacity and capability that is proportionate to the threat, including evidence of investment in skills, awareness, and supervision. The capability gaps identified, particularly limited awareness of key resources such as Authorised Professional Practice and the Fraud Investigation Model, point towards future inspections focusing on training, guidance, and professional standards. Forces that can evidence structured training (initial and continuing), scenario-based learning, accessible investigative models, and supervisor competence in fraud decision-making are likely to be better positioned. Importantly, capability is likely to be assessed not only within specialist teams, but also at the point of first contact, where classification, triage, victim care, and early investigative actions are decided.
7. Finally, forces will be expected to contribute meaningfully to fraud prevention and public protection. HMICFRS is likely to view prevention activity as both achievable and necessary. Through the intelligent use of communications channels, targeted messaging, and local community awareness activity, forces will be expected to demonstrate that they are taking tangible steps to reduce vulnerability and prevent repeat victimisation.

CONCLUSION

This chapter has argued that fraud now represents a core policing challenge, not only because of its scale and prevalence, but because its cyber-enabled and organised nature increasingly disconnects offending from geography and traditional investigative assumptions. Against that backdrop, fraud performance will, from 2025, be judged through the lens of PEEL, with HMICFRS scrutiny likely to intensify. While the UK response architecture is extensive, supported by national reporting, intelligence functions, and specialist capabilities led by the City of London Police, recent HMICFRS reporting has repeatedly highlighted persistent weaknesses in local ownership, clarity of responsibility, and the effective use of available resources. The central message is therefore that "good" fraud policing will not be defined by attempting to investigate everything, but by evidencing a coherent, disciplined local system that can triage demand intelligently, safeguard victims, and take proportionate investigative action where opportunities exist.

In practical terms, the chapter concludes that forces seeking to be inspection-ready should focus on seven interlocking requirements: demonstrable ownership of fraud at frontline and supervisory levels; consistent investigation supported by APP and the Fraud Investigation Model; clear roles, governance, and accountability across the operating model; credible demand analysis that informs resourcing and service design; the operational use of intelligence products to drive activity, not merely reporting; sustained investment in capability, training, and supervision from first contact through to specialist teams; and visible prevention and public protection activity informed by local risk. The identity fraud typology and case studies illustrate why knowledge and scenario-based learning matter: when staff understand the distinctions in behaviour, complexity, and investigative pathways, forces are better positioned to make defensible decisions, reduce duplication, improve victim support, and contribute meaningfully to the national response to fraud.

REFERENCES

Cifas. (2025). Fraudscape 2025. Retrieved June 26, 2025, from https://www.fraudscape.co.uk/

City of London Police. (2022). Fraud investigation policy (including the Fraud Investigation Model). Retrieved June 2, 2025, from https://www.cityoflondon.police.uk/foi-ai/city-of-london-police/publication-scheme/our-policies-and-procedures/2020/march/fraud-investigation-policy/

Crowe. (2023) Annual Fraud Indicator 2023. University of Portsmouth. Retrieved June 26, 2025, from https://crowe1.co.uk/s/abd437ed45dcd1e8a4ec3685053a0fc3044c2d98

Experian. (2023). Types of fraud: How 1st, 2nd & 3rd party fraud are changing. Retrieved June 26, 2025, from https://www.experian.co.uk/blogs/latest-thinking/fraud-prevention/what-is-first-second-and-third-party-fraud/

Gordon, G. R., Rebovich, D. D. J., & Choo, K. S. (2007). *Identity fraud trends and patterns*. Center for Identity Management and Information Protection, Utica College.

His Majesty's Inspectorate of Constabulary and Fire & Rescue Services. (2019). Fraud: Time to choose—An inspection of the police response to fraud. Retrieved June 2, 2025, from https://hmicfrs.justiceinspectorates.gov.uk/publications/an-inspection-of-the-police-response-to-fraud/

His Majesty's Inspectorate of Constabulary and Fire & Rescue Services. (2021). Spotlight report: A review of Fraud: Time to choose. Retrieved June 2, 2025, from https://assets-hmicfrs.justiceinspectorates.gov.uk/uploads/a-review-of-fraud-time-to-choose.pdf

His Majesty's Inspectorate of Constabulary and Fire & Rescue Services. (2023). PEEL Assessment Framework (PAF) 2023–2025. Retrieved June 18, 2025, from https://assets-hmicfrs.justiceinspectorates.gov.uk/uploads/peel-assessment-framework-2023-2025.pdf

Interpol. (2024). US$257 million seized in global police crackdown against online scams. Retrieved December 15, 2025, from https://www.interpol.int/News-and-Events/News/2024/USD-257-million-seized-in-global-police-crackdown-against-online-scams

King, J., & Doig, A. (2016). A dedicated place for volume fraud within the current UK economic crime agenda? The Greater Manchester Police case study. *Journal of Financial Crime*, *23*(4), 902–915.

National Crime Agency. (2024). *Operation Russian Coms (Operational update).* National Crime Agency.

National Crime Agency. (2025). Fraud. Retrieved June 2, 2025, from https://www.nationalcrimeagency.gov.uk/threats-2025/nsa-fraud-2025

National Policing. (2019). National Policing Fraud Strategy 2019. Retrieved June 2, 2025, from https://www.cityoflondon.police.uk/SysSiteAssets/media/downloads/city-of-london/about-us/national-policing-fraud-strategy-2019.pdf

Office for National Statistics. (2022). Office for National Statistics. [Statistical release on fraud losses in 2021]

Office for National Statistics. (2024). Crime in England and Wales. Retrieved June 18, 2025, from https://www.ons.gov.uk/peoplepopulationandcommunity/crimeandjustice/bulletins/crimeinenglandandwales/latest#fraud

Police Foundation. (2018). Fraud is not prioritised by the police, report finds. Retrieved June 26, 2025, from https://www.police-foundation.org.uk/news/policing-fraud/

Police Professional. (n.d.). New report calls for overhaul of fraud policing. Retrieved June 26, 2025, from https://policeprofessional.com/news/new-report-calls-for-overhaul-of-fraud-policing/

PricewaterhouseCoopers. (2024). Future of fraud: A UK view from the 2030s. Retrieved June 26, 2025, from https://policeprofessional.com/news/new-report-calls-for-overhaul-of-fraud-policing/

Public Sector Fraud Authority. (2025). Fraud reform programme: SRO appointment letter for Duncan Tessier (March 2025). Retrieved June 2, 2025, from https://www.gov.uk/government/publications/home-office-major-projects-appointment-letters-for-senior-responsible-owners/fraud-reform-programme-sro-appointment-letter-for-duncan-tessier-march-2025-accessible#:~:text=The%20Fraud%20Reform%20Programme%20is,parliament%20(30%20May%202024)

Public Sector Fraud Authority. (2025). National Fraud Initiative strategy. Retrieved June 26, 2025, from https://www.gov.uk/

UK Government. (2024). Cross Government Counter Fraud Functional Strategy 2024–2027. Retrieved June 26, 2025, from https://assets.publishing.service.gov.uk/media/65f01d1f9812270011f61283/Cross_Government_Counter_Fraud_Functional_Strategy_2024-2027.pdf

Section 4
Legitimacy

Chapter 25
Police Legitimacy

Scott Keay
http://orcid.org/0000-0002-3913-1679
Edge Hill University, UK

ABSTRACT

This chapter summarises key theoretical ideas on police legitimacy and explores how elements of the HMICFRS PEEL assessment framework may influence police practices that affect legitimacy. While PEEL inspections reference legitimacy, chief officers often prioritise trust and confidence, which are linked but not identical concepts. Legitimacy is complex, shaped by internal and external factors, with no single solution. It is best understood as a by-product of police behaviour and activity (Hough, 2020; McGregor, 2024; O'Reilly, 2024), and remains a topic more widely examined in academic than operational contexts. This chapter offers an overview and highlights how PEEL may help identify areas for improvement. For a deeper analysis, further reading is recommended.

INTRODUCTION

This chapter provides a foundational anchor for this section of the book regarding police legitimacy. It will summarise some of the theoretical ideas regarding police legitimacy and aspects of His Majesty's Inspectorate of Constabularies and Fire and Rescue Services (HMICFRS) PEEL (Police Effectiveness, Efficiency, and Legitimacy) assessment framework (HMICFRS, 2021) that might go some way to influence the practical benefit of police activity that can impact on legitimacy. The PEEL inspections refer to the notion of legitimacy but in reality, it might be argued that chief officers do not consider police legitimacy in its own right and tend to focus on aspects of trust and confidence (both of which are linked to legitimacy). Police legitimacy is a complex issue and there are a number of influencing factors,

DOI: 10.4018/979-8-3373-2757-0.ch025

both internally and externally. Therefore, there is no 'silver bullet' that can address issues of legitimacy. Police legitimacy is a by-product of police behaviour and activity (Hough, 2020; McGregor, 2024; O'Reilly, 2024). Indeed, this is an area of policing that is perhaps discussed more in academic circles than in operational policing matters. This chapter will offer an overview of police legitimacy and how PEEL inspections may help forces consider areas for improvement. In regard this theme, there are numerous academic sources that offer more a more in-depth appraisal on police legitimacy – there simply is not enough room here to do this any justice. Recommendations for further reading are included at the end of this chapter.

POLICE LEGITIMACY

Police legitimacy "is about authority – the right of the police, granted by the public, to tell people what to do, and to expect people to obey them" (O'Reilly, 2024, p. 28). Legitimacy refers to how the public perceive the police (both police officers and the police as an organisation) to have authority to exercise their power in pursuit of enforcing the law. Hough notes that authority "is the legitimate right of one person or group to exercise power over another" (2020, p. 13). A police officer's right to enforce the law, use reasonable force, and protect the vulnerable, when necessary, is most often unchallenged (Wood et al., 2024). This is due to the public recognition that the police are justified, i.e., legitimate, in their use of authority and power. The public accept the police's right to dictate appropriate behaviour not only when they feel a duty to comply with police officers, but also when they believe that the organisation acts in a manner that is in accordance with a shared moral purpose, e.g., enforce the law to improve public safety (Jackson et al., 2012; Tankebe, 2013). Indeed, this stems from the original Peelian principles that note "the police are the public and that the public are the police" (Gov.uk, 2012, p. 8). In this context, Bowling et al. (2019, p. 92) refer to the police as "citizens in uniform". This notion reflects the ideal that the police are representative of the public, and that it is this that affords them the legitimacy they need to undertake their work (Wood et al., 2024). However, to be considered as being legitimate when exercising authority, there are two concepts that are often discussed in relation to legitimacy: *policing by consent*, which is essential to legitimacy as it refers to public cooperation, and *procedural justice*, which refers to whether the police deal with the public in a fair and respectful manner. A summary of these concepts will now be discussed.

Legitimacy, Procedural Justice, and Policing By Consent

What is considered successful or popular policing will vary across individuals, communities, governments, and even police forces. However, *procedural justice* is a measure of the extent to which the public may deem policing to be legitimate (Tyler, 2025; Wood et al., 2024). Procedural justice refers to the transparency and fairness of process when the police enforce the law, whilst also offering the public a voice in how they are handled. The public expect fair treatment based on shared values, respect, neutrality, and voice (O'Reilly, 2024). The public are more inclined to comply with the law and view the police as legitimate if they perceive law enforcement as fair, transparent, and impartial (Tyler, 2009). Therefore, legitimacy is based on a trust that ensures the consensual (between the police and the pubic) application of the law, including reasonable force when necessary. Indeed, Tyler (2004) argues that procedural justice can increase legitimacy, in which O'Reilly (2024, p. 28) neatly sums up as "the police can and do affect their own legitimacy through the way that they behave". This leads on to *policing by consent* which is the second concept linked to legitimacy.

Policing by consent suggests that the public *conform* to being policed when they view police officers to be legitimate in their actions. The College of Policing (2023, p. 1) note that "the police can only successfully carry out their work with the support and cooperation of the public". This relies on the police conducting themselves in a proportionate, lawful and accountable way, with the ethical and transparent use of police powers and legislation, decision-making and their use of discretion (College of Policing, 2023). Policing by consent is an important part of police legitimacy and police officers must operate within moral boundaries if they are to be truly legitimate (McGregor, 2024; Wood et al., 2024). Increasingly, police officers must take into account a number of different or contradictory moral considerations in order to make professional decisions. Combined, these three concepts, legitimacy, procedural justice and policing by consent, form the basis for how the public have confidence and trust in the police to carry out their duties. However, there are numerous factors that influence confidence and trust in practice. There are internal factors and external factors, some of which the police have no control over, e.g., "the systemic context of policing", such as how the police operate within the criminal justice system (McGregor, 2024, p. 35).

Internal Factors

The internal factors include those that McGregor (2024, p. 41) refers to as, "the practice of policing". This refers to the conduct and behaviour of police officers in the pursuit of their duty (McGregor, 2021). Consequently, police officers need to consider their own actions and behaviour to assess if they are legitimate or not (Bryant et al., 2013; Tankebe, 2019). It is the everyday interactions that can make a significant difference to members of the public: it is, "the way police treat victims of crime and deal with the kind of low-level issues that comprise the bulk of their workload" (Bradford et al., 2013, p. 87). This includes interpersonal skills, active listening, and explaining decisions, all of which are crucial to maintaining legitimacy. It is equally important that the "institution of policing" (McGregor, 2024, p. 44) is able to support and sustain ethical policing in practice. Addressing police leadership (at all levels), structures and processes to treat people in a fair manner are essential to improving legitimacy. This includes how police forces look after their staff, but also in how staff are recruited, selected, and trained. Simply staffing a force to be representative of the communities the police serve is not enough. For example, having shared values means having the same beliefs and standards and yet not all communities will have the same moral compass or shared values. Therefore, the *institution* and *practice* of policing must be open to reflective and critical thinking on their actions, particularly as external factors, are in constant flux.

External Factors

Policing is often about context and situations in which policing may be inadvertently placed. Police legitimacy is not the sole responsibility of the police as its influences include institutional and systemic problems that are beyond the control of the police, e.g., societal, judicial, and political contexts (McGregor, 2024). External factors are those that can influence policing (both the institution and practice), but also that of the wider public and how they may come to perceive policing. These factors can have a significant impact on trust, confidence, and therefore, on legitimacy (O'Reilly, 2024). For example, the Criminal Justice System (CJS) and politics have an influencing factor on policing as a whole, which can then influence how policing is perceived by the public, e.g., the outcome of a high-profile criminal case. The CJS needs to be resourced to provide adequate service that can support policing. An efficient and effective CJS will go some way to ease pressure on policing for protecting and safeguarding the most vulnerable, public safety, and crime reduction (McGregor, 2024).

The influence of politics is also a significant factor that the institution of policing is acutely aware of. Hough (2020), argues that politicians have ignored legitimacy in place of being tough on crime. This has filtered through to local Police and Crime Commissioners (PCC) that often represents party politics that is not always aligned to the incumbent government. Since 2012 (and until 2028), it is the PCC that holds Chief Constables to account (Cooper, 2021). After 2028, when PCCs will be abolished, regional mayors and new policing and crime boards will be responsible for holding police chiefs to account (Mitchell & Shuttleworth, 2025). It is anticipated that this will include council leaders, meaning political agendas may still be an undercurrent regarding police accountability. Political undertones can also shape the public perception of policing. Therefore, increasing the distance between policing and politics would help steer the practice of policing away from the potential harms associated with the political landscape (McGregor, 2024).

Means Vs Ends

The internal and external factors can be carefully addressed through Goldstein's original concept of problem oriented policing (Goldstein, 1977, 1979, 1990).

In his work, Goldstein (1979) has referred to the 'means over ends' syndrome within policing. He argued that the police had become preoccupied in the institution of policing (i.e., structures and processes) that they had neglected the ends of policing, i.e., the outcomes of police work: what are they wanting to achieve, such as improved community safety. Goldstein (1979), argued that as a result of this, police forces had lost sight of their core responsibilities in improving public safety and reducing crime as they focussed on internal mechanics of the police organisation.

Politicians lack of understanding and concentrating in the *means* (in stark contrast to Goldstein's ideas) ensures that legitimacy is precarious at best and invisible from policy at worse. Pease (2023) regarded the UK Government's 2021 crime policy statement *Beating Crime Report* as political nonsense. Reducing crime is but a small part of the police role and there are other factors, and agencies, that are involved in crime reduction, therefore the police should not be solely held to account for crime reduction. Pease (2023) argued that the government had failed to recognise how the use of research can improve police efficacy and effectiveness, which can be essential to developing an evidence based approach that will help support police legitimacy (Sherman, 1998, 2013). For policing to enhance legitimacy it needs to focus on what it aims to achieve in a transparent and robust manner that involves a degree of community consultation. Crime reduction is not necessarily the best measure for which policing is judged. McGregor (2024, p. 302) argues that "when the public expects the police to reduce crime there is a greater chance of legitimacy being revoked on the basis of ineffectiveness". Therefore, public safety is a more plausible barometer for police legitimacy.

Legitimacy in Crisis

Some scholars posit that police legitimacy is in crisis (Deuchar et al., 2021; Dick et al., 2013; McGregor, 2024). It might be argued that it always has been to some extent (O'Reilly, 2024). History is littered with examples of poor behaviour and actions of police officers, but this chapter will not list these numerous events here, there are other sources where these are discussed in more detail (see suggested reading at the end of this chapter). In summary, there have been recent events, particularly in the UK and the USA, where police legitimacy has been called into question, many of these through police acts and behaviour in themselves. Further, some historical issues still resonate with contemporary police forces as they seemingly struggle to learn from past mistakes. For example, a key message from the Casey Report (Baroness Casey, 2023) is that 30 years on from the murder of Stephen Lawrence in 1993, Black minority communities in London continue to be over-policed and under-protected (Wood et al., 2024). The rise of social media and technology has added to this. Many people have a voice in one way or another, and arguably not always for the best. Indeed, policing 'in a smartphone world' has added to the precarious nature of police accountability and legitimacy (Shaw, 2023). Police actions and demeanour are often captured in everyday encounters and officers must be conscious of their surroundings and the situations that they find themselves in. Social media has magnified these encounters and the video recording of police interactions have almost become an everyday occurrence across social media platforms (Walsh & O'Connor, 2019).

Technology is increasingly intertwined with police accountability, transparency, and trust, which influences police legitimacy. Some argue that police technology fundamentally shapes the modern police role and has been linked to success in some police reforms (Rossler, 2019). Police adoption of emerging technological tools has altered the way police interact with local communities, and can, in some instances, mitigate negative social media encounters posted by members of the public. For example, there are indications that innovations such as the use of police body worn video cameras (BWC) can enhance police accountability and legitimacy. This might be through the deterrent effect it has on potential police misconduct or the influence it has on police-community interactions (Rossler, 2019). Further, the growing emphasis on predictive policing and algorithmic decision-making argue that policing is attempting to adopt a more objective and ethical approach to their business. However, there are questions over whether these approaches merely magnify existing issues of human bias and may call into question police accountability (Alikhademi et al., 2022; Ferguson, 2017).

Yet, to preserve public trust and the legitimacy of each respective police force, accountability is essential (Kochel & Skogan, 2021). So how can the HMICFRS PEEL inspections be of value to improving police legitimacy when all around there appears to be challenges to the same? Perhaps these constant challenges are not necessarily a bad thing as they may act as reminders to policing about the constantly changing world in which they operate. The public is the best form of police governance there is. Despite UK oversight from HMICFRS, the local PCC, the College of Policing,

The Home Office, Independent Office for Police Conduct (IOPC), local Professional Standards Departments (PSD), all of which can pressure the institution of policing, the public are the best judge of character. They are the communities that must work with the police to ensure public safety and guide policing to areas of need.

HMICFRS PEEL INSPECTIONS AND LEGITIMACY

HMICFRS use the PEEL inspection programme to assess the performance of police forces in England and Wales (HMICFRS, 2023). PEEL inspections are used as a governance framework for police forces with a view to ensuring public trust and confidence in policing. This framework considers building trust, transparency, and accountability, with a focus on public engagement, partnership working and victim services. In the words of the HMICFRS:

> *"Our police efficiency, effectiveness and legitimacy (PEEL) inspections assess the performance of all 43 [territorial] police forces in England and Wales. Its main aim is to promote improvements in policing. We provide graded judgments on aspects of forces' performance. We identify where forces need to improve and help the public understand how well their force is performing" (HMICFRS, 2024, p. 5).*

The PEEL Inspection framework reviews the institution of policing, i.e., the organisation and its capacity and capability to carry out its responsibilities. The inspections assess each forces capability and capacity to investigate and reduce crime, increase public safety, and reduce community harm, which is based on a set of core base questions[1] that are used to grade each force: the grading ranges across 4 categories: outstanding, good, requires improvement, or inadequate[2]. Legitimacy, one of the core pillars of PEEL, focuses on how well a force is perceived by the public and whether they see it as fair and legitimate in its actions. However, this is not directly covered within the inspection question set. The judgement criteria (HMICFRS, n.d.) only mentions legitimacy 4 times in the 20 page document: once in the introduction section (p.1), and then in relation to the police use of force (p.13), stop and search (p.14), and in regards to the police force maintaining an ethical culture (p.15). Therefore, it is difficult to directly relate the inspection process to legitimacy per se. It should be argued that the real test of police legitimacy rests with the public and this will be (partly) assessed based on how well each police force may be judged throughout the whole PEEL inspection process as opposed to discrete elements of it. As legitimacy is a complex concept, and this chapter has discussed a number of influencing factors, not all of which the police have control over, there are areas in which the *institution* of policing and police *practice* can be improved to have a positive influence on police legitimacy. The PEEL inspections do not cover these as acutely as they might. Trust and legitimacy cannot be solely developed through an inspection process, they have to be earned (Bradford et al., 2013), which is where this chapter now turns.

Education, Recruitment, Selection, and Training of the Police

One approach to enhance a sense of community engagement, and thus improve trust, confidence, and legitimacy, is through having a professional work force that can deliver a better and more effective service (Hough, 2020). Education, recruitment, selection, training, and critical thinking by police officers will be essential to addressing future issues of trust, confidence and accountability – all of which can foster legitimacy. Getting the best out of those already in service and identifying the next generation of officers who can challenge poor practice and induce a positive influence should be a priority for police forces, especially considering the issues around the National uplift in officer recruitment (Williams & Sondhi, 2022). Indeed, having an effective and efficient workforce is essential as policing has an increasing complexity that requires officers to exercise greater autonomy and critical thinking (Asquith et al., 2017; Bolger et al., 2021; Keay, 2023; LGA, 2024).

Hough (2020) argues that embedding procedural justice in policing is essential to ensuring legitimacy with the public. He further points out four key factors that can support this (Hough, 2020, p. 63):

- Clear leadership and advocacy of procedural fairness principles (Herrington & Colvin, 2016),
- Adoption of internal management that are consistent with the principles of organisational justice, which should include the "fostering of self-legitimacy among front-line staff" (Hough, 2020, p. 67),
- Training for front-line staff and supervisors, particularly in de-escalation skills in handling conflict (Bennell et al., 2021),
- Effective community consultation, which is also a key feature for effective problem-oriented policing (Goldstein, 1979; Hinkle et al., 2020).

All of these key factors are within reach and achievable for all police forces but they will require a significant cultural shift to achieve these aims (Hough, 2020). It has been argued that having a post A-level qualification is part of the professionalisation process and might be a means to improve legitimacy (Andrews, 2024; Neyroud, 2011; Norman & Fleming, 2021), but this is yet to evidenced (Hough, 2020). Police officers with a Higher Education qualification can offer the "police service a degree of intellectual space" to improve the effectiveness of policing (Bryant et al., 2013, p. 393). This is important for critical thinking, the use of discretion, and decision-making, all of which can influence policing by consent and procedural justice, and ultimately, legitimacy. Andrews (2024, p. 7) surveyed, via electronic questionnaire, 535 participants and found that:

> *"Whilst at first glance it appears that a two-thirds majority of the public do not believe a police officer needs a degree, when that question is extended to some form of post A-Level qualification, the number supporting that rises to an overwhelming 91%."*

One of his respondents is quoted as saying "having an accredited 'police' certification would help to develop a universal standard of best practice and vet out staff that are intellectually inept" (Andrews, 2024, p. 6). Collaboration with Higher Education Institutions in the police recruitment process was seen by College of Policing as an opportunity to reshape police culture (Eason & Starr, 2024). This has not developed as originally envisioned (Wood, 2020). However, there is evidence that new recruits with a police degree education have demonstrated strong critical thinking and problem-solving skills (Belur et al., 2020). It could be argued that enhanced police education can provide an objective way to improve critical thinking learning that can challenge embedded police culture, which in turn may positively influence more procedurally just policing. There is no doubt that the public expect the highest possible standards from policing, not just in what they do, but also in how they act and interact with the communities they serve. This should include a constant ambition of police forces to be as effective and efficient as possible, especially in ensuring that what they do is having a positive impact (Sherman, 1998).

CONCLUSION: THE FUTURE FOR BUILDING AND MAINTAINING LEGITIMACY

Not all the public will have an interaction with the police, but all members will have a view on policing and whether they feel policing is just. Police legitimacy is, and will continue to be, an ongoing debate with a consideration of shared values being between the police and the public, something that will be varied from person and community, but also a key element in police-public interactions (O'Reilly, 2024). Legitimacy is partly about perceptions and partly about reality and can be fuelled by technology and social media. It is not always about the good news stories that the police believe can improve how they are viewed. The police need to ensure that they understand community concerns, that they can be relied upon to respond to such concerns and do this through clear and transparent consultation (Muir, 2024). As such, improving legitimacy goes beyond PEEL inspections and governance, it should be inherent in all things that police officers, and the institution of policing does. This will come from having the right people with the right education, training, knowledge, and experience, that are supported by a professional organisation that consistently strives for delivering a better service. So long as police officers and the institution of policing do the right things for the right reasons and in a transparent fashion, then even if the outcome is not what is wanted, the public may still maintain their trust in policing.

It is the aim of this section to consider ways in which police forces may address police legitimacy, but forces should remember that legitimacy is precarious, and external factors can be unpredictable and yet play an important role in how the police are perceived. Legitimacy will be a constant struggle for policing due to the many moving parts that affect policing internally and externally. By understanding what affects legitimacy on a number of levels, will help ease the burden that a changing world, and therefore, changing context in which the police operate influences trust, confidence and accountability: police legitimacy. Police forces that excel in developing their workforce, engage with technological advancements, and providing a supportive management framework will embrace features that are essential to improving police legitimacy. But there is more to this than simply evolving internal factors. This chapter has offered a gentle discussion to lead the way for more in-depth examples of how the institution of policing can improve. The following chapters will address legitimacy through building trust, public engagement, partnership working, and the delivery of a victim focused service.

REFERENCES

Alikhademi, K., Drobina, E., Prioleau, D., Richardson, B., Purves, D., & Gilbert, J. E. (2022). A review of predictive policing from the perspective of fairness. *Artificial Intelligence and Law*, *30*(1), 1–17.

Andrews, T. (2024). Public expectations of police education in England and Wales. *Policing. Journal of Policy Practice*, *18*, paad101.

Asquith, N. L., Bartkowiak-Théron, I., & Roberts, K. A. (2017). *Policing encounters with vulnerability*. Springer.

Baroness Casey. (2023). *Baroness Casey review: Final report. An independent review into the standards of behaviour and internal culture of the Metropolitan Police Service*. https://www.met.police.uk/SysSiteAssets/media/downloads/met/about-us/baroness-casey-review/update-march-2023/baroness-casey-review-march-2023a.pdf

Belur, J., Agnew-Pauley, W., McGinley, B., & Tompson, L. (2020). A systematic review of police recruit training programmes. *Policing. Journal of Policy Practice*, *14*(1), 76–90.

Bennell, C., Blaskovits, B., Jenkins, B., Semple, T., Khanizadeh, A.-J., Brown, A. S., & Jones, N. J. (2021). Promising practices for de-escalation and use-of-force training in the police setting: A narrative review. *Policing*, *44*(3), 377–404.

Bolger, M. A., Lytle, D. J., & Bolger, P. C. (2021). What matters in citizen satisfaction with police: A meta-analysis. *Journal of Criminal Justice*, *72*, 101760.

Bowling, B., Reiner, R., & Sheptycki, J. W. (2019). *The politics of the police* (5th ed.). Oxford University Press.

Bradford, B., Jackson, J., & Hough, M. (2013). Police futures and legitimacy: Redefining "good policing.". In Brown, J. M. (Ed.), *The future of policing* (pp. 79–99). Routledge.

Bryant, R., Cockcroft, T., Tong, S., & Wood, D. (2013). Police training and education: Past, present and future. In Brown, J. M. (Ed.), *The future of policing* (pp. 383–397). Routledge.

College of Policing. (2023). *Building trust and a fair culture*. https://www.college.police.uk/about/corporate-strategy-2022-2026/building-trust-and-fair-culture

Cooper, S. (2021). Police and crime commissioners: A dislocated expectation? *Policing. Journal of Policy Practice*, *15*(3), 1916–1932.

Deuchar, R., Crichlow, V. J., & Fallik, S. W. (2021). *Police–community relations in times of crisis*. Bristol University Press.

Dick, P., Silvestri, M., & Westmarland, L. (2013). Women police: Potential and possibilities for police reform. In Brown, J. M. (Ed.), *The future of policing* (pp. 134–148). Routledge.

Eason, A., & Starr, R. (2024). "Rolling with resistance": The challenges of HEI in police education. In Eason, A., & Starr, R. (Eds.), *The university beat: Critical reflections on the delivery of police education in England and Wales* (pp. 3–14). Palgrave Macmillan.

Ferguson, A. G. (2017). *The rise of big data policing: Surveillance, race, and the future of law enforcement*. New York University Press.

Goldstein, H. (1977). *Policing a free society*. Ballinger Publishing Company.

Goldstein, H. (1979). Improving policing: A problem-oriented approach. *Crime and Delinquency*, *25*(2), 236–258.

Goldstein, H. (1990). *Excellence in problem-oriented policing*. Police Executive Research Forum.

Gov.uk. (2012). *Definition of policing by consent*. https://www.gov.uk/government/publications/policing-by-consent/definition-of-policing-by-consent

Herrington, V., & Colvin, A. (2016). Police leadership for complex times. *Policing. Journal of Policy Practice*, *10*(1), 7–16.

Hinkle, J. C., Weisburd, D., Telep, C. W., & Petersen, K. (2020). Problem-oriented policing for reducing crime and disorder: An updated systematic review and meta-analysis. *Campbell Systematic Reviews*, *16*(2), e1089. PMID: 37133256

HMICFRS. (2021). *What is PEEL?* https://hmicfrs.justiceinspectorates.gov.uk/peel-assessments/what-is-peel/

HMICFRS. (2023). *PEEL assessments 2023–2025*. https://hmicfrs.justiceinspectorates.gov.uk/peel-assessments/what-is-peel/peel-assessments-2023-2025/

HMICFRS. (2024). *Proposed policing inspection programme and framework 2025–29: An inspection programme and framework under Schedule 4A to the Police Act 1996*. https://s3-eu-west-2.amazonaws.com/assets-hmicfrs.justiceinspectorates.gov.uk/uploads/hmicfrs-policing-inspection-programme-consultation-2025-29.pdf

HMICFRS. (n.d.). *HMICFRS judgement criteria*. https://assets-hmicfrs.justiceinspectorates.gov.uk/uploads/PEEL-2018-judgment-criteria.pdf

Hough, M. (2020). *Good policing: Trust, legitimacy and authority*. Policy Press.

Jackson, J., Bradford, B., Hough, M., Myhill, A., Quinton, P., & Tyler, T. R. (2012). Why do people comply with the law? Legitimacy and the influence of legal institutions. *British Journal of Criminology*, *52*(6), 1051–1071.

Keay, S. (2023). *How do the police define, identify, and respond to vulnerability?* (Doctoral dissertation, University of Central Lancashire).

Kochel, T. R., & Skogan, W. G. (2021). Accountability and transparency as levers to promote public trust and police legitimacy: Findings from a natural experiment. *Policing*, *44*(6), 1046–1059.

LGA. (2024). *Right care, right person.*

McGregor, R. (2021). Four characteristics of policing as a practice. *Policing. Journal of Policy Practice*, *15*(3), 1842–1853.

McGregor, R. (2024). *Recovering police legitimacy: A radical framework*. Routledge.

Mitchell, M., & Shuttleworth, K. (2025). *The abolition of police and crime commissioners*. Institute for Government. https://www.instituteforgovernment.org.uk/explainer/police-and-crime-commissioners

Muir, R. (2024). A new mode of protection: The case for redesigning our policing and public safety institutions. *The Political Quarterly*, *95*(3), 409–413.

Neyroud, P. (2011). *Review of police leadership and training*. Home Office.

Norman, J., & Fleming, J. (2021). Studying a police-specific degree. *Police Science and Management*, *24*(2), 162–174.

O'Reilly, C. (2024). *Neighbourhood policing*. Policy Press.

Pease, K. (2023). Beating crime or marking time? Crime research and crime policy: A personal view of the UK government's approach. *Crime Prevention and Community Safety*, *25*(2), 117–130.

Rossler, M. T. (2019). The impact of police technology adoption on social control, police accountability, and police legitimacy. In Rabe-Hemp, C. E., & Lind, N. S. (Eds.), *Political authority, social control and public policy* (pp. 209–224). Emerald Publishing Limited.

Shaw, D. (2023, July 28). The police are struggling to operate in a smartphone world. *Spectator (London, England)*.

Sherman, L. W. (1998). Ideas in American policing. *Policing*, •••, 1–16.

Sherman, L. W. (2013). The rise of evidence-based policing: Targeting, testing, and tracking. *Crime and Justice*, *42*(1), 377–451.

Tankebe, J. (2013). Viewing things differently: The dimensions of public perceptions of police legitimacy. *Criminology*, *51*(1), 103–135.

Tankebe, J. (2019). In their own eyes: An empirical examination of police self-legitimacy. *International Journal of Comparative and Applied Criminal Justice*, *43*(2), 99–116.

Tyler, T. R. (2004). Enhancing police legitimacy. *The Annals of the American Academy of Political and Social Science*, *593*(1), 84–99.

Tyler, T. R. (2009). Legitimacy and criminal justice: The benefits of self-regulation. *Ohio State Journal of Criminal Law*, *7*, 307–359.

Tyler, T. R. (2025). Legitimacy-based policing. *Criminology & Public Policy*, *24*(2), 165–187.

Walsh, J. P., & O'Connor, C. (2019). Social media and policing: A review of recent research. *Sociology Compass*, *13*(1), e12648.

Williams, E., & Sondhi, A. (2022). A narrative review of the literature on the recruitment of younger police officers in age and in service: What are the implications for the police in England and Wales? *Policing. Journal of Policy Practice*, *16*(4), 648–662.

Wood, D., Bradshaw, S., Dickens, T., Parker-McLeod, J., & Davis, C. (2024). *Blackstone's handbook for policing students*. Oxford University Press.

Wood, D. A. (2020). Embedding learning and assessment within police practice: The opportunities and challenges arising from the introduction of the PEQF in England and Wales. *Policing. Journal of Policy Practice*, *14*(2), 374–382.

1 The base question set used in the inspections can be found here: https://hmicfrs.justiceinspectorates.gov.uk/peel-assessments/what-is-peel/peel-assessments-2023-2025/ [accessed 17 January 2025].

2 A table exploring these in more detail can be found at https://assets-hmicfrs.justiceinspectorates.gov.uk/uploads/PEEL-2018-judgment-criteria.pdf [accessed 24 April 2025].

Chapter 26
Strategies for Building Trust, Legitimacy, Confidence, and Satisfaction

Johannes Pieter Oosthuizen
http://orcid.org/0000-0001-6422-6015
University of North Georgia, USA

ABSTRACT

This chapter traces the rise and recent decline of public confidence in policing in England and Wales, using Crime Survey data, PEEL inspection findings, and Dorset Police's Project Genesis. It links falling trust to misconduct scandals, budget cuts, and the routine abstraction of neighbourhood officers, which erodes visible engagement. Forces graded "outstanding" protect neighbourhood resources, employ two-way communication, and embed structured problem-solving. Project Genesis found community engagement occupied under five percent of recorded activity, prompting 44 evidence-based recommendations that later boosted HMICFRS ratings. The chapter contends that sustained, evidence-led investment in local engagement, clear accountability metrics, and protected staffing are vital to restore legitimacy, satisfaction, and confidence, and to future-proof policing against changing public expectations and fiscal pressures.

INTRODUCTION

According to the College of Policing (2015a, p. 2), public trust and confidence in policing are considered to be key indicators of the effectiveness of policing strategies

DOI: 10.4018/979-8-3373-2757-0.ch026

in serving their communities. In England and Wales, this trust is mainly measured through national surveys, such as the Crime Survey for England and Wales (CSEW), and assessments conducted by organizations like HM Inspectorate of Constabulary and Fire & Rescue Services (HMICFRS). Over recent decades, public trust in the police has fluctuated (Hough M., 2003), reflecting broader societal trends and specific challenges within the policing sector and whilst survey data from the early 2000s showed relatively high levels of trust in police fairness and respectfulness, recent findings have reported a decline in these measures (HMICFRS, 2024; Bradford & Jackson, 2024; IOPC, 2025). Understanding the reasons for the decline invite an appreciation of the history behind foundational concepts, such as policing by consent and reassurance policing.

Policing in England and Wales is commonly understood as being grounded in the principle of policing by consent, an ethos associated with the establishment of the New Police in 1829 (Reiner, 2000). While the historical centrality of consent has been debated, it remains a powerful normative framework shaping expectations of police legitimacy and public compliance (Torrible, 2022, p. 10), and consent-based policing reflects a view of the police as operating through public approval rather than coercion, recognising that legitimacy is essential to maintaining social order (Brogden & Nijhar, 2013).

The later development of reassurance policing (Bahn, 1974) further extended this focus by emphasising public perceptions of safety and confidence, rather than solely objective crime measures (Millie, 2014). Although reassurance policing has been criticised for privileging visibility over substantive outcomes, it contributed to the evolution of neighbourhood policing as a model combining visibility, engagement and problem-solving as mechanisms for building trust and legitimacy (Millie, 2014; Fitzgerald et al., 2002).

POLICE TRUST AND CONFIDENCE: POLICY, INSPECTION FRAMEWORKS AND PUBLIC LEGITIMACY

In England and Wales, public trust, confidence and satisfaction are primarily measured through national surveys, notably the Crime Survey for England and Wales (CSEW), alongside police-commissioned surveys and HMICFRS PEEL inspections (UK Data Service, 2020). The CSEW provides long-term data on victimisation and public perceptions, while PEEL assessments evaluate police effectiveness, efficiency and legitimacy, offering an inspection-based account of how forces engage with and treat the public (College of Policing, 2025; HMICFRS, 2024).

Policing in England and Wales is rooted in the concept of policing by consent. This relates to methods of policing designed to maintain the approval, respect and affection of the public. Police officers are considered an essential part of the social fabric of communities they serve, but as Rosenbaum et al. (2005) argue, without the trust and confidence of the public, the police will be seriously limited in their ability to do their job. A 2023 Home Office review of research and literature (Hanway & Hambly, 2023) into public perceptions of policing, identified confidence and trust as distinct concepts and defined them in different ways, and an understanding of the differences can provide greater insight into public perceptions of policing.

Confidence and trust represent related but distinct dimensions of public perceptions of policing. Confidence reflects generalised support for the police as an institution, including among those without direct contact, whereas trust relates more closely to perceptions of police integrity, fairness and ethical conduct, shaped by both past experiences and expectations of future encounters (Cao, 2015; Jackson et al., 2011). Research consistently demonstrates that procedural justice and effective crime control are central to sustaining trust, and that deficits in either trust or confidence can undermine police legitimacy and public cooperation (Hohl et al., 2013; Sergeant, 2017).

Although long-term survey data indicate periods of stability in public trust and confidence, recent years have seen marked declines, particularly since 2019/20. These shifts reflect a combination of high-profile misconduct cases, perceptions of declining institutional performance, and broader reductions in trust across public sector institutions. Evidence suggests that these changes are cyclical rather than linear, with fluctuations shaped by factors such as organisational performance, media scrutiny and demographic variation, resulting in what has been described as a 'new normal' of volatile public trust in policing (Bradford & Jackson, 2024; HMICFRS, 2024). This has been supported by the HMICFRS (2024), who have stated that trust in the police, notably the perception about whether officers behave in a lawful, ethical and fair manner, is influenced by these factors and that confidence in understanding and dealing with the issues that matter to local communities, has continued to be in decline. Consequently, as Bradford & Jackson (2024, p. 444) claim, there could now be a 'natural' flux in public trust in police and a decline in trust in many state institutions, including the police, and has arguably resulted in a 'new normal', where trust in this particular institution shifts upwards and downwards in response to short- and medium-term trends in public opinion.

Changes in levels of confidence in policing may also to be linked to a rise and then a fall in indicators of community connection (reliability, local understanding and dealing with local problems) and therefore not directly linked to perceptions of police treatment (fairness, respectfulness, and trust) which have remained more consistent. (The Police Foundation, 2022, p. 50). Another likely explanation is the rise and fall of the numbers of officers in neighbourhood policing roles and after the introduction of the National Neighbourhood Policing Programme (NPP) in England and Wales in 2008, indicators of public confidence rose alongside increased police visibility. However, once neighbourhood policing numbers started to decline, there was a fall public confidence (The Police Foundation, 2022, p. 51) and this correlation is consistent with research (Cook, 2024; Bradford & Jackson, 2024) that demonstrate links between public confidence, police visibility and numbers, indicating that the relationships are mediated by the quality and quantity of local police engagement, particularly when neighbourhood policing is the vehicle for delivery (Sindall & Sturgis, 2013).

DELIVERING LEGITIMACY THROUGH NEIGHBOURHOOD POLICING: COMMUNITY ENGAGEMENT AND PEEL EVIDENCE

According to the College of Policing (2025), neighbourhood policing significantly improves public confidence and trust in the police when implementing three components, namely: 1) a structured program of community engagement activities; 2) a systematized approach to problem-solving strategies; 3) and a targeted visible police presence. It is the latter that often gets, and continues to get, the attention of the media (McLennan, 2018) and CSEW data has shown that trust in community engagement and problem-solving initiatives has been increasing gradually between 2005/06 and 2013/14, before remaining relatively stable for the following four years. A decline started in 2017/18 (College of Policing, 2025) and can most likely be attributed toward a lack of, or inefficient use of, community engagement methods.

According to a review of the evidence on effective community engagement (Lloyd & Foster, 2009), the key ingredients of successful engagement are understanding that the public are more interested in engaging than police officers are, and in the poorest and most challenging areas, sustained work may be needed before residents will participate. It is also clear that finding ways to engage individuals and groups who do not get consulted and whose needs might be ignored, should be a priority. The evidence also suggests that the attitudes of the police towards engagement are vital, and a lack of commitment or interest is recognized by the public and reduces satisfaction and confidence. An example of this is sexual violence against women and girls. According to Bradford & Jackson (2024, p. 443), trust in the police has decreased among women over the past few years, especially in London and since 2020, fifty-seven per cent of women believed that the police did not treat sexual assault seriously enough. By 2024 this increased to sixty-seven per cent and according to Morton (2021), the police response to the murder of Sarah Everard by a serving Metropolitan police officer in 2021 was a key factor. This suggests that when the police perform poorly in investigating crimes and supporting victim-survivors and seem incapable of rooting out misogyny and sexual violence within their own ranks, the effect on women's confidence in policing is particularly significant. It becomes essential therefor to consider the best practice of police forces who have demonstrated excellence in dealing with these challenges and the initiatives of Humberside and Cambridgeshire will now be considered.

PEEL assessments across all forty-three police forces in England and Wales from 2021/22 and 2023/25 aimed to provide practical and measurable ways to strengthen evidence for structured community engagement strategies. These inspections used professional judgement to assess performance and grade each force as outstanding, good, adequate, requires improvement or inadequate. Several forces were graded as outstanding in 2021/22 and 2023/25 and a summary of one force in each period is set out below.

Humberside: PEEL Assessment 2021/2022 (HMICFRS, 2022)

1. *Community Engagement* - The force effectively engages with diverse communities through face-to-face events and social media, to reach different demographics.
2. *Targeted Communication* - Utilizing platforms like My Community Alert and Next Door, the force ensures its messages connect with the intended audience.
3. *Advisory Groups* - Independent advisory groups, including youth and violence against women, provide valuable community insights and the information gathered helps to maintain ward profiles and set monthly policing priorities.
4. *Safety Initiatives* - Notable initiatives include surveying women and girls to enhance safety and implementing Operation Contract for nighttime safety, as well as Operation Nova, which supports military personnel and veterans with essential services.

Cambridgeshire: PEEL Assessment 2023-2025 (HMICFRS, 2024)

1. *Diverse community engagement*: Officers train with community input, improving understanding of cultural reactions and addressing disproportionality in stop and search.
2. *Disproportionality training*: '#HavingTheConversation' training educates officers on stop and search biases, helping them understand reactions of diverse and vulnerable groups.

One of the most notable aspects of these examples is the deliberate utilisation of resources in areas of community engagement, to develop, protect and strengthen innovative initiatives to enhance their community engagement efforts and thereby increase the potential for improved public satisfaction and confidence levels. This is a critical strategic decision as there have been ongoing concerns for some time now about abstracting neighbourhood police officers from their core role and the impact this could have on levels of public satisfaction and confidence (Bradford & Jackson, 2024, p. 447). Although it was predicted that the Police Uplift Programme (PUP) of 2019 would provide additional officers in neighbourhood policing teams by 2023, the PEEL report of 2021/22 stated that nearly one-third of all police forces in England and Wales were graded as either inadequate or requiring improvement and most forces reported having real challenges in having enough people to respond to expected demand (HMICFRS, 2023, p. 16). In addition, the PEEL report criticised many forces for displaying a tendency to remove neighbourhood officers from their usual duties to deal with emergency response incidents and leave PCSOs as the main neighbourhood resource.

Recent developments have indicated that British politicians may have heeded the warnings, as the UK government announced a significant financial investment in neighbourhood policing to provide 13,000 additional police officers, community support officers and volunteer special constables to patrol communities (Home Office, 2024). This echoed a similar government commitment from 2007, when the implementation of Neighbourhood Policing under the National Reassurance Policing Programme (NRPP) was announced and 16,000 Police and Community Support Officers (PCSO) were introduced (Association of Police Authorities, 2008, p. 5). Significant commitments such as these provide the parameters for neighbourhood policing and have been increasingly considered by police forces and academics alike as a major paradigm shift from the professional centralized, bureaucratic command-like model of policing to an inclusive philosophy that promotes community based problem-solving strategies. This, according to Wakefield & Fleming (2009), encourages partnerships between the police and communities in a collaborative effort to solve crime and disorder.

In contrast, the consequences of failing to protect neighbourhood policing resources could have significant and far-reaching consequences. Establishing what the activities of neighbourhood policing are, in detail, and understanding their priorities is essential to addressing any weaknesses in community engagement strategies and an examination of an evidenced-based approach to this is worth review. An example is the following case study of Dorset Police, who in 2013-2015 conducted a strategic review of their neighbourhood policing model to establish why they experienced a significant drop in public satisfaction and how their neighbourhood police officers were engaging their communities.

CASE STUDY: PROJECT GENESIS: DORSET POLICE

Dorset Police, one of the smallest forces in England and Wales, introduced neighbourhood policing in 2006, investing heavily in neighbourhood policing teams (NPTs) (HMIC, 2008), before public austerity measures reduced NPTs by eight percent and a quarter of all neighbourhood officers and PCSOs by 2014. Under their policy of Total Resource Management (TRM), neighbourhood officers were regularly abstracted to response duties to meet savings targets, with Dorset Police seeking to deliver around eighty percent of required savings from pay budgets - higher than most forces (HMIC, 2013, p. 7).

Between June 2012 and June 2013, public confidence declined markedly, with Dorset Police falling from 1st to 20th nationally for perceptions of doing a good or excellent job, although confidence in local policing recovered slightly by August 2014 (Dorset Police, 2013, p. 1). In response, senior leaders commissioned an independent evidence-based policing study (Project Genesis) to understand the potential reasons for the decline and solutions to reverse the trend.

Quantitative data showed community engagement activity was consistently minimal. Across shifts, engagement rarely exceeded thirteen percent, with PCSOs achieving less than half this rate. When analysed across the full observation period and by role, community engagement was the lowest activity type and in some urban stations, up to ninety-seven percent of neighbourhood officer and PCSO activity was unrelated to community engagement.

Table 1. Pattern of activities of neighbourhood policing teams: by type of shift and officer Source: (Oosthuizen, 2025, p. 15)

Main Activity	PC shifts		PCSO shifts		All types of officers	
Public facing work	**weekend**	**weekday**	**weekend**	**weekday**	**weekend**	**weekday**
Patrol	9.0%	12.8%	36.4%	35.7%	24.3%	25.2%
Attendance & incidents	21.7%	21.0%	11.7%	8.8%	16.2%	14.6%
Post incident work	11.0%	18.6%	21.1%	10.4%	16.5%	14.1%
Community Engagement	13.0%	10.9%	2.5%	5.3%	7.2%	7.9%
Total public facing	54.7%	63.3%	71.7%	60.2%	64.2%	61.8%

Qualitative interviews with eighteen NPT sergeants reinforced these findings. Supervisors reported a drift away from meaningful engagement and widespread abandonment of Police and Community Together (PACT) meetings. Across all observed shifts, community engagement activity never exceeded five percent.

Table 2. Qualitative data collected from 18 interviews with NPT sergeants, 6 from rural areas; 12 from urban areas. This represented 86% of all 21 NPT sergeants in Dorset Police. Source: (Oosthuizen, 2025)

Frequency of PACT	**2 weeks**	**Monthly**	**2 months**	**3 months**	**6 months**	**Never**
Rural NPTs	1	2	0	1	0	5
Urban NPTs	0	2	2	1	3	4
Combined PACT	**1**	**4**	**2**	**2**	**3**	**9**

Project Genesis provided operational-level evidence of challenges that have been widely identified at a national level but rarely measured in detail. While rooted in Dorset Police, the findings illuminate broader structural tensions within neighbourhood policing across England and Wales, particularly the impact of abstraction, performance prioritisation, and reduced supervisory focus on community engagement. National research and typologies have shown that pressures on resources and shifting strategic priorities have fragmented neighbourhood policing, often diluting its community engagement function (Higgins, 2017). In addition, HMICFRS PEEL assessments have consistently pointed to limited or unclear engagement strategies across forces, undermining local problem solving and legitimacy (HMIC, 2017) and Parliamentary inquiries have also highlighted how abstraction of neighbourhood officers to reactive duties erodes relationships that build trust and confidence (House of Commons Home Affairs Committee, 2023). Furthermore, evidence on public perceptions has demonstrated that poor quality engagement and contact reduce police legitimacy and confidence, reinforcing the importance of sustained community engagement for effective policing (Home Office, 2023). As such, the Dorset case study strengthens the national evidence base by demonstrating how strategic pressures translate into day-to-day reductions in engagement activity, with implications for legitimacy, confidence, and long-term policing effectiveness.

A valid concern about what any future challenges for improving public trust and confidence in policing is worth examining. One such emerging area is the use of facial recognition technology (FRT) and according to Bradford & Jackson, (2024, p. 447), along with several other 'new technologies' in policing, there is now a significant push for police to use facial recognition technology more frequently and with higher intensity. Live facial recognition has proven to be a highly controversial development (Sky News, 2025; Oxley et al, 2024), primarily because of the increased levels of surveillance (Boffey & Wilding, 2025) and although the current lack of evidence for its effectiveness as a policing tool is a concern, some studies by the Home Office have shown general support for the concept (Home Office, 2025; The Policy Institute, 2025). These early results suggest the levels of support for the use of FRT varies according to the extent to which respondents trusted in the police (the greater the level of trust in the police, the more support there is for the strategy). Interestingly, even those respondents who indicated that they did not trust the police at all, only a minority were opposed to the use of FRT and may suggest that initiatives explained and aimed at making the public feel safer can also garner public trust.

CONCLUSION

This chapter has demonstrated that public trust and confidence are central to police legitimacy and effectiveness and are closely linked to the quality of neighbourhood policing and community engagement. National survey data, academic research, and HMICFRS PEEL assessments consistently show that declines in confidence are associated with reduced neighbourhood capacity, abstraction of officers, and weakened engagement strategies. The Project Genesis case study provides rare empirical evidence of how these national pressures translate into frontline practice, revealing that abstraction, performance prioritisation, and limited supervisory focus can significantly reduce meaningful community engagement and contribute to declining public satisfaction. Collectively, the findings underline that rebuilding confidence requires more than increased visibility or officer numbers; it demands the deliberate protection of neighbourhood policing, clear accountability for engagement, and sustained investment in skills and partnerships. As policing faces future challenges, including the adoption of new technologies, maintaining public trust through effective, community-centred neighbourhood policing remains fundamental to legitimacy and long-term effectiveness.

REFERENCES

Association of Police Authorities. (2008). *The police authority role in neighbourhood policing: Ensuring sustainability*. Association of Police Authorities.

Bahn, C. (1974). 'The Reassurance Factor in Police Patrol'. *Criminology, 12*(5), 338–345.

Boffey, D., & Wilding, M. (2025, May 24). *Live facial recognition cameras may become 'commonplace' as police use soars*. Retrieved from The Gaurdian: https://www.theguardian.com/technology/2025/may/24/police-live-facial-recognition-cameras-england-and-wales

Bradford, B., & Jackson, J. (2024). Trust in the Police: What is to be Done? *Police Quarterly, 95*(3), 442–449.

Brogden, M., & Nijhar, P. (2013). *Community Policing: National and international models and approaches*. Routledge.

Cao, L. (2015). Differentiating confidence in the police, trust in the police, and satisfaction with the police. *Policing*.

College of Policing. (2015a). *Delivering Neighbourhood Policing - a practice stocktake*. College of Policing Limited.

College of Policing. (2025). *Improving public confidence in the police: An evidence-based guide*. Retrieved from College of Policing: https://assets.college.police.uk/s3fs-public/2025-01/Improving-public-confidence-in-the-police-guide.pdf?VersionId=XpjDwAk0rd7AjDXNdBY75ImCNWDJJ_7k

Cook, A. (2024). *State of Policing: The Annual Assessment of Policing in England and Wales 2023*. HMICFRS.

Dorset Police. (2013). *Declining confidence in Dorset Police? - an emerging issue*. Winfrith: Business Change Department.

Dorset Police. (2013a, April 6). *Our Priorities*. Retrieved July 8, 2014, from Dorset Police: https://www.dorset.police.uk/Default.aspx?page=293

FitzGerald, M., Hough, M., Joseph, I., & Qureshi, T. (2002). *Policing for London*. Willan.

Hanway, P., & Hambly, O. (2023, August 28). *Public perceptions of policing: A review of research and literature*. Retrieved from GOV.UK: https://www.gov.uk/government/publications/public-perceptions-of-policing-a-review-of-research-and-literature/public-perceptions-of-policing-a-review-of-research-and-literature#:~:text=this%20literature%20review.-,Key%20findings,confidence%20in%20future%2

Higgins, A. (2017, April 2). *Neighbourhood policing: a police force typology*. Retrieved from The Police Foundation: https://www.police-foundation.org.uk/publication/neighbourhood-policing-a-police-force-typology/?utm_source

HMIC. (2008, September 1). *Her Majesty's Inspectorate of Constabulary*. Retrieved August 6, 2014, from HMIC Inspection Report: Dorset Police: Neighbourhood Policing: Developing Citizen Focus Policing: http://www.hmic.gov.uk/media/dorset-phase2-neighbourhood-policing-citizen-focus-20080830.pdf

HMIC. (2013). *Dorset Police's Response to the funding challenge*. HMIC.

HMIC. (2017, March). *PEEL: Police effectiveness 2016: A national overview*. Retrieved from HMICFRS Justice Inspectorates: https://assets-hmicfrs.justiceinspectorates.gov.uk/uploads/peel-police-effectiveness-2016.pdf?utm

HMICFRS. (2022, November 17). *Dorset PEEL Assessments 2021/2022*. Retrieved from HMICFRS: https://hmicfrs.justiceinspectorates.gov.uk/peel-reports/dorset-2021-22/

HMICFRS. (2022, November 25). *Engaging with and treating the public with fairness and respect*. Retrieved from Humberside PEEL Assessments 2021/2022: https://hmicfrs.justiceinspectorates.gov.uk/peel-reports/humberside-2021-22/

HMICFRS. (2023, March 17). *Avon and Somerset PEEL Assessments 2021/2022*. Retrieved from Engaging with and treating the public with fairness and respect: https://hmicfrs.justiceinspectorates.gov.uk/peel-reports/avon-and-somerset-2021-22/

HMICFRS. (2023, July). *Police Performance: Getting a Grip*. Retrieved from PEEL Spotlight Report: https://assets-hmicfrs.justiceinspectorates.gov.uk/uploads/peel-spotlight-report-police-performance.pdf

HMICFRS. (2024, July 19). *State of Policing: The Annual Assessment of Policing in England and Wales 2023*. Retrieved from HMICFRS: https://hmicfrs.justiceinspectorates.gov.uk/publication-html/state-of-policing-the-annual-assessment-of-policing-in-england-and-wales-2023/

HMICFRS. (2024, March 12). *Police powers and treating the public fairly and respectfully*. Retrieved from Cambridgeshire PEEL Assessment 2023–2025: https://hmicfrs.justiceinspectorates.gov.uk/peel-reports/cambridgeshire-2023-25/

Hohl, K., Stanko, B., & Newburn, T. (2013). The effect of the 2011 London disorder on public opinion of police and attitudes towards crime, disorder, and sentencing. *Policing. Journal of Policy Practice*, *7*(1), 12–20.

Home Office. (2023, August 28). *Public perceptions of policing: A review of research and literature.* Retrieved from GOV.UK: https://www.gov.uk/government/publications/public-perceptions-of-policing-a-review-of-research-and-literature/public-perceptions-of-policing-a-review-of-research-and-literature?utm

Home Office. (2025). *Public attitudes to police use of facial recognition technology.* The Home Office.

Home Office. (2025). *Accredited official statistics: Police funding for England and Wales 2015 to* 2026. Retrieved from GOV.UK: https://www.gov.uk/government/statistics/police-funding-for-england-and-wales-2015-to-2026/police-funding-for-england-and-wales-2015-to-2026#:~:text=Note:%20Separate%20to%20these%20annual,Annex%20A%20of%20this%20bulletin

Hough, M. (2003). Modernization and public opinion: Some criminal justice paradoxes. *Contemporary Politics*, *9*(2), 143–155.

House of Commons Home Affairs Committee. (2023, October 25). *Policing priorities: Fifth Report of Session 2022–23.* Retrieved from Committees Parliament Publications: https://committees.parliament.uk/publications/42000/documents/208864/default/

IOPC. (2025, June 17). *Public perceptions tracker summary report - 2024/25.* Retrieved from Independent Office for Police Conduct: https://www.policeconduct.gov.uk/publications/public-perceptions-tracker-summary-report-202425

Jackson, J., Bradford, B., Hough, M., Kuha, J., Stares, S., Widdop, S., & Galev, T. (2011). Developing European indicators of trust in justice. *European Journal of Criminology*, *8*(4), 267–285.

Lloyd, K., & Foster, J. (2009). *Citizen Focus and Community Engagement: A Review of the Literature.* The Police Foundation.

McLennan, W. (2018, April 13). *Police numbers: how cuts have made officers 'less visible' on the streets of Camden.* Retrieved from CamdenNewJournal: http://camdennewjournal.com/article/police-numbers-how-cuts-have-made-officers-less-visible-in-camden

Millie, A. (2014). Reassurance Policing and Signal Crimes. In Bruinsma, G., & Weisburd, D. (Eds.), *Encyclopaedia of Criminology and Criminal Justice* (pp. 4327–4335). Springer.

Morton, B. (2021, September 30). *Sarah Everard: How Wayne Couzens planned her murder.* Retrieved from BBC News: https://www.bbc.com/news/uk-58746108

Oosthuizen, J. P. (2025, May 2). *A Comprehensive Analysis of Daily Activities and Operational Effectiveness of Neighbourhood Policing officers in Southern England [PowerPoint Slides].* Tuscon, Arizona: Presented at *The American Society of Evidence-Based Policing Conference.*

Oosthuizen, J. P. (2025). Time on Duty A Quantitative Observational Study of Community Police Officer Activities and Time Management: An English Case Study. *The Pursuit Journal*, *8*(2), 10.

Oxley, G., Uwazuruike, A., Lalic, M., Samuel, H., & Downs, W. (2024, November 11). *Police use of live facial recognition technology.* Retrieved from House of Commons Library: https://commonslibrary.parliament.uk/research-briefings/cdp-2024-0144/

Reiner, R. (2000). *The Politics of the Police* (3rd ed.). Oxford University Press.

Rosenbaum, D. P., Schuck, A. M., Costello, S. K., Hawkins, D. F., & Ring, M. K. (2005). 'Attitudes toward the police: The effects of direct and vicarious experience'. *Police Quarterly*, *8*(3), 343–365.

Sergeant, E. (2017). Policing and collective efficacy: The relative importance of police effectiveness, procedural justice and the obligation to obey police. *Policing and Society*, *27*(8), 927–940.

Sindall, K., & Sturgis, P. (2013). Austerity policing: Is visibility more important than absolute numbers in determining public confidence in the police? *European Journal of Criminology*, *10*(2), 137–153.

Sindall, K., & Sturgis, P. (2013). Austerity policing: Is visibility more important than absolute numbers in determining public confidence in the police? *European Journal of Criminology*, *10*(2), 137–153.

Sky News. (2025, December 4). *Police to ramp up use of 'out-of-control' facial recognition technology amid privacy warnings.* Retrieved from Sky News UK: https://news.sky.com/story/police-to-ramp-up-use-of-out-of-control-facial-recognition-technology-amid-privacy-warnings-13479217

The Police Foundation. (2022, March). *The Police Foundation.* Retrieved from A New Mode of Protection: Redesigning Policing and Public Safety for the 21st Century: https://www.police-foundation.org.uk/policingreview2022/wp-content/uploads/srpew_final_report.pdf

The Policy Institute. (2025, September). *King's College London.* Retrieved from Police use of facial recognition technology in the UK: What the public think: https://www.kcl.ac.uk/policy-institute/assets/police-use-of-facial-recognition-technology-in-the-uk.pdf

Torrible, C. N. (2022). Trust in the police and policing by consent in turbulent times. *Safer Communities*, *21*(3), 171–183.

UK Data Service. (2020, December 18). *British Crime Survey, 1982: England and Wales Data.* Retrieved from UK Data Service: https://beta.ukdataservice.ac.uk/datacatalogue/studies/study?id=1869#:~:text=Up%20to%202001%2C%20the%20BCS,and%20it%20became%20the%20CSEW

Wakefield, A., & Fleming, J. (2009). *The Sage Dictionary of Policing*. Sage Publications Ltd.

Weisburd, D., & Eck, J. (2004). What Can Police Do to Reduce Crime, Disorder & Fear. *The Annals of the American Academy of Political and Social Science*, *593*, 42–65.

Chapter 27
Public Engagement

Dion Glass
http://orcid.org/0009-0004-4842-3093
University of Portsmouth, UK

ABSTRACT

This chapter critically examines how police forces in England and Wales engage with the public in ways that are fair, appropriate, and respectful, as framed by PEEL Q2. It explores the role of Neighbourhood Policing Teams (NPT), procedural justice, and community involvement in fostering legitimacy and trust. Drawing on empirical research, national surveys, and key reviews such as the Lammy and Casey Reports, the chapter analyses current practices, identifies barriers to effective engagement, and highlights opportunities for reform. Particular attention is given to the experiences of minoritised communities and the perspectives of police practitioners. The chapter incorporates recent developments in conflict management training, unconscious bias awareness, and the evolving expectations outlined in the HMICFRS 2025–29 consultation. It concludes by proposing future directions grounded in co-production, cultural competence, and sustainable leadership.

INTRODUCTION

Public engagement is a cornerstone of effective policing, directly influencing trust, legitimacy, and cooperation between the police and communities (Bradford et al., 2014; Tyler, 2006). Research indicates that positive interactions between police and the public contribute to higher levels of compliance and voluntary cooperation, reinforcing the legitimacy of law enforcement institutions (Bradford et al., 2014). While broader policing models shape public perceptions, Neighbourhood Policing Teams (NPT) serve as a key mechanism for fostering sustained engagement and trust (Cosgrove & Ramshaw, 2015; Skogan, 2006). Unlike response-driven approaches,

DOI: 10.4018/979-8-3373-2757-0.ch027

NPT prioritises community partnerships, problem-solving, and local presence, leading to increased trust and social cohesion (Hough et al., 2010). However, challenges arise when NPT is treated as a hybrid function rather than a dedicated, embedded approach, leading to inconsistencies in engagement and fluctuating levels of public confidence (Ralph et al., 2024). This chapter explores public engagement within policing, considering the role of NPT alongside general policing strategies.

Objectives of this Chapter

- To understand the broader significance of public engagement in policing.
- To examine how different policing models, including NPT, deliver fairness, appropriateness, and respect.
- To identify barriers to effective engagement and strategies for overcoming them.
- To explore how NPT and general policing approaches can work in tandem to build public confidence.

THE ROLE OF PUBLIC ENGAGEMENT IN POLICING

Public engagement is a fundamental measure of police effectiveness, influencing the degree to which the public perceives law enforcement as legitimate, ethical, and responsive to community needs. The way officers interact with the public significantly shapes public trust and confidence, ultimately impacting the willingness of individuals and communities to cooperate with the police (Bradford et al., 2014). When engagement is conducted fairly, appropriately, and respectfully, it fosters positive relationships and reinforces the notion that the police operate as a service rather than solely as an enforcement agency (Tyler & Huo, 2002). Conversely, poor engagement, characterised by perceived bias, excessive force, or a lack of transparency, can lead to distrust, reluctance to report crimes, and heightened tensions between the police and the communities they serve (Myhill & Quinton, 2010).

The Importance of Public Engagement

Public engagement is vital for enhancing procedural justice, a concept that refers to how individuals perceive the fairness of interactions with authorities, irrespective of the outcomes of those interactions (Tyler, 2006). Studies have consistently shown that when people believe they are treated with dignity and respect, they are more likely to view the police as legitimate and to comply with the law voluntarily (Tyler & Jackson, 2014). Engagement also plays a crucial role in increasing public confidence in policing by ensuring that officers are seen as accessible, responsive, and accountable.

Effective engagement fosters trust by demonstrating a commitment to serving the needs of diverse communities (Bradford, 2014). Strategies such as problem-oriented policing, community meetings, and school liaison programmes have been found to enhance relationships between officers and the public, leading to greater collaboration in crime prevention efforts (Skogan, 2006). By contrast, policing models that emphasise enforcement over dialogue (such as aggressive stop-and-search practices) have been linked to deteriorating trust, particularly among marginalised groups (Hough et al., 2013).

Fairness, Appropriateness, and Respect in Public Engagement

Fairness

Fairness in policing means treating all individuals equitably, regardless of factors such as race, socio-economic background, or previous contact with law enforcement. Research indicates that perceptions of fairness are closely tied to public attitudes toward the police and that officers who demonstrate fairness in decision-making and communication foster higher levels of trust (Tyler & Jackson, 2014). In practical terms, fairness in public engagement can be assessed through the proportional use of police powers, transparency in decision-making, and efforts to address systemic disparities in law enforcement practices (Bradford et al., 2014).

Appropriateness

Appropriateness refers to the ability of officers to tailor their engagement to the context and needs of different communities. Effective policing recognises that a one-size-fits-all approach is often insufficient in diverse societies (Myhill & Quinton, 2010). Instead, officers must develop cultural competence, adapt their communication styles to different audiences, and employ conflict resolution techniques that prioritise de-escalation over force. Neighbourhood Policing, which emphasises proactive problem-solving and sustained officer presence, is particularly effective in ensuring that police interactions remain context-sensitive and responsive to community concerns (Cosgrove & Ramshaw, 2015).

Respect

Respect in policing is demonstrated through the way officers communicate, listen, and respond to public concerns. Studies have shown that the perception of respect during police encounters significantly influences public willingness to cooperate with police institutions and the criminal justice system (Murphy et al., 2014). This extends beyond verbal communication to include non-verbal cues such as body language, tone of voice, and active listening techniques (Bradford, 2014). Officers who engage respectfully are more likely to elicit cooperation, reduce hostility, and create an environment in which individuals feel comfortable seeking police assistance.

By embedding these principles into daily practice, police forces can foster stronger relationships with the public, improve compliance, and enhance overall community safety. Engaging with the public in a fair, appropriate, and respectful manner is not merely a strategy for increasing police legitimacy; it is a fundamental component of democratic policing and a critical factor in the long-term success of law enforcement institutions and policing by consent.

Public Perspectives on Engagement and Trust

Understanding public engagement in policing requires close attention to the lived experiences of diverse communities. Data from the Crime Survey for England and Wales (CSEW) consistently shows that public confidence in the police is unevenly distributed across demographic lines. While overall levels of trust in the police have remained relatively stable in recent years, disparities persist between ethnic groups. According to the CSEW (2023), White respondents were significantly more likely to express confidence in the police (71%) compared to Black (54%) and Mixed ethnicity respondents (58%), suggesting a critical trust gap that needs to be addressed through engagement practices that are inclusive, transparent, and responsive.

This disparity is compounded by the findings of the Lammy Review (2017), which highlighted the overrepresentation of Black individuals in the criminal justice system and the long-standing perception of racial bias in policing. The review concluded that many Black, Asian, and Minority Ethnic individuals feel over-policed yet under-protected. Such perceptions are shaped not only by current experiences but also by a history of systemic disadvantage, overuse of stop-and-search powers, and a lack of community representation in law enforcement.

More recently, the Casey Review (2023) into the Metropolitan Police found that institutional racism, misogyny, and homophobia were endemic within the force, further undermining public trust, particularly among minoritised and marginalised communities. Casey's report reinforced the view that meaningful public engagement must go beyond surface-level consultation to address deep-seated inequalities and power imbalances. When engagement is perceived as tokenistic or procedural rather than authentic and responsive, it risks further alienating communities who already feel disenfranchised. At the same time, inspection evidence and public confidence data indicate that trust is not uniform across England and Wales, with some forces demonstrating measurable improvements where sustained neighbourhood presence, transparent engagement, and leadership accountability have been prioritised.

Public engagement must therefore be framed within a broader social and historical context. For many communities, particularly Black, Asian, and migrant populations, the police are not always seen as a source of protection, but rather as an institution linked to surveillance, control, and criminalisation (Bowling & Phillips, 2007; Long, 2018; Shiner et al., 2018). This historic distrust cannot be overcome through short-term initiatives alone; it requires a sustained commitment to building relationships based on mutual respect, cultural understanding, and accountability (EHRC, 2020; Casey, 2023; Tyler & Jackson, 2014). This includes adapting engagement strategies for specific groups such as young people, older adults, disabled individuals, and LGBTQ+ communities, whose interactions with police may be shaped by distinct vulnerabilities and access barriers.

Efforts to rebuild trust should include co-produced engagement strategies, investment in diverse recruitment, and the amplification of community voices in policing decisions (College of Policing, 2021; HMICFRS, 2021; Lammy, 2017). Importantly, listening to public feedback, acknowledging harm, and demonstrating change through action are vital for bridging the gap between the police and the communities they serve (Home Office, 2022; Rowe, 2020). By integrating public perspectives -particularly those from underrepresented groups - into the heart of engagement strategies, policing can become more equitable, inclusive, and effective in serving the diverse needs of the UK population (IOPC, 2021; Bradford et al., 2020).

ASSESSING CURRENT PRACTICES IN PUBLIC ENGAGEMENT

Evaluating Fairness in Policing

Assessing fairness in policing requires a critical review of decision-making processes to ensure impartiality and the equitable treatment of all individuals. In this context, fairness is better understood through the principle of equity rather than equality, recognising that different individuals and communities may require different approaches or levels of support to achieve substantively fair outcomes. One approach involves fairness audits, which systematically examine stop-and-search data, use-of-force incidents, and arrest records to identify patterns of disproportionate policing (Bradford et al., 2013). Additionally, police forces increasingly rely on community perception surveys to measure public trust and confidence in law enforcement. These surveys capture insights into how different groups - particularly marginalised communities - experience police interactions (Tyler & Jackson, 2014).

Measuring Appropriateness in Police Interactions

Appropriateness in policing is evaluated through the extent to which officers adapt their approaches to specific situations. De-escalation techniques, such as verbal persuasion and non-threatening body language, are essential indicators of appropriate policing, particularly in situations involving vulnerable individuals (Hough et al., 2013). Moreover, culturally sensitive policing ensures that officers understand and respect the backgrounds and needs of diverse communities (Myhill & Quinton, 2010). Many police forces conduct structured reviews of body-worn camera footage to assess whether officers' actions align with best practices in de-escalation and community engagement. In line with this, officers are taught structured communication models during personal safety training, including the 5-Step Appeal process - simple appeal, reasoned appeal, personal appeal, final appeal, and action - and the LEAPS model (Listen, Empathise, Ask, Paraphrase, Summarise). These models provide a framework for verbal resolution before resorting to force, and their consistent application forms a measurable aspect of appropriate engagement in operational policing (College of Policing, 2020).

Gauging Respect in Public Interactions

Respect is a key determinant of police legitimacy and public cooperation. Police forces measure respect through citizen feedback mechanisms, such as structured interviews and focus groups, which allow individuals to describe their experiences with officers (Murphy et al., 2014). Additionally, observational studies - where researchers or supervisors analyse officer interactions - offer valuable insights into communication styles, tone, and non-verbal behaviour (Bradford, 2014). By embedding respect into daily practice, police can improve public perceptions and strengthen community partnerships. By systematically assessing fairness, appropriateness, and respect, law enforcement agencies can develop targeted strategies to enhance public engagement and foster stronger relationships with the communities they serve.

STRATEGIES TO IMPROVE PUBLIC ENGAGEMENT

Strengthening Training and Education

Effective public engagement starts with comprehensive training and education for officers at all levels. Research has shown that integrating principles of fairness, appropriateness, and respect into police training curricula leads to improved public perceptions and increased legitimacy (Tyler & Huo, 2002). Training should not only focus on technical skills but also on interpersonal competencies, including active listening, empathy, and conflict resolution (Bradford et al., 2014). Although many forces now offer unconscious bias training, HMICFRS (2018) found that few officers could articulate how they apply this in practice. Where forces achieved stronger outcomes, this training was paired with scenario-based supervision and reflective practice sessions that built deeper awareness of public impact.

A key strategy in improving engagement is the use of scenario-based learning and role-playing exercises. These methods allow officers to practice handling complex social interactions, such as de-escalating tense encounters or engaging with vulnerable individuals in crisis (Hough et al., 2013). Furthermore, ongoing professional development ensures that officers remain updated on best practices in community policing and procedural justice (Tyler & Jackson, 2014).

Enhancing Community Involvement

Strengthening public engagement also requires active participation from communities. One effective approach is the establishment of advisory boards composed of community leaders, local organisations, and police representatives. These boards provide a platform for open dialogue, allowing communities to express concerns, co-develop policing strategies, and contribute to decision-making processes (Skogan, 2006).

Another strategy involves citizen-led problem-solving initiatives, where community members and police collaborate to address local safety concerns (Myhill & Quinton, 2010). Such initiatives may include neighbourhood watch programs, youth engagement projects, and restorative justice circles, all of which empower communities to take an active role in shaping public safety (Cosgrove & Ramshaw, 2015). Research suggests that when the public feels included in policing decisions, trust and cooperation improve significantly (Bradford, 2014).

Increasing Transparency and Accountability

Transparency and accountability are essential for maintaining public confidence in the police. One way to enhance transparency is through open access to policing data, including stop-and-search statistics, use-of-force reports, and complaints against officers (Tyler & Jackson, 2014). Providing communities with real-time information on police activity fosters trust and ensures that law enforcement agencies remain accountable for their actions (Hough et al., 2010).

Technology also plays a crucial role in improving accountability. The use of body-worn cameras has been shown to reduce complaints against officers and improve officer conduct (Ralph et al., 2024). Similarly, digital engagement platforms, such as police social media accounts and online reporting tools, create direct channels for community feedback and enhance police responsiveness (Murphy et al., 2014).

By embedding these strategies - strengthening training, increasing community involvement, and enhancing transparency - police forces can build sustainable, trust-based relationships with the communities they serve. Long-term public engagement efforts not only improve perceptions of legitimacy but also lead to greater cooperation, reduced crime, and enhanced community safety.

Practitioner Perspectives on Engagement

While public trust and community outcomes are central to engagement strategies, the perspectives of frontline officers offer equally valuable insights. Police practitioners are the bridge between policy intentions and community experience. According to HMICFRS (2018), strong leadership is vital to embedding fairness and respect in everyday policing encounters. Leaders who model procedurally just behaviour influence cultural norms within the force, enabling frontline officers to reflect these values in community engagement. However, the capacity for officers to engage fairly, appropriately, and respectfully is shaped by structural conditions, organisational culture, and the demands of frontline work.

According to HMICFRS (2022), many officers express a desire to build positive relationships with communities, but report being hampered by limited resources, heavy caseloads, and the dominance of reactive tasking models. A frontline officer quoted in the inspection report noted, *"We're constantly moved around based on demand - there's little chance to build relationships with the same community."* This lack of continuity undermines efforts to create trust-based policing, especially in communities already sceptical of law enforcement.

Burnout is another critical factor influencing engagement. Officers frequently report feeling emotionally exhausted, unsupported, and overwhelmed by rising public expectations and increased scrutiny. According to research by the Police Federation of England and Wales (2021), over 77% of officers reported experiencing symptoms of work-related stress, with many citing public hostility, negative media portrayal, and pressure to meet performance targets as contributing factors. These conditions can foster a culture of cynicism and detachment - both of which undermine respectful, empathetic engagement.

Organisational culture also plays a significant role in shaping officer attitudes and behaviours. While official policies often promote community engagement and procedural fairness, officers working in high-pressure environments may internalise unspoken norms that prioritise enforcement, risk aversion, or operational efficiency. The College of Policing (2020) acknowledged that "tick-box" approaches to engagement can discourage genuine interaction and lead to a perception that engagement is a distraction from "real policing." This view is particularly prevalent in teams where performance is measured primarily by arrests, response times, or other quantitative outputs.

New officers entering the service often report a gap between the inclusive principles taught in training and the realities of operational policing. Without consistent role modelling and supervisory support, these values can be quickly eroded. As one probationary officer interviewed in a College of Policing qualitative study explained, *"There's what you learn in training and there's what actually happens out there. You don't want to rock the boat when you're new."* (College of Policing, 2020, p.17).

Recognising these practitioner experiences is essential for designing engagement strategies that are sustainable and realistic. This includes providing dedicated time for community engagement, rewarding relationship-building efforts, and reforming performance metrics to reflect relational policing goals. Support for officer well-being, supervision that reinforces fairness and respect, and leadership that models inclusive values are all key to shifting engagement from a procedural requirement to a cultural norm. Evidence from forces that have embedded these approaches suggests that officers report greater role satisfaction alongside improved community relationships, reinforcing the sustainability of engagement-led policing.

Leadership, Culture, and Accountability in Public Engagement

Leadership plays a decisive role in shaping how principles of fairness, appropriateness, and respect are translated into everyday policing practice. While training and policy frameworks set expectations, it is senior leadership that determines whether engagement values are embedded, modelled, and sustained. HMICFRS inspections consistently identify leadership behaviour and organisational culture as critical factors influencing how officers engage with the public.

Leaders who actively demonstrate procedurally just behaviour, encourage reflective practice, and prioritise ethical decision-making create conditions in which frontline officers are more likely to engage respectfully and confidently. Conversely, where performance cultures prioritise enforcement outputs, response times, or risk avoidance over relational policing, engagement is often marginalised or treated as secondary.

The gap frequently identified by officers between training ideals and operational realities reflects not a failure of individual commitment, but a failure of organisational alignment. Without visible leadership endorsement and accountability mechanisms, engagement principles taught during training risk being eroded by informal norms and pressures. Embedding engagement therefore requires leaders to reinforce expectations through supervision, promotion criteria, and performance frameworks that value relationship-building alongside operational effectiveness.

Effective leadership in public engagement also involves accountability. Transparent decision-making, openness to community scrutiny, and responsiveness to public feedback signal institutional commitment to legitimacy. Where leaders acknowledge shortcomings and demonstrate learning, trust is more likely to be rebuilt. In this sense, leadership is not simply a structural function but a relational one, central to how policing is experienced and judged by the public.

THE ROLE OF NEIGHBOURHOOD POLICING IN PUBLIC ENGAGEMENT

How NPT Strengthens Engagement

Neighbourhood Policing is particularly effective in building trust due to its consistent, localised presence. Officers working within specific communities develop familiarity and rapport, leading to more effective collaboration. Research indicates that sustained engagement through NPT results in higher public confidence, increased crime reporting, and greater voluntary compliance with the law (Bradford et al., 2014). The emphasis on problem-solving and community partnerships differentiates NPT from other policing models, making it a cornerstone of public engagement efforts (Hough et al., 2010).

HMICFRS inspections of forces including Dorset, Hampshire, and Cheshire illustrate how sustained neighbourhood policing models, where abstraction is minimised, are associated with higher public confidence and more consistent engagement outcomes. While approaches vary by force, these findings highlight the importance of structural commitment to neighbourhood policing rather than its use as a supplementary function.

Challenges Faced by NPT

Despite its benefits, NPT is often compromised when treated as a secondary function. One of the most significant challenges is frequent abstractions, where officers are reassigned from neighbourhood duties to other operational priorities, disrupting continuity and weakening public trust (Ralph et al., 2024). Inconsistent funding and resource allocation further exacerbate these issues, leading to a lack of sustained engagement in some communities (Cosgrove & Ramshaw, 2015).

Comparative Insights

- In fully embedded NPT models, officers have dedicated roles and consistent interaction with the community, leading to higher trust levels and stronger police-community relationships (Skogan, 2006).
- In hybrid models, where NPT functions as an add-on to response policing, engagement is often less sustained and less effective, as officers are frequently diverted to other duties (Hough et al., 2013).

By ensuring that NPT remains a dedicated and well-supported function, police forces can maximise its effectiveness in enhancing public engagement, reducing tensions, and strengthening trust-based policing relationships.

CHALLENGES AND OPPORTUNITIES IN PUBLIC ENGAGEMENT

Barriers to Effective Engagement

Despite the clear benefits of public engagement, several barriers hinder its full implementation in policing.

- Resource Constraints: Many police forces operate under financial and staffing limitations that affect their ability to maintain sustained engagement initiatives. Budget cuts often lead to the reallocation of officers from Neighbourhood Policing to reactive roles, reducing the effectiveness of community-based approaches (Cosgrove & Ramshaw, 2015). Limited personnel also mean that proactive initiatives such as community meetings, outreach programmes, and trust-building activities are deprioritised in favour of immediate law enforcement tasks (Bradford, 2014).
- Public Perception Issues: Negative media coverage, historical grievances, and instances of police misconduct have led to public scepticism regarding law enforcement's commitment to engagement (Myhill & Quinton, 2010). In communities that have experienced over-policing or racial profiling, trust is difficult to rebuild without consistent and transparent efforts to demonstrate fairness and accountability (Tyler & Jackson, 2014).
- Institutional Challenges: Internal resistance to community-led policing models remains a significant barrier. Some officers and departments prioritise enforcement-oriented strategies, viewing engagement efforts as secondary or non-essential (Ralph et al., 2024). Organisational cultures that re-

sist collaborative, problem-solving approaches can undermine the success of Neighbourhood Policing and other engagement strategies (Hough et al., 2013).

Opportunities for Improvement

While challenges exist, there are several opportunities to strengthen public engagement and integrate it more effectively into policing strategies.

- Institutional Commitment to Engagement: To prioritise engagement, police leadership must embed community relationships into policing strategy. This includes developing officer incentives for engagement work, allocating dedicated resources for outreach programmes, and establishing internal performance measures that assess public trust levels (Bradford et al., 2014).
- Digital Engagement Strategies: Expanding police outreach through social media, virtual town halls, and mobile applications offers new avenues for engagement. Digital platforms allow the police to share real-time updates, gather community feedback, and build trust remotely (Murphy et al., 2014). Research suggests that interactive digital engagement, rather than one-way communication, leads to greater public satisfaction and increased cooperation (Ralph et al., 2024).
- Sustained Investment in Neighbourhood Policing: Ensuring that NPT remains a core function rather than a supplementary role is key to improving engagement outcomes. Stability in neighbourhood policing teams, long-term presence in communities, and collaborative problem-solving approaches lead to higher public confidence and reduced crime rates (Cosgrove & Ramshaw, 2015). Investment in NPT should focus on training, recruitment, and officer retention, ensuring that community officers are not frequently reassigned to other duties (Bradford, 2014).

By addressing these challenges and capitalising on opportunities, police forces can develop a more robust, effective, and community-centred approach to public engagement that enhances trust, reduces crime, and fosters long-term cooperation.

FUTURE DIRECTIONS FOR PUBLIC ENGAGEMENT

As policing in England and Wales faces complex and evolving demands, the future of public engagement must shift from procedural compliance toward sustainable cultural transformation. While traditional indicators of fairness and respect

- such as stop and search data, use of force, and community surveys - remain central, emerging priorities highlight the need to embed legitimacy across all aspects of police strategy, training, and practice.

The PEEL 2018 Judgment Criteria made clear that excellence in public engagement requires more than community presence; it demands visible leadership commitment, a culture of fairness, and meaningful co-production with the public. Forces deemed 'Outstanding' were those able to demonstrate how public feedback shaped local priorities and how officers had internalised training on procedural justice and unconscious bias. Yet, the translation of training into practice has remained inconsistent. According to HMICFRS (2018), few officers could articulate how bias awareness, or ethical frameworks informed their daily interactions. Future improvements must move beyond one-off inputs and toward embedded, experiential learning, supported by reflective supervision and peer-led modelling.

The HMICFRS 2025–2029 (HMICFRS, 2024) consultation offers a strategic opportunity to redefine engagement for the next generation of policing. Under the revised PEEL assessment framework, three core questions - leadership, public treatment, and workforce development - will frame how legitimacy is evaluated. This signals an important shift: fairness and respect will no longer be marginal concerns, but central components of force performance. Inspectors will consider not only whether officers treat the public fairly, but whether senior leaders foster a culture that enables this consistently. In this future landscape, public engagement will also be shaped by technological developments. National thematic inspections will explore how forces use biometrics, facial recognition, and digital contact methods, raising critical questions around digital legitimacy, transparency, and consent. Public trust will hinge not just on physical presence in communities, but also on how respectfully and ethically data is gathered, shared, and acted upon.

Moreover, future engagement must respond to trauma and vulnerability, both in the public and within the workforce. With expanded attention to safeguarding and violence against women and girls, there is a clear imperative to integrate trauma-informed and gender-sensitive practices into engagement strategies. These must go beyond protecting victims and also address how policing itself may retraumatise those it seeks to serve. Effective public engagement in this context will require officers who are culturally competent, emotionally literate, and supported by policies that prioritise wellbeing, dignity, and repair.

Looking ahead, advances in artificial intelligence and predictive analytics are likely to further reshape the relationship between police and the public. While such technologies may offer efficiencies in risk identification, resource deployment, and crime prevention, their use raises significant questions for public engagement. Decisions about how data is collected, analysed, and acted upon increasingly require public understanding, consent, and trust. Without transparent communication and meaningful engagement, the expansion of algorithmic decision-making risks eroding legitimacy, particularly among communities already sceptical of police power. Future public engagement strategies must therefore extend beyond traditional face-to-face contact to include dialogue about digital policing, data ethics, and the limits of automated authority, ensuring that technological innovation is accompanied by democratic accountability.

Finally, future directions must be grounded in public co-ownership of policing strategies. Forces that excel will not only consult the public but share power - through citizen panels, community accountability forums, and collaborative problem-solving. As the HMICFRS strategy affirms, forces must move from "promising practice" to institutionalised partnership, embedding community voice at the heart of inspection, design, and decision-making. Public engagement in the years ahead will require adaptability, authenticity, and a deep commitment to equity. The forces that rise to this challenge will not only build legitimacy but help shape a policing model that is truly responsive to the needs, values, and rights of all communities.

CONCLUSION

Effective public engagement in policing requires a multi-layered approach that balances broad organisational strategies with localised, community-based initiatives. While traditional policing models provide essential oversight, Neighbourhood Policing Teams (NPT) plays a crucial role in fostering long-term trust and legitimacy by embedding officers within communities and prioritising relationship-building over enforcement. Sustaining effective engagement necessitates a commitment to reducing officer abstractions, maintaining consistent police presence, and investing in training that emphasises fairness, appropriateness, and respect. By reinforcing community partnerships and adopting digital engagement tools, law enforcement agencies can improve public perceptions, increase voluntary cooperation, and create safer, more cohesive communities. Ultimately, embedding engagement at all levels of policing ensures that interactions between police and the public remain transparent, accountable, and community-oriented, strengthening public confidence in law enforcement and fostering long-term cooperation.

REFERENCES

Bowling, B., & Phillips, C. (2007). Disproportionate and Discriminatory: Reviewing the Evidence on Police Stop and Search. *The Modern Law Review, 70*(6), 936–961. DOI: 10.1111/j.1468-2230.2007.00671.x

Bradford, B. (2014). Policing and social identity: Procedural justice, inclusion and cooperation between police and public. *Policing and Society, 24*(1), 22–43. DOI: 10.1080/10439463.2012.724068

Bradford, B., Jackson, J., & Hough, M. (2014). *Police legitimacy in action: Lessons for theory and policy.* https://academic.oup.com/edited-volume/34517/chapter/292870924

Bradford, B., Yesberg, J. A., Jackson, J., & Dawson, P. (2020). Live facial recognition: Trust and legitimacy as predictors of public support for police use of new technology. *British Journal of Criminology, 60*(6), 1502–1522.

Casey, L. (2023). *The Baroness Casey Review: A review into the standards of behaviour and internal culture of the Metropolitan Police Service.* https://www.met.police.uk/SysSiteAssets/media/downloads/met/about-us/baroness-casey-review/update-march-2023/baroness-casey-review-march-2023a.pdf

College of Policing. (2020). *Conflict management skills.* https://www.college.police.uk/guidance/conflict-management/conflict-management-skills

College of Policing. (2021). *Engaging communities: A guide for police officers and staff.* https://www.college.police.uk/guidance/neighbourhood-policing/engaging-communities

Cosgrove, F., & Ramshaw, P. (2015). It is what you do as well as the way that you do it: The value and deployment of PCSOs in achieving public engagement. *Policing and Society, 25*(1), 77–96. DOI: 10.1080/10439463.2013.802787

Equality and Human Rights Commission. (2020). *Tackling racial inequality: A statement from the Commission following the death of George Floyd and Black Lives Matter protests.* https://www.equalityhumanrights.com/en/our-work/news/tackling-racial-inequality-statement-commission-following-death-george-floyd-and

His Majesty's Inspectorate of Constabulary and Fire & Rescue Services. (2018). *PEEL assessment framework: Judgment criteria.* https://hmicfrs.justiceinspectorates.gov.uk/peel-assessments/peel-2018/

His Majesty's Inspectorate of Constabulary and Fire & Rescue Services. (2021).

His Majesty's Inspectorate of Constabulary and Fire & Rescue Services. (2024).

Hough, M., Jackson, J., & Bradford, B. (2013). *Legitimacy, trust and compliance: An empirical test of procedural justice theory using the European Social Survey*. https://papers.ssrn.com/sol3/papers.cfm?abstract_id=2234339

Hough, M., Jackson, J., Bradford, B., Myhill, A., & Quinton, P. (2010). Procedural justice, trust, and institutional legitimacy. *Policing. Journal of Policy Practice*, *4*(3), 203–210.

Independent Office for Police Conduct. (2021). *IOPC impact report 2020/21*. https://www.policeconduct.gov.uk/sites/default/files/documents/IOPC_Impact_Report_202021.pdf

Lammy, D. (2017). *The Lammy Review: An independent review into the treatment of, and outcomes for, Black, Asian and Minority Ethnic individuals in the criminal justice system.* https://www.gov.uk/government/publications/lammy-review-final-report

Long, L. J. (2018). *Perpetual Suspects: A Critical Race Theory of Black and Mixed-Race Experiences of Policing*. Springer International Publishing., DOI: 10.1007/978-3-319-98240-3

Murphy, K., Mazerolle, L., & Bennett, S. (2014). Promoting trust in police: Findings from a randomised experimental field trial of procedural justice policing. *Policing and Society*, *24*(4), 405–424. DOI: 10.1080/10439463.2013.862246

Myhill, A., & Quinton, P. (2010). Confidence, neighbourhood policing, and contact: Drawing together the evidence. *Policing. Journal of Policy Practice*, *4*(3), 273–281.

Ralph, L., Elliott, I. C., Murphy, J., & Glennon, R. (2024). Navigating the digital beat: A review of social media as a public engagement tool in policing. *International Journal of Emergency Services*, *13*(3), 201–214.

Rowe, M. (2020). *Policing the police: Challenges of democracy and accountability*. Policy Press. https://books.google.com/books?hl=en&lr=&id=ZjDNDwAAQBAJ&oi=fnd&pg=PR7&dq=Rowe,+M.+(2020).+Policing+the+police:+Challenges+of+democracy+and+accountability&ots=Ibbq6Ga9q0&sig=NvjnxfLk7ca-rpZJ4utlJtDiAn8

Shiner, M., Carre, Z., Delsol, R., & Eastwood, N. (2018). *The colour of injustice: 'race', drugs and law enforcement in England and Wales*. https://eprints.lse.ac.uk/100751/

Skogan, W. G. (2006). *Police and community in Chicago: A tale of three cities.* Oxford University Press., https://books.google.com/books?hl=en&lr=&id=j0QOBsB3tUIC&oi=fnd&pg=PR9&dq=Skogan,+W.+G.+(2006).+Police+and+community+in+Chicago:+A+tale+of+three+cities.+Oxford+University+Press.&ots=bpSKV9sodc&sig=phWVMvg5VD567LjjAW-ldspFNnI

Tyler, T. R. (2006). *Why people obey the law.* Princeton university press. https://books.google.com/books?hl=en&lr=&id=77G9sCO_MKIC&oi=fnd&pg=PP13&dq=Tyler,+T.+R.+(2006).+Why+people+obey+the+law.+&ots=_yjbFI3ogk&sig=WV9aBmvQFbENvse42gIYnhcwfbo

Tyler, T. R., & Huo, Y. J. (2002). *Trust in the law: Encouraging public cooperation with the police and courts.* Russell Sage Foundation. https://books.google.com/books?hl=en&lr=&id=wAeGAwAAQBAJ&oi=fnd&pg=PR7&dq=Tyler,+T.+R.,+%26+Huo,+Y.+J.+(2002).+Trust+in+the+law:+Encouraging+public+cooperation+with+the+police+and+courts.&ots=T1EbR1M23P&sig=fLqu_4PQER-3RWDzN6v7XOfNvW4

Tyler, T. R., & Jackson, J. (2014). Popular legitimacy and the exercise of legal authority: Motivating compliance, cooperation, and engagement. *Psychology, Public Policy, and Law, 20*(1), 78.

Chapter 28
Whole Systems Partnership Working

David Rowlands
http://orcid.org/0000-0002-4201-7754
University of Leeds, UK

ABSTRACT

The chapter explores the shift towards whole systems partnership working in UK police forces, and how partnership approaches are helping to address HMICFS PEEL assessment criteria. In discussing this issue, the chapter focuses on three inspection questions: (1) How good is the police force at preventing and deterring crime, antisocial behaviour and reducing vulnerability (2) How good is the police force at protecting vulnerable people; and (3) How good is the police force at managing offenders and suspects. The need for whole systems partnership responses is contextualised with reference to the growing demand on police to respond to situations involving individuals with complex needs and the emergence of partnership and public health approaches. Whilst challenges remain, broadly, collaborative interventions are considered in relation to improved provider relationships, knowledge exchange, strategic and operational support that improve police efficiency, effectiveness and legitimacy.

INTRODUCTION

This chapter examines how ideals and shifts towards whole systems partnership working in UK police forces is helping to address HMICFS PEEL assessment criteria. For the purposes of this discussion, the chapter focuses on inspection questions concerning how good the force is at: (1) preventing and deterring crime, antisocial behaviour and reducing vulnerability (2) protecting vulnerable people;

DOI: 10.4018/979-8-3373-2757-0.ch028

and (3) managing offenders and suspects. The need for whole systems responses is contextualised through an exploration of increased demand on policing from individuals with complex needs, the emergence of partnership and public health approaches, and their benefits and challenges. Benefits of collaborative interventions are considered in relation to improved provider relationships, knowledge and skills exchange, strategic and operational support, and how such collaborative mechanisms work to improve police efficiency, effectiveness and legitimacy.

SHIFTING BOUNDARIES OF POLICING

The past decade has seen a growing prevalence of police contact with individuals facing multiple and complex problems (Home Affairs Committee 2023; HMICFRS 2023). These 'vulnerabilities may underpin or directly contribute to behaviours leading to criminal justice involvement yet often fall outside the traditional remit of law enforcement. Presentations such as mental ill health, substance intoxication and homelessness often involve non-crime incidents but may still require a police response, especially situations posing immediate danger that may require the use of force. This positions the police as *de facto* responders to social crisis (College of Policing 2015; HMICFRS 2020). Even where crimes occur, many victims, or indeed suspects, have histories of trauma or marginalisation, pointing to wider structural, experiential, and health-related factors that influence behaviour.

This reality challenges the conventional boundaries of policing. While restoring social order and enforcing the law are core police functions, officers are increasingly expected to recognise, assess, and respond to complex vulnerabilities. Such tasks require skills, resources, and expertise beyond traditional police training, amplifying the risk of mismanagement (Bartkowiak-Theron et al. 2017). For example, an encounter involving a person in mental health crisis may be escalated rather than de-escalated if inappropriate interventions are used. This shift in police demand has led to growing recognition of the need for collaborative responses that span policing, health and social services, along with youth, third sector providers and the private sector. Indeed, such networked responses are now integral to pluralised models of community safety (Crawford and Evans 2017).

This shift is not new, as Crawford and Cunningham (2015) and van Dijk et al. (2019) document, calls for integrated service delivery have spanned decades. However, austerity measures and the disinvestment in social care since 2010 have intensified policing challenges, with officers increasingly called upon to fill the gaps left by under-resourced services, which in turn risks distorting their role and undermining legitimacy (see Bradford *et al*. 2024; Bradford and Jackson 2024).

Vulnerability and policing

In parallel with the increase in police contact with people with complex problems, vulnerability has become a central theme in UK policing policy. The 1999 Macpherson report and HMICFRS's development of the Protecting Vulnerable People (PVP) framework in 2006 marking pivotal moments. The framework originally focused on domestic abuse, child protection, the management of violent and sexual offenders, and missing persons. Since then, the scope of 'vulnerabilities' has expanded, informed by frameworks such as the National Vulnerability Action Plan (VKPP, 2023), which align closely with the PEEL effectiveness indicators. This enhanced focus and knowledge from police and partners concerning people's vulnerabilities is producing examples of good practice which are supporting more positive outcomes for police encounters.

Nonetheless, significant issues remain, Enang et al. (2022) contending that no consistent national framework exists for defining vulnerability or presenting it as a broad and dynamic concept. Indeed, UK police forces vary in how they respond to vulnerability. Recent assessments by HMICFRS (2022) reflect this, noting wide variation in the quality of vulnerability provision across forces. While some forces demonstrate good practice in identifying and supporting vulnerable individuals, others fall short, resulting in inconsistent practice. This inconsistency undermines the effectiveness of efforts to protect vulnerable people, a core concern of the PEEL framework. As Bartkowiak-Theron and Asquith (2021) point out, the challenge for policing lies not only in recognising vulnerability, but also in knowing how to respond. Lack of appropriate skills is further compounded by officers often having to act in ambiguous and high-pressure environments, navigating tensions between safeguarding, public safety, and enforcement roles.

Whole Systems Responses

In this context, whole system and public health approaches to policing have emerged as promising frameworks, advocating for multi-agency, preventive and harm-reduction-focused responses grounded in shared responsibility, shared objectives, and collective accountability. These service provision networks reflect the complex causes of social harm and highlight how safeguarding concerns emerge at multiple points, requiring coordination that no single agency could provide (HMIC 2008).

Thus, the principle behind whole systems working is straightforward: where problems are multiple and complex, solutions must be collaborative and integrated. Yet achieving this in practice remains challenging. Much of the current discourse on *vulnerability* circulates within a narrow public-health framework (Crawford et al., 2017), reinforcing crisis-management logics rather than addressing the structural conditions that produce harm. A more productive reading of whole systems working instead situates it within a systemic paradigm that sees vulnerability as a product of institutional design, resource allocation and political economy.

Drawing on Gilmour (2025), this perspective encourages actors to address the root social determinants of harm rather than its symptoms. Accordingly, Gilmour's account of *systems leadership* emphasises the moral ecology necessary for effective collaboration. Coxhead and Holyoak's (2025) concept of *Teamership* similarly promotes inter-agency reflexivity grounded in shared moral purpose rather than metric-driven compliance.

Taken together, these insights recast whole system policing as an adaptive ecology rather than an assemblage of silos. In so doing, the emphasis shifts from measuring discrete agency outputs to fostering collective capacity for prevention, collaboration and justice. Indeed, inspection regimes that isolate performance by agency risk privileging procedural compliance over meaningful social outcomes. What is required is a systemic recalibration of how *success* itself is defined.

An effective system response demands that services across the police, health, housing, social care, and the third sector work as a cohesive network. Such networked governance does not mean diluting the core function of policing - the public expects and wants the police to respond to crime and situations of social disorder presenting danger (Bradford et al. 2025). Rather, whole systems models call for a repositioning of the police within a broader system of care and intervention. This means recognising when the police are the right service to respond and when they are not (Rowlands et al. Forthcoming). The recent *Right Care, Right Person* initiative in England and Wales represents an effort to respond to this issue, setting clearer parameters for a police response to mental health-related incidents. Despite criticisms of how the policy was implemented (Health and Social Care Committee 2023) and its implications for health and social care provision (Jefferson et al. 2024), the initiative has stimulated a more open discussion about the role of the police in responding to vulnerable individuals.

In recent years, promising multi-agency strategies and initiatives have emerged. The Law Enforcement and Public Health (LEPH) model promotes a proactive, evidence-based framework for joint responses, focusing on early intervention and harm reduction. Public health approaches to violence prevention, such as those pioneered in Glasgow (Williams and Donnelly 2014) and later adopted nationally (Home Office, 2018) demonstrate how shifting focus from enforcement to prevention helps to reduce reoffending and improve outcomes for vulnerable individuals and communities.

Nevertheless, tensions remain between enforcement and support roles, especially when public health responses are underfunded. Officers may be forced to detain a vulnerable person not necessarily because it is the most appropriate response, but because custody is perceived as the safest or only available place to provide oversight and a minimum amount of care (Solar & Smith 2022). That research highlights instances where vulnerability increases the likelihood of negative police encounters (Friedman et al. 2021) underscores the need for training, accountability, and trauma-informed frameworks within policing cultures.

That being said, it is important to recognise that police occupy a particularly difficult position within partnerships, sometimes having to make decisions outside of partnership remits due to their role in serving multiple publics (e.g., people experiencing street homelessness and shop owners). Creating something of a policing dilemma, such situations may undermine partnership working agreements in certain circumstances. This complexity is further compounded by the dynamics of plural policing, where involvement of private sector entities introduces additional challenges. While addressing resource constraints, the integration of private security firms into public safety strategies can blur accountability lines and complicate the coordination of whole system responses (Crawford 2017). Such partnerships may lead to inconsistencies in service delivery and raise concerns about the equitable provision of policing services (Lister & Jones 2015). Similarly, different police and private security objectives and operational cultures can thwart cohesive strategy implementation. These dynamics emphasise the need for clear governance structures and accountability mechanisms in collaborative policing models (White 2014).

While vital to efficient and effective service provision, for whole systems collaborations to work requires clear roles and service accountability. Furthermore, the lack of shared definitions, objectives, and evaluative frameworks across services limits the ability to measure the impact of partnership work. In the current service provision landscape success is often judged from the perspective of individual agencies rather than collective outcomes. This weakens the effectiveness and legitimacy of multi-agency approaches. To address this, scholars such as Enang et al. (2021) advocate for shared learning environments and interdisciplinary exchange. However, evaluations should prioritise shared outcomes, not individual organisational targets, if genuine system change is to be achieved.

The PEEL framework's emphasis on protecting the vulnerable, preventing crime, and managing suspects provides a useful lens for assessing how well police forces are doing in this space. However, assessments need to acknowledge the broader system within which policing operates. Policing must operate in concert with other services, sharing responsibility and resources, operating with clearly defined roles and relationship building to establish trust between sectors.

WHOLE SYSTEMS APPROACHES TO CRIME AND VULNERABILITY: GOOD PRACTICE

Recognising benefits of integrating law enforcement with health, social care and community organisations in providing holistic and preventative response to crime and vulnerability, contemporary policing in the UK increasingly emphasises whole system, partnership-based approaches. A review of academic literature provides insights into best practices, challenges and opportunities associated with these approaches.

One significant area of innovation has been the development of Multi-Agency Safeguarding Hubs (MASHs). Shorrock et al. (2019) explored the role of MASHs in facilitating rapid, coordinated responses to vulnerable individuals. The work emphasises knowledge sharing benefits of co-located agencies and shared information systems. However, their findings also highlighted variability in referral quality and the absence of standardised assessments, which impacted decision-making. Similarly, McGuire et al. (2021) revealed the importance of integrating adult safeguarding practices with policing to support vulnerable adults at risk of exploitation or harm. The evaluation affirmed the need for robust governance, inter-agency training and shared goals to ensure effective collaboration.

The Police Foundation evaluation of a multi-agency violence reduction project in Slough (Hales & Higgins, 2015) highlights the importance of commitment and resources among participating agencies to effective collaboration. Despite improved professional relationships and more effective case tracking, the initiative struggled to deliver measurable reductions in violent crime, partly due to inconsistent engagement from health and probation services.

Local context and leadership also play a crucial role, as demonstrated by Leicestershire Police's whole system approach to serious violence and vulnerability (College of Policing, 2022). The Leicestershire model emphasises the strategic alignment of police, local authorities, health service, and voluntary sector. A shared data dashboard and joint strategic meetings were key innovations, allowing for evidence-based interventions and more efficient resource deployment. While the approach yielded positive results in addressing high-risk individuals and 'hotspot' localities, considerable effort was required to overcome data sharing, information governance, and siloed working.

Further demonstrating the benefits of local area-based intervention strategy, Davies and Biddle (2018) explored localised responses to domestic abuse focused on perpetrator accountability through multi-agency partnerships. These involved police, probation, health services, local authorities, housing providers and domestic abuse charities working through a coordinated community response (CCR) model. Features of the partnership included shared case management, multi-agency meetings, and the involvement of IDVAs to support victims and coordinate services. While the approach improved offender monitoring and victim-survivor support, inconsistent healthcare, probation and children's services engagement and lack of funding impeded sustainability and wider implementation.

A nuanced picture emerges from other studies focusing on domestic abuse and the protection of vulnerable individuals. Cleaver et al. (2019) explored Multi-Agency Risk Assessment Conferences (MARACs), their findings emphasising the benefits of shared risk frameworks and co-location of services, resonating with Shorrock et al. (2019). However, they also reported inconsistencies in case selection and difficulties in sharing sensitive information, which undermined MARAC effectiveness.

A crime prevention study by Barton and Valero-Silva (2013) analysed Nottingham's partnership between police and housing services. Focused on environmental improvements - including upgraded house security, improved street lighting, and communal regeneration - The Decent Homes Programme reduced crime in targeted areas while also improving perceptions of safety and community cohesion. The collaboration demonstrates the potential of place-based, preventative strategies when anchored in inter-agency cooperation.

Whole System Vulnerability Responses to Perpetrators of Crime

Recent research conducted by the author with the Vulnerability and Policing Futures Research Centre (VPRC) (Engelmann et al. 2025) aligns with and reinforces findings within the wider literature. Reflecting Davies and Biddle (2018), our ongoing Greater Manchester domestic abuse research highlights a strong commitment among police and partner agencies to respond collaboratively to the complex needs of victim-survivors. Mirroring the work of others, the research illustrates the successes of MARACs in managing high-risk cases and the potential of devolved responses anchored in local priorities and inter-agency collaboration, with benefits of service co-location.

However, Greater Manchester's collaborative ethos becomes more contentious when extended to perpetrators. While there is an emerging recognition among some stakeholders of the need to address the root causes of perpetration, such as trauma and adverse childhood experiences (ACEs), to reduce reoffending, this remains a divisive issue. Framed through a victim-survivor lens, the argument that a vulnerabilities-informed approach to perpetrators is essential to reduce victimisation is gaining traction; nonetheless, Greater Manchester police's approach to perpetrators remains enforcement-focused, emphasising the need for swifter criminal justice consequences.

Other services, in particular certain victim-survivor services, adopted this approach, expressing concerns about multi-service intervention weakening criminal accountability. Resistance to a holistic approach to perpetrator intervention stemmed from concerns over offenders' lack of responsibility, poor engagement with services, and manipulation of systems to evade consequences. These dynamics contribute to scepticism toward more rehabilitative models, which are sometimes perceived as being politically unpalatable or 'soft on crime'. Such resistance, particularly from within police ranks and victim advocacy organisations, obstructs the effectiveness and coherence of whole system responses to domestic abuse. The challenge, then, lies in achieving a nuanced understanding among partners that enables a balancing criminal accountability and consequences with approaches that address root causes to foster long-term behavioural change and reduced victimisation.

Collaborative Dialogue and Coordinating Around Shared Objectives

Reflecting the above literature, the author's research in Bradford exploring service provision for vulnerable people in contact with the police demonstrates the value of collaborative models characterised by joint funding initiatives, co-location and shared operational activities, such as outreach and community event days (Engelmann et al. 2024). Knowledge exchange, skills development, strengthened inter-agency relationships, and enhanced operational support afforded through service collaboration were reported to deliver significant benefits to the service efficiency and effectiveness of police and partner organisations. The presence of sustained, open dialogue was viewed by practitioners as critical to success, facilitating mutual understanding and aligned objectives, particularly in relation to reducing harm under the shared concept of 'vulnerability'. Indeed, seeing that police officers were sighted on 'vulnerability' and open to addressing the different factors influencing crime and disorder helped to strengthen previously difficult relationships.

Despite improved police and support service relationships, challenges, nonetheless, remain. While at the strategic level, police, local authorities and larger third sector partnership in Bradford have improved service coordination, as has been identified in other studies (e.g., Hales & Higgins 2015; Davies & Biddle 2018), mental health services were marginalised from the partnership. This was experienced as a significant gap in the whole systems response. Furthermore, smaller specialist agencies were often excluded from strategic networks, undermining service delivery by limiting access to valuable local expertise. This exclusion was especially apparent in case study areas outside of the city centre, where local identity, embedded in a history of marginalisation, manifested in distrust toward statutory services. Such sentiments fostered community resistance to external interventions and fragmented local responses. These challenges were further amplified by intergenerational hostile police-community relations, underlining the need for a police and partnerships focus on building trust and relationships to improve legitimacy over time with alienated communities and historically overpoliced vulnerable populations.

The research also examines Bradford's response to city centre homelessness, identifying good practice of the Homeless Outreach Partnership (HOP). Coordinated by a third sector housing support service, the partnership facilitates a multi-agency collaboration, bringing together police, local authority, housing support and drug and alcohol services, while also engaging local private sector organisations. Based around principles of knowledge exchange, shared objectives and person-led intervention, the partnership supports an assertive outreach service model to engage marginalised individuals experiencing street homelessness. Key to the success of the HOP model is its investment in inter-sector relationship-building and dialogue, instrumental in fostering a local police approach increasingly aligned with welfare intervention that prioritises individual, needs-led support over enforcement. The initiative has been instrumental to developing positive relationships with local policing, their engagement improving service perceptions, effectiveness, efficiency and legitimacy among both service providers and service users.

Still, certain tensions are observed in responding cohesively to street homelessness, with demands on police in serving multiple publics: supporting individuals with acute vulnerabilities such as homelessness and addiction while simultaneously addressing the concerns of local businesses and the wider public. This dilemma reveals the friction between compassionate intervention and visible public safety enforcement. Helping to address this issue, housing support service dialogue with local shops and restaurants was seen as mutually beneficial in improving outcomes for vulnerable individuals while helping to maintain public order. Additional local partnerships between private sector, local authority and police, such as *Pubwatch*, provide platforms to discuss concerns and identify effective responses addressing the multiple needs of those involved.

Broadly, the author's research illustrates demonstrable benefits of close partnership working based on continuous interservice dialogue and joint operations in facilitating shared understanding and objectives to enhance service coordination. Nonetheless, with smaller specialist organisations excluded from strategic partnerships and entrenched community distrust in marginalised areas, challenges of unmet need among those most vulnerable to crime remain (Engelmann et al. 2024).

Collectively, studies affirm that whole system, partnership approaches are critical to modern policing, particularly in addressing crime and the complex needs of vulnerable individuals and communities. While beneficial practices such as co-location, shared data systems, and coordinated decision-making have shown promise, challenges remain in ensuring consistent implementation, securing sustainable funding, promoting partnership inclusivity, and fostering inter-agency and community trust. The success of these models is contingent on a clear strategic vision, adequate resources, multi-sectoral partnerships, person-led interventions, commitment to shared values and continuous evaluation. Continued research and evaluation are essential in refining these approaches and enhancing their impact.

DISCUSSION IN RELATION TO PEEL QUESTIONS

1. How good is the force at preventing and deterring crime, anti-social behaviour, and reducing vulnerability?

The evidence suggests that forces engaged in whole system approaches are increasingly effective at prevention, particularly when partnerships are strategically embedded and co-produced with communities. The Nottingham case study (Barton & Valero-Silva, 2013) shows that environmental improvements combined with police involvement can significantly reduce crime and anti-social behaviour. Similarly, the Leicestershire model (College of Policing, 2022) demonstrates how cross-agency collaboration can proactively address risk factors before they escalate. However, resource limitations, uneven partnership engagement, and data-sharing challenges present barriers to consistent implementation across forces.

2. How good is the force at protecting vulnerable people?

Protection of vulnerable individuals is strongest where MASHs and MARACs are well-resourced and embedded in wider service networks. Studies by Shorrock et al. (2019) and Cleaver et al. (2019) point to the benefits of co-located services and standardised risk assessments. Yet, inconsistent referrals, information silos, and high caseloads present challenges to effectiveness. The author's research in West Yorkshire reinforces these findings, identifying innovative practices but also systemic weaknesses due to under-resourcing and lack of service provider participation. Exclusive partnerships and poor partnership engagement impede effective service delivery and protection. In particular, police and third sector practitioners identified lack of strategic involvement from mental health services as a gap in the system (Engelmann et al. 2024). High Mental Health and Social Care access thresholds were seen to burden police officers in responding to vulnerable people in crisis, referring to insecurely funded third sector organisations as a singular recourse.

The above issues notwithstanding, research identifies significant benefits of inclusive whole system approaches, building multi-sectoral partnerships, drawing on local assets, and engaging communities. Protection of vulnerable people is best when police forces are able to work in synchrony with health, housing and social care, not least of which since such collaborations help foster trauma-informed, person-centred police practice.

3. How good is the force at managing suspects and offenders?

The research literature indicates that effective offender management is closely linked to the quality of multi-agency coordination. Davies and Biddle (2018) show that localised, perpetrator-focused interventions in domestic abuse cases can improve outcomes by aligning police, probation and support services. Similarly, Hales & Higgins (2015) illustrate the promise of managing high-risk individuals through case conferencing. Challenges include inconsistent engagement, lack of performance metrics and insufficient follow-through. Police forces that excel in this area have developed shared risk management protocols and mechanisms for accountability across agencies.

CONCLUSION

UK police forces that embrace whole systems, partnership-led models show promising results in crime prevention, protection of vulnerable populations and offender management. However, these approaches are complex and resource intensive. Systems leadership requires attending to the underlying social determinants of harm and cultivating a moral ecology that enables agencies to work collaboratively. This demands inter-agency reflexivity grounded in common values rather than narrow performance targets.

Taken together, these orientations frame whole systems partnerships as an adaptive ecology rather than a collection of organisational silos, shifting emphasis from discrete outputs to collective capacity for prevention, collaboration and justice. Scaling up such practices therefore depends on strategic leadership, sustainable funding, integrated data systems and, crucially, a genuine commitment to inter-agency cooperation. Ultimately, whole systems models are not quick fixes; they represent a forward-thinking recalibration of what success in policing looks like, towards more compassionate, equitable and effective social outcomes.

REFERENCES

Asquith, N. L., & Bartkowiak-Théron, I. (2021). *Policing practices and vulnerable people*. Palgrave Macmillan.

Barton, H., & Valero-Silva, N. (2013). Policing in partnership: A case study in crime prevention. *International Journal of Public Sector Management, 26*(7), 543–553.

Bradford, B., & Jackson, J. (2024). Trust in the Police: What is to be Done? *The Political Quarterly*, *95*(3), 442–449.

Bradford, B., Jackson, J., & Taylor, E. (2024). Policing the permacrisis-Guest editors' introduction. *The Political Quarterly*.

Bradford, B., Rowlands, D., Weirich, C. A., & Crawford, A. (2025). What service should police provide? Towards a minimum policing standard. *Policing and Society*, *35*(7), 1001–1018. DOI: 10.1080/10439463.2025.2535667

Cleaver, K., Maras, P., Oram, C., & McCallum, K. (2019). A review of UK based multi-agency approaches to early intervention in domestic abuse: Lessons to be learnt from existing evaluation studies. *Aggression and Violent Behavior*, *46*, 140–155.

College of Policing. (2015). Mental health and policing: Picking up the pieces. https://www.college.police.uk

College of Policing. (2022). Whole system approach case study – Leicestershire Police. https://www.college.police.uk

Coxhead, J., & Holyoak, J. (2025). The Lack of Leadership and the Need for 'Teamership' in British Policing. In *Special Topics in Policing: Critical Issues and Global Perspectives* (Vol. 3, pp. 97–110). Springer Nature Switzerland.

Crawford, A. (2017). Temporalities in security: long-term sustainability, the everyday and the emergent in the Anthropocene. In *Criminology and the Anthropocene* (pp. 153–180). Routledge.

Crawford, A., & Cunningham, M. (2015). Working in partnership. *Police leadership–rising to the top*, 71-94.

Crawford, A., & Evans, K. (2017). *Crime prevention and community safety*. Oxford University Press.

Davies, P. A., & Biddle, P. (2018). Implementing a perpetrator-focused partnership approach to tackling domestic abuse: The opportunities and challenges of criminal justice localism. *Criminology & Criminal Justice*, *18*(4), 468–487.

Enang, I., Murray, J., Dougall, N., Aston, E., Wooff, A., Heyman, I., & Grandison, G. (2022). Vulnerability assessment across the frontline of law enforcement and public health: A systematic review. *Policing and Society, 32*(4), 540–559.

Engelmann, L., Rowlands, D., Crawford, A., & White, A. (2024). *Service provision for vulnerable people in contact with policing: a strategic view from Bradford.* Vulnerability and Policing Futures Research Centre.

Engelmann, L., Rowlands, D., Yardimci, O., Walklate, S., Westmarland, N., & Fitz-Gibbon, K. (2025). *Responding to family violence, domestic abuse: lessons from Greater Manchester (UK) and Victoria.* Summary Report, Vulnerability and Policing Futures Research Centre.

Friedman, J., Syvertsen, J. L., Bourgois, P., Bui, A., Beletsky, L., & Pollini, R. (2021). Intersectional structural vulnerability to abusive policing among people who inject drugs: A mixed methods assessment in California's central valley. *The International Journal on Drug Policy, 87*, 102981. PMID: 33129133

Gilmour, S. (2025). Violence-informed approaches to preventing criminalisation. *LinkedIn.* Available at: https://www.linkedin.com/pulse/violence-informed-approachespreventing-professor-stan-gilmour-kpm-c95re

Hales, G., & Higgins, A. (2015). Evaluation of the Slough multi-agency violence reduction project. The Police Foundation. https://www.police-foundation.org.uk/publication/evaluation-of-the-slough-multi-agency-violence-reduction-project

Health and Social Care Committee. (2023). Right care, right person: Policy review and impact on mental health services (HC 1243). House of Commons.

Her Majesty's Inspectorate of Constabulary and Fire & Rescue Services (HMICFRS). (2020). *Policing and mental health: Picking up the pieces.* HMICFRS.

Her Majesty's Inspectorate of Constabulary and Fire & Rescue Services (HMICFRS). (2022). *State of policing: The annual assessment of policing in England and Wales 2022.* HMICFRS.

Her Majesty's Inspectorate of Constabulary and Fire & Rescue Services (HMICFRS). (2023). *Policing vulnerable people: The PEEL effectiveness assessment 2023.* HMICFRS.

Her Majesty's Inspectorate of Constabulary (HMIC). (2008). *Thematic inspection report: Leading from the front.* HMIC.

Home Affairs Committee. (2023). Policing priorities and challenges: Eighth report of session 2022–23 (HC 947). House of Commons.

Jefferson, L. A., Doran, J., Gilburt, H., Dale, V. M., & Bloor, K. E. (2024). Exploring Health and Social Care perspectives on the implementation of 'Right Care, Right Person', under the National Partnership Agreement.

Lister, S., & Jones, T. (2015). Plural policing and the challenge of democratic accountability. In *Accountability of policing* (pp. 192–213). Routledge.

Macpherson, W. (1999). *The Stephen Lawrence Inquiry: Report of an inquiry by Sir William Macpherson of Cluny*. The Stationery Office.

McGuire, J., Evans, E., Kane, E., McGuire, J., Evans, E., & Kane, E. (2021). Multi-agency safeguarding for vulnerable and at-risk adults. *Evidence-Based Policing and Community Crime Prevention*, 261-297.

Shorrock, S., McManus, M. A., & Kirby, S. (2019) Investigating the Characteristics of Vulnerable Referrals Made to a Multi-Agency Safeguarding Hub. Policing, 13 (2). pp. 201-212. ISSN 1752-4512

Solar, C., & Smith, M. (2022). Austerity and governance: Coordinating policing and mental health policy in the UK. *Policy Studies*, *43*(2), 352–369.

van Dijk, A., Hoogewoning, F., & Punch, M. (2019). *What matters in policing? Change, values and leadership in turbulent times*. Policy Press.

VKPP (Vulnerability Knowledge and Practice Programme). (2023). National Vulnerability Action Plan (NVAP). https://www.vkpp.org.uk

White, A. (2014). Post-crisis policing and public–private partnerships: The case of Lincolnshire Police and G4S. *British Journal of Criminology*, *54*(6), 1002–1022.

Williams, D. J., & Donnelly, P. D. (2014). Is violence a disease? Situating violence prevention in public health policy and practice. *Public Health*, *128*(11), 960–967. PMID: 25443389

Chapter 29
Between the Police and Public:
A Unique Perspective on Rebuilding Trust and Confidence – A Case Study

Poppy Josephine Caitlin Murray
http://orcid.org/0009-0000-5776-1044
BE LADS, Guernsey

ABSTRACT

This chapter details the author's personal journey of working with the police to rebuild public trust and confidence, particularly in relation to violence against women and girls (VAWG). It explores the turning points, challenges, and insights gained along the way, while offering practical recommendations drawn from first-hand experience, public engagement, and campaign development. With a professional background in journalism and marketing, alongside working in partnership with the police as a conduit to the public, the author educates and inspires with the message that one person can make a difference.

INTRODUCTION

"Do you trust the police?" I'll never forget the moment I was asked that question live on air by a BBC Radio Guernsey host. Given that I was being interviewed about an upcoming presentation I would be delivering at the 2023 HeForShe UK Police

DOI: 10.4018/979-8-3373-2757-0.ch029

Ally Event, the question itself didn't surprise me. What did surprise me was the speed and intensity with which my gut instinctively answered: *"no"*.

Thankfully, I kept that instinctive "*no*" to myself and took a moment to consider my response more carefully. I didn't want to say "*no*," but I also wasn't willing to be dishonest. Instead of giving a direct answer, I responded in a way that felt like I'd make a better politician than campaigner. I spoke about the complex reasons why trust in the police is so difficult to establish and sustain - particularly for women - and acknowledged the very real concerns that contribute to this reluctance. At the same time, I expressed my belief that the police are making genuine efforts to rebuild public trust and confidence.

As I drove away from the studio, I gave a silent prayer of thanks that I hadn't been pushed to give a "yes" or "no" answer. As a journalist myself, I certainly would have noticed the avoidant nature of my answer and was grateful that the host had been satisfied with it. For the rest of the drive, I debated what my answer would be if I were ever asked to give a definitive response.

I considered the ramifications of saying "*no*." As someone actively campaigning to end violence against women and girls (VAWG) and to rebuild public trust in the police, a direct "*no*" would have placed me in clear opposition to the very institution I aimed to influence - potentially undermining my ability to work constructively with them. On a personal level, I also feared that publicly expressing distrust might affect how I'd be treated if I ever needed their help. In Guernsey's close-knit community, this fear is common. Many hesitate to criticise public institutions - be it police, healthcare, or education - out of concern for potential repercussions.

But saying "yes" would have been dishonest. I worried that encouraging others, especially women, to trust the police prematurely could put them at risk. If harm followed, I'd feel complicit.

By the time I got home, I'd made myself a promise: I wouldn't answer that question until I could say "yes" and truly mean it. It would take two more years - and countless hours of working with police forces and organisations - before I reached that point.

Since 2021, I've held a unique and privileged position that few civilians experience: seeing the other side of trust and confidence in policing. Through these experiences, combined with my background in journalism, marketing, and VAWG campaigning, I offer a civilian's perspective on rebuilding public trust. I hope it contributes meaningfully to ongoing efforts. In this chapter, I share how my journey began, and offer practical advice based on my own experience of learning to trust the police again. For brevity, I've included just a few key examples to highlight the power of authentic engagement and transparency, though there are many more I could tell.

ISSUES IMPACTING PUBLIC TRUST AND CONFIDENCE IN THE POLICE

My instinctive answer that I did not trust the police came from a mix of personal experience, the experiences of friends and family, and the seemingly endless stream of news about police officers abusing their power, committing crimes, or failing so significantly that justice is never delivered. My lack of trust was reflective of recent data which demonstrates that public trust in policing has fallen sharply. The Office for National Statistics' 2025 report on perceptions of the police found that only 49% of people rated their local force as doing a 'good' or 'excellent' job. This marks a substantial decline from 2015, when the figure stood at 62%. The trend is clear: confidence in policing has eroded over the past decade, reflecting a growing public concern about effectiveness, fairness and accountability.

This lack of trust does not only relate to violence against women and girls. From the disproportionate use of stop and search powers against Black, Asian, and minority ethnic communities, to persistent failures in handling mental health callouts, to widely reported cases of corruption, misconduct and institutional discrimination, public confidence in policing has been eroded on multiple fronts. Black people in England and Wales are still around seven times more likely to be stopped and searched than white people, according to Home Office figures. High profile scandals, including officers sharing photographs of murder victims, the repeated mishandling of rape and domestic abuse cases, and officers sexually abusing members of the public, have further damaged the legitimacy of policing in the eyes of the public.

Layered onto this is the steady decline in successful criminal prosecutions, meaning many victims across all crime types see little chance of justice. Together, these failures create a broader environment in which trust is not simply fragile but has been actively deteriorating.

PEEL inspections consistently find significant variations in the quality of investigations, with many forces criticised for slow progress, poor supervision, and inconsistent victim follow-up. Inspections have also identified weaknesses in how forces identify and safeguard vulnerable people, including victims of rape, high-risk missing persons, and those with mental health vulnerabilities. A common finding is that forces lack the capacity to fully meet demand, leading to backlogs and reduced public confidence in the ability to deliver justice.

BE LADS CAMPAIGN

My journey of working in partnership with the police began when Sarah Everard went missing - a case that shook the nation and further fractured already fragile trust in policing.

As time has passed, it's easy to forget that the public interest in Sarah's disappearance began before it was known that her kidnap, rape, and murder were committed by a serving police officer. Tragically, Sarah was neither the first nor last woman to vanish while walking alone. Yet her story captured public attention in a way most women's stories don't. What struck me was that, for once, it was impossible to imply, directly or indirectly, that she was in any way to blame.

To be clear, a victim is never to blame. But that doesn't stop the media or public from suggesting, subtly or overtly, some form of contributory negligence. When 20-year-old India Chipchase was raped and murdered by 52-year-old Edward Tenniswood, headlines read:

- *"India Chipchase 'downed six Jägerbombs' on the night she died"* (Daily Mail)
- *"Rugby WAG 'downed six Jagerbombs' and vanished from club before being 'raped and murdered'"* (Daily Star)
- *"Barmaid 'was very drunk' before her rape and murder"* (Express)

Such commentary implies blame and also offers women like me a false sense of security. The unspoken message becomes: *If you want to stay safe, don't drink like that.* As if a cautionary tale for victims, not a condemnation of the perpetrator. But India wasn't killed because she drank. She was killed because Tenniswood chose to rape and murder her. Yet the narrative shifted blame to India. When victims' stories are framed like this, public sympathy is eroded and responsibility moved away from the perpetrator.

When it came to Sarah Everard, the media and the public had no blame to assign. Sarah was not overly intoxicated, she was not dressed in a way that anyone could suggest was provocative, she took the safest, most well-lit route, a friend knew where she was, and she had been on the phone to her partner for most of her walk. Sarah did all the things that I, and most women, would have done believing it would be enough to keep us safe. But it wasn't enough.

As all the possibilities of what Sarah could have done differently – and therefore what other women could do differently in future – were quickly ripped away, '#SarahEverard' started trending. Women flooded social media with their own stories of feeling, or being, unsafe while walking alone, along with the everyday precautions we take to feel safer: holding our keys between our knuckles, sharing our live location, staying on the phone, wearing only one earphone (if any), and choosing the safest route home - even if it means a longer route.

When the public learned that Sarah's 'mistake' was trusting a serving police officer, the collective shock deepened. The very figure we're taught to seek help from had used that trust to cause unimaginable harm.

As women shared their stories, '#NotAllMen' started trending higher than Sarah's name. The hashtag accompanied comments from men feeling vilified by the action of Wayne Couzens. They viewed Sarah's murder as an outlier, while women saw it as a story which irrefutably validated long-held fears.

Amidst the noise, I saw a comment that simply asked: *'What can I, as a man, do to help?'* The question caught my attention - not only as a rare and genuine attempt by a man to bridge the growing divide between men and women on these issues, but also because, when I saw it, no one had replied. Feeling compelled to find an answer, I began researching to answer my own question: *Where do you signpost the men who, upon learning of women's fears about walking alone, genuinely want to help alleviate them?* I found countless personal safety and prevention campaigns directed at victims and some, though not many, aimed at perpetrators to think about the consequences of their actions. I couldn't, however, find any campaign directed at the men who wanted to help. So, I made one. I sat in my room with a notepad and pen, and I created the BE LADS Campaign – with "BE LADS" being an acronym for simple advice men could follow to help women feel safer walking alone:

- Be visible
- Ease the tension by making a phone call
- Look away, don't stare
- Active bystander intervention
- Distance yourself
- Share the walk*

*Either physically or by staying on the phone, or location sharing.

On my 29th birthday – eight days after Sarah Everard's body was found – I posted BE LADS on Facebook. My only thought at that time was that, if just one man followed one piece of advice, and one woman felt safer on her walk as a result, then it was worth the time spent creating the campaign.

In the months that followed, I spoke with the local media in my home of Guernsey, I met with the island's politicians and with teachers. By October, a BE LADS lesson had been added to the curriculum for all 16-year-olds on the island. By the following February, the BE LADS message had been delivered as training to over 1,000 staff at a construction company in Ireland, in a community that had been shaken by the murder of Ashling Murphy (who was raped and murdered while jogging alone).

BE LADS WITHIN POLICING

By the end of 2022, an article about BE LADS had been published in the ISPCC Practitioner Magazine and Police Oracle Magazine, identifying the campaign as a crime prevention initiative to tackle violence against women and girls. Then, in April 2023, I stood in front of over 70 police officers and staff as the first civilian speaker at the annual HeForShe UK Police Ally Event.

The event took place less than a month after The Baroness Casey Review had been released, and institutional misogyny within policing remained headline news. I found myself in the unexpected position of being the only civilian in a room of police officers and staff who were sitting in the shadow of one of the most damning reports of policing in recent history.

As much as I wanted those officers to listen to me, I wanted to listen to them more. I wanted to know what the other side of the story was. But I didn't hear another side. What I heard was speaker after speaker express that the Casey Review of the Metropolitan Police Service ("MPS") could have easily been about their own force. I heard officers from the MPS tell us that the issue was not a case of 'bad apples', the issue was a culture – the entire orchard - that desperately needed to change. I heard disappointment, disillusion, and heartbreak.

As I listened, barriers were broken down. I realised I was in a room with ordinary people - parents, children and siblings - who just happened to be police officers and staff, and who were just as concerned about the state of UK policing as I was. I stood in front of them and asked for their help. I promised, if they continued to be driven by a desire to help people, that they would find more and more people who appreciate and respect that help. I urged them to understand that they each had far more power than I did, and that they could use it to do more than I had; the same message I want to share with everyone reading this.

After my presentation, countless officers thanked me, invited me to their forces, and offered to help me in any way that they could. Since then, I have delivered BE LADS to over 2,000 police officers and staff across the UK. I had the privilege of presenting BE LADS at New Scotland Yard to a group of women committed to making their communities safer. I also met one of the officers who had worked on Sarah's case, before presenting BE LADS to his department. On the same day, a Guernsey Police officer, Aaron Cusack, was sentenced to two-and-a-half years in prison for pressuring a vulnerable woman into dropping a rape complaint - a stark reminder of the scale of work still to be done.

BE LADS has been well-received by police forces across the UK and Channel Islands, with testimonials including: *"The BE LADS campaign is doing something different; it speaks to men and boys and gives them an active role in keeping women and girls safe. For too long, the focus has been on what women and girls should be doing to keep safe rather than on what men and boys could be doing. The campaign provides a straight-forward approach that can easily be adopted by anyone. I would not hesitate to recommend Poppy as a speaker and her campaign as a tool to raise awareness of violence against women and girls and the role men and boys have to make others feel safer. We are sharing Poppy's campaign with police forces across the UK." (Louise Crawford, HeForShe Programme Manager for UK Policing)*

"I met Poppy at a national event in Wales and her delivery addressed some of the societal issues we have with male violence against women. Her input balances practical advice about what men can do to help women feel safer and what women can do to safeguard themselves too. Poppy should be so proud of what she has achieved so far on her journey to make the world a safer place for women with her thought-provoking delivery." (Terry Mole, HeForShe Coordinator for Gender Equality, Metropolitan Police Service)

CASE STUDY: CITY OF LONDON POLICE

City of London Police (CoLP) has shown the highest proportional uptake of the BE LADS Campaign of any UK police force, with one third of its officers having attended the training. Through online training sessions, officers and staff have engaged with the campaign's practical approach to tackling sexual harassment and violence against women and girls, providing very positive feedback on both the content and delivery.

The collaboration began after City of London Police ("COLP") Lead Public and Personal Safety Trainer, Garry Shuttleworth, saw me present BE LADS at the 2023 HeForShe Police Ally Event for UK Policing. I had met Garry the evening before, along with several other officers, and he shared a series of dramatic stories from his career. To me, these stories were harrowing; to the officers around the table, they seemed entirely routine. Garry hadn't shared them to shock me. In fact, he was enthusiastically encouraging me to consider a career in policing, emphasising that being able to help the public still made the job worthwhile, even in the face of heavy criticism and scrutiny.

At the end of the event the following day, Garry joined a long queue of officers waiting to speak to me – a moment that still feels surreal when I think back on it. One by one, officers I had never met offered words of support, encouragement and commitment to helping turn BE LADS into something bigger than I ever imagined. Garry could easily have slipped away; instead, he stayed in that queue so long that he missed his scheduled train home and had to take a later one. When he finally reached the front, he looked at me with seriousness and sincerity and said: "Forget everything I said last night. Don't join the police – you're doing exactly what you're meant to, and I'm going to do whatever I can to help you."

Posting on social media that evening, Garry said: "*The highlight of the event was listening to the compelling, extremely thought-provoking, and passionate talk by Poppy Murray who put across her presentation about BE LADS to a large group of police officers perfectly. The fact you could see eyes watering from those in attendance really showed that what she said hit home. I would – and will – encourage every man and boy to look up BE LADS and understand that it's not all men but is all women.*"

Garry then attained the support of CoLP Detective Superintendent Kate MacLeod and online training sessions (one-hour each) were then arranged for CoLP police and staff, with Garry and Kate's enthusiasm contributing to the high attendance rates. Garry also went on to partner with me to deliver BE LADS workshops to at-risk students at the Chelsea FC Foundation's Standing Together Event. Garry's contributions in the session demonstrated the police's willingness to work in partnership with the community, and he directly helped to address concerns regarding trust in the police when raised by the students. This partnership helped to shift attitudes amongst young people about VAWG and also contributed significantly to rebuilding the students' trust and confidence in the police.

In December 2025, Garry won the Equity, Diversity, and Inclusion Award at the City of London Police Force Awards, with his contributions to the delivery of BE LADS forming part of his nomination. To this day, Garry mentions BE LADS – and me – in rooms I am not in. He continues to champion the campaign on his social media, and he is unfailingly at the end of the phone whenever I need advice or a sounding board for new presentations. He not only fulfilled his promise to elevate the campaign; he helped rebuild something I had quietly lost. His support has played a significant part in restoring my trust and confidence in the police.

PRACTITIONER EVALUATION: BE LADS PROGRAMME (CITY OF LONDON POLICE)

Source: Detective Superintendent Kate MacLeod, City of London Police

Context: Evaluation of three BE LADS sessions delivered to City of London Police

Having reviewed the feedback from three BE LADS sessions delivered to City of London Police, I can say with confidence that this initiative has had a profound and measurable impact on our organisation. The responses highlight not only strong engagement from participants, but also a genuine shift in understanding about women's safety and the role men can play in creating safer environments.

What stood out most was the number of attendees who described the sessions as thought-provoking, informative, and essential. Officers and staff repeatedly commented that they had never previously considered how their everyday behaviour might affect women, nor how simple actions such as crossing the road, announcing their presence, or making a phone call could significantly reduce fear for women walking alone. Many stated that they would immediately begin adjusting their behaviour as a result. One participant reported putting the advice into practice on the same evening as the training, becoming more aware of how their presence might be interpreted and taking active steps to reduce anxiety for women nearby.

Participants were particularly struck by the campaign's non-accusatory tone. The sessions provided space for honest reflection rather than blame, enabling officers and staff to engage openly with the material. Several attendees described the shark analogy as a "brilliant" and accessible way to illustrate why women's fear is rational, even when most men pose no threat. Others noted that BE LADS gave them practical tools they could share with colleagues, friends, and family members, including daughters who regularly navigate public spaces after dark.

The feedback also revealed how powerfully the sessions resonated with women within the force. Many expressed that they strongly identified with the examples shared, describing the content as validating and long overdue. Several commented that the initiative should be mandatory for all officers and staff, particularly given the policing context and our responsibility to safeguard women and girls. As one participant observed, "we should be championing campaigns such as this."

The sessions additionally prompted reflection among managers and leaders. Some highlighted how BE LADS could be incorporated into broader efforts to challenge misogyny, improve inclusivity, and strengthen our organisational response to violence against women and girls. There was a clear recognition that these conversations must continue, not only as part of professional development but as a wider cultural shift within policing.

While the majority of feedback was overwhelmingly positive, a small number of participants felt the content was less personally relevant or that they were already aware of the material. Even in these cases, however, the importance of the topic was acknowledged. Importantly, no feedback disputed the campaign's value; rather, responses reflected differing starting points in knowledge and experience.

Overall, the evaluation demonstrates that BE LADS is an effective, accessible, and impactful programme that resonates with both men and women across the force. Participants left with increased awareness, practical tools, and a stronger understanding of how their behaviour can influence the safety and comfort of women. From a

City of London Police perspective, BE LADS aligns strongly with our commitment to tackling violence against women and girls, rebuilding trust and confidence, and equipping our workforce with the insight needed to effect meaningful change. Based on the feedback received, I would wholeheartedly endorse the continuation and expansion of this programme across other police forces.

LESSONS LEARNED FROM LISTENING

No matter where I am, or which force I present to, I always feel I gain more by listening than I give by speaking. I listen to officers tell me, "*Everyone knew he was a problem*" about ex-colleagues imprisoned for offences against women. I listen to senior leaders express regret that the officers who "*need to be in the room to hear this*" are, too often, the ones who do not attend. And I listen - time and again - as every force speaks of being under-resourced.

I also listen when officers tell me that they are scared to admit they are police officers. That they would be hesitant to approach a lone woman in case they appear threatening. And how difficult their job has become – not only for them, but for their loved ones too - under the seemingly relentless barrage of scrutiny from the public and the media.

The more I listen, the more I have come to understand that David Carrick was not an MPS problem. Michael Darbyshire was not a West Mercia Police problem. Aaron Cusack was not a Guernsey Police problem. The problem is policing culture, which allows the wrong people to be in the right place to commit these offences.

I understand that for every David Carrick, Wayne Couzens, Michael Darbyshire, Aaron Cusack, and Adam Provan, there are many more Terry Moles, James Foxes, Jake Wrights, Garry Shuttleworths, Damian Kitchens, Matthew Edwardses, and James Sutherlands. I've met countless men and women who embody exactly what a police officer should be. But we, the public, rarely hear about them.

BE LADS placed me in a unique position between the police and the public. Without all the answers about policing, yet too informed to see things purely from a public perspective. It's a position I never sought, but one for which I'll always be profoundly grateful. It is only from this unique viewpoint that I can say, with absolute confidence, that the public and the police are all saying the same thing. Both sides know that the problem is systemic. Both sides want things to change and improve. Both sides have been let down and want trust and confidence to be restored. Unfortunately, that will not happen while the public and police continue to be presented as being on opposing sides.

What do I think needs to happen for things to change? The answer has become blindingly clear to me. What needs to happen is for everyone – police and public – to accept and remember three simple truths:

- Power is held by ordinary people.
- Change is not as difficult to bring about as we are led to believe.
- If you can help, you should.

These three undeniable truths should, in my view, guide all attempts to restore public trust and confidence in the police.

POWER

One of the most unsettling aspects of the Sarah Everard case was the question it left behind, particularly for women: "What can I do differently?" We cannot, and must not, allow the answer to become "Don't trust the police."

The real answer is: "Know your rights." And this is something the police should actively and consistently promote. Police officers hold significant power over the public - this is well understood. What is less often recognised is the power the public holds when they are informed. Educating people about their rights when dealing with the police is a vital step in rebuilding trust and confidence. To support this approach, I created an infographic [see figure 1] for Guernsey Police to help inform the public of their rights during police interactions. While seemingly simple, the information on this infographic plays a hugely important role in empowering the public to trust the police.

Figure 1. Be LADS in Partnership with Gurnsey Police.

TWO DRINK DRIVING SUSPECTS

In conveying the impact of this infographic, I've found it useful to flip the narrative: *Imagine you're a police officer who has pulled over two drivers, both of whom you suspect may be drink driving. You ask each of them the same question. One replies: "I haven't been drinking - you can trust me." The other says: "I haven't been drinking - you can trust me, and I'm happy to take any sobriety tests you need to carry out.'*

Which driver are you more inclined to believe? Both could be telling the truth or lying. But only one has actively invited you to validate their claim. That offer of transparency changes the dynamic entirely.

An officer who says, *"You can trust me,"* may well be telling the truth. But an officer who also invites the civilian to call the station to verify their identity shows a willingness to be held accountable. That simple offer of transparency builds trust and helps the public feel safer and more in control.

While this approach adds some administrative burden for both the officer and the colleague answering the call, the potential value in restoring trust and confidence is significant.

MEDIA RELATIONS

In many ways, I can relate to police officers who feel nervous about revealing their profession. I've often hesitated to admit to police officers that my background is in journalism. 'Reporter' can feel just as taboo in policing circles as 'police officer' does in a newsroom.

Through my work with police forces, I've seen first-hand the extraordinary behind-the-scenes efforts to tackle violence against women and girls - work that is rarely, if ever, shared with the media. Time and again, I've heard the same refrain: *"What's the point in telling the media? They'll only twist it."*

I've been on the other side of that dynamic. I've been encouraged by editors to make headlines more inflammatory, to dig for controversy in police press releases, or to find members of the public willing to offer an opposing view. I've also experienced the frustration of not being able to speak to officers directly, relying instead on airbrushed, impersonal statements from communications teams, which often left me sceptical of the full story.

The relationship between the police and the media is as strained, if not more so, than the relationship between the police and the public. If public trust is to be rebuilt, this relationship must be repaired. The media has little to gain by fixing it. The police have everything to gain.

Whether or not that seems fair, the responsibility to lead this change lies with the police.

In my experience, there are three key steps the police can take to strengthen their relationship with the media:

1. *Invite journalists into the police station* – let them see the people behind the uniform and gain insight into the realities of day-to-day policing.
2. *Proactively engage the media with regular press releases* – set aside fears of stories being manipulated and share every success, initiative, and community engagement story, not just crisis responses.
3. *Identify and train a small group of officers to speak confidently and consistently to the media* – building a trusted, informed bridge between policing and the public.

The third point is likely to be the most contentious within policing. It's a long-standing rule that officers should not, and often are prohibited from, speaking to the media. While this stems from understandable concerns about misreporting or loss of control over narratives, the unintended message it sends to both journalists and the public is striking: *If the police don't even trust their own officers with words, why should we trust them with our safety?*

I'm not suggesting that every officer should have free rein to speak to the press. But there should be designated officers who are trusted to speak openly, without hiding behind pre-approved statements or scripted media releases. The authenticity that comes from officers speaking in their own words can only strengthen the relationship between the police and the public.

CASE STUDIES:

Detective Sergeant Thomas Lowe

I met DS Lowe while developing the 'Guernsey Guide to Reporting Spiking' – a document I created to dispel myths and encourage victims of spiking to come forward. I immediately warmed to DS Lowe, not because he had all the answers, but because he was honest when he didn't, and committed to finding them. So, when I launched my next project - training night-time economy staff to respond to spiking and sexual violence - he was one of the first people I contacted.

At the project's launch, DS Lowe attended a media opportunity with me, without the presence of the States of Guernsey's Senior Media & Communications Officer. It was notable - whether by choice or circumstance - that DS Lowe had been entrusted to speak directly to the press. Reporters picked up on this too, each waiting their turn to speak with him. What followed was a genuine, unscripted message on behalf of Guernsey Police that strengthened public support for the project.

Chief Officer Damian Kitchen

2024 marked a period of significant change for Guernsey Police, with the retirement of both the Chief Officer and Deputy Chief Officer - and a second DCO set to retire in 2025. The impact of this full leadership transition was not lost on the public. I was particularly interested in how the new leadership would approach rebuilding trust and confidence.

Damian Kitchen, formerly Head of Operations at the National Police Coordination Centre, was appointed as Chief Officer. A few months into his role, I was introduced to him through a mutual contact. In his first email to me, Chief Officer

Kitchen expressed a desire for Guernsey police to make commitments and be held to account.

When we met, Chief Officer Kitchen made no grand promises, but demonstrated a clear understanding of the issues, shared personal insights, and outlined specific focus areas. He also remarked that he preferred to write his own media quotes and speak directly to the public. Since then, I've seen him give interviews with sincerity and authenticity.

PUBLIC RELATIONS

Communication between the police and the public extends far beyond traditional media. From public meetings to social media, websites, and informal interactions, police forces have considerable control over the messages they choose to share.

In my experience, however, communication is too often reactive rather than proactive, shaped by a "don't ask, don't tell" approach. Even seemingly trivial information can become contentious if the public feels it has been withheld. This applies not only when information is missing, but also when it's available yet difficult to find or understand.

The PEEL Framework identifies that forces "should use two-way community engagement showing that [the force] understands, listens, and responds to what matters to its communities" and should "empower local people to become involved in local policing activity".

There are simple steps that could help forces to implement this recommendation, such as social media polls to gauge public feedback on certain topics, holding community engagement meetings with a different topic each session (such as have been held in Guernsey through 2025), or online and paper surveys or other communications. In a meeting with Guernsey Police in early 2025, where I shared recommendations on restoring public trust, particularly around VAWG, I expressed a simple aspiration: to reach a point where I'm bored by how frequently I see updates about this work on their website and social media.

One of the most valuable lessons I've learned through working in media, marketing, and alongside police forces is this: Perception will always trump reality.

You can be doing the best work in the world, but if no one knows about it, it's as though it never happened. That's why I encourage forces to share regular updates across all digital channels. These should cover not only VAWG-related efforts, but all areas of community safety, meetings held, conferences attended, reviews undertaken, and actions taken.

I often hear officers say their work is "not worth shouting about." I urge you to remove that phrase from your vocabulary. Whether something is worth sharing depends on who's listening. What feels routine to the police may be deeply meaningful to a member of the public it impacts.

It's also essential that police messaging is accessible, especially via official websites. Having reviewed several police sites, I've noticed recurring issues that can undermine both usability and public trust:

- Outdated or inconsistent photography, particularly of personnel.
- No "quick exit" button for users.
- No translation options for non-English speakers.
- Long PDF documents with no hyperlinks or navigation.
- Poorly designed user journeys that make information hard to access.

An external review of your website and social media can help identify simple ways to improve transparency and reinforce public confidence.

CASE STUDY: GUERNSEY POLICE

Over the last year in particular, Guernsey Police has noticeably increased its public communication around sexual assault and violence against women and girls, working in alignment with the messaging promoted by local charities.

Social media posts with strong and consistent messaging have helped to build confidence that Guernsey Police is taking violence against women and girls, and sexual assaults, seriously. For example, on 30 May 2025, Guernsey Police posted:

"This week we've had two successful prosecutions progress through the Magistrate's Court for sexual assault – both men groping women in nightclubs. The first person was sentenced to two months in prison and given a five-year notification order in Court for his offences. The second was found guilty at trial and will be sentenced next month."

"Tackling violence against women and girls and inappropriate behaviour in the night-time economy remains a top priority for Guernsey Police, and we will continue to rigorously pursue offenders who think they can get away with it. Groping someone is not just "something that happens" in a night club. It is a criminal offence, and we will take any reports seriously."

"If you've been the victim of a sexual assault in the night-time economy, please report it so we can put the offender in front of the Courts" [Followed by contact information]

Guernsey Police also routinely tags local support services in its social media posts, including Victim and Witness Support, Willow House (the Sexual Assault Referral Centre), Safer (the domestic abuse charity) and SafetyNet Guernsey (the night-time economy safety charity). This demonstrates a commitment to signposting victims to specialist help and reinforces the message that support is available across the island, even for those who do not wish to report an incident to the police.

According to the Guernsey Police 2024 Annual Report, reports of sexual offences rose by 46% compared to the prior year. This rise should not, in my view, be interpreted as an increase in offending; it most likely signals a meaningful change in public willingness to report. It is reasonable to speculate that increased visibility of support services, clearer messaging from the police and increased community discussions around sexual violence have all contributed to more victims feeling able to seek help.

TRUST AND CONFIDENCE IN THE PUBLIC BY THE POLICE

When we talk about trust and confidence, the focus is almost always on the public's trust in the police. Rarely do we examine the reverse: the police's trust in the public. I don't mean that officers lack belief in the public when it comes to allegations, evidence, or requests for help - far from it. What I've observed is a notable absence of trust from the police that the public genuinely respects them. In my view, this is a critical part of the wider problem.

With the perfect storm of unfiltered social media, 24/7 news cycles, high-profile cases of police abuse, and algorithms that reinforce pre-existing views, the police are now under more intense and constant scrutiny than ever before.

Expanding public relations efforts inevitably brings the possibility of negative feedback. Public commenters frequently use police posts to air unrelated concerns, and if they cannot criticise the content directly, they will often redirect their criticism elsewhere. Unsurprisingly, this can have a demoralising effect on officers and staff and make them less willing to communicate openly with the public, perhaps feeling as though it is impossible to do the "right" thing in the eyes of the public. It is, therefore, hugely important that police officers and staff are given perspective on public trust and confidence, to enable and empower them to take criticism less personally.

THE DIFFERENCE WITH POLICING

I often hear the argument from police officers that: *"One bad doctor doesn't lead the public to distrust all healthcare professionals, so why should one bad police officer taint the whole profession?"*. I can only offer my own observation, in the hope that it helps explain what makes policing different in the eyes of the public.

Most people accept they'll need medical assistance at some point. It's much easier to believe you might never need the police. No one plans to become a victim of crime, and those committing one hope to avoid police altogether. It's easier to doubt, or criticise, a service you don't expect to need, than one you rely on.

There's also a key difference in how these professions operate. A GP often works alone, behind closed doors. Police officers often work in pairs, within a wider team. That contrast shapes public perception. It seems plausible that a rogue GP could go unnoticed, but far harder to believe that a dangerous police officer could act unchecked. So, when such cases do occur, the public doesn't just question the individual, they question the culture that enabled it.

When raising awareness of VAWG and promoting the BE LADS Campaign, I use an adapted analogy first shared with me by a teacher at an all-boys college where I was delivering a presentation.

SHARK ANALOGY

- *There are an estimated 500 species of shark in the world's oceans.*
- *Of these, only four are classified as "man-eaters".*
- *Most people can't identify shark species by a fin alone.*

Imagine you're swimming and you see a fin approaching. Despite the odds being overwhelmingly in favour of it belonging to a harmless species, your instinct is likely fear. Why? Because you simply don't know which kind it is.

Now imagine that 97% of people like you have been attacked by sharks in your area. In assessing the risk to your safety, would you find more comfort in the statistic that only 0.8% of sharks are dangerous, or would the 97% figure weigh more heavily?

This is the reality for women. With 97% of women aged 18-24 in the UK (AAPG, 2021). and 97% of women in Jersey (Bailiwick of Guernsey Law Enforcement, 2024), reporting experiences of sexual harassment - and with men making up most perpetrators (European Union agency for Fundamental Rights, 2014)- it is entirely understandable that women may view any man as a potential threat, even while knowing that most men are not.

Just as not all men are threats, neither are all police officers. In fact, in a strikingly similar statistic to the man-eating shark analogy, just 0.7% of police officers in the UK were accused of violence against women and girls, including sexual harassment, between October 2021 and April 2022 (NPCC, 2023).

While this is a small minority, and not all allegations will have been substantiated, the frequency and prominence of media reporting creates a perception that such incidents are far more common. (Perception will always trump reality.)

In sharing this analogy, I hope to emphasise that most women do recognise that most police officers are not a threat. However, the statistics stacked against women as victims of sexual harassment, combined with high-profile cases like Wayne Couzens and David Carrick, make it entirely reasonable for some women to feel fearful or hesitant, even when interacting with officers who pose no danger. By understanding and accepting this rationale, police officers can begin the work of rebuilding trust, particularly with women, and re-establishing confidence in the communities they serve.

CONCLUSION

I was recently taken aback when Guernsey Police Chief Inspector Andrew Hockey (now retired) expressed his hope that VAWG could one day become "self-policing." Sensing my surprise (perhaps assuming he was being flippant) CI Hockey went on to explain.

He recalled how apprehensive police had been about enforcing Guernsey's public smoking ban. Yet to their surprise, enforcement wasn't needed. The public policed it themselves. Almost overnight, smoking indoors became socially unacceptable, and anyone who tried to light up quickly found themselves out of step.

Once CI Hockey shared this perspective, I felt encouraged. Misogyny and VAWG may still be far too common, but like smoking indoors in public, we can reach a point where such behaviour is no longer tolerated, where the public plays an active role in holding one another accountable. But that will only happen if more of us take personal responsibility for creating change.

Before the sceptics among you dismiss this as unrealistic, please remember that BE LADS and my subsequent work with the police - and even this chapter - started with one person trying to help.

I had no personal connection to Sarah Everard. I had no personal connection to the man who posted the question asking what he could do to help women. I had no personal connection to the police. I was simply someone who tried something because I felt strongly enough to help.

If you're reading this and you work within policing, you're already starting from a far stronger position than I did. You hold a role within an institution with immense influence and inherent authority. I urge you to use your voice. Share these messages. Help drive change.

I've seen firsthand how quickly change can happen. I've seen how much power we each hold. I've seen what happens when you try to help.

To create lasting and meaningful change, all it takes is for enough people to realise that they can be someone who tries something. That's all I did. And that's all it will take.

REFERENCES

Bailiwick of Guernsey Law Enforcement. (2024). [Law enforcement publication]. States of Guernsey.

European Union Agency for Fundamental Rights. (2014). Violence against women: An EU-wide survey—Main results report. Publications Office of the European Union. https://fra.europa.eu/en/publication/2014/violence-against-women-eu-wide-survey-main-results-report

National Police Chiefs' Council. (2023). *Tackling violence against women and girls: Policing performance and insights (Insights report, March 2023)*. NPCC.

Taskforce on Violence Against Women and Girls. (n.d.). *The issue of violence against women and girls in Jersey*. Government of Jersey.

Chapter 30
Delivering Victim–Focused Services

Tony Blockley
Leeds Trinity University, UK

ABSTRACT

This chapter examines how police forces in England and Wales deliver victim-focused services, drawing on procedural justice theory, trauma-informed policing, and evidence from PEEL inspections. It explores how forces support victims from initial contact through investigation and aftercare, highlighting practices such as effective call handling, timely updates, accurate crime recording, and personalised victim care. The chapter showcases innovations like digital case tracking portals and victim liaison officers, and stresses the importance of transparency, empathy, and communication in building trust. Barriers such as limited resources, inconsistent crime recording, and poor follow-up are discussed alongside strategies to improve performance. Recommendations include greater use of technology, enhanced officer training, and integration of victim feedback to ensure fairer, more responsive, and supportive policing services.

INTRODUCTION

Police forces are judged by how effectively they support victims of crime. Focusing on the victim helps build trust and confidence in policing, provides appropriate support, and improves the likelihood of achieving just outcomes. The PEEL inspection framework assesses how police forces manage victim contact, crime recording, investigation standards, and overall victim care. Although it does not issue a final score, research shows that high-performing forces tend to follow procedural justice principles, apply effective safeguarding systems, and comply with

DOI: 10.4018/979-8-3373-2757-0.ch030

legislation protecting victims' rights (Bradford et al., 2022). This chapter examines evidence-based policing practices, highlights best practices from high-performing forces, and explores the systemic challenges that hinder progress. It also provides recommendations on how forces can improve their victim-focused services.

THEORETICAL AND EVIDENCE-BASED CONTEXT

The research underscores the importance of procedural justice in shaping victims' satisfaction with police interactions. Procedural justice theory argues that how authorities make decisions and treat individuals directly impacts their willingness to engage with the justice system (Tyler, 2006; Sunshine & Tyler, 2003). When victims believe police actions are fair, transparent, and respectful, they are more likely to report crimes, cooperate with investigations, and engage in the justice process (Bolger & Walters, 2019; Murphy & Barkworth, 2014).

Recent studies also show that repeat victimisation remains a key concern, where a small number of victims experience a disproportionate amount of harm (Bowers & Johnson, 2018). Addressing this requires early identification of repeat victims and proactive interventions. Furthermore, restorative justice approaches can empower victims by facilitating dialogue, repair, and closure (Sherman & Strang, 2012). These approaches can enhance trust and support emotional recovery, particularly for victims of property and interpersonal offences.

Procedural justice focuses on the way police make decisions, and the respect victims feel during those interactions. Studies show that when victims feel their concerns are heard, decisions are clearly explained, and they are treated respectfully, they are more likely to support investigations and share helpful information (Heron & Eisma, 2021). This is especially crucial for vulnerable victims, such as those experiencing domestic violence or sexual assault, where the relationship between the victim and the officer plays a key role in building trust and cooperation.

Transparency is also a key aspect. When police actions are transparent, and victims understand why decisions are being made, it reduces feelings of alienation and suspicion, making victims more willing to cooperate (Tyler & Huo, 2002). When victims feel respected and their cases are handled fairly, they are more likely to report future crimes, trust the police, and engage with the justice system (Murphy & Barkworth, 2014).

High-performing police forces demonstrate procedural justice principles in their practices. For example, West Midlands Police introduced a domestic abuse support desk, allowing victims to interact with trained professionals via video calls. This initiative resulted in greater satisfaction and trust and increased victim engagement in justice (HMICFRS, 2023a). By making these services fair, respectful, and transparent, the force created a more cooperative environment, showing how vital procedural justice is to improving police effectiveness and public trust.

These real-world examples align with Tyler's (2006) assertion that fairness and transparency lead to greater cooperation and legitimacy in policing, particularly when victims feel heard and respected.

TRAUMA-INFORMED POLICING

Victims of crime, especially those dealing with domestic abuse, sexual violence, or hate crimes, often experience long-term psychological trauma (Guay et al., 2019). Trauma-informed policing is about recognising how crime affects victims emotionally and adjusting police responses to reduce harm and support recovery. This approach addresses not just the immediate crime but also the emotional and psychological needs of victims (Birch, 2024). These principles are particularly important when working with child victims, whose voices must be actively heard and supported in line with the Victims' Code and UN Convention on the Rights of the Child (NSPCC, 2023).

Trauma-informed policing is grounded in several core principles that guide how officers interact with victims to minimise harm and support recovery:

1. The principle of safety underscores the importance of ensuring that victims feel both physically and emotionally secure throughout their engagement with police.
2. Creating a safe environment is essential to building trust and encouraging cooperation.
3. Equally important is the principle of choice, which involves providing victims with clear, accessible information about their rights and options, allowing them to make informed decisions at their own pace.
4. Collaboration is also central to trauma-informed practice. It emphasises the need for coordinated efforts between police, victim advocacy organisations, mental health professionals, and other support services to ensure that victims receive comprehensive, wraparound care.
5. Finally, the principle of empowerment focuses on helping victims regain a sense of control over their situation. This is achieved by equipping them with the necessary resources, guidance, and emotional support to navigate the justice process confidently and autonomously.

Police forces rated highly in PEEL inspections often integrate trauma-informed care into their victim support strategies. For instance, Thames Valley Police launched a Digital Citizens Portal, where victims can track the progress of their cases. This tool allows victims to feel more in control and empowered, improving engagement and safety (HMICFRS, 2023b). By utilising technology, the force aligns with the principle of empowerment, where victims regain a sense of control and security. Similarly, West Midlands Police employs trauma-sensitive interviewing to reduce re-traumatisation. Such initiatives reflect a growing focus on equality, diversity, and inclusion (EDI), recognising how intersecting identities, such as gender, ethnicity, disability, and digital access, influence victims' experiences and expectations of justice (Home Office, 2023). Trauma-informed policing not only improves victim satisfaction but also enhances the effectiveness of investigations. By addressing victims' emotional and psychological well-being, forces create environments where victims feel respected and supported, which leads to more successful outcomes for investigations.

PROCEDURAL JUSTICE IN PRACTICE

The Code of Practice for Victims of Crime (Home Office, 2021) outlines police obligations to support victims. These include regular updates, referral to support services, and the right to make a Victim Personal Statement (VPS). The VPS allows victims to express the emotional impact of crime, ensuring their experiences are heard in court decisions (Kunst et al., 2021). Forces that perform well ensure strong compliance with the Code and consistent updates to victims (HMICFRS, 2023c). However, compliance alone is insufficient: embedding empathy and emotional intelligence into every stage of engagement remains vital for procedural legitimacy.

These rights help maintain victim confidence in the justice process by ensuring that victims are informed and supported from the moment they report the crime until the case is concluded (Home Office, 2021). The Victims' Code stresses that victims should be kept informed at every stage of the investigation or trial, and it mandates that police forces provide access to victim support services such as counselling and legal advice, especially for victims of serious crimes like domestic abuse and sexual assault (Home Office, 2021).

One important element of the Victims' Code is the Victim Personal Statement (VPS), which allows victims to describe the emotional and psychological effects of the crime on their lives. This statement gives victims a voice in justice and helps ensure their experiences are considered in sentencing and parole decisions (Kunst et al., 2021). By incorporating the VPS into case files, police forces not only fulfil legal obligations but also make sure that the court takes the emotional toll of crime into account when deciding on justice outcomes.

Forces that perform well in PEEL assessments ensure strong compliance with the Victims' Code. They inform victims, ensure they receive necessary support services, and regularly update them on case progress (HMICFRS, 2023c). For example, Greater Manchester Police implemented a robust victim care programme with check-ins and a dedicated support hotline, leading to high levels of satisfaction among victims (HMICFRS, 2023a). On the other hand, forces that underperform often fail to communicate effectively with victims, which can lead to disengagement and undermine trust in the system. A study by Koster et al. (2016) found that victims who felt unsupported were less likely to cooperate with investigations, significantly hindering the chances of successful prosecution.

CALL HANDLING AND VICTIM CONTACT

The first point of contact a victim has with the police, typically through a 999 or 101 call, plays a significant role in shaping their overall experience. The speed and quality of the police response can strongly influence whether a victim feels supported and is willing to remain engaged in the justice process. High-performing forces tend to exhibit key practices that underpin effective initial contact. Prompt response times are crucial, as they enhance victim satisfaction and help secure evidence and prevent further harm (Tyler, 2006). Equally critical are structured risk assessment procedures that enable early identification of vulnerability, ensuring that victims' immediate needs are met and appropriate resources are deployed (HMICFRS, 2023d). Furthermore, empathetic and clear communication during call handling is essential for establishing trust and making victims feel heard and supported throughout their initial interaction with the police (Sweeney, 2022). Increasingly, first contact now occurs through online or digital channels. This shift has introduced new forms of vulnerability, such as online fraud, image-based abuse, and cyberstalking, which require tailored triage and safeguarding responses (Europol, 2024). Forces must also recognise that digital exclusion and language barriers can compound vulnerability, particularly for victims from minority or marginalised backgrounds (Home Office, 2023).

Effective call handling helps identify vulnerability from the first point of contact. Vulnerability can come from many factors, including age, mental health, or the nature of the crime itself, such as domestic violence or sexual assault. By identifying these vulnerabilities early, the police can respond in a way that feels sensitive and appropriate to the victim's circumstances (McGuire et al., 2021). For children and young people, effective call handling must also ensure that their voices are heard and interpreted accurately. The NSPCC (2023) highlights that children's disclosures of abuse or neglect are often missed or minimised during initial contact, underscoring the need for trauma-informed questioning and immediate safeguarding action.

West Midlands Police has made significant strides in improving how it handles high-risk domestic abuse cases. To better meet the needs of victims, a multi-agency risk assessment conference (MARAC) process was introduced. Although there was significant demand for these services, the force introduced a triage system to filter cases, ensuring that resources were used efficiently while safeguarding vulnerable victims. For example, 20 out of 253 cases were triaged in Coventry to ensure the right level of care was given to each case.

In addition, the introduction of a domestic abuse support desk where victims could engage with trained professionals via video calls showed strong early results. Victims who used the service reported feeling more confident about their engagement with the justice process, with 76% of victims saying they preferred video calls over telephone or home visits (HMICFRS, 2023d). However, the force acknowledges that there are still challenges, including a backlog of cases. These issues must be tackled to ensure vulnerable individuals receive timely and appropriate support. Addressing these challenges requires integrated digital, procedural, and emotional responses. Effective early contact sets the foundation for victim trust, procedural fairness, and trauma-informed investigation, themes explored further in the next section.

CRIME RECORDING AND INVESTIGATION QUALITY

Accurate and timely crime recording is fundamental to effective victim support, appropriate resource allocation, and the delivery of thorough and well-structured investigations. Within the PEEL framework, particular emphasis is placed on whether crimes are correctly classified and recorded without delay (HMICFRS, 2023c). It also examines the extent to which victims are kept informed through regular updates on the progress of their case (Altan & Baudin-Naniex, 2024) and whether investigations are conducted in a structured and proportionate manner that reflects the seriousness and complexity of the offence (Prince et al., 2021).

Accurate crime classification helps police allocate resources properly and track patterns, which supports victims and protects the public. Furthermore, keeping victims informed throughout the investigative process is essential for fostering trust and maintaining victim cooperation (Tyler, 2006; Kunst et al., 2015). Repeat victimisation remains a persistent challenge for forces, with a small number of victims accounting for a disproportionate share of offences (Bowers & Johnson, 2018). Embedding repeat victimisation analysis into recording systems allows forces to prioritise prevention and allocate safeguarding resources more effectively. In parallel, forces should ensure that crime data captures protected characteristics, so EDI outcomes can be monitored and addressed transparently (Home Office, 2023).

High-performing forces tend to have robust oversight and monitoring mechanisms to ensure crime is recorded accurately, investigations are victim-centred, and resources are allocated where they are most needed. This focus on accuracy and victim engagement builds trust and ensures the investigation moves in the right direction. Greater Manchester Police made notable progress in improving crime recording and the quality of investigations. They introduced a comprehensive quality assurance system, which improved the accuracy of crime recording and ensured that resources were used efficiently. As a result, victims were more satisfied because they received regular updates and felt that their concerns were being addressed effectively. In parallel with these procedural improvements, restorative justice initiatives are increasingly used to support emotional recovery. Evidence shows that allowing victims to participate in restorative processes can increase satisfaction and promote closure, particularly when linked to robust investigative practice (Sherman & Strang, 2012).

In addition, Greater Manchester Police adopted a victim-centred approach to investigations. Victims were kept informed throughout the investigative process, increasing satisfaction. Supervisors also played an active role, regularly reviewing investigations to ensure that all lines of inquiry were explored and that the investigations were completed on time (HMICFRS, 2023a). These approaches demonstrate that accurate recording, procedural fairness, and restorative engagement are interconnected. Together, they underpin consistent, victim-centred service delivery and prepare the ground for more holistic forms of victim support.

VICTIM ENGAGEMENT AND SUPPORT

Providing practical support to victims involves far more than simply investigating the crime; it requires ongoing, proactive engagement to ensure victims feel supported at every stage of the justice process. Police forces that perform highly in PEEL assessments typically demonstrate excellence in several key areas of victim care. One such area is the provision of specialised support services tailored to victims of domestic abuse, sexual violence, and other serious offences. These services enable victims to access the personalised care they need during investigations, contributing to improved experiences and outcomes (HMICFRS, 2023c). In addition, Body-Worn Video (BWV) has proven valuable in reducing the emotional strain of repeated recounting of traumatic events. BWV helps preserve critical evidence and spares victims the distress of having to relive their experiences multiple times during the investigative process (HMICFRS, 2023c). High-performing forces also invest in officers' effective victim communication and safeguarding training. This training equips officers with the skills to engage compassionately and professionally with vulnerable individuals, strengthening the trust and cooperation essential for successful investigations. Ensuring inclusivity in victim support requires recognising that experiences of crime and engagement with police are shaped by gender, age, ethnicity, and disability (Home Office, 2023). Children and young people often require adapted communication methods to ensure that their voices are heard and understood in line with the Victims' Code and safeguarding legislation (NSPCC, 2023). Forces demonstrating excellence in this area incorporate youth advocates or family liaison officers to help interpret and represent the child's perspective throughout investigations.

Thames Valley Police has been praised for introducing the Digital Citizens Portal, a tool that enables victims to track their case progress online. This digital innovation has improved victim engagement by providing real-time updates on the case status. This helps victims stay informed and feel more in control of the process. Victims can also communicate directly with investigating officers, contributing to greater satisfaction and trust in the police response (HMICFRS, 2023b). Digital platforms such as the Citizens Portal also provide new opportunities to support victims of online crime, including cyberstalking and image-based abuse, by allowing rapid reporting, case updates, and evidence uploads (Europol, 2024). To remain inclusive, however, forces must mitigate risks of digital exclusion by maintaining multiple contact routes for victims without stable internet access or digital literacy.

In addition, Thames Valley Police introduced personalised victim support programmes. These programmes are tailored to meet each victim's specific needs, helping to enhance their experience and increase their cooperation with law enforcement. By adopting technology such as the Digital Citizens Portal, Thames Valley Police has improved victim support while increasing transparency and reducing the emotional burden on victims. Taken together, these developments demonstrate that effective victim engagement combines technological accessibility, empathetic communication, and inclusivity. When integrated consistently across forces, such approaches create a policing culture that not only records crime effectively but sustains the victim's trust throughout the justice journey.

CHALLENGES AND BARRIERS

While many police forces have made notable progress in enhancing victim-centred service delivery, several persistent challenges undermine effectiveness. One of the most significant barriers is resource constraints. Many forces face understaffing, contributing to slower response times and lower-quality investigations. This problem makes it harder for them to prevent crime and manage cases efficiently, often resulting in delays and reduced victim engagement (HMICFRS, 2023c). Another challenge lies in the variability of crime recording practices. Inconsistencies in classifying and logging incidents can lead to incomplete or inaccurate data, which weakens the reliability of crime trend analysis and disrupts the appropriate allocation of resources. Such inaccuracies may compromise police responses and the quality of investigative outcomes (Alderden & Ullman, 2012). Additionally, a lack of consistent follow-up with victims remains a critical issue. When victims do not receive timely updates or feel left out of the process after reporting a crime, their trust in the justice system diminishes. This erosion of confidence often leads to disengagement, making successful prosecution less likely and weakening the overall effectiveness of victim support efforts (Holder & Englezos, 2024). These systemic barriers do not affect all victims equally. Evidence from recent inspections shows that victims from marginalised or digitally excluded groups, as well as children and young people, are more likely to experience inconsistent follow-up and lower satisfaction rates (HMICFRS, 2023c; NSPCC, 2023). Where online victimisation or coercive control is involved, these weaknesses can be compounded by a lack of specialist digital investigation capacity (Europol, 2024). Addressing these disparities requires stronger equality monitoring and closer integration of child-safeguarding principles within all victim-service frameworks (Home Office, 2023).

Forces rated 'Requires Improvement' tend to struggle more with these issues. Insufficient resources, poor communication, and inconsistencies in crime recording contribute to higher case attrition rates, where victims disengage from investigations due to delays or lack of support (HMICFRS, 2023c). On the other hand, high-performing forces have managed to overcome these challenges by developing strong structures and processes. They excel in providing specialised victim support, maintaining clear communication with victims, and ensuring accurate crime recording. This consistency leads to better victim engagement, higher satisfaction, and improved cooperation, which ultimately helps to achieve better outcomes for victims and the justice process (HMICFRS, 2023c). These findings suggest that victim-centred practice depends not only on resource availability but also on leadership culture, digital capacity, and inclusion strategy. Future progress will require forces to embed equality impact assessment and child-voice feedback mechanisms within performance frameworks to ensure that improvements benefit all victims, not just those most visible to the system.

FUTURE DIRECTIONS AND RECOMMENDATIONS

The role of technology in the delivery of victim services is set to expand significantly, as police forces increasingly adopt digital tools to streamline processes, enhance transparency, and improve victim experiences. Technological advancements will likely become central to service provision in the coming years. One such development is the use of artificial intelligence (AI) to support call handling. AI-assisted systems can improve efficiency by conducting more effective risk assessments at the point of contact, enabling forces to prioritise cases, assess threat levels, and identify vulnerabilities faster and more accurately (HMICFRS, 2023b). In parallel, digital evidence submission portals are emerging as a key tool to reduce the burden on victims. By allowing individuals to upload information remotely, these platforms support investigative processes while minimising the need for repeated in-person contact, reducing potential re-traumatisation (HMICFRS, 2023b). Automated case tracking systems also offer significant potential benefits. These systems allow victims to monitor the status of their case in real time, promoting transparency, increasing trust, and ensuring individuals remain informed throughout the justice journey (Russell & Pappas, 2018). While digital innovation offers clear benefits, forces must also consider accessibility and inclusivity. Not all victims have equal access to digital tools, and overreliance on technology risks excluding those without reliable internet access or digital literacy (Home Office, 2023). Equally, online engagement presents specific safeguarding challenges for children and young people, particularly where offences involve digital exploitation or grooming (NSPCC, 2023; Europol, 2024). Embedding equality and safeguarding audits within technology implementation is therefore essential to ensure that these systems serve all victims effectively.

In addition to new technologies, more forces are recognising the need to professionalise victim services to improve consistency and quality. Specialist training for police officers in trauma-informed care is crucial for those working with victims of domestic abuse and sexual violence, equipping them with the knowledge and sensitivity required to manage emotionally complex cases (Millar et al., 2022). Mandatory refresher courses on victim communication help maintain these skills, ensuring that officers remain empathetic, responsive, and well-prepared to address victims' emotional and practical needs (HMICFRS, 2023c). Professionalisation also depends on embedding equality, diversity, and inclusion (EDI) within training content. Officers must understand how intersecting factors such as gender, race, disability, and sexual orientation shape victim experience, perceptions of fairness, and access to justice (HMICFRS, 2023c; Rock, 2023). Building these competencies fosters a service culture that treats difference as integral to effectiveness rather than an afterthought. Expanding the use of victim liaison officers provides an additional route to strengthening victim support, offering consistent, personalised guidance, timely updates, and emotional support that significantly enhance victims' experiences throughout the justice process (Rock, 2023).

The PEEL 2023–2025 framework is expected to emphasise holistic approaches to victim care. A stronger focus on safeguarding outcomes will be central to this, ensuring that vulnerable victims are protected throughout the investigative process and beyond, particularly those who are repeat victims of domestic abuse or sexual violence (HMICFRS, 2023c). The integration of victim feedback into the assessment framework is also likely to become more prominent, allowing forces to adapt their approaches to the lived experiences of those they serve (Kunst et al., 2015). Finally, there will be an increased emphasis on early intervention. Proactive engagement with repeat victims can prevent further harm and enable more tailored responses, ensuring that individual needs are met before trauma is compounded (Bowers & Johnson, 2018). Taken together, these developments point toward a model of policing that is technologically empowered, trauma-informed, and socially aware. The challenge ahead lies not only in adopting digital tools but in ensuring they are used ethically, inclusively, and in ways that reinforce procedural justice for every victim.

CONCLUSION

This chapter has outlined how police forces can strengthen victim-focused services by applying evidence-based practices, learning from high-performing forces, and addressing persistent barriers. Key priorities include investing in technology, enhancing officer training, and embedding trauma-informed approaches. However, genuine professionalisation also requires that equality, diversity, and inclusion principles, the voice of the child, and recognition of repeat and online victimisation are systematically embedded within victim policy and practice. These priorities are essential for meeting PEEL standards and building a sustainable culture of procedural justice and care. By adopting these measures, police forces can move beyond compliance towards a model of policing that is technologically empowered, trauma-informed, and socially aware — one that ensures every victim is respected, supported, and safe throughout their engagement with the justice system.

REFERENCES

Alderden, M. A., & Ullman, S. E. (2012). Creating a more complete and current picture: Examining police and prosecutor decision-making when processing sexual assault cases. *Violence Against Women, 18*(5), 525–551. PMID: 22814891

Altan, L., & Baudoin-Naneix, S. (2024). Transforming how we communicate with victims: moving beyond information provision to a communication system. REVISTA INTERNACIONAL DE VITIMOLOGIA E JUSTIÇA RESTAURATIVA, 2(2).

Birch, P. (2024). Trauma-informed policing: Enhancing law enforcement practices through empathy and sensitivity. Abuse. *An International Impact Journal, 5*(2), 1–21.

Bolger, P. C., & Walters, G. D. (2019). The relationship between police procedural justice, police legitimacy, and people's willingness to cooperate with law enforcement: A meta-analysis. *Journal of Criminal Justice, 60*, 93–99.

Bowers, K., & Johnson, S. D. (2018). *Repeat victimisation and crime prevention: From theory to practice*. Oxford University Press.

Bradford, B., Aston, E., O'Neill, M., & Wells, H. (2022). *'Virtual policing', trust and legitimacy*. Eleven International Publishing.

Europol. (2024). *Internet organised crime threat assessment (IOCTA) 2024*. The Hague, Netherlands: Europol. https://www.europol.europa.eu

Guay, S., Beaulieu-Prévost, D., Sader, J., & Marchand, A. (2019). A systematic literature review of early posttraumatic interventions for victims of violent crime. *Aggression and Violent Behavior, 46*, 15–24.

Heron, R. L., & Eisma, M. C. (2021). Barriers and facilitators of disclosing domestic violence to the healthcare service: A systematic review of qualitative research. *Health & Social Care in the Community, 29*(3), 612–630. PMID: 33440034

His Majesty's Inspectorate of Constabulary and Fire & Rescue Services. (2023a) PEEL 2023–25 Police effectiveness, efficiency and legitimacy An inspection of Greater Manchester Police. Available at: https://hmicfrs.justiceinspectorates.gov.uk/peel-reports/greater-manchester-2023-25/

His Majesty's Inspectorate of Constabulary and Fire & Rescue Services. (2023b) PEEL 2023–25 Police effectiveness, efficiency and legitimacy An inspection of Thames Valley Police. Available at: https://assets-hmicfrs.justiceinspectorates.gov.uk/uploads/peel-assessment-2023-25-thames-valley.pdf (Accessed: 04 February 2025).

His Majesty's Inspectorate of Constabulary and Fire & Rescue Services. (2023c) Meeting the needs of victims in the criminal justice system. An inspection of how well the police, the Crown Prosecution Service and the Probation Service support victims of crime. Available at: https://hmicfrs.justiceinspectorates.gov.uk/publication-html/meeting-the-needs-of-victims-in-the-criminal-justice-system/

His Majesty's Inspectorate of Constabulary and Fire & Rescue Services. (2023d) PEEL 2023–25 Police effectiveness, efficiency and legitimacy An inspection of West Midlands Police. Available at: https://assets-hmicfrs.justiceinspectorates.gov.uk/uploads/peel-assessment-2023-25-west-midlands.pdf (Accessed: 04 February 2025).

Holder, R. L., & Englezos, E. (2024). Victim participation in criminal justice: A quantitative systematic and critical literature review. *International Review of Victimology*, *30*(1), 25–49.

Home Office. (2021). *Code of Practice for Victims of Crime*. Retrieved from https://www.gov.uk/government/publications/victims-code-of-practice

Home Office. (2023). *Victims and prisoners bill: Policy paper.* London, United Kingdom: His Majesty's Stationery Office. https://www.gov.uk/government/publications/victims-and-prisoners-bill

Koster, N. S. N., Kuijpers, K. F., & Kunst, M. J. J. (2016). Crime victims' perceptions of police behavior, legitimacy, and cooperation: A review of the literature. *Taylor & Francis Victims &...*, *1*(1), 1-20. DOI: 10.1080/15564886.2015.1065532

Kunst, M., de Groot, G., Meester, J., & van Doorn, J. (2021). The impact of victim impact statements on legal decisions in criminal proceedings: A systematic review of the literature across jurisdictions and decision types. *Aggression and Violent Behavior*, *56*, 101512.

Kunst, M., Popelier, L., & Varekamp, E. (2015). Victim satisfaction with the criminal justice system and emotional recovery: A systematic and critical review of the literature. *Trauma, Violence & Abuse*, *16*(3), 336–358. PMID: 25352031

McGuire, J., Evans, E., Kane, E., McGuire, J., Evans, E., & Kane, E. (2021). Victim Counselling and Support: A Review of Police, Community and Therapeutic Interventions. Evidence-Based Policing and Community Crime Prevention, 361-415.

Millar, A., Saxton, M., Øverlien, C., & Elliffe, R. (2022). Police officers do not need more training, but different training. Policing domestic violence and abuse involving children: A rapid review. *Journal of Family Violence*, *37*(7), 1071–1088.

Murphy, K., & Barkworth, J. (2014). Victim willingness to report crime to police: Does procedural justice or outcome matter most? *Victims & Offenders*, *9*, 178–204.

National Society for the Prevention of Cruelty to Children (NSPCC). (2023). *How the system responds to children disclosing abuse: Learning from case reviews.* London, United Kingdom: NSPCC. https://learning.nspcc.org.uk

Prince, H., Lum, C., & Koper, C. S. (2021). Effective police investigative practices: An evidence-assessment of the research. *Policing*, *44*(4), 683–707.

Rock, P. (2023). The Role of Victim Advocacy in Criminal Justice Reform in England and Wales. *Annual Review of Criminology*, *6*(1), 499–527.

Russell, B. L., & Pappas, N. (2018). Officer involved domestic violence: A future of uniform response and transparency. *International Journal of Police Science & Management*, *20*(2), 134–142.

Sherman, L. W., & Strang, H. (2012). *Restorative justice: The evidence*. The Smith Institute.

Sunshine, J., & Tyler, T. R. (2003). The role of procedural justice and legitimacy in shaping public support for policing. *Law & Society Review*, *37*(3), 517–548.

Sweeney, K. (2022). Understanding emotion as a strategy in policing. *The Police Journal*, *95*(3), 473–491.

Tyler, T. R. (2006). *Why people obey the law*. Princeton University Press., DOI: 10.1515/9781400826752

Tyler, T. R., & Huo, Y. J. (2002). *Trust in the law: Encouraging public cooperation with the police and courts*. Russell Sage Foundation.

About the Contributors

Kate Benson is a Lecturer in Criminology and Criminal Justice at Brunel University of London and a former police detective. Kate is a Senior Fellow of the Higher Education Academy, recognised for her sustained record of effective leadership in teaching and learning in higher education. As former Head of Delivery for the Police Education Qualifications Framework (PEQF) and current commercial contract lead, Kate has been instrumental in advancing the PEQF since its inception in 2021. Drawing on nearly a decade of frontline policing and specialist detective experience, she brings extensive professional insight through her leadership of strategic initiatives which centre on curriculum design, quality assurance, and learner development.

Ross Campbell is a senior police officer with twenty-six years of service, with extensive experience in operational policing, workforce leadership, vetting, and professional standards. He holds a Master's degree in Criminal Psychology and a degree in Policing, and is a PhD student researching psychometric and psychological considerations in policing. His research focuses on how cognitive and behavioural assessment can strengthen recruitment, vetting, and leadership across the service. Ross has led major national reform programmes centred on ethical leadership and public trust, leading the policing response for police vetting following publication of Part One of the Angiolini Inquiry. This work will ensure a more consistent and transparent approach to vetting across UK policing. He has also held significant roles locally and nationally in inclusion and disability, championing psychologically safe and supportive working environments. His advocacy for neurodivergent colleagues and those with disabilities has been recognised through national awards for inclusion. Ross's career reflects a long-term commitment to ethical, evidence based, and inclusive policing that is capable of meeting modern expectations and strengthening public confidence.

Sophie Curtis-Ham, PhD, is an honorary research associate at the University of Waikato and senior researcher at New Zealand Police. She has previously worked as an intelligence analyst in the UK and NZ. Her research interests span the fields of evidence-based policing, investigative and forensic psychology and environmental criminology. She has innovated tools for analysing crime harm, police effort, and crime investigation suspects' locations, to support strategic and investigative decision-making.

Naomi Davis-Crane is a Senior Lecturer in policing at Liverpool John Moores University. She left policing in 2023 in a senior leadership role as the Head of Analysis for Counter Terrorism Policing Borders Operations having had a 13-year career in a diverse range of intelligence roles. Naomi now lectures in police leadership and organisational behaviour, terrorism, and intelligence practice. She is shortly to complete her doctoral study examining the interplay between police culture, leadership and employee motivation; and is actively researching civilian experiences of police culture, barriers to female advancement into senior and executive leadership in policing, and opportunities to evaluate organisational climate in policing.

Larissa Engelmann is a Research Fellow at the Economic and Social Research Council funded Vulnerability and Policing Futures Research Centre at the University of Leeds, exploring how the police and other services can best be harnessed to prevent and reduce vulnerabilities. Her interests span subjects and sectors such as the prevention of online child sexual victimisation, the service provision for vulnerable populations in contact with the police, and domestic abuse responses. She is a mixed-methods researcher and works collaboratively with local practitioners and communities. Her passion is police learning and development within the law enforcement and public health realm. Her projects on police learning and education have mainly been focussed in Scotland, where she completed her PhD at Edinburgh Napier University. She is currently exploring and supporting police-academic partnerships in the UK and central Europe through her role as co-chair of the European Society of Criminology Working Group on Policing. Her work influences policy and practice locally and nationally to support police and partner organisations, communities, as well as higher education institutions, to collaborate and develop effective and sustainable services. She is a board member of the Global Law Enforcement and Public Health Association (GLEPHA) promoting research, understanding and practice at the intersection of law enforcement and public health.

Rob Ewin is a Detective Inspector currently specialised in digital forensics and the investigation of major and organised crime. His work is grounded in a strong academic foundation, holding a PhD in the relationship between vulnerability and witnesses, and an LLM in Qualifying Law from Liverpool John Moores University. Dr. Ewin's legal scholarship focuses on evidential procedures, particularly the challenges of disclosure and hearsay in criminal proceedings. His LLM and PhD praised for its analytical rigour and clarity, explored the intersection of hearsay evidence and human rights, offering critical insights into procedural fairness and the treatment of vulnerable witnesses.

Stephanie Kewley is a Professor of Forensic and Criminal Justice at Liverpool John Moores University, currently seconded to the Centre for expertise on child sexual abuse as a Principal Research and Evaluation Officer. She has for over two decades worked across Criminal Justice and Forensic Psychology research, educational, and correctional contexts; holding academic, practitioner and managerial roles. The central focus of her professional experiences has been to support, advocate and promote the safe and healthy functioning of marginalised and stigmatised populations involved in and/or incarcerated by criminal justice structures and systems. Stephanie is a board member of the National Organisation for the Treatment of Abusers (NOTA), Co-Editor for the Journal of Sexual Aggression, and academic advisor for several international projects.

Denise Martin is a Professor of Criminology and Policing at the University of Northumbria. She has been involved in researching police and policing for over 20 years. She has worked with a range of organisations including the Home Office, Police Scotland, the Mayors Office for Police and Crime and Skills for Justice. Her main areas of research are on Police Professionalisation, Police Organisational Culture and Police Misconduct. She was an Associate Director of the Scottish Institute of Police Research between 2016 and 2024, is currently a member of the board for Global Law Enforcement and Public Health Association and a Liaison for the European Society of Criminology Police Working Group and Co-convenor of the BSC Police Misconduct Forum. She is editor of 4 book and has published a number of articles on police related issues.

Poppy Murray is a writer, public speaker, and campaigner from Guernsey, specialising in violence against women and girls (VAWG), night-time economy safety, and rebuilding trust and confidence in the police. She was a UN Women UK Delegate for the Commission on the Status of Women in 2024 and 2025, Runner Up in the "Making Safer Spaces" category at the 2024 National Police Chiefs' Council VAWG Recognition Event, and 2025 Winner of the Crimestoppers Guernsey Award for Outstanding Achievement. Poppy motivates and inspires audience with her message that one person can make a difference.

JP Oosthuizen is an Assistant Professor at the University of North Georgia (UNG), where he teaches undergraduate and Ph.D.-level courses in Intelligence Studies, Homeland Security, and Criminology. Prior to joining UNG in August 2022, Dr. Oosthuizen held academic positions at several universities, including Rabdan Academy in Abu Dhabi (U.A.E.), where he taught criminology, intelligence gathering, police leadership, and community safety. He also served as a senior lecturer in Criminology and Program Leader for the MSc in Applied Criminology at the University of Winchester (UK), as well as holding teaching roles at the University of West London and Greenwich University in London. Dr. Oosthuizen has a distinguished background with over 24 years of service in the military and law enforcement. He served in the South African National Defense Force and later as a police officer with Dorset Police in the UK. As part of his professional achievements, he was a UK College of Policing Research Scholar at John Jay College of Criminal Justice in New York City and held the position of Director of the Institute of Policing at the University of Winchester. Academically, Dr. Oosthuizen holds a Professional Doctorate in Criminal Justice from the University of Portsmouth. He also earned a Master's degree (with merit) in Criminology and Criminal Justice, a Bachelor's degree (with honors) in Policing, an Associate (Foundation) degree in Policing, and a Certificate in Education from Canterbury Christ Church University (UK). Dr. Oosthuizen's work has been recognized through several awards, including the Student-Led Teaching Award (2016, University of Winchester), the Divisional Commander's Commendation (2013, Dorset Police), the Community Champion Award (2011, Poole Borough Council, UK), and the John Jay Community Safety Award (2010, Poole Borough Council, UK). At UNG, Dr. Oosthuizen serves on the Senate and Curriculum Committees, as well as the National Security Committee for the university's Strategic "Big Bets" initiatives.

Jeremy (Jerry) Pearson is a Senior Lecturer in Policing at the University of Sunderland and a former police officer. After a 30-year career in policing with Northumbria Police, Jerry retired as a Detective Superintendent in 2020 and later the same year began working as an academic. He has a significant background in the field of organisational ethics and has previously led large scale counter corruption and misconduct enquiries as well as possessing extensive experience in both the overt and covert investigation of serious and organised criminality. He is a former Head of the National Police Chiefs' Council (NPCC) International Crime Coordination Centre (ICCC) and prior to the UK's exit from the EU, led the UK police contingency planning team, working alongside colleagues from the National Crime Agency (NCA), the Home Office and policing agencies across Europe. As an Independent Lead Reviewer, Jerry has worked with local authorities in the completion of Local

Child Safeguarding Practice Reviews and conducts safeguarding work for the Football Association (The FA) and UK Athletics.

Sarah Pemberton is an Associate Professor in Criminology and Head of College for Law, Social and Criminal Justice at Birmingham City University. Her research focuses on domestic abuse, sexual violence, and the criminal justice system's response to these issues. She has a particular interest in policing and the management of individuals convicted of sexual offences, exploring the tensions between public protection and rehabilitation. Her work also examines the role of police in supporting desistance and preventing sexual harm through trauma-informed and positive criminological approaches.

David Rowlands is a Research Fellow with the Vulnerability and Policing Futures Research Centre (VPRC) at the University of Leeds. His research interests include the intersection of vulnerabilities and policing, identity processes influencing encounters with law enforcement, and processes of desistance and rehabilitation.

Hannah Jane Simpson is a criminologist with a Master of Laws (LLM) in Criminal Justice and Penal Change from the University of Strathclyde. With over a decade of experience in criminal justice, she has worked extensively in police custody, courts, and policy reform. Whilst serving with Police Scotland, she was instrumental in implementing key initiatives, including Scotland's first juvenile and women-only custody suite and virtual custody courts during the COVID-19 pandemic. Her academic research focuses on penal reform, youth justice, and domestic abuse interventions. She has contributed to scholarly discourse through ongoing research projects; and policy-oriented analyses on youth justice reform and police custody disposals in domestic abuse cases.

Ann Stevens has worked in Criminal Intelligence and Financial Crime for 30 years in both Public and Private Sector roles. Ann was a police officer and intelligence officer (FIO) for Merseyside Police and later moved to Global Security Financial Crime and Intelligence positions in the private sector. With a focus on Intelligence Investigations, taking a proactive approach to crime reduction and risk mitigation, Ann has leveraged global networks and joint agency collaboration to effectively respond to crime, disorder, serious and complex organized crime. Ann has been the Director of Professional Development for IALEIA, she has also developed and instructed Financial Crime and Intelligence Programs for the past 14 years. Ann's education and professional profile includes an MSc Counter Fraud & Counter Corruption, Certified Fraud Examiner, (CFE) Certified Anti-Money Laundering Specialist (CAMS), Certified Geographic Profiling Analyst (GPA),

Certified Criminal Analyst (CCA) Accredited Counter Fraud Specialist (ACFS) and Accredited Counter Fraud Trainer (ACFT).

Steven Wadley is a Senior Lecturer in Policing at Birmingham City University and is undertaking a PhD examining the impact of working as a Special Constable, alongside being a full-time policing student.

Andy Wilson is a PhD student researching in the area of controlled drugs markets, specifically County Lines responses. He is a retired police sergeant with Police Scotland, retiring from the Learning and Development Department, where he worked on the introduction of the Scottish Modern Apprenticeship in Policing.

Index

A

B

C

D

E

F

G

H

R

S

T

V

W

www.ingramcontent.com/pod-product-compliance
Lightning Source LLC
LaVergne TN
LVHW061528290926
849162LV00004B/707